THE INSIDERS' GUIDE TO
RENO & LAKE TAHOE

THE INSIDERS' GUIDE TO

LAKE RENO & TAHOE

by
Jeanne Lauf Walpole
and
Mike Carrigan

The Insiders' Guide®
An imprint of Falcon® Publishing, Inc.
A Landmark Communications company
P.O. Box 1718
Helena, MT 59624
(800) 582-2665
www.insiders.com

Sales and Marketing: Falcon Publishing, Inc.
P.O. Box 1718
Helena, MT 59624
(800) 582-2665
www.falcon.com

•

FIRST EDITION
1st printing

•

©1999 by Falcon Publishing, Inc.

•

Printed in the United States
of America

•

Cover photos, K. Markgraf

Publications from *The Insiders' Guide*® series are available at special discounts for bulk purchases for sales promotions, premiums or fundraisings. Special editions, including personalized covers, can be created in large quantities for special needs.
For more information, please contact Falcon Publishing.

ISBN 1-57380-104-6

Preface

The commuter plane bumped along the rough air above Lake Tahoe in the Sierra Nevada mountain range bordering California and Nevada. Molly Gale, a precocious 9-year-old, pressed her face against the oval window, trying desperately to see her new home in Reno, about 25 miles east of the sapphire-blue lake.

"I see buildings down there," she blurted out to her parents, as the plane dipped into the valley. "That must be it. That must be Reno, but it looks like someone planted all the fields with Rice Krispies."

Yep, that's Reno in the summer, and in the fall, and in the winter and in the spring — a painter's palette where most of the hues are brown with just a splash of green dotting the banks along the Truckee River, the waterway that snakes from Lake Tahoe through Reno to Pyramid Lake. But, as all Insiders will tell you when you first arrive, Reno's unique beauty will grow on you. And it does — especially at sunrise when the sun peeking over the eastern mountain range casts purple shadows that seem to stretch forever — or at dusk when you can stand anywhere in the city and have an unobstructed view of an awe-inspiring sunset that bounces golden rays from the tops of the snow-sprinkled mountains.

Visitors soon learn that water is definitely a precious commodity in the Reno area, which has been riddled with droughts over the years, though a short 45-minute drive over the mountains and through the pine trees will bring you to the shores of Lake Tahoe, one of the deepest lakes in the world. In fact, Lake Tahoe is so deep that if you emptied it into California, the lake's water would completely cover the state to a depth of two feet. These extremes are just one example of Reno/Tahoe's diversity, a diversity that often makes the area one of the most misunderstood in the United States. Don't fret though. We Insiders will help you understand the area's idiosyncrasies, and we'll guide you through the maze of things to see and to do here.

To those who have never visited Reno/Tahoe, the misconception might be that it is an area with acres and acres of slot machines, buckets full of liquor and rooms so thick with smoke you have to chop your way through them with a machete. Those who have visited the area know that Reno is an uncluttered place with friendly people where we still call our elected officials by their first names and where we still sit down at a neighborhood cafe and share the newspaper. They know that to drive the 72 miles around Lake Tahoe takes the better part of the day, and during that drive they will see multimillion dollar homes, double-wides in trailer parks and miles and miles of pristine beaches. This variety makes the Reno/Tahoe area difficult to describe, but it is why we love it here.

Although best known for our gaming and entertainment, Reno/Tahoe is a popular recreation area, too. You name it, we've got it. You can golf, hike, fish, boat and do just about any other summer activity. And if snow skiing is your pleasure, Lake Tahoe boasts the largest concentration of ski resorts in North America. Because of its plethora of outdoor recreation activities, the Reno/Tahoe area earned Rand McNally's (the road atlas people) highest rating as America's No.1 place for outdoor fun.

And if it's quality of life you're looking for, the Reno/Tahoe area was ranked in 1997 as one of the top 50 places to raise a family, and Reno was ranked in 1997 as the No. 1 literary city by the National Endowment for the Arts.

Varied? Yes. Remote? Maybe. But no one can dispute that the area is packed with excitement. Here, the saying goes that the outdoor fun lasts all day long and so does the nightlife. We don't roll up our sidewalks at sunset. If you have a craving for a steak at 3 AM, you'll have no trouble finding one (and no one here will make you feel guilty for eating it). And, of course, if it's gaming you want, the area has more than 60 gaming establishments.

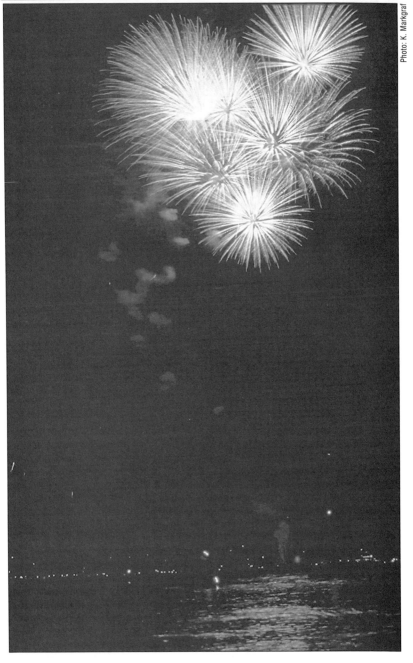

Photo: K. Markgraf

Fireworks burst into the night sky above Lake Tahoe.

Since the choices here are so diverse and so numerous, we figure this Insiders' Guide will come in mighty handy. We hope we've compiled a guide to the area that not only divulges the well-known places but also will lead you to the real Reno/Tahoe, the Insiders' Reno/Tahoe — from the tiny Mexican cafe with zero atmosphere but with the best burritos this side of Mexico City to the best fishing spot on the Truckee River (which just happens to be about five minutes from downtown Reno).

We hope you use this guide as a road map to trek off the typical tourist path. We have slipped to you in this one guide the totality of our 30 combined years of living in one of the truly spectacular areas of the United States. We offer to you our Insiders' choices of the best restaurants, the prettiest campsites and the toughest and easiest golf courses. We lead you to the best downhill and cross-country ski resorts. We give you options for choosing the right healthcare facility. We discuss the area's newspapers and magazines and radio and television stations. We even tell you about the local school districts and the boom in the real estate business. Our wish is that you toss this guide into your car's glove compartment along with your area maps and proof of car insurance (required by Nevada law) so you'll be able to whip it out when you continue on your quest for something to do or see in the Reno/Tahoe area.

And this is a good time to address any rumors you might have heard about prostitution in Nevada — because the rumors are true. Prostitution is legal in Nevada, but only in the rural counties. The Reno/Tahoe area is not in a rural county so you will not find any legal bordellos here.

We'd like to end this preface with a few words from Mark Twain, who, by the way, began his writing career in Virginia City, only 20 miles from downtown Reno:

"Throw away the bowlines, sail away from the safe harbor. Catch the trade winds in your sails. Explore, dream, discover."

Now, come visit us!

About the Authors

Jeanne Lauf Walpole

Born and raised in northwestern Montana, Jeanne Lauf Walpole first moved to Nevada after graduating from Washington State University in Pullman, Washington. She taught high school Spanish and geography and, together with her husband, established several family-owned casinos in Fallon, 60 miles east of Reno. After some years, the pressure of this 24-hour-a-day enterprise became grueling. They sold the business and moved to Sun Valley, Idaho, with their three sons, Chris, Scott and Kevin. In this mountain paradise the family was able to fully indulge in their love of the outdoors. But after four years, Jeanne longed for the "real world" again.

She moved to Memphis, Tennessee, where she received her master's degree in journalism from the University of Memphis. She then returned to Reno to build a career in publishing and freelance writing.

Jeanne has written for a variety of publications and was editor of *Active Times*, a regional senior publication in Memphis, and editor/publisher of *Golden Gateways*, a travel newsletter for mature travelers. She was also a contributing writer for the book *Reno & Tahoe Country: An Illustrated History of Western Nevada*.

Community service has played an important role in her life, and she has served on numerous boards and been elected to public office. In the past several years, her commitment to those in need drew her to Crisis Call Center where she serves as president of the board of directors and answers calls of those in crisis.

Her passion for travel began before she could read, as some of her earliest childhood memories are of looking at pictures in *National Geographic* magazine. She has traveled in more than 60 countries and lived in Bogota, Colombia, as a Fulbright Scholar and in Mexico City as a summer school student.

When not facing deadline, she can be found hiking or backcountry skiing with James and their dogs, Shelby and Inka.

Mike Carrigan

Mike Carrigan graduated from the United States Naval Academy in 1973 and spent the next 18 years gallivanting around the world at the government's expense. He circumnavigated the globe three times, visiting more than 70 countries. He lived for four years in Brazil, where he trekked down the Amazon River, trudged through the Brazilian rain forest, and tramped along the country's sand-duned northeastern coastline.

In 1991 he retired from the U.S. Navy and settled down in Nevada. He began his second career in 1992 in print journalism, working for the *Lahontan Valley News*, a daily newspaper in Fallon, Nevada. During his four years as a general assignment reporter, he roamed over, around and through northern Nevada, searching for a Pulitzer Prize–winning story. He never found one, but he did manage to win 21 writing awards from the Nevada Press Association and to earn a master's degree in journalism from the University of Nevada, Reno. His fiction writing appeared in *Nevada Sampler*, a book introducing 11 new Nevada writers, and his short story, "The Chessmen," won first place in *Anthology Magazine*'s 1997 writing contest.

He hung up his reporter's notebook and pen in 1996 and now teaches journalism at UNR. He was elected to the Sparks City Council in 1999.

He lives in Sparks with his wife Cora, an elementary school teacher, and their 17-year-old daughter Molly. Ashley, their 22-year-old daughter, is a senior at UNR majoring in international affairs. The Carrigan family cannot shake the wanderlust and still travels extensively during their summer vacations. Their ever-vigilant border collie Emma stands guard over the backyard, hoping one day for a lapse in security so that she too can roam the Reno/Sparks area.

Acknowledgments

Jeanne Lauf Walpole

Writing about this special corner of the world has been delightful; after all, most people enjoy talking about the things they love (writers especially!). But compiling the immense amount of information needed to make this book as useful and accurate as possible required the help of countless sources. Although it's impossible to list them all, my thanks go to every one of those people who answered phone calls, gave tours and interviews and mailed written materials in my pursuit of up-to-date information about the Reno/Tahoe area. I'm deeply grateful they shared their thoughts and knowledge with me.

A few individuals went above and beyond the call of duty to help: Larry Herman shared his passion for big cats at the Sierra Safari Zoo; Jenny Mercer took me on an indoor safari at the Safari Suite in the Peppermill Hotel Casino Reno; Rick Sorensen explained slot machines from A to Z at International Game Technology; and the staff at North Tahoe Regional Park zipped around the trails on snowmobiles to measure the exact number of ski-able kilometers.

And last, but by no means least, thanks to James, Shelby and Inka for your patience in missed walks as I worked to meet the periodic deadlines.

Special thanks go to our proofreader, Marilyn King, for her sharp eye and tireless dedication in preparing this book for the printer at long last.

Mike Carrigan

Whew! What a project. Writing this guide turned out to be as monumental a task as the Donner Party's trek over the Sierra. Like that pioneer wagon train, we had our breakdowns and setbacks, but unlike them, we weathered the storms with only a little gnashing of teeth.

This guide was definitely a team effort so my first thanks goes out to my writing partner Jeanne. She was the beacon of light who kept me from running aground with her sage advice and wonderful words of wisdom.

Next, my thanks go out to Doug and Robyn Moore, my dear Aussie friends, whom I dragged around the Reno/Tahoe area during their "hols." And a special thanks to Doug for accompanying me on the greatest golfing tour of my life.

To the Richards brothers, Steve and Mike, probably two of the best fishermen and hunters in Nevada, for sharing their secrets and their great fishing and hunting stories. Especially the ones that began with, "You should have been here last week . . ."

A special thanks goes out to the late Mike Land of the University of Nevada, Reno. He was my writing teacher and my friend. Without his definitive book on the history of Reno, our history chapter would have been lacking many interesting facts and figures.

And my last thanks go out to Cora, Ashley and Molly. During the writing of this guide, I disappeared for hours at a time researching and banging on my computer. As always, they supported me 110 percent and never complained.

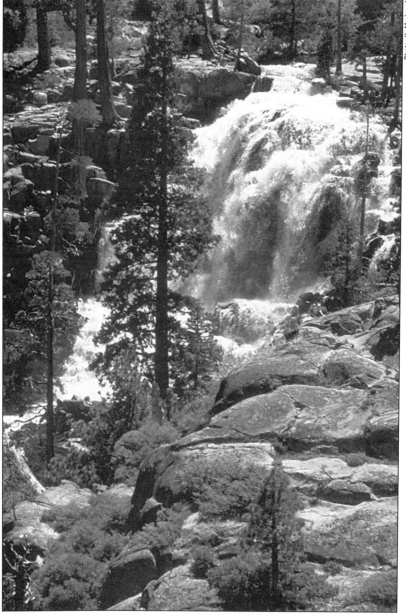

In June, the waterfall near Lake Tahoe, at Emerald Bay,
spills through the rocky gorge toward the lake.

Table of Contents

Directory of Maps

RENO/TAHOE AREA

RENO/SPARKS, NEVADA

NORTH SHORE LAKE TAHOE

To Truckee & I-80

Northstar–at–Tahoe Ski Area

267

Tahoe Vista

Kings Beach

Carnelian Bay

To Steamboat

431

Incline Village

Crystal Bay

Brockway

Lake Tahoe–Nevada State Park

28

Marlette Lk.

To I-80

89

Lake Forest

△*Tahoe SRA*

Tahoe City

CALIFORNIA

NEVADA

28

To Carson City

Tahoe Pines

NORTH SHORE LAKE TAHOE

50

Homewood

Glenbrook

Tahoma

Sugar Pine Pt. St. Park

△

Meeks Bay

LAKE TAHOE

N

89

To South Lake Tahoe

50

To South Lake Tahoe

SOUTH SHORE LAKE TAHOE

We enjoy all 365 days of the year here, and on the Nevada side of the area we offer entertainment that lasts 24 hours per day.

How to Use This Book

You won't have to flip through many pages of *The Insiders' Guide® to Reno & Lake Tahoe* to realize that we've crammed tons of information into this 400+ page book. But don't let its length discourage you. Look over our Table of Contents and you'll get a feel for how easy we made it for you. We have organized the guide in such a way that you don't have to read every chapter. In fact, pick and choose only those chapters that you find useful. We know that if you're just passing through on that well-earned vacation, the Neighborhoods and Real Estate or Healthcare and Wellness chapters might not interest you. But if you are planning a move here, we think these chapters are a must-read.

We do feel that our History chapter is one you should spend an extra few minutes reading. After all, the Reno/Tahoe area is steeped in history. Here, the infamous Donner Party wintered on its ill-fated journey to California. Here, two drunken Irishmen discovered that in a glob of blue-ish mud rested millions of dollars worth of silver. Here, Mark Twain got his literary start. Only a few books recount the history of our area and we've tried to synthesize them down to a few pages so that you can quickly learn about the beginnings of one of the best places to vacation or live in the United States.

No other place in America offers the diversity of the Reno/Tahoe area. We enjoy all 365 days of the year here, and on the Nevada side of the area we offer entertainment that lasts 24 hours per day.

In this book we guide you through what we consider the best restaurants, golf courses, ski resorts, vacation rentals and just about any-

thing else we think would interest visitors and those who are relocating to our paradise.

If you're planning a move here and want to know about our school districts, flip to the Education and Child Care chapter. Then spend some time in our Area Overview chapter; it gives you a feel for the quality of life here plus a quick look at your new neighbors.

If you're here to enjoy the multitude of sports available, turn to our Winter Sports chapter or our Recreation chapter. Since the Nevada side of the area is known for its casinos, we have included a chapter dedicated to the gambling scene, including information on the basics of the games of chance we play here: turn to our Casino Nightlife chapter for all of this.

Because the Reno/Lake Tahoe area is so large we have divided it into four geographical regions: Reno, Sparks, North Shore Lake Tahoe and South Shore Lake Tahoe.

Reno and Sparks make up the only two incorporated cities in the Truckee Meadows, the area that borders the Truckee River from the California state line to a few miles east of Sparks. Each city has its own infrastructure but are so close together they are only separated by a street sign and a zip code.

We define the North Shore of Lake Tahoe as that area from Meeks Bay on the southwestern shore clockwise to Spooner Lake on the northeastern shore. The South Shore is that area from Spooner Lake clockwise back to Meeks Bay.

Our chapters begin with a short introduction, a quick look at what's to come. Then we orient you to the various offerings by dividing most chapters into these four standard geo-

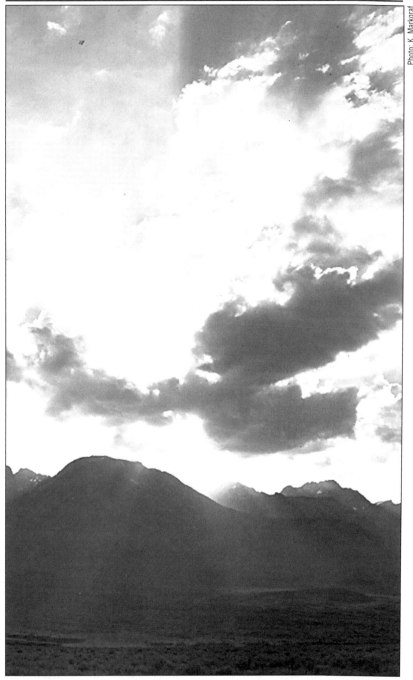

Photo: K. Markgraf

Sunset in the desert sends shafts of color onto the mountains surrounding Reno.

graphical areas — Reno, Sparks, North Shore Lake Tahoe and South Shore Lake Tahoe.

If you're a golfer, for instance, and you want to find a recommended course in Sparks, turn to the Golf chapter and thumb through it until you see the subheading of Sparks. Here we have listed the courses available for public play in Sparks, including length of the course, greens fees, and so on.

Exceptions to this standard geographical breakdown include the Recreation chapter, which is organized by activity, the Restaurants chapter, which is first organized by type of food, several chapters where Reno and Sparks have been combined, and some chapters that are narrative only.

You'll also notice throughout the guide that with every address and telephone number, we have listed the city, state and the area code. We did this because we cover a large area that spans two states and five counties. When making phone calls, remember that the California area code around Lake Tahoe is (530) and that the area code for all of northern Nevada is (775) as of May 1999. We tried to list the toll-free (800, 888 and 877) numbers when possible to help cut down on your long distance phone bills, too.

Throughout this guidebook, we have scattered Insiders' Tips on the bottom of the pages. Some are helpful, some are fun facts and some are just plain interesting area trivia. Whatever they are, we had fun arm-wrestling other Insiders for their well-guarded tips. You'll also find Close-ups throughout the book highlighting information about unique people, events and places around the Reno/Tahoe area. Spend a little time on these because we think they are fun and interesting.

Now, we have tried to include all the information and tips you will need to make your visit or stay in the Reno/Tahoe area enjoyable but we must include this disclaimer: we probably left something out. After all, even Insiders don't know everything. So if you discover a restaurant we overlooked or a daytrip we failed to mention, let us and the publisher know and maybe we'll include it in the next edition. Write to Insiders' Guides, Falcon Publishing, PO Box 1718, Helena MT 59624. Or visit our website at www.insiders.com. Our publisher welcomes all criticisms and comments and we authors welcome all compliments.

Our last recommendation is to buy a road map to accompany this guidebook. Together they will lead you through one of the most spectacular areas in our country.

And don't be afraid to dog-ear the pages or write notes in the margins. (We expect one of you to doodle in the white spaces while the other is driving the car up the Mt. Rose Highway looking for that ski resort — and we don't expect you to color inside the lines either!) This is your guide, so do with it what you want.

We sincerely hope you like the Reno/Tahoe area as much as we do.

Lake Tahoe, North America's largest alpine lake, straddles the state line with two-thirds of it sitting in California and one-third sitting in Nevada.

Area Overview

The down-home attitude and the openness of our citizens make the Reno/Tahoe area a very attractive place not only to live but also to visit. Our climate is moderate (even though snow has been known to fall in June), our views are spectacular and our small-town friendliness is unsurpassed in the United States.

We've grown since the early days and continue to grow, that's for sure, but the rate of growth is tolerable. If you've never been here before, don't expect a northern replica of Las Vegas. We have only a handful of buildings that reach more than three stories high, and we are a heck of a lot more friendly.

The area of coverage for this guide incorporates a large territory (we have a lot of land here) so we have divided it into four locations: Reno, Sparks, North Shore and South Shore of Lake Tahoe.

Reno and Sparks are sister cities that butt up against each other in the Nevada county of Washoe, which stretches from the northeastern tip of Lake Tahoe to the Oregon border.

Lake Tahoe, North America's largest alpine lake, straddles the state line with two-thirds of it sitting in California and one-third sitting in Nevada. The lake is bordered by Placer and El Dorado counties in California and Washoe, Carson and Douglas counties in Nevada. More than 60 creeks flow into Lake Tahoe but only the Truckee River flows out of the lake, on its meandering route through Reno and Sparks to eventually empty into Pyramid Lake, north of Reno.

We have defined the North Shore of Lake Tahoe as that area from Meeks Bay on the southwestern side of the lake clockwise to Spooner Lake, near the intersection of Nev. Highway 28 and U.S. Highway 50. The South Shore is defined as the area from Spooner Lake clockwise around Lake Tahoe back to Meeks Bay.

We'll describe these four areas in a little more detail later in this chapter, but first, some general information on the Reno/Tahoe area as a whole:

Statistics for the Reno/Tahoe area:

Median Age: 36.5
Percent White: 78.9%
Percent Latino: 11.6%
Percent Asian/Pacific Islander: 5.3%
Percent African American: 2.5%
Percent Native American: 1.7%
Percent Male: 50.4%
Percent Female: 49.6%
Average Annual Income: $29,528
Average Cost of a Home: $132,000
Number of Hotel/Motel Rooms: 28,313
Number of Golf Courses in the Area: 31
Average Mean Temperature: 53 degrees

Population Growth

Nevada continues to lead the western states in percentage of population growth. The state grew from 1.6 million in 1995 to 1.8 million in 1998 and is predicted to add about 100,000 new residents each year, mostly in the south. Now, to some in Nevada, leading the western states in population growth is not something to be proud of, but when you think about it, some U.S. cities have bigger populations than the entire state of Nevada so the numbers aren't that scary. Besides, the population is scattered across 110,000 square miles of land making the overall population density only 16 people per square mile — and that isn't so bad.

Most of the population is concentrated in Las Vegas, Reno and Sparks. Reno and Sparks have a combined population of 223,000, with another 90,000 living in the unincorporated communities of Washoe County, including the Nevada side of Lake Tahoe.

The California side of Lake Tahoe boasts a population of about 25,000, with most of the people living in South Lake Tahoe, California. The growth rate around the California side of the lake sits at 2 percent a year, a rate that has remained the same for several years.

New Arrivals and Ethnicity

New arrivals to the Reno/Tahoe area include singles, young families, executives and senior citizens. The male-to-female ratio is almost 50–50. And if being an outsider has you worried, it shouldn't. Only 12 percent of the population on the Nevada side are native-born. Of the rest, 49 percent have lived here more than 11 years, 24 percent between 4 and 10 years and 15 percent of the population has lived here less than 3 years. The numbers on the California side are about the same.

People older than 55 make up more than 20 percent of our population, and to cater to this large percentage of seniors in the community, dozens of services and facilities are scattered throughout the area. They include services in nutrition, legal matters, volunteer programs, transportation, employment and educational opportunities (see our Retirement chapter for more information on services and facilities).

The ethnic characteristics of the area are divided among Whites, Blacks, Native Americans, Asian and Pacific Islanders, and Latinos.

Local Politics

The political makeup of the area sometimes confuses the first-timer, too, because very few voters stick to the so-called "party line." In other words, most of us vote for the person we think will do the best job rather than voting a strictly one-party ticket. The spring candidate's ideas, personality and character mean more to voters here than the political party affiliation. Voters will cross party lines to elect those they think will do the best job and usually support referendums which benefit individual freedoms.

Reno and Sparks

The cities of Reno and Sparks remain a crossroads for travelers just as they were in the late 1800s, but the two cities also have blossomed into prime locations not only for gaming establishments but for corporation headquarters, manufacturing and distribution. We are definitely pro business. Nevada has no corporate income tax, personal income tax, unitary tax, inventory tax, franchise tax on income, franchise fee, estate tax or gift tax. Because of their prime location (and with help from these other incentives), Reno and Sparks can truly be called "The Industrial Hub of the West."

Reno and Sparks are located in the Truckee Meadows, the area that borders the

www.insiders.com

See this and many other **Insiders' Guide®** destinations online.

Visit us today!

INSIDERS' TIP

On St. Patrick's Day, the 1,600 white light bulbs on the Reno Arch are replaced by green bulbs as a tip o' the hat to the area's Irish-American heritage.

Even modern streets in Reno retain traces of the area's history.

Truckee River from the California border to just east of Sparks, at an elevation of 4,400 feet above sea level in a high desert plateau east of the Sierra Nevada mountain range. Daily temperatures on the whole are mild, with a yearly average of 53 degrees. However, during the summer, the difference between the high and low can be as much as 45 degrees, which sometimes causes health problems for people who are not used to such a dramatic temperature range. The humidity is low during the summer (about 25 percent) and moderate during the winter (about 60 percent). The sun shines an average of 300 days a year.

A real problem for some people, though, is the pollen count. When the sagebrush and the cottonwood trees are in bloom, people who have a tendency to suffer from allergies sometimes have it rugged here. And at times during the winter, when the wind is stagnant, a haze layer will hang over the Truckee Meadows. Both the cities of Reno and Sparks restrict wood burning in fireplaces during this hazy period because the fireplace smoke adds to the already less-than-optimum air quality. But as soon as the wind kicks up again, it blows the haze layer away.

Employment

In Reno and Sparks, jobs are plentiful and as varied as our population. The unemployment rate is one of the lowest in the country, at 3.7 percent. The pay scale ranges from very good to minimum wage, but living expenses are low here, especially when compared to California cities like San Francisco and Sacramento. The only area of some concern is that people say the price of housing is too expensive when compared to the average wage.

The gaming industry (casino owners prefer the word "gaming" instead of gambling) provides about one-third of the employment opportunities, but Reno and Sparks are also

INSIDERS' TIP

The area boasts more than 15 ski resorts within 60 miles of Reno.

the leading distributing and warehousing locations in the west. These types of jobs account for a large percentage of employment, too. The area also has a rapidly growing manufacturing sector which is continually hiring. Nevada's Right to Work law also prevents unions from establishing closed shop policies here. In other words, non-union personnel are not precluded from working. The choice of joining a union is up to the worker.

Even though the majority of jobs here are blue collar and service-industry related, we have our fair share of white-collar, executive jobs, too. Just whip open any of our local phone books and you'll see a long list of doctors, dentists and especially attorneys. Plus, with all of our industry, supervisory positions are plentiful if you are qualified. So you see, finding employment in the Reno/Tahoe area isn't a big problem.

Reno

The downtown area of Reno is, without a doubt, the most famous part of town. Its motto, "The Biggest Little City in the World," is recognized around the globe. A stretch of land 3 blocks wide from the Truckee River bridge on First Street north to Interstate 80 is home to the majority of the casinos, but several others are located outside of downtown. The City of Reno has plans to renovate the area along the Truckee River downtown and has already ordered the destruction of several old buildings to make way for a complex of retail shops, restaurants, art galleries and a gigantic movie theater complex.

The majority of people work in Reno because that's where most of the businesses and commercial complexes in the Truckee Meadows are. Several strip malls dot its landscape and many mom-and-pop businesses are scattered around the city. The Truckee Meadows' largest mall, Meadowood, with almost 1,000,000 square feet of retail space, is located in Reno at the intersection of S. Virginia Street and McCarran Boulevard.

Even though the city is growing, the people in Reno still demonstrate that old Western hospitality that most visitors find charming and refreshing — especially if they come here from some of the more populated and hurried cities around the United States.

Sparks

In the early days, when Reno was making its mark as the sin capital of the United States because of the legalization of gambling, the old saying went: "Reno is so close to hell you can see Sparks." Today that rivalry still exists between the two cities, but it's all in fun.

Most of Sparks, about two-thirds, is residential area, with the other third zoned for commercial property, mostly warehouses. The majority of the people who live in Sparks work in Reno. Sparks has about three strip malls and the city fathers say they will OK the building of more to help develop a business base in the "Rail City." But for now, most Sparks residents do their shopping and entertaining in Reno.

Sparks is trying to foster more eating establishments and businesses to help keep residents from leaving the city limits. To accomplish this feat, the City of Sparks continues its redevelopment of Victorian Square, a 6-block entertainment complex in the downtown area along Victorian Avenue, where most of Sparks's casinos are located. When the complex is complete, it will feature tree-lined walkways, fountains, theme shops and an 1880s-

INSIDERS' TIP

The names for some of the silver mines in Virginia City were as diverse as their owners. Some of the names included: The Bonanza, the Monarch, the Gray Eagle, the Columbiana, the Branch Mint, the Maria Jane, the Universe, the Root-Hog-or-Die, the Samson and Delilah, the Treasure Trove, the Golconda, the Sultana, the Boomerang, the Great Republic, the Grand Mogul, the Golden Eagle and the Sarah Jane.

type central plaza for concerts and community events. In the spring of 1998, developers completed Phase One, which includes a 14-screen, state-of-the-art, digital-sound movie theater and a 740-space parking garage.

The city is also developing an old gravel pit into a multi-use park. Sparks Marina Park, as it is known now, used to be called Helm's Gravel Pit. But during the flood of 1997, the pit filled up with water. With the help of a court settlement, the city began to transform the former eyesore into a complex that will feature an outdoor amphitheater, 2 miles of trails, a sandy beach area, shops and restaurants along the water's edge and a trophy trout lake. The city opened the lake to fishing in April of 1999 before construction began on any of the structures. The Nevada Department of Wildlife stocks the lake with 2- to 3-pound trout, and some local anglers have already proclaimed it a good place to fish. We Insiders do like our fishing (see our Fishing and Hunting chapter for some tips on where to cast your line).

Lake Tahoe

Lake Tahoe sits tucked into the Sierra Nevada mountain range at an average elevation of 6,200 feet above sea level. The lake is 22 miles long and 12 miles across, with about 72 miles of shoreline. The higher elevation makes its temperature slightly cooler than the Truckee Meadows. During the summer, most people opt for casual wear like T-shirts and shorts, but sweaters and lightweight jackets are usually worn during the cooler evenings. The sun shines an average of 274 days a year here, but the weather can be unpredictable so a varied wardrobe is advisable when visiting the lake. It's not unusual for snow to fall in every month.

The Lake Tahoe area continues to be the undisputed year-round resort area in the United States. The crystal waters of the country's largest alpine lake and its location, tucked between mountain ranges high in the Sierra Nevada, make it one of the most beautiful spectacles in the West and one of the most favored vacation destinations for Americans for more than 100 years. No other U.S. lake can boast an average water visibility of 125 feet or a 99.7 percent water purity rate — cleaner than drinking water in most U.S. cities.

In the winter, the 20 feet of average snowpack and annual snowfall of up to 40 feet make it a skiers' paradise (see our Winter Sports chapter for details). And starting in the spring when the snow melts away, Lake Tahoe becomes the perfect place to sail, swim, windsurf, fish and play on the countless white beaches (see our Recreation chapter for more). The sun shines a lot here and, as the Lake Tahoe Resort Association says, "Lake Tahoe kids smell like summer. It's the combination of fresh mountain air, sunscreen, dirt, sweat, popsicles and frantic child energy."

Employment

From our description of the year-round activities, you can see that the No. 1 industry here is outdoor adventure, so the majority of jobs involve catering to tourists year-round.

North Shore and South Shore Communities

The communities along the North Shore and South Shore of Lake Tahoe are varied: small and big, sleepy and bustling. One exists for every mood and every perspective. The North and South shores' communities range from one with an Old West flavor to one with a heart-pounding nightclub atmosphere and, of course, two of the communities depend on the gaming scene.

North Shore
On the California side, the area from Meeks

The Reno Arch

Ask visitors what one thing they remember the most about their trip to Reno and five out of six will say the "Reno Arch" — unless they happened to be the newest $16-million MegaBucks slot machine winner. This famous trademark with its neon lights and slogan, "The Biggest Little City in the World," tends to stick in one's mind.

The arch spans Virginia Street at Commercial Row just south of the railroad tracks and welcomes visitors to the downtown casino area. The current arch with its 800 feet of red neon tubing spelling out "Reno" and its 1,600 light bulbs spelling out the city's slogan is actually the fourth to be hoisted over Virginia Street.

Even though historians will argue that the first arch spanning the street welcomed home Nevada's volunteer cavalry from the Spanish-American War in 1899, they acknowledge that the first to advertise the city with a crown of lights went up in late 1926. The city built the arch to celebrate and advertise the completion of the transcontinental highway system through Reno. It commemorated the completion of the Lincoln Highway and was erected at one of Reno's greatest municipal celebrations with "Reno Transcontinental Highway Exposition" painted across the arch.

The world-famous slogan came later as a result of a 1929 contest held by city fathers to give Reno a motto. Entries included: "Reno: Nevada's Silver Lily"; "Reno: Where Life's Worth Living"; "Reno: The Town Without a Frown"; and "Reno: The Great Divide." But a man from Sacramento, California, offered "The Biggest Little City in the World" and won. The man blatantly copied the slogan advertising the Jeffries–Johnson

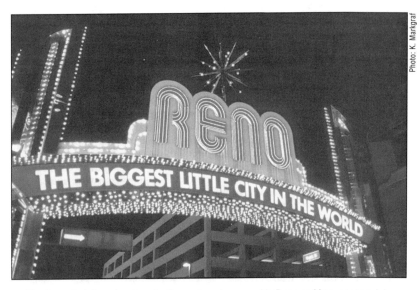

The Reno Arch is a signature for the casino playground in Reno and has appeared in movies, postcards and advertising.

heavyweight title fight that took place in Reno in 1910. That slogan read "The Biggest Little City on the Map," and even though the similarity was obvious, the appraisal committee selected the man's entry and awarded him the $100 prize. Some people still feel that it was a rigged contest.

The arch went dark for several months during the Great Depression when the city could not afford to keep it lighted. But after years of neglect, city workers gave the arch an overhaul in 1935. The structure was reinforced and the light bulbs forming the lettering were replaced with neon lights. Also, the crown and festoon of lights above the city name were removed. This arch lasted until 1964. It now hangs on the Lake Street side of the National Automobile Museum (which is located at 10 Lake Street in Reno).

In 1963 a publicist for Harolds Club, which was the casino located closest to the arch, pushed to raise $100,000 for a new, more modern arch. Reno residents met the challenge and raised the money from business and private citizen donations. The city unveiled the new arch on New Year's Eve in 1963 to help bring in the new year. This arch lasted more than 20 years.

On August 4, 1987, Reno revealed its newest and current arch as part of a multi-million dollar city revival plan called "RENOvation." At that time critics wanted to remove the "tacky" arch and slogan, but proponents called them a friendly way to boast about the city. Today, the debate whether to keep or remove the sign remains. At least once a year during a Reno City Council meeting, someone rekindles the debate over the Reno Arch. In 1999, there was even talk about hiring a stuntman to jump a motorcycle over it.

So the story of the Reno Arch seems to be a never-ending chapter in Reno's history. But though the debate continues, the arch remains a cultural icon and one of the most recognized city symbols in the world.

Bay to Tahoe Pines has the "Old Tahoe" feel to it, with gorgeous mansions tucked away in the woods and expansive white beaches with some of the prettiest scenery along the lake. Old Tahoe–style architecture emerged from the early 20th century when people traveled here by train, men went for groceries in dog sleds and women carried shotguns to scare away the wild animals. The architecture included a rustic look with a mix of native wood and stone on the exterior and a touch of 1890s San Francisco style, plenty of wood on the interior, including the floors, and at least one stone fireplace. This area is home to the Erhman Mansion at Sugar Pine Point State Park, which was the filming location for the movie, *Godfather II*.

Traveling clockwise around the North Shore, the next little community is Tahoe City. This town is noted for its dam, Fanny Bridge (see our Attractions and Kidstuff chapters), and as the birthplace of the Truckee River. But when night falls, it transforms itself into a place where everyone seems to go for nightlife action on the California side of Lake Tahoe. Why? Because it has some of the best spots to go dancing on the North Shore where some of the hippest bands around play (see our Nightlife chapter). The atmospheres of some of its smaller night spots are renowned around the lake as some of the most romantic, too.

This little hamlet is followed by Carnelian Bay, Tahoe Vista and Kings Beach. These towns line a flat stretch along the North Shore

---

INSIDERS' TIP

Weddings and divorces have long been major industries in Nevada, due to the state's short residency requirements.

that is very popular because of its wide, public beaches and easy access to the lake. The stretch also has a variety of small stores that run along the edge of Calif. Highway 28. Carnelian Bay and Tahoe Vista are known for their great restaurants (see our Restaurants chapter) and their unsurpassed views of the lake. Kings Beach, the site of a 7-acre state beach and park of the same name, is the last stop on the California side of the North Shore.

At the extreme northern end of the lake is Crystal Bay, a community of hotels and casinos straddling the Nevada–California border. This is the location of the Cal–Neva Resort, so called because it is built half on the California side and half on the Nevada side of Lake Tahoe. This casino-resort was made famous by one-time owner Frank Sinatra and his "Rat Pack." Frequent visitors in the old days included the Kennedys and some underworld figures. Crystal Bay is also home to the Tahoe Biltmore and the Crystal Bay Club, other noted landmarks on the lake (see our Resorts and Hotels and Motels chapters).

Continuing in a clockwise direction, you come upon Incline Village, Nevada, an upscale community set on a mountainside. In addition to its panoramic views of the lake and its great beaches, the village boasts one of the finest championship golf courses at Lake Tahoe (see our Golf chapter). The cost of housing here is some of the most expensive around the lake (see our Neighborhoods and Real Estate chapter). It is also home to Sierra Nevada College, known to Insiders because of its fifth-year teacher education program (see our Education and Child Care chapter).

From Incline Village to the intersection of U.S. Highway 50, Nev. Highway 28 winds its way around the lake, revealing gorgeous, pristine beaches and sapphire-blue water. The Ponderosa Ranch, film location for the TV series *Bonanza*, sits just off the highway on the way out of town; down the road from the ranch is Sand Harbor, part of Lake Tahoe–Nevada State Park and home to summer music concerts and a Shakespeare festival in August (see our chapters one Parks, Recreation, Annual Events and The Arts).

South Shore

Spooner Lake sits near the intersection of U.S. 50 and Nev. 28 and is the first landmark to define Lake Tahoe's South Shore on our clockwise tour. Down U.S. 50, Cave Rock is the next landmark: you have to drive through a 25-yard tunnel carved from solid rock.

Zephyr Cove sits along the shoreline and is home to a mile of sandy, white beach. Zephyr Cove Beach is one of the best areas around the lake to bring the family to enjoy tons of water activities, including parasailing, water skiing and Jet Skiing (see our Recreation and Kidstuff chapters). It is also the home port of the M.S. *Dixie II*, a paddle wheel vessel which cruises the lake.

At Lake Tahoe's extreme south shore, on the Nevada side of the California-Nevada border, sits Stateline, the major casino center on the lake, with quality hotel-resorts featuring great dining, big-time entertainment and, of course, gambling. Caesar's Tahoe, Harrah's Lake Tahoe, Harvey's Resort Hotel/Casino and the Lake Tahoe Horizon Casino Resort sit snugly along U.S. 50 here, waiting for those of you who feel lucky (see our Resorts and Casino Nightlife chapters for more information). Edgewood Golf Course is located here as well (see our Golf chapter).

Traveling over the California state line, you'll come upon Heavenly Ski Resort in the town of South Lake Tahoe. The resort sits high in the mountains, providing panoramic views of the Nevada desert and the entire lake. A tram runs year-round to transport passengers straight up the mountainside to enjoy skiing in the winter and lunch and the view, all year. South Lake Tahoe is the largest town on the lake and has one of the only two small airports serving Lake Tahoe. Many shops, restaurants, bars and motels line U.S. 50, which cuts through the heart of town.

Continuing around the lake, you come upon Emerald Bay State Park, a sparkling green inlet, secluded and framed by mountain peaks. Nestled on its shores is one of the most photographed spots in America — Vikingsholm Castle. The 38-room mansion was built in 1920, and some call it the finest example of Scandinavian architecture in the United States. This spot is also the jumping-off point for hikers burning to explore the high oounliy and the 130 mountain lakes of the Desolation Wilderness, a 63,500-acre nationally designated wilderness area. Hikers have been known to walk the trails of this area for weeks before coming back to "civilization." (A wilderness area is one in which the government has restricted access to only hiking and horseback riding; no motorized vehicles are allowed.)

So take the best in entertainment, gaming, dining and accommodations, mix them with real, down-home Western hospitality and every outdoor activity you can name and what do you have? The premier vacation and living location in the United States — if not in the world. Read on to discover why we think the Reno/Tahoe area is the ultimate playground.

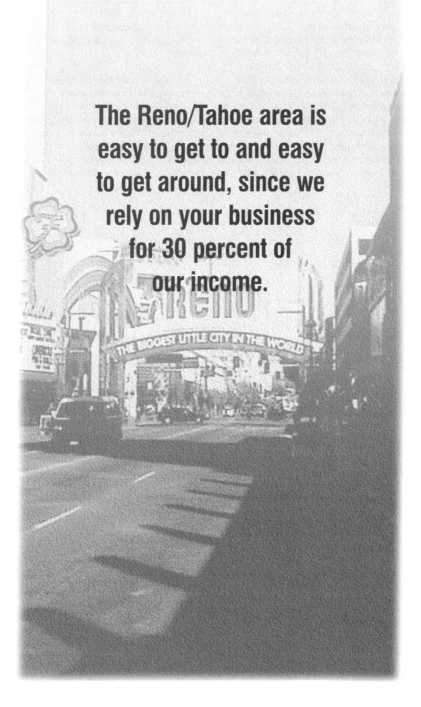

The Reno/Tahoe area is easy to get to and easy to get around, since we rely on your business for 30 percent of our income.

Getting Here, Getting Around

The Reno/Tahoe area is easy to get to and easy to get around. We make sure of that, since we rely on your business for 30 percent of our income. So we have plenty of plane, bus and train services that get you here and plenty of ground transportation to whisk you around. If you use any of these commercial modes of transportation to get here, we definitely recommend renting a car or an SUV once you arrive. You'll need to be mobile so you can visit the many fascinating sights waiting for you around the area.

Lake Tahoe sits about 45 minutes to an hour away from Reno/Sparks and if you're planning to visit the lake, it's more convenient for you if you have your own car. That way, you can stop and smell the pine trees at your leisure. But if you don't like to drive, especially during our snowy winter months, don't worry, because we have gobs of commercial ground transportation to get you around.

Reno/Sparks

The Reno/Tahoe Visitors' Information Center likes to call the cities of Reno and Sparks the hub of an extensive transportation area. The teenagers here like to call the same area an island. And even though the teenagers are partially correct (Reno and Sparks are somewhat isolated from the rest of the West), getting here is extremely easy.

The area is accessed by two major highways, many commercial and commuter airlines, bus transportation and train service. And the blessed thing to remember when you get here is that traveling around the city is even easier. We have no rush hour to speak of and

the only traffic backups occur downtown on Virginia Street in front of the casinos (though these delays are more fun than they are tiresome). Most of the congestion is caused by revelers charging across the street, flitting from one casino to another, and by drivers cruising up and down the little strip watching the people parade.

The one driving problem we do have, though, is potholes. We seem to grow them here like Iowa farmers grow corn. The local daily newspaper even runs a section warning drivers of the latest road construction schedule and pothole alert. The phenomenon is horrendous during the winter and just plain terrible during the summer when road construction crews clog some streets attempting to fix the holes.

On a happier note, the Reno/Tahoe International Airport is the easiest international airport in the United States to get to, park at and fly out of. Several access routes are available to whisk travelers in and out, and we have never heard of anyone missing a flight because of backed-up traffic. The new three-story parking garage makes finding a parking spot easy, and local lore holds that hassles are few and far between.

The Regional Transportation Commission's (RTC's) Citifare bus line provides the Reno/Sparks area with its public transportation service, and Amtrak provides daily east- and westbound train service.

Highways

The location of the general highway system entering and leaving the Reno/Sparks area hasn't changed much since the 1860s when the east–west emigrant trail converged with the north–south trail at Lake's Crossing in downtown Reno. Today, the area is situated on two major highway corridors: Interstate 80 and U.S. Highway 395.

Heading westbound, I-80 links the area to California through Donner Pass in the Sierra Nevada mountains. Sacramento is about 133 miles away and San Francisco lies beyond at 224 miles from downtown Reno. I-80 eastbound transverses the entire northern part of the state, pops you out at Wendover, Nevada, and leads on to Salt Lake City, Utah, some 520 miles from Reno.

U.S. 395 south leads from Reno to southern California trekking through Nevada's capital, Carson City, and the mountain town of Bishop, California, and eventually to Los Angeles about 472 miles down the highway. Heading north on U.S. 395, you slice through the extreme northeastern part of California and on into Oregon at Goose Lake about 240 miles away.

Now you see why the teens facetiously call Reno an island: every other big city is quite a few miles down the road from the area.

Surface Streets

If Reno is the heart of northern Nevada, then Virginia Street is its major artery. This main drag bisects Reno in a north–south direction and terminates north and south of the city where it converges with U.S. 395. Virginia Street, where it crosses the Truckee River at the old site of Lake's Crossing, is also the location of most of the casinos in Reno and the zero-zero point for the street-numbering system, which is set up as a grid. For example, Fourth Street west of Virginia Street is called

W. Fourth Street and switches to E. Fourth Street, you guessed it, east of Virginia Street. The north–south roads are similarly split, using the Truckee River as their boundary, so streets are labeled north on the north side of the river and labeled south on the south side. The higher the address number, the farther it is from downtown, the Truckee River and Virginia Street.

Another major thoroughfare that literally encircles Reno/Sparks is McCarran Boulevard. This four-lane road loops metropolitan Reno/Sparks and is about 23 miles in length. Insiders use the boulevard to quickly travel from one part of the area to another and avoid the many smaller cross streets and traffic signals. The speed limit is 45 miles per hour, and it's a convenient way to avoid downtown congestion. McCarran is called N. McCarran north of its intersection with I-80 and S. McCarran south of the intersection.

The casinos use a 24-hour, three-shift schedule for their employees, but most of the other working folks here are locked into a normal day-shift. Even though the rush hour here is minimal, a prudent driver will stay away from the intersection of I-80 and U.S. 395 during the early morning and late afternoon. Insiders call the eight on- and off-ramps of the two converging roadways the Spaghetti Bowl and even though traffic rarely comes to a halt, it does slow to a crawl for 15 or 20 minutes during the commute times. We suggest you use McCarran Boulevard rather than I-80 or U.S. 395 because McCarran will get you to where you need to go even if it adds a few miles to your journey during heavy traffic.

The driving rules of the road here are not complicated, but there are a few things to be aware of. Pedestrians in the casino area of

INSIDERS' TIP

Telephone the California Department of Transportation for road reporting service in California 24 hours a day at (530) 445-7623. In Nevada, call the Nevada Department of Transportation anytime, day or night, at (775) 793-1313.

downtown Reno and in the Victorian Square area of Sparks are notorious for charging in front of vehicles, while avoiding crosswalks and ignoring stop signs and red traffic lights. Special care must be taken when driving around foot traffic in these areas.

A big no-no here is failure to observe the speed limit in a school zone. Usually a flashing yellow light and a marked sign will alert drivers to the mandatory 15 mile-per-hour limit. A lapse will cost you about $250.

Speed limits here often prove to be a problem for the visitor who is not accustomed to the faster speeds allowed on our interstate. On the rural highways, the limits range from 55 to 65 miles per hour, but on sections of I-80 drivers are allowed to drive at 70 miles per hour, so due care must be observed.

One last note about driving in Reno: Nevada laws on driving under the influence (DUI) of alcohol or drugs are tough. If chemical tests show that a motorist has a blood alcohol concentration of .010 or more, or any detectable amount of a controlled substance, the first offense brings with it a revoked driver's license for 90 days, a mandatory jail sentence of 2 days to 6 months and a fine of $200 to $1,000. The second DUI within 7 years yields a revoked driver's license for 1 year, a mandatory jail sentence of 10 days to 6 months and a $500 to $1,000 fine. If a motorist is convicted of a third DUI in Nevada, regardless of which state the first two were in, the mandatory sentence is 1 to 6 years in the Nevada State Prison, a revoked driver's license for 3 years and a $2,000 to $5,000 fine. A DUI conviction causing death or serious injuries will result in a prison term of up to 20 years.

Basically the rule of thumb here is: one drink, take a taxi. From one end of Reno to the other is only about a $20 cab ride. So listen to the Insiders on this one — the odds are against you if you drink and/or do drugs and drive.

Airports

Reno/Tahoe International Airport
2001 E. Plumb Ln., Reno, Nev.
• **(775) 328-6400**

As we said before, the Reno/Tahoe International Airport is the easiest international airport in the United States to get to, park at and fly out of. The airport provides for 127 daily departures with nonstop service to 23 destinations in the United States and Canada, making it a snap to catch a plane here. The airport provides a full range of aviation services for the Reno/Sparks area, western Nevada and northeastern California. It is within the Reno city limits and butts up against the City of Sparks. The commute time to the airport from the majority of the hotel/casinos in the area is about 15 minutes and the drive is less than an hour from Lake Tahoe.

Driving to the airport from anywhere in the Reno/Sparks area is a breeze. The easiest access is to take U.S. 395 (either north or south, depending on your starting location) to the airport exit and follow the signs to the terminal area. If you're in downtown Reno, follow Virginia Street, Wells Avenue or Kietzke Lane (or any other north–south street) until you hit Plumb Lane. Go east on Plumb Lane until it ends at the airport, then follow the signs to the terminal.

The airport is classified a medium hub, primary commercial airport by the FAA and is served by most major commercial and two commuter airlines, including Reno Air, the area's hometown airline. Reno Air (recently acquired by American Airlines) and Southwest Airlines provide for most of the passenger service here.

Reno/Tahoe is also used by cargo carriers, general aviation and military aircraft. The airport served more than 150,000 takeoffs and landings in 1997 and handled more than 1.8 million passengers, 4.5 million pounds of mail and 18.2 million pounds of cargo.

The airport covers some 1,400 acres and is staffed 24 hours per day. The terminal space includes U.S. Customs and Immigration offices and 22 second-level gates on two concourses. The airport is designated a landing rights and Port of Entry airport. It has one set of parallel runways, the longest at 11,000 feet, and one crosswind runway at 6,100 feet in length. Three fixed-wing operators provide a full range of services for private aircraft.

The airport is also home to the Nevada Air National Guard (NANG), the "High Rollers," who gained fame during the Persian Gulf War flying RF-4 Phantom reconnaissance aircraft.

Today the High Rollers fly the C-130 Hercules transport aircraft to provide rapid pickup and airlift duties. The squadron currently has 12 C-130s based at Reno/Tahoe airport.

Thanks to a new $31 million project to increase parking by 25 percent and improve the roadway in front of the terminal, dropping off and picking up passengers is stress-free and extremely easy. The 2,400 space, three-story parking garage also takes the hassle out of finding a parking space.

The garage offers long-term, short-term and valet parking. The long-term fees are $2 per hour, with a daily maximum of $7. In short-term parking, the first 20 minutes are free, then the fees creep to $1 per hour, with a daily maximum of $12. Valet parking is $5 for the first two hours, up to a daily maximum of $10. Although valet parking is a little more expensive, it's well worth it: when you step off the plane, you can pick up their direct line to summon your car. It will be parked in front of the terminal, with the engine running and the heater or air conditioning on, when you step out of the building. Airport officials say the $12 maximum in short-term parking is to keep the section relatively free from long-term parkers, making it easier to find a parking space.

See our Rental Car and Other Ground Transportation sections in this chapter for information on renting cars at the airport and other ways to get to and from the airport.

Reno Stead Airport
4895 Texas Ave., Reno, Nev.
• **(775) 328-6570**

The Reno Stead Airport is a general aviation airport located 9 miles north of downtown Reno off U.S. 395. The airport has two asphalt runways (8,090 feet and 7,601 feet), lights, hangars and full services. General aviation pilots have a choice of two fixed-based operators — Aviation Classics Limited and General Aviation Services. The airport has an unstaffed tower with a UNICOM frequency of 122.8. Pilots are not charged landing fees.

Aviation Classics Limited charges $5 per day for tie-down fees and provides Jet A and 100 LL (low-lead) fuel. General Aviation Services has a tie-down fee of $4 per day and provides 80-87 octane and 130 octane fuel. Both companies provide cut rates on monthly tie-down fees beginning at $36, depending on the size of the aircraft.

The Nevada Army National Guard has a facility located about 1 mile from the airport out of which military helicopter activities are conducted. Reno Stead Airport is also home

Photo: Reno/Tahoe International Airport

The Reno/Tahoe International Airport is known for its easy-to-get-into and -out-of facility.

to the annual Reno Air Races in September, closing the airport to all general aviation aircraft (see our Annual Events chapter for details about the Reno Air Races).

Rail Service

The railroads literally put Reno and Sparks on the map and today, the Union Pacific Railroad still provides cargo shipments by rail through the Truckee Meadows. (The railroad is a somewhat controversial subject in the Reno/Sparks area since further plans call for more than 20 freight trains a day to pass through downtown. Some residents fear the resulting disruption of traffic and emergency services. Sinking the tracks into a multimillion dollar train trench is a favored solution, according to some, including the mayor of Reno.)

Reno/Sparks's railroad heritage notwithstanding, if you're wishing to experience the old-fashioned, unhurried method of passenger train transportation these days, you have to look to Amtrak, America's train service.

Amtrak
135 E. Commercial Row, Reno, Nev.
• **(775) 329-8638, (800) 872-7245**

Amtrak provides passenger train service through Reno, west to the Bay Area and east to Chicago. The west- and eastbound California Zephyr make one daily stop each in the Truckee Meadows. The westbound California Zephyr, train number 5, stops at the downtown Reno station at mid-morning on its way to the Bay Area. The eastbound California Zephyr, train number 6, stops at the Reno station in the late afternoon on its way to Chicago. Call Amtrak for exact departure times.

The one-way coach fare to the Bay Area from Reno runs anywhere from $41 to $88 depending on the time of year. The coach fare from Reno to Chicago can vary from $117 during the low season (August and September) to $213 during the rest of the year.

The California Zephyr offers sleeping cars, dining cars and a sightseeing lounge. The trip to the Bay Area is about 8 hours. The Chicago run takes about 48 hours.

Buses

The old joke around here is that not a lot of visitors arrive by bus but after a bad night at the craps tables, a lot return home on one. The fact is that riding a bus may not be the fastest and the most sophisticated method of travel, but it is usually the cheapest.

Greyhound Bus Line
155 Stevenson St., Reno, Nev.
• **(775) 322-2970, (800) 231-2222**

Greyhound offers about 22 daily arrivals and departures from Reno, heading to all parts of the United States. Most departures and arrivals are between the hours of 6 AM and 6 PM but the station stays open 24 hours per day, with one bus straggling in around midnight. One-way fares west range from $20 to Sacramento to $32 to San Francisco. The one-way fare to Salt Lake City is $43 and to Las Vegas the fare jumps to $72. Tickets may be purchased at the station at the time of departure, but Greyhound offers discounts if tickets are purchased three to 21 days in advance.

Mass Transit

Citifare
2050 Villanova Dr., Reno, Nev.
• **(775) 348-7433**

Citifare, the public transit service for the area, operates 24 fixed routes in Reno and Sparks. Routes originate at the Citicenter Transit Center in downtown Reno and the Citistation Transit Center in downtown Sparks. Buses travel outbound from these two hubs and go to outlying neighborhoods. The buses run

---

INSIDERS' TIP

Visitors wishing to rent cars here need only a valid driver's license from any state. Non–U.S. citizens usually need an international driver's license.

seven days per week from about 4:30 AM to midnight, though some routes run 24 hours.

Bus fare is $1.25 for a one-way ticket. Seniors older than 60, disabled people and Medicare recipients pay 60¢. Youth between the ages of 5 and 17 ride the bus for 90¢. Children younger than 5 ride free. Citifare does not charge for transfers.

Frequent passengers may purchase daily, weekly and monthly passes, which are good for unlimited riding. Fares for a Daily Pass are: Adult, $3.50; Youth, $2.70; Senior/Disabled/Medicare, $1.80. For a 7-Day Pass, it's Adult, $12.50; Youth, $9; Senior/Disabled/Medicare, $6. For a Monthly Pass, costs are as follows: Adult, $40; Youth, $29; Senior/Disabled/Medicare, $19.

Taxis

On any given day, about 400 taxis buzz up and down the streets of Reno and Sparks. Riders may hail a cab, but a phone call ahead is the best way to guarantee a ride when you need one. Most taxis cluster around the big hotel/casinos and the airport.

Two of the three local companies — Reno-Sparks Cab, (775) 333-3333, and Whittlesea Checker Taxi, (775) 322-2222 — charge $1.80 for a step-in fee for the first one-sixth of a mile, then $1.65 per additional mile.

The Yellow/Deluxe Cab Company, (775) 355-5555, charges $1.65 for a step-in fee for the first one-sixth of a mile then $1.50 per additional mile. This company also offers luxury cabs like Cadillacs and Lincolns at no extra charge.

None of the companies charges extra for additional passengers, but the maximum per taxi is five. On average, a taxi ride from the airport to downtown Reno is about $7, and from the airport to downtown Sparks the fee is about $11.

Limousines

Traveling in the plush comfort of a limousine is the most comfortable and decadent way to cruise the streets of Reno/Tahoe. Heads turn when you pull up in your Lincoln Town car with the darkened windows, and everyone strains their necks trying to capture a glimpse of who might be riding in unabashed style. If you think you would relish this type of transportation, Reno has three limousine services to accommodate you.

Most of the stretch limos have a wet bar and a stereo but some come equipped with a television, cellular phone and a sliding moonroof. But the biggest attraction, as far as we are concerned, is that the vehicle is driven by someone else. These chauffeurs are not only the most competent drivers in the area, but they are also the most knowledgeable. If a limo chauffeur doesn't know where to find something or how to get someplace, it probably doesn't exist.

The average cost for these luxury automobiles with drivers is $42 per hour without a wet bar and $55 per hour with a wet bar. Operators include Bell Luxury Limousine, (775) 786-3700, Sierra West Limousine, (775) 329-4310 and Executive Limousine, (775) 333-3300. Executive Limousine requires a two-hour minimum for their vehicles, and all of the operators say that there's a three-hour minimum for a trip from Reno to Lake Tahoe.

A number of the larger hotels, motels and casinos have courtesy limousine and bus service on call. Check with your hotel/motel or casino for details.

If a less formal mode of transportation is more to your liking and pocketbook, Bell Luxury Limousine also operates a 20-passenger bus with a $40 per hour rental rate.

Rental Cars

We really wish we could tell you that a car is not necessary when you visit Reno/Tahoe, but we can't. Sure, you can get along without one if all you want to do is hang around your hotel or a casino day and night. But to really enjoy all that the area has to offer, you need to be mobile. You'd be missing so much of the fun if you didn't have a convenient way to get around. We think that renting a car is the best way to see Reno/Tahoe. Plus, a rental car will allow you to experience some of the daytrips we suggest later in this guide.

Rates vary from agency to agency but the average cost for an economy car with unlimited miles starts at $18 per day. The big thing to remember when you rent a car here, though, is that every government agency wants a piece of the rental-car action. So, above and beyond the daily rate, renters have to pay a 10 percent airport surcharge, a 7 percent Nevada sales tax and a 6 percent Department of Motor Vehicle license tag fee, for a whopping total of 23 percent tacked on to the price of your rental car. Most companies also offer a $10 per day collision damage waiver. Some companies will let you use a cash deposit when renting, but most will want to see a major credit card, a valid driver's license and a second piece of picture I.D. Most companies here require the driver to be at least 25 years old.

The majority of the rental agencies maintain rental booths in the Reno/Tahoe airport just off the baggage-claim area. These companies are:

Advantage, (775) 825-9191, (800) 777-5500
Alamo, (775) 323-7940, (800) 462-5266
Avis, (775) 785-2727, (800) 331-1212
Budget, (775) 785-2545, (800) 527-0700
Dollar, (775) 348-2800, (800) 800-4000
Hertz, (775) 785-2554, (800) 654-3131
National, (775) 785-2576, (800) 227-7368
Resort, (775) 348-1535
Thrifty, (775) 329-0096, (800) 367-2277

Some of the other companies that are away from the airport and are very reliable include:

Agency, (775) 828-3772
Enterprise, (775) 329-3773
Lloyds International, (775) 348-4777
U-Save, (775) 323-0880

Lake Tahoe

Even though Lake Tahoe rests high in the Sierra Nevada range, tucked in neatly between the borders of California and Nevada, it is quite easy to reach as long as the weather is cooperative. But during the winter months, large amounts of snowfall can make getting here quite a challenge. Be sure to check road conditions before setting out in the winter: for California roads call (530) 445-7623 and for Nevada call (775) 793-1313.

A four-wheel-drive vehicle is ideal for all road conditions and chains may be required on cars in the winter. (See our Winter Sports chapter for more about winter driving.)

Be aware that traffic in and out of the Lake Tahoe Basin is very heavy at certain times of the year and hours of the day. The days immediately before and after holidays and weekends (when everyone seems to arrive and leave all at once) sometimes see stalled traffic. Accidents and snowfall can further complicate driving conditions.

Traffic out of ski resorts is very heavy from 3 to 4:30 PM, especially from Alpine Meadows, Squaw Valley USA and Northstar–at–Tahoe ski resorts. To avoid the congestion you may want to stay away from these areas at that time of day if you're not skiing.

Traveling to and from Lake Tahoe earlier or later than the masses is advised if possible. But usually the 72 miles around the lake can easily be traveled by car with little or no problem. A number of mass transit vehicles afford you cheap and reliable transportation if you don't care to drive yourself.

Highways

Six highways lead into Lake Tahoe, and from the Reno/Sparks area you have the option of using five of the six. The most reliable and easiest way out of the Truckee Meadows to Lake Tahoe is the I-80 route.

This route uses I-80 west from Reno to the California town of Truckee. From Truckee, Calif. Highway 267 cuts south past Northstar–at–Tahoe to the northern part of the lake. The highway will pop you out at Kings Beach.

If you stay on I-80 through Truckee, you can pick up another scenic route to the lake. Just before Donner Memorial State Park, Calif. Highway 89 juts south to the lake. This highway passes by Squaw Valley and Alpine Meadows ski resorts and brings you out at Tahoe City.

The Reno-to-Tahoe route traveled by most Insiders is over the Mt. Rose summit. To reach this route, you want to travel out of Reno on U.S. 395 south until the road intersects with Nev. Highway 431. The highway climbs over the summit to the lake and brings you out just north of Incline Village. A word of warning here: this route is by far the most scenic but it is also the most dangerous. The highway is loaded with switchbacks and climbs steeply up the mountain from 4,400 feet to more than 8,000 feet at the summit, then rushes down to the lake. In the summer, driving the skinny two-lane road can be heart-pounding and in the winter, it can be treacherous. Even though the highway is tight and winding, Insiders will fly up and down it no matter what the road conditions. So if you find yourself with a death-grip on the steering wheel and holding up more than three cars, look for a pullout and let the faster traffic pass. We will also give you odds that four out of five Insiders will not know where Nev. 431 is located. We know it as the Mt. Rose Highway. (See our Attractions chapter for details about this scenic drive.)

Another route to Lake Tahoe from Reno involves driving to Carson City via U.S. 395 south. Outside of Carson City, U.S. Highway 50 heads west over Spooner Summit to the lake. U.S. 50 brings you out just north of Zephyr Cove, just a short drive from Stateline.

If you continue out of Carson City on U.S. 395, you can travel another scenic route to Lake Tahoe. U.S. 395 continues south until it intersects Nev. Highway 88 near Minden. Nev. 88 intersects with Nev. Highway 207, known to Insiders as the Kingsbury Grade. This highway stretches over Daggett Pass to the lake. The highway intersects U.S. 50 just north of Stateline. Once again, this road is scenic but treacherous, especially during the

winter. Great care should be used when driving this road.

From Sacramento, two routes exist to Lake Tahoe, the I-80 route to Truckee and the U.S. 50 route up the south side of the lake. The I-80 route is the much faster way but U.S. 50 is the more scenic. U.S. 50 passes Echo Lake and the Upper Truckee River and brings you out at South Lake Tahoe.

Surface Streets

Only one highway encircles the entire lake, but it changes its designation four times. Beginning at Kings Beach and heading clockwise, the highway is Nev. Highway 28 until it intersects with U.S. 50 near Spooner Lake. It's called U.S. 50 until outside of South Lake Tahoe, where it changes to Calif. 89 to Tahoe City. From Tahoe City to Kings Beach it is Calif. Highway 28. Most of the other streets in the little towns that dot the lake are easy to find with the help of a good local map.

Airports

Reno/Tahoe International Airport
See write-up earlier in the chapter.

Truckee Tahoe Airport
10356 Truckee Airport Rd., Truckee, Calif.
• (530) 587-4119

The Truckee Tahoe Airport is a general aviation airport located between Truckee and Kings Beach. The airport offers a full range of airport services for corporate and private aircraft. The airport has a 24-hour UNICOM year-round on frequency 122.8 and has an Automated Weather Observation System (AWOS) on frequency 118.0 or by phone at (530) 587-4599.

The airport has two paved runways (7,000 feet and 4,650 feet) and offers 24-hour aircraft fueling with 80 octane, 100LL (low lead) and

---

INSIDERS' TIP

If you're a new resident to the area, you have one month to get a Nevada driver's license and register your vehicles.

Jet A fuel. It has 210 paved aircraft tie-downs at $8 per night and up, depending on the size of the aircraft. The airport offers scenic flights, summer biplane and glider rides, aircraft charters, aircraft rentals, instruction and aircraft maintenance. Rental cars are available at Airport Auto Rental, (530) 587-2688. The airport also offers seasonal ground transportation.

Lake Tahoe Airport
1901 Airport Rd., South Lake Tahoe, Calif.
• **(530) 542-6180**

The Lake Tahoe Airport is a single runway, general aviation airport located just south of the "Y" intersection of Calif. 89 and U.S. 50. The 8,544-foot runway is paved and the airport's tower is staffed on frequency 118.4 from 8 AM to 8 PM daily. The airport is served by Tahoe Air, (888) 824-6324, a full-service all-jet airline with flights to Los Angeles (LAX) and San Jose, California.

The airport does not charge a landing fee for private aircraft but charges $10 per day and up for overnight tie-down fees, depending on the size of the aircraft. Jet A and 100 LL (low lead) fuel is available from Oasis Aviation, (530) 541-2110. Charter and sightseeing flights as well as aircraft rentals are offered by Alpine Lake Aviation, (775) 588-4748.

Rail Service

Amtrak
10065 Donner Pass Rd., Truckee, Calif.
• **(530) 587-3822, (800) 872-7245**

The California Zephyr makes two daily stops in Truckee, which serves as a jumping-off point for Lake Tahoe. The westbound California Zephyr, train number 5, pulls into the Truckee station in the late morning on its way to the Bay Area. Passengers have just a few minutes to board. The eastbound California Zephyr, train number 6, arrives in Truckee on its way to Chicago at mid-afternoon. Again, passengers only have a few minutes to board. Call Amtrak for ticket price information and specific departure and arrival times.

Buses

Greyhound Bus Lines
Horizon Casino, U.S. Hwy. 50, Stateline, Nev. • **(775) 588-4645**

Greyhound provides three daily departures to Sacramento and San Francisco from the Stateline station. The bus station hours are from 8 AM to 6:30 PM, Monday through Friday.

No Stress Express
Carson City, Nev. • **(775) 333-6955, (877) 829-4864**

This bus line provides daily service from the Reno/Tahoe airport to both North and South Lake Tahoe. Tuesday, Wednesday and Saturday, one bus runs to the North Shore and one to the South Shore; three buses run each route on other days. The company uses vans and mid-sized buses. The one-way fares start at $32 to both shores. Tickets may be purchased at the company's desk behind National Rental Car in the baggage claim area of the airport.

Tahoe Casino Express
(775) 785-2424, (800) 446-6128

This company runs 14 departures from the Reno/Tahoe airport to Lake Tahoe's South Shore hotel/casinos only. The one-way fare is $17 for the 1-hour-and-45-minute drive. Passengers may buy tickets from the Welcome Center at the airport.

Mass Transit

Mass transit is not a problem around the lake. About eight different modes of transpor-

INSIDERS' TIP

Amtrak's California Zephyr stops in Sparks for about 10 minutes but the station is not staffed. Insiders find boarding easier and less stressful at the downtown Reno station. It is staffed and open from 8:30 AM to 5:30 PM, seven days a week.

tation are available to whisk you from one little town to the next and all the beaches and parks in between.

Bus Plus
(530) 542-6077

This service is a 24-hour-a-day ride-share program within the South Lake Tahoe and Stateline areas. Using minivans, this door-to-door service is only $3 per person one-way.

Nifty 50 Trolley
(530) 542-6077

These trolleys resemble open-air San Francisco trolleys but on wheels. They appear June through Labor Day, ferrying passengers from Stateline west to Kiva Beach and from the tram at Heavenly Ski Resort east to Zephyr Cove. Drivers are in early-1900s costume and provide interpretive information and narration about sites and scenes along their routes. The fare for each one-hour route is $2 for adults and $1 for children between 4 and 7 years old. Children younger than 4 ride free. The price for both routes is $3. The trolley operates from 10 AM to 11 PM.

South Tahoe Area Ground Express (STAGE)
(530) 542-6077

This public bus system weaves in and out of the residential districts of the South Shore area from the "Y" intersection of U.S. 50 and Calif. 89 to the casinos at Stateline. The general fare is $1.25 for a one-way passage and $2 for an unlimited day pass. A seniors day pass is $1 and children younger than 8 ride free. Monthly passes are available for $40. The buses operate from 6 AM to midnight.

Tahoe Area Regional Transit (TART)
(530) 581-6365, (800) 736-6365

This public bus service runs from Incline Village to Sugar Pine Point State Park near Meeks Bay and offers shuttle service from Tahoe City to Truckee. Buses on these routes are equipped with racks for bicycles and snow skis. The one-way adult fare is $1.25. Children 5 years old and younger ride for free. All-day passes are $3 for adults, $2 for seniors and $1 for disabled passengers. TART buses operate every hour from 6:30 AM to 6:30 PM, seven days a week.

Tahoe City Trolley
(530) 587-6128

This trolley service operates between Stateline and Tahoe City from late June to Labor Day. The trolley runs a day route from 10:30 AM to 6 PM, serving the west shore to Stateline, and a night route from 6 PM to midnight, serving Squaw Valley to Stateline. The cost is $2.50 per person (including children) for an all-day pass.

Taxis

Taxi companies dot the entire shore of Lake Tahoe.

On the **North Shore** try:
Sunshine Taxi Company, (530) 831-8294
Tahoe Truckee Taxi, (530) 583-8294
Yellow Cab, (530) 546-9090
ZZ Cab, (530) 581-0222
On the **South Shore** try:
All Company Dispatch, (800) 441-8294
Paradise Taxi, (530) 577-4708
Sunshine Taxi Company,(530) 588-5555
Tahoe Keys Taxi, (530) 544-8294

Limousines

The following companies offer limousine service around the lake:
Aladdin Limousines, (530) 544-3333, (800) 546-6009
All Seasons Tahoe Limousine Service, (530) 577-2727, (800) 334-1826
Luxury Limousine of Tahoe, (530) 542-2277, (800) 458-9743

INSIDERS' TIP

Take advantage of riding taxis with a group and splitting the fare. The charge is the same for one to five passengers.

Royal Limousine Service, (775) 825-3900, (800) 660-4546

Sierra Shuttle Service, (530) 550-1777

Sierra West Limousine, (775) 588-1079

Truckee Tahoe Limousine, (530) 587-2160, (800) 255-2160

Rental Cars

North Shore rental agencies include:

A and A Perkins Auto Rental, Truckee, (530) 587-7823

A and A Auto Rental, Truckee, (530) 582-8282

Airport Auto Rental, Tahoe Truckee Airport, (530) 587-2688, (800) 200-2688

Alpine Car Rental, Incline Village, (775) 833-4424

Incline Village Rent-a-Car, Incline Village, (775) 831-3726

South Shore rental agencies include:

Avis, Stateline, (775) 588-4450

Hertz, Stateline, (775) 785-2554

National, Stateline, (775) 588-3629

Tahoe Rent-a-Car, (530) 544-4500

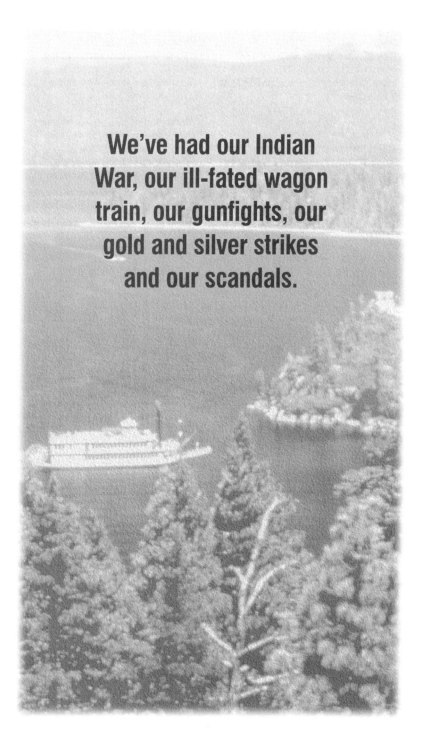

We've had our Indian War, our ill-fated wagon train, our gunfights, our gold and silver strikes and our scandals.

History

The cities in northern Nevada aren't like other cities around the United States, that's for sure. Here you can play slot machines in grocery and convenience stores, visit elephants who live in a casino's parking lot or watch a 60-foot-tall indoor mining rig pump out spendable dollar tokens. Most of the cities are somewhat eccentric with a splash of the fantastic thrown in, and they all have a way of grabbing your attention. Like the rest of Nevada, the Reno/Tahoe area is steeped in history. We've had our Indian War, our ill-fated wagon train, our gunfights, our gold and silver strikes and our scandals. These colorful pieces of history are what make the area so fascinating.

Col. H.B. Maxson, an early Reno/Tahoe pioneer, wrote in his autobiography the following about his introduction to Reno:

"I was reared in a strict Baptist community in New York and was taught to be respectful to all, but sociable with few without being properly introduced. My first lesson in western hospitality was received on a train to Reno.

"A very pleasant man passed through the car addressing everyone as 'my son' and extending the greetings of the day. This was contrary to my teachings and I declined to answer him. But later I observed that everybody spoke to him so I asked the conductor who the old gentleman was and he said with a laugh, 'That's the governor of Nevada.' For the first time I realized that the customs of the West were certainly different from the teachings of the East.

"At the first opportunity I apologized and told the governor that I was taught not to talk with strangers and had heard that the trains out West were filled with confidence men who parted innocent eastern travelers from their money. Whereupon, the governor laughed and told everyone on the train that he had been taken for a three-card monte sharp and when we got to Reno he treated the house at the Old Depot Hotel bar and paid for me to stay in the best room in the house."

And as Insiders, we can assure you things really haven't changed since then.

The First Nevadans

Long before trailblazer John C. Fremont tramped his expedition through the Truckee Meadows (the area bordering the Truckee River from the California state line to just east of what is now Sparks), Native Americans inhabited the state. Although anthropologists claim that more than 27 tribes roamed the Nevada wilderness, only two — the Washoes and the Northern Paiutes — gathered seeds, fished and hunted in the Reno/Tahoe area. These tribes had to search for food constantly, making survival of the individual family their highest priority. The search for food kept them perpetually on the move with little time for leisure.

These two tribes were more fortunate than most of the others in Nevada because, for part of the year, they had two abundant lakes to fish. The Washoes had Lake Tahoe, one of the deepest and highest alpine lakes on the continent, and the Northern Paiutes fished Pyramid Lake, a starkly beautiful watershed 25 miles northeast of present-day Reno. Both tribes also became adept at decoy making and at hunting the waterfowl that used Tahoe and Pyramid lakes as landing zones on their southern migratory trek. The Indians fashioned decoys from wood and tules (long reed-like plants that grow in the wetlands) to attract the birds and used their hunting skills to kill them for food.

The Indians' handicrafts not only included fashioning these elaborate decoys but also included basket weaving. These baskets were not for decoration but were essential tools, a means of carrying food and water.

Their decoy- and basket-making became legendary around Nevada. Experts consider the Washoes to be the best basket makers in the United States; Dat-So-La-Lee, a Washoe Indian who died in 1925, was thought to be the best of the best. She would spend as much as a year working on a single basket. Some of her work can be seen in the Nevada State Museum in Carson City and at the Nevada Historical Society in Reno (see our Attractions and Daytrips chapters).

These early inhabitants of the Reno/Tahoe area didn't plant crops. They were gatherers, so they used their hand-crafted baskets to carry the pine nuts they harvested to supplement their food supply through the sometimes harsh winters. During late fall, they would gather at the piñon groves for the harvest. The men would beat the seed-filled pinecones to the ground with long poles, and the women would collect the cones in their baskets. After the nuts were removed from the cones, cleaned and roasted, the Indians would enjoy a family reunion. So even though the recreational activities of these two tribes were limited, they did make time for personal enjoyment and are even credited with establishing a long-standing Reno/Tahoe tradition — gambling.

That's right, the Washoes and the Northern Paiutes would bet on just about anything, including running games and games of strength and agility. Their wagers sometimes consisted of everything they owned, including their blankets, baskets, jewelry, feathers and even their prized rabbitskin robes. These gambling games would sometimes go on for days and while a few families would walk away rich with new possessions, others were left with literally just the skins on their backs.

These two tribes remained in the area to greet the first white explorers, but soon found them more of a threat to their civilizations than the harshest winter or drought-ridden summer.

Trailblazers, Mapmakers and Risk Takers

"The beaver are so plentiful a man has no

need for traps. The little varmints just jump into your tote-sack."

That's the legend that Jedediah Smith, a trapper with the Rocky Mountain Fur Company, heard in 1827. So he and 15 other trappers blazed a trail into the Reno/Tahoe area to prove the legend of the beaver and to find the mythical San Buenaventura River that supposedly flowed from the Rocky Mountains to the Pacific Ocean. Unfortunately, they found neither.

Smith is credited, however, with being the first white man to cross the present state of Nevada near Reno and the first to encounter and write about the Indian tribes in the area. Because of his early encounter and friendship with the Indians, other early Nevada explorers owed Smith a great deal—especially John C. Fremont, a pathfinder for the U.S. Army engineers.

Even though several pioneers like John Bidwell, John Bartleson and Joseph Chiles crossed northern Nevada before him, Fremont is credited with the exploration of the Reno/Tahoe area. In 1844 he led an expedition through northeastern Nevada to Pyramid Lake and finally to the Truckee Meadows. Fremont, along with legendary scout and frontiersman Kit Carson, charted the new territory and, as Smith attempted years before, searched for the San Buenaventura River. When Fremont first saw a river emptying into Pyramid Lake he thought it might be the Buenaventura, but he realized that it was too small to be the mythical river. He was glad, however, to see his new find teeming with fish. Fremont's band had endured many months in the sparse high desert, living off small game and birds, and the feast of fresh-caught fish was a welcome respite. Fremont's small band filled up on their catch and called the swift river the Salmon-Trout River after the tasty fish. Historians agree that later mapmakers changed the stream's name to the Truckee River after a Paiute chief who served as a guide for other expeditions.

Fremont, Carson and their group pressed on from the Truckee Meadows and first saw Lake Tahoe from the top of Red Lake Peak, now called the Carson Pass. Fremont first

The tremendous impact of mining in the history of the Reno/Tahoe area is memorialized at Miners Park in nearby Virginia City, Nevada.

named this magnificent body of water Lake Bonpland after a botanist but referred to it as Mountain Lake on his maps. The name was later changed to Lake Bigler after a California governor and finally, in 1945, the California Legislature changed the name to Lake Tahoe from a bastardized Indian word meaning "big water."

Fremont's expedition circumnavigated northern Nevada and proved that no such river as the San Buenaventura existed. But, more importantly for scientists, they also determined that the Great Basin of northern Nevada has no outlet and that all the rivers flow inward. Fremont's importance to the area is best summed up by his wife Jesse: "From the ashes of my husband's campfires have sprung cities."

Fremont paved the way for other American pioneers to trek through the Truckee Meadows, but without a doubt the most famous emigrants to the Reno/Tahoe area were members of the ill-fated Donner Party. In 1846, George Donner and his brother, Jake, led an 87-member wagon train from Fort Hall, Idaho, on the Oregon Trail to the Truckee Meadows. The two had read a book by Lansford Hastings, who described a shortcut through the Sierra Nevada mountain range to the promised land

— California. The two Donner brothers persuaded the impatient families that the shortcut was the better route.

After many setbacks suffered during the trek through the treacherous high desert, the Donner Party arrived in the Truckee Meadows in mid-October. After the stark, vast Nevada desert, the plush campsites along the Truckee River were a welcome sight and enticed the party to stay for several days to rest up. This luxury proved fatal.

Fort Hall locals, who knew about the harsh Nevada winters, had warned both brothers to cross the Sierra Nevada before the first snowfall, but members of the weary party easily convinced the leaders to stay. After all, they argued, what harm can a few more days make? But by the time they reached the mountain pass (now called the Donner Pass) between Nevada and California, heavy snows forced them to turn around and to head back toward the Truckee Meadows. As fate would have it, deep snow prevented them from reaching the docile meadows. Instead, the party was forced to pitch camp along a frozen lake (now Donner Lake) to weather out the winter.

The party had no game to hunt and a dwindling food supply. They struggled to stay alive through the harsh winter by eating their pack animals, their shoes and their leather harnesses. But their most gruesome act, the one remembered throughout history, was cannibalism. When their supplies ran out and some of the old people and babies starved to death, members of the Donner Party ate them. When rescuers finally reached the lake in April 1847, they found only 47 of the original 87 members alive. (See our Daytrips Chapter for more information on Donner Memorial Park in Truckee.)

Although the Hastings Cutoff garnered a reputation as a death route, pioneers continued to use the shortcut to reach California, even more so when gold was discovered outside of Sacramento in 1848. This gold strike soon made the Truckee Meadows a jumping-off point for prospectors heading into California. Wagon train after wagon train poured into the Reno area, and it soon became "an important crossroads where the north–south, east–west emigrant trails met," according to local historian Mike Land.

You only have to glance at the variety of names in local telephone books to realize the international flavor of the Reno/Tahoe area. Adding to the melting pot begun with the first Native Americans, early settlers represented such diverse cultures as Cornish, Irish, Scottish, English, Chinese, French, Mexican and Basque. They mined silver, built canals, herded sheep and constructed railroads from the 1850s on. The French and Spanish Basques were especially influential, settling all over northern Nevada and assuming positions of power and leadership in their communities. To indulge in the cuisine of this delightful ethnic mix of peoples, see our Restaurants chapter, and for details about the many groups that celebrate various cultures see our chapter on The Arts.

Lake's Crossing Becomes Reno

Myron Lake knew a good deal when he saw one. A capable businessman who was both energetic and visionary, Lake knew when he saw Charles W. Fuller's bridge across the Truckee River in 1861 that Fuller was on to something. After all, travelers on the north–south and east–west trails had to cross the swift, little river, and the choices were few — wade, swim or use the rickety toll bridge.

But Fuller's bridge had a flaw — every time the river rose, the bridge washed away. He rebuilt the bridge several times between 1859 and 1861, but Fuller was a Missouri settler, not an architect, so in 1861 he decided to sell out and move on to better business deals, and Lake was ready to buy him out. Just as it has happened so many other times in this area, one man's misfortune turned out to be another man's jackpot.

Lake first rebuilt the bridge (much sturdier this time) and added a trading station, inn and bar. He also bought up the land 14 miles north and 3 miles south of his bridge. Lake was a veteran of the Mexican War and still kept up on Washington, D.C., politics. He calculated that railroads would soon be crossing the country linking the east and west coasts, and he guessed they would have to come through the Truckee Meadows. He was right.

Lake held all the aces and knew he had a winning hand. The railroad was coming, and the discovery in 1859 of the Comstock Lode in Virginia City had silver seekers flocking to the Truckee Meadows. The only road to the silver-rich city just happened to be across Lake's new bridge, and he grew richer and richer from the tolls paid by those supplying the miners in Virginia City. And he charged for every single thing crossing his bridge: horses, cattle, wagons, chickens, pigs, sheep, and even the men. If it crossed the bridge, he got money for it.

Lake expanded his holdings, buying more land and constructing more buildings. Besides his river property, he owned a gristmill and a livery stable and continued to buy up range land. By 1864, the area that would eventually be the City of Reno was known as Lake's Crossing. But Lake's greatest business deal came four years later with Charles Crocker of the Central Pacific Railroad.

The Central Pacific and Union Pacific railroads raced each other across the west, laying track to see which company acquired the good right-of-way land. The Central Pacific headed east from California, and the Union Pacific headed west from Nebraska. The Central Pacific reached the Truckee Meadows first,

VACATION RENTAL EXPERTS

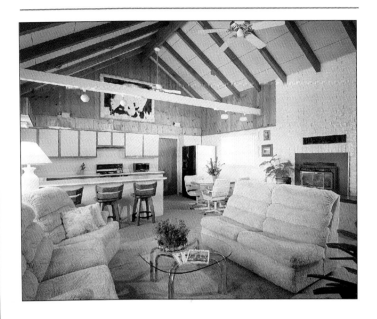

"We arrange great
indoors so you
can enjoy the
great outdoors"

Enjoy the perfect
Tahoe vacation by
selecting from one of
our condominiums,
homes, cozy cabins or
elegant mountain
chalets. We have the
perfect vacation
property to fit your
needs and budget.

1-800-344-9364

2516 LAKE TAHOE BLVD.
SOUTH LAKE TAHOE, CA 96150

www.tahoelodging.com
E-MAIL astation@aol.com

ACCOMMODATION
STATION

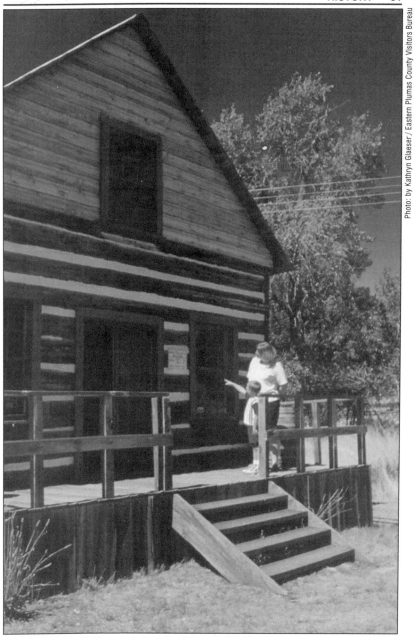

Photo: by Kathryn Glaeser / Eastern Plumas County Visitors Bureau

The Jim Beckwourth Museum in Portola, California, offers a glimpse into the colorful past of those who setttled the frontier of the Reno/Tahoe area and its surrounding mountain and desert towns.

even though the railroad took five years to cross the Sierra Nevada, but the length of time didn't bother Lake. He was waiting for the railroad when it reached Lake's Crossing in March 1868.

Lake had already struck a deal with Crocker of the Central Pacific, asking only that a train depot be built on his property. In return, Lake promised to deed 400 acres to the railroad. Crocker liked the deal, surveyed the land and divided it into building lots. To thank Lake, Crocker had the railroad deed back 127 lots to Lake. The two then auctioned off the city six weeks later.

The railroaders decided that the new town should be called "Argenta," a poetic term meaning silver. After all, the discovery of the Comstock Lode in Virginia City had really put the Truckee Meadows in the annals of history. But Crocker wanted to honor an old family friend, Union General Jesse Lee Reno, who was killed at the battle of South Mountain, Maryland, in 1862. At first, the name met with resistance since Reno had never stepped foot in Nevada; however, Comstock miners and the new town's citizens admitted that the simple name "Reno" had a good ring to it, and the name stuck.

Silver Puts Reno/Tahoe on the Map

"Can you shoot?"

That's the first question the editor of the *Gold Hill Daily News* on the Comstock asked Wells Drury when he applied for the job of a newspaper reporter in 1874.

"Will you stand without hitching? You can write what you please. Nobody will censor it. But you have to defend yourself if anybody has a kick," the editor said throwing a shooting-iron down on his desk. "We call this six-shooter the 'family bible.' You may need it. You may not."

Drury got the job and later that day covered "one murder, two fatal mine accidents, and a runaway stage coach." He also gained a reputation as a gunfighter when he pointed the "family bible" at a town bully and blew off the man's left ear. Those were the days when Virginia City and Gold Hill on the Comstock

Lode were the "hell-raisingest" mining camps in the world. And a history of Reno/Tahoe would be remiss if it didn't mention the silver find that gave birth to these two towns just 20 miles away from Reno on the slopes of Mount Davidson. The Comstock Lode put Reno on the map and made Lake Tahoe the center of a logging empire which supplied the towns with timber to shore up their mines, build their structures and lay their railroad tracks.

Brothers Hosea and Ethan Grosh staked their claim in Gold Canyon on the southern slope of Mount Davidson in 1853. They were looking for gold and although they didn't find much, they did identify the "messy blue mud" that got in the other gold prospectors' way. It was silver, and for the next three years the brothers tried desperately to find the financial backing they needed to properly examine the silver deposits. Unfortunately, both brothers died in 1857 before profiting from their discovery. In fact, their find remained a secret.

After the brothers died, a shifty con man named Henry Comstock, for whom the silver-find would be named, moved into their cabin and announced to the other miners that he had been made the Groshs' partner in exchange for keeping their land free from would-be claim jumpers. According to historian Mike Land, "Comstock had no idea about the silver-find. He was just a lucky little man who was in the right place at the right time."

Not far from Comstock's cabin, Patrick McLaughlin and Peter O'Riley discovered more gold flakes surrounded by the blue-black mud. The two men staked a claim and prospected the gold while throwing away the silver-rich earth. Comstock heard about the find and conned McLaughlin and O'Riley into believing that they were trespassing on his land. He offered to make them and an old prospector named James Finney partners for an equal share in their claim. They agreed, and the four formed the Comstock Company and began pulling out gold from a mine they named Ophir, after one of King Solomon's mines. The partners still knew nothing of the silver they were throwing away until some ore wound up in the Truckee Meadows.

The blue-black mud interested two ranchers in the Truckee Meadows who collected some and sent it off to a mining office in California. The sample was assayed and was found to be loaded with silver. Before the two ranchers had a chance to act on the welcome news, James Walsh and Joseph Woodward, two insiders who worked in the assay office, scurried to the Ophir Mine to buy out the four prospectors before they could hear about the wealth of silver. Three of the owners sold their shares outright for $2,500 apiece, but Comstock held out for $11,000, thinking he was the better businessman. In reality, the four sold their rights to $310,000,000 worth of silver for $18,500. When Walsh and Woodward returned to California, they spread the word of their find and the great silver rush on the Comstock Lode began.

Virginia City and Gold Hill grew up from the Ophir Mine; the silver boom helped fatten the coffers of Reno as well. And while Lake Tahoe was pretty much a myth up to this time (known only to Indians and a few hardy explorers), the rush to riches beginning in 1860 put it literally on the map. When word of the enormous silver deposit in Nevada reached settlers in nearby California, hordes of aspiring millionaires saddled their horses and hit the hair-raising trail over the Sierras to the mines. Choked daily with hundreds of mule teams, stagecoaches and riders, the narrow path took travelers right past Lake Tahoe. To accommodate these first travelers to the area, waystations sprang up, including Yank's Station near Echo Summit and Lake House, Tahoe's first lakeshore hotel near present day Al Tahoe in South Shore Lake Tahoe.

But in addition to providing the ever-important route to the silver fields, the Lake Tahoe area also offered a resource critical for the development of the mines: the towering virgin forests yielded massive timbers to shore up mine shafts and wood to drive steam engines. The Comstock's insatiable appetite for wood fueled the wholesale plunder of Tahoe's timberlands by lumbermen eager for huge profits. Mills that opened near Glenbrook on the east side of the lake used an innovative flume system to transport the timbers over the mountains to the mines.

Lumber was hauled by rail to the top of Spooner Summit and then shot down a V-flume to Carson City where it was hauled by rail to Virginia City. Near Incline Village, logs were hauled to the top of the mountain via a 4,000-foot tramway and then dumped into a flume that carried them to their pickup point for the railroad. The town of Incline Village derives its name from this tramline. To ensure a steady supply of water to float timbers in the flumes, the lumber companies built dams and created Spooner and Marlette lakes (see our Recreation and Winter Sports chapters for present-day fun in these lakes).

The Virginia and Truckee Railroad began operations in 1869, linking Carson City with the Comstock and later with Reno and the Central Pacific Railroad. The V&T Railroad carried the silver-rich ore down to Carson City and supplied the mines with goods from Reno.

In May of 1860, the Pyramid Lake Paiutes met to discuss the miners who were pouring into the Truckee Meadows. The Indians had weathered the explorers, mapmakers and pioneers who were just passing through, but they could not tolerate the miners who took their land, cut down their piñon trees and kidnapped their women. On May 12, the Paiutes won the first Battle of Pyramid Lake by luring a scraggly band of volunteers into an ambush. Of the 105 white men who fought in the skirmish, 76 died and 29 were wounded. By June, 1,550 volunteers and four companies of regular Army soldiers marched on Pyramid Lake. The Paiutes, guided by Chief Numaga, didn't engage the white men but retreated to the shores of the lake. The white men were thus the new masters of the Truckee Meadows, and the Indians, by treaty, remained at the lake.

The silver extracted from the Comstock Lode also convinced the U.S. Congress to admit Nevada as the 36th state on

INSIDERS' TIP:

The first train robbery in the West occurred seven miles east of Reno in November of 1870. "Smiling Jack" Davis of Virginia City pulled the stickup.

October 31, 1864, to help finance the Civil War on the side of the Union.

Thus from the awful blue-black mud loaded with silver sprang a state, two boomtowns, one Indian war, a railroad and a host of colorful characters, the most famous being Samuel Clemens, who joined the editorial staff of the *Territorial Enterprise* newspaper in Virginia City in 1862 and in 1863 began using his famous pen name, Mark Twain.

The mines petered out in the late 1880s and the populations of Virginia City and Gold Hill fell from 10,900 in 1880 to 2,500 in 1900. Gold Hill eventually disappeared and Virginia City turned into an almost-ghost town. However, Reno and Lake Tahoe thrived. The little town on the Truckee River became the most important city in Nevada, and Lake Tahoe turned to tourism and began building resorts and inns.

Reno/Tahoe Outgambles Two Depressions

In mining vocabulary inherited from Mexico, the opposite of the Bonanza (the big strike) is the Borrasca (the worst of bad luck). Reno/Tahoe learned that Spanish word all too well in the early 1880s. The Comstock mines had provided the major source of income to most Nevadans, but by 1881 most of the silver mines were played out. One by one they closed down and miners left the state in droves, looking for the next "glory hole." From 1880 to 1900, the population of the state dropped from 62,000 to 42,000, and the U.S. Congress even contemplated abolishing Nevada's statehood. Although it had never been done before, Congress was ready to try. It never came to pass, however, and Reno and Lake Tahoe managed to weather a 20-year depression.

The little town on the Truckee River came to be the most important city in Nevada. The railroads took financial hits from the closing of the Comstock mines, that's for sure, but their Nevada runs continued, this time supplying the growing cattle and sheep ranches. These ranches operated successfully because the railroads were able to transport their stock to California, Nebraska and other yards around the United States. So Reno continued as the railroad center of Nevada.

Lake Tahoe, meanwhile, diverted its attention from logging to tourism. Although barren mountains remained as the legacy of lumbering and mining (50,000 acres had been cut by the 1890s), the silver rush was responsible for the beginnings of summer tourism in the Lake Tahoe Basin. Exposed to thousands of commercial travelers in the 1860s and 1870s, the grandeur of the lake was a secret no more. In spite of the decline of the Comstock mines, travelers continued to arrive in the basin, but now it was for pleasure rather than for business. Waystations, resorts and hotels flourished all around the lake, introducing wealthy customers to lazy alpine summers in one of the world's loveliest settings.

Resorts like Tahoe Tavern and the Grand Central Hotel near Tahoe City, the Glenbrook Hotel in Glenbrook and the Tallac Hotel (see our chapters on Attractions, Annual Events and The Arts) near South Lake Tahoe pampered guests with extraordinary luxury in the midst of this rustic mountain setting. Not content to reside in resorts, some notables constructed elegant summer residences, such as Vikingsholm, built by Mrs. Lora Knight (see our Attractions and Kidstuff chapters) and the Thunderbird Lodge, constructed by real estate magnate George Whittell. Less luxurious digs also thrived, including Camp Richardson which emphasized (as it still does today) a family-oriented experience in the great outdoors.

Because of the absence of roads, steamers like the *Tahoe*, *Meteor* and *Tod Goodwin* carried passengers and freight from one area of the lake to another. And while the lumber

---

INSIDERS' TIP:

The oldest schoolhouse in Nevada is the Glendale School in Sparks, built in 1864. The building was used until 1958. It is now part of the Heritage Park and Museum in downtown Sparks.

barons pillaged the mountainsides, the first tourists plundered the lake through unbridled overfishing. Because the supply of fish was believed to be inexhaustible, anglers were encouraged to catch as many as they could, with the average running around 20 per person for a four-hour outing. Fortunately, in later years concern for the environment and natural resources became a priority, with public and private groups working successfully to restore the forests and fish populations.

The second gold rush began in Nevada in 1900, when an old prospector named Jim Butler went looking for his wayward mule near the town of Tonopah, Nevada, and discovered pockets of gold and silver. This time the state grew by 50,000 fortune seekers. During the next 10 years, Reno's population grew from 4,500 to almost 11,000, and Sparks, Reno's sister city, was born.

In 1902, swampland and ranch land made up most of the area 4 miles east of Reno, but by 1904 a new town of 1,000 people sprang up, thanks to the Southern Pacific Railroad. The SP Railroad succeeded the Central Pacific as the owners of the railroad tracks across northern Nevada, and in order to straighten the rails and snip a few miles from the route, the SP Railroad decided to move its maintenance yard and roundhouse from Wadsworth, Nevada, to be closer to Reno. The railroad bought up the ranch land, filled in the swampland with railway carloads of dirt and rock and moved its employees there. As an incentive, the company gave each family a plot of land on which to build a house. The new town was an instant success and was named after John Sparks, a miner, cattleman and eventual governor of Nevada.

Reno real estate investors bought up other ranch properties for more housing projects, and the City of Sparks became incorporated in March 1905. In the beginning, Southern Pacific Railroad officials ruled Sparks's politics with an iron hand, making it a company town and giving Sparks the nickname of Rail City, because it relied on the railroad for its existence. Sparks weathered the Great Depression better than other Nevada cities. During the 1930s, Sparks's city government put unemployed men to work on street, sidewalk and sewer repair and construction projects.

Reno and Sparks have had an on-again, off-again romance with gambling. Throughout its history, the Truckee Meadows has attracted settlers who like to take risks. Nowhere in the United States have more fortunes been won and lost. Gambling has always been part of Reno's history, but anti-gambling factions came to town, too, along with the faro dealers and three-card monte sharks. From the 1860s to the 1930s, Reno's gambling laws were controversial at best.

In 1861, the Territorial Legislature outlawed games of chance, but the law was ignored. So in 1879 the law was repealed, and the state tried to cash in on gambling by requiring a license to operate any gambling establishment. But after heavy betting on the famous Jim Jeffries and Jack Johnson heavyweight prizefight in Reno in 1910, the lid slammed down again on gambling. The *San Francisco Examiner* proclaimed in a headline that "Legalized Gambling Has Drawn Its Last Breath in the United States." It was true, almost — "legal" gambling did stop, but the betting continued, only now it was moved to the backrooms of saloons and other secret places. Two short knocks and a "Joe sent me" could get a person into a high-stakes game that was usually held at night with full permission of the local police force. The only thing the ban seemed to do was to bring in a time of gangsterism to Reno.

The two biggest hoods in Reno were "Big Bill" Graham and Jimmy "The Cinch" McKay. These two "gentlemen" owned the infamous Bank Club and had friends from back East who found Reno a great place to hide from the FBI and to launder stickup money. Gangsters like Pretty Boy Floyd, John Dillinger and Baby Face Nelson visited the Truckee Meadows in the late 1920s and early 1930s. Graham and McKay ruled downtown Reno for years, but they went too far one day and were sentenced to nine years in prison for mail fraud. Still, illegal gambling went on.

To erase the stigma, Reno Mayor E. E. Roberts called for a repeal of the anti-gambling law during his reelection campaign in 1931. "You cannot legislate morals," he said. "You can't stop gambling, so let's put it out in the open."

The people reelected Roberts, and on

March 19, 1931, Nevada repealed its anti-gambling law. The reaction around the United States, however, was more vicious than expected. The *Los Angeles Times* called Nevada "a new Babylon," and The *Kansas City Star* called Reno a cross between "Sodom, Gomorrah and Hell." Once again, legislators in some states called for the repeal of Nevada's statehood. But Nevada survived the threat, and Reno survived the two depressions because of its legalized gambling and because it cashed in on a new business — divorce.

About the same time Roberts was hoping legal gambling would bring a new bonanza to Nevada, Governor Fred Balzar gave promoter Norman Biltz the green light to try to populate the state with millionaires. Citing the tax advantages offered by the state, Biltz found wealthy people from around the country who managed to survive the stock market crash of 1929 and wined and dined them in elaborate style at Lake Tahoe. Many of them were favorably impressed, including Jim Stack, E. L. Cord, Max Fleischmann and Cornelius Vanderbilt III. They were the first of many influential people to invest in real estate around the lake.

Divorce City

No one really paid much attention to Nevada's residence requirements to become a voting citizen: it was only six months because itinerant miners made up most of the state's population and if the requirements were made any stricter, not very many citizens would be eligible to vote. No one looked hard at Nevada's liberal divorce laws either, until a Reno lawyer advertised quickie divorces in New York and California newspapers.

Nevada's short residency requirements and wide range of grounds for divorce soon made Reno the divorce capital of the world. In fact, the business became so lucrative that the Nevada Legislature dropped the required residency period down to three months and later in 1931 dropped it further to only six weeks. Now the rich and famous flocked to Reno to shed their undesirable mates. Some old-timers swore that they found more gold in the Truckee River beneath the Virginia Street bridge, where new divorcees threw in their wedding bands, than in all the mines on the Comstock.

The new divorce phenomenon also provided another business for Reno — dude ranches. Neil West was the first to recognize that those seeking a divorce needed somewhere to stay during the six-week period. So he built cabins on his cattle ranch near Reno and rented them to the "dudes." Other ranchers followed West's lead. Even Lake Tahoe followed suit, and resorts and inns sprang up all over the Nevada side of the lake. Nearly every community around the lake today owes its existence to a resort or a hotel.

The flip side of the divorce coin provided another lucrative business for Reno — weddings. Since Reno had no waiting period to get married, just the time it took to buy a marriage license, wedding chapels popped up around Reno. The business bloomed in the war years of the 1940s, and by 1952 Reno weddings outnumbered divorces.

The Biggest Little City in the World

In the 1950s and '60s, the Reno/Tahoe area got down to the business of expanding. After all, Reno's slogan, "The Biggest Little City in the World," had been made world-famous since the summer of 1928 when a Sacramento man won $100 for suggesting it, and the city fathers wanted to live up to the saying. But two families can really be credited with putting Reno on the map — the Smiths and the Harrahs. Raymond "Pappy" Smith and his son Harold started the world-famous Harolds Club and Bill Harrah began Harrah's.

In 1942, Harolds Club came up with the slogan, "Harolds Club or Bust," incorporated it with the drawing of a Conestoga wagon and plastered the signs along the highways of the United States. More than 2,000 signs adorned the roadways of America, reminding travelers to visit Reno, the "biggest little" gambling spot in the country. At that time, Reno and Harolds Club were the most popular tourist attractions in the United States. Some of the signs reportedly found their way to Australia, Europe, Asia and even Africa. The club prospered and along with it, Reno.

Harrah began his operation with only a few hundred dollars and no partners, but his willingness to take risks, like so many Reno pioneers before him, enabled his empire to grow. After World War II, he began buying up all the Reno property and clubs he could — and couldn't — afford. He also expanded his holdings to the South Shore of Lake Tahoe. Harrah continued his philosophy of using profits to expand properties and to build newer and bigger casinos. He was one of the first casino owners to feature Hollywood celebrities to attract customers to his showrooms. (For more information on Harrah's, see our Resorts chapter.)

The building boom began again, and more and more entrepreneurs flooded into the area. Lake Tahoe experienced unregulated growth in the '50s and '60s with the development of gambling on its South Shore. The Winter Olympics of 1960 in Squaw Valley added to the urbanization of the lake. Developers drained and filled marshland for waterfront homes, and hotels and motels sprang up around the lake.

As the Lake Tahoe Basin experienced more and more growth, the influence of the Washoe Tribe almost completely disappeared. By 1870 only about 500 Indians were known to still frequent the area. What was once the Indians' ancestral summer home became a playground for the rich, the famous and almost anybody who could manage to get there. Accessible only in summer because of heavy snow for many years, it became a year-round resort in 1947 when U.S. Highway 50 was opened as an all-season roadway. Today the Washoes are returning to the lake, beginning with their 30-year permit to run Meeks Bay Resort which was awarded by the U.S. Forest Service in 1998.

The casinos continued to bring in visitors by the millions, pumping megadollars into the area's economy, but nonetheless some anti-gambling activists convinced the Reno City Council to restrict the building of casinos to a small, downtown area. The council literally drew a red line on a map around a 5-square block area. This, they said, would be the only section of Reno to allow casinos. The area outside of the red line would cater to "businesses, homes, churches, banks, schools and all other entities that represented normal life."

The "red-line district" worked for the first two decades, but in 1955, one of the owners of the Primadonna Casino challenged the restriction. The Reno City Council relented and casinos expanded past the red-line area and some even sprang up in Sparks. The ordinance was not officially repealed, however, until 1972.

After word spread about how much profit Nevada casinos could provide their owners, corporations poured into the Reno/Tahoe area looking to cash in on the lucrative business. The eccentric Howard Hughes even bought out the Smiths and acquired Harolds Club. Hughes's presence in Reno spurred even more corporations to invest in Reno and Lake Tahoe. Hilton Hotels, MGM, Ramada Inn, Holiday Inn, Circus Circus, Caesars, Sahara and the Del Webb corporation all own or owned a casino property in the Reno/Tahoe area.

And, the rest, as they say, is history.

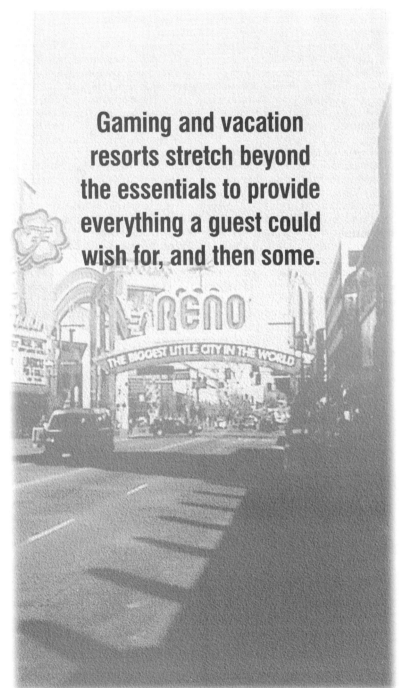

Gaming and vacation resorts stretch beyond the essentials to provide everything a guest could wish for, and then some.

Resorts

Because tourism is the lifeblood of the Reno/Tahoe economy, visitors to the area have a tantalizing array of accommodations to choose from. In our Vacation Rentals chapter we tell you how to rent or lease a home away from home, ranging from cabins and condos to large sumptuous houses. In our Hotels and Motels chapter we describe more conventional lodging, such as luxury hotel/casinos and back-to-basics motels. In this chapter we give you a rundown on gaming and vacation resorts that stretch beyond the essentials to provide everything a guest could wish for, and then some.

Gaming Resorts

Since gaming's legal in Nevada, Lady Luck plays a prominent role in available accommodations in the Reno/Tahoe area. But casino gambling's not legal in this part of California, so all the gaming resorts we recommend in this chapter are in Nevada.

Restricted gaming in Nevada (slot machines only) is found in a variety of locations, such as grocery stores, drug stores and bars. You can even pay for your groceries at the checkout and hopefully win your money back at the slots before leaving the store. Unrestricted gaming (table games, sports books and keno together with slot machines) is limited to casinos.

While most small casinos do not offer overnight lodging, the large gaming establishments do. And because of increased competition in recent years, many large casinos have evolved from just hotel/casino properties into themed gaming resorts offering a diverse array of comforts and amusements for their guests.

Although it can be difficult to distinguish between a hotel/casino and a gaming resort, we believe a gaming resort offers more than just the minimum in food, lodging and unrestricted gambling. Reno/Tahoe gaming resorts provide a comprehensive package to guests, including multiple options in rooms, restaurants and entertainment. You can bed down in a variety of accommodations, from a standard room to a luxurious penthouse suite, all with full-service hotel amenities. You can satiate your appetite at a lavish buffet, a casual coffee shop or an elegant gourmet dining room. And you can entertain yourself with nonstop casino action, dazzling stage revues, headliner entertainers, intimate piano bars, swinging discos and lively video arcades — all without ever leaving the building.

In their quest to satisfy guests' every need, some gaming resorts also provide upscale shopping arcades, theaters, swimming pools, health clubs and spas. Many provide convention facilities, group rates and shuttle transportation. And if you finally tire of the on-site recreation, many gaming resorts will arrange for skiing, golfing and other area activities.

A gaming resort can be a destination in and of itself, a place to stay and play and truly pamper yourself for several days. For details on casino entertainment, see our Casino Nightlife chapter; for detailed descriptions of some dining options, see our Restaurants chapter.

As each gaming resort offers every amenity imaginable, choosing between them can be difficult. But if location and atmosphere are important, then differences do exist. For visitors who prefer the quiet ambiance of an elegant gaming establishment, the Reno Hilton is a good choice. But for families with children, or those who want to be in the middle of the action, Circus Circus fits the bill.

To help you distinguish between the properties we recommend, in this chapter we describe the general flavor of the resort as well as all its amenities. All gaming resorts accept credit cards and offer nonsmoking accommodations. Children are welcome; in fact, many resorts make special provisions for them. In most cases, though, it's a good idea to leave Rover at home because the resorts don't provide kennels. Also, most accommodations are wheelchair accessible, but be sure to confirm this when making reservations.

If you're lucky enough to be flexible in your travel plans, it can be a distinct advantage when booking lodging in a Reno/Tahoe gaming resort. Rates and availability vary a great deal with the time of the year; some resorts go so far as to double rates during peak holidays. Accommodations at all these resorts are more expensive and difficult to obtain if the bookings include Martin Luther King Jr. Day, Presidents Day, Memorial Day, the Fourth of July, Thanksgiving, Christmas and New Year's. High season at Lake Tahoe resorts also includes January to mid-April and mid-June to mid-September.

Bookings at gaming resorts in the Reno area are also affected by special events that draw large numbers of visitors (see our Annual Events chapter). The most heavily booked week of the year is during Hot August Nights (usually in early August), when rooms in some gaming resorts are sold out a year in advance. Other major events are the Reno Rodeo, the last week of June; the Nevada State Fair, the third week of August; The Nugget Best in the West Rib Cook-off, Labor Day weekend; the National Championship Air Races, The Great Reno Balloon Race, Street Vibrations and the Virginia City International Camel Races in September; and the National Senior Pro Rodeo Finals in November. If you're planning to attend any of these events, it's wise to book as far ahead as possible.

In general, high season in the Reno area is July to mid-October, mid-season is April to June and low season is mid-November through December (excluding Christmas and New Year's) and January to March. But because high and low seasons are not always the same at Lake Tahoe as they are in the Reno area, it's possible to find accommodations in one area during its low season and still enjoy the activities of the other during its high season. For example, if you can't find lodging at Lake Tahoe during peak ski season, you may have better luck finding it in Reno; and if you're shut out of a room during Hot August Nights in Reno, you can try finding lodging at Lake Tahoe. With less than an hour separating the two areas, plus shuttle transportation that's available from some gaming resorts, getting from place to place is pretty easy, so this would definitely be an attractive option.

When booking, be sure to inquire about any packages that might result in savings and convenience. Also ask about any special events that might be going on, such as gaming tournaments, which could result in additional perks or benefits for resort guests. Also be aware that some resorts have minimum stay requirements during high season.

For reservations at any of the following gaming resorts, you can either call them direct or call the Reno/Tahoe Visitors Information Center, (800) 367-7366.

Price Code

Each resort's listing includes a symbol that represents the price range for a standard room for one weekend night during high season. The figure is based upon double-occupancy and excludes tax.

$	$69 to $99
$$	$100 to $149
$$$	$150 to $200
$$$$	More than $200

Reno

Atlantis Casino Resort
$$ • 3800 S. Virginia St., Reno, Nev. • (775) 825-4700, (800) 723-6500

The only thing missing in this lush tropical paradise is Tarzan and Jane swinging from a vine over the 21 tables. With its thatched canopies, floral carpet and jungle foliage, Atlantis is a touch of Tahiti in southwest Reno. Like many gaming resorts, it started small. In 1972, it was the Golden Road Motor Inn and had one restaurant, the Copper Kettle. But with steady growth and major expansion, today Atlantis offers 1,000 rooms, seven restaurants and a full array of entertainment options.

If you like the tropics, you'll love Atlantis; the jungle theme seems to envelop you. From the colorful parrots talking at the buffet to the exotic fish swimming in the steakhouse, this resort is fully themed. Even the names of the restaurants — Purple Parrot and Toucan Charlie's — reflect the tropics. You can't miss the signature landmark, the huge glass Skyway that connects the parking area with the main casino. With twin Grecian columns shooting flames high into the sky, the Skyway depicts the Lost City of Atlantis and offers Reno's only gaming with a view.

Guests can choose from rooms or Jacuzzi suites in the hotel towers or from comfortable standard guest rooms in the economy motorlodge. All accommodations feature 24-hour room service, in-room keno and deluxe amenities. Some tower rooms have mountain or city views. And, for the comfort of all guests, Atlantis has a high-tech environmental control system that creates an almost smoke-free atmosphere.

In addition to all the excitement of the casino games, nightlife includes free cabaret entertainment and dancing in the Atlantis nightclub. For relaxation in the casino area, guests can choose from seven different lounge areas. Other amenities include a swimming pool with large sun deck, a health club and spa, free valet parking and the Entertainment Fun Center with the latest in video arcade games.

Atlantis has won several "Best" awards from local newspapers, and we can certainly see why. Toucan Charlie's Buffet & Grille offers the "Best Sunday Brunch," a feast sure to please even the most hardcore gastronomes. It's not only the quantity but also the quality that makes this international buffet truly an event in eating around the world. And the Atlantis Seafood Steakhouse, with its exotic undersea decor and exquisite food, is easily one of the top dining spots in Reno. The resort also features five other restaurants: Cafe Alfresco for delicious pasta and salads, the Purple Parrot for American favorites, the Snack Bar & Soda Fountain for quick snacks, the Oyster Bar for fresh seafood and an Italian ristorante for delectable Italian specialties.

Atlantis is popular with both locals and visitors because of its frequent slot, blackjack and keno tournaments. Locals also perceive its nightclub and restaurants as good values and "in" places to be. It's just down the street from

INSIDERS' TIP

Reno/Tahoe is not like Las Vegas, so don't expect gaming resorts here to be as flamboyant and ostentatious as the mega-resorts there.

the Reno/Sparks Convention Center, so convention attendees find Atlantis a very convenient home base. But before you reserve a room here, be aware that it's about 3 miles from downtown Reno, and the next nearest casino is several blocks away.

If you're a skier, be sure to inquire about ski packages.

Circus Circus Hotel/Casino–Reno
$ • 500 N. Sierra St., Reno, Nev.
• (775) 329-0711, (800) 648-5010

Circus Circus Hotel/Casino–Reno opened in 1978 with the same family-oriented entertainment concept as the immensely successful Circus Circus in Las Vegas. From its original 104 hotel rooms, the resort has grown to encompass 4 city blocks, including 1,572 rooms and suites. Connected by skybridges to Silver Legacy Resort Casino and the Eldorado Hotel/Casino, Circus Circus is part of a tri-property complex that offers 21 restaurants and more than 200,000 square feet of gaming space.

Circus Circus has been a family destination for years because of its live circus acts on the Midway Stage and its carnival-style arcade (see our Attractions chapter for details). While recent renovations have toned down the original hot pink decor in favor of a classic turn-of-the-century European motif, it's still a three-ring circus complete with clowns, balloon sculptures and brightly colored stuffed animals everywhere.

Circus Circus not only has entertainment for the whole family but affordable accommodations and meals too. It has five restaurants: the Hickory Pit Steak House, the Big Top Buffet, the Main Street Deli and Ice Cream Shoppe, the 3 Ring Restaurant and Art Gecko's Southwest Grill. The resort offers free shuttle service to and from Reno/Tahoe International Airport and complimentary garage and valet parking on the property. Although this resort is best known for its family appeal, it's also popular with adults because of its choice VIP and executive suites.

Eldorado Hotel/Casino
$ • 345 N. Virginia St., Reno, Nev.
• (775) 786-5700, (800) 648-4597

When it opened in 1973, the Eldorado Hotel/Casino's location north of the world famous Reno Arch was considered dubious. The heartbeat of downtown Reno gaming was several blocks south, literally on the other side of the railroad tracks. But today the Eldorado is in the center of the action, part of a tri-property complex that also includes the Silver Legacy Resort Casino and Circus Circus gaming resorts.

Family-owned and -operated, the Eldorado's success is a testament to hands-on personal management. The attention to detail is everywhere, from the plush linens in the rooms to the elegant interior appointments to the creative culinary delights in its eight restaurants. Rising 25 stories above N. Virginia Street, the Eldorado has 817 rooms and suites that range from deluxe king rooms to luxurious penthouse suites with whirlpool tubs and sitting and dining areas.

The unobstructed view of the Sierra Nevada mountains from many of the rooms is a delightful plus. But with such diverse entertainment available just downstairs, most guests don't spend a lot of time contemplating the luxury of their rooms. After checking in, you can try your luck at one of the more than 2,000 slot machines, 90 table games and three keno lounges in the street-level casino. If you're a sports aficionado, you can place your bet and quench your thirst at the Race & Sportsbook and Stadium Bar, which features a huge selection of beers from all over the world.

Moving up to the mezzanine level, you can stroll along a European-style promenade lined with an eclectic array of shops, restaurants and bars. The specialty boutiques offer fine collectibles, souvenirs and apparel for the most ardent shoppers. The restaurants serve cuisine from around the world in everything from a casual buffet setting to an elegant formal atmosphere. You can enjoy fine Italian dining in one of three settings at La Strada: a courtyard terrace, an authentic wine cellar or a countryside villa. You can sip beer made on-site, watch your favorite sporting event and dance the night away in the upbeat environment of the Brew Brothers microbrewery.

At the far end of the promenade you can treat yourself to a taste of Paris in Bistro Roxy by the Fountain of Fortune in the Grand Plaza. Although it seems a bit gaudy to some people

— five ornate figures spew water toward a colorful painted sky — the fountain helps set the mood of a European sidewalk cafe. Other restaurants at the Eldorado include the Chef's Pavilion, for a sumptuous buffet; Choices, for express snacks and meals; Tivoli Gardens, for American, Asian and Mexican entrees; the Seafood Buffet, for delectable fish; and The Grill, for wood-roasted meats and fish. The quality of food and the choice of wines at the Eldorado are considered some of the best in the Reno area. The owners of this resort are also part-owners of the Ferrari–Carano winery in Napa, California, so their interest in fine cuisine is well documented.

If you've come to Reno/Tahoe to see world-class entertainment, you won't be disappointed at the Eldorado. Broadway shows and headliners are regularly featured in the state-of-the-art Eldorado Showroom. And if this isn't enough, the resort further pampers its guests with a health spa, swimming pool, video arcade and free valet parking.

When it's finally time to bed down for the night, Insiders know it's very important to remember where you've booked your room. Since the Eldorado is connected to Silver Legacy and Circus Circus via the promenade, it's easy to stroll from one to the other without realizing it, and it's not uncommon to see guests at any of these three resorts wandering around lost because they can't find the particular elevator that delivers them to their room. The Eldorado is decidedly upscale and appeals to guests who want to be downtown where all the action is.

Harrah's Reno
$$ • 219 N. Center St., Reno, Nev.
• (775) 786-3232, (800) 427-7247

It's hard to speculate what casino gaming would be like without the influence of the late Bill Harrah, founder of Harrah's Casino Hotels. When he arrived in Reno in 1937 at the age of 26, Harrah learned that legalized gambling was a rough business not far removed from the card rooms and saloons of the wild wild West. But he opened his first club, a one-room bingo parlor with six employees, and began a style of management and growth that would become industry standards over the years. Harrah reasoned that the comfort of his guests was the first priority, so customer service has always been the watchword at Harrah's. Although guests may not be aware of this philosophy, they do know that the attention to the little things makes their stay more enjoyable.

From that inauspicious beginning in 1937, Harrah's Reno has grown and prospered during the years and is now a four-star destination gaming resort. Harrah's Entertainment, Inc. is also a publicly traded corporation that operates casino resorts in 10 different states, including Harrah's Lake Tahoe.

Guests at Harrah's Reno can choose from 565 deluxe guest rooms and suites, each with a 100 percent satisfaction guarantee and 24-hour room service. Amenities include an extensive health club, a swimming pool, in-house massage services and a beauty shop.

Adjacent to and also owned by Harrah's is the Hampton Inn at Harrah's, including 408 superior yet moderately-priced rooms. This Hampton Inn is a cut above most others of the same name because, in addition to the usual complimentary breakfast, it also offers valet parking, an original art exhibit, a fitness center and a bell desk. The Hampton is very popular because the rooms are much cheaper than Harrah's, and it's right next to all the casino activity.

Harrah's Reno has always been known for its award-winning cuisine, and with six restaurants to choose from, guests will never go hungry. The Steakhouse, with its impeccable service and outstanding entrees, provides a first-class dining experience for any occasion. It's

---

INSIDERS' TIP

Most casinos have players clubs that entitle members to special perks and events. When booking a room, or even upon arrival, ask about the benefits to determine whether it would be an advantage to join.

also popular with locals for power lunches. A variety of fine food is also available at Planet Hollywood, Cafe Andreotti, the Fresh Market Square Buffet, the Sports Deli and the Garden Room.

Bill Harrah was also a pioneer in using celebrity entertainers to attract casino customers. The Headliner Room in Harrah's Reno has showcased literally hundreds of top-name entertainers since it first opened in 1966. Until just a few years ago, the dinner shows were legendary events because they afforded guests as well as locals a chance to dress up and "do the town." Although the attire is more casual now, and only cocktails are served, the quality of entertainment remains just as high with either headliners or stage revues playing nightly. The Headliner Room was renamed Sammy's Showroom in 1991 in honor of the late Sammy Davis Jr., who performed there more than 30 times from 1967 to 1989.

Harrah's downtown locale makes it easy for guests to walk from casino to casino and also to stroll along the Truckee River, which is just a block away. It's also close to the National Automobile Museum which houses a portion of Bill Harrah's original collection of vintage cars (see our Attractions chapter for details).

Peppermill Hotel Casino Reno
$ • 2707 S. Virginia St., Reno, Nev.
• (775) 826-2121, (800) 282-2444

Back in 1971, the Peppermill was a popular coffee shop known for the enormous servings of fresh fruit that accompanied almost all of its menu selections. The fresh fruit is still served today, but the coffee shop is just a small part of the full-service gaming resort that offers a tantalizing choice of first-class accommodations, entertainment and dining options.

For lodging, guests can choose from 1,070 luxurious rooms featuring 24-hour room service, telephones with e-mail, in-room movies and keno, and minibars. Suites with Jacuzzis and fax machines are also available. Premier dining choices include the Peppermill, the original 24-hour coffee shop with an international menu; the Island Buffet, with a Polynesian theme; the Steak House for American favorites in a casual setting; and the White Orchid, for elegant dining in an intimate, romantic en-

vironment. At press time the resort announced plans for a three-phase expansion to include a new showroom, additional convention space and a 17-story hotel addition.

The outdoor pool at the Peppermill is especially beautiful; it's tucked at the base of a waterfall that cascades down a replica of a Sierra Nevada mountain. Other amenities of this first-class resort include a health club, gift shop, beauty salon, full-service concierge desk and a free shuttle to and from downtown and the airport. Besides the casino with its more than 1,400 slot and video poker machines and wide variety of table games, the Peppermill offers free entertainment in the casino cabaret.

The casino area of this resort is particularly busy and surrounds you with a dazzling display of flashing lights and clanging bells. For an island of calm away from this din, try the Fireside Lounge (ask for directions because it's hidden in the sea of slot machines). With its circular gas fireplace/fountain and plush couches, it's a lovely oasis, one at the top of the list of Insiders' favorite romantic hideaways: the Fireside Lounge is well known as a great place for marriage proposals.

The Peppermill is close to the Reno/Sparks Convention Center and to shopping at Meadowood Mall (see our Shopping chapter). If you're in the mood to walk and commune with nature, Virginia Lake with its 1-mile walking path is just a block away.

Reno Hilton
$ • 2500 E. Second St., Reno, Nev.
• (775) 789-2000, (800) 648-5080

Sprawling over 148 acres inside the city limits of Reno, the Reno Hilton is pretty hard to miss. In fact, if you arrive by air at Reno/Tahoe International Airport, you often get a marvelous bird's-eye view of the resort just before touching down. When it roared into town in 1978 as the MGM Grand–Reno (complete with a real lion), it dwarfed everything else around. It had the world's largest casino, with more than 2,000 slot machines. It had the world's largest stage, with a DC-9 jet as a prop in the extravaganza, *Hello Hollywood, Hello*. And it had more than 1,000 hotel rooms, which quickly doubled to more than 2,000. It was owned briefly by Bally Manufacturing and re-

Photo: John Ascuaga's Nugget

Resort amenities like this pool-side atrium are a bonus to busy visitors.

named Bally's Reno, but it has been owned by Hilton Hotels Corporation and named the Reno Hilton since 1992.

Although it has since been eclipsed in size by other gaming resorts in Nevada, the Reno Hilton still entertains its guests in grand style. Built around a Hollywood theme, it oozes opulence, from its enormous chandeliers to the signed pictures of movie stars lining the walls. The carpets are plush and the ambiance is quiet elegance, quite a contrast to the earsplitting din of many other casinos.

A stay at this resort is entertainment personified. Besides all the usual casino games, sports book enthusiasts rave about the huge SuperBook that has set new standards of technological sophistication not found in other casinos. In addition to a vast array of huge TV screens showing live sporting events from all over the country, it has 188 seats with individual color monitors and writing desks.

If you should tire of the nonstop action in the full-service casino, try bowling in the 50-lane bowling alley or a game of tennis on the indoor/outdoor courts or shopping in the large upscale shopping mall. You can even practice your golf swing at Nevada's only aquatic golf driving range on Lake Hilton and win prizes by shooting at the floating greens.

The Reno Hilton also has a large swimming pool, health club and Fun Quest Family Amusement Center. One of the favorite stops for locals at this resort is the movie theater, which is reminiscent of private Hollywood screening rooms. For ultimate comfort you can relax on cozy couches equipped with end tables for your refreshments.

And when the sun goes down, the world-class fun really begins — the Reno Hilton is in the forefront for nightlife (see our Nightlife and Casino Nightlife chapters for specifics). You can let your imagination run free in the lavish stage productions in the Reno Hilton Theater. You can laugh with the country's top comics in the Improv Comedy Club. You can dance the night away with top-name bands in the Aspen Lounge. And during the summer months, you also can see headliners in the resort's outdoor amphitheater.

And speaking of outdoors, the strange

looking contraption in the northwest corner of the parking lot is the Hilton's Ultimate Rush Thrill Ride. If you can't find enough excitement within the building, you can be hoisted 180 feet to the top and freefall 60 feet. It might be especially appealing if you've just lost a bundle in the resort's casino (see our Attractions and Kidstuff chapters for more information).

To satisfy your every eating whim, the Reno Hilton has a variety of restaurants. Designed around a replica of the Grand Canyon, the Grand Canyon Buffet offers breakfast, lunch and dinner, all for a moderate price. For a more formal dinner setting, the Steak House specializes in gourmet continental and American cuisine. Andiamo serves luscious Italian entrees in a contemporary neoclassic setting. Chevy's Fresh Mex offers Mexican food in a Southwestern-themed setting, and Johnny Rocket's offers a trip back to the 1940s with its diner motif and great hamburgers and shakes.

When booking a room at the Reno Hilton, it's important to remember it's not within walking distance of other casinos or the downtown area. But with all the amenities the resort offers, maybe that's not important. It's a favorite place for all who enjoy elegance without the hustle and bustle so common to many other resorts.

Silver Legacy Resort Casino
$ • 407 N. Virginia St., Reno, Nev.
• (702) 329-4777, (800) 687-7733
When Silver Legacy Resort Casino opened in 1995, it redefined the Reno skyline. Its 38 floors of gleaming glass and concrete make it a vivid landmark, but it's the massive sphere alongside it that really catches your attention. Initially criticized by local residents as being ugly, tasteless and ordinary, the big globe is the world's largest composite dome and measures 180 feet in diameter. To find out what happens inside the dome, see our description

of the Mining Machine at Silver Legacy in the Attractions chapter.

As part of the tri-property complex that also includes Circus Circus Hotel/Casino–Reno and the Eldorado Hotel/Casino, Silver Legacy's street-level exterior takes you back to the 1800s with turn-of-the-century storefront facades. This same theme is carried out inside the resort where you'll find rich, dark woods and vibrant furnishings reminiscent of Nevada's silver-mining days.

If you take the time to really look around the public areas of the property, you'll be surprised at the number and quality of antiques and collectibles that are casually displayed everywhere. You'll see an authentic Wells Fargo stagecoach, complete with leather baggage holders and straps; a colorful carousel that was handmade in 1910; and countless smaller items, such as bronze streetlights, old-time model planes and antique cash registers. But you really can't miss the 43 pieces of the Mackay Silver Collection that are beautifully displayed in the grand hotel lobby. The entire 1,300-piece collection was commissioned in 1876 by the late John W. Mackay, a silver baron, for his wife, Marie Louise. Mackay sent a half ton of silver from a Comstock mine in Virginia City, Nevada, to Tiffany & Company in New York, where it took 200 men two years to craft the service. The dies were later destroyed so the pattern would truly be one of a kind.

Sprawling over 2 blocks of downtown Reno, Silver Legacy has 1,711 guest rooms and suites. Amenities include an outdoor swimming pool and sun deck, health spa, beauty salon and a tantalizing array of upscale shops. The five restaurants offer a tempting variety of cuisine, such as the fresh shellfish served at Fairchild's Oyster Bar and the melt-in-your-mouth steaks at Sterling's Seafood Steakhouse. Silver Legacy also has three lounges and a large exhibition hall where head-

INSIDERS' TIP

When driving south on U.S. Highway 395 near the Del Monte Lane exit, the enormous, turreted structure you see to the right is not a gaming resort. It's the private residence of John Harrah, son of the late gaming pioneer, Bill Harrah.

How Suite it Is!

Most resorts and hotels offer suites, which often simply means that a separate sitting area and a few extra amenities are thrown in. But in addition to these basic suites that many guests can afford to rent, a lot of Reno/Tahoe resorts have taken the suite concept to new heights in size and richness by offering "super suites." Costing millions of dollars to construct and furnished with almost outrageous elegance, these suites are designed to dazzle even the highrollers and celebrities for whom they're reserved.

With 4,200 square feet, three bedrooms, five and a half bathrooms, two bars and 10 television sets, the Super Safari Suite at the Peppermill Hotel Casino Reno is larger than most people's homes — and certainly a lot more ostentatious. But don't look for the kitchen; there isn't one. When guests check in here, they'll be sweating in a sumptuous Jacuzzi underneath a changing domed sky, not over a hot stove. When hunger pangs strike, gourmet cuisine is just a phone call away. The attentive staff will deliver and serve it on the suite's stunning glass-and-wood dining room table that was handcrafted in Italy.

At a cost of $1.5 million, no expense was spared in creating this essence of elegance. The safari theme begins at the heavy, handcarved wood door that showcases an elephant with protruding tusks. Each room in this massive penthouse eloquently elaborates on the unique artistry of Africa, from the striking zebra-design carpets to the sculptures of native water carriers surrounding the Jacuzzi to the plush leopard-patterned fabrics on the walls.

It's not the jungle, but the Super Safari Suite at the Peppermill Hotel Casino in Reno.

Photo: Jeff Ross

The designer spent nearly a year combing the globe for just the right accouterments to exquisitely carry out the safari theme. The feel of Africa is authenticated in the tribal masks, shields and drums used as decorative art pieces. And the theme is carried out to the last detail, including the gold elephant heads that serve as tiebacks for the window coverings.

But what would a safari be like without animals? When you first walk into this suite, you'll be stunned to see a full-sized rhinoceros casually standing by the pool table — so lifelike, it looks almost as if it's charging the table to take the next shot. And then there's an elephant in the foliage surrounding the Jacuzzi that appears to be guarding the pool as its own private watering hole. Although they look real, the monstrous

— continued on next page

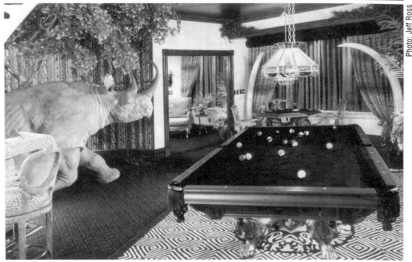

Photo: Jeff Ross

The Super Safari Suite at the Peppermill Hotel Casino Reno
includes a one-of-a-kind pool room.

animals were sculpted from fiberglass along with several other pieces of animal artwork displayed in the suite.

The rooms sprawl across the top two floors of the hotel, and a beautiful circular staircase connects the separate levels. The five full bathrooms are beautifully appointed with handmade tiles, and all feature steam showers. The largest steam shower, which accommodates 12 people, can simulate a tropical rainstorm and also has a large TV screen built into the wall.

In addition to the Jacuzzi, the main living room has state-of-the-art entertainment equipment, including a VCR, a stereophonic sound system and an immense television screen.

So what does all this cost? If the resort charged, it's estimated the Super Safari Suite would cost $5,000 a night. But it's actually free to highrollers as long as they gamble large sums of money. So if you're envious, don't be. You can take comfort in knowing there's no "free lunch" since anyone who stays here has had to "earn" the right to do so.

liners perform, plus the Catch a Rising Star comedy club (see our Nightlife chapter). Remember, when you stay at any of the three resorts in this tri-property complex, you can easily wander from one to the other because they're all interconnected with skywalks.

Insiders know this is definitely the liveliest place in Reno — it's noisy, it's crowded and it's exciting.

Sparks

John Ascuaga's Nugget
$ • 1100 Nugget Ave., Sparks, Nev.
• (775) 356-3300, (800) 648-1177

From a 60-seat coffee shop across the street from its current location, John Ascuaga's Nugget has grown since 1955 into one of the largest gaming resorts and convention centers in the Reno/Tahoe area. Its twin 29-story towers dominate the skyline east of downtown Reno.

While this resort doesn't have an obvious theme, luxury still abounds, from the gorgeous, year-round rooftop spa to the colorful Basque decor of its most recently opened restaurant, Orozko. A family owned and -managed property, the Nugget prides itself on personalized service. It offers 1,600 deluxe rooms and suites, and all provide stunning views of the Sierra Nevada mountains or the valley.

The resort is also home to the only golden rooster declared an object of art by a jury in a highly publicized trial against the U.S. Government. Weighing 206 troy ounces and standing more than 9 inches tall, the rooster was crafted to promote a new restaurant in the casino. And even though the resort had obtained permission from the San Francisco Mint to create the bird, the government prosecuted the Nugget, declaring that individuals are not allowed to have more than 50 ounces of gold unless it is an object of art. Anyway, the government lost the case; the jury declared that the rooster is art and now he is free as a bird and can be seen near the hotel entrance.

Well known for its quality cuisine, the resort can satisfy any taste in food with its eight restaurants. A longtime Insider favorite is John's Oyster Bar, where you can sit at the bar and watch the seafood (which is flown in fresh daily) being prepared in a variety of mouthwatering ways. The Steakhouse Grill has some of the best steaks in town, and Trader Dick's provides a fully themed Polynesian dining experience, complete with an enormous saltwater aquarium over the bar, loaded with gorgeous fish.

The Nugget is also a hot spot for entertainment. Headliners share the stage in the Celebrity Showroom with the famous elephant Angel. We tell you all about this highly trained pachyderm in our Kidstuff chapter. Headliners also appear in the larger Rose Ballroom. The Casino Cabaret showcases musical lounge acts and Trader Dick's features dance music popular with the 40 and older crowd.

As Victorian Square is right across the street, the Nugget is an especially lively place during special events that take place there,

such as the Best in the West Nugget Rib Cook-off (see Annual Events). Victorian Square also plays host to some events connected with Hot August Nights. (See our Attractions chapter for a description of this 6 block area of Victorian Square, and our Annual Events chapter for more about Hot August Nights.)

North Shore Lake Tahoe

Cal–Neva Resort
$$ • 2 Stateline Rd., Crystal Bay, Nev.
• (775) 832-4000, (800) 225-6382

It was once owned by Frank Sinatra. And Marilyn Monroe and John F. Kennedy were frequent guests. Known as the "Lady of the Lake," the Cal Neva Lodge (now the Cal–Neva Resort) was a favorite playground for Hollywood's biggest stars during the 1940s and '50s. But when the Nevada State Gaming Control Board learned Sinatra was also entertaining people with questionable backgrounds, it rescinded his gaming license. The lodge fell upon hard times until a succession of new owners revived it beginning in the 1980s.

Today the Cal–Neva Resort retains the romance, history and elegance of its past. It has all the touches and amenities of a modern full-service casino resort. Since the California–Nevada state line bisects the property, you can swim from state to state in the lovely outdoor pool overlooking Lake Tahoe or stand with one foot in each state in front of the enormous rock fireplace in the Indian Room. Used for special events, the Indian Room also showcases the history of Lake Tahoe with displays of Washoe Indian artifacts and pictures of early settlers.

The main lodge of the resort has been restored to its original 1937 design, including open-beamed ceilings and hardwood floors. A focal point is the Circle Bar with its domed ceiling that contains 7,000 pieces of glittering multicolored German crystal. It's hard to beat this favorite watering hole's view of the lake at sunset. But lake views are a given here since all the private rooms as well as public areas of the lodge have large windows facing the water.

You can choose from hotel rooms in the tower or cabins and chalets on the lakeshore, including a variety of accommodations once used by celebrities. Fireplaces and patios are also available. Besides the 24-hour casino, other amenities include two restaurants, two bars, tennis courts, a video arcade and a full-service European health spa and fitness facility.

Romance, however, is still the name of the game for this grand old dame. The Cal–Neva is one of the hottest spots for weddings at Lake Tahoe. With three wedding chapels and a complete bridal and honeymoon service on-site, the resort specializes in personalized weddings performed in exquisite surroundings overlooking the lake.

For a taste of Old Tahoe with all the comforts of today, the Cal–Neva is a fun place to stay. It's in the center of Crystal Bay, where you can walk to three other casinos and several more restaurants.

Hyatt Regency Lake Tahoe Resort & Casino

$$$$ • Country Club Dr. at Lakeshore Dr., Incline Village, Nev.
• (775) 832-1234, (800) 233-1234

If you've stayed in Hyatts anywhere in the world, you know they offer the utmost in luxury. The Hyatt Regency Lake Tahoe Resort & Casino is a top-of-the-line mountain retreat that appeals to families, couples and groups. Tucked away in a splendid forest of pine trees on the shore of Lake Tahoe, the resort has 458 deluxe alpine guest rooms, suites and beachfront cottages.

Decorated in a warm, woodsy style, the guest rooms have private butler servibars, two phones, in-room safes and cable TV that includes more than 100 movies to choose from. The suites are larger and offer either a lake or mountain view plus parlor rooms that separate the bedrooms.

Two-bedroom cottages situated on the resort's private beach are also available and include fireplaces in the parlor rooms, private decks overlooking the lake and wet bars. Several units also have kitchens.

Like many Hyatts, this resort also has a Regency Club with VIP services and amenities such as morning newspaper delivery, nightly turndown, bathrobes and access to the Regency Club Lounge.

A stay at this resort can be as relaxed or as fast-paced as you want it to be. With magnificent views of the lake and mountains, many guests are perfectly content to just unwind and enjoy the scenery from a comfortable chair on the beach. But for those looking for more activity, the Hyatt provides enough variety to keep guests entertained around the clock. Besides the casino, the resort offers tennis courts, a 24-hour outdoor heated pool and spa, a health club, a video game room and shops.

If this resort is in your price class, it can be a great choice for families because Camp Hyatt offers a comprehensive, supervised activity program for children of guests (see our Kidstuff chapter for details). The restaurants offer three distinct dining styles — Pacific Rim food is served in Ciao Mein, casual cuisine in the Sierra Cafe and hearty American entrees in the Lone Eagle Grille.

A favorite with locals, the Lone Eagle Grille is a must-stop, if only for a drink. With two huge rock fireplaces and a cathedral-like beamed ceiling, it's Old Tahoe personified. The interior is warm and the view of the lake, dazzling. On cold days, it's a special treat to bundle up and sip your favorite drink by the outdoor firepit on the grille's lakeshore deck.

The Hyatt is close to the Ponderosa Ranch, Diamond Peak Ski Resort, golf courses at Incline Village and a variety of hiking trails.

South Shore Lake Tahoe

Caesars Tahoe

$$$ • 55 U.S. Hwy. 50, Stateline, Nev.
• (775) 588-3515, (800) 648-3353

Directly across from the prestigious Edgewood Tahoe Golf Course, Caesars Tahoe affords lovely views of lush green fairways (in

INSIDERS' TIP

When checking in at a gaming resort, ask about show reservations. Many resorts give preferential reservations to their guests.

the summer) with Lake Tahoe shimmering in the background. If you want the convenience of walking to other resorts, restaurants and shopping, Caesars is a great location. Although you don't have to wear a toga to fit in, some of the resort's employees do because of the decidedly Roman theme.

The hotel has 440 rooms, and many have in-room Roman tubs or Jacuzzis. Its 37 themed suites are lavish depictions of Hollywood, ancient Rome, the Orient and the Bahamas. Winter or summer, Caesars has a full complement of activities to entertain guests, including a full-service casino with race and sports book, and a health club with a lagoon-style indoor pool.

One of the best views of Lake Tahoe is from its middle, and Caesars makes it easy for guests to see by offering cruises on its private yacht, the *Odyssey*. Two-hour trips on this 58-foot Hatteras boat depart year round at 10 AM and take guests across the lake to lovely Emerald Bay. When the sun goes down, Caesars's live entertainment kicks into high gear, including headliners appearing in its Circus Maximus showroom and all-night dancing in Nero's 2000 dance club (see our Casino Nightlife and Nightlife chapters). The resort has eight restaurants offering an eclectic variety of cuisine, such as Cantonese in the Empress Court, northern Italian in the Primavera and California-style in Planet Hollywood. Other amenities include a complete wedding service, three lounges and a galleria of shops. Although you don't really have to leave the building to be entertained, Caesars is close to other casinos in Stateline and just a few miles from the base of Heavenly Ski Resort.

Harrah's Lake Tahoe

$$$$ • U.S. Hwy. 50, Stateline, Nev.
• (775) 588-6611, (800) 427-7247

When the late legendary gaming pioneer Bill Harrah first set eyes on the Gateway Club in Stateline, he was amazed that such a small rundown establishment could be making so much money. But location was the key, as the club sat on the border between California and Nevada at beautiful South Shore Lake Tahoe. Harrah bought it, remodeled it and reopened it as Harrah's Lake Tahoe in 1955. The rest is history, as the saying goes. With his unique management style, Harrah crafted a five-star resort that has been called the Cadillac of gaming resorts. (See our listing for Harrah's Reno in this chapter for details about Mr. Harrah.)

The hotel is a vision of luxury. Each room includes a bay-like window, telephones, TVs and two bathrooms. Although it's an 18-story high-rise, the hotel's earthen colors blend perfectly with the surrounding Lake Tahoe landscape. The natural textures of the interior also reflect the mountains, giving guests the feeling they are in a splendid alpine lodge.

But the luxury doesn't stop there. In typical Harrah's style, the cuisine in its seven restaurants is also world-class. At Friday's Station Steak & Seafood Grill on the 18th floor, you can enjoy a moderately priced dinner with a million-dollar view of Lake Tahoe. There is an equally spectacular view from the top floor at the Forest Restaurant, where you can enjoy a bountiful buffet. Or, if your idea of a view is a river, you can eat in a grove of aspens with a river running through it in the American River Cafe.

But the shining star of all the restaurants, including both a setting and a menu sure to please even the most discriminating gourmet, is The Summit. It's intimate, it's exclusive and it's difficult to get in, but if you're lucky enough to get a reservation, we guarantee you won't be disappointed. Set in the penthouse suite where Sammy Davis Jr., Frank Sinatra and Wayne Newton stayed when they appeared in the show room, The Summit provides a dining experience you will not soon forget.

And what would a casino resort be like without live entertainment? The South Shore Room has been a must-stop for celebrity entertainers since it opened in 1959; the roll call of past and present performers reads like a list of "Who's Who in Entertainment." Although it used to include dinner and dressing up, the shows are now more casual and include drinks only. Outside the South Shore Room, the show rocks on as live bands perform nightly on the Casino Center Stage.

Harrah's Lake Tahoe is a great place for families. You can even bring the family pet along because it's one of the few resorts that provides kennels. Children can enjoy the Family Fun Center, where they'll find the latest video games, virtual reality and an indoor playscape.

Other amenities at the hotel include a large, dome-covered swimming pool and spa, a health club and a variety of shops. Its location in the heart of Stateline makes Harrah's Lake Tahoe appealing to guests who want to be in the center of the action. This resort is first-class in every respect, but be aware that it can be very busy, especially during high season.

Harveys Resort Hotel/Casino
$$ • U.S. Hwy. 50, Stateline, Nev.
• (775) 588-2411, (800) 427-8397
Founded in 1944 by the late Harvey Gross, Harveys Resort Hotel/Casino has the distinction of being South Shore Lake Tahoe's original casino property. From its humble beginnings as a one-room gambling club, it has grown to a full-service resort with the largest hotel at Lake Tahoe. Its modern glass towers and slick decor present a striking contrast to the woodsy ambiance of most other Lake Tahoe resorts.

The contemporary theme is carried through to the 740 rooms and suites, most of which offer a view of the mountains or Lake Tahoe. The rooms are large and luxurious, with all the extras expected of an award-winning property. Resort amenities include a shopping galleria, health club, swimming pool, spa and video game arcade.

Harveys casino is the largest at Lake Tahoe — 88,000 square feet of gaming. The Emerald Theater features stage revues, and headliners appear in its outdoor arena during the summer. It's not hard to find great food at Harveys as the eight restaurants offer enough variety to fit any mood and taste. Locals particularly prefer the Sage Room because of absolutely mouthwatering steaks served in a casual Western environment, or Llewellyn's, where you're treated to delectable continental fare with a gorgeous view of Lake Tahoe.

Since Harveys is directly across U.S. Highway 50 from Harrah's Lake Tahoe, guests at either of these resorts can easily walk from one to the other. This area of Stateline is the busiest at South Shore Lake Tahoe, so if you want to be in the center of the action, this is definitely the place.

Lake Tahoe Horizon Casino Resort
$$ • U.S. Hwy. 50, Stateline, Nev.
• (775) 588-6211, (800) 648-3322
Of the four gaming resorts in Stateline —

Caesars Tahoe, Harrah's Lake Tahoe, Harveys Resort Hotel/Casino and the Lake Tahoe Horizon Casino Resort — the latter is the least expensive and the least lavish. Formerly the Sahara Tahoe, it was refurbished in 1995 with pleasant pastel colors and light woods.

Accommodations include deluxe and standard rooms and, for that very special occasion, the suite formerly used by Elvis Presley. Amenities at the Horizon include the largest outdoor heated swimming pool at Lake Tahoe, three outdoor hot tubs, a shopping arcade, an amusement center and a fitness center.

Claiming to have the "friendliest tables in Tahoe" in its 24-hour casino, the Horizon has a casual and laid back atmosphere. If you're looking for dining bargains, the restaurants at the Horizon are a good place to start. Josh's serves lobster at a very reasonable cost, and the Four Seasons specializes in a one-pound New York steak for a surprisingly low price. Bars include the Tahoe Mountain Brewery, which serves microbrews, Sato Sushi and the Cabaret Bar. The Aspen Lounge features live entertainment, a large-screen TV and dancing. The Horizon is within walking distance of other casinos and shopping, and it's also close to Heavenly Ski Resort.

Vacation Resorts

Northstar-at-Tahoe and the Resort at Squaw Creek in the North Shore Lake Tahoe area do not have casinos since they're in California. But except for gaming and its inherent nightlife, these resorts offer every other year-round amenity you can think of. For an explanation of high and low seasons and general booking information, refer to the beginning of this chapter.

North Shore Lake Tahoe

Northstar-at-Tahoe
$$ • Calif. Hwy. 267, 6 mi. north of Lake Tahoe • (530) 562-1010,
(800) 466-6784
With its impressive array of activities and amenities, Northstar-at-Tahoe has been in a class of its own since it opened in 1972. From the wooded slopes of Mt. Pluto, where you

Photo: Harrah's Reno

Luxury rooms, excitement in lavish casinos, restaurants to indulge your every whim, and special places to relax and unwind await resort visitors in the Reno/Tahoe area.

can hike, bike and ski down a dormant volcano, to the pristine meadows of Martis Valley, where you can golf and hike, Northstar offers a mountain vacation that is hard to beat.

Its 260 lodging units range from hotel-type rooms to condominiums to spacious mountain homes. Accommodations feature fireplaces, color TVs, VCRs and telephones. All units, except rooms in the Village Lodge, have fully equipped kitchens.

Winter sports include downhill skiing and snowboarding on 2,420 acres of mountain terrain, cross-country skiing on 65 kilometers of groomed trails, sleigh rides and snowmobile tours (see our Winter Sports chapter for details).

The resort shifts gears in the summer, but the fun doesn't stop. Guests can enjoy golf at Northstar's challenging 18-hole course (see

our Golf chapter), mountain biking in the park, free tennis on its 10 outdoor courts, horseback riding and guided nature hikes on mountain trails and fly fishing at Sawmill Lake. Northstar also has two outdoor heated swimming pools, spas, saunas and a fitness center. It's the perfect place for families because all activities have special provisions for children, including special ski and golf packages, an adventure camp and the Minors' Camp child care center.

During the winter the resort serves breakfast and lunch in several locations on the mountain, including the Summit Deck & Grille, with a lovely view of Lake Tahoe, and the Big Springs Day Lodge at the top of the gondola. In the base village you can enjoy a drink and gourmet dining in the Timbercreek Restaurant and Lounge, buy groceries and deli items in

INSIDERS' TIP

Gaming resorts are usually generous with giveaways, so don't hesitate to ask about coupons for gambling, dining and drinking.

Vacation resorts offer lodging plus a whole range of summer and winter activities.

the Village Food Company or treat the family to pizza at Pedro's. The clubhouse at the golf course offers casual dining in the summer and Basque dinners on weekends during the winter. The village also has shops where you can buy upscale activewear and rent sporting equipment.

Insiders agree that one of the best features of Northstar is the free shuttle that continuously runs throughout the resort. So if you arrive by car, you can just park it and leave it. When you're ready to ski, you simply call the shuttle. You'll be picked up practically at your door and transported to the base of the mountain. No more struggles through crowded parking lots with all your ski equipment. The shuttle will take you anywhere in the resort — to dinner, to the tennis courts or to the golf course.

When booking lodging at Northstar, be sure to inquire about special packages. There's such a variety, you're bound to find one that will save you money and make your stay more

convenient. You can also reserve lodging at Northstar through some of the rental agents listed in our Vacation Rentals chapter. They rent a number of additional privately owned properties at the resort that might not be available through resort reservations. But when using an off-site rental agent, be aware that resort packages might not be available.

We highly recommend this resort at any time of the year for adults and families. Because of the variety of activities available on-site and the range of lodging from moderate to deluxe, it has something for everyone.

Resort at Squaw Creek
$$$$ • 400 Squaw Creek Rd., Olympic Valley, Calif. • (800) 327-3353

Everything about the Resort at Squaw Creek is delightfully discriminating — its location in Olympic Valley, surrounded by the magnificent jagged peaks of Squaw Valley USA; its lavishly appointed accommodations, offer-

---

INSIDERS' TIP

The concierge at a gaming resort can assist in arranging show reservations and local tours.

ing the optimum in comfort and luxury; and the endless variety of year-round activities that are conveniently available just outside.

When it opened in 1990, this resort set new standards of elegance for the North Shore Lake Tahoe area. And it has been winning prestigious awards for excellence from publications ever since, including *Conde Nast Traveler, Gourmet* and *Wine Spectator* magazines.

All guest rooms have gorgeous views of either the snow-dusted peaks or the pristine mountain meadow. They also feature custom furnishings, original artwork, refrigerators, minibars and spacious windows that open to the fresh mountain air. Of the 405 accommodations, 200 suites are available, some with fireplaces, sitting areas and complete kitchens.

But the stunning decor is by no means confined to the rooms — the public areas of this resort are simply gorgeous. The tasteful combination of wood, stone and glass used to construct the buildings blends beautifully with the surrounding mountain terrain. In summer, the exterior areas are especially enjoyable; the stone terraces and pool area offer lovely views of the landscape, including the cascading waterfall that runs through the property.

Winter activities at this premier resort include downhill skiing, snowboarding, cross-country skiing, ice-skating, sledding, sleigh rides, dogsled rides and snowshoeing. Squaw Creek also has its own lift that gives skiers access to the lifts at Squaw Valley USA, the site of the 1960 Winter Olympics (for details on winter activities at Squaw Valley see our Winter Sports chapter).

Summer activities include golf on the 18-hole Robert Trent Jones Jr. golf course (see our Golf chapter for more information), tennis,

horseback riding, rafting, boating, hiking, mountain climbing and biking. The resort also has a three-pool water garden with a 120-foot waterslide and four spas, plus a complete health and fitness center. Additional summer activities are available at Squaw Valley USA. A variety of supervised children's programs are also offered summer and winter.

Dining can also be an exceptional experience at Squaw Creek with five restaurants to tempt your palate. Cascades offers a relaxed buffet with special regional dinners. Ristorante Montagna specializes in California Italian cuisine. Sweet Potatoes Deli serves delectable breakfasts and lunches and will even pack a picnic basket or backpack lunch for you to take along on a hike through the valley. Bullwhackers Pub and Restaurant serves steaks, fish and burgers in a lively microbrew atmosphere. And the resort's four-diamond signature restaurant, Glissandi, offers exceptional gourmet dining in an intimate, luxurious setting.

If you're arriving by air at Reno/Tahoe International Airport, Squaw Creek provides transportation to the resort. It also operates a free shuttle to Squaw Valley USA. And whether you're booking winter or summer, be sure to inquire about packages because the resort offers a large assortment.

Although you can easily spend your entire vacation right on the property, Squaw Creek is just 5 miles from Lake Tahoe. If you can afford to stay at the resort, it offers the optimum in elegance. But even if you can't afford the rooms, drop by for a drink or dinner; you can still enjoy the gorgeous views. And don't be surprised if you're rubbing elbows with TV and movie stars since the Resort at Squaw Creek is a well-known celebrity destination.

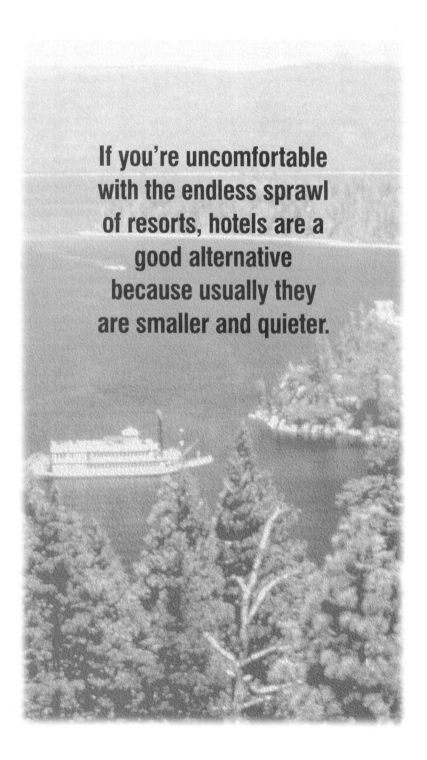

If you're uncomfortable with the endless sprawl of resorts, hotels are a good alternative because usually they are smaller and quieter.

Hotels and Motels

Because many visitors come to Nevada to gamble, most Nevada hotels in the Reno/Tahoe area have casinos. Casino owners learned years ago that by providing rooms for their patrons, they would have captive players for their gaming tables and slot machines. With the exception of the McCarran House in Sparks, all the Nevada hotels we recommend in this chapter have gaming. And since casino gambling's not legal in the California area of Reno/Tahoe, the hotels there don't have casinos.

The hotels in this chapter are really scaled-down versions of the gaming and vacation resorts we tell you about in our Resorts chapter. Although the hotels provide a variety of amenities, they don't offer the same level of comprehensive options as the resorts do. But if you don't want all the extras of a full-service resort, why pay for them? And if you're uncomfortable with the endless sprawl of resorts, hotels are a good alternative because usually they are smaller and quieter.

For accommodations that are more back-to-basics, motels are a good choice. While a few motels have restaurants and bars and many have swimming pools and other extras, in general they're in the business of just providing you with a clean, comfortable room for the night and not entertaining you. Notable exceptions to this are the Western Village Inn/Casino in Sparks, Nevada, and the Lakeside Inn & Casino in Stateline, Nevada, which have

casinos as well. Many motels are cheaper than hotels or resorts and their rooms may also be more readily available, especially during high season.

Our list of recommended motels is not meant to be exhaustive but as Insiders we have singled out examples of the kinds of accommodations that are available. You can find out about additional motels in the Reno/Tahoe area by calling the 800 numbers below.

The hotels and motels in this chapter accept credit cards and most have nonsmoking accommodations and rooms that are accessible to the disabled. Since rates and availability vary with special events as well as the season of the year, check out our Resorts chapter for our Insiders' advice about the easiest and most difficult times to book rooms. Be aware that during holidays and sometimes on weekends, some properties may require a minimum stay of more than one night. You can reserve accommodations by calling any of the hotels or motels directly or also by calling The Reno/Tahoe Visitors Information Center, (800) 367-7366, or Lake Tahoe Reservations, (800) 288-2463.

To avoid confusion about the physical addresses of some of the properties at Lake Tahoe, it's important to know that some highways are called by street names within the towns. Along North Shore Lake Tahoe, Nev. Highway 28 is called Tahoe Boulevard in Incline Village, and Calif. Highway 28 is called

N. Lake Boulevard in Brockway, Kings Beach and Tahoe City. Along Lake Tahoe's west shore, Calif. Highway 89 is also called W. Lake Boulevard. In South Lake Tahoe, California, U.S. Highway 50 is also known as Lake Tahoe Boulevard. Now, with that said, let's take a look at some of the accommodations that are available.

Price Code

Each hotel or motel listing includes a symbol representing a price range for a standard room for one weekend night during high season based upon double-occupancy and excluding tax.

$	$38 to $55
$$	$56 to $79
$$$	$80 to $99
$$$$	$100 to $149
$$$$$	More than $149

Hotels

Reno

Best Western Airport Plaza Hotel
$$ • 1981 Terminal Wy., Reno, Nev.
• (775) 348-6370, (800) 648-3525

Right across the street from Reno/Tahoe International Airport, the Airport Plaza Hotel is very convenient for visitors arriving by air. Its 270 rooms are clean and comfortable, and a free shuttle is available to and from the airport. The restaurant has a cozy intimate atmosphere and is a great place for lunch, especially if you like sumptuous salad bars.

With its rich wood paneling, the lounge has the feel of a library, offering a quiet place to relax after a harried day of travel or fun. Other amenities include a small casino with slot machines only, an outdoor pool and a health club. Pets are welcome. Although you can walk to the airport, you'll need transportation to get to other casinos and attractions.

Boomtown Hotel Casino Reno
$$$ • I-80, 7 mi. west of Reno, Nev.
• (775) 345-6000, (800) 648-3790

A last outpost as you head west over the summit on Interstate 80, Boomtown Hotel Casino Reno has always catered to travelers. Originally a bareboned truck stop called Bill and Effie's, it has provided truckers and travelers alike a much needed shelter to wait out the winter storms which frequently close I-80.

Boomtown has continued to boom over the years and today it's a large hotel/casino with a Hollywood western theme. It appeals to families and people traveling on a budget, but is still a hangout for truckers because where else are they treated so special? With private dining digs, accommodations and perks for truck drivers, no wonder the parking lot is jammed with 18-wheelers, with or without a snowstorm.

Although not elegant, Boomtown's 300-plus rooms are pleasant and modestly priced. The hotel also features 29 suites and minisuites, most with Jacuzzi baths and enclosed balconies. Hotel amenities include a newly refurbished indoor swimming pool and patio. Since the management of this resort uses modest food prices to attract both locals and travelers, eating in any of the four restaurants is a bargain.

Boomtown is a great place for families, not only because of the low prices, but also because it has a huge Family Fun Center that kids simply adore. Its focal point is a large antique carousel built by Herschell–Spillman in 1908. But the rest of the amusements are modern and high-tech, such as the latest video games, miniature golf, virtual reality, movies and a dynamic motion theater (see our Kidstuff chapter for more information).

For adult entertainment, Boomtown has a full-service casino with live entertainment in the Boomtown Lounge nightly except Mondays. RVers have also found that the RV park at this resort is a great base camp because it's in between Reno and Lake Tahoe. We tell you more about it in our Camping and RVing chapter.

When staying at Boomtown, keep in mind

www.insiders.com
See this and many other **Insiders' Guide®** destinations online.
Visit us today!

it's not within walking distance of other casinos or shopping because it's 7 miles west of Reno, though there is a shuttle to the downtown area.

Boomtown is poised to boom again as future construction plans will add 2,000 hotel rooms, an 18-hole golf course, a large multiuse entertainment center and an interactive working history museum. When complete, the expansion will make Boomtown the largest gaming resort in northern Nevada.

Fitzgeralds Casino/Hotel Reno
$$$ • 255 N. Virginia St., Reno, Nev.
• (775) 785-3300, (800) 648-5022

If you've always wanted to visit the Emerald Isle but never made it, you can sample Irish hospitality in the Nevada desert at Fitzgeralds Casino/Hotel Reno. The luck of the Irish is alive and well in this Irish-themed hotel that's situated right beside the world famous Reno Arch in downtown.

Constructed in 1976, the 351 rooms are spacious and comfortable and offer stunning city and mountain views. The Fitz, as Insiders call it, has three restaurants —Mollys Garden Restaurant, Limericks Pub & Grille and O'Luckys Buffet/Showroom. Bars include the Fitz Showbar, Blarney Stone Sports/Pub, Luckys Bar and Limericks Pub. You can easily walk to other downtown casinos and restaurants when staying at the Fitz. (See our Nightlife chapter for more information.)

Flamingo Hilton
$$$ • 255 N. Sierra St., Reno, Nev.
• (775) 322-1111, (800) 648-4882

In the heart of downtown Reno, the ambiance at the Flamingo Hilton reminds you of Las Vegas in the 1950s. It's bright, it's noisy and even a little gaudy. But the more than 600 rooms are beautifully furnished, and the hotel offers a number of amenities, including in-room movies, 24-hour room service, a language interpreter, free valet parking and a complimentary airport shuttle.

Be sure to catch the show in the Flamingo Showroom: it's always first-class (see our Casino Nightlife chapter for details). The hotel has five restaurants that offer a broad spectrum of culinary delights, but the most popular with locals is The Top of the Flamingo Hilton Restaurant — Reno's only rooftop dining area. With its gorgeous panoramic view of downtown and the surrounding mountains, The Top of the Hilton (as it's known by Insiders) is a lovely dining spot for special occasions. Its adjoining lounge, which features easy listening dance music, is an "in" spot for the older crowd.

The Flamingo has a busy convention and meeting business but does not go out of its way to appeal to families. If you want the excitement of downtown it's a good choice, since it's within walking distance of other casinos and restaurants.

Holiday Inn & Diamond's Casino
$$$ • 1000 E. Sixth St., Reno, Nev.
• (775) 786-5151, (800) 465-4329

It's hard to tell what you'll get at a Holiday Inn these days as there doesn't seem to be a generic standard for them anymore. But the Holiday Inn & Diamond's Casino is a cut above most, including 286 comfortable rooms in a high-rise that affords gorgeous mountain views. The hotel also has two restaurants, an outdoor swimming pool, a bar and an airport shuttle. It's even OK to bring your pet along.

Just down the street from the Reno Livestock Events Center, it's a great location if you're attending events there, such as the Reno Rodeo or the Nevada State Fair (see our Annual Events chapter for details about these events). But it's a little remote from downtown, so don't expect to walk to other casinos or attractions.

Pioneer Inn Hotel/Casino
$$ • 221 S. Virginia St., Reno, Nev.
• (775) 324-7777, (800) 879-8879

Two blocks south of the Truckee River in

INSIDERS' TIP

Boomtown Hotel Casino Reno's cowboy boot collection on display in Waddies Steak and Dinner House is legendary. Almost as legendary is their scrumptious Strawberry Tall Cake, which you can indulge in for only $1.

downtown Reno, the Pioneer Inn Hotel/Casino has 252 moderate rooms. Amenities include a swimming pool, three restaurants, a bar and live entertainment. The Iron Sword restaurant is well known to locals as a great place for steak at a reasonable price. You can easily walk to other casinos and downtown attractions from this hotel.

Sundowner Hotel/Casino
$ • 450 N. Arlington Ave., Reno, Nev.
• (775) 786-7050, (800) 687-5490

With its cowboy logo, the Sundowner Hotel/Casino is a modern facility with an Old West theme. Amenities for its 593 rooms include an outdoor swimming pool, three restaurants, a lounge and a shuttle to the airport. It has a convenient downtown location close to other hotels, casinos and restaurants.

Sparks

McCarran House
$$ • 55 E. Nugget Ave., Sparks, Nev.
• (775) 358-6900, (800) 548-5798

If you don't want to fight your way through the slot machines to find guest registration, you can find your comfort zone at McCarran House. Absent a casino, it's just a regular hotel. But the 220 rooms are clean and modern and hotel extras include an outdoor swimming pool, spa, health club, restaurant, bar and a free 24-hour shuttle to the airport and around Sparks. It's just down the road from Victorian Square, where special events are held (see our Annual Events chapter for a list).

Silver Club Hotel/Casino
$ • 1040 Victorian Ave., Sparks, Nev.
• (775) 358-4771, (800) 905-7774

You can't get much closer to the action at Victorian Square in downtown Sparks than the Silver Club Hotel/Casino. It offers 206 moderate rooms, three restaurants, five bars, live entertainment in the casino and an airport shuttle. If you're in town Labor Day weekend for the Best in the West Nugget Rib Cook-off, it's right outside the door (see our Annual Events chapter).

North Shore Lake Tahoe

Sunnyside
$$$$$ • 1850 W. Lake Blvd., Tahoe City, Calif. • (530) 583-7200, (800) 822 2754

It's warm, it's romantic, it's cozy. Sunnyside is everything you could hope for in an intimate Old Tahoe lodge. Insiders know it as a favorite watering hole and place to be seen, especially during summer on the large deck overlooking the marina.

If you're lucky enough to book one of the 23 unique rooms here, your stay is bound to be a delightful alpine experience. The ambiance of both the public areas and the individual rooms can best be described as rustic elegance. While the rock fireplaces and heavy wooden beams give it a snug atmosphere, the overall feeling is light and open because large windows face Lake Tahoe and afford gorgeous views of the water and mountains.

The small lounge on the mezzanine level is especially delightful; you can curl up in a comfortable chair away from the people below and drink in the beauty of the lake.

There's a full-service restaurant and bar, and hotel guests are treated to a complimentary continental breakfast. Even if you can't book a room here, stop by to eat or drink since it's a great people-watching place. But don't be discouraged by the difficult parking situation, particularly in the summer — just be creative as it's well worth the effort. Sunnyside is 2 miles south of Tahoe City on Calif. Highway 89.

Part of the excitement of downtown Reno is the Flamingo Hilton, reminiscent of the 1950s with all the exciting casino amenities.

Tahoe Biltmore

$$$ • 5 Nev. Hwy. 28, Crystal Bay, Nev.
• (775) 831-0660, (800) 245-8667

Built in 1946 as the Tahoe Biltmore, this hotel has had a succession of names during the years, including the Cal–Neva Biltmore and the Nevada Lodge. In 1986, the present owners took back the original name — Tahoe Biltmore.

One of the oldest hotel/casinos at Lake Tahoe, the Biltmore boasts an interesting history of celebrity appearances by big name stars like Rowan and Martin, Regis Philbin and Phyllis Diller, who reportedly shocked theatergoers with her vivid green hair. The hotel also claims to have a resident ghost — a showgirl named Mary who was murdered in her room and whose spirit has reportedly been seen by employees and guests throughout the years.

Although its heyday as a showcase for celebrities is over — outshined by larger, glitzier gaming resorts in the Lake Tahoe area — it still offers comedy, dance music and stage revues in its Aspen Cabaret. Refurbished in 1997, the main casino tower has 47 rooms with room service, bell service and lake views. The other 45 rooms are motel-style accommodations to the rear of the property.

Besides the full-service casino, amenities include a swimming pool, 24-hour coffee shop and a sports bar. The Biltmore is known by Insiders to offer some of the best values in rooms and food at Lake Tahoe. It's also within easy walking distance to several other casinos and restaurants. Be sure to ask about membership in Club Biltmore, a cash-back players club that entitles members to prizes and perks at the hotel.

South Shore Lake Tahoe

Embassy Suites

$$$$$ • 4130 Lake Tahoe Blvd., South Lake Tahoe, Calif. • (530) 544-5400, (800) 988-9820

Perched right on the California–Nevada

state line, Embassy Suites has 400 luxurious suites with separate living rooms, minibars, microwave ovens and coffee makers. The restaurant serves lunch and dinner, and the lounge offers pizza as well as all your favorite beverages. Guests can also enjoy a complimentary breakfast each morning and a free cocktail reception each evening.

On-site recreational facilities include an indoor pool, whirlpool, sauna, fitness center and outdoor sundeck. The hotel also has heated valet parking and several shops. If it's convenience you want, Embassy Suites is a good choice because it's in the center of all the casino action and just down the road from Heavenly Ski Resort. It's a beautiful upscale property sure to please most any visitor to Lake Tahoe.

Motels
Reno

Adventure Inn
$$$$ • 3575 S. Virginia St., Reno, Nev.
• (775) 828-9000, (800) 937-1436

If you're in the mood for romance, Adventure Inn can help set the stage. The 45 themed rooms and suites can transport you to a variety of fantasylands such as space, the jungle, a cave or ancient Rome. Nothing is ordinary here, from the 8-foot round- or heart-shaped beds to the in-room spas and rain forest showers. There's even stretch-limo service to and from the inn (radius of 10 miles) and free champagne in the rooms. It's not surprising that the inn also has an on-site wedding chapel.

Best Inn and Suites
$$ • 1885 S. Virginia St., Reno, Nev.
• (775) 329-1001, (800) 626-1900

On one of the busiest corners in southwest Reno across from Park Lane Mall, the Best Inn and Suites has 103 moderate rooms, a dining room and a delightful outdoor pool area.

The lounge has live music for dancing and is a favorite weekend hangout for the older crowd. It's several miles south of downtown, so don't expect to walk to the casinos.

Bonanza Motor Inn
$$ • 215 W. Fourth St., Reno, Nev.
• (775) 322-8632, (800) 808-3303

With 57 moderate rooms and an outdoor pool, the Bonanza Motor Inn is within walking distance of downtown casinos and attractions. It's also OK to bring your pet along.

Colonial Motor Inn
$$ • 232 West St., Reno, Nev.
• (775) 786-5038, (800) 255-7366

Just a couple of blocks from all the casino action on S. Virginia Street, the Colonial Motor Inn has 100 rooms and an outdoor pool. You can just park your car and walk most anywhere downtown from this location. It's also close to the Truckee River Walk, the paved path along the Truckee River (see our Attractions chapter).

Days Inn
$$ • 701 E. Seventh St., Reno, Nev.
• (775) 786-4070, (800) 448-4555

If you're a Reno Rodeo fan, the Days Inn is a good location; it's just a couple of blocks from the Reno Livestock Events Center. On-site amenities for its 137 rooms include the Chicago Deli, which is a full-service restaurant, and an outdoor swimming pool. Pets are OK, but you'll need transportation to casinos and attractions.

La Quinta Inn
$$ • 4001 Market St., Reno, Nev.
• (775) 348-6100, (800) 531-5900

If you're arriving by air, La Quinta Inn is convenient since it's just across from Reno/Tahoe International Airport. Its 130 rooms are pleasant and modern. The inn has an outdoor swimming pool, a restaurant and an airport shuttle. Pets are allowed.

Reno Central Travelodge
$$ • 2050 Market St., Reno, Nev.
• (775) 786-2500, (800) 648-3800

Formerly a Rodeway Inn, the Reno Central Travelodge has 211 moderate rooms and an outdoor swimming pool. It's close to the Reno Hilton and Reno/Tahoe International Airport. But when staying here, be aware you'll need transportation to get to restaurants and casinos. Pets are welcome.

Reno Travelodge Downtown

$ • 655 W. Fourth St., Reno, Nev.
• (775) 329-3451, (800) 578-7878

With clean moderate rooms and an outdoor swimming pool, the Reno Travelodge Downtown is within walking distance of many casinos and restaurants. You can also share your room with your pet.

Super 8 Motel

$$ • 5851 S. Virginia St., Reno, Nev.
• (775) 825-2940, (800) 797-7366

A former Holiday Inn, the Super 8 Motel has a restaurant, lounge, outdoor swimming pool, airport shuttle and live entertainment. Its 153 rooms are clean and comfortable, and you can bring your pet along. But it's not close to attractions or casinos, so you'll need your car or other transportation to get around.

Truckee River Lodge

$ • 501 W. First St., Reno, Nev.
• (775) 786-8888, (800) 635-8950

You can fall asleep to the sound of a running river at the Truckee River Lodge; the Truckee River is right across the street. The only completely nonsmoking hotel/motel facility in Reno, this lodge is a healthy place to stay. Its on-site restaurant specializes in healthy foods, and you'll also find bike rentals and a health club. You can just park your car in the covered parking area and leave it because downtown casinos and restaurants are within easy walking distance.

University Inn

$ • 1001 N. Virginia St., Reno, Nev.
• (775) 323-0321

For economical lodging right at the University of Nevada, Reno campus, the University Inn has 173 moderate rooms. It's especially convenient if you're attending sporting or musical events at Lawlor Events Center. Availability is sometimes limited, however, by what's happening at the university. It's easier to book in the summer and any time classes are not in session. The on-site restaurant is open weekdays only, and the inn is close to downtown casinos and restaurants.

Vagabond Inn

$$ • 3131 S. Virginia St., Reno, Nev.
• (775) 825-7134, (800) 552-1555

The Vagabond Inn has 129 basic rooms and provides an airport shuttle and outdoor swimming pool. It's south of downtown, just a few blocks from the Peppermill Hotel Casino Reno. If you're ambitious and want an interesting outdoor walk, Virginia Lake with its mile-long path is close by.

Sparks

Inn Cal

$ • 255 N. McCarran Blvd., Sparks, Nev.
• (775) 358-2222, (800) 550-0055

The Inn Cal has 133 modest rooms and is close to John Ascuaga's Nugget and Victorian Square (see our Nightlife, Attractions and Kidstuff chapters for information on these).

Motel 6 Sparks

$$ • 2405 Victorian Ave., Sparks, Nev.
• (775) 358-1080, (800) 466-8356

The 95 rooms at this Motel 6 are clean, comfortable and economical. There's an outdoor swimming pool, and pets are welcome.

Western Village Inn/Casino

$ • 815 E. Nichols Blvd., Sparks, Nev.
• (775) 331-1069, (800) 648-1170

At the east end of Sparks, right off I-80, the Western Village Inn/Casino has 280 economy rooms plus a number of amenities not usually found with basic motels. It offers a casino, three restaurants, lounge, entertainment and an outdoor swimming pool in a down-home Western atmosphere. It's close to Victorian Square and right next to Sparks Marina Park

---

INSIDERS' TIP

Guests at Fitzgeralds Casino/Hotel Reno can earn "O'Lucky Bucks" by using The Fitzgeralds Card when they play slot machines, table games and keno. The bucks are immediately redeemable for gifts, hotel rooms, food and beverages.

(see our Parks chapter). You'll need transportation to downtown Reno and other area attractions.

North Shore Lake Tahoe

Cal Neva Inn
$$$ • 9937 N. Lake Blvd., Brockway, Calif. • (530) 546-3341, (800) 648 2324

Sitting on the California–Nevada state line across from the Cal–Neva Resort, the Cal Neva Inn has 90 comfortable, casual accommodations. It's clean, but not exactly luxurious. Some family units, decks and patios are available. It offers an outdoor swimming pool but no access to Lake Tahoe. You can easily walk to casinos and restaurants in Crystal Bay, Nevada.

Crystal Bay Motel
$ • 24 Nev. Hwy. 28, Crystal Bay, Nev. • (775) 831-0287

With 18 economy units, the Crystal Bay Motel provides clean rooms in a woodsy location in the heart of Crystal Bay. It's within easy walking distance to casinos and restaurants but has no beach access.

Pepper Tree Inn
$$ • 645 N. Lake Blvd., Tahoe City, Calif. • (530) 583-3711, (800) 624-8590

Even though the Pepper Tree Inn is not right on Lake Tahoe (it's across the street), many of its rooms still have unobstructed lake views. You can also enjoy great views of the lake and all the action in downtown Tahoe City from the swimming pool deck and the upper level sundeck. The rooms are pretty basic, but the location is within walking distance of the paved path along the Truckee River, Fanny Bridge, the Tahoe City Marina and the Tahoe City Golf Course.

Sun 'n Sand Lodge
$$ • 8308 N. Lake Blvd., Kings Beach, Calif. • (530) 546-2515, (800) 547-2515

The accommodations at the Sun 'n Sand Lodge are average, but the location is definitely upscale since it sits right on its own private beach. A walkway outside the rooms provides a great place to sit and enjoy your morning coffee or evening drink while taking in a million-dollar view of Lake Tahoe. It's within walking distance of a movie theater, restaurants, shops and a golf course/snowmobile track in Kings Beach.

Tahoya Shores Lodge
$$$$ • 7610 N. Lake Blvd., Kings Beach, Calif. • (530) 546-2571

Since it was built to accommodate athletes who competed in the 1960 Winter Olympics at Squaw Valley USA, the units at Tahoya Shores Lodge are like minicondominiums and include small sitting areas, microwave ovens and bars. You can enjoy the large common deck overlooking Lake Tahoe and a lovely swimming cove below. But because the lake temperature is usually quite cold, the heated swimming pool and spa provide welcome relief.

Although each unit is individually owned and decorated, some are available for rent. The lodge offers great access to the lake, but you'll need transportation to casinos and most restaurants.

The Cottage Inn at Lake Tahoe
$$$$ • 1690 W. Lake Blvd., Tahoe City, Calif. • (530) 581-4073, (800) 581-4073

Ideal for a sentimental getaway, the cottages at The Cottage Inn at Lake Tahoe were built in 1938 in Old Tahoe style, with warm woods and knotty pine throughout. Each unit is unique, such as the Romantic Hideaway with its two-story fireplace and natural rock Jacuzzi with waterfall, or the Enchanted Cottage, with its life-size indoor tree.

Nestled amidst huge pines, The Cottage is just steps from a gorgeous beach where you can swim, sunbathe, picnic, play volleyball or just enjoy one of the most glorious views on the planet. Country breakfast is included, and you can either enjoy it in the dining room, on the outdoor deck at the main lodge or in your room. Wine, cookies and coffee are available in the sitting room of the lodge, and there's also a sauna.

The Cottage is delightful since it exudes country charm with a touch of elegance, all in a kicked-back natural setting. Two miles south of Tahoe City on Calif. Highway 89, it's close to restaurants along the west shore of the lake and in Tahoe City and to skiing at Homewood, Alpine Meadows and Squaw Valley USA. The paved bike path that runs along the lake is right outside the door.

South Shore Lake Tahoe

Econo Lodge
$$$ • 3536 Lake Tahoe Blvd., South Lake Tahoe, Calif. • (530) 544-2036, (800) 895-7304

The Econo Lodge has 36 clean, comfortable accommodations, including suites, and some even have fireplaces. Pets are welcome, and other amenities include a swimming pool, hot tub and sauna. It's close to hiking and biking in the summer and skiing at Heavenly Ski Resort in winter. Lake Tahoe is just a short stroll away.

Holiday Inn Express
$$$$ • 3961 Lake Tahoe Blvd., South Lake Tahoe, Calif. • (530) 544-5900, (800) 544-5288

The winner of several awards for its recent upscale renovation, the Holiday Inn Express offers luxury at a reasonable price. Each of the 89 rooms and suites has a refrigerator, coffee maker, ice and large remote control TV. Some suites have fireplaces, fully equipped kitchens and private spas. Other amenities include a free continental breakfast, an indoor spa and sauna and an outdoor swimming pool. It's a little removed from the casino action at Stateline, Nevada, but it's right across from Lake Tahoe.

Homewood Marina Lodge
$$ • 5180 W. Lake Blvd., Homewood, Calif. • (530) 525-6728

On the quiet west shore of Lake Tahoe, the Homewood Marina Lodge has cottages and motel rooms; some include kitchens and fireplaces. You'll find an on-site restaurant and bar as well as a private beach with an expansive lawn area.

Inn by the Lake
$$$ • 3300 Lake Tahoe Blvd., South Lake Tahoe, Calif. • (530) 542-0330, (800) 877-1466

Across from sandy El Dorado Beach, all the beautifully appointed rooms and suites at the Inn by the Lake have private balconies. Some units have fireplaces, kitchens, wet bars and refrigerators. It's a great location for skiers because Heavenly Ski Resort is just a mile away. A continental breakfast is offered daily and there's a year-round heated swimming pool with spa and sauna. In summer, you'll enjoy the miles of hiking and biking trails that are just outside the door.

Lakeside Inn and Casino
$$$ • 168 U.S. Hwy. 50, Stateline, Nev. • (775) 588-7777, (800) 624-7980

The Lakeside Inn and Casino has many of the amenities, but not the hubbub or size of larger properties at South Shore Lake Tahoe. It's a little off the beaten path and several blocks from the heart of the action near Harrah's Lake Tahoe in Stateline, Nevada. But don't sell it short; it boasts two restaurants in addition to a casino, bar, outdoor swimming pool, arcade and gift shop.

The 124 rooms are comfortable and spacious but not elegant. Insiders know that the Timber House Restaurant is a great place for prime rib at a reasonable price.

Lazy S Lodge
$$ • 609 Emerald Bay Rd., South Lake Tahoe, Calif. • (530) 541-0230, (800) 862-8881

The Lazy S Lodge has cozy rustic cottages with fireplaces and kitchenettes, and studio units with wet bars, microwave ovens and refrigerators. You'll also find a swimming pool, hot tub and large lawn with barbecues and picnic tables.

Quality Inn & Suites
$$ • 3838 Lake Tahoe Blvd., South Lake Tahoe, Calif. • (530) 541-5400, (800) 245-6343

Tucked away in tall pines, Quality Inn & Suites has 121 standard rooms, suites and condos, with some kitchens available. If you're too tired to drive to a restaurant after a full day's activities at Lake Tahoe, you can have a savory Indian dinner at the on-premises restaurant, the Taj Mahal. And after a hard day of skiing the bumps at Heavenly Ski Resort, you can relax with an aprés-ski drink in the Fireside Lounge.

Other amenities include complimentary continental breakfasts as well as a year-round

Photo: Tahoe Biltmore

The Tahoe Biltmore is one of the oldest hotels in the area and boasts a history of celebrity guests and appearances.

hot tub, swimming pool, courtesy shuttle to ski resorts and casinos, picnic and barbecue area and a billiard and video game room. This establishment is about a half-mile from the casinos at Stateline, Nevada.

Royal Valhalla Motor Lodge
$$$ • 4104 Lake Shore Dr., South Lake Tahoe, Calif. • (530) 544-2233, (800) 999-4104

You can't get much closer to Lake Tahoe than the Royal Valhalla Motor Lodge — it's right on the shore and has its own private beach. The lodge offers accommodations that include kitchenettes and balconies, and you'll

also enjoy continental breakfasts, a hot tub and a swimming pool.

Tahoe Chalet Inn
$$ • 3860 Lake Tahoe Blvd., South Lake Tahoe, Calif. • (530) 544-4069, (800) 821-2656

The Tahoe Chalet Inn is a touch of European elegance right in the heart of South Shore Lake Tahoe. From its standard rooms to themed suites to chalets, you are sure to feel pampered and at home. One of the themed suites is the Marie Antoinette Room (no, it doesn't have a guillotine) featuring lovely antique-style furnishings and a roaring fireplace.

INSIDERS' TIP

Two people have been known to swim across Lake Tahoe. Fred Rogers of South San Francisco, California, made it across in 1955. Earline Christopherson, who was 16 years old at the time, crossed in 1962 in 13 hours and 37 minutes.

The inn also provides complimentary continental breakfasts, an indoor spa and sauna room, a heated seasonal swimming pool and a fitness/video game room. You also can walk to the casinos, shops and restaurants in Stateline, Nevada.

Tahoe Tropicana Lodge
**$$ • 4132 Cedar Ave.,
South Lake Tahoe, Calif.**
• **(530) 541-3911, (800) 447-0246**
The Tahoe Tropicana Lodge has great ski packages for Heavenly Ski Resort, Squaw Valley USA, Northstar-at-Tahoe, Kirkwood, Alpine Meadows and Sierra-at-Tahoe. Just a half-block from the casinos at Stateline, Nevada, and three blocks from Lake Tahoe, it's convenient to nightlife, restaurants and shopping. The on-premises Greenhouse Restaurant and Bar has a cozy atmosphere of lush green plants and European stained glass. Amenities include free champagne, a hot tub and free shuttle service to casinos and ski areas.

For your home away from home you can rent a cozy cabin tucked away in the forest, or a luxurious condominium on the beach, or a private residence with a spectacular view of Lake Tahoe.

Vacation Rentals

For accommodations in the Nevada cities of Reno and Sparks, we recommend hotels, motels and gaming resorts (see our related chapters for these). But if you're planning on staying anywhere in the Lake Tahoe Basin, you can choose from a large selection of vacation rentals in addition to hotels, motels and resorts. Vacation rentals include condominiums, homes and cabins that typically offer more privacy, space and amenities not always available in more traditional accommodations. Vacation rentals have particular appeal for visitors planning to stay longer than just a night or two. They are also popular with large groups of people such as families or several couples who are traveling together. While their biggest appeal may be a greater degree of comfort, vacation rentals can also be more economical in certain situations. Some vacationers find it cheaper to rent a home or condo rather than several hotel rooms, especially if the cost is split between several couples.

The variety of properties available is immense. For your home away from home you can rent a cozy cabin tucked away in the forest, or a luxurious condominium on the beach, or a private residence with a spectacular view of Lake Tahoe. The choice is yours, depending upon your budget and your expectations. Vacation rentals include fully equipped kitchens, linens, color televisions and telephones. Many also include fireplaces, VCRs, private

decks, hot tubs, saunas, microwave ovens and washers and dryers. Some have security systems, parking garages and access to private beaches, tennis courts, spas and pools. Many accommodations are wheelchair accessible, and some with secure yards allow pets. Ski in/ski out properties and no smoking accommodations are also available.

The cost of rental usually depends upon the sleeping capacity, the view, the location, the amenities and the degree of luxury. It also varies with the season of the year. Rates can range from as low as $60 a night to as high as $2,000 or more. Top prices are charged during high season, January to mid-April and mid-June to mid-September, and premium rates also apply for bookings that include Martin Luther King Jr. Day, Presidents Day, Memorial Day, the Fourth of July, Thanksgiving, Christmas and New Year's. Insiders know you can expect lower rates at Lake Tahoe in the fall and late spring.

Most properties also require a minimum stay of two to five nights. The required length depends upon the time of year as well as the particular property requested. For longer stays, some properties can be rented on a weekly rate.

A reservations deposit is usually requested at the time of booking, and full payment plus a security deposit is due before arrival. Since cancellation policies vary, it's wise to inquire when booking. Most properties accept credit cards, but be sure to confirm this when you reserve.

Although size and amenities are considerations in choosing a vacation rental, location can be equally important in the Lake Tahoe Basin. Depending upon the season of the year and the activities you'll be pursuing, you'll want to choose a rental that is most convenient for you. If you're a nonskier you probably won't want to pay a premium price for a ski in/ski out location in the winter. But if watersports are your main interest, you may want to pay more to be right on the beach in the summer. And if nightlife is important to you, you may want to be close to the casinos in Stateline, Nevada, or the clubs in Tahoe City. But if your idea of a vacation is hiking and cooking dinner in, you may be more comfortable in laid-back communities at the lake such as Homewood or Kings Beach. The weather can also dictate your level of comfort. A secluded cabin in the woods may be wonderfully private during the summer but extremely challenging to reach in the winter, especially without a four-wheel-drive vehicle

Because vacation rentals are in such demand during holidays and high season, we recommend you plan as far ahead as possible. If you decide the week before Christmas

to pack up the family and spend the holidays in a winter wonderland at Lake Tahoe, don't be surprised if there's no room at the inn. For holiday and premium season bookings it's usually necessary to reserve six months ahead, and for specific properties, particularly homes, many visitors reserve a year in advance. Although it's easier to book during low season, we still recommend arranging your accommodations as soon as you can to avoid being disappointed.

The Lake Tahoe Basin is composed of a variety of communities, each offering its own particular personality and appeal. When choosing a vacation rental as your home base it's a good idea to consider the ambiance and amenities of each area.

Community Overviews

North Shore Lake Tahoe

Incline Village and Crystal Bay, Nev.

An exclusive community of about 10,000 year-round residents, Incline Village is home to a growing number of people who can live

Some vacation rentals are convenient to area golf courses or may have a golf package included in the rental fee.

anywhere — airline personnel, computer experts and entrepreneurs who work from home offices. The governing arm, the Incline Village General Improvement District (IVGID), owns and manages several parks, golf courses and a ski resort for residents and visitors to enjoy. The fees and access extended to residents are occasionally available to those staying in vacation rentals as well.

Just 2 miles from Incline Village, Crystal Bay is smaller and offers less shopping and fewer restaurants. But this short stretch of the Lake Tahoe shoreline seems to have it all — sandy beaches, golf, skiing, casino nightlife and hiking. It is home to the world-famous Ponderosa Ranch, the Incline Village championship and executive golf courses and Diamond Peak Ski Resort. It's a great place for exploring the hidden beaches and coves of the lake's undeveloped east shore. Vacation rentals can be anything from posh lakefront homes to condos with a view to modest cabins.

Kings Beach and Brockway, Calif.

Kicked back and unpretentious, Kings Beach and Brockway are less ritzy than some other areas along the lake. But if casual is the name of your game, you're bound to feel comfortable here. Skiing, golfing and nightlife are nearby and restaurants are decidedly informal. Vacation rentals include quiet condos in the pines, lakeview homes and secluded chalets.

Tahoe City, Calif.

About the same size as Incline Village, Tahoe City is especially appealing to young singles because of its nightlife, shopping and close proximity to Squaw Valley USA and Alpine Meadows ski resorts. It's a lively community any season of the year, as visitors and residents alike use it as a jumping off point for river rafting, biking and winter sports. While some other communities along the North Shore seem to roll up the sidewalks at night, the night spots in Tahoe City rock on into the wee hours. Rentals include luxury home condos in the Dollar Point area, with its private beach and summer amenities.

South Shore Lake Tahoe

Stateline, Nev., and South Lake Tahoe, Calif.

Stateline, Nevada, and South Lake Tahoe, California, may seem like one community, but they're actually two since the state line runs through the middle of the area. But most visitors don't notice unless they spot the separate visitors centers and law enforcement agencies. With a combined permanent population of about 35,000, which can triple during holidays, this area of the Lake Tahoe Basin is easily the most densely populated.

Stateline is home to glitzy casinos such as Harrah's Lake Tahoe, Harveys Resort Hotel/Casino, Caesars Tahoe and the Lake Tahoe Horizon Casino Resort. If it's nightlife you're after, this is the place — the fun goes on 24 hours a day. You'll find both Heavenly Ski Resort, which also straddles the California–Nevada state line, and Kirkwood ski area close by (see our Winter Sports chapter for details). This area of the Lake Tahoe Basin is probably a good choice for visitors looking for a more fast-paced environment. During high season, however, traffic can be a problem and parking can sometimes require creative ingenuity. Vacation rentals run the gamut, from condos on the Nevada side of Heavenly Ski Resort to luxurious executive homes on the lake to less pretentious cabins in the woods.

www.insiders.com

See this and many other **Insiders' Guide®** destinations online.

Visit us today!

INSIDERS' TIP

Guests who book lodging through Lake Tahoe Accommodations receive a welcome kit of toilet articles and a complimentary bottle of its private-label wine.

Old Tahoe Communities

Considered "Old Tahoe" because of their rustic charms, Homewood, Meeks Bay, Rubicon, Sunnyside and Tahoma are small west shore communities that appeal to outdoor enthusiasts. Nightlife here may consist of a barbecue at the beach while watching the sun go down or dinner in one of the fine restaurants along the lake. The pace is slow as visitors are intent on soaking up the spectacular environment that surrounds them. For skiers, Homewood ski area, Squaw Valley USA and Alpine Meadows are close by (see our related chapter on Winter Sports). Summer visitors delight in the sandy beaches, numerous hiking trails and historic sites in this area. A variety of vacation rentals is available, but multiunit complexes are smaller than in the Stateline and South Lake Tahoe area.

Outside Lake Tahoe

Northstar–at–Tahoe
6 mi. north of Lake Tahoe
on Calif. Hwy. 267

Although it's not on Lake Tahoe, Northstar-at-Tahoe's lovely mountain setting offers skiing, golfing, horseback riding, tennis and hiking.

See our detailed description of Northstar in our Resorts and Winter Sports chapters. Vacation rentals at Northstar include cozy ski condos and luxurious golf-course homes.

Squaw Valley USA and Alpine Meadows
3–6 mi. north of Lake Tahoe
on Calif. Hwy. 89

Not just a world-class ski resort, Squaw Valley USA is a year-round playground offering an amazing array of activities for any season. Alpine Meadows ski resort, just over the ridge from Squaw, offers a quieter environment with world-class skiing in the winter and hiking in the summer. Vacation rentals at these resorts can include affordable mountain hideaways, posh condominiums and large homes. See our detailed descriptions of these resorts in the Winter Sports chapter.

Individual Properties

Because the sheer number and variety of vacation rentals available in the Lake Tahoe Basin is exhaustive, we can't begin to list them all. But to give you a better idea of the kinds of properties you can rent, we'll take a peek at some of the individual accommodations.

Photo: Dan Coffey/Northstar-at-Tahoe

Condominiums that belong to winter ski enthusiasts are often available
as rentals during the off-season months.

North Shore Lake Tahoe

Tahoe Edgelake Beach Club
7680 N. Lake Blvd., Tahoe Vista, Calif.
• **(530) 546-3324**

In the laid-back Kings Beach area, Tahoe Edgelake Beach Club has lakefront and lakeview accommodations along its private sandy beach. Boat owners can also take advantage of its pier and buoys.

Club Tahoe
914 Northwood Blvd., Incline Village, Nev. • **(775) 831-5750**

Centrally located in beautiful Incline Village, Club Tahoe provides guests with a vast array of on-site amenities including tennis courts, spas, a swimming pool, a game room, an exercise area, a lounge and volleyball facilities. Each fully equipped two-bedroom condo will sleep up to six people. These modestly priced accommodations appeal both to families and couples.

Lakeside Tennis and Ski Resort
955 Tahoe Blvd., Incline Village, Nev.
• **(800) 821-4912**

Lakeside Tennis and Ski Resort is the ideal place to perfect your tennis game. With its 12 championship courts, tennis clinics and pro shop, it has been selected by the U.S. Tennis Association as one of the country's top-20 tennis clubs. It's also convenient to skiing and all the other activities available to visitors in the North Shore area. The apartments are fully equipped to make your vacation a memorable experience during any time of year.

INSIDERS' TIP

If you're on a ski vacation, be sure to inquire whether your vacation rental provides ski storage and shuttle service to the ski resorts. If you are driving, an enclosed garage means you don't have to unload equipment each day after returning from the slopes.

Chinquapin
3600 N. Lake Blvd., Tahoe City, Calif.
• (530) 583-6991

Secluded along a mile of lakefront property, Chinquapin offers luxurious condos with one to four bedrooms. Although close to the hustle and bustle of Tahoe City, the complex is a quiet oasis for enjoying the beauty of the lake and the surrounding forest

South Shore Lake Tahoe

An Angel's Haven Resort
3357 Lake Tahoe Blvd., South Lake Tahoe, Calif. • (530) 544-9297, (800) 588-6754

Far from bare-boned condos, the accommodations at An Angel's Haven Resort will pique your imagination with a variety of themes. You can imagine yourself on safari in "Out of Africa," a dramatic hideaway with all the comforts of home accented with black velveteen and leopard prints. You can create your own romantic fantasy in "Cupidon," where cherubic fabrics and Italian decor set just the right mood. You can dream about another place and another time in "Sistine Madonna," with the elegance of its European renaissance decor art and antiques. All accommodations are close to south shore casinos and to Heavenly Ski Resort.

Inn at Heavenly
1261 Ski Run Blvd., South Lake Tahoe, Calif. • (530) 544-4244

Hidden among two acres of pines, the Inn at Heavenly offers guests country mountain decor with a touch of luxury. Although constructed of logs, the Inn is anything but rustic as the fireplaces are meticulously crafted and the woodwork is hand-stenciled. You can enjoy breakfast in your own complete kitchen or join guests in the nearby lodge for a gourmet spread. The Inn has the ambiance of an upscale bed and breakfast plus many of the amenities of a condominium.

Lakeland Village Beach & Ski Resort
3535 Lake Tahoe Blvd., South Lake Tahoe, Calif. • (800) 822-5969

In the heart of the South Shore area, Lakeland Village Beach & Ski Resort has all the amenities for a perfect vacation — a private, sandy beach, tennis courts, swimming pools

INSIDERS' TIP

Many vacation rental complexes offer special skiing and golfing packages which include lift tickets and rounds of golf.

and beachside games. The underground parking garage is especially convenient in the winter, and the resort runs free shuttles to ski areas and casinos.

Pine Cone Resort
601 U.S. Hwy. 50 E., Zephyr Cove, Nev. • (800) 568-2463

It's quaint, it's rustic and it has all the comforts of home. In a lovely forest overlooking Lake Tahoe, Pine Cone Resort is a small complex of just 22 units. While not luxurious, it's a favorite for families, especially in the summer.

PineWild
600 U.S. Hwy. 50 E., Zephyr Cove, Nev. • (800) 544-3234

With 28 landscaped acres and a quarter-mile private beach, PineWild offers guests an ultraluxurious vacation in a gorgeous natural setting. All these townhouses have wood-burning fireplaces and two private decks. Some units also have free boat mooring right outside the door and a second fireplace in the master bedroom. Gated for security, PineWild appeals to the discriminating vacationer.

Tahoe Seasons Resort
3901 Saddle Rd., South Lake Tahoe, Callf. • (800) 540-4874

At the base of the tram on the California side of Heavenly Ski Resort, Tahoe Seasons Resort provides easy access to skiing as well as all the activities in the South Shore area. In addition to all the amenities of a condominium, it has a restaurant, room service, a fireside lounge and a gift shop. And you can choose from a variety of lodging packages tailored to meet your individual needs.

The Ridge Tahoe
400 Ridge Club Dr., Kingsbury, Nev. • (775) 588-3553

Perched high above Lake Tahoe on the Nevada side of Heavenly Ski Resort, The Ridge Tahoe is the ultimate in convenience for skiers. With its own gondola connecting the condo complex to the ski resort lifts, skiers can be on the slopes in a matter of minutes. Although its location on the eastern side of the mountain range blocks a view of Lake Tahoe, many units have panoramic vistas of the Carson Valley to the east. Just 10 minutes from the casinos at Stateline, the two-bedroom units at The Ridge Tahoe are a handy location all year round.

Camp Richardson Resort
1900 Jamesen Beach Rd., South Lake Tahoe, Calif. • (800) 544-1801

A favorite for families because kids have plenty of room to roam, Camp Richardson has rustic accommodations near historic sites, hiking trails and beaches. Its corrals offer pack trips into nearby wilderness areas, and it has a complete outdoor sports center for a variety of summer activities.

The Role of the Rental Agency

Although you can contact individual properties directly, we recommend using a rental agency because they have large lists of every type of property available. With your budget and specific needs in mind, they can find the accommodation that is exactly right for you. Rental agencies can also assure you that your property is clean and well-maintained and that everything included is in good working order. Most agencies have conveniently located offices for check-in and check-out, eliminating a lot of the hassle typically involved in arrival and departure. Some are also full-service real estate offices and are described in more detail in our Neighborhoods and Real Estate chapter.

Space doesn't permit us to list all the rental agencies in the Lake Tahoe area, but here's a few to help you find that perfect vacation hideaway.

Rental Agencies

Accommodation Station
2540 Lake Tahoe Blvd., South Lake Tahoe, Calif. • (530) 542-5850, (800) 344-9364

This agency handles rentals in the South Shore Lake Tahoe area for 85 condos and homes priced from $90 to $600 per night.

Many resort areas have vacation rental units listed in their accommodation hotlines.

Coldwell Banker
120 County Club Dr. #3, Incline Village, Nev. • (775) 831-4800, (800) 748-5919

Coldwell Banker manages about 65 cabins, condos and homes in Incline Village that rent for $85 to $650 nightly.

Lake Tahoe Accommodations
(530) 581-5210, (800) 544-3234

One of the largest rental agencies in the Tahoe area, this company has 400 units ranging in size from studio apartments to seven-bedroom homes. The properties are scattered all around the lake and nightly rates run anywhere from $99 to $1,700.

Lake Tahoe Lodging
292 Kingsbury Gr., Stateline, Nev. • (775) 588-5253, (800) 654-5253

With more than 150 properties ranging from studio apartments to large homes, this company specializes in high-end luxury homes in the South Shore Lake Tahoe area. You can bed down for the night in digs costing anywhere from $65 to $3,000 per night.

Lakeshore Realty Property Management
954 Lakeshore Blvd., Incline Village, Nev. • (775) 832-3341

Lakeshore Realty Property Management has about 50 condominiums, homes and cabins in Crystal Bay and Incline Village. Rentals cost $99 to $525 per night.

Northstar–at–Tahoe
(530) 562-1010

About 250 rental units are available at Northstar, and they range from hotel-type rooms to condominiums to mountain and golf course homes.

South Lake Tahoe Reservation Bureau
599 Tahoe Keys Blvd., South Lake Tahoe, Calif. • (530) 544-5397, (800) 698-2463

This large reservation bureau has about 200 condos, homes and cabins in the South Shore Lake Tahoe area, with a price range of $100 to $600 a night.

Squaw Valley USA
(530) 583-5585

Although it may be difficult during high season to get through on this number, it provides direct access to vacation rentals in the Squaw Valley area.

Tahoe Rental Connection
2241 James Ave., South Lake Tahoe, Calif. • (530) 542-2777

The Tahoe Rental Connection handles property on the California side of Lake Tahoe only. Its 120 units rent for $85 to $600 nightly.

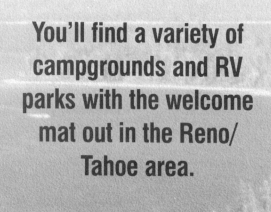

You'll find a variety of campgrounds and RV parks with the welcome mat out in the Reno/ Tahoe area.

Camping and RVing

"Camping and RVing" incorporates everything from a simple sleeping bag flung on the ground to a fully equipped motorhome complete with a satellite dish. Whatever your idea of "home away from home," you'll find a variety of campgrounds and RV parks with the welcome mat out in the Reno/Tahoe area. They run the gamut in terms of amenities and luxuries, from sites with just a water spigot to luxury minineighborhoods with swimming pools and convenience stores.

Although most of the RV parks in Reno/Sparks are in urban areas, many have trees and attractive landscaping and some even provide access to the Truckee River. Conveniently located to casinos and major attractions, they offer RVers attractive accommodation options at considerable savings over hotels and motels. However, if you're looking for more of a bonafide back-to-nature experience (especially if it includes a tent), you'd best head to the campgrounds and RV parks in the Lake Tahoe Basin. Around the lake you'll find a few snazzy facilities with all the comforts of home, but most campgrounds are geared toward enjoying an awesome night sleeping under the stars.

The camping and RV facilities in the Reno/Sparks area are privately owned and are open year-round. Rates vary from season to season, with the highest fees charged in July and August and during special events (see our Annual Events chapter for details). Facilities in the Lake Tahoe area are owned either privately or by government entities. They are open usually from Memorial Day weekend through October, with the exception of General Creek campground at Sugar Pine Point State Park and Zephyr Cove Resort, which are open all year.

For general information on campgrounds in the Lake Tahoe Basin you can contact California State Parks at (530) 525-7232, Nevada State Parks at (775) 831-0494 and the U.S. Forest Service at (530) 573-2694. Ask for a copy of the *Lake of the Sky Journal* from the Forest Service: it has a grid showing services available at most area campgrounds plus hiking and backcountry information. You can also log onto www.reserveusa.gov for Forest Service information and onto www.reserveamerica.com for California campgrounds. We strongly recommend that you reserve space as soon as you can because the demand for campsites is heavy. Also be aware that the central reservation sytems used by some campgrounds may be difficult to reach, in particular (877) 444-6777 for the Forest Service facilities and (800) 444-7275 for California state sites.

We organize this chapter in the usual four geographical areas: Reno, Sparks, North Shore Lake Tahoe and South Shore Lake Tahoe. We give you a thumbnail sketch of some of the camping and RVing facilities you'll find, listing the basic amenities offered and describing their general ambiance. We give you approximate ranges of rates, but keep in mind that fees may have changed by the time you book space. Our listing isn't meant to be all-inclusive but rather a sample of the kinds of options you can choose from. For campgrounds located in parks, such as D.L. Bliss, see our Parks chapter for a complete description of activities and surrounding terrain.

If you really want to get away from it all, you can strap on a pack and head to the backcountry where you can make your own camp in an exquisite alpine setting of your own choosing. We tell you about where and how to do this in our Recreation chapter.

Reno

Boomtown Hotel Casino Reno
I-80, 7 mi. west of Reno, Nev.
• (775) 345-6000, (800) 648-3790

In spite of its easy access to Interstate 80, the RV park at Boomtown Hotel Casino Reno is quiet and almost in a world of its own. Hugging a bluff above the Truckee River, the park offers eye-catching desert and mountain views. Daily rates range from $20 to $25, depending on the time of year, and weekly fees are around $118. Monthly rates of about $360 are available from October 1 to May 31. If you're a member of Good Sam or AARP be sure to show your card for a discount. The maximum stay during the summer months is 28 days, and during the rest of the year it's 84 days.

The park offers the basic services, including sewer, water, electric and cable TV hookups. There are also shower and laundry facilities, a year-round hot tub and a seasonal swimming pool. Pets are okay, but no tents are allowed.

You'll find plenty of entertainment at the Boomtown Casino right next door (see the description in our Hotels and Motels chapter). Just minutes from downtown Reno and Truckee, California (the gateway to Lake Tahoe), this park is also a convenient jumping-off spot for many other sights in the area.

Keystone RV Park
1455 W. Fourth St., Reno, Nev.
• (775) 324-5000

The Keystone RV Park has 102 RV sites just across the street from the Truckee River near downtown Reno. Daily rates range from about $20 to $24, depending upon the size of your RV. Weekly rates are $114, monthly from $315 to $335. Discounts are given for Good Sam members and for paying in cash. There's no maximum on the number of days you can stay.

The park provides water, electric, sewer, cable TV and phone hookups. You'll find all the basics, including propane, at nearby stores. Amenities also include laundry and shower facilities. Pets are accepted upon approval, but no tents are allowed.

Reno Hilton
2500 E. Second St., Reno, Nev.
• (775) 789-2000, (800) 648-5080

You can take advantage of many of the same amenities hotel guests enjoy, such as a gorgeous swimming pool and health club, when you park your rig at the RV park at the Reno Hilton. Daily rates run from about $15 to $40, depending on the time of year. The maximum allowable stay is 28 days and rates are by the day only.

The park provides water, sewer and electrical hookups but no cable TV or propane. Other amenities include a minimart along with laundry and shower facilities. Pets are welcome, and the cancellation policy is 24 hours. The 230 spaces are for RVs only, with no tent camping allowed. You'll be right in the middle of the action here: the Reno Hilton is a major gaming resort, with all the bells and whistles for a fun-filled stay (see our Resorts and Casino Nightlife chapters for more about this classy resort).

Reno RV Park
735 Mill St., Reno, Nev. • (775) 323-3381

Reno RV Park offers a tree-shaded park for 46 RVs just a few blocks from all the casino action downtown. Daily rates run around $21, weekly $133, and monthly from $350 to $488, depending on the time of year. Discounts are available for Good Sam, AAA and Golden Age members.

On-site services include sewer, water, electric and extended cable hookups, along with laundry and shower facilities. You can fill your

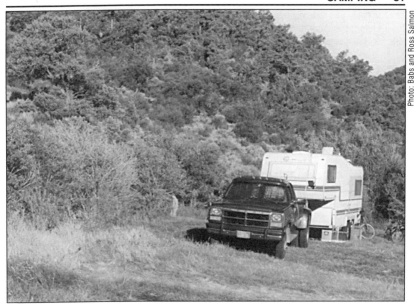

Photo: Babs and Ross Salmon

With so many great facilities in the Reno/Tahoe area, campers have a variety of different areas — and camping styles — to choose from.

propane tank at the park, and the nearest mini-mart is less than a block away. Pets that have been approved have a large grassy area for exercise. Since the park is in demand in the summer, we recommend you call ahead for bookings during that time of year. Be aware they have a 24-hour cancellation policy. No tents are allowed.

Shamrock RV Park
260 E. Parr Blvd., Reno, Nev.
• **(775) 329-5222**

Shamrock RV Park offers 121 sites just off U.S. Highway 395 north of Reno. Daily rates are around $23 and weekly about $150. Monthly rates are about $300 but aren't usually available during the summer months.

You'll find all the basic necessities, including hookups for electricity, sewer, water, tele-phone and cable TV. There are also shower and laundry facilities, a swimming pool and propane provided on-site. The park is generally very quiet even though you can easily walk to the nearby Bonanza Casino. No tents are allowed. Pets are okay upon approval.

Sparks

River's Edge RV Park
1405 S. Rock Blvd., Sparks, Nev.
• **(775) 358-8533**

It's pretty hard to beat this idyllic setting in an urban area. Nestled along the banks of the Truckee River, River's Edge RV Park provides 164 RV spots in a grassy wooded environment. Daily rates are around $18, with discounts available for Good Sam and AAA mem-

INSIDERS' TIP

Don't be surprised if you're treated to a free headliner concert when staying in the RV park at the Reno Hilton in the summer: the outdoor amphitheater is just around the corner.

bers. Weekly and monthly rates are available from October to April and run around $116 and $385 respectively.

In addition to the standard amenities of sewer, water and electric hookups, the park also has shower and laundry facilities. Propane and a few basic necessities are available on-site. To make the most of your stay in this lovely spot, we recommend a picnic on one of the tables scattered amongst the trees or a relaxing afternoon around the beautiful swimming pool. For a more ambitious endeavor, head west toward Reno on the Truckee River Walk just outside your door and enjoy all the delights the river has in store for you. You can check in with your pet (on approval), but no tents are allowed. The only disadvantage to River's Edge is noise from aircraft using Reno/Tahoe International Airport.

Victorian RV Park
205 Nichols Blvd., Sparks, Nev.
• **(775) 356-6400, (800) 955-6405**

One of the newest RV parks in the area, Victorian RV Park is a great location if you're attending events such as Hot August Nights at Victorian Square (see details in our Annual Events chapter). Clean and well-maintained, the park has 92 sites strictly for RVs. Daily rates are around $17 and monthly about $364. Members of Good Sam, AARP and AAA are offered discounts. The basic essentials such as sewer, electric, water and cable TV are provided along with shower and laundry facilities. Park guests are allowed to use the swimming pool across the street at the Thunderbird Resort. And don't forget Fido since he's welcome, too.

North Shore Lake Tahoe

Granite Flat
Calif. Hwy. 89, 1 mi. south of Truckee, Calif. • **(530) 587-3558, (877) 444-6777 for reservations**

You can almost cast your fishing line into the Truckee River right from your camp site at Granite Flat campground: many of the 72 RV and tent sites sit right on the banks of the rushing water. Granite Flat is also especially wheelchair-friendly, with 17 accessible camp sites and a wheelchair-accessible river trail. Basic services for the $12 fee include piped water and vault toilets. Pets are okay on leashes. Since the campground is just off the highway, it's noisy sometimes and also lacks the seclusion of more isolated sites.

Lake Forest
Lake Forest Rd., 2 mi. northeast of Tahoe City, Calif.
• **(530) 583-3796, ext. 29**

With the only public boat ramp in the North Shore Lake Tahoe area, the campground at Lake Forest is a great location for boaters. The 20 tent and RV sites rent for $12 a night on a first come, first served basis. You can bring Fido along, but be sure he also brings his leash. Amenities include flush toilets, piped water, picnic tables and barbecue pits. A public swimming beach, shops and restaurants are nearby. To get to the campground from Tahoe City, head northeast on Calif. Highway 28 for about a mile, turn right onto Lake Forest Road and follow it to the lake. The campground is near the U.S. Coast Guard Station.

Martis Creek
Calif. Hwy. 267, 7 mi. north of Kings Beach, Calif. • **(530) 639-2342**

Tucked on the edge of Martis Creek Lake in an 850-acre wildlife preserve, Martis Creek campground offers marvelous opportunities to view birds and animals, such as Canada geese, ducks, coyotes and deer. It's also an angler's dream with a reservoir well stocked with Lahontan cutthroat and German brown trout.

With 25 RV and tent sites, the campground offers the basics of piped water, chemical toilets, barbecues and picnic tables. The daily fee is $10 and there are no reservations. Pets are allowed but should be leashed on the campground property. Even though it's just off Calif. Highway 267, about halfway between Kings Beach and Truckee, California, the campground is peaceful and quiet, with great views of Martis Peak and Mt. Pluto. There's a wonderful world of outdoor fun all around (see our description of Truckee in our Daytrips chapter for more details), including all the amenities of Northstar–at–Tahoe. Be sure to ask the on-site ranger about tours of the dam and campfire programs.

Mt. Rose Campground
Nev. Hwy. 431, 20 mi. southwest of Reno, Nev. • (775) 882-2766, (877) 444-6777 for reservations

Surrounded by gorgeous alpine hiking terrain, Mt. Rose Campground is nestled in the trees at 8,900 feet in elevation. If it's hot in Reno or at Lake Tahoe, you can always beat the heat up here. Amenities for the 24 RV and tent sites include piped water, flush toilets, picnic tables and fire pits. Although some sites are first come, first served, most are on the reservation system. Because this campground is the only one along the Mt. Rose Highway (Nev. Highway 431), we recommend that you reserve ahead. The daily rate is $9, but it's half-price for those with Golden Age and Golden Access Passports. If you intend to use those memberships for the discount, be sure to mention it when you book the reservation.

At this elevation snow is often on the ground until late spring, but the campground opens by the first of June and closes in September. Whatever time of year you're here, be sure to bring along warm clothing because nighttime temperatures can be cold all year long. This area is an especially great place for dogs since there's plenty of room for them to roam in the surrounding wilderness.

If your idea of camping involves a pristine mountain setting, you won't be disappointed here. You can wade through knee-high wildflowers in Tahoe Meadows, conquer the summit of windswept Mt. Rose and hike through stands of tall timber for magnificent views of Lake Tahoe. Or you can just sit around a blazing campfire and listen to the coyotes howling at the moon (see more about Tahoe Meadows and Mt. Rose in our Recreation, Attractions and Winter Sports chapters).

Sandy Beach Campground
6873 N. Lake Blvd., Tahoe Vista, Calif.
• (530) 546-7682

Just across the street from Sandy Beach (a public beach on Lake Tahoe), Sandy Beach Campground offers a lake view along with close proximity to restaurants and shops in Tahoe Vista and Kings Beach. The 44 sites are divided about equally between tenters and RVers. Daily rates run from $15 to $20 and services include full hookups, flush toilets, piped water, showers, tables and stoves. Dogs are okay for $1.50 each. The campground is open May to October; reservations are advised during July and August.

Tahoe State Recreation Area
Calif. Hwy. 28, Tahoe City, Calif.
• (530) 583-3074, (800) 444-7275 for reservations

The good news at Tahoe State Recreation Area is that you're right on the lake and close to restaurants and shops. The bad news is the noise from the nearby highway. But if you don't mind the swish of cars, you can enjoy great views of the lake. It's probably a better location for RVers than tenters since the noise is less noticeable inside a vehicle. Amenities at this 38-site campground include piped water, flush toilets, showers and swimming. You can bring your dog for $1 per day.

William Kent
Calif. Hwy. 89, 2 mi. south of Tahoe City, Calif. • (530) 583-3642, summer only; (877) 444-6777 for reservations

You can be in the middle of all the action around Sunnyside Resort but still enjoy seclusion in a deep forest at William Kent camp-

---

INSIDERS' TIP

D.L. Bliss State Park, Eagle Point, General Creek and Tahoe State Recreation Area allow leashed dogs in the campgrounds but not on trails or beaches.

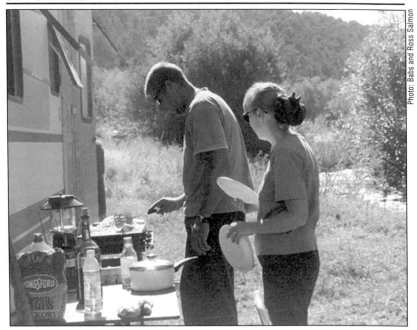

Photo: Babs and Ross Salmon

In the desert or on the shores of a lake, there's nothing like breakfast outdoors.

ground. Just across the road from William Kent Beach and Sunnyside, the campground gives easy access to Lake Tahoe and all water sports. To get around you can use the extensive system of bike trails or hop on a Tahoe Area Regional Transit (TART) bus nearby.

The daily fee is $15 and amenities for the 95 sites (40 are suitable for RVs) include piped water, flush toilets, picnic tables and fire rings. Pets are okay, but must be leashed.

South Shore Lake Tahoe

Camp Richardson Resort
1900 Jameson Beach Rd., South Lake Tahoe, Calif. • (800) 544-1801
You can enjoy all the amenities of a full-service mountain resort when you set up camp at Camp Richardson Resort. Its four fabulous sandy beaches offer endless opportunities for every kind of watersport imaginable. You can also ride horses into the nearby mountains, pedal along the lakeshore bike trail and hike into neighboring alpine lakes.

Camp Richardson is close to the casino action at Stateline, Nevada and to Tallac Historic Site with its enchanting arts programs (see our Attractions and The Arts chapters for details).

The campground has 112 sites with hookups, fire rings, picnic tables, showers, piped water and flush toilets available. You can buy supplies in the convenience store, launch your boat at the boat ramp and eat dinner out (complete with live music) in the on-site restaurant.

Although families love Camp Richardson, don't bring the dog since they aren't allowed at the resort. Daily rates run from $17 to $25.

D.L. Bliss State Park
Calif. Hwy. 89, 9 mi. north of South Lake Tahoe, Calif. • (530) 525-7277, (800) 444-7275 for reservations

With heavily wooded, secluded sites along the spectacular west shore of Lake Tahoe, camping at D.L. Bliss State Park is pure bliss. Of all the camping options in the Lake Tahoe area, Bliss is premier. You can swim and sunbathe on one of Tahoe's largest white sand beaches, you can hike the ruggedly picturesque shoreline to beautiful Emerald Bay and you can bike to Tahoe City on the area's longest paved bike path (we tell you much more about the park in our Parks chapter).

Basic services for the 172 sites include piped water, showers, group sites and flush toilets. Daily fees range from $16 to $20, and pets are okay on leashes. This campground is mostly for tenters since only 21 sites are suitable for RVs.

Eagle Point at Emerald Bay State Park
Calif. Hwy. 89, 6 mi. north of South Lake Tahoe, Calif. • (530) 525-7277, (800) 444-7275 for reservations

Hugging the rocky cliffs above Emerald Bay, Eagle Point campground offers gorgeous views of one of the loveliest spots in all of Lake Tahoe. With easy access to the Desolation Wilderness, there's hiking galore and the beach at Emerald Bay is a short quarter-mile walk away (see our Parks chapter for more details about Emerald Bay State Park).

Services available for the 100 RV and tent sites include showers, piped water and flush toilets. Dogs are okay, and daily rates run around $16.

Fallen Leaf
Calif. Hwy. 89, 2 mi. south of South Lake Tahoe, Calif. • (530) 573-2674, (877) 444-6777 for reservations

Fallen Leaf campground has 205 sites for tenters and RVers, providing picnic tables, flush toilets, fire rings and piped water. Daily fees are about $14, and pets are allowed on a leash. The sites are scattered amongst the tall pines just a short distance from lovely Fallen Leaf Lake. It's also close to trailheads leading into the Desolation Wilderness.

General Creek at Sugar Pine Point
Calif. Hwy. 89, 1 mi. south of Tahoma, Calif. • (530) 525-7982, (800) 444-7275 for reservations

As part of Sugar Pine Point State Park, General Creek campground enjoys a lovely tree-shaded setting along the west shore of Lake Tahoe (see our Parks chapter for more details about the park). Services for the 175 tent and RV sites include piped water, showers (summer only), flush toilets, fire rings and picnic tables. It's open all year and because of heavy summer use, we recommend getting reservations during July and August.

Although the park extends across Calif. Highway 89, there are no campsites on that side. But you can still enjoy swimming, biking and hiking in the area. Daily fees are around $16, and pets are okay on leashes.

Nevada Beach
Elks Point Rd., 1 mi. northeast of Stateline, Nev. • (775) 588-5562, (800) 280-2267, (877) 444-6777

Nevada Beach campground is on a lovely sandy beach but still close to all the casino action at Stateline. Of the 54 sites, 30 are okay for RVs. Daily rates run $14 to $16, with services including flush toilets, piped water, picnic tables and fire rings. With its location right on the lakeshore, activities at the campground are water-oriented, such as swimming and boating.

Tahoe Valley
1175 Melba Dr., South Lake Tahoe, Calif. • (530) 541-2222

The largest camping facility in the Reno/Tahoe area, Tahoe Valley offers just about everything you'd ever want to make your camping/RVing experience enjoyable. You'll find all the basics of piped water, flush toilets, cable TV, barbecues, fire rings, picnic tables, showers and complete hookups for any size recreational vehicle. Amenities also include a swimming pool, convenience store, tennis courts, recreation hall, sports courts, storage facilities and a tourist information center. Shuttle service to Stateline, Nevada, casinos runs from

Photo: Greg Gilman/Eastern Plumas County Visitors Bureau

Though you don't need to leave the immediate area to find picturesque places to camp, the state parks and national forests in eastern California offer views like this one.

11 AM to midnight. Daily fees range from $22 to $30. The facility is usually open from April through October and you can stay as many nights as you like during that time. Pets are okay on leashes.

The 413 sites at Tahoe Valley are sprinkled amongst the tall pine trees bordering the Upper Truckee River near the Factory Stores at the "Y." You'll find biking, hiking, horseback riding and golf nearby. Look for the campground at the intersection of U.S. Highway 50 and C Street.

Zephyr Cove Resort
U.S. Hwy. 50, Zephyr Cove, Nev.
• **(775) 588-6644**

You can camp all year round at the campground at Zephyr Cove Resort. Although peaceful during the fall and winter, it's a beehive of activity during the summer months. We strongly recommend getting reservations at this popular family resort during July and August.

The campground has 170 sites for tenters and RVers, with full hookups, piped water, flush toilets and showers available. Daily rates range from $17 to $26. Other amenities include a minimart, horseback riding, snowmobiles, lake cruises, a swimming beach and restaurants. Pets are allowed on leashes.

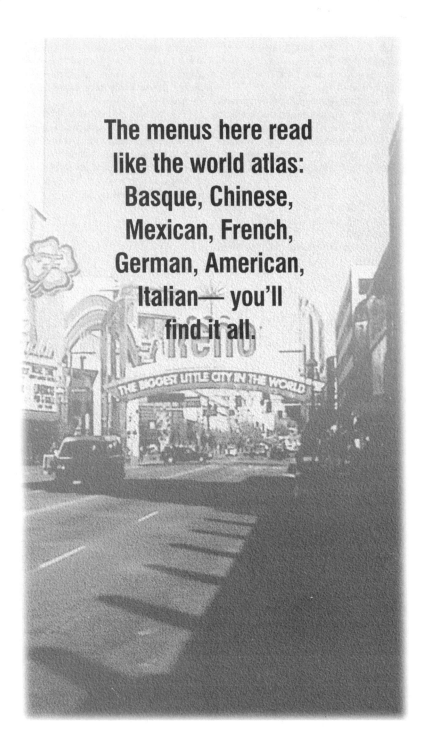

The menus here read
like the world atlas:
Basque, Chinese,
Mexican, French,
German, American,
Italian— you'll
find it all.

Restaurants

Nowhere is the Reno/Tahoo area's character and diversity more apparent than in its restaurants. The menus here read like the world atlas: Basque, Chinese, Mexican, French, German, American, Italian — you'll find it all. And we're going to brag a little and tell you that the food prices are reasonable, too. We guarantee that a family of four can go to dinner and the bill won't leave Dad wondering who'll have to wash dishes to pay for the meal.

You can thank the area's casinos for the low prices. They have seen to it that menu prices stay at reasonable levels. Most serve inexpensive food in order to entice their patrons to stay put so that the casinos reap bigger monetary rewards from them at the gaming tables. So casinos are accustomed to operating their restaurants at a loss, which helps everyone out in the pocketbook department. This philosophy forces restaurants outside of the casinos to stay with reasonable prices, too, in order to remain competitive and in business.

But just because the prices are reasonable, don't assume the restaurants hedge on quality. We won't let them. Our ever-changing population here expects only the finest in cuisine. Some critics have compared our restaurants to those in San Francisco. In fact, many Bay Area restaurateurs are reaching out into the Reno/Tahoe market. So the definite upside to this highly competitive market is a plethora of fine restaurants that are reasonably priced.

We're sure you've heard already that every hotel/casino has its own signature steakhouse, gourmet dining room, coffee shop or cafe, and we're confident that you will discover these gastronomical delights on your own, so we've concentrated this chapter on restaurants located away from the bright lights of the casinos. We'll take you on a gourmet tour of restaurants off the beaten path, into the back alleys of towns, into the strip malls,

into the Insiders' neighborhoods. We'll take you to the locals' favorite eating establishments. We'll give you a list of restaurants to die for.

Other venues we'll not be suggesting are chain restaurants and fast-food joints. Sure, we have most of the chains and most of the fast-food places, but we feel you're already familiar with these so we'll concentrate on what's unique to these parts.

We've arranged this chapter a little differently than the others. It's divided into two main regions — Reno/Sparks and Lake Tahoe Area — and then broken down by type of restaurant (American, Italian, Mexican, etc.) and then by our standard geographical areas. So, for instance, if you're in Reno and are hankering for Mexican food, it'll be easy to browse through the Reno/Sparks "Mexican" section until you find the taqueria that strikes your fancy (or the one closest to you). Or if you'll be heading to the Lake Tahoe area and want to plan a special evening with that special someone, you can look through the listings around the lake to find just the right place.

Most of the restaurants have very casual dress requirements so don't be surprised at any meal to see someone dressed up in a coat and tie next to someone wearing a pair of shorts and a T-shirt.

Most of the restaurants listed accept the major credit cards, but we'll let you know those that don't.

You should realize that many of the restaurants that serve both lunch and dinner will open between 11 and 11:30 AM and then close for a few hours before reopening again for dinner. Also, some of the restaurants around Lake Tahoe have different schedules during high season than during the off-season. And, of course, hours and days of operation change from time to time. If a particular time or day is important to you, we suggest that you call to confirm the restaurant's hours.

One important fact to remember in the

Reno/Tahoe area is that the laws on smoking in restaurants are very different in Nevada than they are in California. In Nevada, smoking is permitted in designated areas and all restaurants have nonsmoking sections. In California, smoking is prohibited in all restaurants.

Price Code

To give you an idea of how much you can expect to pay, we've coded the entries in this chapter using the following system. Our price-code rating reflects the average cost of entrees for two, without cocktails, appetizers, wine, dessert, tax and tip.

$	less than $20
$$	$21-$50
$$$	$51-$100

So loosen your belts a notch and prepare to take a guided tour of the gastronomical haunts of the Reno/Tahoe area's Insiders.

Oh, and one last thing: "Bon Appetit, Hon."

Reno/Sparks

American

Reno

The Aero Club
$$ • 442 Flint St., Reno, Nev.
• (775) 324-1629

With its collection of aviation memorabilia from the 1920s, '30s and '40s, The Aero Club is one restaurant in Reno that's packed with people when the National Championship Air Races come to town. But it's not only the flying machines that provide a peek into the past: the restaurant itself is historic, housed in a turn-of-the-century mansion that takes you back to the early days of Reno. You can dine indoors in lovely wood-paneled elegance or enjoy the wooded grounds at a table in the garden, weather permitting. The customized menu is eclectic, including specialties such as Jamaican jerk pork medallions and Lafayette Escradrille jambalaya. The restaurant is open for lunch and dinner Tuesday through Saturday.

Archie's Famous Grill
$ • 2195 N. Virginia St., Reno, Nev.
• (775) 322-9595

If you want just plain, good food, try Archie's. It's located across the street from the University of Nevada, Reno, and is a student hangout so you know the prices are reasonable. Breakfasts are huge here and include tons of home-style grilled potatoes, and Archie's can whip up a mean sourdough French toast. Its lunch special is a $1/3$-pound hamburger on a fresh, soft bun. For dinner, most patrons recommend the Jamaican chicken. Archie's has an outdoor patio which is a great place to be when the balloon races are in town. Archie's sits across the street from Rancho San Rafael Park where the hot air balloons take off and is open for breakfast, lunch and dinner seven days a week, but it closes at 4 PM Sunday, Monday, and Tuesday.

Amelia's Restaurant and Flightline Bar
$$ • 655 S. Rock Blvd., Reno, Nev.
• (775) 858-7316

The best thing about this restaurant is that its bar overlooks the runways at the Reno/Tahoe International Airport and the Sierra Nevada mountains so you get a great view of takeoffs and landings and a fantastic view when the sun ducks behind the mountains. It's open 8 AM to 5 PM Monday, and Tuesday through Friday 8 AM to 8 PM. The food is fine, but the real drawing card of this restaurant is the view and atmosphere. The sandwiches are the forte so lunch tends to be better than dinner. And, yes, it's named after Amelia Earhart.

Blue Skies Back-Door Cafe
$ • 10 Lake St., Reno, Nev.
• (775) 348-2583

You won't find a more delightful place in Reno for lunch than Blue Skies: it offers indoor and outdoor seating smack on the banks of the Truckee River next to the National Automobile Museum.

Enjoy a sunny lunch while you watch the ducks and joggers go by. With names like Rolls-Royce and Edsel, the salads, sandwiches, soups and pasta entrees reflect the car collection next door. If you're visiting the museum, we suggest making lunch at Blue Skies a part of your outing, especially if it's a nice day. The restaurant is open for lunch daily and periodically showcases local entertainers and musicians on the outdoor patio. (For more information about the museum see our Attractions chapter.)

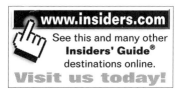

www.insiders.com

See this and many other **Insiders' Guide®** destinations online.

Visit us today!

Blue Star Cafe
$ • 6350 S. Virginia St., Reno, Nev.
• (775) 852-2111

The food here is average but this '50s style diner is a fun place to eat. It serves about 10 different types of burgers and a large selection of sandwiches. The best things on the menu are the homemade soups and, believe it or not, the baked meat loaf. The Blue Star brags that its shakes and malts are the best in town. This diner has original Seeburg jukeboxes at each of its booths, giving it that *Happy Days* feel. It's open every day for breakfast, lunch and dinner.

Cafe Soleil
$$ • 4796 Caughlin Pkwy., Reno, Nev.
• (775) 828-6444

As its name suggests, a meal at Cafe Soleil will bring sunshine into your life. A popular hangout for professionals living in the Caughlin Ranch area, it's not a typical tourist stop. But for innovative food that blends American and Pacific Rim flavors, we recommend you venture away from the hotel zone and enjoy a delicious meal here. With its sunny decor and warm Mediterranean ambiance, Cafe Soleil is a classy place. If the dining room is full, you can eat at tables in the lounge or at a bar where you can watch the food being prepared. Reservations are advised, and be sure to ask about tables with a city view. It's open daily for dinner and for brunch on Sunday.

Christmas Tree Restaurant
$$ • 20007 Mt. Rose Hwy., Reno, Nev.
• (775) 849-0127

For dinner in the mountains (but close to Reno), the Christmas Tree Restaurant offers delightful cuisine from its perch high above the valley. The warm, woodsy ambiance is comfortable year-round, but is especially inviting when snow turns the surrounding landscape into a winter wonderland. Although the mahogany-grilled meats are legendary in these parts, the menu also includes such taste delights as Pasta Conchiglia and shrimp scampi. On the way to Mt. Rose–Ski Tahoe ski resort, the bar is a popular après-ski hangout. The bar opens at 3:30 PM and dinner is served from 5 PM nightly. If you head up here in the winter, be sure to check the weather and road conditions.

Famous Murphys Restaurant Grill & Oyster Bar
$$ • 3127 S. Virginia St., Reno, Nev.
• (775) 827-4111

Although the name and decor are decidedly Irish, the cuisine is American, featuring prime rib, steaks, seafood, chicken and pasta. You can eat in the main dining rooms or, for lighter fare in a more casual environment, you can try the grill and oyster bar. Local sports fans know that the bar at Murphys is a great place to enjoy fresh oysters on the halfshell while watching their favorite sporting event. The restaurant serves dinner nightly and lunch Monday through Saturday; it opens at 5 PM on Sunday.

Hilltop Bar & Eaterie
$ • 4792 Caughlin Pkwy., Reno, Nev.
• (775) 826-2665

The panoramic city view from the Hilltop Bar & Eaterie is impressive whether you're grabbing a quick lunch, enjoying a drink with friends or relaxing over a leisurely dinner. And the best part is that almost any seat in the house will give you good visibility. The stunning view is the star in this place: the menu and decor are simple and laid-back. You'll find an interesting selection of soups, salads and sandwiches for lunch and chicken and pasta entrees for dinner. Live music is offered periodically (call for dates and times) which attracts the older singles crowd around the bar area. Tucked in the same shopping mall as Cafe Soleil (see our previous entry), the Hilltop is open for lunch and dinner Monday through Saturday.

Millie B's
$ • 1555 Vassar St., Reno, Nev.
• (775) 329-3831

This breakfast and lunch hole-in-the-wall (the owner doesn't mind if you call it that) is a closely guarded secret among Insiders. Why? Its homemade cinnamon rolls and beignets with vanilla sauce might just be the best in the state. Other menu items are good, but Millie's is renowned around the area for these two items which are worth the drive to sample. It's open for breakfast and lunch, Monday through Friday.

The 19th Hole
$$ • 1200 Razorback Rd., Reno, Nev.
• (775) 825-1250

Perched above Lakeridge Golf Course (see our Golf chapter), the 19th Hole offers diners lovely golf course and city views over the tops of huge trees. Although it's a favorite with golfers, you don't have to play the game to appreciate the rich ambiance and good food in this restaurant. Dinner selections include a wide variety of veal, pasta, chicken, seafood and steak entrees. There's a separate bar, usually crowded with golfers replaying their rounds over favorite drinks. The restaurant is open for dinner Tuesday through Saturday and for lunch Monday through Friday. It's closed the first two weeks of January each year.

Peg's Glorified Ham & Eggs
$ • 425 S. Sierra St., Reno, Nev.
• (775) 329-2600

Peg's is close to downtown and is a favor-ite hangout for Reno attorneys. Open seven days a week for breakfast and lunch, Peg's specializes in, of course, egg dishes. The house specialty is Huevos Rancheros, served in a tortilla, smothered in sauce with plenty of hash browns. The portions are huge here, and the service is very friendly. A great place to go for a quick breakfast or lunch if you're downtown or if you're looking for legal representation.

PJ & Co. Restaurant Saloon
$$ • 1590 S. Wells Ave., Reno, Nev.
• (775) 323-6366

PJs is located kitty-corner from the Rapscallion Restaurant (see subsequent entry under "Seafood") and next door to Corrigan's Irish Pub (see our Nightlife chapter). PJs has been around for about 13 years and is casual, homey and a favorite local hangout, especially on Friday nights. Breakfast is served every day from 7 AM to noon, and locals keep coming back for its eggs Benedict and veggie omelets. PJs features gigantic burgers and homemade fries for lunch and specializes in Tex-Mex cooking for some of its dinner items, but the pork back ribs keep most diners happy. PJs has an outside area for dining and a full bar that offers eight different beers on tap. The kitchen stops serving at 9 PM. It also has three TVs which are always tuned to some sports channel. The restaurant and bar are only separated by a wooden railing so it can get noisy, especially on Friday nights after work. Say "hi" to Larry the bartender if you visit.

Skyline Cafe
$$ • 3005 Skyline Blvd., Reno, Nev.
• (775) 825-5611

Nestled in an upscale residential area, Skyline Cafe is a popular locals' hangout. You can enjoy delicious seafood and pasta entrees along with panoramic views of the city. Seating on the patio is available when weather permits, and there's a small bar up front to

---

INSIDERS' TIP

The best food bargains in the Reno/Tahoe area are the lavish buffets available at most casinos.

meet and greet friends. The bar opens daily at 4 PM and dinner is served from 5 to 10 PM. Reservations are advised.

Sparks

Cozy's Coffee Shop
$ • 2258 Oddie Blvd., Sparks, Nev. • (775) 359-8008

Cozy's serves down-home American food and lots of it — so don't come here expecting finger-food and small, dainty portions. Every day, for breakfast, lunch and dinner, its cooks prepare rich, flavorful food from scratch using only fresh produce and top-quality meats. Its specialties include pot roast, just like grandma used to make, with a gravy to kill for. But you can't go wrong ordering that old standby T-bone steak with Cozy's special sauteed mushrooms. If you'd rather have breakfast — a big breakfast — try the chicken-fried steak with three eggs and hash browns smothered in country gravy. If you have room for dessert (and we're betting you won't, but don't let that stop you!), tell your waitress to slice a generous portion of one of Cozy's homemade fruit pies. The atmosphere inside reminds you of being in a friend's kitchen, and the waitresses are some of the nicest and friendliest in town. The restaurant is located in a strip mall between ShopKo and Albertson's market. You can't miss the hot pink and violet exterior.

Freddie's Roost Grille and Sports Bar
$$ • 7755 Spanish Springs Rd., Sparks, Nev. • (775) 626-1000

For an establishment that calls itself a grille and sports bar, Freddie's has exceptional food and eye-catching views of Red Hawk Golf Course's 18th hole and wetlands (see our Golf chapter for details about the course). Freddie's is a great place to go if you want good food, a lively sports bar and friendly service. But don't think of this place as your typical sports bar and grille. Sure, it has big-screen TVs for watching your favorite sporting events but it also has its share of indoor and outdoor fireplaces and intimate, secluded corners to cuddle in. Every night, something special goes on at Freddie's. During NFL season on Monday night, Freddie's offers appetizers at half price. Tuesday is usually "Parents' Night Out" where it puts on a G-rated movie for the kids on a big-screen TV in the rear dining room and offers them pizza and ice cream for about $5 so parents can enjoy a relaxing dinner by themselves. Friday is seafood special night. Sunday, Freddie's hosts a champagne brunch.

If the weather permits, dining on the wooden outside deck is popular and if the weather gets a little brisk, you'll see patrons grouped around the outdoor fireplace. Freddie's serves the standards like grilled chicken and Reuben sandwiches but also whips up gourmet delights like mustard and garlic crusted lamb with a Cabernet demiglace. And don't pass up a chance to try Freddie's desserts; some are topped with a drizzle of white and black chocolate. Diners have been seen licking the plate while sampling these desserts. Freddie's is open for lunch and dinner every day of the week.

Great Basin Brewery
$$ • 846 Victorian Ave., Sparks, Nev. • (775) 355-7711

This microbrewery not only makes fresh, handcrafted beers right before your eyes in its special, glass-enclosed brewroom, it also serves up a wide variety of excellent food. Yes, most patrons come here and crowd around the L-shaped bar to savor one of their favorite brews but when you walk in, take a look around and you'll see a packed dining room, too. The brewery's beers are among the best in America and have won numerous awards at the Great American Beer Festival, but some Insiders think this brewery also has the best fish and chips in the Reno/Tahoe area. Its secrets are the fish and batter. Instead of frozen fish, it uses hand-cut Alaskan cod and deep fries it in Wild Horse Ale batter (Wild Horse Ale is one of the brewery's signature beers).

Other unique specialties are the garlic fries made with real pieces of garlic scattered throughout the potatoes and its adaptation of an Old World pub fare favorite called Shepherd's Pie. The pie is made with tender, braised lamb, veggies and gravy surrounded by mashed garlic potatoes. If pub grub is your preference, try the sausage sampler, which includes all of the brewhouse's four kinds of sausage. Every night, Great Basin has a dinner special (Monday is all-you-can-eat fish and chips), and on the weekends the brewery has entertainment (see our Nightlife chapter). Located just a few blocks from Victorian Square Plaza, this is a local hangout before and after the movies. During the summer, it has an outside sitting area with a stage presenting free entertainment. The wait for a table on Fridays and Saturdays can be lengthy, especially if Victorian Square is hosting a special event. Great Basin serves lunch and dinner seven days a week.

Landrum's Cafe
$ • 415 S. Rock Blvd., Sparks, Nev.
• (775) 359-8686

The owners of this cafe call it the area's last real diner and when you walk through the door you may agree. The decor is 1950s, the service is fast and friendly, and the menu is short and without regard for cholesterol or calories. Landrum's has been in the Reno/Sparks area since 1947, and Insiders say it hasn't changed its menu. In fact, most patrons don't even look at the menu when they order, and the cook still prepares everything in plain sight of diners sitting on stools. You can still order its original hearty chili-cheese omelet or its biscuits and home fries smothered in country gravy loaded with hunks of pork sausage.

This is a locals' hangout that only serves breakfast and lunch. Landrum's is noted for its Early Bird Special served from 6 to 7:30 AM every day which consists of two eggs, any style, bacon or sausage and potatoes for under $3. For a real treat, try the $1/3$-pound hamburger, cooked the way you want it and topped with a thick slice of grilled Bermuda onion — and don't forget one of its signature milk shakes. An Insiders' favorite is the rich and thick homemade chili. And, yes, rock 'n roll music is definitely on the jukebox. This diner is packed during Hot August Nights (see our Annual Events chapter), so be prepared.

Rapscallion's Roadhouse Grille
$$ • 1250 Disc Dr., Sparks, Nev.
• (775) 626-7066

This restaurant is owned by the same people who run Rapscallion's in Reno (see our subsequent entry under "Seafood"), and the quality at this one is on par with its Reno sister. Specialties are steaks, steaks, and steaks, but the menu also features chicken and wood-fired pizza. The Roadhouse is home to the 72-oz Sirloin — if you think you can eat a 4½-pound steak. Locals flock here for its 2-for-1 drink Happy Hours where appetizers are only $1.95. Open for lunch and dinner every day, it's a real nice neighborhood spot to unwind in.

Asian

Reno

Bananas! Restaurant & Bar
$$ • 2323 S. Virginia St., Reno, Nev.
• (775) 825-5500

With a menu featuring meals from Thailand, the Mediterranean and the Caribbean, it's hard to categorize this restaurant. Since the cuisine is spicy like much Asian food, we've put it in that section. From the whimsical monkeys dancing across the menu pages to the jungle green decor, Bananas! is a fun place. If your tastebuds lean toward the Caribbean, you can try Short Ribs Ocho Rios or Jamaican jerk chicken; for Mediterranean fare you can choose honey mustard lamb or smoked salmon seasoned rice; and if you prefer Thai cuisine you can enjoy Chili Roughy or Pud Thai noodles. The separate bar up front offers beers from around the world, a reasonable wine list and entertainment periodically. Bananas! is open daily for lunch and dinner.

Bangkok Cuisine
$$ • 55 Mt. Rose St., Reno, Nev.
• (775) 322-0299

If you love the vibrant flavors of Thailand — lemon grass, peppers and curries — Bangkok Cuisine should please your palate. Be sure to ask about how spicy the food is, and order it according to your taste: many entrees served at this restaurant are very hot. The decor is pleasant, with black lacquered furniture and souvenirs of Thailand lending a slight Asian feel to the place. The menu is extensive, with chicken, fish, meat and vegetables prepared in a variety of Thai styles.

Photo: John Ascuaga's Nugget Casino Resort

"Extraordinary" is the only word to describe the buffet selections in Reno.

Bangkok Cuisine is a hangout for the Bangkok Consortium, a group of locals who discuss politics while feasting on Thai cuisine. The restaurant is open for lunch and dinner Monday through Saturday.

Cafe de Thai
$$ • 3314 S. McCarran Blvd., Reno, Nev.
• (775) 829-8424

We think the authentic Thai cuisine served at Cafe de Thai is some of the best Asian food in the Reno/Tahoe area. You'll find all the typical Thai dishes here, offered in varying degrees of spice from zesty to mild. The ambiance is quiet and comfortable but not sumptuous.

Although it's away from the major hotels and casinos, Cafe de Thai is easy to find on S. McCarran Boulevard. It's open for lunch and dinner Wednesday through Saturday.

Kyoto Restaurant
$$ • 915 W. Moana Ln., Reno, Nev.
• (775) 825-9686

For mouthwatering Japanese tempura, sushi, teriyaki and sukiyaki, we highly recommend the authentic cuisine at Kyoto Restaurant. The food is delightful, the prices are reasonable and the contemporary ambiance is relaxing and enjoyable. You'll find all your Japanese favorites on the menu plus a selection of tantalizing daily specials. Kyoto is open for lunch and dinner Monday through Saturday.

INSIDERS' TIP

If you will be in the area for a few days, pick up *Entertainment '99* (or *2000*); it's chock full of Restaurant options.

Palais de Jade
$$ • 960 W. Moana Ln., Reno, Nev.
• (775) 827-5233

An extremely well-decorated and sophisticated Chinese restaurant which is constantly voted No. 1 by Reno Insiders, Palais de Jade has a wide variety of plates including noodles and vegetable entrees. Specialties are the Kung-Pao chicken and pan-fried noodles. The menu sports about 100 different entrees. The cooking styles are mostly Cantonese and Mandarin, but a few dishes are cooked in the Szechuan style. The best thing about this restaurant, besides the food and friendly service, is the lazy susan tables. The spinning shelves make it easier to sample everyone's entrees, and you can enjoy them and the great food every day from 11 AM to 10 PM .

Pho 777
$ • 201 E. Second St., Reno, Nev.
• (775) 323-7777

Pho 777 derives its name from the north Vietnamese broth (*pho*) and a Vietnamese belief that 7 is a lucky number and that three of any thing is extremely lucky. The owner will tell you that the three 7s are extraordinarily lucky because when you add them together they equal 21 and if you add the 2 plus the 1, you get 3 again. We're not sure how lucky the name is for the owner, but diners are lucky to have such a tastefully inexpensive noodle shop for lunch and dinner seven days a week. The restaurant only has room inside for about 20 diners and it's so popular, you'll often see people waiting outside for a seat. And for good reason: Pho 777 combines warm broth with soft noodles to concoct a low-calorie, extremely tasteful meal, all for under $5. The restaurant has about 14 different *phos* listed on its menu, as well as eggrolls, shrimp and pork flame-broiled over rice, pork slices and fried rice combinations. And none of the dishes is prepared spicy because each table is equipped with its own condiment tray so you can add as much of the hot pepper sauce as you wish. But take care when adding the chili sauce from the small jar: it's fire.

Rickshaw Paddy
$ • 4944 S. Virginia St., Reno, Nev.
• (775) 828-2335

Nicknamed "an Asian bistro," Rickshaw Paddy offers a tour of Asian taste treats based upon the legend of Seamus McGillicuddy, an Irishman who collected recipes as he traveled throughout Asia. You can savor the flavors of China, Thailand, Japan, the Philippines and Malaysia in a variety of luscious dishes, such as curry roast duck, Nasi Goreng, Malaysian chicken and grilled Mongolian lamb chops. The atmosphere is not the thing here, but the food is to die for. Because it's sometimes crowded during peak meal times, we suggest you try to eat earlier or later than most people. Lunch is served from 11:30 AM to 2:30 PM and dinner from 5 to 10 PM, daily except Sunday.

Sparks

Shanghai Restaurant
$$ • 1269 Baring Blvd., Sparks, Nev.
• (775) 358-1122

This may be the best Chinese restaurant in Sparks, though it's often overlooked by visitors because it sits tucked away in a remote corner of Baring Village Shopping Center. It has attractive Chinese decor, and the menu is extensive with reasonable prices. The waiters and waitresses are extremely friendly, and it's easy to see why Sparks locals love this place. The food is tasty, especially the General's Chicken and the sesame beef. The owner has a master's degree in journalism from the University of Nevada, Reno, but said he found owning this restaurant more fun and lucrative. After you try his food, we're positive you'll thank him for his career change. Shanghai Restaurant is open every day for lunch and dinner.

Barbecue

Sparks

B.J.'s Bar-B-Q
$ • 754 N. McCarran Blvd., Sparks, Nev.
• (775) 355-1010

This tiny restaurant is located in the Silver State Plaza in Sparks and just could be the best barbecue joint in the area. The interior of the restaurant is Spartan with a few tables and chairs. But you won't care about the atmosphere when you sink your teeth into any of the entrees topped with the restaurant's special sauce. This barbecue sauce has won several awards and is a local favorite. The smoked pork barbecue sandwich is worth writing home about. B.J.'s is open every day but Sunday from 11 AM to 9 PM.

Rutherford's Ol' South Restaurant & Bar
$$ • 55 E. Nugget Ave., Sparks, Nev.
• (775) 685-7777

Open every day for breakfast, lunch and dinner, Rutherford's combines Texas and Southern barbecue with a touch of Gulf Coast seafood, a combination some Insiders find irresistible. Located next door to the McCarran House, this restaurant is easy to spot from I-80. It uses natural wood-burning ovens and slow cooks all of its meats for at least 18 hours. If barbecue is your favorite, try the Killer Platter, a combination plate loaded with spareribs, chicken, beef, pork and sausage. If you prefer seafood, the Fisherman's High Tide Platter combines shrimp, scallops, crab cakes, frog legs, fish and clam strips and is big enough for two. All in all, Rutherford's has 99 items on its menu. At one end of the restaurant, some tables are situated around a fireplace for a more romantic feel; otherwise, the restaurant is open and airy. Rutherford's offers this challenge to anyone: if you can eat its special 6-pound steak, you can have it for free. If you fail to eat it at one sitting, you have to pay $42.50. Good luck.

Basque

Reno

Louis' Basque Corner
$$ • 301 E. Fourth St., Reno, Nev.
• (775) 323-7203

Dinner at Louis' is one of the most spectacular dining experiences in the Reno/Tahoe area; it really shouldn't be missed. When you enter this Reno icon, you walk into the Basque Country of northern Spain and southern France. Basque sayings line the walls, as well as pictures from the Pyrenees, pottery from Cibourne and other Basque pieces. But this

Photo: Caesars Tahoe

From casino restaurants to river-walk eateries, visitors will find every kind of dining in Reno.

restaurant's drawing card is its food cooked in the Basque way — and plenty of it (no one has ever left Louis' hungry). All dinners include soup, salad, French bread, Basque beans, French fries, a first course (shellfish, beef, tongue, oxtails, chicken), a main course (roast pork, steak, lamb chops, rabbit, calamari, paella), a bottle of wine, milk, coffee, tea and dessert. This restaurant serves dinner family-style at long tables where you may be seated next to strangers if you don't have at least eight in your party. The owners, Louis and Lorraine Erreguible, have been overseeing this restaurant for more than 30 years and often say their diners enter as customers and leave as friends. Before dinner, try one of Louis' Picon Punches. It's an alcoholic concoction where one is plenty and two's too many. Basque Corner is open for lunch and dinner every day.

Buffets

Most casinos/hotels in the area have at least one buffet. And why shouldn't they? The concept of the buffet was invented in Nevada in the 1940s. Prices for these buffets start at $6.99 and go up to $19.99. So if you're into lavish productions with carved ice sculptures, all-you-can-eat prime rib and shrimp and a list of food selections that tops 40 per meal, from salads to homemade desserts, try one of the following buffets:

Reno

Big Top Buffet, Circus Circus Hotel/Casino–Reno, 500 N. Sierra Street, Reno, Nevada, (775) 329-0711

Boomtown Silver Screen Buffet, Boomtown Hotel Casino Reno, I-80 at Boomtown, Reno, Nevada, (775) 345-6000

Chef's Pavilion, Eldorado Hotel/Casino, 345 N. Virginia Street, Reno, Nevada, (775) 786-5700

Flamingo Room Buffet, Flamingo Hilton, 255 N. Sierra Street, Reno, Nev., (775) 322-1111

Fresh Market Square Buffet, Harrah's,

Reno, 219 N. Center Street, Reno, Nevada, (775) 786-3232

Peppermill Island Buffet, Peppermill Hotel Casino Reno, 2707 S. Virginia Street, Reno, Nevada, (775) 689-7236

The Grand Canyon Buffet, Reno Hilton, 2500 E. Second Street, Reno, Nevada, (775) 789-2000

The Victorian Buffet, Silver Legacy Resort Casino, 407 N. Virginia Street, Reno, Nevada, (775) 329-4777

Toucan Charlie's, Atlantis Casino Resort, 3800 S. Virginia Street, Reno, Nevada, (775) 824-4433

Sparks

The N.Y. Steak Buffet, Silver Club Hotel/Casino, 1040 Victorian Avenue, Sparks, Nevada, (775) 358-4771

Rotisserie Buffet, John Ascuaga's Nugget, 1100 Nugget Avenue, Sparks, Nevada, (775) 356-3300

Triple Crown International Buffet, Baldini's Sports Casino, 865 S. Rock Avenue, Sparks, Nevada, (775) 358-0116

Coffee Houses

Reno

Deux Gros Nez
$ • 249 California St., Reno, Nev.
• (775) 786-9400

When you walk through the door of this coffee house, you get the feeling that you've passed through a time portal back to the 1960s. There's a bicycle motif, with several hanging from the walls, as well as several other bike-riding pieces including posters of the Tour de France. Two Big Noses, the translation of the French name, features a wide variety of items on its menu but most regulars swear by the focaccia, which comes with several different toppings. Its coffees and lattes are good, too. The best way to describe this place is: "Like totally far out, man." It's open every day for breakfast, lunch and dinner.

Emerald City Espresso & Tea Cafe

$ • 3594 W. Plumb Ln., Reno, Nev.
• (775) 322-1525

Named for Seattle, the city that spawned the current coffee craze, Emerald City is a relaxing spot to enjoy your favorite designer coffees and teas while you chat with friends or read the morning newspaper. On snowy winter days, it's especially inviting to cozy up on the comfy couches around the blazing fireplace. This casual eatery/coffee house is a hangout for students as well as residents of the upscale Caughlin Ranch area. You can order homemade soups, salads, sandwiches, quiches and pastries daily for breakfast, lunch and snacks. During summer months it's open weekdays from 6:30 AM to 4 PM and until 7 PM other months. Saturday hours are from 7 AM to 3 PM and Sunday from 8 AM to 3 PM.

Continental

Reno

Adele's at the Plaza

$$$ • 425 S. Virginia St., Reno, Nev.
• (775) 333-6503

If you're on a budget you might not be comfortable at Adele's at the Plaza: it's one of the most expensive places in town. But if you're in the mood to splurge or to celebrate a special occasion, you've come to the right place. The dinner menu features imaginative meat and fish entrees with luscious appetizers that include caviar and foie gras. For lunch you can choose from a great selection of lighter fare, such as sandwiches, salads and fresh fish entrees. The richly appointed decor creates a classy romantic mood. The bar features a huge selection of Scotch whiskies, and the wine list is extensive. Adele's is open for dinner nightly and for lunch Monday through Friday.

Bricks Restaurant & Wine Bar

$$ • 1995 S. Virginia St., Reno, Nev.
• (775) 786-2277

Named for the Comstock-era bricks used in its construction, Bricks is a classy dining experience even for the most discriminating palates. Each menu selection is almost a work of art, from the colorful design of the food on the plates to the exquisite aromas and tastes each course embodies. With entrees including fresh fish, pasta and meats, you can indulge yourself in such culinary delights as trout stuffed with crab, venison medallions in wine sauce and pork tenderloin with carmelized apples. Bricks is also well known for its superb choice of wines by the glass and its variety of single malt Scotches. The ambiance is one of Old World elegance, crisp white linens contrasting with dark brown woods. The restaurant is open Monday through Friday for lunch and dinner and dinner only on Saturday.

French

Reno

Pimparel's La Table Francaise

$$$ • 3065 W. Fourth St., Reno, Nev.
• (775) 323-3200

This is one of the most sophisticated and charming restaurants in the Reno/Tahoe area. It's also one of the most expensive but well, well worth the price. Yves Pimparel, the owner/chef, serves both classic and contemporary French dishes in a country inn atmosphere, decorated in white. The menu changes frequently so don't be afraid to try this restaurant more than once during your stay here. Pimparel was born in the Champagne region of France and began his career as a chef saucier at Pruniers Restaurant in Paris. He was also chosen to be one of the chefs to cook for

INSIDERS' TIP

If you're on a food budget, try eating your main meal at lunch when many restaurants serve the same entrees as at dinner but at cheaper prices. (From a health standpoint, this may be better for you, too.)

Queen Elizabeth II when she toured France. He later moved to the United States as chef to the Ambassador of France and stayed to cook for several well-known restaurants in New York, San Francisco and then Reno. His menus are always tantalizing, and some of the favorites are smoked duck Carpaccio, sauteed veal with porcini mushrooms, and succulent marinated rack of lamb. He prepares everything to order so don't be impatient. This restaurant is located about 2 miles west of Reno in a quiet, rustic setting and is open Tuesday through Saturday for dinner only. Reservations are recommended.

German

Reno

Bavarian World
$$ • 595 Valley Rd., Reno, Nev.
• (775) 323-7646

A unique restaurant, deli and bakery rolled into one, Bavarian World specializes in the food and beer of southern Germany. The restaurant is noted for its sauerbraten and its pork roast, and the bakery specializes in crusty German breads and rolls (its rye bread comes highly recommended). The deli offers the largest selection of cold cuts and sausages in the area and features more than 12 different kinds of liverwurst. Bavarian World also has an Alpine Boutique which sells hats, children's clothes and dresses. The restaurant section has a huge dance floor and an intimate bar tucked away in the back. It is also home to Helmut Gebhard, a German recording artist, who specializes in yodeling. Not only does he yodel Alpine tunes, but he has been known to yodel some country and western tunes as well. A fun restaurant with excellent food, Bavarian is open every day except Sunday and holidays for breakfast, lunch and dinner.

Indian

Reno

Sapna Indian Restaurant
$ • 3374 Kietzke Ln., Reno, Nev.
• (775) 829-1537

The delicious aroma of curry greets you at the door of Sapna Indian Restaurant. Whether you're vegetarian or not, you'll relish the variety of choices on their tantalizing menu offering cuisine from both northern and southern India. You can choose from a variety of tandoori and masala curry dishes prepared either vegetarian or with meats, fish or fowl. You can complete your meal with a tempting array of freshly made *nan*. Don't expect great atmosphere here: it's just so-so. The food, however, is sure to please. The restaurant is open for lunch and dinner Monday through Saturday and from 5 to 9 PM on Sunday.

Italian

Reno

Pane Vino
$$ • 3446 Lakeside Dr., Reno, Nev.
• (775) 829-9449

Tucked in the Moana West Shopping Center, Pane Vino offers the regional cuisine of Italy in an Old World environment. Its intimate ambiance reminds us of many of the small ethnic restaurants sprinkled all over San Francisco. As expected in any Italian eatery, you'll find lots of pasta dishes on the menu along with veal, game hen, seafood and beef prepared in traditional ways. With personable, friendly service, the staff at Pane Vino makes you feel almost like family. Reservations are advised since the place is quite small. It's open

---

INSIDERS TIP

Almost every casino in northern Nevada has a cabaret bar with free, live entertainment.

for lunch Monday through Friday and dinner daily.

Johnny's Ristorante Italiano
$$ • 4245 W. Fourth St., Reno, Nev.
• (775) 747-4511

A long time local favorite, Johnny's serves up delectable Italian cuisine with a touch of elegance. With classy high-backed chairs and a marble sculpture that dominates the room, the dining area is reminiscent of a lovely old Roman villa. Some menu selections tend to be on the rich side, but low-fat entrees are also included. You'll find a tantalizing variety of fresh seafood, pastas and meats to choose from. If you're looking for lighter fare, we suggest pizza and salad in the delightful Italian contemporary bar up front. The pizza is low-fat and absolutely delicious. Located right next to the Glory Hole (see our listing under "Steakhouses" in this chapter), Johnny's is open for dinner Tuesday through Saturday and is closed the first two weeks of January each year.

LaVecchia Varese Ristorante
$$ • 3501 S. Virginia St., Reno, Nev.
• (775) 825-1113

With colorful stained-glass windows, white lace curtains and warm brick walls, LaVecchia Varese Ristorante creates a comfortable, intimate setting for enjoying the innovative Italian cuisine on its menu. Intimate and elegant (but at the same time laid-back), the ristorante is the perfect choice for a romantic dinner for two. The owner and chef, who hails from Varese, Italy, takes pride in serving only foods that are freshly prepared on the premises.

This restaurant is anything but the usual spaghetti house: the menu is unique with entrees that combine the flavors of various cultures, including a selection of low-fat dishes. It's open for lunch Monday through Friday and for dinner Monday through Saturday. You can also enjoy jazz Wednesday evenings. Since

it's just a stone's throw from the Truckee River, we suggest a stroll along its banks either before or after dinner, weather permitting.

At press time, future plans indicated a possible move to a new location on S. Virginia Street, so be sure to call to confirm their whereabouts.

Luciano's
$$ • 719 Virginia St., Reno, Nev.
• (775) 322-7373

Luciano Parisi, the owner/chef of this fine Italian restaurant, hails from Bologna, Italy, and has brought with him some excellent family recipes. He offers a great selection of appetizers, soups, salads and more than a dozen pastas along with meat, chicken and fish dishes. Every day, he has at least 10 specials listed on a chalkboard as you walk in, so don't forget to look. The porcini mushroom ravioli is the signature dish.

The interior is intimate and often crowded so be sure to call for reservations. This restaurant is the favorite of a University of Nevada, Reno, Italian professor. What more can we say? Oh, it's open for lunch 11:30 AM to 2 PM Tuesday through Friday and for dinner Tuesday through Sunday from 5 PM to 9 PM. It's closed on Monday.

Viaggio
$$ • 309 Kietzke Ln., Reno, Nev.
• (775) 828-2708

The Reno/Tahoe area has an abundance of Italian restaurants but this one, located in Franktown Corners, has by far the best selection of wines. Almost half of this place is a wine shop where you can sample about 25 good to excellent wines by the glass. The other half is an intimate restaurant with a modern motif and an open kitchen in the back. Viaggio makes all of its pastas from scratch, including the ravioli. It serves all of the Italian favorites: Osso Bucco, fettuccine Alfredo, Saltimbocco — but its forte is its extensive wine list with

---

INSIDERS' TIP

Smoking is permitted in designated areas in all Nevada restaurants, but it is prohibited in all California restaurants.

more than 500 selections. Viaggio's is open weekdays for lunch and dinner and for dinner only on weekends.

Mexican and Southwestern

Reno

Cantina Los Tres Hombres
$ • 7111 S. Virginia St., Reno, Nev. • (775) 852-0202

At Cantina Los Tres Hombres you'll find all your Mexican favorites served in a typical south-of-the-border environment. A child-friendly establishment with good food at reasonable prices, it's a great place to take the whole family. The bar up front is a popular meet-and-greet hangout for young singles. You can watch sporting events on the big screen TVs and laugh at the antics of local comics on weekends. The cantina is open daily for lunch and dinner.

Sparks

El Sazon
$ • 2290 Oddie Blvd., Sparks, Nev. • (775) 351-2352

This Mexican restaurant started in a five-table space in Greenbrae Shopping Center in Sparks but was so popular it quickly outgrew such modest surroundings. El Sazon is the most authentic Mexican restaurant in the Reno/Tahoe area. A good sign of a great Mexican restaurant is when you hear Spanish being spoken by a majority of the diners, and it happens a lot at El Sazon. The restaurant is open every day for breakfast, lunch and dinner and the waiters and waitresses are friendly and helpful if you don't know what to order. Everything is homemade on the premises: no canned refried beans here. Its specialties include the Carne Asada (marinated, grilled rib-eye steak), the Chuletas de Puerco (marinated pork chops) and the Langosta a La Mexicana (Mexican broiled lobster just like in Baja California). Even the tortillas are homemade here so you can't go wrong ordering any of the standbys, like tacos and enchiladas. And, of course, on Saturday and Sunday, it serves the traditional Menudo (tripe stew). Don't miss this restaurant if you want authentic Mexican food.

Salsa Dave's
$ • 2855 N. McCarran Blvd., Sparks, Nev. • (775) 331-7777

If you like salsa, try this little restaurant located in Sparks Mercantile Shopping Center on the corner of Pyramid Way and McCarran Boulevard. Homemade salsa here comes in mild, medium and your-mouth's-on-fire. And Dave Pegasus, the owner, suggests that you try his salsa on everything on the menu. You can't miss Dave either. He's usually wearing a colorful shirt with matching hat. He was raised in Mexico so the food here is authentic, though not as heavy as Mexican food usually is. Dave's has a bar with tall tables and chairs where you can drink and sample his salsa, and it also has regular tables. Dave's wife Beverly suggests the fish tacos, made with batter-fried cod and topped, of course, with Dave's salsa. Dave's is open seven days a week for lunch and dinner.

Seafood

Rapscallion Seafood House & Bar
$$ • 1555 S. Wells Ave., Reno, Nev. • (775) 323-1211

Known for some years as "Reno's Official Seafood Restaurant," Rapscallion Seafood House & Bar prides itself on its selection of freshly caught fish. With historical memorabilia tastefully displayed on the dark wood walls, the dining and bar areas have the look and feel of turn-of-the-century San Francisco. Weather permitting, you can also enjoy outside seating on the surrounding deck. The bar is a popular meet-and-greet hangout, espe-

---

INSIDERS' TIP

Dining outdoors on a patio or deck? Don't forget the sunscreen.

cially on Wednesday nights. Rapscallion is open daily for lunch and dinner and also serves a special brunch on Sunday.

Plumb and Kietzke lanes with plenty of parking on the side. It's open daily for lunch and dinner.

Steakhouses

Reno

Glory Hole
$$ • 4201 W. Fourth St., Reno, Nev.
• (775) 786-1323

When you get a hankering for a mouth-watering steak served Nevada-style, head for the Glory Hole. The finest cuts of beef, grilled to perfection, are served with loaded baked potatoes, rice or pasta and a trip to the yummy salad bar. The dark wood and Victorian light fixtures give a laid-back, comfortable feel to the place. If you happen to blow in the door on a cold winter's night, try warming up in front of the roaring fire in the lounge before diving into that juicy steak dinner. It's a bit off the beaten path for tourists, but don't let that deter you. The Glory Hole is open daily for dinner at 5 PM.

Jeremiah's Steakhouse
$$ • 800 E. Plumb Ln., Reno, Nev.
• (775) 827-2080

If you've got a big appetite, the large portions at Jeremiah's Steakhouse will go a long way toward satisfying it. Since it specializes in steaks with all the delectable trimmings, many entrees at this popular eatery can be a real cholesterol blowout. But if you're into more healthy eating, look closer at the menu and you'll also find chicken and seafood selections. With lots of warm woods and leathers, the Western motif creates a comfortable laid-back atmosphere for a casual lunch or dinner. The restaurant is easy to find at the corner of

Vegetarian and Natural

Reno

Einstein's Quantum Cafe
$ • 6135 Lakeside Dr., Reno, Nev.
• (775) 825-6611

Mention the word "vegetarian" and many people think of food that's probably good for you but ultimately without taste and appeal. Einstein's Quantum Cafe explodes that myth with a menu chock full of gourmet vegetarian food that's not just for vegetarians. You can be good to yourself by choosing from their savory selection of wraps, pitas, salads and soups. Although not as healthy for you, the desserts are divine and so are the wines. Tucked in a small neighborhood shopping mall, Einstein's is a little off the beaten path for tourists but is easy to find from S. McCarran Boulevard. It's open for lunch and dinner Tuesday through Sunday. Periodically the restaurant also features live entertainment, such as jazz groups.

The Blue Heron Natural Foods Restaurant & Bakery
$ • 1091 S. Virginia St., Reno, Nev.
• (775) 786-4110

As the name denotes, The Blue Heron Natural Foods Restaurant & Bakery emphasizes healthy, natural foods in all its menu items. Although it's strictly vegetarian, we think you'll enjoy the tasty selection of menu items combining vegetables and grains. Don't expect great atmosphere here because you won't find it. What you will find is delicious food that

---

INSIDERS' TIP

If you're too tired to go out to eat, you can call the Delivery Diner for the Reno/Sparks area at (775) 828-3463. You can choose tasty items from more than 20 restaurants, including Casablanca, Cantina Los Tres Hombres, Giorgio's Pizza & Pasta, Kyoto and Bangkok Cuisine.

even your doctor would approve of your eating. The restaurant is open for lunch and dinner Monday through Saturday.

Lake Tahoe Area

American

North Shore Lake Tahoe

Austin's
$$ • Country Club Dr., across from the Hyatt Regency Lake Tahoe Resort & Casino, Incline Village, Nev.
• (775) 832-7778

If you miss your mother's cooking, you just might find it at Austin's: the restaurant is well known to Insiders for serving huge portions of good home-cooked food. Tucked into a rustic log cabin reminiscent of an old hunting lodge, the hearty food and casual decor suit the mountain environment to a "t." What better way to fuel the body for a day on the ski slopes or mountain trails than with a Bear Feast breakfast at Austin's, an all-in-one meal with eggs as the basic ingredient? For lunch you can choose from substantial hot entrees, a variety of burgers and super salad bowls. Dinner offerings include steaks and fish, along with such down-home favorites as liver and onions, meatloaf and grilled pork chops. With delicious homemade pies displayed prominently up front, Austin's is not the place for dieters. Forget the calories and dive into a meal only mothers know how to prepare — you can always ski or hike it off during the day. Austin's is open for breakfast, lunch and dinner daily.

Big Water Grille
$$ • 341 Ski Wy., Incline Village, Nev.
• (775) 833-0606

Combining American contemporary with Mediterranean and Pacific Rim influences, the cuisine at the Big Water Grille offers a delightful culinary experience to the most discriminating diners. But throw in spectacular panoramic views of Lake Tahoe and a classy Tahoe decor that incorporates upscale art-

works, and you have a truly memorable evening. You can celebrate a romantic special occasion here or just stop by after skiing (Diamond Peak Ski Resort is just up the road). The roaring fire in the cozy bar up front is especially inviting on a cold winter's evening. Menu selections include such delights as grilled venison flank with wild rice and Szechuan pepper whiskey sauce, Tataki marinated fresh Hawaiian fish, and Sonoma duck breast with confit leg (where the leg of the duck is slow roasted and preserved in its own juices and then cooked with the breast). Be sure to take a look at the petroglyph designs and etched glass that make the atmosphere so unique. During high season the restaurant is open for dinner nightly, but it closes one day a week during slack. Be sure to call ahead.

Gar Woods Grill and Pier
$$ • 5000 N. Lake Blvd., Carnelian Bay, Calif. • (530) 546-3366

Named for the elegant mahogany boats developed in the 1920s by Garfield Wood, Gar Woods Grill and Pier celebrates fine food along with Tahoe's classic wood boating era. Nestled on the lakeshore right next to Sierra Boat Company, Gar Woods is a beehive of activity during the Concourse de Elegance in August when all the woodies are on display. The dinner menu at this laid-back eatery features a variety of pasta, fresh seafood and steaks. If you arrive by boat (except in winter) you can take advantage of valet boat parking at the Gar Woods pier. The view of the lake (either from the deck or the indoor dining area) is lovely and the people watching can't be beat. It's open for lunch and dinner daily during high season; lunch is served weekends only during low season.

Glissandi
$$$ • Resort at Squaw Creek, 400 Squaw Creek Rd., Olympic Valley, Calif. • (530) 581-6621

Indisputably one of the finest mountain resorts in America, the Resort at Squaw Creek is in a class by itself. Anything you do here is special, but dining at Glissandi is a treat even for the most sophisticated palates. Featuring American food with a French flair, the menu will entice you with such delights as herbcrusted Angus tenderloin, roast breast of squab, and Broken Arrow Ranch Wild Boar. Appetizers are equally tantalizing and include warm asparagus and shiitake mushrooms with Yukon Gold potato, and smoked golden trout with potato pancake. You can also sample the best the chef has to offer with a special prix fixe menu created nightly that includes an appetizer, salad, entree and dessert.

Awarded the "Best of Award of Excellence" by *Wine Spectator* magazine, the restaurant is a wine lover's Utopia: it features more than 350 labels, with each wine carefully selected to complement the creative cuisine. It has also been awarded the AAA Four-Diamond Award and named one of the best restaurants in Northern California by the *Gault-Millau Restaurant Guide*.

With tall tapers glowing against the snow-white tablecloths and warm mahogany accents, the simple elegance of the decor enhances the lush meadow and granite peaks of Olympic Valley as seen through the floor-to-ceiling windows. Dining with this spectacular view, any season of the year, is extraordinary to say the least.

Glissandi is open for dinner Tuesday through Saturday during peak season and closes several days a week during off season. Be sure to call ahead for reservations and to verify hours and days. Also ask about special wine and dine events held in the restaurant periodically. Because this resort and Squaw Valley USA are unique, we suggest you spend some time here. Come for the day and enjoy all the activities and scenery. If you're just coming for dinner, allow time enough to see a little of the valley. We tell you all about activities offered here in our Recreation, Resorts, Winter Sports and Golf chapters.

Jake's on the Lake
$$ • 760 N. Lake Blvd., Tahoe City, Calif.
• (530) 583-0188

A classy but casual eatery, Jake's on the Lake is tucked on the lake side of the Boatworks Mall with lovely views of the water. It's especially convenient if you've been browsing the shops in the mall. With its woodsy ambiance, you'll love the laid-back Old Tahoe feeling of this place. We suggest enjoying sundown in the bar over an appetizer and your favorite drink. Outdoor seating is available in the summer, and some tables in the indoor dining area offer views of the lake. The dinner menu features steaks, chicken and seafood; sandwiches and salads are available in the bar.

Like many Insiders, we've enjoyed the fine food and great atmosphere at Jake's for years. But over and above that, it's also a place that offers service beyond the call of duty. When our doggie bag was mistakenly thrown out one night, the staff replaced it with an entire steak dinner, cooked to order with all the trimmings, for our dogs. Needless to say, the restaurant has now become a favorite with our canines. Jake's is open for lunch and dinner daily.

Lone Eagle Grille
$$ • Country Club Dr. at Lakeshore
Blvd., Incline Village, Nev.
• (775) 832-3250

From simply a decor standpoint, the Lone Eagle Grille is one of the most outstanding restaurants in the Reno/Tahoe area. With enormous vaulted ceilings, two-story rock fireplaces, huge wrought-iron chandeliers and mammoth windows facing Lake Tahoe, it creates the luxury of an elegant hunting lodge that's equal to none. Just being here and soaking up the environment is special. From an Insiders' viewpoint, however, it may not give you the best value for your money: it's expensive and the service is just so-so. If you don't feel like splurging, come here for lunch or enjoy drinks and appetizers in the bar — the view is the same as in the dining room. You can also take your drink to the firepit on the beach just in front of the restaurant. The dinner menu features grilled beef, veal, lamb, fowl, fresh seafood and pasta. The restaurant is open daily for lunch and dinner. Although it's part of the Hyatt Regency Lake Tahoe Resort & Casino, you won't find it in the main hotel building: look for the large log structure right on the lakeshore.

Steamers Beach Side Bar and Oven
$ • 8290 N. Lake Blvd., Kings Beach,
Calif. (530) 546-2218

For a kicked-back, inexpensive lunch or

dinner, you can't beat the pizza, oven-baked sandwiches and calzones served up at Steamers Beach Side Bar and Oven. With an amazing array of ingredients to choose from, you can design your own pizza just the way you like it. For lighter fare, choose from a tasty selection of soups and salads, including Steamers own clam chowder. Nestled on a beautiful sugary beach, Steamers is a great place to feed the whole family. It's open daily for lunch and dinner.

Sunnyside
$$ • 1850 W. Lake Blvd., Tahoe City, Calif. • (530) 583-7200

The spacious outdoor deck at Sunnyside is the place to be for drinks, lunch or dinner in the summer: you can soak up a gorgeous panoramic view while watching all the boats coming and going. The cozy indoor dining room and bar, with a roaring fire and huge timbered ceiling, is just as popular in the winter: you can warm up and relax after a hard day on the slopes, enjoying a hot mulled wine followed by a gourmet dinner. The menu is typical American, with steaks, seafood, chicken and pasta. If you're lucky enough to have booked a room in the lodge here, you can look forward to a delightful Old Tahoe stay indeed (see our Hotels and Motels chapter for more information about lodging). The restaurant serves lunch and dinner daily and also breakfast during the summer.

Sunsets On The Lake
$$ • 7320 N. Lake Blvd., Tahoe Vista, Calif. • (530) 546-3640

Sunsets On The Lake boasts a winning combination: a diverse cuisine served in a traditional Tahoe environment. Hugging the lakeshore, the restaurant offers spectacular views from the dining areas as well as the Island Bar, which hangs right over the water. A blend of California and continental, the cuisine features fresh food prepared in a variety of enticing ways. For starters try a sashimi appetizer or the halibut taco accompanied by

the appropriate wine from the impressive wine list. Valet parking is available and you can also arrive in your boat. Sunsets is a Tahoe tradition — don't miss it. It's open daily for lunch and dinner during high season but closed from November 1 to December 15.

The Moose's Tooth Cafe
$$ • 400 Brassie Ave., Kings Beach, Calif. • (530) 546-9495

Nestled in a lovely log structure on the Old Brockway Golf Course (see our Golf chapter for more information about the course), The Moose's Tooth Cafe serves up hearty cuisine that will stay with you the whole day through. Start with a breakfast of tofu veggie scramble or crab cake Benedict, and take a break for a Moose Spiced Burger or portobello mushroom sandwich for lunch; then dive into a slab of Danish baby back ribs or a platter of Cajun fish for dinner. The decor is comfortable Old Tahoe, with a roaring fire and peeks of the lake.

The restaurant is easy to find at the intersection of Calif. highways 28 and 267: just look for the log building on the first fairway (it's also the golf pro shop). It's open for breakfast, lunch and dinner daily during high season but closed several days a week during low season. We suggest calling to verify hours and days during off season.

For a very interesting backcountry ski outing, you can ski to the restaurant from North Tahoe Regional Park. It's a pretty moderate run of just several miles, but you'll need cars at both ends of the trek. See our Winter Sports chapter for details about the park, where you can pick up maps showing ski trails in the area.

South Shore Lake Tahoe

Edgewood Restaurant
$$ • 180 Lake Pkwy., Stateline, Nev. • (775) 588-2787

If decor is an important element in your

INSIDERS' TIP

To save money, check for dining and happy hour coupons in local newspapers.

dining experience, you won't find anything more majestic than Edgewood Restaurant at the Edgewood Tahoe Golf Course (see our Golf chapter for more information about the course). Renovated in 1992 for more than $5 million, the restaurant/clubhouse perfectly reflects the grandeur of Lake Tahoe in its customized cathedral-like design. From the dramatic central cupola resting on 20-foot timbers to the wooden window dormers with intricate panes, the structure is a testimony to the beauty of custom woodworking. The blend of cedar, ash, teak and granite lends power and luxury to the natural ambiance of the building. And all this with an awesome view: the turquoise waves are lapping at the white sand beach right outside with the snowcapped Sierra Nevada mountains directly across the lake.

But aside from gawking at the surroundings, you're here to eat, right? The dinner menu features such delightful entrees as fresh sea bass, roast loin of elk, fresh sturgeon and ahi tuna, all served with fresh seasonal vegetables. Edgewood is open for dinner daily, lunch Monday through Friday and brunch on Sunday during the summer. It serves dinner Wednesday through Sunday during the winter and is closed the month of November. Reservations are advised.

As it's one of the most spectacular and romantic sites along the lakeshore, we highly recommend your visiting Edgewood, even if it's just for drinks and looks.

Evan's American Gourmet Cafe
$$ • 536 Emerald Bay Rd., South Lake Tahoe, Calif. • (775) 542-1990

Tucked in a charming little house surrounded by pines, Evan's American Gourmet Cafe offers gourmet cuisine in an intimate romantic atmosphere. You can enjoy such taste treats as tournedos of beef on polenta croutons and crispy fried veal sweetbreads served with just the right wine. And speaking of wine, Evan's has received the "Award of Excellence" from *Wine Spectator* magazine along with three stars in the Mobil Travel Guide and three diamonds in the AAA Guide. It's open daily for dinner, but call to verify during off season. Reservations are advised.

Nepheles
$$ • 1169 Ski Run Blvd., South Lake Tahoe, Calif. • (530) 544-8130

After navigating one last run down Gunbarrel at Heavenly Ski Resort, load up your skis and head down the road to Nepheles. The bar opens at 2 PM and you can relax over your favorite drink and discuss the best (or worst) runs of the day with your skiing buddies. Or how about popping into a hot tub in one of their private spa rooms, where you can enjoy cocktail service and stereo music while soothing your sore muscles? Then stick around for dinner: you can choose from a variety of creative California cuisine items, such as wild boar chops, grilled portobello mushrooms and escargot au natural. It all sounds like the perfect ending to a perfect day to us. Be sure to call for information and reservations for the spa. Nepheles is open year-round with dinner served nightly.

Asian

South Shore Lake Tahoe

Hunan Garden
$ • 900 Emerald Bay Rd., South Lake Tahoe, Calif. • (530) 544-7268

If you've got a healthy appetite but a small budget, try the luncheon and dinner buffets at Hunan Garden restaurant. You can eat all you want of their distinctive Chinese cuisine at very affordable prices. You can also order from their full menu of selections, including beef, pork, chicken and seafood entrees, vegetarian dishes, chow mein and mu shu. If your children like Chinese food it's an economical place for the whole family to enjoy dinner out. Hunan Garden is open for lunch and dinner daily.

Samurai Restaurant
$$ • 2588 U.S. Hwy. 50, South Lake Tahoe, Calif. • (530) 542-0300

It's hard to diet if you're on vacation, but dining at Samurai Restaurant will help you eat healthy: most entrees are high in nutrition and low in fat and cholesterol. The traditional Japanese menu includes such favorites as teriyaki, tempura, nabemono, shioyaki and sashimi. All dinner entrees include miso soup or salad and rice. For a lighter meal you can mix and match maki sushi and nigiri from their wide selection. The restaurant is open daily for dinner.

Buffets

As we mention in the Reno/Sparks portion of this chapter, buffets are a mainstay of casinos and gaming resorts. On the South Shore of the lake, try the following buffets:

Garden Buffet, Harveys Resort Hotel/Casino, U.S. Hwy. 50, Stateline, Nevada, (775) 588-2411

Le Grande Buffet, Lake Tahoe Horizon Casino Resort, U.S. Hwy. 50, Stateline, Nevada, (775) 588-6211

The Roman Feast, Caesars Tahoe, U.S. Hwy. 50, Stateline, Nevada, (775) 588-3515

Continental

North Shore Lake Tahoe

La Fondue
$$ • 120 Country Club Dr., Incline Village, Nev. • (775) 831-6104

Although it used to be the rage back in the 1970s, it's hard to find fondue anymore, so for something different we suggest you try this Swiss/French restaurant. It's also a fun, relaxing way to enjoy dinner with good friends and family. So if you're up to managing that pot of hot oil in the middle of the table, you can order beef, meatballs, chicken, lamb, prawns and scallops to cook and then dip in luscious homemade sauces. Or you can try a typical Swiss cheese fondue or a delectable chocolate and ice cream fondue dessert. The restaurant is open for dinner daily except Tuesday and is closed for three weeks in both May and November.

The Soule Domain
$$ • Stateline Dr., next to the Tahoe Biltmore, Brockway,Calif.
• (530) 546-7529

Voted "Best Place to Take a Date" for six years by *Action Magazine*. The Soule Domain is intimate, romantic and elegant. Nestled in a historic log cabin surrounded by pines, it specializes in continental/nouveau and creative American cuisine. Tantalizing menu selections include Thai curry scallops, smoked pheasant sausage salad, smoked sturgeon appetizer plate, and grilled quail. In the winter it's especially cozy to eat at a fireside table and in the summer patio dining is available, weather permitting. It's open for dinner nightly, and we recommend calling for reservations as seating is limited. Look for The Soule Domain in Crystal Bay, just 10 yards across the state line in California.

South Shore Lake Tahoe

Swiss Chalet Restaurant
$$ • 2544 Lake Tahoe Blvd., South Lake Tahoe, Calif. • (530) 544-3304

An institution in the South Shore Lake Tahoe area for more than 40 years, the Swiss Chalet Restaurant is the next best thing to dining in Switzerland. You'll need to throw your diet out the window to enjoy most of the cuisine here, but it's worth it since everything is absolutely delicious. Specialties of the house include Swiss veal, curry Stroganoff, German sauerbraten and, of course, that old favorite, Wienerschnitzel. It's open for dinner Tuesday through Sunday throughout the year.

The Greenhouse Restaurant & Bar
$$ • 4140 Cedar Ave., South Lake Tahoe, Calif. • (530) 541-3235

When they named this place The Greenhouse, they weren't kidding: it's absolutely lush with green foliage. The abundance of flourishing plants along with the European stained

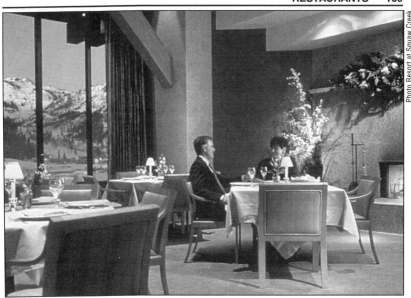

The Reno/Tahoe area has a tantalizing variety of restaurants with a view.

glass and warm woods creates a comfortable environment for fine dining. You can enjoy familiar entrees from the continent such as roast duckling a l'Orange, Langouste et Veau du Chef and filet mignon Bearnaise. The restaurant is open daily for dinner, and reservations are recommended. You'll find it conveniently located near Harveys Resort Hotel/Casino.

The Summit
$$$ • Harrah's Lake Tahoe, U.S. Hwy. 50, Stateline, Nev. • (775) 588-6611

When Sammy Davis Jr. was a regular headliner in the South Shore Room of Harrah's Lake Tahoe, he stayed in the posh Star Suite tucked away on the 16th floor of the hotel. Other celebrities who made the suite their home away from home included Frank Sinatra, Neil Sedaka and Liza Minnelli. It was used as a set in the film *Things Change*, starring Don Ameche, and was where Paul Anka composed many of his most famous hit tunes.

Affording gorgeous views of the lake, the Star Suite is a vision of loveliness, with an enormous two-story fireplace, an intimate bar and a cozy mezzanine overlooking the main living space. Wouldn't you love to sit back and relax over a gourmet dinner in this very penthouse? Well you can since now it's The Summit, ranked one of the top 10 restaurants in the country by the American Academy of Restaurant Sciences.

But aside from its unique atmosphere and history, this award-winning restaurant features cuisine absolutely to die for: choices include venison roulade, roast rack of lamb with anise crust, grilled antelope loin with exotic grains, and individual prime beef Wellington. The chef's selection menu offers a multicourse dinner which can also be served with a selection of fine wines.

Although we don't typically feature casino restaurants in this chapter since you're sure to find them on your own, you might not dis-

---

INSIDERS' TIP

The buffet dinner originated in Nevada in the 1940s.

cover The Summit. Intimate and exclusive, it's not as widely known as many other restaurants in casinos. For an exceptional dining experience (especially that romantic special occasion), we highly recommend this restaurant. If you're lucky enough to get a reservation (be sure to call well ahead), expect a very leisurely and memorable evening.

The restaurant is open daily for dinner during high season and from Wednesday through Monday the rest of the year. For reservations call (775) 588-6611, ext. 3000, before 4 PM and ext. 2196 after 4 PM.

French

North Shore Lake Tahoe

Engadine Cafe at Rainbow Lodge
$$ • Rainbow Rd. Exit, I-80, west of Truckee, Calif. • (530) 426-3661

Although it's a little far afield (unless you're cross-country skiing at Royal Gorge), Rainbow Lodge is worth the drive for a memorable

dining experience. Built in the 1920s of hand-hewn timber and granite, the lodge oozes the history of the Sierras. You can step back in time and imagine what winters were like when heavy snow made skiing the only possible mode of transportation. Tucked deep in the pines along the American River, the setting is exquisite any time of the year.

The cuisine in the Engadine Cafe features fine French and California entrees such as swordfish on rice noodles with hoisin glaze and salmon with sun-dried tomato beurre blanc. Because the lodge is popular with health-conscious hikers and skiers, you'll also find vegetarian selections.

You can soak up Sierra history along with gourmet food for breakfast, lunch and dinner daily during high season, but the lodge and restaurant are closed Tuesday and Wednesday during off season. Dinner reservations are advised during high season, and we suggest you call to verify hours during off season. For details about cross-country skiing at Royal Gorge, see our Winter Sports chapter.

To get to the lodge from Kings Beach take Calif. 267 north to Truckee (about 6 miles)

Photo: Roger Brotherton

The beautiful architecture of the Old First National Bank is the unique home of Planet Hollywood.

and then travel west on I-80 for about 10 minutes to the Rainbow Bend Exit.

Le Petit Pier
$$$ • 7238 N. Lake Blvd., Tahoe Vista, Calif. • (530) 546-4464

Easily one of the most splendid restaurants in the Reno/Tahoe area, Le Petit Pier is divine indeed. Every detail speaks to elegance, from the edible flowers dusting the salad greens to the 300-plus vintage wines on the wine list. Entrees are very French, and you may find yourself asking the waiter to explain them to you. The cuisine is unique: not many restaurants serve lavender orange glazed Muscovy duck breast with huckleberry sauce, for example. With comfortable pastel colors accenting warm woods in three cozy dining areas, the restaurant exudes the atmosphere of a classy old country inn. Needless to say, the service is impeccable.

On a warm summer evening try to get a window table (the restaurant almost hangs over the lake). Toward sundown, flocks of Canada geese gather below, waiting for bread to be tossed down to them. Parking is sometimes difficult so take advantage of their valet service.

Although an evening here is expensive, it's well worth every penny. The restaurant is open Wednesday through Monday for dinner, with seatings at 6 and 9 PM during high season. Times may vary during off season. Reservations are strongly recommended.

Italian

North Shore Lake Tahoe

Azzara's Italian Restaurant
$$ • 930 Tahoe Blvd., Incline Village, Nev. • (775) 831-0346

A great favorite with locals, Azzara's will more than satisfy your craving for first-class pasta. Other entrees include steak Toscano, paella and Osso Buco. The sea green wallpaper and white lace curtains create a laid-back comfortable atmosphere, perfect for enjoying a meal with friends or the whole family. If you have to wait for a table (which is likely since

it's a popular place), just have a seat in the bar area and talk skiing, golf or hiking with the locals. Conveniently located in Raleys Incline Center, Azzara's is open for dinner Tuesday through Sunday.

Lanza's
$ • 7739 N. Lake Blvd., Kings Beach, Calif. • (530) 546-2434

With its casual decor and reasonable prices, Lanza's is a good choice for families with children. You can relax in its family-friendly atmosphere after a hard day skiing or hiking. From its varied selections of pasta, pizza, chicken and veal you're sure to find everybody's favorite. If you're just too tired to eat in a restaurant, you can give them a call and order from their takeout service. Lanza's is open for dinner daily throughout the year.

South Shore Lake Tahoe

Ivano's at the Lake
$$ • 290 Kingsbury Gr., Stateline, Nev. • (775) 586-1007

Featuring classic Italian recipes along with Ivano's original entrees, Ivano's at the Lake serves food prepared with only the freshest ingredients. Just reading the extensive menu will whet your appetite with such offerings as penne Arrabbiata, linguine Puttanesca, Bistecca della Mamma and Petto di Pollo alla Salvia. You'll find just the right wine to accompany your entree from the more than 70 on their wine list. The ambiance is casual elegance and romantic enough for a special evening with a special someone. Ivano's is open for dinner Monday through Saturday.

Scusa! on Ski Run
$$ • 1142 Ski Run Blvd., South Lake Tahoe, Calif. • (530) 542-0100

One of the most popular Italian restaurants in the South Shore Lake Tahoe area, Scusa! on Ski Run specializes in typical Italian fare, such as pasta, calamari, eggplant, veal and chicken entrees. The ambiance is comfortably casual, with white walls and tablecloths, accented by black furniture and splashes of bright color in accent touches. It's conveniently located on the road to Heavenly Ski Resort and has plenty of parking. You'll be able to dine nightly here during high season, but call for days and hours during low season. Reservations are advised.

Seafood

North Shore Lake Tahoe

Captain Jon's Restaurant & Grill
$$ • 7220 N. Lake Blvd., Tahoe Vista, Calif. • (530) 546-4819

Only the freshest fish prepared in imaginative ways is served at Captain Jon's Restaurant & Grill. You can choose from seared sea scallops served around a bed of linguini gremolata, or seafood Udon, an assortment of fresh fish in a ginger broth. If you're not in the mood for fish, give the butternut ravioli or marinated flank steak served with bordelaise sauce a try. If you're arriving by boat, you can tie up at Captain's Jon's dock just outside the restaurant. A perfect start to the evening (weather permitting) is enjoying your favorite libation at the dockside bar while the sun sinks golden into the waters of Lake Tahoe. Then adjourn to the restaurant where you can continue to enjoy the view from their outside dining area or move to cozy quarters indoors. The restaurant is open daily for dinner during high season and for lunch at the pier Tuesday through Sunday during the summer. Hours and days vary during off season so be sure to call ahead. (See also our Nightlife chapter.)

South Shore Lake Tahoe

The Fresh Ketch
$$ • 2435 Venice Dr. E., South Lake Tahoe, Calif. • (530) 541-5683

What better place to enjoy scrumptious fresh seafood than right on the water? At The Fresh Ketch you can feast on fish in the upstairs dining room, in the seafood bar or on the patio, all overlooking lovely Lake Tahoe. Menu items include fresh oysters, steamed New Zealand clams, Alaskan king crab, cioppino and mixed seafood grill. The restaurant is easy to find in the Tahoe Keys Marina.

It's open daily for lunch and dinner and reservations are recommended.

Steakhouses

North Shore Lake Tahoe

Crystal Bay Club Steak & Lobster House
$$ • Nev. Hwy. 28, Crystal Bay, Nev. • (775) 831-0512

One of the best-kept dining secrets in the North Shore Lake Tahoe area is the steakhouse tucked in the corner of the Crystal Bay Club. Unpretentious and almost hokey, the casino doesn't seem at first glance to be the likely site of fine cuisine with a French flair. But take our word for it: the food is melt-in-your-mouth, the service is impeccable, the decor is tasteful and the prices are unbelievably reasonable. So wend your way through all those clanging slot machines and step into this little corner of gentility to enjoy a luscious dinner of steak, seafood or fowl served with just the right wine. It's open for dinner daily.

Old Range Steakhouse
$$ • 7081 N. Lake Blvd., Tahoe Vista, Calif. • (530) 5464800

You know this restaurant has something to brag about: the prime cuts of meat are proudly displayed as you walk in the door. The Old Range Steakhouse is a meat-eater's paradise, with every cut of beef served every way imaginable. It's all delicious, it's all tender and it's all juicy.

For those wanting lighter fare, you'll also find vegetarian selections on the menu. What more could you want? Well, try views of Lake Tahoe, just across the road, and a warm homey Western ambiance you can just sink down into. Do we like this place? You betcha. You can ride the range for dinner Thursday through Tuesday.

If you want to add an artistic element to your evening out, come a little early and drop into the Vista Gallery upstairs, enjoy the view from the deck and have a drink before settling into a succulent steak. See our chapter on The Arts for more information on the gallery.

Photo: David Madison for Royal Gorge

What better way to spend a romantic evening
than in a quiet "Old Tahoe" restaurant with your favorite person?

South Shore Lake Tahoe

Lake Tahoe Chart House
$$ • 392 Kingsbury Gr., Stateline, Nev.
• (775) 588-6276

High in the forest above Lake Tahoe, the Lake Tahoe Chart House specializes in fine steaks, prime rib and seafood served in a comfy woodsy environment. You may not get past the appetizers on this menu, however, since starters include such yummy choices as Creole shrimp beignets, herb-steamed artichoke, and lobster cakes. It's convenient to find up Kingsbury Grade on the way to the Nevada side of Heavenly Ski Resort. The Chart House is open daily for dinner; reservations are advised.

Tea Rooms

North Shore Lake Tahoe

Lady Margaret's Tea Room & Treasures
$ • 774 Mays Blvd., Incline Village, Nev.
• (775) 831-2544

When Mrs. Lora Knight was in residence at Vikingsholm, she had tea every day on tiny Fannette Island (see our Attractions and Recreation chapters for the history of this quaint castle). You won't find high tea in the middle of Emerald Bay anymore, but you can enjoy it in all its Victorian splendor — complete with fine china and all the very proper accouterments — at Lady Margaret's Tea Room & Treasures. Reminiscent of a time when etiquette was everything, Lady Margaret's serves delicious soups, quiches, salads and sandwiches or scones, shortbread and decadent desserts for either lunch or tea. It's all accompanied by a piping hot pot of tea (snuggled in a decorative cozy) and served in elegant drawing-room surroundings. Lady Margaret also caters special events and offers later afternoon tea by reservation. You can also shop for one-of-a-kind consignment clothing and collectibles in the treasures portion of her shop (see our Shopping chapter for details).

Lady Margaret's is open Tuesday through Saturday from 11 AM to 3 PM for lunch and snacks and from 2:30 to 4:30 PM for afternoon tea. It's closed one week in March and October so be sure to check during those months.

Nevada gaming establishments have refined casino nightlife to an art form designed to dazzle the senses of even the most discriminating casino patrons.

Casino Nightlife

With casinos springing up on riverboats and Indian reservations all over the country, you don't have to come to Nevada to gamble anymore. But because the Silver State has been in the business of legalized gambling longer than any other entities (since 1931), Nevada gaming establishments have refined casino nightlife to an art form designed to dazzle the senses of even the most discriminating casino patrons.

You can literally lose yourself (but hopefully not all your money) in a virtual world of gourmet dining, lavish stage revues, celebrity performances and lively games 24 hours a day. Aside from running out of money, many visitors complain they don't have time to sleep because the action never stops. If you've come to the Reno/Tahoe area to gamble, remember that casino gambling is legal only in Nevada and not in California. But if you're bedded down in California lodging, don't despair since the Nevada casinos aren't very far away from wherever you might be staying.

While many people hit the casinos with the hope of breaking the bank (the casinos', not theirs), the chances of that happening are slim because the odds on the machines and table games are in the casinos' favor. For example, if you expect to hit a MegaJackpot on Megabucks, your chances are only about 200,000 to 1 after putting about $25 in the machine. (We tell you more about MegaJackpots in the Close-up in this chapter.) And though the house or casino advantage on other games is not as daunting as Megabucks, it's still about 5 percent on roulette and 22 percent on keno, for example. Remember that casinos make money when you lose, and in the long run most players eventually do.

The healthiest way to approach gaming is to think of it as entertainment. Don't expect to win big, but do hope to have a good time. Gamble only the amount of money you can realistically afford to lose, and then know when to quit. The best time to quit is when you've won, and if you don't win before your budgeted amount is gone, walk away. To avoid being stuck without money to get home (it happens more often than you'd think), set aside enough for the trip home, and don't touch it until you leave town.

If you're a novice at gambling, it's a good idea to learn something about it before you plunk down your hard-earned cash. After all, you wouldn't invest in a business without finding out about it first, would you? Most casinos have free lessons to teach you the games, or you can go to the Reno Tahoe Gaming Academy for instruction (see details in our Attractions chapter). If you have questions about slot machines, most casino slot employees can answer them for you. And while some dealers on the table games are happy to answer questions, keep in mind that your fellow players may not appreciate your holding up the game if the action is particularly hot and heavy. To help you get started, we'll give you a few basics of the most popular games found in Reno/Tahoe casinos. Good luck!

Is Lady Luck with You?

Blackjack or 21

The object of Blackjack or 21 is to draw cards totaling 21 or closer to 21 than the dealer. Each player receives two cards face down, and the dealer receives one card face down and one face up. Cards are counted as their face value, except face cards (which are 10) and aces (which are either 1 or 11). After receiving the first two cards, players can take additional cards or "hits" or choose to "stand" with the first two cards. If you exceed 21, or go "bust," you lose.

The dealer has specific rules for playing his hand, and these are posted on the table. If the dealer's hand exceeds 21 after he takes one or more hits, all players who didn't exceed 21 prior to the dealer hitting will be paid. Otherwise the player must be closer to 21 than the dealer. If the player and the dealer have the same count, it's a "push" and no money is exchanged. Other rules include buying insurance, splitting bets and doubling down; these are best learned when practicing the game.

Craps

One player throws the dice and is the "shooter," while the other players bet either with or against him. If the shooter throws a 7 or 11 on the first throw or "come out," bets on

the "pass line" are paid and bets on the "don't pass line" are collected. If the first throw totals 2, 3 or 12, the dealer collects pass-line bets, and if it totals 3 or 12, he pays don't-pass-line bets. A total of 2 on the don't-pass-line is neither paid nor taken. If the shooter throws a total of 4, 5, 6, 8, 9 or 10, that number becomes the "point."

On each subsequent roll, if the shooter throws the point before a 7 is thrown, pass-line bets are paid and don't-pass-line bets are collected. But if the shooter rolls a 7 before the point is thrown again, the don't-pass-line bets are paid and the pass-line bets are collected. To add excitement to the game, a variety of other bets can be made, including "come," "don't come," "any craps," "hard way" and "field." But because of their complexity, we suggest you learn these finer points while actually playing or observing a game in progress.

Keno

In each keno game, 20 balls are randomly selected from a pool of 80 numbered balls. Players try to pick some of these 20 winning numbers in a variety of combinations. Winnings are determined by the number of balls chosen correctly or the "catch."

Since payouts and combinations differ from casino to casino, players need to consult the keno brochures at the individual gaming establishments. You can play keno while enjoying dinner or a drink at the bar because the results are displayed on large boards throughout the clubs, and keno runners will collect your tickets and deliver your winnings.

Roulette

The numbers on a roulette wheel are numbered 1 to 36 and alternately colored red and black. There's also a 0 and a 00, which are green. Players can bet on as many numbers

INSIDERS' TIP

Don't even think about drinking and driving in the Reno/Tahoe area as the DUI laws in Nevada and California are strictly enforced.

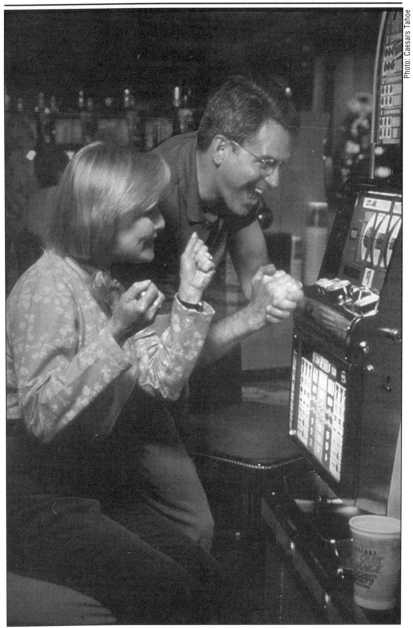

Photo: Caesars Tahoe

You too can experience the thrill of gaming for mere pocket change at the slot machines where winners are awarded a waterfall of coins, bright lights, loud buzzers and the admiration of other hopeful contestants.

as they want and in a variety of combinations. The dealer spins the white ball in the opposite direction of the wheel, which rotates counter-clockwise, and bets can be placed until the ball is about ready to drop into the wheel. Pays vary from 35 to 1 for 0 or 00 to 2 to 1 for a column of 12 numbers.

Gaming Machines

Gaming machines come in a variety of colors, shapes and sizes, with high-tech sound and visual effects designed specifically to attract your attention and money (see our Closeup on Hometown Machines in this chapter for a brief history of them). You can drop coins in one at a time or up to 20 at a time in some multiple-coin machines.

When playing a multiple-coin machine, be sure to check the payoff table; usually, the more coins you put in, the higher the jackpot. For large jackpots, look for progressive machines; the more they're played, the more the jackpots increase. And to take advantage of skill as well as luck, try the video poker machines since they allow for more player interaction than some of the other machines.

If you're a real dyed-in-the-wool slot player, check out the free players clubs offered by most casinos. As with frequent flyer benefits awarded by airlines, you earn perks the more you gamble. A player tracking system monitors your play through the membership card you insert in a machine when you play it. Because there's such a variety of machines, don't be surprised if you don't know how to play all of them. But you'll have more fun (and maybe win more) if you understand the basics, so just ask.

It's Showtime!

Casino nightlife is not just about gaming, however. Insiders know you can always be a winner when you see the shows since the odds are definitely in your favor that you'll have a good time. With such a tantalizing array of choices, it's safe to say there's something to please everybody. You can be amazed by daring highwire performers and amused by the country's top comics. You can delight in the antics of live elephants and dance to your fa-

vorite rock group. And if it's celebrities you want, just choose the venue. You can worship them from afar in a large outdoor arena or up-close and personal in a cozy theater.

Whichever shows you decide to take in, we do recommend calling for reservations. Since the Reno/Tahoe area is a popular convention destination, shows are frequently sold out to visitors attending meetings. Hotel/casinos and gaming resorts frequently give reservation preferences to their guests, so be sure to ask about this when you check in. Some of the best show deals in town are dinner/show and room/show packages offered by some casinos.

And remember, all seats are not equal, so check out where yours will be located if they're assigned when you book. If they're not assigned, arrive early for the show. Sometimes you can get the best seats by tipping the maitre d' $10 or $15.

If you have trouble getting a reservation, ask the hotel concierge to help. Although jackets, ties and cocktail dresses were the order of the evening some years ago, the attire now is more casual. Almost anything goes, except bathing suits, tank tops and bare feet. You won't be served dinner as part of the show (unless it's a special event), but drinks can be purchased either at your table or at a nearby self-service bar.

Some performances are not suitable for children so if you're planning to take the whole family, be sure to ask if there are any age limitations to the show you want to attend.

For current Reno/Tahoe show information, check out "Best Bets," a weekly entertainment supplement to the *Reno Gazette–Journal*. Entertainment guides are also published in *Showtime* and the *Reno News & Review*, which you can pick up free at casinos, hotels and restaurants. In the South Shore Lake Tahoe area, look for free copies of *Lake Tahoe Action* and in the North Shore Lake Tahoe area, for *North Shore Truckee Action*.

All the gaming establishments we tell you about in this chapter have full-service casinos, with hundreds of gaming machines and dozens of table games. But to round out your Reno/Tahoe experience, we hope to whet your appetite for all the other kinds of live entertainment available. So now, let's hit the town!

Reno

Atlantis Casino Resort
3800 S. Virginia St., Reno, Nev.
• **(775) 825-4700**

Voted "Best Late Night Hang-Out" by readers of the local daily newspaper, Atlantis Casino Resort has one of the classiest dance spots in the Reno/Tahoe area (see our Nightlife chapter). With its exotic undersea setting, the quiet elegance of the Atlantis Seafood Steakhouse gives way to the dazzling excitement of the Atlantis Nightclub around 10 PM. State-of-the-art sound and lights create a romantic atmosphere that's popular with couples and singles of all ages.

Atlantis also books a variety of concerts and reviews in its Grand Ballroom such as the *Thunder from Down Under All-Male Dance Revue* and the Absolut Swing and Dance Concerts. The prices at this casino for a typical big show run about $20 to $25. Free entertainment is also offered in the Center Stage Cabaret in the main casino area.

Boomtown Hotel Casino Reno
I-80, 7 mi. west of Reno, Nev.
• **(775) 345-6000**

The Boomtown Cabaret features top lounge acts nightly except Monday. You can have a seat in the lounge area, where there's no cover or minimum charges, or also watch the show while you play slots or table games.

Eldorado Hotel/Casino
345 N. Virginia St., Reno, Nev.
• **(775) 786-5700**

When the owners of the Eldorado Hotel/ Casino decided they needed a new theater, they spared no expense and effort in creating a high-tech showroom equal to none in the Reno/Tahoe area. Decorated in a 1940s art deco style, the 580-seat Eldorado Showroom is warm, elegant and intimate. Plush comfortable seats are steeply tiered to permit unobstructed viewing from almost every vantage point. And because the technical components, such as acoustics, lighting and audio, are state-of-the-art, the quality of production is truly amazing.

The room usually showcases Broadway hits such as *Smokey Joe's Café* and *Spirit of the Dance*, which was voted best in Reno for two years running and combines Irish dance, tap, jazz, Flamenco and ballet with a story line of a spirit searching for her true love. When booking a reservation, try to avoid seats on the sides of the upper level as the view of the stage is not nearly as clear as from middle-section seats.

Also at the Eldorado, The Brew Brothers is one of the most popular dance spots for the younger crowd. Live musical groups, ranging from rock to soul, take to the stage at this casual microbrewery on Friday and Saturday nights (see our Nightlife chapter for more details). And for a quiet change of pace, Bistro Roxy has a romantic piano bar in a French country setting.

Flamingo Hilton
255 N. Sierra St., Reno, Nev.
• **(775) 322-1111, (775) 785-7080 ticket information**

The electrifying shows at the Flamingo Showroom, such as *American Superstars* and *Carnival of Wonders*, have all the elements expected of polished stage revues. The productions are always snazzy, with first-class music, dancing and special effects. You'll appreciate the comfort of this theater: almost all the seats have good visibility of the stage.

If you're in a romantic mood, catch the elevator to the Top of the Flamingo Hilton Restaurant, where you can enjoy a lovely view of the city while you dance the night away in the intimate lounge (see also Restaurants). On balmy summer evenings, you can enjoy colorful downtown skyline and listen to up-and-coming musical groups at the hotel/ casino's outdoor concerts.

INSIDERS' TIP

To find out everything you want to know about gambling, visit the Gambler's Bookstore at 4001 S. Virginia Street in Reno, or call them at (775) 825-7778.

Photo: Reno Hilton

Lavish shows at venues like the Reno Hilton Theater add unforgettable excitement to the casino nightlife experience in the Reno/Tahoe area.

Harrah's Reno
219 N. Center St., Reno, Nev.
• **(775) 786-3232**

The legendary Bill Harrah, founder of Harrah's Reno and Harrah's Lake Tahoe, believed that first-class live entertainment was a vital part of a successful gaming establishment (we tell you more about Mr. Harrah in our Resorts and History chapters). That tradition continues in Sammy's Showroom at Harrah's Reno with exciting production shows, adult revues and celebrity performers. At 7 PM nightly except for Thursday, the showroom features *Cirque Berserk*, a parody of the circuses in Europe with mystery, illusion and the occasional bizarre.

At 9:30 PM, the room lights up to the sounds of hypnotic Latin tempos and exciting dance routines of *Skintight*, an adult revue, which translates into partial nudity so no children are allowed.

With 440 seats, the room is intimate enough to make you feel close to the performers but large enough to showcase full-size productions. The most comfortable seats in the house are the circular booths, so when you arrive be sure to ask the maitre d' if any are available.

Holiday Inn & Diamond's Casino
1000 E. Sixth St., Reno, Nev.
• **(775) 786-5151**

Small stage revues and musical groups are featured in the Holiday Inn Showroom at the Holiday Inn & Diamond's Casino. It has been recently renovated, though it's not as

---

INSIDERS' TIP

When you win a jackpot, it's customary to tip the change person 5 to 10 percent of it if she or he has given you efficient and friendly service.

Hometown Machines

Have you ever dreamed of becoming an instant millionaire? MegaJackpot gaming machines manufactured by International Game Technology make that dream come true for a lucky slot machine player somewhere in North America on the average of once a month.

Headquartered in a state-of-the-art manufacturing facility in South Meadows Business Park in Reno, IGT sells more gaming machines than all other United States manufacturers put together.

When gaming was first legalized in Nevada in 1931, table games (such as 21, craps, roulette and poker) accounted for about two-thirds of the casinos' gross revenues. Serious gamblers (who were usually male) preferred the tables, but casinos installed rows of slot machines to amuse the wives and girlfriends of their "real" players.

Based upon the original Liberty Bell slot machine designed by San Franciscan Charlie Fey in 1895, the early slots were mechanical machines, with three spring-loaded reels that would freely spin when the handle was pulled. With 20 symbols on each reel, 8,000 combinations were possible, and jackpots were paid for symbols that lined up on the pay line. The "hold" for the house (the amount the casino kept) was around 20 percent of the total money put into the machine.

Machines were designed to accept pennies, nickels, dimes or quarters. Because the handles were frequently hard to pull, ardent slot players back then probably suffered from tennis elbow even before the term was coined. But slot machines have come a long way since then.

With the advent of computer technology, IGT developed the first video poker machines in the 1970s, starting the gaming revolution that eventually rendered the old mechanical slots obsolete. Driven by microprocessors and equipped with high-tech sound and graphics, today's machines offer a sophisticated array of games to casino patrons. You can play a hand of poker or take a spin at the Wheel of Fortune or try your luck at a progressive machine whose jackpot increases with each pull of the handle.

With so many options, just walking into a casino can be downright bewildering since you're confronted with a veritable barrage of clanging bells and blinking lights, all designed to entice you to play. If you're interested in winning big, there's nothing like Megabucks and Super Megabucks, which are networks of progressive machines that link casinos throughout an entire state to a huge progressive jackpot. Beginning at $5 million for Megabucks and $10 million for Super Megabucks, the MegaJackpots increase every time one of the machines is played in any of the casinos linked to the network.

The changes brought about by advanced technology have not been limited to the kinds of games that are played, however. With increased variety, higher levels of complexity and larger jackpots, today's slot machines have broader appeal so that Nevada casinos now report that more than half their gross revenues come from machines. Yes, "reel" men now play slots. And no, the handles are no longer hard to pull. In fact, many machines don't have handles at all, but come equipped with buttons to push that are much easier on players' elbows.

In the middle of this gaming revolution, casinos also realized that if they could train slot players to pump dollars into the machines instead of smaller coins like quarters,

— continued on next page

Photo: Peter Walker

Think it's just a game? Think again. All IGT slot machines are tested in the anechoic chamber for the emission of radio waves which could interfere with casino security systems.

they could afford to pay out jackpots more often. By setting a dollar machine to hold only 5 percent instead of 20 percent, they could make the same amount of money because 5 percent of $1 is the same as 20 percent of a quarter. When players began winning more often (even though they were probably spending more money), slot machines became even more popular.

But the gaming revolution is still evolving; IGT believes that new products are continually needed to keep slot machine players stimulated. With dozens of new games under development at any given time, the company introduces about 25 each year to players around the world. And each year, more than 100,000 gaming machines roll off the assembly line in IGT's 1 million–square-foot plant. So when you play the slots in Reno/Tahoe (or anywhere else in the world), it's a good bet that you're playing a hometown machine that was conceived, developed and produced at IGT in Reno.

large and flashy as the major casinos in town: it's low-key and comfortable.

Peppermill Hotel Casino Reno
2707 S. Virginia St., Reno, Nev.
• **(775) 826-2121**

Surrounded by banks of slot machines in the middle of the casino, the Cabaret in the Peppermill Hotel Casino Reno is hard to miss. It sets the tone for this fast-paced club since the live entertainment is an integral part of the action. You can enjoy the free show and keep an eye on the casino happenings at the same time. Their lounge acts seem to be the best in Reno, and the employees seem to be the friendliest. The Convention Showroom also features large orchestras and stage revues. Ticket prices vary but usually hover around $20.

Reno Hilton
2500 E. Second St., Reno, Nev.
• **(775) 789-2000, (775) 789-2285 ticket information**

If you're looking for a downright dazzling entertainment experience, the lavish shows at the Reno Hilton Theater will no doubt fit the bill. Not just the usual flash and dash of pretty costumes and intricate dancing, most shows challenge the imagination with breathtaking athletic feats. The recent production of *Aireus* presented some of the best trapeze artists and gymnasts in the world in surrealistic flying sequences that made you feel like you could swoop and soar right alongside them. And no theater is better suited to these shows than the Hilton's because its cavernous size gives exciting depth to the productions.

But Insiders know there are some very bad seats in this house, with some theatergoers actually facing away from the stage. When making a reservation, it's best to actually view the seating chart at the box office. Since individual seats in the booths are also assigned, be especially careful of those seats in booths toward the outside of the room that cause you to sit with your back to the stage.

For more down-to-earth entertainment, the Hilton features top comics in the Just For Laughs Comedy Club (see our Nightlife chapter). And for listening and dancing pleasure, you can enjoy first-rate lounge acts in a forest of 60 aspen trees in the Aspen Lounge. Summer visitors have the added choice of seeing headliners outside the building in the Hilton Pavilion. Concerts here are especially memorable when the full moon presents a backdrop to the action on stage. If you are comfortable in the middle of the crowd, the level seating is okay. But if you want a better vantage point of the stage, ask for seats in the bleachers in the back. Since this is a large amphitheater, it's a good idea to take binoculars if you want to get a good look at your favorite star. Tickets run between $30 and $50, depending upon the entertainers.

Silver Legacy Resort Casino
407 N. Virginia St., Reno, Nev.
• **(775) 329-4777**

Some of the hottest entertainers in the country play the Grande Exposition Hall at Silver Legacy Resort Casino, the newest and grandest hotel/casino in Reno. The shows are first-class, but the setting is not. Because it's not a theater but a hall that's used for a variety of events, it's less than ideal in a concert situation. Seating is on one level only, in rows of straight-back chairs with no tables or arm rests for your drinks. If you're sitting any farther than four rows back from the stage, your best view of the performance is on the video screens hung all around the room. But if you're not fussy about the surroundings, you can see some of the best acts offered in the area. Tickets are steep here when compared to the rest of Reno and Sparks. The range usually starts at $25 and goes up to $75 depending upon the talent.

If you're in the mood for laughs, you can see the country's top upcoming comics perform at Catch A Rising Star Comedy Club (see Nightlife). Silver Legacy also has live entertainment in the Silver Baron's Bar & Lounge and in the Legacy Saloon.

Sparks

John Ascuaga's Nugget
1100 Nugget Ave., Sparks, Nev.
• **(775) 356-3300**

If you're not prepared for it, the opening act every night in the Celebrity Showroom at

John Ascuaga's Nugget is a real surprise. As the curtains open, Angel takes center stage and proceeds to delight the audience with her amazing repertoire of tricks and stunts. But the headliners who regularly play the room don't mind being upstaged by this talented act since she's considered to be one of the most talented elephants in the world. We tell you all about this gifted pachyderm in our Kidstuff chapter.

Aside from the elephant, the Celebrity Showroom hosts top-name entertainers in a luxurious theater setting that's just intimate enough to give you that up-close and personal experience. On a larger scale, the Nugget showcases celebrity performances in the Rose Ballroom. Prices in the ballroom range from $35 to $50. For dancing, there's also rock groups in the Casino Cabaret and mood music in Trader Dick's.

Silver Club Hotel/Casino
1040 Victorian Ave., Sparks, Nev.
• (775) 358-4771

Lounge acts play nightly in the casino at the Silver Club Hotel/Casino. The general ambiance is down-home and decidedly casual: don't expect the elegance offered by glitzier casinos here.

North Shore Lake Tahoe

Cal–Neva Resort
2 Stateline Rd., Crystal Bay, Nev.
• (775) 832-4000, (800) 225-6385

The Cal–Neva Resort, owned by Frank Sinatra in the 1960s and frequented by Sinatra's "Rat Pack" and the Kennedys, is teeming with history. Marilyn Monroe was supposed to have had a midnight rendezvous with JFK here in the early 60s. But now the Cal–Neva, named so because it straddles the Cali-

fornia and Nevada state line, is relatively quiet. It still manages, from time-to-time, to book big names in its Frank Sinatra Room. Most of the time the room is dark, but the likes of Jimmy Cliff have performed here lately.

Crystal Bay Club
Nev. Hwy. 28, Crystal Bay, Nev.
• (775) 831-0512

Small, laid-back and decidedly unpretentious, the Crystal Bay Club has been pleasing customers with its no-frills atmosphere for years. Tucked away in the back of the casino, the lounge features small combos that play upbeat music for dancing. It's not fancy, but if you're in the mood to boogie on down it's a great spot to be (see our Nightlife chapter for more details).

Hyatt Regency Lake Tahoe Resort & Casino
111 Country Club Dr. at Lakeshore Dr., Incline Village, Nev. • (775) 832-1234, (800) 233-1234

The Casino Stage Bar at the Hyatt Regency Lake Tahoe Resort & Casino features live bands four to six nights a week, depending upon the season of the year. The Lakeside Grand Ballroom provides a venue for its occasional concerts and is home to one of the lake's jazz festivals. Like Hyatts all over the world, it's posh, but since this is Tahoe, it's also laid-back (see our Nightlife chapter for more information).

Tahoe Biltmore
5 Nev. Hwy. 28, Crystal Bay, Nev.
• (775) 831-0660

The Tahoe Biltmore features standup comics, dance groups and small stage revues throughout the year in the Aspen Cabaret. The shows are usually very entertaining. Check out our Nightlife chapter for more information.

INSIDERS' TIP

Since you have to be 21 years old to gamble in Nevada, you can't have your children with you while you play slot machines or table games. They can walk through casinos on their way to video arcades, restaurants, hotel rooms and shows but cannot loiter around the games.

Photo: Reno Hilton

Flying through the air with the greatest of ease, daring young men and women on the flying trapeze will certainly entertain you.

South Shore Lake Tahoe

Caesars Tahoe
55 U.S. Hwy. 50, Stateline, Nev.
• **(775) 588-3515**

Headliners regularly appear in the Circus Maximus Showroom's plush 1,500-seat theater. The likes of Dolly Parton, The Beach Boys, The Judds, Huey Lewis and the News, David Cassidy and Vince Gill have all performed here. This resort seems to target the younger crowd. Tickets range from $50 to $75. The showroom has also booked championship fights. It's comfortable, it's first-class and a winning way to spend an evening at Lake Tahoe.

But live entertainment at Caesars doesn't stop here. If you're in an all-night mood, you can dance the night away on the largest dance floor at the lake at Nero's 2000 nightclub (see our Nightlife chapter for more details). Or for a slower change of pace, you can relax to easy listening music in Cleo's Lounge.

Harrah's Lake Tahoe
U.S. Hwy. 50, Stateline, Nev.
• **(775) 588-6611**

Harrah's South Shore Room, which opened in 1959, prides itself on performing two shows nightly except Tuesdays. The shows usually change about three times a year but you can always count on one for the entire family and one for mature audiences, meaning partial nudity is guaranteed. Two of its shows that received rave reviews were *New York, New York* and *Erocktica 2000*. *New York, New York* delivered comedy, singing and dancing under the premise of four sailors on leave

INSIDERS' TIP

About 3 percent of Americans who gamble are compulsive gamblers. To get help for this addiction you can call (775) 356-8070.

In the high-limit rooms, the stakes are higher and the excitement is palpable.

in New York for 24 hours. *Erocktica* had everything: classic rock 'n roll, swing music, visual effects, dancing and a cast of partially clad men and women. Tickets for the shows range from $15 to $23. Harrah's occasionally books the likes of The Smothers Brothers and Art Garfunkel in its showroom. If you're planning on attending a show during high season, be sure to call for reservations as soon as possible because tickets sell out well in advance.

It's a comfortable theater with high-quality sound and lighting, so any production you see here is first-class in every way. In the casino area of the resort you can also enjoy live bands at the Casino Center Stage.

Harveys Resort Hotel/Casino
U.S. Hwy. 50, Stateline, Nev.
• **(775) 588-2411**
If you want the glitter and glamour of a full-scale stage revue, try the productions at the Emerald Theater at Harveys Resort Hotel/Casino. With vivid costumes, electrifying dancing and exciting music, they're guaranteed to stimulate your senses. Harveys is home to Tahoe Live's *Rockin' Blues Revue*, a show which has a tribute to the Blues Brothers, plenty of soulful blues, swing, a little dose of disco and a lot of comedy. Occasionally, during the summer months when the weather is obliging, the casino will book a big name and hold a concert in its parking lot. Tickets for blues events are $20. The big-name tickets are usually higher. You can also relax to the mellow piano in Llewellyn's, with its elegant decor and lovely lake view at the top of the hotel.

Lake Tahoe Horizon Casino Resort
U.S. Hwy. 50, Stateline, Nev.
• **(775) 588-6211**
Once hostess to many of the world's brightest stars in the Grande Lake Theater, the Lake Tahoe Horizon Casino Resort has recently downsized its entertainment package. You can enjoy typical lounge acts in the Golden Cabaret, dance to easy listening music in the Aspen Lounge and see first-run movies in the former Grande Lake Theater.

And If That's Not Enough . . .

Other Reno casinos that have lounge entertainment include Fitzgeralds Casino/Hotel Reno, 255 N. Virginia Street, (775) 785-3300; the Pioneer Inn Hotel/Casino, 221 S. Virginia Street, (775) 324-7777; and the Sands Regency Hotel Casino, 345 N. Arlington Avenue, (775) 348-2200. The Rail City Casino at 2121 Victorian Avenue in Sparks, (775) 358-4771, also has live entertainment in the casino area.

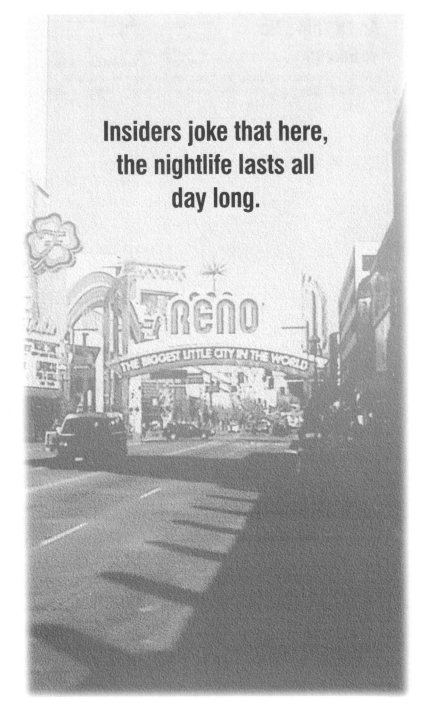

Insiders joke that here,
the nightlife lasts all
day long.

Nightlife

$2$4–7–365:that's what Insiders say about the nightlife in the Reno/Tahoe area. It's rocking 24 hours a day, 7 days a week, 365 days a year.

The only city in the world that can outdo the Reno/Tahoe area for nighttime entertainment is our big sister to the south. But being second still puts us way, way ahead of other cities. We do an outstanding job of keeping visitors and locals alike hip-hopping to the night scene. In fact, Insiders joke that here, the nightlife lasts all day long.

Throughout the year, the area jumps and jives from the sounds of big-time production numbers in the casino showrooms to the local punk band pounding out tunes in its first gig at one of those three-stooled, dimly lit dives. But if you want a cozy place where you can snuggle next to a fire, we've got that, too. In fact, we've got just about every kind of nightlife scene covered. And remember, all of our casinos have cabarets or lounges where some of the best Insider talent performs just about every hour of every night of the week and the best thing is, the lounge entertainment is free.

We have major performing artists like Patti LaBelle, Tony Orlando, Dwight Yoakam, Trisha Yearwood, The Doobie Brothers, Howie Mandel, Chuck Berry, Jerry Lee Lewis and Little Richard constantly popping in and out of the area. We've got comedy stores. We've got pubs and microbreweries. We've got nightclubs. So you can see that we won't let you whine that there's nothing to do at night here.

That's the magnificent thing about this area: no matter what the season or what the weather, you can play hard all day and party hard all night. In this chapter, we'll toss out our favorite picks of the night scene in the Reno/Tahoe area. We'll point you in the right direction no matter what your tastes happen to be. We'll guide you to the best karaoke bars, nightclubs, brewpubs, country and western dance halls and other nightlife that the

area has to offer. See our Casino Nightlife chapter for a run-down of the entertainment offerings in the casino showrooms.

We've decided to divide this chapter by type of establishment, then by our geographical locations to help you find just the right place that tickles your fancy.

We would, however, like to put in a disclaimer here: the Reno/Tahoe area is dotted with hundreds of bars, but we have listed only our Insiders' choices, most of which have entertainment, both live and recorded. As far as the rest of the bars are concerned, you're on your own.

Just heed these words of warning: on the California side of the area, bars usually open at 6 AM and close at 2 AM but on the Nevada side of the area, our liquor laws allow 24-hour-a-day drinking if you're 21 or older. So pace yourself and beware of our driving under the influence law (see our Getting Here, Getting Around chapter for a detailed explanation of the law). The one place we guarantee to be a drag during the night is our county jails so behave in a responsible manner.

Also remember that the night scene changes constantly here so to keep up on what's happening, grab one of our weekly entertainment guides (see our Media chapter for a list). Now, let's party.

Comedy Clubs

Reno

Catch a Rising Star
Silver Legacy Resort Casino, 407 N. Virginia St., Reno, Nev. • (775) 325-7454
This national chain of comedy clubs has bolstered the careers of such stars as Robin Williams, Jerry Seinfeld, Brett Butler and Billy Crystal. This theater has a 200-seat capacity

and books established comedians. The format generally calls for two 80-minute shows nightly, six nights per week. Each 7:30 PM and 10 PM show features two comedians. Tickets run from $13 during the week to $15 on the weekends. Wednesday is locals' night, where they offer two-for-one tickets with a Nevada driver's license.

Improv
Reno Hilton, 2500 E. Second St., Reno, Nev. • (775) 789-2078

The Improv's theater is cozier than the theater at the Silver Legacy. In fact, most of the seats are super-close to the stage, which sets up an atmosphere that screams, "Heckle me." The format is also a two-comedian show with show times of 8:30 PM during the week and 8:30 PM and 10:30 PM on the weekends. Prices start at $15 and go up to $18 on the weekend. Insiders seem to prefer this club to the other two.

www.insiders.com
See this and many other
Insiders' Guide®
destinations online.
Visit us today!

Just for Laughs
Sands Regency, Fourth and Arlington sts., Reno, Nev. • (775) 348-2200

One of the three comedy clubs in Reno, Just for Laughs's show times are 8:30 PM, Wednesday through Sunday, plus a second show at 10:30 PM on Friday and Saturday. Tickets run about $10 but they also have a dinner and show package for $16, which is the best deal. The format usually includes two comedians per show.

Country and Western Dancing

Reno

Lone Star Lounge
9275 Lemmon Dr., Reno, Nev. • (775) 677-9129

Definitely not a nightclub for Urban Cowboys, this club caters to folks who like country/western music in a small setting. Tucked away in a little shopping center in Lemmon Valley, the Lone Star has live country music on the weekend and a Thursday night karaoke party. On Sunday, they usually host horseshoe and volleyball tournaments and on Monday, they have a potluck, bring your own dish night. Most cowboys and cowgirls here are the real McCoy.

Rodeo Rock
1537 S. Virginia St., Reno, Nev. • (775) 323-1600

This country and western dance hall bills itself as "a whole nuther kinda country." C&W music is prevalent throughout the week and there's always something fun going on, including free dance lessons, pool, darts and family night every Sunday. A lot of Urban Cowboys hang out here. But on Tuesdays, radio station KRZQ turns it into Club KRZQ with alternative music for the younger set. The Rodeo Rock has one of the largest wooden dance floors around. It's capable of handling 200 dancers. Oh yeah — it also has a mechanical bull.

Microbreweries

Reno

Brew Bothers
Eldorado Hotel/Casino, Fourth and Virginia sts., Reno, Nev. • (775) 786-5700

Located inside of the Eldorado Hotel/Casio, the Brew Brothers' clientele is usually about 50 percent visitors and 50 percent locals. This brewpub is always crowded, especially on Friday nights. The reason: the beer. Try the Redhead Amber or the Double Down Stout. Prices range from $1.25 for a small glass to $2.50 for a pint during happy hour (4 PM to 6 PM daily). It has local bands performing during the week and headline bands on the weekend. Ages vary from early 20s up to the late 40s. The pub food here is very good, too.

Sparks

Great Basin Brewery
846 Victorian Ave., Sparks, Nev.
• (775) 355-7711

This is the most popular night spot in Sparks and is located just off Victorian Square. Besides having great food (try the fish and chips or the sausage sampler), Great Basin brews its own beers and, for its effort, has been awarded gold, silver and bronze medals in the 1994, 1995, 1997 and 1998 Great American Beer Festival. It has also been voted the Truckee Meadows' best brewpub three years in a row. Besides outstanding beer (Insiders recommend the Jackpot Porter or the Nevada Gold), Great Basin features wines and spirits, brewery tours, outdoor dining and free, live music. Every Wednesday is jazz night, and during the summer on Sunday, catch the Great Basin Players performing one-act plays on the south-side stage.

South Shore Lake Tahoe

The Brewery at Lake Tahoe
3542 U.S. Hwy. 50, South Lake Tahoe, Calif. • (530) 544-2739

The South Shore's only microbrewery, it features great home-brewed beer and an outside deck to enjoy it on. The brewery is open from noon to midnight during the summer and mixed hours during the winter. There are no hours set aside to get "happy," and the brewery doesn't have any entertainment. This establishment is for drinking home brews only. Its signature beer is the Bad Ass Ale. Give it a try if you like strong, English-type ale.

Nightclubs

Reno

Alturas Bar and Nightclub
1044 E. Fourth St., Reno, Nev.
•(775) 324-5050

Don't come here unless you like Harley Davidsons, the American flag and can sing two bars of Nevada's state song. The Alturas Bar bills itself as "biker friendly with no attitudes." The bar is an Insiders' hangout which turns to live blues on Saturday night with catering by Big Ed's Bar-B-Que, next door. This is really a great place if you are into the biker scene and love the blues.

Atlantis Nightclub
Atlantis Casino Resort, 3800 S. Virginia St., Reno, Nev. • (775) 825-4700

This nightclub comes complete with a mirrored ball, an eight-foot animatronic octopus and laser-shooting sharks. And, if you like the music of the late 70s and early 80s, Thursday night is "Disco Inferno" at this high-tech nightclub. Doors open at 10 PM every night with a $5 cover charge on Thursday, Friday and Saturday.

Blue Max
3611 Kings Row, Reno, Nev.
• (775) 747-4300

The Max is a little bar is tucked away in a small shopping center in northern Reno. It's clean, well-lighted and caters to the college crowd. The Max has DJ music during the week and will occasionally have live music on the weekend. It is a diverse nightclub, playing hip-hop on Tuesday, techno on Thursday, and salsa, merengue and cumbia on the weekend. UNR students frequent here. It is definitely off the beaten path but worth finding. Sometimes it charges a $3 cover.

Cantina Los Tres Hombres
7111 S. Virginia St., Reno, Nev.
• (775) 852-0202

The Cantina is a typical Mexican restaurant decorated with an adobe facade and sporting an outdoor patio shaded from the sun with colorful umbrellas. On the weekend, it has live music and is a popular choice of Insiders. The music usually starts at 10 PM and features all types, including reggae. Located way down Virginia Street, the Cantina usually does not charge a cover.

Confetti's
50 E. Grove St., Reno, Nev.
• (775) 829-9477

Live Latin and Mexican music rocks this

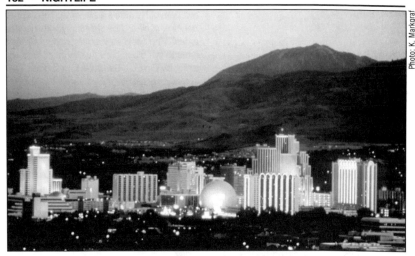

Reno lights up at night with all the glitz and color of the casinos in action.

joint on Friday and Saturday night. It's open from 9 PM to 5 AM with a cover charge of about $7. On Sunday, it features teen dances and live concerts, but you'll have to call ahead to find out exactly what's lined up each Sunday. Confetti's is located close to the downtown area.

Continental Lounge
1885 S. Virginia St., Reno. Nev.
• **(775) 324-7737**

It's called "Reno's Little Jewel," because it has been around some 30 years. The lounge is home to live jazz, blues, swing and Terry Scott, one of Reno's greatest guitarists. Live dance music flows Tuesday through Saturday, usually attracting the older crowd. And, the owners say, this is Reno's most intimate and cozy lounge. Most Insiders think they're right.

Del Mar Station
701 S, Virginia St., Reno, Nev.
• **(775) 322-7200**

If you know what an emo-band is then you will know what kind of a place Del Mar Station

is. If you don't, we suggest you stay away. A good example of what kind of bands jam here is GWAR, a soul-searching group which projectile vomits during its show. Other groups like Redrum, Banana Hammock and Enuff Z'Nuff have performed here, with tickets running from $5 to $15.

Einstein's Quantum Cafe
6135 Lakeside Dr., Reno, Nev.
• **(775) 825-6611**

This eclectic cafe is something new to the Reno area, a neighborhood restaurant which features live music toward the end of the week. From Thursday through Saturday, the cafe presents various jazz artists. And, on Sunday for a special treat, Reno's nonprofit jazz society jams here from 6 to 9 PM. The best thing about it is that it's free. (See also our Restaurants chapter.)

Fourth Street Jazz Club
302 E. Fourth St., Reno, Nev.
• **(775) 323-3007**

This new little club in town makes its home across the street from Reno's famous Louis'

INSIDERS TIP

Casual attire is the mode for most nightclubs in the Reno/Tahoe area.

Basque Corner Restaurant on Fourth Street (see our Restaurant chapter). This jazz club is housed in a quaint brick 1920s-style corner building. It's open Tuesday through Saturday, from 8 PM until the last die-hard patron leaves. On Wednesday, the little club has live jazz with a $3 cover charge. This is getting to be a popular Insiders' joint.

Hacienda Restaurant & Bar
10580 N. McCarran Blvd., Reno, Nev.
· (775) 746-2228
Another Mexican restaurant that has a nice place to listen to or dance to live music on Friday night, the Hacienda usually charges a $5 cover. Insiders' favorite night is Wednesday for ladies' night, which is billed as Chicks and Salsa Night.

Lilly's Jazz and Supperclub
Plumas St. and McCarran Blvd., Reno, Nev. · (775) 829-5074
This supper and jazz club is located at Reno's prestigious Lakeridge Tennis Club. The club features live jazz on Wednesday and Friday night. The clientele are mostly members of the tennis club. Need we say more? (See our Recreation chapter for more about Lakeridge.)

Little Waldorf Saloon
1661 N. Virginia St., Reno, Nev.
· (775) 323-3682
The Little Waldorf is the hangout of the University of Nevada, Reno's entire student body or so it seems. Since it's right across the street from the university, everything at this saloon is geared to the college crowd. The club has live music on Friday night, usually starting at 10 PM with no cover. The Wall, as it's called by Insiders, has a long, well-stocked bar, pool tables, several big-screen TVs for watching sporting events plus a good little restaurant. Prices are reasonable, but don't come here if you don't like younger crowds and the "F" word. The saloon is a favorite bar for Wolf Pack (UNR's mascot) fans of all ages after the university's home football games on Saturday.

Reno Live
210 N. Sierra St., Reno, Nev.
· (775) 329-1952
Someone got the bright idea in 1999 to convert a dying downtown casino into five different dance clubs, each with its own theme. It sounded harebrained at the time but it worked. Now, Reno Live is divided into these clubs: Sharkey's, playing 90s hits; Gen X, playing rave and techno; Hip Cat Lounge, playing hits of the 70s; Retro, playing the 80s kind of music; and Eddie's, playing hits of the 50s and 60s. The best thing about this place, besides the variety of music and patron ages, is that a $5 cover charge will get you into all five nightclubs. Reno Live is open from Thursday night through Sunday night from 9 PM to 5 AM. You must be 21 years old or older to enter.

The Zephyr Lounge
1074 S. Virginia St., Reno, Nev.
· (775) 324-9853
At the new Zephyr Lounge, the owners say the excitement comes from not knowing who you might see here — a banker, a veteran, a pacifist or a teacher. And its music is as varied as its clientele. Some nights there is jazz, some nights blues, and some nights swing music. The Zephyr also transforms itself into a comedy club, an improvisational theater and a forum for poetry readings — so it truly has something for just about everyone. You must call ahead to see what the owners have in store; it changes all the time.

Sparks

Hard Hat Bar & Grill
950 Glendale Ave., Sparks, Nev.
· (775) 359-0411
A fairly new club to the Sparks scene, Hard Hat is located in the industrial section of the city, hence its name. The club features a live band on Friday and Saturday night beginning at 9 PM with a $5 cover. Call to see what kind of music is playing. Also, on Sunday, it doesn't sell alcohol and caters to the 19-and-under crowd with a DJ starting music at 9 PM.

Oasis
2100 Victorian Ave., Sparks, Nev.
· (775) 359-4020
This little club is situated way west of Sparks and features Mexican music twice a week. Usually, a local band plays on Friday night and a band from Mexico stars on Satur-

day night. The club charges a $4 cover, and the music goes from 9 PM to 5 AM.

Sidelines Bar
1237 Baring Blvd., Sparks, Nev.
• (775) 355-1030

This little bar is tucked away in a shopping center on Baring Boulevard. It's definitely a neighborhood bar that caters to its regular customers. The best thing about this bar is the clientele. They're friendly, respectful and fun. The Sidelines has live music on Saturday with no cover charge.

North Shore Lake Tahoe

Captain Jon's Restaurant & Grill
7220 N. Lake Blvd., Tahoe Vista, Calif.
• (530) 546-4819

This is the North Shore's best seafood restaurant and a favorite of Lake Tahoe Insiders. The Captain provides live music Thursday through Saturday in the lounge. Captain Jon's is a very laid-back establishment, so go here if you are feeling romantic — and don't forget to stroll on the pier. (See also our Restaurants chapter).

Crystal Bay Club and Casino
14 Nev. Hwy. 28, Crystal Bay, Nev.
• (775) 831-0512

This casino is not much to look at, but it provides live music almost every night of the week. This is the kind of place that you might think twice about because of its looks — but trust us: the music in the lounge is good and people are friendly. Furthermore, the restaurant is excellent.

Elevation
877 N. Lake Blvd., Tahoe City, Calif.
• (530) 583-4867

Voted year after year as the best place to go dancing at Lake Tahoe, this club is one of the reasons Tahoe City has the reputation of

an all-night party town. There is a band playing here every night of the week. Usually, every night is a different theme. For instance, Thursday is hip-hop night, Friday is rock 'n roll night and on Tuesday, reggae music is performed. This is a must if you like to dance and are looking for a great time. Its only drawback is that cover charges sometimes run anywhere from $12 to $15.

Gar Woods Grill and Pier
5000 N. Lake Blvd., Carnelian Bay, Calif.
• (530) 546-3366

Gar Woods is one of the most crowded establishments around the lake but well worth coming to if only to take a look at its architecture. It has huge picture windows, multiple levels and an outdoor deck. The restaurant's fantastic but the wait is sometimes long. Gar Woods provides live music on Friday and Saturday from 7 PM to about midnight. Try a "Wet Woody," the bar's signature drink. (See also our Restaurants chapter.)

River Ranch Lodge
Calif. Hwy. 89 and Alpine Meadows Rd.,
3.5 mi. north of Tahoe City, Calif.
• (530) 583-4264

Located 3.5 miles away from Tahoe City, River Ranch Lodge is another reason Insiders call their city the party capital of the lake. You have to go here during the summer because the lodge holds its dances on an outside patio that overlooks the Truckee River. It usually books big-name entertainment so the music is great. But the atmosphere is so romantic, we guarantee that you wouldn't notice if a musician hit a sour note.

South Shore Lake Tahoe

The Beacon Restaurant
1900 Jameson Beach Rd., South Lake Tahoe, Calif. • (530) 541-0630

This restaurant sits beachfront at historic

Camp Richardson and not only provides great music on Wednesday, Saturday and Sunday but also provides a fantastic view of Lake Tahoe. The music varies between blues, folk and jazz and is performed on the outside deck. There are not enough O's in romantic to describe this place. If you're looking for intimacy, you've got to try the Beacon. (See our Recreation and Vacation Rentals chapters for more information about Camp Richardson.)

Island Cafe
4093 U.S. Hwy. 50, South Lake Tahoe, Calif. • (530) 542-1142

One of the newer places in South Lake Tahoe, this little club is located a short walk from the casinos at Stateline. The cafe is usually crowded because live music is offered here almost every night of the week beginning at 9 PM. This is turning out to be one of South Shore's hottest night spots.

Hoss Hoggs
2543 Lake Tahoe Blvd., South Lake Tahoe, Calif. • (530) 541-8328

Hoggs gained its reputation with visitors because of its great American cuisine of ribs, steaks and chicken. But it's also known as a fun time because it offers live music every night of the week except Wednesday. Monday night, patrons get the chance to show off their singing prowess with an open mike competition. Beer drinkers will enjoy its beer garden.

Nero's 2000
Caesar's Tahoe, U.S. Hwy. 50, Stateline, Nev. • (775) 586-2000

Nero's 2000, located inside Caesar's Tahoe, books live concerts with world-class reggae, alternative, Motown and rock groups at least once or twice per week. It has nightly promotions and contests and when a live band isn't playing, you can dance the night away in a disco-type atmosphere. Nero's is a very happening place and very popular all year long.

Cover charges range from $4 to $10 depending on the entertainment. This place rocks from 9 PM until the early morning.

Rojo's Tavern
3091 Harrison St., South Lake Tahoe, Calif. • (530) 541-4960

Rojo's has that Old Tahoe feel to it with its rustic look. Besides being a very good restaurant, the tavern adds live music in its downstairs cabaret from Thursday through Saturday night. If you want a get a feel for the Lake Tahoe of the 1920s and 30s, give Rojo's a visit.

Turtles
Embassy Suites, 4130 Lake Tahoe Blvd., Stateline, Calif. • (530) 543-2135

Literally only an alley away from Nevada, this California club rocks every night with dancing and food and drink specials. Music is supplied by DJs. Turtles usually has some sort of contest every night in a sports bar atmosphere.

Pubs

Reno

Corrigan's Bit O'Ireland
1526 S. Wells Ave., Reno, Nev. • (775) 322-1977

To give you a sense of the kind of atmosphere here, Corrigan's has an electric sign counting down the days until St. Patrick's Day and a placard that reads, "England get out of Ireland." The owner is really named Corrigan, and you can get Harp and Guinness on draught. What more do you need know about this Irish pub? This is an Insiders' hangout, though its clientele changes often. One day it might be students from the local university, the next it might be the construction workers from across the street. One thing's for certain,

---

INSIDERS TIP

What a difference a state makes! Nevada's nightclubs and bars allow smoking, but smoking is prohibited in California nightclubs and bars.

don't come here on St. Patrick's Day unless you like crowds. It's SRO only. But you wouldn't expect less from an Irish pub.

Foley's Irish Pub
2780 S. Virginia St., Reno, Nev.
· (775) 829-8500

The owner of Foley's used to be a bartender at Corrigan's. You can't miss him — he's the one with the real Irish brogue. This pub sits right across the street from the Peppermill Hotel Casino Reno. Foley's has the good Irish stout on tap and the good Catholic whiskey behind the bar (okay, it also has the fairly good Protestant whiskey, too). It also has a kitchen which prepares pub food. This pub has room for a small band and books real Celtic musicians once in a while.

Limericks Pub and Grille
Fitzgeralds Casino Hotel Reno, 255 N. Virginia St., Reno, Nev. · (775) 785-3677

Once again a good place to find Guinness on tap and for a reasonable price. The reason we recommend this pub is because during the summer months, Fitzgeralds hires college students from Ireland to work in this bar and its restaurant. It's almost like being in Ireland, and the kids are great conversationalists.

The Flowing Tide Pub
10580 N. McCarran Blvd., Reno, Nev.
· (775) 747-7707

A newer pub that caters to both the young and old crowds, this pub has a boatload of beers on tap and supplies live music on the weekend. Needless to say, it's a favorite of the university crowd, but it is also the home of the news people from a local television station. The atmosphere is friendly and so are the bartenders and waitresses.

South Shore Lake Tahoe

McP's Irish Pub
4090 Lake Tahoe Blvd., South Lake Tahoe, Calif. · (530) 542-4435

Located about one block from Stateline, this pub has Irish food and drink, a dart board, pool and live music seven nights per week.

There always seems to be someone from Britain in here.

Mulligan's Irish Pub
3600 Lake Tahoe Blvd., South Lake Tahoe, Calif. · (530) 542-1095

Another of South Tahoe's Irish pubs, Mulligan's has Guinness on tap and provides live music Wednesday through Sunday in the summer and on Friday and Saturday during the winter. What more can you ask?

The Tutor English Pub
1041 Fremont St., South Lake Tahoe, Calif. · (530) 541-6603

The Tutor bills itself as a typical English pub complete with draught ales, live music four nights per week and, of course, darts. Give this a try if you like your ale.

Sports Bars

Reno

Bully's Sports Bar & Grill
2005 Sierra Highlands Dr., Reno, Nev.
· (775) 746-8006
Bully's Sports Bar & Grill Too
18156 Wedge Pkwy./Mt. Rose Hwy., Reno, Nev. · (775) 851-7400
Bully's Sports Bar & Grill No. 3
2955 N. McCarran Blvd., Sparks, Nev.
· (775) 352-8400

Bully's has been voted the No. 1 sports bar in the Reno/Tahoe area for the last several years and for good reason. These three bars are the epitome of what sports bars should be — big screen TVs, friendly employees and everyone screaming for their favorite team. These sports bars are equipped with scrolling score boards to keep patrons up to date on all the games. Good luck trying to find a seat in any of these bars on Friday and Saturday night.

Fourth Turn Bar & Grill
2285 Kietzke Ln., Reno, Nev.
· (775) 825-7223

This sports bar has a racing car decor, complete with Indy and NASCAR replicas adorning the walls. It's your standard friendly bar that specializes in burgers and beer and has numerous TVs on which to enjoy your sports.

Knucklehead's Sports Bar
405 Vine St., Reno, Nev.
• **(775) 323-6500**

Enjoy your favorite game on one of this bar's five TV screens. Happy hour is happening from 4 to 7 PM here with drinks as low as $1.25.

Sullivan's
1290 E. Plumb Ln, Reno, Nev.
• **(775) 829-7854**

Sullivan's was voted the second best sports bar in Reno, right behind Bully's. You'll find 38 beers here and sports memorabilia scattered about besides numerous TVs.

Sparks

Freddie's Roost Grille and Sports Bar
7755 Spanish Springs Rd., Sparks, Nev.
• **(775) 626-1000**

This is an upscale sports bar located on Red Hawk Golf Course in the Wingfield Springs area of Sparks. The clientele is mostly locals who live around the golf course. The bar reflects a country-club atmosphere. (See our Golf chapter for more about the course.)

Luckie's Sports Bar & Deli
608 E. Prater Wy., Sparks, Nev.
• **(775) 331-3321**

Luckie's is open 24 hours a day and has a middle-aged, working-class clientele. TVs are in place for watching your favorite games, and it even has a small dance floor if you get bored with the sports.

Sparky's Sports Bar & Grill
1450 E. Prater Wy., Sparks, Nev.
• **(775) 356-6969**

Softball is king in Sparks, with about 7,500 people signed up to play in several leagues around the city. On any given night of the week, you'd swear that every one of these players is in Sparky's. It is rapidly becoming the place to go after that hard-played game. The atmosphere is loud and if you don't like seeing sweaty people in softball uniforms, stay away. Definitely an Insiders' hangout.

South Shore Lake Tahoe

Goal Post
290 Kingsbury Gr., Stateline, Nev.,
• **(775) 588-6563**

Football is the word of the day at this sports bar. TVs line the walls and the clientele is as varied as the games on TV. It's a good little bar to watch your favorite sports.

Gay-Friendly Nightclubs

Below we've listed the clubs and bars that advertise that they're friendly and accommodating to gay men and lesbians. The kind of entertainment and the clientele range across the spectrum; for a more complete rundown on each establishment's clientele, style and entertainment, pick up a copy of the area's gay newspaper, the *Reno Informer* (see our Media chapter).

Reno

Carl's, 3310 S. Virginia Street, Reno, Nevada, (775) 829-8886

The Five Star Saloon, 132 West Street, Reno, Nevada, (775) 329-2878

INSIDERS TIP

Don't drink and drive in the Reno/Tahoe area. The first offense is usually 3 days in jail and a $650 fine. The third DUI conviction in Nevada within a 7 year period is a felony with mandatory prison time.

Photo: Caesars Tahoe

Elaborately themed nightclubs are one of many options for nightlife in this happening part of the world.

The Patio, 600 W. Fifth Street, Reno, Nevada, (775) 323-6565

The Quest, 210 W. Commercial Row, Reno, Nevada, (775) 333-2808

Visions, 340 Kietzke Lane, Reno, Nevada, (775) 786-5455

1099 Club, 1099 S. Virginia Street, Reno, Nevada, (775) 329-1099

South Shore Lake Tahoe

Faces Nightclub, 270 Kingsbury Grade, Stateline, Nev., (775) 588-2333

Karaoke Bars

Insiders feel the karaoke scene here is more popular than it is in Japan. So we've listed as many places as we could find that accommodate those of you who feel the urge to sing in public. Most of the places listed have the same format: sign up, build up courage and then belt out that song.

Some of the places listed are clubs, some are bars and some are restaurants. Be aware, though, that a producer at our local cable-access TV station roams the area's karaoke bars with a camera and be advised that you just might be singing for the entire cable-viewing crowd.

Reno

The Break Away, 10 E. Ninth Street, Reno, Nevada, (775) 324-6200; Saturdays at 9 PM.

Ichiban Japanese Steakhouse, 210 N. Sierra Street, Reno, Nevada, (775) 323-5550; Saturdays, 10 PM to 2 AM

INSIDERS TIP

Most night spots on the Nevada side of the Reno/Tahoe area have video poker machines built into their bars.

Longnecks, 200 Lake Street, Reno, Nevada, (775) 323-6004; Tuesday through Saturday

Porky's, 3372 S. McCarran Boulevard, Reno, Nevada, (775) 825-3777; Saturdays, 10 PM to 1 AM

Shooters, 434 N. Virginia Street, Reno, Nevada, (775) 329-9646; Thursday and Friday, 9 PM to 1 AM

West Second Street Bar, 118 W. Second Street, Reno, Nevada, (775) 348-7976; nightly at 9 PM

Sparks

Salsa Dave's, 2855 N. McCarran Boulevard, Sparks, Nevada, (775) 331-7777; Friday and Saturday at 9:30 PM

Sidelines, 1237 Baring Boulevard, Sparks, Nevada, (775) 355-1030; Sundays at 8 PM and the first and third Saturdays of each month at 9:30 PM

South Shore Lake Tahoe

Harveys El Vaquero Restaurant, U.S. Highway 50, Stateline, Nevada, (775) 588-2411; Saturdays, 10 PM to 1 AM

Men's Clubs

Reno didn't acquire the nickname "Sin City" by gambling alone. Its adult entertainment scene, especially the men's clubs, help add to this nefarious handle. These men's clubs are found all over Reno and, unlike those in Las Vegas, they can serve alcoholic beverages. Listed below are the more popular and reputable clubs in the Reno/Tahoe area. Always expect to pay a cover charge for admittance or a two drink minimum instead of a cover charge. Depending upon the club, drinks for patrons can range from $5 to $10. Drinks for the dancers are more.

Reno

Ed's Fantasy Girls, 1095 E. Fourth Street, Reno, Nevada, (775) 324-7877

The Men's Club, 270 Lake Street, Reno, Nevada, (775) 786-7800

Empire Club, 2457 E. Second Street, Reno, Nevada, (775) 329-8480

Spicehouse Cabaret, 310 Spokane Street, Reno, Nevada, (775) 786-1299

Wild Orchid, 515 S. Virginia Street, Reno, Nevada, (775) 324-1010

Extraordinary growth
over the past several
decades has caused a
retail explosion, with
new shopping centers
seeming to gobble up
every piece of
vacant land.

Shopping

Since the first pioneers arrived in the 1800s, the Reno/Sparks area has been a regional trading center, serving the shopping needs of local residents as well as people living in rural parts of northern Nevada and California. While it will never rival glitzy shopping meccas like San Francisco, Dallas or New York, the Truckee Meadows is viewed as a lucrative market of about one-half million eager shoppers by retail marketers.

Extraordinary growth over the past several decades has caused a retail explosion, with new shopping centers seeming to gobble up every piece of vacant land. Along S. Virginia Street, a concrete/asphalt retail row has replaced the peaceful pastures, once home to cattle lazily grazing on the tall green grasses. North of downtown Sparks, shopping centers and housing subdivisions blanket the previously unspoiled desert landscape. Many locals lament this rapid urbanization and the inherent loss of the wide-open spaces. But for shoppers it means more stores, bigger stores and stores with ever-increasing choices of treasures to buy.

While shoppers once flocked to downtown Reno to browse the upscale stores sprinkled amongst the casinos, now they head to the myriad of malls strung along major streets and sprawling in between housing developments. As in many cities and towns, shopping in Reno moved from the downtown to outlying areas when malls came into vogue. The movement began in the late 1960s when Park Lane Mall opened its doors at the corner of Plumb Lane and S. Virginia Street. Meadowood Mall, the area's largest shopping mall, pushed development further south to the corner of S. McCarran Boulevard and S. Virginia Street. While Reno has experienced robust growth in all directions, the lion's share has been to the south with retail establishments now stretching clear up Nev. Highway 431 (the Mt. Rose Highway).

With the preservation of Victorian Square, Sparks has maintained a small town shopping ambiance in its core downtown (see our Attractions chapter for more about Victorian Square). The square has an interesting collection of specialty shops that are especially appealing to visitors. Other shopping is clustered in malls along major streets, such as McCarran Boulevard, Prater Way and Oddie Boulevard. You can buy the basics, but if you're looking for glitz you won't find much here. All that is about to change, however, as Sparks is growing up. With the opening of the Rialto Trade and Commerce Center in the fall of 2000, Sparks will draw shoppers from all over the region. The upscale mall, located about 2 miles north of McCarran Boulevard on Pyramid Lake Road (Nev. Highway 445), will rival Meadowood Mall in size and variety of stores.

While you can shop for all the necessities as well as niceties of life in the Reno/Sparks area, shopping in the Lake Tahoe Basin is more tourist-oriented. There are plenty of boutiques to browse that offer tantalizing one-of-a-kind specialty items. But if you're looking for essentials at a reasonable price, your choices are apt to be slim. You can't beat the selection of outdoor clothing and ski equipment, but don't expect to find many three-piece suits to wear to the office. In contrast to the megamarts and chain stores so prevalent in the Reno/Sparks area, shops in the Lake Tahoe region are mostly mom-and-pop establishments, highly individualized and unique in their merchandise and character. They're easy to spot, clustered in a few minimalls around the lake or tucked next to restaurants and hotels. Most shopping in the South Shore Lake Tahoe area is found at the "Y" (the junction of U.S. Highway 50 and Calif. Highway 89) and around the California–Nevada state line. Construction beginning in 1999 by the Park Avenue Redevelopment Project will add to shopping options with a village-like walking mall on the east side of U.S. 50 and a gondola to Heavenly Ski Resort.

To help you maximize your shopping experience in the Reno/Tahoe area, we've organized this chapter by our regular four geographical regions, Reno, Sparks, North Shore Lake Tahoe and South Shore Lake Tahoe. Within each of these regions we start with an overview of the main malls and a sampling of the shopping centers. (We don't describe all the stores in the main malls because they all have a large variety of shops that will meet most of your shopping needs.) Then we tell you about some individual stores in the following categories: antiques, books, casino shopping, consignment, gifts and souvenirs, kidstuff, pawn shops, sporting gear and women's clothing.

www.insiders.com
See this and many other
Insiders' Guide®
destinations online.
Visit us today!

Most malls are open seven days a week, but since store hours can vary, we've included a main number when it's available so you can call to verify hours before heading out.

Our listing of stores isn't meant to be all-inclusive. We hope to merely whet your appetite so you can discover other shopping delights on your own. For a more complete listing of stores you can consult local telephone directories. So put on your walking shoes, grab your credit card and let's shop 'til we drop.

Reno

Malls and Shopping Centers

Airport Square–Costco Center
E. Plumb Ln. and Harvard Wy., Reno, Nev. • (775) 823-6986

If you're searching for bargains, you've found the promised land in this shopping center. Anchored by Costco (who among us hasn't been the proud purchaser of a 50-year supply of something here?), the center caters largely to discount shoppers who are very price savvy. Pull into the parking lot and you know you've

arrived, since it's swarming with people packing bulk quantities into the backs of pickup trucks and trunks of cars. So grab a handtruck and let's load it up at Costco, Office Depot or PetSmart, to name a few.

Arlington Gardens Mall
606 W. Plumb Ln., Reno, Nev.
• (775) 826-0337

Owned by the Junior League of Reno (a nonprofit community service group), Arlington Gardens is where "women who lunch" meet and greet. With picturesque cobblestone floors and tiny boutiques nestled around the Country Garden Restaurant, it's a cozy getaway from the busy-ness of the day. You can meet your friends for breakfast or lunch and then browse the specialty shops for a relaxed shopping outing. Although the food in the restaurant is delicious, the service is often sporadic. But keep in mind it's a garden (and certainly not McDonald's!) so there's no reason for you to feel hurried.

Fire Creek Crossing Shopping Center
S. McCarran Blvd. and Kietzke Ln., Reno, Nev. • (949) 757-7776

It's the era of the megastore and Fire Creek Crossing exemplifies it. Many stores here are big, big, big — almost overwhelming customers with their available choices. If variety is the name of the game for you, you'll love shopping in such stores as Circuit City, Gart Sports, Home Store and Michael's Arts & Crafts. Located in the heart of Reno's retail row, Fire Creek Crossing can be a jumping off point to neighboring malls, such as Meadowood Mall and Smithridge Plaza.

Franktown Corners
2309 Kietzke Ln., Reno, Nev.
• (775) 825-1500

Complete with a quaint clock tower, Franktown Corners exudes the ambiance of an intimate village. Although the center is relatively small, the specialty shops and restaurants are intriguing and upscale. It's a great place to kill time while your car is getting decked out at the adjoining Franktown Hand Car Wash & Express Detailing. For wining and dining we recommend Viaggio Italian Cuisine (see our Restaurants chapter). You can also catch a quick meal at Fourth Turn, a sports bar/restaurant with an auto racing motif (see our Nightlife chapter).

Meadowood Court
S.W. Corner of S. McCarran Blvd. and S. Virginia St., Reno, Nev.

Barnes & Noble, Best Buy, Petco and Casual Male go head-to-head with other retailers in their new superstores at Meadowood Court. When you're tired of shopping, you can take a load off in two restaurants: Macaroni Grill and On the Border.

Meadowood Mall
S. Virginia St. and S. McCarran Blvd., Reno, Nev. • (775) 827-8450

Anchored by Macy's, JCPenney and Sears, Meadowood Mall is Reno/Tahoe's largest shopping center. With more than 95 stores, eateries and services, Meadowood stores include 25 locations for women's clothing, 21 for cards and gifts, 10 for sporting goods, 19 for shoes and 18 for men's apparel. The Palms Food Court offers everything from hot dogs on a stick to sizzling Cajun food to Mrs. Field's cookies. You can also take a welcome break from shopping in the restaurant on the second floor of Macy's North (the women's and children's store).

Amenities available at the mall include strollers, wheelchairs and an information booth. Citifare Shopper bus service is available to Meadowood from the downtown Reno bus depot at Fourth and Center streets, City Station-Sparks on C Street, Atlantis Casino/Resort and The Peppermill Hotel Casino Reno. Call Citifare at (775) 348-7433 for details.

If you're an ardent shopper, you're sure to enjoy Meadowood. It's clean and well maintained with an interesting mix of stores that provides something for everybody.

Park Lane Mall
Plumb Ln. and S. Virginia St., Reno, Nev. • (775) 825-9452

As Reno/Tahoe's first real mall, Park Lane Mall had its heyday beginning in the 1960s. Since then its glory has been eclipsed with larger retail outlets, like Meadowood Mall and Fire Creek Crossing, that have been built further south. When Park Lane lost its anchor stores, Weinstock's and Sears, the future of the mall looked dim. But with the addition of Gottschalks department store and the Century 16 Park Lane Theaters, the center seems to be on the comeback trail. At press time mall tenants were hoping for an even bigger shot in the arm from Jethro's Beverly Hillbillies Mansion & Casino, a project planned adjacent to the mall. Although the City of Reno has approved the construction of a 280-foot oil derrick with a 70-foot flame on top, Max Baer (who played Jethro in the TV series) is still working to finalize the deal.

But for now you can take in a movie, browse the 70+ shops and have a bite to eat at the Metro Grill. To make your shopping more comfortable, the mall offers complimentary strollers and wheelchairs, security escorts and an information booth. If you need a free place to exercise you can also join Park Lane's mallwalkers at 7 AM every day.

Redfield Promenade
S. Virginia St. and Kietzke Ln., Reno, Nev.

In the busiest shopping corridor in the Reno/Tahoe area, the new Redfield Promenade boasts four glitzy megastores: Bed Bath & Beyond, Borders Books, Cost Plus World Market and The Good Guys. Just opened in the spring of 1999, these bright new stores seem to bombard your senses with the variety of choices they offer.

INSIDERS' TIP

Most area golf courses and ski resorts have retail shops that carry a great variety of upscale equipment and apparel. Watch for end-of-the-season sales for the best prices.

Shopper's Square Mall
E. Plumb Ln. and S. Virginia St., Reno, Nev. • (775) 323-0430

With about 50 stores and six restaurants, you can certainly while away a few hours in this mall. The biggies are Marshalls Department Store, Sheplers Western Wear, Ben Franklin Crafts and Sav-On Drugs. It's located right across Plumb Lane from Park Lane Mall, so you can easily hit both malls in the same day. Planned expansion of Shopper's Square will double its size plus add an entertainment center and a five-story parking structure.

Smithridge Plaza
S. McCarran Blvd. and Smithridge Dr., Reno, Nev. • (775) 823-6986

If you're on your way to Meadowood Mall, you can also comparison shop at Smithridge Plaza, directly across the street. It offers great deals at such stores as Stein Mart, Mac Frugal's Bargains Close-Outs, Pier 1 Imports and Trader Joe's. There's also a Toys R Us, with a store called Parent Teacher Aids right next door. When it's time for lunch (or dinner), try a tasty Mexican meal at Chili's restaurant, right on the corner.

Southwest Pavilion
8175 S. Virginia St., Reno, Nev. • (775) 356-6118

Southwest Pavilion offers one-stop shopping with an up-to-date Scolari's supermarket surrounded by upscale shops, such as At The Ritz, Golf USA, High Desert Herbs, Scandia Down and Talbots. The exterior is tastefully constructed of soft pink stucco, a standout amongst the other businesses along the street.

Town Center Mall
100 N. Sierra St., Reno, Nev. • (775) 333-2828

With a focus on vintage clothing, antiques and crafts, Town Center Mall is a fun place to peruse the funky little shops. You can shop for one-of-a-kind gifts created by the different vendors in Antique Alley and the Crafters Gallery or choose art deco collectibles at Romaine's Collectibles or select gaming memorabilia at Sage of Nevada. Just steps from the Truckee River Walk in downtown Reno, try combining a stroll along the river

with a cruise through this unique mall. If you're driving you can park free in the River Gallery Garage just across the street: the mall will validate your ticket.

Antiques

All "R" Yesterdays
125 Gentry Wy., Reno, Nev. • (775) 827-2355

Within easy walking distance of both Atlantis Casino Resort and the Peppermill Hotel Casino Reno, All "R" Yesterdays offers everything from A to Z in collectibles and antiques.

Unique to this store is a collection of 1930s and 1940s vintage clothing. You can also shop for Christmas items year-round in their Christmas House. If you like the excitement of shopping via an auction, check out the antique and estate auctions held by Anchor Auctions in the rear of the building. For information about dates and merchandise call them at (775) 827-1801.

Antique Center of Nevada
1251 S. Virginia St., Reno, Nev. • (775) 324-4141

With more than 100 dealers showing their wares, the Antique Center of Nevada has an amazing assortment of collectibles, decor items and furniture just waiting for you to buy. Spread out over three malls, this eclectic assortment of fine and funky treasures varies in price all the way from 50¢ to $10,000. There's no hassle to park: just head into the parking lot on the corner of Arroyo and S. Virginia streets.

Reno Antiques
677 S. Wells Ave., Reno, Nev. • (775) 322-5858

If you're driving down Wells Avenue you can't miss Reno Antiques: the front yard is completely full of the vintage bathtubs so highly prized by antique collectors. Once inside you'll encounter an intriguing mix of antiques and collectibles. As one of the oldest antique stores in the area (since 1974), the business prides itself on always offering merchandise at a fair price. It's a "one-horse" show, according to the owner, since he does all the buying and selling himself.

Books

Adventist Book Center
1095 E. Taylor St., Reno, Nev.
• **(775) 322-2305**

If you're looking for information about a healthy physical and spiritual lifestyle, stop by the Adventist Book Center. Owned and managed by the Nevada–Utah Conference of Seventh-day Adventists, the store has a large selection of Adventist and Christian books, games and videos for adults and children. There's even a health food store, complete with vegetarian cookbooks, to get you on the track to a meatless diet. One of the oldest bookstores in the area, it's been pleasing customers since 1953.

Barnes & Noble
5555 S. Virginia St., Reno, Nev.
• **(775) 826-8882**

Comfortably ensconced in a huge new megabookstore, Barnes & Noble is a major literary presence in the Reno/Tahoe area. Much more than purveyors of books and avant-garde magazines, modern bookstores are cultural centers, selling music, videos and gourmet coffee in addition to a huge variety of reading materials. And to further whet your intellectual appetite, they also sponsor special events (see our chapter on The Arts for details). If you like to read, you'll simply love this store. It's a browser's delight: hanging out and perusing the shelves is expected and encouraged.

Black & White Books
3378 Lakeside Ct., Reno, Nev.
• **(775) 828-3445**

Back in the early 1990s, the owners of Black & White Books decided they either had to have an enormous garage sale or open a bookstore because they'd accumulated literally thousands of books. They opted to go into business, and Black & White Books was born in 1994. The store carries more than 100,000 new, used, out-of-print and rare books that span the spectrum of interests for all ages.

Known as one of the West's better bookstores, the store frequently supplies other book vendors from around the world and Internet sellers, such as Amazon.com. Come enjoy the world of books by the picturesque fountain just inside.

Borders Books
4995 S. Virginia St., Reno, Nev.
• **(775) 448-9999**

This new Borders Books is a cultural superstore. You'll find a gourmet coffee shop, a great selection of videos and music in addition to zillions of books. The store is bright and spacious, perfect for a relaxed shopping outing. Like Barnes & Noble, the store also sponsors cultural activities (see our chapter on The Arts for details).

Family Tree Books
1274 E. Plumb Ln., Reno, Nev.
• **(775) 826-8733**

A locally-owned independent bookstore, Family Tree Books sells books written by and for members of the Church of Jesus Christ of Latter Day Saints (LDS). It also offers a large variety of religious gift items. The owners pride themselves on their comfortable personalized service: all the employees are very well-read and are familiar with everything that's sold in the store. The store is conveniently located in the Airport Square–Costco Center.

Gambler's Bookstore
4001 S. Virginia St., Ste. 8, Reno, Nev.
• **(775) 825-7778**

Everything you've ever wanted to know about gambling is right here in the more than 1,000 books offered for sale at the Gambler's Bookstore. You can learn how to play casino games, explore the history of Nevada gaming or unravel the mysteries of sports betting. One of the few bookstores in the country devoted entirely to the subject of gambling, it also sells videos and computer software. It's easy to find on the first floor of Old Town Mall.

Paperback Exchange
131 Vesta St., Reno, Nev.
• **(775) 322-8822**

With more than 70,000 titles to choose from, it's pretty hard to say you can't find anything to read in the Paperback Exchange. As the name suggests, the merchandise is exclusively paperbacks, which the store both sells and trades. It's a little tricky to find (the street is only one block long), but look for it behind Rapscallion Restaurant off Wells Avenue.

Silver Sage Bookstore
1557 S. Virginia St., Reno, Nev.
• **(775) 348-0022**

Silver Sage Bookstore has a fascinating mix of metaphysical and New Age books. To enhance your spiritual exploration you can choose from books on Eastern and Western philosophies as well as on health, healing, astrology and addictions. The store also sells videos, tapes, candles and gifts. It's easy to find in the South Virginia Plaza shopping center.

Sundance Bookstore
1155 W. Fourth St., Reno, Nev.
• **(775) 786-1188**

Tucked in the Keystone Square Shopping Center, Sundance Bookstore is a favorite with longtime residents since it's owned and managed by locals. You can buy a cup of espresso at the cart up front and then relax in the cozy, intimate atmosphere of this very personal store. If you're looking for books about Nevada and the Sierra or works by local and regional authors, you'll find one of the best selections in the area right here. The store is also able to order obscure titles that large chain bookstores are unable to get. Don't be surprised if the service here is impeccable: it always is since the owner is likely to wait on you.

Waldenbooks
Meadowood Mall, Reno, Nev.
• **(775) 825-7544**
Park Lane Mall, Reno, Nev.
• **(775) 826-1234**

You can buy books to your heart's content at both these Waldenbooks stores, but don't expect the bells and whistles of the new mega-

bookstores. They're just about books, books and more books. Located in major malls, both Waldens in Reno are well stocked and comfortable to shop (see our previous descriptions of these malls). The Meadowood store is slightly larger and includes a Waldenkids.

Casino Shopping

Reno Hilton
2500 E. Second St., Reno, Nev.
• **(775) 789-2000**

From fine art to upscale clothing to typical tourist souvenirs, the Reno Hilton shopping arcade offers about 30 classy shops to tempt your wallet. You'll find a few shops on the casino level near the hotel check-in area, but the majority are one level down where you'll also find the movie theaters. With its deep-carpeted quiet ambiance, the Hilton is an especially fun place for a leisurely browse.

Eldorado Hotel/Casino
345 N. Virginia St., Reno, Nev.
• **(775) 786-5700**

You can shop for fine jewelry, resortwear, collectibles, specialty gifts and logo items in the snazzy shops that line the European-style mezzanine that connects the Eldorado Hotel/Casino to the Silver Legacy Resort Casino. Overlooking the casino areas and lined with bars and restaurants, the mezzanine is bright, brassy and a bit noisy, but the upbeat gaming atmosphere makes buying a fun experience for many customers.

Consignment

Katie Magoo's
912 S. Virginia St., Reno, Nev.
• **(775) 329-8553**

With six rooms packed full of period costumes and vintage clothes, Katie Magoo's offers a captivating shopping experience that's

---

INSIDERS' TIP

A favorite daytrip for Insider shoppers is going to Truckee for its quaint downtown shops and factory outlet stores (see our Daytrips chapter for details).

unique to the area. Clothing ranges in age from the late 1800s to the 1970s and is priced to fit almost everyone's budget. If you're looking to get all decked out for a special event, it's a must stop. You'll love this funky old house. Hours vary so be sure to call ahead.

Labels Consignment Boutique
3350 Lakeside Dr., Reno, Nev.
• **(775) 825-6000**
A favorite stop for women who love great clothes at bargain prices, Labels Consignment Boutique sells designer clothes at a fraction of their full retail price. You don't need to worry about damaged goods because everything on the racks is top quality. The store is beautifully appointed, like an upscale retail establishment in any large city.

Little People Mommies Too
565 Keystone Ave., Reno, Nev.
• **(775) 324-1494**
Although many consignment clothing stores focus on women's apparel, you can outfit the entire family at Little People Mommies Too.

The store offers men's, women's and children's clothing for all seasons and occasions, with a small selection of vintage items and maternity clothes. New parents can realize significant savings with the store's little people's furniture. The store is conveniently located in the Keystone Shopping Center, right off Interstate 80.

The Recycle Closet
115 Thoma St., Reno, Nev.
• **(775) 323-2294**
Tucked in a little brick house with a purple bathtub out front, The Recycle Closet sells women's clothing from casual to cocktail and men's apparel from boots to suits. You're sure to find the right size since they range from 2 to 32 for women and from small to big and tall for men.

The store specializes in current styles within the past five years and also classic clothing. You'll also find an interesting assortment of costume jewelry and Western wear. Parking is a breeze right next to the store and can be accessed from Center Street.

Gifts and Souvenirs

Country Gourmet
606 W. Plumb Ln., Reno, Nev.
• **(775) 829-9559**
Tucked in the Arlington Gardens Mall (see our previous description of the mall), the Country Gourmet is a cook's delight with unique kitchen items and gourmet foods. If you want a gift typical of Nevada, try the shop's specialty, a Nevada gift basket.

Jungle Love Artistry
2303 Kietzke Ln., Reno, Nev.
• **(775) 828-0944**
Jungle Love Artistry is simply irresistible. Where else can you special order an angel, complete with a halo and wings, in the image of your favorite pet? Your first step into this tiny store puts you into another world. With the sound of running water and serene music in the background, take your time and enjoy the lovely artist-made gifts from artisans all over the world. The emphasis is on animals and on crafts representing different cultures. Don't miss this store, especially if you're an animal-lover. Jungle Love Artistry is nestled in the middle of Franktown Corners shopping center.

Lucky 7
229 N. Virginia St., Reno, Nev.
• **(775) 324-4970**
For Reno and Lake Tahoe logo T-shirts at reasonable prices, try the Lucky 7 souvenir shop near the casinos in downtown Reno. Open since 1985, the store stocks a wide variety of typical tourist items.

Millenium Awards
130-B Plumb Ln., Reno, Nev.
• **(775) 826-9118**
You don't have to travel all the way to Egypt or Pakistan to buy their exotic crafts and artworks. Stop by Millenium Awards and choose from all of the lovely mother-of-pearl and brass gift items imported from these countries. The store also offers custom embroidery and laser engraving on almost anything you purchase or bring in.

Pure Country Americana
1300 E. Plumb Ln., Reno, Nev.
• **(775) 826-1800**

The warmth of country living exudes from this shop in the Airport Square–Costco Center shopping plaza. It boasts the largest collection of Dept. 56 decorative villages in the Reno/Tahoe area, along with the largest selection of Boyd's Bearstones. As you might guess from the store's name, it also features Americana items in red, white and blue or with stars and stripes. Enjoy a leisurely browse with a cup of delicious espresso purchased from the coffee counter up front.

Kidstuff

Carty's Kid Stop
6137 S. Virginia St., Reno, Nev.
• **(775) 852-7700**

With such adorable merchandise available for kids, it's great fun shopping for them. You'll have a ball at Carty's Kid Stop, northern Nevada's largest children's store. Everything you ever wanted to buy for the little ones is here, and then some. You can indulge your tots from their lovely selection of upscale clothing, fun-filled toys and designer furniture. Carty's also has all the necessary extras for safe parenting, such as strollers and car seats. The store is conveniently located next to ShopKo.

Gymboree Store
5180 Meadowood Mall Cir., Reno, Nev.
• **(775) 829-9724**

The windows of Gymboree Store are easily the most colorful and cheerful displays in Meadowood Mall, since the store is full of brightly-colored clothing that kids just love. Kids like the look and fit of the clothes, but parents appreciate their durability. The store guarantees that their merchandise is kid-tough and the tags on all the clothes attest to it. You can also shop for accessories, such as sunglasses especially designed for children, or furniture, like Gym Rockers.

Morgan's Closet
606 W. Plumb Ln., Reno, Nev.
• **(775) 827-8829**

If you love dressing your child to the nines, Morgan's Closet is a must stop. Their clothing is distinctly upscale, with such high-quality brands as Cakewalk, Petit Bateau and Ruth of Carolina. The store offers one of the largest selections in the area of special events apparel, including communion dresses and wedding clothes. You'll find clothing for infants to about 9 years old. Since the store is located in Arlington Gardens Mall (see our previous description), you can treat your child to breakfast or lunch in the Country Garden Restaurant as part of your shopping outing.

Once Upon A Time Children's Boutique & Books
5000 Smithridge Dr., Reno, Nev.
• **(775) 825-1620**

Open since 1981, Once Upon A Time Children's Boutique & Books offers one-stop shopping for your children. The store carries a wide variety of upscale clothing, from casual to formal in sizes infant to 16. About half the store is devoted to hardbound books, toys, gift items and accessories. It's easy to find, next to The Men's Wearhouse in the Smithridge Plaza shopping center.

Pawn Shops

Palace Jewelry and Loan Co, Inc.
300 N. Virginia St., Reno, Nev.
• **(775) 322-2863**

With two GIA-certified gemologists on staff, the Palace Jewelry and Loan Co., Inc. guarantees all jewelry purchases. In business since 1958, the company deals in new merchandise as well as items that have been lost to pawn. You'll find a good mix of items to buy, including musical instruments, electronics and guns. If you're looking for cash, the company will loan up to $1 million.

Superpawn
190 N. Center St., Reno, Nev.
• **(775) 323-2352**
350 N. Virginia St. • (775) 322-4373
641 S. Rock Blvd. • (775) 331-4044

A family-owned and -operated business dating from the 1930s, Superpawn began with a single location in downtown Reno and has expanded to 30 stores in Arizona and Nevada. If you need money you can get instant cash by pawning almost anything of value. But if you're shopping, you can find incredible bargains in such things as jewelry, coins, electronics, musical instruments, tools and sporting goods. The best selection of tools and musical instruments is found at the Rock Boulevard store. For high-priced jewelry try the N. Virginia Street location.

Sporting Gear

Bobo's Mogul Mouse Ski & Patio
515 E. Moana Ln., Reno, Nev.
• (775) 826-9096

If you need to rent equipment, you can choose from Reno's largest ski and snowboard rental department at Bobo's. Friendly, professional service combined with a large variety of inventory makes shopping here a pleasure. You'll find everything you need to buy for the entire family for fun in the snow.

Eclipse Running
960 W. Moana Ln., Reno, Nev.
• (775) 827-2279

Eclipse Running is a running store run by runners. More than just selling shoes, the owners are committed to helping customers become lifelong runners. They offer personalized service that includes help with training and injuries. The store has been open since 1995 and also offers a selection of snowshoes and swimming apparel and accessories.

Gart Sports
4813 Kietzke Ln., Reno, Nev.
• (775) 828-1234

A megastore with seemingly unlimited choices, Gart Sports is Reno/Tahoe's largest sporting goods store. You can completely outfit yourself for any sporting activity in all major brands of equipment and apparel. In spite of its size, the store maintains personalized service. Salespersons are hired because of their knowledge of a particular sport: if you're buying skis, a skier will help you select them. The store has oodles of parking and is conveniently

located in the Fire Creek Crossing Shopping Center.

Harley-Davidson of Reno
2295 Market St., Reno, Nev.
• (775) 329-2236

If you're a Harley-kind-of-person, you've found your Eden. Harley-Davidson of Reno will light your fire with its large selection of riding gear, accessories and Buell bikes. It's better if you arrive on a Harley, but cars are okay.

Nevada Bob's Discount Golf
4112 Kietzke Ln., Reno, Nev.
• (775) 826-2245

Dubbed the "Nordstrom's of golf shops," Nevada Bob's Discount Golf is the area's largest and oldest golf shop. The warm woods and plush carpets in this classy store give an air of elegance not usually found in golf shops. But in spite of the rich decor, you don't have to be rich to shop here. Prices are very competitive and the store stands behind all its products. You'll find all major brands of golf clothing and equipment, and you can even have your clubs custom-fit by the professionally trained staff.

Play It Again Sports
651 E. Moana Ln., Reno, Nev.
• (775) 825-6311

As the name suggests, not all used sporting equipment is relegated to the trashbin. Play It Again Sports buys, sells, trades and consigns both used and new sports gear of all kinds. You can recover some of your initial investment in equipment by trading or selling outright. In the store's 12 departments you'll find everything from baseballs to golf clubs to exercise machines.

Reno Fly Shop
294 E. Moana Ln., Reno, Nev.
• (775) 825-3474

There's not much question about the owner of Reno Fly Shop knowing his business: he won the prestigious Jackson One-Fly fishing

INSIDERS' TIP

Reno is a great place to do your Christmas shopping while you are on vacation contest in Jackson Hole, Wyoming in 1994. The sales force is equally knowledgeable with several fly fishing books to their credit. Open since 1978, this store is a full-service fly shop, offering fly tying, rodbuilding and fly fishing lessons; Nevada and California guide service; and a complete line of clothing and equipment. You can buy top-of-the-line Simms Gortex waders to go with your Sage, Scott, Orvis or Winston fly rod. It's a great specialty store for the ardent fly fishing enthusiast (and this is no fish story).

Reno Mountain Sports
155 E. Moana Ln., Reno, Nev.
• **(775) 825-2855**

You can buy all the gear and clothing you'll need for skiing, backpacking, hiking, climbing and kayaking at Reno Mountain Sports. With a professional staff that's sports-oriented, you can be assured that equipment is suited to your ability and body size. Well-stocked with all the best-known sporting goods brands, the store is great fun for browsing. For equipment rentals and service, drive around to the back of the building and use the rear entrance.

Snowind Sports
2500 E. Second St., Reno, Nev.
• **(775) 323-9463**

Tucked away in the lower level of the shopping arcade in the Reno Hilton, Snowind offers sales and rentals for mountain bikes, inline skates, skis and snowboards. If your skis need tuning, you'll get the best tune in town here. The easiest access to the store is from the parking lot adjacent to the driving range by the lake.

Women's Clothing

Concepts By Fine 'N Funky
228 Vassar St., Reno, Nev.
• **(775) 853-1400**

You know Concepts By Fine 'N Funky is

special the minute you see the store. Off the beaten path in a semiresidential neighborhood, the ambiance of this charming green and white cottage a la the 1800s is lovely. The store specializes in top-quality merchandise not sold anywhere else in the area, such as Lucky, Big Star and Diesel jeans; Trina Tarantino jewelry; and Kiehls natural hair and skin products. The clothes are classy and range from casual to cocktail. You can also shop for men and children. The store has another location at the Boatworks Mall in Tahoe City, California, (530) 583-1400 (see our description of the mall later in this chapter).

Laurel's Fashions and Bridal Boutique
3430 Lakeside Dr., Reno, Nev.
• **(775) 827-1150**

Exceptional personal service is the hallmark of Laurel's Fashions and Bridal Boutique. You want to look your absolute best for that very special occasion, and their tailoring service will ensure that clothing fits perfectly. Besides formal wear, the store carries casual and funky apparel. When you're finished shopping, stop in for dinner at one of the fine restaurants in the Moana West Shopping Center, such as Kyoto Restaurant and Pane Vino. The store is closed Sunday and Monday.

Pendleton of Reno
300 N. Center St., Reno, Nev.
• **(775) 323-1119**

It might seem strange to shop for woolens in a bowling facility, but one of the largest Pendleton stores in the country is located in the National Bowling Stadium. This bright airy store is full of men's and women's sweaters, jackets, slacks and shirts. There's also a large selection of lovely Indian blankets. The best time to find bargains is in July and January during the store's seasonal clearance sales. You can park in the stadium's parking garage off Fourth Street. Be sure to validate your ticket at the information booth to avoid a fee.

INSIDERS' TIP

Last-minute shoppers will be happy to know you can buy high-quality Reno/Tahoe souvenirs in the shops at Reno/Tahoe International Airport.

Ross Stores Inc.
4825 Kietzke Ln., Reno, Nev.
• (775) 826-2000

Ross is a discounter's delight, but be prepared to work for your bargains. Since the real treasures are often well hidden, you've got to paw the racks to ferret out the good stuff. Real shoppers enjoy the challenge of the hunt, however, and just roll up their sleeves and plunge in. The store is easy to find in Fire Creek Crossing shopping center.

Stein Mart
5069 S. McCarran Blvd., Reno, Nev.
• (775) 826-7222

Some of the best clothing values in the area are found at Stein Mart, the mini department store in Smithridge Plaza. The store has a wonderful variety of top-quality, name brand clothes for 25 to 50 percent off regular retail prices. Stein Mart is a cut above most discount stores, with classy merchandise and upscale decor. In addition to its great selection of women's apparel, the store has fine men's and children's departments.

Talbots
8155 S. Virginia St., Reno, Nev.
• (775) 851-7777

Talbots is a class act, selling classic casual, classic business and classic formal clothing. To help you build your wardrobe the classic way, the store offers personal shopping service, wardrobe consulting and appointment shopping. If you don't find what you want in the store, help is merely a phone call away. Just pick up the Red Line Phone in the shop and order your merchandise directly from Talbots catalogue. Talbots is conveniently located in the Southwest Pavilion mall.

William Fur & Leather
3370 Lakeside Ct., Reno, Nev.
• (775) 828-0995

Although fur and leather can be a sensitive subject these days, if you're going to buy and wear it you want it to be top-quality. William Fur & Leather is Reno/Tahoe's most complete full-service salon. All merchandise is personally selected by William on his frequent trips to the best international sources of merchandise. Like the coats themselves, the shop is luxurious, with deep carpeting and a wine bar tucked cozily in one corner. The store also offers trade-in, layaways, consignments, cold storage, repairs and cleaning. Service is personalized, with William helping you to select just the right purchase and celebrating it with a glass of champagne.

Sparks

Malls and Shopping Centers

Greenbrae Shopping Center
Greenbrae Dr. and Pyramid Wy., Sparks, Nev.

With a large bowling center and an eight-screen movie theater, Greenbrae Shopping Center offers entertainment in addition to shopping. The stores include Hancock Fabrics, Ben Franklin Crafts, Pet City and Thrift Depot. If you think you're paying too much to see movies, give the New Greenbrae Theaters a try. When films have been pulled from first-run theaters, they're shown here for just a fraction of what you'd pay in other theaters. As one of the oldest shopping centers in the area, Greenbrae isn't glitzy, but it's clean.

Iron Horse Shopping Center
S.W. Corner of Prater Wy. and N. McCarran Blvd., Sparks, Nev.

The Iron Horse Shopping Center offers one-stop shopping with Albertson's Food & Drug, Payless Shoesource, Target, The Wherehouse, Party Universe (discount party supplies) and Mother Lode Bicycles. For lunch or dinner at a reasonable price try Applebee's Neighborhood Grill & Bar.

McCarran Plaza
N.W. Corner of Prater Wy. and N. McCarran Blvd., Sparks, Nev.

Along with a sprinkling of casual eateries, McCarran Plaza offers Mac Frugal's Bargains Close-outs, Foot Locker, Eagle Valley Frames, Movie Max and a Longs Drug Store. The plaza is just across the street from the Iron Horse Shopping Center.

Silver State Plaza
680 N. McCarran Blvd., Sparks, Nev.

Anchored by Safeway and Sav-On Drugs, Silver State Plaza serves most of the basic needs of nearby residents. Stores include Vicks' Books, Radio Shack, Mervyn's California Department Store, Jo-Ann Fabrics & Crafts, Dollar Tree (everything for $1 or less) and the General Nutrition Center.

Victorian Square
Victorian Ave., Sparks, Nev.

With its quaint turn-of-the-century motif, Victorian Square is a delight to shop. You'll find a fun mix of specialty shops perfect for browsing. It's the center of activity for downtown Sparks, so you can also attend special events, take in a movie at the Century Sparks 14 theaters or play in the interactive fountain (see our description of the square in our Attraction and Kidstuff chapters).

Antiques

Sandy's Attic Collectibles & More
2160 Victorian Ave., Sparks, Nev.
• (775) 331-3188

With a little bit of everything from soup to nuts, Sandy's Attic Collectibles & More makes the most of its tiny little house. Merchandise changes all the time so you never know what you'll find in the way of furniture and collectibles. The owner constantly searches estate sales and storage auctions for unusual items.

Victorian Square Emporium
834 Victorian Ave., Sparks, Nev.
• (775) 331-2288

Not many antique stores can boast a collection of authentic gaming memorabilia. The Victorian Square Emporium has original oil artworks, felt gaming layouts, cards, dice and clothing from area casinos. Antiquers know these items are hard to come by so be sure to ask about them when you're in the store.

Like the historical goodies inside, the emporium's physical location also has a past. It was built in the early 1900s by the Southern Pacific Railroad and served as a hotel during Sparks's heyday as a railroad stopover. Today it's packed with the treasures displayed by about 40 antique dealers and crafters. You'll find everything from A to Z, including furniture, antique glassware, jewelry, paintings and collectibles.

The emporium hosts a monthly Nostalgia Fair on the street outside, showcasing resident and visiting dealers' merchandise. Call for dates and times and also ask about their periodic antique auctions.

Books

His Word Christian Book Store
810 Holman Wy., Sparks, Nev.
• (775) 359-7940
7689 S. Virginia St., Reno, Nev.
• (775) 853-2665

Although the mainstay of both locations of His Word Christian Book Store is Christian books, the stores are also minimarts offering a wide selection of other religious items. You can shop for gifts, such as Seraphin angels and Precious Moments figurines. Or you can browse the aisles for pictures, cards, videos, music and tapes. As in many bookstores, the ambiance is comfortable and relaxed. Be sure to sample the coffee at His Ground, the coffee nook in the Reno store.

New Life Christian Book Store
546 Greenbrae Dr., Sparks, Nev.
• (775) 331-1155

It's probably the only post office in the country that will pray for your mail to arrive on time. Tucked in the back of the New Life Christian Book Store, the postal substation is a full-service post office equipped to handle all of your mailing needs.

Up front, the store has the only large selection of used, out-of-print and hard-to-find Christian books in the area. You'll be delighted to discover their reasonable prices: most everything ranges from $1 to $3. The store also carries new books, gifts, pictures, plaques, T-shirts, hats and jewelry.

The Book Gallery
1203 N. Rock Blvd., Sparks, Nev.
• (775) 356-8900

To peruse all the titles at The Book Gallery is a daunting task. With more than 200,000 books in stock, the inventory spills into three buildings. The store buys, sells and trades used paperbacks and hardbound books of all categories. You'll also find a selection of videos.

Gifts and Souvenirs

Art Dogs and Grace II
1921 Victorian Ave., Sparks, Nev.
* **(775) 331-8554**

Art Dogs and Grace II is the home of hand-dipped incense. If you can't find just the right scent and shape on the shelf, you can ask the store to specially dip incense for you. It's a fun shop for the whole family, with imported crafts from Bali and Indonesia, Grateful Dead memorabilia and an eclectic array of medium-priced artwork and jewelry.

Peggy O'Neill's
2855 N. McCarran Blvd., Sparks, Nev.
* **(775) 359-1999**

Oozing country charm, Peggy O'Neill's is a bright and cheery shop just chock-full of unusual gifts and goodies for the home. Browse to your heart's delight among the displays of furniture, paper goods, candles, tapestries and ceramics. When you've found just the right gift, the store will giftwrap it free for you. You can find this quaint shop in the Mercantile Center.

The Gift Cottage
225 Fifth St., Sparks, Nev.
* **(775) 359-3400**

It's easy to spot the Gift Cottage on Fifth Street: just look for a 1930s white bungalow trimmed in luscious burgundy. Once past the little front porch, you'll love perusing the upscale gift items. But don't look for kid's stuff or Beanie Babies because this shop focuses on collectibles cherished by older folks. You'll find a lovely selection of ceramics, dolls and bears. The shop is one of the few sources for Wee Forest Folk, tiny resin figures that are meticulously hand painted.

Pawn Shops

Metro Pawn
254 E. Glendale Ave., Sparks, Nev.
* **(775) 359-5151**

You can buy watches, jewelry, cameras, VCRs, TVs and electronics at Metro Pawn. They're never far away, with four locations in the Reno/Tahoe area. You can shop at the location above or at 800 W. Fifth Street, (775) 322-1030; 51 E. Grove Street, (775) 828-0770; or 6150 S. Virginia Street, (775) 828-5454 in Reno.

Pacific Pawnbrokers
1246 Victorian Ave., Sparks, Nev.
* **(775) 359-7761**

With four locations in the Reno/Tahoe area, Pacific Pawnbrokers offers a huge selection of jewelry, musical instruments and electronics.

The largest store is the address above, with smaller stores at 701 Ryland Avenue in Reno, (775) 348-2525; 920 Victorian Square in Sparks (775) 359-6222; and 3908 Lake Tahoe Boulevard in South Lake Tahoe, (530) 542-6494 (see our description below). The stores also have Spanish-speakers on the staff.

Sporting Gear

House of Arrows Archery Pro Shop
2166 Victorian Ave., Sparks, Nev.
* **(775) 356-6614**

The House of Arrows Archery Pro Shop does more than just meet your archery needs: it also offers a unique display of handmade long bows dating from the 1920s. But if the historical equipment isn't your cup of tea, you can buy the latest in new or used, custom-fit to your skill level and goals.

Catering to what the owner dubs, "the local archery 3-D junkie," the store specializes in upper-end and hard-to-find bows and arrows. It's also an information center for archery meets and competitions held around the country.

Sierra Mountaineer–Rocksport– Indoor Climbing Center
1901 Silverada Blvd., Sparks, Nev.
• (775) 358-4824

At Sierra Mountaineer you can find whatever clothing and equipment you'll need to help make your mountain outing safe and fun. The store also has a good selection of backcountry ski equipment for rent. Be sure to take a look at their climbing center, where it's fun to watch the climbers inching like Spiderman up the perpendicular walls.

The Gilly Fishing Store
1111 N. Rock Blvd., Sparks, Nev.
• (775) 358-6113

An old-fashioned store with new ideas, The Gilly Fishing Store offers customers personalized service along with the latest merchandise. You'll find the largest selection of fishing tackle in the Reno/Tahoe area, plus clothing, float tubes, rods and reels. The store also sells custom rods, does repairs and rents fishing videos. You can also hear your share of fish stories here since it's the meeting place of the Great Basin Bassers, a local bass fishing club.

Women's Clothing

Mervyn's California Department Store
520 N. McCarran Blvd., Sparks, Nev.
• (775) 358-8800

Mervyn's California Department Store offers good quality clothing suitable for most occasions. You won't find wild funky clothes, but it's a good source for wardrobe basics. It's easy on the pocketbook since most merchandise is reasonably priced. You'll also find goodies for your home along with clothing for the rest of the family in this full-service department store.

North Shore Lake Tahoe

Malls and Shopping Centers

Boatworks Mall
760 N. Lake Blvd., Tahoe City, Calif.
• (530) 583-1488

With any view of Lake Tahoe at a premium, the Boatworks Mall is special indeed. Hugging the shoreline in Tahoe City, the mall offers a lovely environmental experience along with a fun shopping outing. In a rustic Tahoe atmosphere with periodic glimpses of the lake, you can shop for fine art, food and wine, books, jewelry, games, clothing and souvenirs. The merchandise is unique and the setting oh so special. When you're through shopping and ready to drop, head into Jake's On The Lake on the first floor of the mall for drinks and dinner. You won't be disappointed.

Christmas Tree Village
868 Tahoe Blvd., Incline Village, Nev.

It almost seems like Christmas every day at the Christmas Tree Village shopping mall. The quaint Tyrolean decor makes it festive all year round. You can buy fine art at Art Attack, children's clothing at Puddin 'N Pie, unique jewelry at Incline Jewelry, collectibles and gifts at The Tahoe Store Emporium and women's and junior clothing at 5th Season Clothing Company. Last but not least, you can experience the sights, sounds and smells of Christmas every day in the Christmas Shoppe.

Cobblestone Center
475 N. Lake Blvd., Tahoe City, Calif.
• (530) 583-1580

Built in 1966, the Cobblestone Center is Tahoe City's oldest mall. Its charming Swiss-Bavarian architecture lends a picturesque touch to the lovely alpine setting. Reminiscent of European villages, the clock in the center's tower chimes on the hour and plays carillon music. The center boasts a movie theater and a restaurant with outdoor dining, plus an interesting mix of shops selling clothing, gifts, art, home furnishings and cosmetics.

Lighthouse Shopping Center
850 N. Lake Blvd., Tahoe City, Calif.
• **(530) 583-3471**

Just a hop, skip and a jump from the Boatworks Mall, the Lighthouse Shopping Center offers vital services such as a post office, video store and a Safeway supermarket in addition to a few specialty shops. You can easily shop both these malls at the same time since they're adjacent to each other.

Raley's Incline Center
930 Tahoe Blvd., Incline Village, Nev.

Anchored by a large Raley's supermarket, Incline Center is the heart of shopping in Incline Village. You can find basic essentials here as well as tourist items. The stores offer upscale clothing, hardware, gourmet foods, video rentals, books, art and gifts. When hunger strikes you can choose from fine Italian cuisine at Azzara's Italian Restaurant or gourmet burgers at Rookies Sports Bar & Grill or fresh bagels at the Sierra Bagel Factory.

Squaw Valley USA
1960 Squaw Valley Rd., Olympic Valley, Calif. • **(530) 583-6985**

Even if you're not skiing, you can browse the quaint shops clustered near the base of the lifts at Squaw Valley USA. As you might expect, most stores are oriented toward skiing and outdoor activity. Since the business is seasonal, some shops are closed during the summer months. While in Olympic Valley,

check out the shops at the Resort at Squaw Creek, just off Squaw Valley Road as you enter the valley (see our descriptions of Squaw Valley and the Resort at Squaw Creek in our Winter Sports and Resorts chapters).

Antiques

Cloth Cottage
700 N. Lake Blvd., Tahoe City, Calif.
• **(530) 581-5772**

At the Cloth Cottage you can pick out the perfect antique, vintage or casual fabrics for your home or office. You'll get plenty of ideas from browsing the lovely room displays of antique furnishings complete with appropriate fabrics. The professional staff will show you how to utilize the fabric yourself or will custom sew any items. The store sells the best quilting fabrics in the area and carries top-quality brands like Waverly and Weathervane Hill. There's also a great selection of antique furniture, collectibles and bedroom ensembles.

Girasole
319 W. Lake Blvd., Tahoe City, Calif.
• **(530) 581-4255**

At Girasole you'll find a lovely selection of antique country pine furniture imported from England, Ireland and Mexico. The store also has gift items for the home, including hand-painted Italian ceramic dinnerware.

Tahoe City Antiques
475 N. Lake Blvd., Tahoe City, Calif.
• **(530) 583-3152**

Once you get past the 1909 vintage canoe right inside the door, you'll find a potpourri of antique rustica at Tahoe City Antiques. Although the store features a little bit of every-

---

INSIDERS' TIP

Alpine Boutique, located in the Bavarian World Restaurant, features a wide selection of Bavarian hats, children's clothes and dresses. Bavarian World also has a German deli noted for its sauerbraten and a bakery that specializes in German breads and rolls. While you are there, catch a performance of Helmut Gebhard, who yodels Alpine tunes as well as country and western favorites. See our Restaurants chapter for more information.

thing, the focus is on Old Tahoe. If you're decorating a vacation hideaway, the furnishings found here will help you bring the ambiance of Lake Tahoe into your home.

Books

Alpine Bookstore
600 N. Lake Blvd., Tahoe City, Calif.
• **(530) 581-4136**

It's quaint, it's intimate and you're sure to feel comfortable browsing the shelves at Alpine Bookstore while sipping a fragrant cup of espresso. You'll find an eclectic mix of new, used and rare books on the shelves at this independently owned bookstore, along with a good assortment of Tahoe guides and history books. The shop is the oldest bookstore in the North Shore Lake Tahoe area and the only one that carries used books. If you can't find what you want in stock they'll order it for you, including out-of-print and hard-to-find editions. The service here is hometown friendly and very personalized.

Bookshelf At The Boatworks
760 N. Lake Blvd., Tahoe City, Calif.
• **(530) 581-1900**

The Bookshelf At The Boatworks has something for everyone, including a children's section. If you want information about local history or the great Tahoe outdoors, you'll find a good collection of books on the Lake Tahoe region right up front.

Northern Light
930 Tahoe Blvd., Incline Village, Nev.
• **(775) 831-7283**

With the soothing sound of New Age music and the sweet scent of incense in the air, shopping at Northern Light is a pleasant interlude in anyone's day. The store sells gifts for the mind, body and spirit, which include books, audiotapes, crystals and candles. Book titles

are provocative, to say the least: *Angel Therapy*, *Arthritis Cure Cookbook*, and *The Journey of Your Soul* are seen on the shelves.

Village Hallmark & Books
930 Tahoe Blvd., Incline Village, Nev.
• **(775) 831-3301**

You can buy cards and logo gifts in addition to books at the Village Hallmark & Books store. Although it doesn't pretend to be a megabookstore, you can find plenty of reading material from their selection of best sellers and Lake Tahoe books.

Consignment

Lady Margaret's Tea Room & Treasures
774 Mays Blvd., Incline Village, Nev.
• **(775) 831-831-2544**

It's oh so British and oh so delightful. Come in for high tea, served on fine china in a Victorian atmosphere, and then shop for one-of-a-kind upscale clothing and jewelry. In the Village Center, the store is a little tricky to find: take Village Boulevard south from Tahoe Boulevard and turn west on Southwood Boulevard and then west on Mays Boulevard.

Gifts and Souvenirs

Cabin Fever
551 N. Lake Blvd., Tahoe City, Calif.
• **(530) 583-8143**

It's easy to get into a Tahoe mood with the lovely display of mountain and wildlife accessories, gifts and home furnishings at Cabin Fever. From the stylish log furniture to the stuffed animals, the merchandise is warm and homey. You can completely decorate your home or just buy gifts for friends in this eclectic shop. There's also an art gallery with wonderful outdoor art.

INSIDERS' TIP

Amazon.com, the Internet bookseller, ships merchandise from a huge warehouse in Fernley, Nevada, about 30 miles east of the Reno/Sparks area.

Gundy of Scandinavia
475 N. Lake Blvd., Tahoe City, Calif.
- **(530) 583-4633**

Festive is the name of the game at Gundy of Scandinavia where it's Christmas every day. How can you resist buying with all the wonderful sights, smells and sounds of the holidays enveloping you? Just indulge and select from quaint ornaments and collectible gifts imported from Scandinavian countries. After all, Christmas comes but once a year — except at Gundy.

The Tahoe Store Emporium
868 Tahoe Blvd., Incline Village, Nev.
- **(775-832-5332**

Leanin' Tree greeting cards, Beanie Babies and Tahoe T-shirts are just a few of the items you'll find in The Tahoe Store Emporium. You can also shop for candles, games and toys. You'll find this shop when you're browsing the Christmas Tree Village.

Kidstuff

Puddin 'N Pie
868 Tahoe Blvd., Incline Village, Nev.
- **(775) 831-5010**

In sizes from infant to 14, the clothing at Puddin 'N Pie covers the gamut. You can buy everything from durable playclothes to formal outfits. Brands include Healthtex, Baby's Own and Sarah Louise. The store also has a gift section with toys, jewelry and baby mementos. It's located in the Christmas Tree Village shopping center, right next to Joanna's Boutique for Women.

Ruffles & Ruffnecks
475 N. Lake Blvd., Tahoe City, Calif.
- **(530) 583-1128**

As the name implies, you can buy everything from lacy dresses for little girls to tough jeans for little boys at Ruffles & Ruffnecks. The shop boasts the largest selection of children's clothing in the North Shore Lake Tahoe area, with medium to upscale fashions in such brands as Cash Cash, Eagle's Eye, Fresh Produce and Guess. You'll also find books, toys,

accessories and Beanie Babies. The store is easy to find in the Cobblestone Mall.

Pawn Shops

Great Basin Pawnbrokers
797 Southwood Blvd., Ste. 4, Incline Village, Nev. • (775) 833-1001

You can shop in a comfortable, relaxed atmosphere at Great Basin Pawnbrokers. Specializing in jewelry, the store has a great selection of diamonds, colored stones and fine watches. There's something in every price range, from $5 to $5,000. If you can't find that extra special piece of jewelry in stock, the store will special order it for you. You can also check out their selection of cameras, electronics, musical instruments and tools. All merchandise is fully guaranteed. The store has a second location at 22 Nev. Highway 28 in Crystal Bay, Nevada, (775) 831-8383.

Sporting Gear

Alpenglow Sports
415 N. Lake Blvd., Tahoe City, Calif.
- **(530) 583-6917**

If you're looking for specialists in all types of mountaineering, head into Alpenglow Sports. They've been in the business since 1979 and can meet your needs for rock climbing, trail riding and all forms of Nordic skiing. You can buy clothing and equipment in such brands as Patagonia, North Face and Black Diamond. The store also features a full-service rental shop.

Olympic Bike Shop
620 N. Lake Blvd., Tahoe City, Calif.
- **(530) 581-2500**

According to local cyclists, Olympic Bike Shop is the number one bike shop in the area. You'll find the area's largest selection of accessories, parts and clothing along with their top-of-the line bikes. Bike brands include Canonndale, KHS, Specialized and Trek. You can also pick up maps and guide books of the area to make your biking outings hassle-free.

Specializing just in biking, the store is open from the first of May until the end of October.

Porter's Ski & Sport
885 Tahoe Blvd., Incline Village, Nev.
• **(775) 831-3500**

Porter's Ski & Sport has been a mainstay sportswear shop in the area since 1964. The store sells alpine skis, snowboards and snowshoes in winter and water-skis and tennis equipment in the summer. You'll find one of the best selections of sportswear in the area, with great clothing for the entire family from Columbia, Nordica and North Face. You can also rent bikes from the store during the summer. The company also has locations in Tahoe City at 501 N. Lake Boulevard, (530) 583-2314 and 100 N. Lake Boulevard, (530) 583-0293. The last store is a discount outlet located right next to Fanny Bridge.

The Back Country
255 N. Lake Blvd., Tahoe City, Calif.
• **(530) 581-5861**

As the name indicates, The Back Country specializes in all your needs for venturing off the beaten path. Avid skiers and bikers themselves, the super-friendly staff is very knowledgeable about the surrounding mountain environment. When you buy or rent equipment here you can select from the very best and latest merchandise. Brands include Dynafit, Garmont, K2 and Rossignol. Their full-service bike shop is open all year.

Village Ski Loft
800 Tahoe Blvd., Incline Village, Nev.
• **(775) 831-3537**

Voted the number one ski shop in the West by readers of *Snow Country* magazine, the Village Ski Loft can meet all of your family's needs for a great winter in the great outdoors. The shop features a huge inventory of equipment to buy or rent, including all major brands. And even if you're skiing/snowboarding skills aren't up to par, you'll look great in the snazzy clothing featured here. During the summer months the store converts to a mountain bike shop.

You'll find a second location of Village Ski Loft at Diamond Peak Ski Resort during the winter.

Village Sports
550 N. Lake Blvd., Tahoe City, Calif.
• **(530) 583-3722**

Village Sports specializes in clothing and footwear for all sporting activities. Look for high-fashion ski outfits in the winter and top-quality swimming and running gear in the summer. The shop also sells alpine ski equipment and snowshoes.

Women's Clothing

Camila's At Tahoe
760 N. Lake Blvd., Tahoe City, Calif.
• **(530) 583-0120**

From casual to cocktail, Camila's At Tahoe can find just the right clothing for any occasion. Brands include Access, Portrait, Le Chic and Telluride. With a complete line of scarves, shoes, belts and handbags to choose from, you can select the perfect accessories for your new outfits. The store is located on the lower level of the Boatworks Mall.

Incline Outfitters
930 Tahoe Blvd., Incline Village, Nev.
• **(775) 831-0432**

Tilley hats, Pendleton shirts and high-quality Tahoe logo apparel adorn the racks of Incline Outfitters. It's the Tahoe look personified — casual, comfortable and stylish. You can shop for the whole family here. Look for this store in the Raley's Incline Center.

Joanna's Boutique for Women
868 Tahoe Blvd., Incline Village, Nev.
• **(775) 831-5010**

With brands like Carole Little, Platinum, Tour de Femme and Jordache, Joanna's Boutique for Women covers the spectrum in clothing. You can shop for a day on the golf course or a night on the town. The shop also carries children's clothing. It's conveniently located in Christmas Tree Village.

INSIDERS' TIP

Don't overlook the possibility of finding treasures at the local pawn shops.

Jeunesse Better Clothing
930 Tahoe Blvd., Incline Village, Nev.
• (775) 831-5600

If you're looking for flashy jeans outfits, glittering with rhinestones, you've come to the right place. Jeunesse Better Clothing will sell you a natty Nevada-style cowboy hat along with better sportswear and dress-up apparel. It's medium-priced so you don't have to break the bank to shop here. The shop is easy to find in the Raley's Incline Center.

TJ's of Tahoe
898 Tanager St., Incline Village, Nev.
• (775) 832-0555

Featuring only clothing made in America, TJ's of Tahoe is a delightful boutique. You'll love the latest fashions from Christine Damen, Fezz, Painted Pony and Sareet. For the total look, the store also carries a complete line of accessories such as belts, hats and shoes. Be sure to browse the gift section where you'll find everything from decorative paperweights to colorful woven throws.

South Shore Lake Tahoe

Malls and Shopping Centers

Crescent V Fashion Center
U.S. Hwy. 50 at Park Ave., South Lake Tahoe, Calif. • (530) 955-1454

The largest mall in South Shore Lake Tahoe, Crescent V Fashion Center has an eclectic mix of shops, including Tee-Shirt Shop, Wonderland Kids, Emerald Bay Trading Company, Alpine Clothing, Side Street Boutique and 1000 Bathing Suits. You can also see first-run movies at the Stateline Cinema and catch a bite at Monk's Pizza, Sizzler or the Water Wheel South Restaurant.

Factory Stores at the "Y"
U.S. Hwy. 50 and Calif. Hwy. 89, South Lake Tahoe, Calif.

Shop for bargains galore at the Factory Stores at the "Y." Outlets include Bass Shoe Factory, Big Dog Sportswear, Home Again, Oneida Factory Store, Sunglass Hut International and Van Heusen Factory Store. As the name tells you, the mall is at the "Y," smack in the middle of the busiest shopping area in the South Shore Lake Tahoe area. You can easily use the outlet as a jumping off point to other nearby stores.

Ski Run Marina Village
970 Ski Run Blvd., South Lake Tahoe, Calif. • (530) 544-9500

You can experience the beauty of Lake Tahoe while you roam the shops at Ski Run Marina Village. Quaint and picturesque, the stores front the lake, affording fabulous views of the water and the mountains beyond. We recommend a leisurely stroll through Cabin Fever, L J's Jewelry, Something Different, Sunglass Time, Village Wear and Weyland Galleries. You can also enjoy dining with a view at Riva Grill on the Lake or the Marina Village Cafe.

Antiques

Auntie Q's Antiques & Treasures
800 Emerald Bay Rd., South Lake Tahoe, Calif. • (530) 542-2169

With four rooms and 2,000 square feet of display space, you'll find everything from furniture to collectibles to jewelry at Auntie Q's. You can buy, sell, trade and browse to your heart's content.

Hanifan's Arts & Antiques
855 Emerald Bay Rd., South Lake Tahoe, Calif. • (530) 542-4663

A must-stop if you're looking for antiques, Hanifan's Arts & Antiques is really three stores in one. We direct you to the address above, but once there be sure to check out the second location at 868 Emerald Bay Road and the third, Michael's Antique Mall, at 854 Emerald Bay Road. Overflowing with collectibles from Europe as well as America, these three shops have the largest selection of antique merchandise in the Tahoe area. You'll find such goodies as Northern European pine furniture, American Victorian oak, Egyptian copper pots and French carved armoires. Local delivery is free and they ship around the world.

Patricia's Fine Gifts & Antiques
U.S. Hwy. 50 and Elks Point Rd., Zephyr Cove, Nev. • (775) 586-1001

From the elegantly simple to the simply elegant, Patricia's Fine Gifts & Antiques is a class act that attracts discriminating buyers. The upscale merchandise includes Haviland and Bristol china, Baccarat and Waterford crystal and Cranberry and Depression glass. The store also carries antique desks, lamps, chairs and specialty items. You'll find the store in the Round Hill Square shopping center.

Books

Mountain Song
2540 Lake Tahoe Blvd., South Lake Tahoe, Calif. • (530) 544-2244

Mountain Song is a gathering place for spirit, mind and body, offering a variety of merchandise along with classes and workshops. You can choose from a mind-expanding assortment of books, gifts, jewelry, CDs and tapes. Escape the hustle and bustle of everyday life, and enjoy a quiet interlude in this spiritual oasis.

Neighbors Bookstore
Caesars Tahoe, Stateline, Nev. • (775) 588-4559

It may be small, but it's a serious little bookstore. The shelves at Neighbors Bookstore are packed with books on all major subjects. You're sure to find just the right book to settle into on your Tahoe vacation. Or how about a book on tape that you can tuck in your beach bag?

Sierra Book & Gift Shop
1072 Emerald Bay Rd., South Lake Tahoe, Calif. • (530) 541-6464

The oldest bookstore in the South Shore Lake Tahoe area, Sierra Book & Gift Shop surprises and delights customers with the wide selection of books it carries. Although minus all the accouterments of the megabookstores, you'll appreciate the personal service and ambiance of a good old-fashioned bookstore. If you simply must browse with your cup of espresso in hand, you can stop at Starbucks, just two doors away.

Casino Shopping

Caesars Tahoe
55 U.S. Hwy. 50, Stateline, Nev. • (775) 588-3515

If you're staying at Caesars and get snowed in, don't worry about shopping opportunities: the galleria of shops will do its part to help you weather the storm. Grab your purse or wallet and head to such shops as Caesars Exclusively for signature clothing, Hot Cha Cha for the latest in women's fashions, Sierra Galleries for fine art and The Sport Shop for your ski and beach needs.

Harrah's Lake Tahoe
U.S. Hwy. 50, Stateline, Nev. • (775) 588-6611

Harrah's Galleria offers a tantalizing array of art work, souvenirs and specialty items. You can buy Harrah's logo merchandise in Extended Play, fine art at Addi Gallery, sports memorabilia in Gallery of Legends (see our description in The Arts chapter), Warner Brothers products at Warner Bros. Studio Store and biker goodies in Harley-Davidson. If you're a member of HOG (Harley Owners Group) be sure to show your membership card: the store has a special section just for you. When you need a break from browsing, stop at Club Cappuccino for your favorite coffee beverage.

Harveys Resort Hotel/Casino
U.S. Hwy. 50, Stateline, Nev. • (775) 588-2411

At Harvey's Resort Hotel/Casino you can have fun buying gifts and souvenirs at the Hard Rock Cafe, Harvey's Gifts and Harvey's Flower Shop. For sporting goods and apparel be sure to stop at Heavenly Sports.

Consignment

Connie's Clothesline
2660 Lake Tahoe Blvd., South Lake Tahoe, Calif. • (530) 544-3001

Called "Tahoe's best kept secret," Connie's Clothesline is a treasure house of upscale fashions for both women and men. You can be assured of good quality when you buy here:

only top-quality items make it to the racks. Sizes range from extra small to full-figured and run the gamut of brands.

Gifts and Souvenirs

Buffalo Trading Post
4039 Lake Tahoe Blvd., South Lake Tahoe, Calif. • (530) 541-7676

You can buy everything from Acoma pottery to Zuni jewelry in the Buffalo Trading Post, the oldest trading post in California. Most of the lovely artifacts are made by American Indians, including masks, dolls and sand paintings.

The colorful merchandise spreads into two stores, offering one of the largest selections of gifts in the South Shore Lake Tahoe area. Don't miss the beauty displayed in this unique shop.

Oneida Factory Store
2016 Lake Tahoe Blvd., South Lake Tahoe, Calif. • (530) 541-0826

If it's made of silver, you can find it at the Oneida Factory Store. What's even better, you can buy it for 30 to 40 percent less than regular retail prices. You can find just the perfect wedding or baby gift from their large selection of silver and crystal merchandise. For that very special event you can have your gifts engraved. The Oneida shop is tucked in the Factory Stores at the "Y" shopping mall.

Paper and Gold
Caesars Tahoe, Stateline, Nev. • (775) 588-4438

Expect the unexpected at Paper and Gold because this shop is truly unique. The owners look at the whole world as a marketplace, buying distinctive crafts directly from the artisans themselves. You'll find a delicious collection of one-of-a-kind treasures that include such things as cameos from Italy, kimonos from Japan and Tibetan singing bowls from Nepal. You can also browse a lovely selection of art glass, jewelry, kaleidoscopes and wooden boxes. You know this store is something special when many customers travel from San Francisco just to do their Christmas shopping here. Paper and Gold is special. Don't miss it.

Sierra Book & Gift Shop
3445 Lake Tahoe Blvd., South Lake Tahoe, Calif. • (530) 541-4222

With a 6-foot ostrich in the front window, you can be sure that Sierra Book & Gift Shop is unique. The tantalizing mix of gifts, books, collectibles and women's fashions constitutes a mini-department store. If you're looking for stationery, you've come to the right place: the store boasts the largest selection in the South Shore Lake Tahoe area. Connecting to the store, Ternullo's Creamery & Cafe is handy for coffee or lunch. The shop's other location on Emerald Bay Road is mostly books (see our description earlier in this chapter).

Kidstuff

Kids Exchange
2520 Lake Tahoe Blvd., South Lake Tahoe, Calif. • (530) 541-7640

If you're on a budget (and who isn't?), you'll appreciate the reasonable prices at Kids Exchange. A full-service children's store, it carries a complete line of clothing for infants through teenagers. You can also shop for toys, books and videos. Moms-to-be will enjoy browsing the maternity section. Kids Exchange has a second location at Calif. Highway 28 and Coon Street in Kings Beach, California (North Shore Lake Tahoe).

Wonderland
3996 Lake Tahoe Blvd., South Lake Tahoe, Calif. • (530) 542-2000

With upscale trendy merchandise filling the racks and shelves, it's fitting that the decor of Wonderland is special. The colorful textured walls and faux-painted pillars form just the right backdrop for showcasing those oh so cute fashions from Baby Guess, Baby Lulu, San Francisco Blues, Quik Silver and Billabong. You can outfit your child from head to toe, and find matching father-son and mother-daughter outfits too.

The store offers everything from swimwear to skiwear to formalwear. You'll also find a full line of dancewear as well as dress-up clothes. Clothes-conscious kids can select with confidence in this store as it carries the latest, most popular clothing.

Pawn Shops

Oliver's Jewelry & Loan
Round Hill Sq., Ste. 206, Zephyr Cove, Nev. • (775) 588-8470

As jewelry brokers, Oliver's Jewelry & Loan boasts one of the largest inventories of jewelry in the South Shore Lake Tahoe area. You'll love their prices: diamonds are 10 percent above their wholesale cost and most other jewelry is 30 to 50 percent less than retail. The store is easy to find in the lovely new Round Hill Square shopping center.

Pacific Pawnbrokers
3980 Lake Tahoe Blvd., South Lake Tahoe, Calif. • (530) 542-6494

Within easy walking distance to South Shore casinos, Pacific Pawnbrokers is a full-service pawn shop. You can shop for such things as jewelry, electronics and musical instruments. If you're looking for used sporting equipment, give this store a try; it always has a great selection.

Sporting Gear

House of Ski
209 Kingsbury Gr., Stateline, Nev. • (775) 588-5935

House of Ski is a total ski shop, with retail sales, rentals and service. The very latest accessories, fashions and equipment are for sale, with package discounts offered on all equipment. You can also rent equipment and whatever clothing you might need. The shop is easy to find on Kingsbury Grade on the way to the Nevada side of Heavenly Ski Resort.

International Discount Golf & Winter Sports
2482 Lake Tahoe Blvd., South Lake Tahoe, Calif. • (530) 544-7888

It's easy to save money when you shop at International Discount Golf & Winter Sports. The store sells name brand sporting equipment at true discount prices. It pays to shop around when you're investing in skis or golf clubs so be sure to price the merchandise here before you buy. You can also save money on Lake Tahoe logo accessories.

Rainbow Mountain
1133 Ski Run Blvd., South Lake Tahoe, Calif. • (530) 541-7961

Voted the "Best Ski Shop" by the *Tahoe Tribune*, this full-service shop on the road to Heavenly Ski Resort can meet all of your skiing and snowboarding needs. You can buy new and used top-of-the-line equipment and apparel. If you're a sometime- or novice skier or snowboarder, not to worry since you can rent any clothing you might need along with equipment that will meet your skill level. The shop also offers a free van shuttle, but call ahead for the schedule.

Tahoe Bike Shop
2277 Lake Tahoe Blvd., South Lake Tahoe, Calif. • (530) 544-8060

Headquartered in a 90-year-old log cabin, Tahoe Bike Shop is South Shore Lake Tahoe's oldest bike shop. Focusing solely on biking, the store offers a complete line of BMX, cruiser, mountain and road bikes. If you're not in a position to buy, you can rent from their large selection of rental bikes. Ardent bikers themselves, the staff is friendly and personal. Don't be surprised if they take you out on a ride to show you the ropes.

Women's Clothing

Bugle Boy Factory Outlet
4008 Lake Tahoe Blvd., South Lake Tahoe, Calif. • (530) 542-2121

You can't go wrong shopping at Bugle Boy Factory Outlet: the casual unisex look is perfect for Lake Tahoe's laid-back lifestyle. The store stocks women's, men's and children's sizes along with a small selection of accessories. Men who forget to pack white shirts or dress slacks for formal events will be happy to know they can also find them here. Bugle Boy is conveniently located in the Crescent V Fashion Center.

Sidestreet Boutique
U.S. Hwy. 50 at Park Ave., South Lake Tahoe, Calif. • (530) 544-9071

Sidestreet Boutique is a breath of fresh air. Clothing is high-end and different from fashions found in most large stores. You can outfit yourself from casual to cocktail in such brands as Custo, Laundry and Solini. For the perfect head-to-toe look, the sales staff will help you select just the right accessories. For weddings, the shop also has a sales and rental department for bridal wear and tuxedos. To keep up your strength while browsing the lovely clothes, treat yourself to a freshly baked scone accompanied by your favorite coffee drink from the in-store cafe.

Pazazz
1004 Ski Run Blvd., South Lake Tahoe, Calif. • (530) 542-4457

Just one-half block from the lakeshore, Pazazz is conveniently located across the street from Embassy Suites Hotel. You can't beat their selection of clothing which appeals to all ages. Stop in for a great afternoon of trying on everything from classic career suits to smart sportswear to smashing cocktail ensembles. When your treasures are nicely bagged, we recommend dinner and drinks down the street at River Grill on the Lake as the sun sets over gorgeous Lake Tahoe.

You can reach for the stars at the Fleischmann Planetarium, journey back to the wild, wild West at the Ponderosa Ranch and take a walk down Main Street America circa 1930 at the National Automobile Museum.

Attractions

When the Nevada State Legislature legalized unlimited gaming in Nevada in 1931, the Reno/Tahoe area became a mecca for people hoping to strike it rich in the casinos. With nonstop entertainment 24 hours a day, the casinos are hard to beat as crowd-pleasing, main attractions. They range in size from the giants, like the tri-property Circus Circus–Silver Legacy Resort & Casino–Eldorado Hotel/Casino complex in downtown Reno, to the smaller, locally oriented establishments, such as the Rail City Casino in Sparks.

Some visitors literally never see the light of day during their entire visit to the area, as the dizzying array of casino amusements becomes their main focus. With the exception of the circus acts at the Midway Stage at Circus Circus and the automated mining machine and laser show at Silver Legacy, we explore the amenities of the casinos in the chapters on Hotels and Motels, Resorts and Casino Nightlife.

But for now let's venture outside and have a look at "the other Reno/Tahoe," a land rich in history, natural beauty and unlimited opportunities for recreation and personal enrichment. You can reach for the stars at the Fleischmann Planetarium, journey back to the wild, wild West at the Ponderosa Ranch and take a walk down Main Street America circa 1930 at the National Automobile Museum. You can pet a deer at the Sierra Safari Zoo, roll a customized bowling ball at the National Bowling Stadium and ride a paddle-wheeler across the pristine waters of Lake Tahoe. Or you can simply drink in the wonder and majesty of one of the most beautiful natural settings on earth.

With Lake Tahoe and the Sierra Nevada Mountains just outside, it might seem redundant to list other attractions. A view anywhere can be a breathtaking attraction in itself. Lake Tahoe has been called "America's Treasure" by politicians, travel writers and nature lovers. And the 72-mile drive along its shoreline has

been named "The Most Beautiful Drive in America." To get the most out of the drive, we suggest picking up a copy of the two-hour audiocassette *Drive Around the Lake* for $9.95 at the Tahoe–Douglas Visitor Center at 195 U.S. Highway 50 in Stateline, Nevada, or call them at (775) 588-4591. This center also has the most complete collection of information on the Lake Tahoe Basin.

You can also pick up information at the local Chambers of Commerce: 969 Tahoe Boulevard in Incline Village, (775) 831-4440; 245 N. Lake Boulevard in Tahoe City, (530) 581-6900; and 3066 Lake Tahoe Boulevard in South Lake Tahoe, (530) 541-5255. The Lake Tahoe Visitors Authority at 1156 Ski Run Boulevard, (530) 544-5050 and the Lake Tahoe Visitors Bureau at 2254 U.S. Highway 50 in South Lake Tahoe, (530) 544-7750, also have tourist information.

Lake Tahoe is the largest alpine lake in North America, and its crystal clear waters reflect an ever changing kaleidoscope of colors depending upon the weather at that particular moment. In this chapter we'll point out some of the must-see attractions in the Lake Tahoe Basin, other than the scenery. For a description of parks, beaches and recreational opportunities, see our Winter Sports, Golf, Parks, Camping and RVing, Fishing and Hunting, and Recreation chapters. And for the ultimate mind-blowing Tahoe experience, we wholeheartedly recommend any view of the lake at sunset, preferably with your favorite person and your favorite libation close at hand.

Reno

Animal Ark
1265 Deerlodge Rd., Reno, Nev.
• (775) 969-3111

Animal Ark is a wildlife sanctuary and nature center that shelters animals that don't have the skills to survive on their own. Disabled and orphaned animals such as gray wolves, bobcats, bears, snow leopards and Arctic foxes live in natural surroundings at the Ark. Aside from the animals, the educational displays scattered around the grounds make it an especially appealing learning experience for kids. (See also our Kidstuff chapter.)

Although most people can't own a wild animal as a pet, you can do the next thing by adopting one at the Ark. Through their adoption program, you can help pay for the care and feeding of such residents as Mignon, the kit fox, or Shere Khan, the tiger, or Whoopi, the peregrine falcon.

The Ark is open daily from 10 AM to 4:30 PM from April 1 to October 31. Admission is $6 for adults, $5 for seniors and $4 for children ages 3 through 12. It's a bit of a drive out of Reno, but well worth it. To get to the Ark take U.S. Highway 395 north to the Red Rock Road exit, turn north on Red Rock Road and drive 11.5 miles to Deerlodge, turn right and continue for 1 mile.

Circus Circus Midway Stage
500 N. Sierra St., Reno, Nev.
• (800) 648-5010

When Circus Circus Hotel/Casino opened in Reno in 1978, casino patrons were astonished to see trapeze artists and high-wire walkers performing right above their heads as they placed their table bets and pulled the handles of slot machines. The age of the total entertainment concept had been born, complete with an enormous clown as a logo and a pink-and-white-striped circus tent enveloping portions of the building.

Although structural changes during the years have made the circus acts less visible from the casino floor, they can be optimally viewed from the Midway section of the casino. Young and old alike are drawn to the carnival-style arcade at the Midway where they can win stuffed toy animals and other prizes at the more than 30 games available. The circus acts are free and can be seen daily throughout the year from 11 AM to midnight. See our Kidstuff chapter for more information.

Fleischmann Planetarium
1650 N. Virginia St., Reno, Nev.
• (775) 784-4812

Perched on a knoll overlooking the campus of the University of Nevada, Reno, Fleischmann Planetarium looks like a saucer-shaped spaceship that has just touched down. Its curious shape is actually a hyperbolic paraboloid canopy that covers the elliptical interior of the building.

Inside you can see such curiosities as all three meteorites ever found within Nevada, or find out what your real weight would be on the planet Venus, or see how a black hole acts in space. These and many other exhibits are on display in the Astronomical Museum. But for many visitors the real space experience takes place in the domed theater on the lower level where you can see spectacular films about nature and the universe. Lean back and relax in the reclining loge chairs while the show unfolds all around you on the Skydome 8/70 screen. For those wanting to view the real thing, however, the telescope of the public observatory is available on clear Friday nights throughout the year from 8:30 to 9:30 PM.

For unusual space treasures, the gift shop is full of educational games, scientific books and also Nevada's largest selection of telescopes, spotting scopes and binoculars. Admission to the museum, gift shop and observatory is free. Theater prices are $6 for persons ages 13 through 59 and $4 for children younger than 13 and persons 60 and older. The building is open Monday through Friday, except holidays, from 8 AM to 8 PM. As features and show times in the theater vary throughout the year, we suggest you call ahead for the listings and schedule. See our Kidstuff chapter for more information.

Mining Machine at Silver Legacy Resort Casino
407 N. Virginia St., Reno, Nev.
• (775) 329-4777, (800) 687-8733

Showcasing Nevada's silver mining heritage, the automated mining machine at Silver Legacy Resort Casino is a working model of how ore might have been processed in the

1800s. Towering 120 feet above the main casino floor, the machine is continuously in motion with pumping bellows, steam engines and running ore wagons. Designed so that human hands wouldn't touch the metal throughout the process, the finished product is coins spewing out near the Silver Baron's Bar and Lounge.

Although the resort created a fictitious tale of a miner named Sam Fairchild to explain the development of the machine, it doesn't have to be historically accurate to be appreciated. From an engineering standpoint alone, it's fascinating to see all the parts working together. But if mechanics don't interest you, stick around, as this is only part of the action. The machine is encompassed by the world's largest composite dome. The interior of the dome reflects the skies of Reno, showing an entire day from sunrise to sunset.

From noon til 11 PM daily, the dome is the backdrop for the *Legend of the Legacy Laser Show*, a spectacular, but also whimsical production of how the West was won, Reno-style. If you don't plan to be in the building for at least several hours, it's best to call ahead to get show times because the laser show alternates with a light show during the day. Admission is free and the best vantage point is around the railing on the mezzanine level.

Mount Rose Highway
Nev. Hwy. 431, from Reno to Incline Village, Nev.

For your first-time-ever view of Lake Tahoe, nothing beats the 25-mile drive up the Mount Rose Highway to Incline Village. In Reno take U.S. 395 south to the junction of Nev. Highway 431 (Mount Rose Highway) and follow the signs to North Shore Lake Tahoe.

Beginning at an elevation of 4,498 feet, the road gradually climbs for a few miles through the desert on the eastern side of the Sierra Nevada mountains. But at about 6,000 feet in elevation, the terrain changes dramatically from high desert to alpine forest. Huge

conifer and red fir trees dominate the landscape as the road begins to twist and turn toward the summit. As you climb higher, you are treated with magnificent views of Reno and Sparks to the north and Washoe Lake to the south. Near the summit is the Mount Rose–Ski Tahoe ski resort with a base elevation of 8,260 feet.

You are rewarded with your first glimpse of Lake Tahoe several miles farther as you pass the sign that reads, "Mt. Rose Summit, Elevation 8,900, Highest Year-Round Sierra Pass." Surrounded by snowcapped peaks, the size and beauty of the lake can take your breath away. As the road descends to lake level at 6,225 feet you'll drive through the Tahoe Meadows, an alpine paradise for hikers, skiers and snowmobilers. See our Winter Sports and Recreation chapters for details of activities here.

The season and weather will have a great deal to do with what you see on this drive. In spring and summer, expect a profusion of wildflowers, such as lupine, paintbrush and larkspur. In the fall you can count on an explosion of color from the aspen trees in several locations. And in the winter you may encounter heavy snowfall, with the road appearing to be nothing more than a trail winding through a tunnel of snow. If you are particularly afraid of heights and high mountain roads, however, this drive may not be for you. The road is narrow and dropoffs on the sides can be very steep.

Since driving in the mountains in winter can be hazardous, it is always wise to call ahead for road conditions. For the most updated information on Nevada roads call (775) 793-1313.

National Automobile Museum
10 Lake St., Reno, Nev. • (775) 333-9300

Nowhere is America's love affair with the automobile more celebrated than at the National Automobile Museum. Housing the most comprehensive public display of cars in the western hemisphere, the museum presents a singular history of the automobile and its role in American society.

Four authentic street scenes representing each quarter of the 20th century take visitors back in time to experience vignettes of American history. The real-life scenes are complete with the cars, architecture and memorabilia of the eras.

On Turn-of-the-Century Street you can see a realistic blacksmith's shop, illustrating the gradual change in transportation from horses to cars. On the 1930s Street you can watch Milton Berle and Ronald Reagan on a vintage television set.

Adjoining galleries contain the remainder of the more than 200 antique, vintage, classic and special interest cars in the collection. Of particular interest to many visitors are the cars previously owned by celebrities, such as Elvis Presley's 1973 Cadillac Eldorado Coupe, John Wayne's 1953 Corvette and James Dean's 1949 Mercury.

The cars in the museum were part of the original Harrah's Automobile Collection, owned by the late William F. Harrah, founder of Harrah's Hotels/Casinos. Following his death in 1978 and the subsequent purchase of the collection by Holiday Corporation, the William F. Harrah Foundation received a gift of 175 cars. The foundation is a public/private partnership that owns and manages the museum. (See our Resorts chapter for more information on Mr. Harrah's ventures.)

Before leaving the building, be sure to stop at the gift shop, where you can buy books and magazines on almost every type of car ever manufactured. And for a relaxing break, try lunch or a snack at Blue Skies Back-Door Cafe which adjoins the museum on the Truckee River (see Restaurants). The museum is open Monday through Saturday from 9:30 AM until 5:30 PM and Sunday from 10 AM until 4 PM. It's closed Thanksgiving and Christmas days. Admission rates are $7.50 for adults, $6.50 for seniors, $2.50 for children ages 6 through 18 and free for children 5 and younger when accompanied by an adult. (See also our Kidstuff chapter.)

On the Lake Street side of the building, be sure to get a look at one of the older Reno Arches with the famous slogan, "The Biggest Little City in the World." A more elaborate version of the arch is on N. Virginia Street and Commercial Row. (See our subsequent entry in this chapter, and the Close-up in our Area Overview chapter, for more about the Reno Arch.)

National Bowling Stadium
300 N. Center St., Reno, Nev.
• **(775) 334-2695**

Described by the American Bowling Congress as the "Taj Mahal of tenpins," the National Bowling Stadium is the world's largest bowling facility. Used primarily for ABC and other tournaments, this ultramodern stadium has 80 Brunswick lanes and state-of-the-art scoring equipment and acoustics.

Although only tournament participants are allowed to bowl here, nonbowlers can enjoy this multipurpose facility as well. You can watch all the tournament action from the plush seats in the spectator section. Or you can shop for clothes in the Pendleton Shop or try out a customized bowling ball in Lane 81 in the retail shopping area. You can satisfy your hunger pangs with an All-American burger in the Big City Stadium Diner and Lounge on the main floor. Or you can take in a movie in the domed giant screen theater.

Admission to the building is free, and free validated parking is available in the garage off the Fourth Street entrance. As tournament schedules vary, we suggest calling prior to your visit to verify dates and times. The building is open daily from 8 AM until 6 PM. Admission to the theater costs $6 for adults and $4 for seniors 60 and older and children 12 and younger. Daily showings are at 1, 2:30 and 4 PM. For specific show titles, call (775) 334-2634.

Nevada Historical Society
1650 N. Virginia St., Reno, Nev.
• **(775) 688-1190**

As Nevada's oldest museum, the Nevada Historical Society provides ongoing support and preservation for the state's fabulous heritage. In its newly renovated building near the Fleischmann Planetarium, you can take a walk on the historical side through fascinating displays of how such things as mining, gaming, ranching and various ethnic groups molded

Photo: K. Markgraf

The Sparks Museum features a large collection of memorabilia from the town's history, much of it railroad-oriented—as the nickname "Rail City" suggests.

the state's unique society. Of special interest is the million-dollar exhibit of rare baskets made by famous Washoe basketmaker, Dat-So-La-Lee (see our History chapter). New to the museum with the remodeling is a diarama of a typical general store, complete with all the goods stocking the shelves.

The research library at the museum is a historian's dream come true. Open to the public, it houses the largest collection of materials relating to the history of Nevada and the Great Basin. You can find long-lost relatives plus delve into the minutiae of the past in the library's books, newspaper files, maps and photographs.

The society also sponsors a provocative variety of ongoing educational events throughout the year, such as lectures, trips and gala exhibits. If you're looking for volunteer opportunities, it's a great place to investigate: volunteers are used in many areas, including the newly expanded gift shop. You can also support the museum by buying an annual membership for about $25.

The museum and gift shop are open Monday through Friday from 10 AM to 5 PM and the library is open Tuesday through Saturday from noon to 4 PM. Admission to the museum is $2 for adults. We recommend combining visits to the museum and the Fleischmann Planetarium since they're adjacent to each other (see our previous entry for details on the planetarium).

Reno Arch
N. Virginia St. and Commercial Row, Reno, Nev.

If you're on N. Virginia Street in downtown Reno, you simply can't miss the Reno Arch. Blazing with 800 feet of neon tubing and 1,600 lights, it welcomes visitors in grand style to "The Biggest Little City in the World." The slogan was the result of a 1929 contest conducted by the mayor to publicize the city.

The slogan stuck and the Arch has been the identifying landmark for Reno ever since.

(You'll find a Close-up on it in the Area Overview chapter.) It has been redesigned and replaced several times; the present structure was erected in 1987. An older arch constructed mainly of steel and lit with neon is at 10 Lake Street next to the National Automobile Museum.

Reno Tahoe Gaming Academy
215 S. Wells Ave., Reno, Nev.
• (775) 329-5665

Do you want to play craps, 21, roulette or poker, but don't have a clue how to place a bet or what the rules of the games are? For a mere $10 and two hours of your time, you can learn the basics behind the scenes where dealers are trained. At the Reno Tahoe Gaming Academy, student trainees practice newly acquired skills in game settings (putting just chips, not money, on the line).

Under the supervision of the training director, visitors can learn to play in a comfortable, risk-free environment. Then, armed with the strategies of the games, you can hit the casino tables with more than just your pocketbook and a desire to win. Visitors are welcome after 1 PM Monday through Thursday throughout the year, but are requested to call ahead for reservations. The cost is $10 for two hours of instruction.

Sierra Safari Zoo
10200 N. Virginia St., Reno, Nev.
• (775) 677-1101

Animal lovers say they have died and gone to animal heaven when visiting this zoo nestled at the base of Peavine Mountain. It offers a rare "up-close and personal" opportunity to interact with more than 200 exotic animals. Distinct from the glitzy, big city zoos of concrete cages and prolific souvenir stands, this zoo is just about animals in a natural setting.

Free to roam behind security fences, most of the animals have been born and handraised in captivity. Many are exceptionally gentle and

---

INSIDERS' TIP

Nevada ranks fourth in the nation as a summer vacation destination, according to a survey of travelers by the Travel Industry Association.

Photo: Roger Brotherton

The Truckee River flows through Reno and the Truckee River Walk is a great place for visitors and residents to enjoy the city.

tolerant to human touch. Visitors can view 40 different species from around the world, including muntjacks (deer from India), rheas (flightless birds from Argentina), audads (sheep from the Middle East) and servals (cats from the African savannas).

Children especially enjoy the petting section of the zoo, where they can wander among the animals to pet and feed them. The signature animal is Hobbs, a 1,100-pound liger. A cross between a lion and a tiger, ligers are unusual because they are born only in captivity and only 40 of them exist anywhere in the world.

Dedicated to the propagation and preservation of animals, the zoo is nonprofit and staffed almost entirely by volunteers. Zoo workers have named all the animals, such as Elvira, the North American alligator who is affectionately known as "the lizard with an attitude," and Crystal and Snickers, the Burmese pythons on display only in the summer months.

To reach the zoo, take the Red Rock Road Exit off U.S. 395 about 8 miles north of Reno. Turn left and go underneath the underpass to the second road and then turn left again. Don't be put off by the seemingly unpretentious appearance of the zoo. It's well worth the visit. Admission is $7 for adults, $5 for children ages 3 through 12 and free to children 2 and younger. The zoo is open daily April through October from 10 AM until 5 PM. If the weather is questionable, you might want to call ahead. (See also our Kidstuff chapter for more information.)

The Wilbur May Center
1502 Washington St., Reno, Nev.
• **(775) 785-5961**

The Wilbur May Center in Rancho San Rafael Park has something for everyone. It's a museum, an arboretum and an adventure park. The son of David May, founder of the May Department Stores Company, Wilbur D. May lived in Reno from 1936 until his death in 1982. A philanthropist dedicated to the welfare of children, Wilbur D. May's legacy lives on through the foundation that built and maintains the center.

Designed as a comfortable ranch-style home, the Wilbur D. May Museum showcases May's eclectic collection of memorabilia gathered from his more than 40 trips around the world. An avid art and antique collector, May acquired such treasures as rare T'ang Dynasty pottery, primitive African artwork and Egyptian scarabs. His life as a rancher is chronicled in the tack room with its elaborate array of western artifacts. And his years as a big game hunter are reflected in the trophy room with dozens of animals from all over the world. Although the contents are professionally displayed and documented, the museum has the ambiance of a home rather than a public building. Visitors almost feel as if May himself had invited them over for a private showing of his residence.

The Wilbur D. May Arboretum and Botanical Garden contains pools, waterfalls and a xeriscape garden of plants indigenous to the high desert climate. And designed especially for children ages 2 through 12, the Wilbur D. May Great Basin Adventure has a petting zoo, pony rides and a log flume ride.

Admission to the museum is $2.50 for adults, $1.50 for seniors and children ages 3 through 12 and free to children younger than 3. Hours are 10 AM until 5 PM Tuesday through Sunday during the summer and Wednesday through Sunday during the winter. The adventure park is open from 10 AM until 5 PM daily, except Monday, from Memorial Day through Labor Day. Admission costs $3 for adults and $2 for children ages 3 though 12. Children younger than 3 are admitted free. There is no charge to view the botanical garden. (See also our Kidstuff chapter.)

Truckee River Walk
Arlington and Island aves., Reno, Nev.

On its route from Lake Tahoe to Pyramid Lake, the Truckee River flows through Reno, bringing much-needed water to the desert environment. The river provides a fertile habitat for a wide variety of wildlife as well as a delightful place for residents and visitors to enjoy the outdoors.

One of the easiest ways to enjoy the river is to take the Truckee River Walk in either direction from Wingfield Park on Arlington and Island avenues. Heading west, the walk meanders past old Victorian homes shaded by huge elms and cottonwoods and then enters Idlewild Park with its rose garden, children's playland and ponds full of waterfowl. From here it continues on for several miles past Oxbow Park to Chrissie Caughlin Park on W. McCarran Boulevard.

Going east through the business section of downtown, the path wanders through a variety of other small parks to finally end near Vista Boulevard east of Sparks. The distance from Chrissie Caughlin Park to Vista Boulevard is about 10 miles. As you walk along, keep your eyes peeled for the many birds that live here, such as flycatchers, mallards, belted kingfishers, hawks and Canada geese. And don't be surprised at the number of anglers trying their luck, as the Truckee is considered a premium fishing stream (see our Fishing and Hunting chapter).

Bikes and RollerBlades are welcome on the path, but motorized vehicles are not. Dogs need to be leashed, and owners are expected to clean up after them. See our Parks chapter for more details about Wingfield and Idlewild parks.

Sparks

Sparks Museum
820 Victorian Ave., Sparks, Nev.
• **(775) 355-1144**

In 1904 Sparks was the busiest railroad terminal between Ogden, Utah, and Sacramento, California. Its location near the base of the Sierra Nevada mountains was strategic for the large steam engines that pulled trains over the mountain passes to the valleys in California. Much of the city's early history is tied to the railroad, including its nickname, Rail City.

The Sparks Museum allows visitors to step back in time and experience those turn-of-the-century railroad days. Much of the memorabilia is railroad oriented, such as the model train collection that begins with the DeWitt Clinton and ends with the last of the steam-driven engines. Other displays include a barbershop with a collection of 200 razors and a full-sized Amish-type carriage, circa 1910. While the displays are not elaborate, history buffs will love the variety and attention to detail.

Hours are 11 AM until 4 PM Tuesday through Friday and 1 till 4 PM Saturday and Sunday. Although admission to the museum is free, donations are welcomed. (See also our Kidstuff chapter.)

Victorian Square
Victorian Ave., Sparks, Nev.

When the citizens of Sparks decided to revitalize their downtown area some years ago, they selected a colorful turn-of-the-century theme appropriate to the Rail City's history. The result was Victorian Square, a four-block area featuring a bandstand gazebo, Victorian-style storefronts and streetlights, park benches, a fountain and a 14-screen movie theater complex.

Also in keeping with the historical theme is the Glendale School at the east end of the square. Constructed in 1864 on a nearby ranch, it is the oldest remaining school building in Nevada. It was relocated to the square in 1993.

Victorian Square is the place to be for special events, such as the Best in the West Nugget Rib Cook-off, Hot August Nights and the Hometowne Christmas. See our Annual Events chapter for details on these. On Thursdays from June through September you can buy fresh produce and enjoy cooking demonstrations and musical events at the Hometowne Farmers Market. Hours for the market are 4 until 9 PM June through August and 4 until 8 PM in September.

To get to the square, take Interstate 80 east and exit on Rock Boulevard. Turn left on Rock and then right on Victorian Avenue.

Wild Island Family Adventure Park
250 Wild Island Ct., Sparks, Nev.
• (775) 359-2927

Wild Island Family Adventure Park has more than enough excitement to keep the family entertained all day long. With eight exciting water adventures, two miniature golf courses and a variety of racetracks in the Formula K

Raceway, it's hard to decide which adventure to tackle first. For more details, see the write-up in our Kidstuff chapter.

North Shore Lake Tahoe

Cablecar at Squaw Valley USA
Calif. Hwy. 89, 6 mi. north of Tahoe City, Calif. • (530) 583-6955, (800) 545-4350

Best known as the site of the 1960 Winter Olympics, Squaw Valley USA is one of America's premier year-round resorts. The Olympic flame still burns brightly as you make the turn into Olympic Valley, but other amenities of the games such as the ski jump and Olympic ice rink have been torn down.

Squaw Valley is a veritable paradise of recreation and activities, which we cover in more detail in the chapters on Resorts, Recreation, Golf and Winter Sports. But whatever your choice of activity, winter or summer, a ride in the tram from the Base Village to High Camp Bath & Tennis Club is a must. From a base elevation of 6,200 feet, the tram rises 2,000 feet to a world-class playground perched high above Lake Tahoe. The unobstructed views are simply awe-inspiring.

You can while away an entire day in this alpine Eden. Enjoy hiking, skiing, ice-skating, swimming, bungee jumping, playing tennis and mountain biking. In the winter it's crowded with skiers, but in the summer it can be a quiet getaway undiscovered by most. If just relaxing in the sun is what you want, you won't find a better place than the decks around the swimming lagoon and spa. And you won't go hungry, as the bars and restaurants at High Camp offer everything from casual fare to fine dining.

During ski season, the tram operates from 9 AM until 9 PM weekdays and from 8:30 AM until 9 PM weekends. Daily hours during the summer are 9:30 AM to 9 PM. Tram-only tickets cost $14 for adults, $12 for seniors 65 and older and $5 for children ages 12 and younger. Ride/skate and bike/swim tickets are $19 for adults and $10 for children ages 12 and younger. The tram is closed from late September until mid-October. In summer, we strongly suggest bringing along sunscreen and also a jacket

M.S. *Dixie II* cruises the waters of Lake Tahoe taking visitors on a guided tour of the lake and its exquisite surroundings.

because the temperature is much cooler here than in the valley. If the weather is questionable, call (530) 583-6985 to check the cablecar operation schedule. (See also our Kidstuff chapter.)

Fanny Bridge
**Junction of Calif. hwys. 89 and 28,
Tahoe City, Calif.**

Fanny Bridge spans the Truckee River where it empties from Lake Tahoe on its journey toward Pyramid Lake. Also at this site is the concrete dam with 17 gates used to raise or lower the level of the lake. While this in itself may not be particularly interesting to visitors, the number of enormous rainbow trout living in the waters around the bridge merit your attention.

Although catching fish is not permitted any-where near the bridge, it's perfectly legal to feed them. Almost any day of the year, groups of people can be seen leaning over the edge of the bridge (fannies sticking out) to feed the fish. The smell of cooking hamburgers typically permeates the air here because several restaurants overlook the bridge. During the summer's daylight hours, their outside dining areas are particularly inviting. (See also our Kidstuff chapter.)

Gatekeeper's Museum
**Junction of Calif. hwys. 89 and 28,
Tahoe City, Calif. • (530) 583 1762**

The gatekeeper of Lake Tahoe was entrusted with the responsibility of monitoring the level of the lake, using a hand-turned winch system to keep the water at prescribed levels. He lived in the gatekeeper's cabin on the south

INSIDERS' TIP

Be sure to stop at area visitor centers for maps and details about attractions and special events.

side of Fanny Bridge. The original cabin, built sometime between 1910 and 1916, was destroyed by fire in 1978. The present cabin was built in 1981 with funds raised by the North Lake Tahoe Historical Society.

Since 1986 the Federal Watermaster's Office in Reno has regulated the level of the lake. Today the gatekeeper's cabin is a museum showcasing Lake Tahoe's past through natural history displays, stories of pioneers and priceless artifacts. Of particular interest are exhibits showing the effects of growth and pollution on the Tahoe Basin.

Tucked away in a forest of ancient conifers, the handcarved, lodgepole pine structure is an exemplary specimen of Tahoe-style architecture. Its interior is cozy and warm, almost inviting you to curl up in front of the fire with a good historical novel. Be sure not to miss the Marion Steinbach Indian Basket Museum, a collection of more than 800 baskets from tribes all over the country, that is on display here.

The museum is open Wednesday through Sunday, May 1 through June 15 and from Labor Day until October 1, and it's open every day from June 16 through Labor Day. The hours are 11 AM until 5 PM. Although admission is free, donations are welcome.

Ponderosa Ranch
100 Ponderosa Ranch Rd., Incline Village, Nev. • (775) 831-0691
More than 500 million television viewers in 86 countries have relived the days of the wild, wild West through the television series *Bonanza*. Filmed at a time when the National Broadcasting Company (NBC) and the Radio Corporation of America (RCA) were eager to show off color television, the Ponderosa Ranch at Lake Tahoe was selected as the setting for the show because of its spectacular scenery.

The saga of the Cartwright family became the most popular TV series ever, producing some 430 episodes during its 13-year run. Since 1967, the ranch has been a popular tourist attraction, with about 40 of its 400 total acres open to visitors.

Step back in time to the post–Civil War era as you wander around the 12-acre downtown. It's authentic to the last detail, including the Silver Dollar Saloon advertising "meals 25 cts.," the Old Time Photo Shop specializing in "tin types" of yesteryear and the gallows reminding everyone that the bad guys don't always win. Of particular interest is the variety of horse-drawn vehicles casually parked everywhere, as if their owners were in town shopping for the day. Antiques abound in the stores and in the streets because the ranch owners are avid collectors.

The highlight of the ranch is the massive log structure used as the Cartwright family home, where many interior scenes for the series were filmed. Visitors will recognize the red-and-white-striped Victorian sofa in front of the massive stone fireplace, the ornate straight-backed chairs in the dining room and the Cartwrights' hats and jackets that are still hanging from a hat rack near the front door — preserved as they existed during the filming.

But the Ponderosa Ranch is all about family fun so there are plenty of activities to keep everyone busy. You can test your skill at the Moonshine Shootin' Gallery, make new friends at the Pettin' Farm, pan for gold at the Lucky Bonanza Mine and ride a horse at the Pony Rides. When it's time to eat, how about an enormous Hossburger for just $3? Or you can start the day with a haywagon breakfast of Ben's Scrambled Eggs, Hop Sing's Sausage, flapjacks and beverages.

The Ponderosa Ranch is affordable family fun: admission prices, including the haywagon breakfast, are just $11.50 for adults, $7.50 for children ages 5 through 11 and $2 for children 4 and younger. Subtract $2 if you'd rather not have the breakfast. (Yes, children ages 4 and younger would then be admitted free.)

The ranch is open 9:30 AM until 5 PM April through October, weather permitting. Breakfast haywagons depart twice daily, Memorial

---

INSIDERS' TIP

Be a weather watcher in the winter and call ahead for updated road conditions. For Nevada roads call (775) 793-1313, and for California roads call (530) 445-7623.

Day through Labor Day, at 8 and 9:30 AM. Since much of the activity at the ranch is outdoors, be sure to wear comfortable shoes and to bring along a jacket if the weather is questionable. (See also our Kidstuff chapter.)

Watson Cabin Living Museum
560 N. Lake Blvd., Tahoe City, Calif.
• **(530) 583-8717**

Built in 1909, the Watson Cabin Living Museum is the oldest building in Tahoe City. Listed in the National Register of Historic Homes, the cabin contains the first indoor private bathroom in Tahoe City, as well as antiques and collectibles from the turn of the century. The cabin is open daily June 15 through Labor Day from noon until 4 PM. Admission is free, but donations are welcome.

South Shore Lake Tahoe

Aerial Tram at Heavenly Ski Resort
Heavenly Ski Resort, end of Ski Run Blvd., South Lake Tahoe, Calif.
• **(800) 243-2836**

For a million-dollar view of Lake Tahoe, it's hard to beat the 1-mile ride on the tram at Heavenly Ski Resort. From this vantage point 2,000 feet above the level of the lake, the size and grandeur of the Lake Tahoe Basin is exquisite.

Once there you can simply relax on the deck or enjoy the view from inside the Monument Peak restaurant and bar. But during the summer, if you're more ambitious, you can take a modest hike along the ridge for a greater variety of views. As Insiders, we definitely recommend being there at sunset when the colors on the lake are their most spectacular. Since Heavenly is a world-class ski resort, we cover the winter amenities in our chapter on Winter Sports.

Tram-only tickets cost $12 for adults and $7.50 for children ages 6 through 12. Children younger than 6 ride free. A ride-and-dine package, which includes dinner in the Monument Peak restaurant, is available for $25.95 a person during the summer. During the summer season, the tram runs weekdays from 10 AM until 9 PM and weekends from 8:30 AM until 4 PM. The tram then runs weekdays from 8:30 AM

until 4 PM during ski season. The tram is closed following ski season until mid-May and from the third weekend in September to the opening of the next ski season. (See our Kidstuff chapter for more information.)

Emerald Bay and Vikingsholm Castle
Calif. Hwy. 89, 5 mi. from South Lake Tahoe, Calif. • **(530) 573-2600**

If there is a signature view of Lake Tahoe, Emerald Bay with tiny Fannette Island would be the No. 1 choice. This narrow arm on the southwestern shore of the lake is especially picturesque with its emerald green water surrounded by sheer granite cliffs. The scenery alone is worth the drive, but the real jewel of this spot is Vikingsholm Castle.

The castle is not accessible by car; it's a 1-mile walk from the Emerald Bay parking lot. Built by Mrs. Lora Knight in 1929 as her summer residence, the home is one of the finest examples of Scandinavian architecture in the western hemisphere. Because the site of the house reminded her of fjords in Norway, Mrs. Knight decided that the house should also be Scandinavian.

Constructed of granite and timber found at the lake, the 38-room mansion is a replica of an 11th-century Viking castle. Although in some ways the interior seems dark and cold, the building can be appreciated for its workmanship and attention to detail. Tours are usually available daily from mid-June through Labor Day from 10 AM until 4 PM, but call ahead to verify specific times and admission prices.

From Vikingsholm, the trail continues for about 2.5 miles along the shore of the bay to Emerald Point on the main body of the lake and from there another 4.5 miles to D.L. Bliss State Park.

Another popular hike from this area is the 1-mile walk to Eagle Lake. The trailhead begins across the road from the Emerald Bay parking lot in the Eagle Falls Picnic Area.

Since this is probably the most visited site at Lake Tahoe, parking in the summer is always difficult. We recommend getting there early in the morning to avoid the crowds. And this section of Calif. Highway 89 is often closed in winter because of heavy snowfall, so be sure to call prior to your visit.

Photo: K. Markgraf

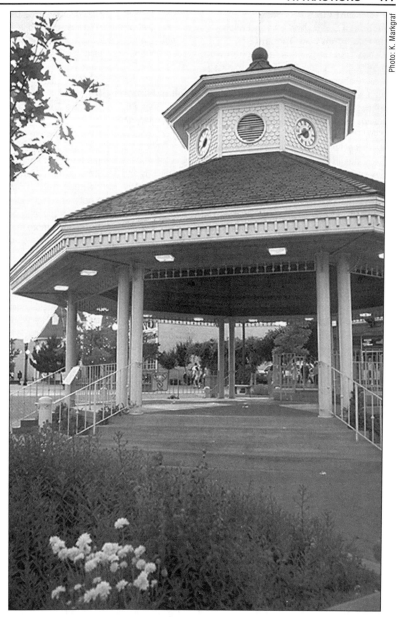

The residents and businesses of Victorian Square in Sparks created a turn-of-the century atmosphere with Victorian storefronts and a gazebo highlighting an entire area of shops, casinos and restaurants for visitors who enjoy the old-time appeal.

Fallen Leaf Lake
Junction of Calif. Hwy. 89 and Fallen Leaf Rd., South Lake Tahoe, Calif.

The second-largest natural lake in the Lake Tahoe Basin, Fallen Leaf was an appendage of Lake Tahoe many years ago. Three miles long, Fallen Leaf Lake is considered by many scientists to be a microcosm of Lake Tahoe. Because it is smaller, researchers are studying the effects of pollution on the lake as they believe the same effects will appear in a similar way later in the larger Lake Tahoe.

A variety of easy hikes begin from the Fallen Leaf Campground about a half-mile from Calif. 89. Other longer hikes begin from the parking lot just past the Fallen Leaf Marina at the end of the lake. The drive alone is worth the trip, though, because the lake is very scenic. Keep in the mind that the going is slow — the road is one-way with few turnouts.

To reach the lake, take Calif. 89 northwest at its junction with U.S. Highway 50 in South Lake Tahoe (the "Y"). Look for Fallen Leaf Road about 3 miles on, turn left and follow it to the lake. Fallen Leaf Lake is frequently not accessible during winter months because of heavy snowfall.

Hornblower's Tahoe Queen
Marina Village, at the foot of Ski Run Blvd., South Lake Tahoe, Calif.
• **(800) 238-2463**

Seeing Lake Tahoe from the deck of an authentic paddle wheeler is an unforgettable experience. *Hornblower's Tahoe Queen* sails from its pier in South Lake Tahoe across the lake and into Emerald Bay daily throughout the year. The cruises last from two to three hours and are available with options that include meals, drinks and dancing.

Departures are from 10:30 AM to 7 PM. The 2 PM trips on Monday and Tuesday are gaming cruises with personnel onboard to teach the rules and strategies of 21, craps, roulette and poker. Prices for the cruise only are typically $16 for adults and $8 for children ages 4 through 12 (see our Kidstuff chapter for more details). Dinner/dance cruises cost about $40 for adults and $28 for children. Since other cruise options are available, we suggest you call for specific prices and times.

Tallac Historic Site
Calif. Hwy. 89, South Lake Tahoe, Calif.
• **(530) 541-5227**

Following the discovery of silver in Nevada, Lake Tahoe became a popular summer retreat for wealthy people from San Francisco, Virginia City and Sacramento. In 1880, Elias J. "Lucky" Baldwin built an opulent resort including a casino and two hotels on this site. For more than 30 years it was *the* place to be at Tahoe. But as the area became more accessible through the use of automobiles, those who could afford it were building their own lavish estates all around the lake.

The Tallac Resort was torn down in 1916, but the foundation is still visible. Visitors to the Tallac Historic Site can see several examples of luxurious old private estates. The Baldwin estate, built in 1921 of handhewn logs, is now the Tallac Museum. The museum is free and is open weekends from 11 AM until 3 PM from Memorial Day weekend to mid-June. The rest of the summer season through Labor Day weekend it is open Wednesday through Sunday from 10 AM until 4 PM. September schedules tend to vary according to available personnel, so call ahead for hours and days of operation.

The Pope Estate, the largest and most luxurious at the site, was constructed in 1894 and has art exhibits and a living history program. The outbuildings have viewing screens which allow visitors to see the opulence of the interior furnishings. The Heller Estate, also known as Valhalla, is a community events center where concerts, art shows and special events are held during the summer.

Aside from offering a peek into Tahoe's past, Tallac Historic Site is a lovely place to enjoy a beautiful, white sand beach bordered

---

INSIDERS' TIP

October is one of the best months to visit the Reno/Tahoe area as the crowds are gone, the scenery is spectacular and reduced rates are sometimes available.

by large pine trees more than 400 years old. Taylor Creek Visitor Center is just a stone's throw away on the Tallac Historic Site Trail.

To reach the site take Calif. 89 northwest for 3 miles past its junction with U.S. 50 in South Lake Tahoe (the "Y"). Parking is available at either the Tallac Historic Site or the Taylor Creek Visitor Center.

Taylor Creek Visitor Center
Calif. Hwy. 89, South Lake Tahoe, Calif.
• (530) 573-2674

Adjoining the Tallac Historic Site, the area around Taylor Creek Visitor Center gives the visitor ample opportunities to experience the Taylor Creek ecosystem and to understand its relationship to Lake Tahoe. With Mt. Tallac rising 9,735 feet in the background, you can wander the paths through this meadow to view the native flora and fauna.

In spring and summer tiny wildflowers spring up everywhere, and in the fall much of the vegetation turns crimson and gold. Flowing from Fallen Leaf Lake to Lake Tahoe, Taylor Creek is a premier spawning ground for kokanee salmon in October. The creek becomes a ribbon of red during the spawn as the fish leave Lake Tahoe to mate and die upstream. Taylor Creek is one of the few places outside Alaska where the salmon spawn can be seen so easily. Visitors can study a diverted section of Taylor Creek through aquarium-like windows at the Lake Tahoe Stream Profile Chamber in the visitor center.

Be sure to pick up brochures and trail maps inside the building; they'll direct you to special events and other hikes in the area. The center is open from Memorial Day weekend until June 20 from 8 AM to 4:30 PM Wednesday through Sunday. From June 20 to the end of September it is open from 8 AM to 5:30 PM and weekends only from 8 AM to 4:30 PM in October. Admission to the stream profile is free. (See also our Kidstuff chapter.)

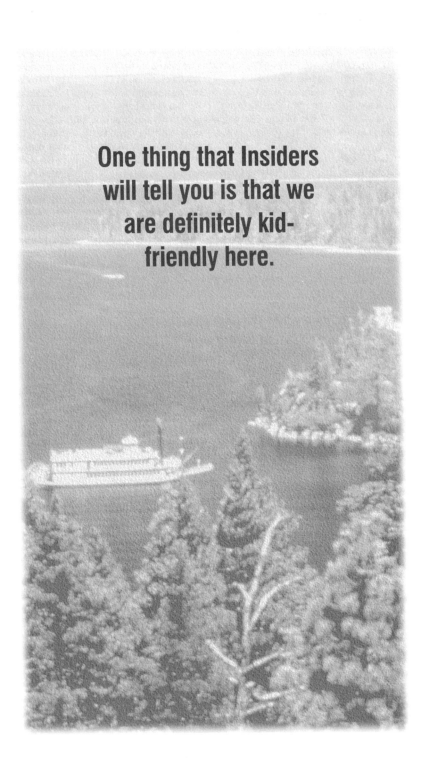

One thing that Insiders
will tell you is that we
are definitely kid-
friendly here.

Kidstuff

Even though the Reno/Tahoe area is normally thought of as an adult's playground because of our many casinos, you'll find plenty of things to do here as a family. One thing that Insiders will tell you is that we are definitely kid-friendly here.

So what do we have to offer? A lot of activities, both indoor and outdoor, to keep you and your kids entertained.

You'll notice that most of the activities we recommend are outside — that's because we are renowned for our beautiful outdoors and we feel it is imperative that you get a taste of the many things to do with your kids away from your hotel or motel rooms. Some of our suggestions keep you inside, though, and some even include things to do in and around the casinos.

On the subject of kids and casinos, heed these words of warning: when traveling through the casinos with your children, don't dilly dally. Kids are allowed to walk through casinos as long as they don't linger, especially near the slot machines or the table games. Also, parents are not allowed to make bets with their children in tow. The best way to traverse the gambling establishments is with your little ones firmly in hand. The hustle and bustle and the bright lights of the casino floor will mesmerize most kids, causing even the least interested to stop and stare.

To help you locate the activities that best fit your interests, we have arranged this chapter by category of things to do and then have further divided the activities by our four geographical areas (Reno, Sparks, North Shore Lake Tahoe, South Shore Lake Tahoe). For other things to do as a family, check out our Recreation, Spectator Sports and Annual Events and Daytrips chapters.

Amusement Parks and Rides

Reno

Boomtown Family Fun Center
I-80 W. and Garson Rd., Reno, Nev.
• **(775) 345-6000, (800) 648-3790**

Boomtown Hotel Casino Reno has one of the best fun centers in Reno. The center is jammed with about 200 video and arcade games where kids can win tickets and turn them in for prizes. It also has a 9-hole miniature golf course, a merry-go-round, an indoor Ferris wheel, a vertical bouncing Rodeo Rider and the only Iwerks 3D Motion Theater in town. The theater has hydraulically activated seats that react with the movie on the screen and special polarized 3D glasses. The center is open every day from 10 AM to 10 PM. The games range from 25¢ to $1.50 and the Motion Theater is usually $4 for a 3D motion movie and $3 for a regular motion ride. All-day unlimited wristbands for the Fun Center are $13.

Circus Circus Hotel/Casino–Reno
500 N. Sierra St., Reno, Nev.
• **(775) 329-0711, (800) 648-5010**

Kids love this casino because it has a circus and a carnival on the second floor — a circus complete with clowns, trapeze artists and tight rope walkers. It also has a large area that houses most carnival games, plus its fair share of video and arcade games. Most of the games cost about $1 to play and most offer standard carnival prizes like stuffed animals; some give out tickets redeemable for prizes.

The circus acts take place every half-hour, starting at 11 AM and continuing until closing. It's open from 10 AM to midnight during the week and 10 AM to 1 AM on the weekends.

The Ultimate Rush Thrill Ride
Reno Hilton, 2500 E. Second St., Reno, Nev. • (775) 786-7005

Insider kids say this is the best ride in the Reno/Tahoe area. They also say it's the most exciting. This ride is like hang gliding, bungee jumping and skydiving rolled into one.

Riders strap into the same kind of harness hang gliders use; up to three people can ride together. The harness is connected to two long poles by cables. Operators pull riders to the top of a 180-foot launch tower. Once riders are at the top, they are released and free-fall toward the ground, clearing it by 6 feet and accelerating to about 65 m.p.h. Riders then swing back and forth until slowed down.

Riders have to be at least 42 inches tall. Weight and age of the rider are not restricting factors.

The only drawback to this ride is that it is expensive — $25 for one person for one ride. But if students ride during the week, the price is cut in half. Insiders say the best time to ride is at night. Make sure you call ahead to see if it's open: sometimes it closes if the weather's bad or it's windy.

Sparks

Wild Island
250 Wild Island Ct., Sparks, Nev. • (775) 359-2927

Wild Island is divided into three activities — a waterpark, a miniature golf course and a raceway. The waterpark is the favorite of most visitors.

This is the only waterpark in northern Nevada, and it is a great place to go in the summer, no matter how old you are. They have three mini slides in the Little Lagoon for small children, or they can ride the Dragon and Frog slides or float around in the Lazy River. Older children and some adults can take their chances with the bigger slides like the Stingray and Shark Bait that twists and turns all the way down. But if you're looking for a more adventurous ride, try a drop down the Red Viper or slide through the dark on the Black Widow. If you think these two slides are too much for one person, you can rent a double-person tube and go down in tandem.

Wild Island also has a place called Hurricane Cove where swimmers can get in water fights at the water gun stations or stand underneath a giant waterfall that dumps 650 gallons of water from a bucket at the top of a tree house. Hurricane Cove also has tube slides and rope climbs.

The best waves in northern Nevada can be found at the Montego Bay wave pool. Swimmers can body surf here or just float around in a tube. This place is fun for most everyone. Kokomo's 21 Club is a spa designed for adults.

The waterpark usually opens in May and stays open all summer until the weather gets cold again. Entrance fees begin at $16.

Wild Island also has two 18-hole miniature golf courses with waterfalls and little rivers running through them. It's a fun place for families and it is open all year. A round is usually $4.50. Inside they also have a game arcade and a booth to trade in tickets for prizes. Both inside and outside are open day and night. Call for the times, as they vary with the season.

Wild Island has the only miniature racetrack in northern Nevada, too. Formula K Raceway has two tracks, one for larger children and one for smaller. The big kids get to drive gas-powered Indy cars and the little ones get to drive electric-powered Sprint cars. Plan on spending about $10 at the racetrack.

Wild Island can also cater birthday parties. Prices vary, so telephone for details.

South Shore Lake Tahoe

Lake Tahoe Amusement Park
2401 Lake Tahoe Blvd., South Lake Tahoe, Calif. • (530) 541-1300

This is a good amusement park that has lots of rides and carnival games. You can buy a book of tickets that lets your kids ride on go-karts, the Superslide, a merry-go-round, a Tilt-A-Whirl and more. It has a snack bar and the park is open from May through September from 11 AM to 10 PM. Family packs of tickets start at $20 for 35 tickets.

Lake Tahoe Balloons
(530) 544-1221, (800) 872-9294

This is the most adventurous thing to do at Lake Tahoe — float above the crystal blue water in a hot-air balloon. These balloons take off and land on a special launch boat on the lake. The only drawback is that it is expensive, about $100 for each person. But it will definitely be an adventure not soon forgotten. You can write Lake Tahoe Balloons at PO Box 19215, South Lake Tahoe CA 96115. For more information on ballooning, see our Recreation chapter.

Arcades and Games

Reno

Reno Hilton Fun Quest
2500 E. Second St., Reno, Nev. • (775) 789-2386

This is a video arcade located inside a casino and it's the favorite of Insider kids because it has more than 200 video and arcade games. Along with these, it also has some of the best interactive games available. Kids can either get into a great game of laser tag on the Q-2000 Laser Tag battlefield or, along with six other pilots, fly an X-Wing fighter in the Galaxian Theater. Several virtual reality games are scattered around as well.

They also have a place called Tumble Town Playground where tiny tots can go to jump and climb on the playground equipment. The arcade is open at 10 AM every day but closes at different times, depending on the day of the week. Most games start at $1 but the Laser Tag, the VR games and the X-Wing fighters are more in the $4 to $5 range.

Sparks

Nugget Skywalk Arcade
John Ascuaga's Nugget, 1100 Nugget Ave., Sparks, Nev. • (775) 356-3300, (800) 648-1177

This is the best arcade in Sparks. It's located on the second floor above the casino and really has two different rooms. One has video and arcade games for younger children, and one room has the most up-to-date video games for older ones. Insider kids say the best thing about this arcade is the prices are the cheapest around. It's a good place to take the kids in Sparks if the weather is bad.

Sparks Indoor Batting Cages
1855 E. Lincoln Wy., Sparks, Nev. • (775) 358-4487

If you want to keep your children in shape for playing baseball or softball or if they just want to hit a couple of balls, this is the place. The indoor cages are right next door to Wild

Island and each cage has a different speed pitch of either softballs or hardballs. After they're finished hitting, the entire family can get something to eat at the grill. According to our sources, the burgers are good here and so are the fries. The prices to hit balls are reasonable — $5 for 20 pitches, or you can rent the entire cage for $20 an hour.

North Shore Lake Tahoe

Hyatt Regency Lake Tahoe Resort and Casino
Country Club Dr. and Lakeside Dr., Incline Village, Nev. · (775) 832-1234

This is a small arcade used mostly by children and teenagers staying at the hotel. It only has about 20 games but they are all state-of-the-art video. The games start at 25¢ for the less complicated and go up to $1 for games such as Alpine Racer II. The arcade is open 24 hours per day but the state's curfew does apply (10 PM for children 18 and younger.)

South Shore Lake Tahoe

Caesars Tahoe
55 U.S. Hwy. 50, Stateline, Nev. · (775) 588-3515

Caesar's arcade is aimed at teenagers. It has 40 up-to-date video games with only a few for the smaller children. Prices per game begin at 50¢ and go up to $1. It has a few pinball machines but most of the games are the interactive, video type. It's open 24 hours except during certain times of the year (check with the arcade attendant for specifics).

Harrah's Lake Tahoe
U.S. Hwy. 50, Stateline, Nev. · (800) 427-7247

The attendant here says this is the best arcade at the lake and Insiders agree. The Family Fun Center has 200 games which include redemption games, video games, skill games and simulators. Kids can win tickets at some of the games and can redeem them for more than 3,000 prizes. This center also has state-of-the-art simulators and a virtual reality batting cage. Smaller children are welcome at the Play Pal area, complete with monkey bars and crawl chutes. Prices start at 25¢ for the older games and go up to $3 for the VR batting cage.

Harveys Resort Hotel/Casino
U.S. Hwy. 50, Stateline, Nev. · (775) 588-2411

Harvey's has more that 160 games in its Virtual Forest Arcade for kids and teenagers. Half of the games are interactive video and half are redemption games. This arcade also has a 12-seat motion theater which runs three different movies a day. Games begin at 25¢ and climb to $1. The motion theater costs $3 per person for the 15-minute ride. It's open 24 hours a day but children 14 and younger must be out of the arcade by 10 PM on weekdays and midnight on weekends.

Boating and Watersports

North Shore Lake Tahoe

Lake Tahoe Parasailing
700 N. Lake Blvd., Tahoe City, Calif. · (530) 583-7245

If you've never tried parasailing before, you've got to try it on Lake Tahoe. You can sail from 10 feet above the water, all the way up to 650 feet where the view is spectacular. The best thing about this outfit is that you never have to get wet. Take-offs and landings are done on the back of a boat on a launch pad. But if you want it, as a part of your 20-minute ride, they'll dunk you in the water. During the hot summer months, getting a little wet is often a great idea. The 20 minutes usually cost about $20.

The owners also run Lighthouse Watersports, (530) 583-6000, about 2 blocks away, where you can rent sail and power boats and WaveRunners. Prices vary depending upon the watercraft rented. (See also our Recreation Chapter for more boat rental information.)

Tahoe Sailing Charters
Tahoe City Marina, Tahoe City, Calif. · (530) 583-6200

If you ever wanted to try sailing, this is the place. They have many different sailboats you

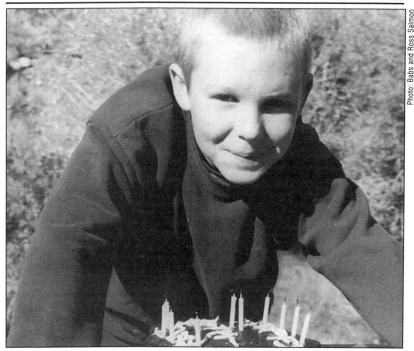

This young birthday boy is having his birthday celebration at a campground. There are special places all around the Reno/Tahoe area for youngsters to have fun.

can rent and all kinds of sailing cruises to try out (prices start at $25). They even give sailing lessons. This is a cool way to see Lake Tahoe on a hot day.

South Shore Lake Tahoe

Cruises

Take the family on a cruise of Lake Tahoe and you'll agree with us that it is the best way to see the lake and its surrounding beauty. Two companies run paddle wheelers on the lake and offer about five different cruises, ranging from a strictly sightseeing cruise to a sunset dinner dance. These paddle wheelers are similar to the ones that used to run up and down the Mississippi River; they provide a stable platform for cruising Lake Tahoe. The boats have different schedules depending on the day of the week so telephone or write for details before you come. Fares begin at $8 for children and $16 for adults for the sightseeing

cruise. On some cruises, children under 12 travel free.

M.S. *Dixie II*, Zephyr Cove, Nev., (775) 588-3508

Tahoe Queen, Marina Village, South Lake Tahoe, Calif., (530) 541-3364, (800) 238-2463

Lake View Sports
3131 U.S. Hwy. 50, South Lake Tahoe, Calif. • (530) 544-0183

This is the place to go on the South Shore to rent just about anything you want to have fun in the lake or around the it. You can rent in-line skates, JetSkis, bikes or mopeds. If you want to rent a boat, they run a shop nearby called Tahoe Key Boat Rentals, (530) 544-8888. Both of these establishments are kid-friendly. (See also Recreation.)

Zephyr Cove Resort
U.S. Hwy. 50, Zephyr Cove, Nev. • (775) 588-6644

This is the one of the best places on the

Photo: Verdi Trails West, Inc.

This young rider from the YMCA of The Sierra Equestrian Camp is getting a great ride.

South Shore to take the family because you can do and rent just about everything here. You can sail, rent boats and JetSkis, or go parasailing at Capt. Kirk's. You can rent snowmobiles in the winter, ride the M.S. *Dixie II* paddle wheeler around the lake, swim and go fishing. Or you can just relax on the beach. Prices vary depending upon the activity you plan, and they charge an entrance fee of $3 to park your vehicle. A great place to spend the day.

Day and Summer Camps

Lake Tahoe's hotels and resorts have excellent reputations for being "kid friendly" and for taking care of children. A few even have summer and day camps available to keep kids occupied while you're off doing grown-up things. Most of these camps require that the children be at least 3 years old and toilet-trained; some have even stricter age guidelines.

The costs for the sessions vary depending upon the length of stay and time of day, but usually half-day programs cost about $28 and full-day programs go up to $70 with meals included. The programs include supervised hikes, swimming, sledding, snowshoeing, arts and crafts, video arcade visits, games, sports, and beach play — all depending upon the time of year.

Here are a few that we think are tops:

North Shore Lake Tahoe

Camp Hyatt
Hyatt Regency Lake Tahoe Resort and Casino, Country Club Dr. and Lakeview Dr., Incline Village, Nev.
• **(775) 832-1234, (800) 553-3288**

This summer camp runs seven days per week from the beginning of June until Labor Day. Its sessions are broken down into five timeframes, with different costs per timeframe: 9 AM to 1 PM, $28; 9 AM to 4 PM, $45; noon to 4 PM, $28; 5 to 9 PM, $28; and 5 PM to midnight, $40. The camp provides supervised activities for children of hotel guests. The age limits are 3 to 12 years old.

During other months of the year, Camp Hyatt is open on the weekends only with the same session times and prices.

Mountain Buddy's Club
The Resort at Squaw Creek
400 Squaw Creek Rd., Squaw Valley,
Calif. • (530) 581-6624

Mountain Buddy's is a year-round program for children 4 to 12 years old. Chaperones take the kids on hikes; supervise arts and crafts; take the kids swimming; and, during the winter months, take them sledding and snowshoeing. This resort program always receives high praise from both parents and children.

The cost for an all-day stay is $70 and for a half-day stay, the price is halved to $35. A full day begins at 9 AM and ends at 5 PM. Half-day programs go from 9 AM to 12:30 PM, 1:30 to 5 PM, and 6:30 to 9:30 PM.

South Shore Lake Tahoe

Kids Camp
Harveys Resort Hotel/Casino,
U.S. Hwy. 50, Stateline, Nev.
• (775) 588-0752

Kids Camp is a perfect place to leave the children if you want a night out. This camp is only open from 6 to 10 PM but it's open seven days per week. Kids 6 to 13 years old are welcome here, and they don't have to be guests of the hotel. Activities include trips to the movies, the video arcade, bowling and other activities depending upon the time of year. The cost for the 4-hour program is $40.

Fishing

Reno

The Truckee River and Virginia Lake

If you or your kids like to fish, you have your choice of one of these two places to go in Reno.

The Truckee River is one special place for anglers because you can actually go fishing for trout right downtown. Any place in the river is good. Some people think that you have to go a long way up or down the river to catch fish, but that's not true. A lot of fish have been caught from Idlewild Park, Mayberry Park and Fisherman's Park. The only problem with the Truckee River is that you have to have a fair amount of skill and experience to catch fish.

If you or your children are beginners, a better place to go is Virginia Lake, which has some big fish (up to five pounds). You and your family have a real good chance of catching some. Bring along a lot of bread, too, because this lake has hundreds of ducks and geese. And if the fish aren't biting, it's fun to see how many ducks and geese you can get to come over and eat. Call the Nevada Division of Wildlife at (775) 688-1500 for more fishing information and see our Fishing and Hunting chapter.

Sparks

Sparks Marina Park
The City of Sparks Parks and Recreation Dept. • (775) 353-2376

The City of Sparks transformed a former gravel pit and community eyesore into one of the best fishing spots in the Reno/Sparks area. Set to reopen in January 2000, this lake will provide outstanding fishing for both adults and children. The city spent more than $35,000 stocking the lake with catchable and trophy-sized trout. No gas-engine propelled boats are allowed on the water, keeping pollution at a minimum. Bank fishing is excellent, as is fishing from float tubes and self-propelled and electric-motor boats. All types of bait are recommended from worms, salmon eggs and Power bait to spinners and flies. There is no charge for fishing but a valid Nevada fishing license is required (see our Fishing and Hunting chapter for details).

INSIDERS' TIP:

Both Nevada and California have 10 PM curfews for children under 18.

South Shore Lake Tahoe

Saw Mill Pond
Saw Mill Rd., South Lake Tahoe, Calif.
• (530) 573-2600

There are lots of places to take kids fishing on and around Lake Tahoe but like we've said before, you have to be a fairly good angler to catch anything (besides, fishing with kids is not as much fun as *catching fish* with kids!). So, if you're looking for fishing spots that cater to the younger anglers, South Shore has two places that are good for kids and fun to try. Saw Mill Pond is one (Tahoe Trout Farm is the other, see the next entry). You have to bring your own gear here, and only children are allowed to fish. Fishing here is free of charge.

Tahoe Trout Farm
1023 Blue Lakes Ave., South Lake
Tahoe, Calif. • (530) 541-1491

Tahoe Trout Farm is the other place especially for kids to fish. They loan the young anglers rods and reels and even supply the bait. It's all free until they catch a fish, then you have to pay for it. Prices vary. This farm usually opens in May and closes in September; hours every day are 10 AM to 7 PM. Give it a try.

Horseback Riding

Reno

High Sierra Stables
3105 Indian Ln., Reno, Nev.
• (775) 677-1477

One of the best ways to see Reno is from a horse. These stables have many horses that are easy to ride, so they're very good for first-time riders. The owners make sure that they have horseback rides for everyone from children to adults. If you and your family are good riders, they'll even arrange private rides for

you. They also have full-moon rides, barbecues, birthday parties and dinner rides, and offer pickup and delivery service from your hotel to their stables. The stables are open all year from 9 AM until the sun goes down. Prices start at $25 an hour.

Verdi Trails
1850 W. Old Hwy. 40, Verdi, Nev.
• (775) 345-7600

This is one of the places to go to horseback riding around the Truckee Meadows. Verdi Trails is only 10 miles from Reno at the foot of the Sierra Nevada mountains. Here, you can go on trail rides and hayrides. Prices begin at $25 for an hour ride.

North Shore Lake Tahoe

North Shore Stables

There are many places to go horseback riding around the North Shore of the lake. All these stables have hourly rides (they start at $20 per hour) and provide guides. All of these stables also offer riding lessons. Some have hayrides during the summer and sleigh rides during the winter. Just call them for the latest info.

Alpine Meadows, Calif. 89, between Tahoe City and Truckee, California, (530) 583-3905

Cold Stream Corral, Donner Lake exit off of I-80, Truckee, California, (530) 587-4121

Northstar Stables, Northstar–at–Tahoe exit off of Calif. Hwy. 267, Truckee, California, (530) 562-1230

Ponderosa Ranch, Nev. 28, Incline Village, Nevada, (775) 831-2154

Squaw Valley Stables, Squaw Valley exit off of Calif. 267, between Tahoe City and Truckee, California, (530) 583-7433

South Shore Lake Tahoe

South Shore Stables

Like the North Shore, the South has many

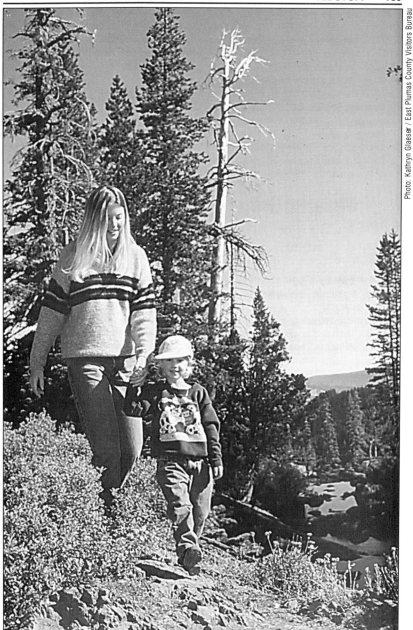

A great way to spend time together while developing an appreciation for nature is to take your kids hiking on the many trails around Reno and Lake Tahoe.

outfits that rent horses. At most of them, you can have lessons, go riding, and take hayrides in the summer and sleighrides in the winter. Check out any of these horseback-riding places. Prices start at $20 per hour.

Camp Richardson, Calif. 89, South Lake Tahoe, California, (530) 541-3113

Cascade Stables, Calif. 89, near Cascade Lake, California, (530) 541-2055

Sunset Stables, U.S. 50, near the airport, South Lake Tahoe, California, (530) 541-9001

Zephyr Cove Stables, U.S. 50, Zephyr Cove, Nevada, (775) 588-5664

Miniature Golf

Reno

Horizon Family Magic Carpet Golf
6925 S. Virginia St., Reno, Nev.
• (775) 853-8837

This miniature golf course is the only one in Reno and it has three different courses that kids find fun to play. The prices start at $4.50 and go up, depending on how many holes you want to play. After you're finished with the miniature golf, there's also a special hole where if you score a Hole-In-One, you win a special prize. The course also has a pizza parlor for those hungry golfers.

North Shore Lake Tahoe

Magic Carpet Golf
5167 N. Lake Blvd., Carnelian Bay, Calif.
• (530) 546-4279

This is a big facility that has three miniature golf courses. They're all fun and prices are reasonable (about $4.50). But these courses are very popular, and they're always crowded. They open when the snow melts and stay open until the snow returns. Call for times.

South Shore Lake Tahoe

Fantasy Kingdom Miniature Golf
U.S. Hwy. 50, South Lake Tahoe, Calif.
• (530) 544-3833

This is one of two places to play miniature

golf at South Shore. This course caters to the younger kids with a fantasy theme of castles and dragons around the course. It's open in the summer from 10 AM to 9 PM. The prices start at $5.

Magic Carpet Golf
2455 Lake Tahoe Blvd., South Lake Tahoe, Calif. • (530) 541-3787

Magic Carpet Golf is the second place to play miniature golf on the South Shore. Here they have two big courses that are less crowded than the Fantasy Kingdom. It is open from April until November. The price hovers around $5.

Movies

If you want movies, we've got movies. In fact, we have more than 50 movie screens in the Reno/Tahoe area, with more projected to be built in the next few years. The newest Century complexes in Reno and Sparks are technologically terrific. These 30 screens feature stadium seating, which means no bad seats in the house: even that tall cowboy with the even taller hat won't bother you in these new theaters. And all of them are equipped with cutting-edge digital sound.

Reno

Century Park Lane 16
Virginia St. and Plumb Ln., Reno, Nev.
• (775) 824-3333

Keystone II Cinema
2500 E. Second St., Reno, Nev.
• (775) 786-4411

Do you like going to the movies but don't like the seats? The Keystone II Cinema in the lower level of the Reno Hilton offers a delightful alternative. With its cozy couches just big enough for two, it's the next best thing to having your own private screening room. Enjoy the classics and foreign films that aren't available in traditional theaters, and the first-run movies you're dying to see anyway.

National Bowling Stadium
300 N. Center St., Reno, Nev.
• (775) 334-2634

Strange as it may seem, this professional

bowling stadium is one of the best places in Reno to see a movie. The screen in this theater is 4 stories high: that's about five times bigger than a regular theater screen. When they show movies here, they're gigantic. Movies change frequently, so call ahead for show subjects and times.

Tickets are $6 for adults and $4 for children. For more details about the stadium, see our Attractions chapter.

Sparks

Century Sparks 14
1250 Victorian Ave., Sparks, Nev.
• (775) 353-7469

El Rancho Drive-In
El Rancho Ave. and Oddie Blvd., Sparks, Nev. • (775) 358-6920

New Greenbrae 8
520 Greenbrae Dr., Sparks, Nev.
• (775) 358-3456

North Shore Lake Tahoe

Brockway Theater
8707 N. Lake Blvd., Kings Beach, Calif.
• (530) 546-5951

Cobblestone Cinema
465 N. Lake Tahoe Blvd., Tahoe City, Calif. • (530) 546-5951

Incline Village Cinema
901 Tahoe Blvd., Incline Village, Nev.
• (530) 546-5951

South Shore Lake Tahoe

Horizon Stadium Cinemas
1057 Emerald Bay Rd., South Lake Tahoe, Calif. • (530) 541-2121

Lakeside Cinema
1054 Emerald Bay Rd., South Lake Tahoe, Calif. • (530) 541-2121

Stateline Cinema
Crecent V Shopping Center, South Lake Tahoe, Calif. • (530) 541-7481

Museums

Reno

Fleischmann Planetarium
N. Virginia St., on the campus of the Univ. of Nevada, Reno
• (775) 784-4811

This one is a great family outing because not only do you get to see a planetarium show with stars and planets but you also get to see a short movie on an educational subject. In the past, the planetarium has shown movies on climbers ascending Mt. Everest and on the Antarctic and penguins.

This planetarium also has different things to do depending on what time of year you visit. In October, they have a show about Nevada ghosts, and during the summer, kids can take classes on how to build model rockets. At the end of the class, the builders get to go outside and launch their rockets. Every Friday night, as long as the sky is clear, they open the sliding roof of their observatory so you can look through their 12-inch telescope. Don't pass up this great place. The planetarium is open all year but call because the times are different every day. Admission is about $5. (For more information see our Attractions chapter.)

National Automobile Museum
10 Lake St., Reno, Nev.
• (775) 333-9300

INSIDERS' TIP

Looking for activities and fun things to do for children while staying in the Reno/Tahoe area? The concierge at a resort will have contacts for area activities and may even offer childrens' events at the resort. Your accommodation can often supply babysitter resources and local daycare information.

Photo: Babs and Ross Salmon

Give a kid a fishing rod and — well, you can see the smile on this young sportsman's face.

If you're a car nut, this is the place for you. The old saying, "They don't make cars like this anymore," really fits here. They have cars on hand like the 1949 Mercury James Dean drove in the movie *Rebel Without a Cause* and an Indy 500 race car that most kids really like.

The museum is set up as different streets with the cars parked along the curbs. There's also an old car placed so you and your family can take a picture with it. They even lend you period clothes to go along with the car. (The use of the clothes and the picture are free.) The museum has more than 200 cars in four different rooms, so there's plenty to see. The museum is open all year except Thanksgiving and Christmas Day. It usually opens at 9:30 AM and closes at 5:30 PM. Admission prices are $7.50 for adults and $2.50 for children. (See our Attractions chapter for more details.)

Wilbur D. May Great Basin Adventure
Rancho San Rafael Park, Reno, Nev.
• **(775) 785-5961**

Wilbur May, a department store mogul, traveled around the world about 40 times, collecting odds and ends. He donated most of his collection to the City of Reno, and now it's housed in a replica of his ranch in Rancho San Rafael Park. Most visitors agree that the most interesting room in this museum is the one with his trophies from big game hunting. But the best thing about this park is that there is something to do for everyone.

The park has a petting zoo, pony rides, an old-fashioned log ride and a mine where kids can pan for gold. There's also a nature walk and a place where children can climb on one-third–size replicas of dinosaurs. The park also has indoor gardens that have two goldfish ponds, many kinds of flowers and plants, and a waterfall. They usually have an exhibit that changes about every six months and plenty of room for picnics and barbecues. This is an entire day trip. The park is open from 10 AM to 5 PM during the summer. Fees start at $5. (See our Attractions chapter for more information.)

Sparks

Sparks Heritage Foundation and Museum
820 Victorian Ave., Sparks, Nev.
• **(775) 355-1144**

Sparks is nicknamed "Rail City" because it used to be a railroad town, so most of the pieces in this museum have to do with trains.

They have a collection of old lanterns used by the trains' brakemen and a stationary train across the street that visitors can walk through. The museum is free, but they ask that you donate $1 per person to the museum fund. (See our Attractions chapter for more details.)

North Shore Lake Tahoe

Donner Memorial Park and Museum
Donner Pass Rd, Truckee, Calif.
• **(530) 587-3841**

This park and museum is outside of North Shore Lake Tahoe. It's a fun place for the family to visit but you have to remember your history here. This is where pioneers tried to cross the Sierra Nevada mountains in winter but were snowed in. After they ran out of food, they ate their horses and cows; eventually they had to eat their saddles and leather harnesses. Some of the pioneers also turned to cannibalism to survive the harsh winter.

The museum shows slides of drawings of the Donner Party's wagon train and their encampment. And in the summer, you can hike on the trail to see where they built their cabins. Times vary, so telephone before coming. (See our Daytrips chapter for more to see and do in nearby Truckee.)

South Shore Lake Tahoe

Vikingsholm Castle
Emerald Bay State Park, South Lake Tahoe, Calif. • (530) 525-7277

Around here we call it a castle but it's really a stone home built at the water's edge. The home was designed with a Scandinavian look and resembles architecture associated with the Vikings, hence its name. The question most visitors ask is how the stones were transported here, since there are only two ways to get to the house: from the water or down a steep dirt path about a mile long. (When you

visit, the rangers will be glad to give you the answer.) The walk makes the visit to this home challenging because you have to walk down that very 1-mile path (the easy part) to get to the house, but then you still have to walk back up (the hard part).

Once at the bottom of the trail, you can swim on the beautiful beach or picnic at one of the many barbecue pits. Don't forget to ask the rangers about the little house the owner built on the island across the water from the main home. They say she had tea there every day. Tours of the main house are offered during the dry months (i.e. the months without snow) on the half-hour. Fees start at $6. (See our Attractions and Parks chapters for more information.)

Outdoor Fun

Sparks

Victorian Square
Victorian Ave., Sparks, Nev.
• **(800) 367-7366**

Victorian Square is the first redevelopment project in Nevada and a good place to take a walk, go shopping, and look at and play in one of the most unique water fountains in the West. The city also puts on a lot of different events here at different times of the year, such as the only Christmas parade in Nevada (read the Annual Events and Attractions chapters of this book for more information).

North Shore Lake Tahoe

Fanny Bridge
Tahoe City, Calif.

This is the bridge that spans the Truckee River where it flows from Lake Tahoe. The Truckee is the only river that leaves the lake and from this bridge you can see the dam that controls the water. When you lean over the rail, you can see the huge trout swimming between the dam and the bridge. They call it Fanny Bridge because so many people are leaning over watching the trout, passers-by can only see the Lookie-Lous' rear ends sticking up. Drive to the "Y" (the intersection of Calif. highways 89 and 28) at Tahoe City and you can't miss it. (See our Attractions chapter for more information.)

Squaw Valley USA
Squaw Valley, Calif. • (530) 583-6955

Squaw Valley is located just up the road from Lake Tahoe and it's definitely worth the drive, not only to ride the cable car up the mountain, but to try all the other things they have around, too.

Near the entrance to the cable car, they have a rock-climbing wall that's about 30 feet tall. It's set up for all kinds of climbers, from beginners to experts, so try it out before you hop on the cable car ride. Once you are at the High Camp (a $5 ride up the mountain for children), you can visit the Olympic Museum. Squaw Valley was home to the 1960 Winter Olympics. There are also places to go ice-skating or bungee jumping, play tennis and volleyball, go horseback riding, mountain biking, swimming or hiking. This is definitely an all-day trip. Prices for the different activities vary. For more information see our Attractions, Resorts, and Recreation chapters.

South Shore Lake Tahoe

Heavenly Ski Resort Aerial Tram
Heavenly Ski Resort, Stateline, Nev.
• (775) 586-7000

This tram takes you up a mountain to about 2,000 feet above Lake Tahoe, and the view from the top is spectacular. There's a good restaurant there with a huge deck where most people gather to try to glimpse a little of the lake. Or you can hike up a mile-long trail through the forest until you come to a clump of large boulders. From here, the view seems never-ending. It's worth the extra walk. Not many people brave the mile hike, but it looks much worse than it really is. See our Attractions chapter for more details.

Lake Tahoe Adventures
• (530) 577-2940

This company provides for the second most adventurous outings around South Shore. (The first is riding in a hot air balloon over Lake Tahoe, see the Lake Tahoe Balloons entry in the "Amusement Parks and Rides" section of this chapter.) This company can arrange four-wheeling trips around the lake's rugged trails. You can opt to travel in an ATV, a jeep or a Hummer. The off-road tours last from about 1 hour to all night if you want to go on one of their camping trips. The best ride is on Rubicon Trail. They have trips that are classified from "easy" all the way up to "difficult." Prices vary but start at $45. Write them at PO Box 11521, South Lake Tahoe CA 96115.

Parks and Playgrounds

Reno

Idlewild Playground
1900 Idlewild Dr., Reno, Nev.
• (775) 329-6008

This playground is in a huge park near the Truckee River, which flows through Reno. The playland has a train, a roller coaster, electric cars and a Tilt-a-Whirl. Most of the rides are for tiny tots but the bigger kids can play soccer, football, volleyball, softball and baseball. And, if they like to run, the park has a jogging path.

It's a great place to have a picnic or a barbecue, and there is plenty of play equipment. This is one of the best places in Reno to go to spend an inexpensive day with the kids. For more to do and see in the park, see our Parks chapter.

Sparks

The City of Sparks Parks and Recreation Department
98 Richard Wy., Sparks, Nev.
• (775) 353-2376

The city has 37 different parks that have

Photo: K. Markgraf

The Reno Rodeo has captured the attention of this young cowpoke.

baseball and softball fields, swimming pools and playgrounds. Plus, the rec department puts on numerous activities for kids throughout the year.

The department has programs in arts and crafts; swimming and other sports like tennis, soccer and, of course, baseball and softball; gymnastics; dance; poetry; drawing; painting; theater; cheerleading; snowboard lessons; and self-defense classes, just to name a few. The department prints a catalog of activities, which is available at their office on Richard Way. The fees vary by activity and are very reasonable.

North Shore Lake Tahoe

Lake Tahoe–Nevada State Park
2005 Nev. Hwy. 28, Incline Village, Nev.
• (775) 831-0494

This is a spectacular park that has about 13,000 acres. There are so many things to do all over the park that a family could spend its entire vacation here. The park has places to go fishing, swimming, picnicking, hiking, camping, mountain biking, scuba diving, boating and horseback riding. A telephone call is a must to see what's going on when you arrive. (See also our Parks chapter.)

Sand Harbor
Nev. Hwy. 28, Incline Village, Nev.
• (775) 831-0494

Although the beaches here are the best around the lake, don't come here if you're trying to get away from other people. These popular beaches are white and sandy, and the water is so clear that you can see the bottom. Besides swimming and boating, there are also nature trails for hiking. Entrance fees are $6 per carload. (See our Parks and Recreation chapters for more details.)

South Shore Lake Tahoe

U.S. Forest Service Lake Tahoe Visitor Center
Calif. Hwy. 89, South Lake Tahoe, Calif.
• (530) 573-2674

This center has a nature walk called "The Rainbow Trail" where hikers can see the plants and animals that live and grow around the lake. You can also visit Taylor Creek Marsh, a protected wetlands. And they have a viewing area where you can see trout swimming in a natural creek. It is a great way for youngsters to learn about the birds, fish, animals and plants around Lake Tahoe. The rangers here are really outstanding, and they love to answer youngsters' questions. (See our Attractions chapter for more information.)

Ranches

North Shore Lake Tahoe

Ponderosa Ranch
100 Ponderosa Ranch Rd., Incline Village, Nev. • (775) 831-0691

Someone in the family will probably remember the TV western show *Bonanza* — at least from the reruns. It was the most popular Western of all time on TV. In the series, the Cartwright family owned a ranch called the Ponderosa, and this is where they filmed the show's outdoor scenes. Now, it is an amusement center.

They've built an entire Western town here, complete with a saloon, general store and an ice cream parlor. They even have the Cartwright's ranch house, like you've seen on TV. Every day they have a hayride through the forest, and after that they serve a big break-

---

INSIDERS' TIP

Traveling with children takes a little extra planning, but looking ahead to the type of adventure planned will pay off. It is a good idea to call ahead and find out if food, beverages, restrooms, and other necessary ammenities for children will be available at the site of the attraction.

fast of sausage and pancakes. They also have a petting farm, a mystery mine and a shooting gallery. Throughout the day, they have fake gunfights between the town's sheriff and the bad guys. And they also have free pony rides. All the attractions are included in one price: $11.50 for adults and $7.50 for kids, including the breakfast.

The ranch is usually open from the end of April until October from 9:30 AM to 5 PM. The breakfast hayride starts at 8 AM and goes until 9:30 AM. (See our Attractions chapter for more details.)

Rock Hunting

Reno Gem & Mineral Society
PO Box 2004, Reno NV 89520

Around the Reno/Tahoe area are numerous places to hunt for rocks and minerals. If you want to take the kids rock hunting, write to the address above and the Society will be glad to send you a map showing you where to go and what kind of rocks and minerals you'll find there. (If you're venturing out into the desert, be sure to read our Daytrips chapter for tips on safety.)

Skateboarding

Reno

Reno Skateboard Park
Idlewild Park, 1900 Idlewild Dr., Reno, Nev. • (775) 334-2270

This 7,000-square foot park is the only one in the Truckee Meadows and is crowded most of the time. It's located at Idlewild Park (see our Parks chapter for more information about the park) and there's no charge for its use.

Both skateboards and in-line skates can be used here but no bikes. However, you'll see several kids whipping in and out on their bikes until park supervisors run them off. The Reno Parks and Rec Department recommends the use of safety equipment, but it doesn't require its use. So it's skate-at-your-own-risk. The park is open all year during the day.

South Shore Lake Tahoe

South Tahoe Skateboard Park
Bijou Park, Al Tahoe Blvd., South Lake Tahoe, Calif. • (530) 542-6055

This skateboard park is considered to be one of the top five in California. It requires helmets and pads and lets you use skateboards and in-line skates, but no bikes are allowed. The park is open from sunup to sunset, weather permitting. There is no charge to use the park.

Skating

Reno

Roller Kingdom
515 E. Seventh St., Reno, Nev. • (775) 329-3472

If your kids like to skate, this is the only place that has inside skating in Reno It's open all year and lets them use in-line skates if they prefer.

The best thing about this rink is that it has special hours every day when only children under 10 years old can skate. No adults or teenagers are allowed to skate for these two hours, though all children must be supervised by a parent. The rink has special times for children, teenagers and adults, so call for the

---

INSIDERS' TIP:

On the Nevada side, children are allowed in establishments that sell liquor as long as the establishments serve food as well. It is always a good idea to check the surroundings to prevent youngsters from being exposed to adult situations.

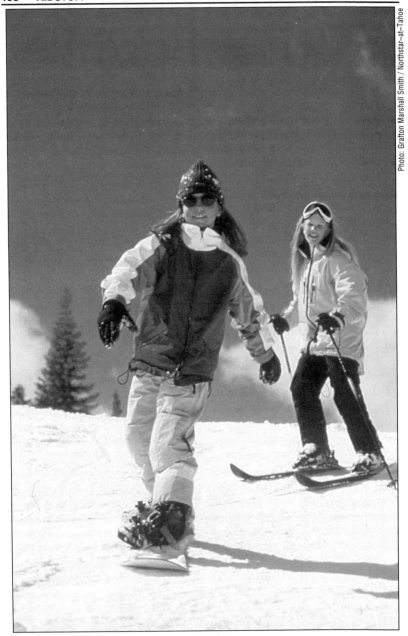

Photo: Grafton Marshall Smith / Northstar–at–Tahoe

Miles and miles of groomed ski runs around the Reno/Tahoe area offer fun and challenge to kids when they get out their snowboard or their alpine skis.

exact times and plan to set aside about $10 per person for this skating adventure.

Sparks

Wingfield Springs Ice Rink
Wingfield Springs, Sparks, Nev.
• **(775) 020-1000**
This is a great place to come during the winter months if you like to ice skate or want to learn how. The rink is usually open in the afternoons, Monday through Thursday; it opens earlier on the weekends. This is a big rink and usually not very crowded. Call for the rink times. The entrance fee is about $10 if you bring your own skates. But if you're going to be around the area for a time, they have season passes. (See our Winter Sports chapter for more information.)

Zoos and Animals

Reno

Animal Ark
1265 Deerlodge Rd., Reno, Nev.
• **(775) 969-3111**
This is a great place to see wild animals. The Ark is a wildlife sanctuary, a place that takes care of animals that can't take care of themselves. The Ark has foxes, mountain lions, bobcats, wolves, bears and even tigers. The best thing about the Ark is that they let the kids get a close-up look at all the animals. The Ark has animal demonstrations and picnic areas and during October, you can even howl with the wolves at night.

The Animal Ark is open from April through October, 10 AM to 4 PM, but doesn't open if the weather is rainy. The Ark is slightly off the beaten path so drive north on U.S. 395 to Red Rock Road (Exit 78), turn right and drive about

11 miles to Deerlodge Road, then look for the Animal Ark sign. The entrance fees are usually around $5. (See our Attractions chapter for more information.)

Sierra Safari Zoo
10200 N. Virginia St., Reno, Nev.
• **(775) 677-1101**
This is Reno's rendition of a zoo and the place where you can see a liger (half lion, half tiger). Besides the liger, the zoo has zebras, kangaroos, buffalo, llamas, camels and other wild animals. The best thing about this zoo is that children can pet, feed and play with some of the animals. The people who run it are very hospitable and will try to answer all your questions. This zoo is open from April 1 to October 31 from 10 AM to 5 PM every day. Admittance is $7 for adults and $5 for children. (See our Attractions chapter for more details.)

Sparks

Bertha and Angel
John Ascuaga's Nugget, 1100 Nugget Ave., Sparks, Nev. • **(775) 356-3300, (800) 648-1177**
Bertha and Angel are the most famous elephants in Nevada. The two animals perform every night on a stage at John Ascuaga's Nugget casino. Bertha weighs 8,000 pounds and Angel, who is younger, weighs 5,000 pounds. When they aren't performing, they live behind the casino in a house called "The Elephant Palace."

Starting at 10 AM every day, you can visit them at their palace. And, usually at 1 PM, you can watch their trainer give them a bath. Viewing is free.

At press time, it was rumored that Bertha would be retiring soon from her onstage performances, but that she'd still be part of special events and would remain at The Elephant Palace.

If you're planning to be in the area for some of our major events like Hot August Nights, the Great Reno Balloon Races, the Reno National Air Races, or the Reno Rodeo, make sure you reserve your hotel or motel rooms early.

Annual Events

We think that the Reno/Tahoe area is a mecca of entertainment for visitors and locals alike. Throughout this book we have tried to convince you, too, by detailing the thousands of things to do, places to go and sights to see. In this chapter, we list for you, by month, the events we feel are the biggest crowd-pleasers. But we also touch on the more time-honored events that we Insiders find just plain charming and down-homey.

We outline the more flamboyant and highly visual celebrations that tend to be the norm on the Nevada side of the area, and we also give you details on the less dramatic but equally entertaining and fun festivals and celebrations that touch on our historical beginnings and our cultural diversity.

Most of the events listed are for visitors, but some are aimed at getting locals involved in the community. No matter which, everyone is welcome.

If you're planning to be in the area for some of our major events like Hot August Nights, the Great Reno Balloon Races, the Reno National Air Races, or the Reno Rodeo, make sure you reserve your hotel or motel rooms early. And we do mean early: in 1998, more than 150,000 visitors flooded into Reno and Sparks to enjoy Hot August Nights, and just about every room in the area was booked almost a year in advance.

We have not included specific dates because most events are associated with just the month, so the dates are fluid. Therefore it

behooves you to call the contact number we've provided to verify the event's actual date and location if you are planning to attend and want to set aside vacation time for the visit. (See our chapter on The Arts for more information on other cultural events.)

Well, let's press on with our Insider's Guide to the Annual Events of the Reno/Tahoe area. (We have also included some events that are outside of our geographical area but we think are definitely worth the time and effort to attend.)

January

Martin Luther King Jr. Birthday Celebration
John Ascuaga's Nugget, 1100 Nugget Ave., Sparks, Nev. • (775) 329-8990

This is a four-day celebration honoring the birthday of America's greatest civil rights leader. The event around the 15th of the month includes free entertainment and culminates with an awards dinner, usually in the $20 range. Past guest speakers have included the Reverend Lewis Anthony.

South Lake Tahoe Winter Celebration
Various locations, South Lake Tahoe, Calif.

A monthlong series of events celebrated in South Lake Tahoe, the Winter Celebration includes a beer festival, parades, downhill ski races, snowboarding competitions and the Celebrity Ski Classic at Heavenly Ski Resort. These events are usually scheduled on the weekends and are a good way to fight off the winter doldrums. Many of the events are free, though some fundraising events will have an admission fee. Call the Lake Tahoe Visitors Authority, (530) 544-5050, for details and schedules.

www.insiders.com

See this and many other Insiders' Guide® destinations online.

Visit us today!

Big West compete for the division championship and a chance to move on to the NCAA Basketball Championship Tournament. Even though UNR is expected to leap to the Western Athletic Conference (WAC) in 1999-2000, the Big West Tournament, usually held in early March, is scheduled here until the year 2001. Ticket prices begin at $5.

Snowfest Winter Carnival
(530) 583-7625

This is a 10-day event held all over North Shore Lake Tahoe and Truckee. Most of the ski areas and businesses on the northern part of the lake participate in the 120 or more events including parades, ski and snowboard races, fireworks, food events and a Polar Bear swim. This is truly a family event and includes many spectator-involved activities. The carnival usually begins in early March and even though some events are free, don't forget to bring money for food and drinks. You can write for information at PO Box 7590, Tahoe City CA 96145.

February

American Bowling Congress Championship Bowling Tournament
National Bowling Stadium, 300 N. Center St., Reno, Nev. • (775) 334-2600

Beginning in mid-February, the bowling stadium hosts American Bowling Congress (ABC) members from across the United States. The 1998 event made it into the record books for the largest bowling tournament ever held. The spectator's fee is usually $2 to $3 per day. This tournament did not happen in 1999, and the Bowling Congress may move the tournament in 2000, so be sure to call ahead.

University Winter Carnival
Univ. of Nevada, Reno, Reno, Nev.
• (775) 784-6589

This weeklong event is oriented toward the university-aged crowd. The event, usually held in the middle of the month, includes a variety of on-campus entertainment open to the public, as well as snow activities that include skiing, snowboarding and tobogganing. Definitely a must for those in the younger generation who enjoy the snow and winter activities.

March

Big West Conference Basketball Tournament
Lawlor Events Center, Univ. of Nevada, Reno, Reno, Nev.
• (775) 784-6900

In an eight-team format, the schools in the

St. Patrick's Day Celebration
Virginia St., Reno, Nev. • (775) 785-3300

March 17th brings a celebration that gives you great Irish music, food and crafts. The majority of the fun happens in front of Fitzgeralds Casino/Hotel Reno near the famous Reno Arch on Virginia Street. The event kicks off with the lighting of the arch after hundreds of the white bulbs have been replaced with green ones. Virginia Street is blocked off during the event so spectators can enjoy the many food stands and craft booths. Admittance is free, but bring money for food and drinks. Almost every bar in Reno with an Irish name is SRO during this celebration.

Annual Mother Earth Awakening Pow Wow
Stewart Indian Museum, Carson City, Nev. • (775) 882-6929

The spring equinox (March 20th or 21st) brings Native American dancers, drummers and singers to this powwow. The three-day celebration includes artisans and craftspeople from all over the West. This is an excellent

Photo: Snowfest! Winter Carnival

The Snowfest! Winter Carnival parade has this crowd enjoying the antics of some costumed participants.

example of an out-of-area event that is worth the drive. The younger visitors especially seem to enjoy this event. The Native American dances and singing are always a hit. From Reno, take U.S. Highway 395 south for 30 miles to Carson City.

other antics associated with these rough-and-tumble pioneers. This is a great, free event for the entire family. From Reno, take U.S. 395 south for 30 miles to Carson City. Call the Carson City Visitors Authority for information: (775) 687-7410 or (800) NEVADA-1.

April

Eagle Valley Muzzleloaders' Spring Rendezvous
Carson City, Nev.

The Eagle Valley Muzzleloaders are a group of Nevadans trying to preserve America's heritage by re-enacting the lives of the rugged mountain men who were among the first white men in the region. In late April, these mountain men gather for a weekend at an encampment along Canyon Road in Carson City to participate in a survival hike, black-powder shoot, strongest man contests and

May

Cinco de Mayo Fiesta Nevada Celebration
Peppermill Hotel Casino Reno, 2707 S. Virginia St., Reno, Nev. • (775) 827-4978

This outdoor event is celebrated as close to May 5th as possible in the parking lot of the Peppermill Hotel Casino Reno. It's Nevada's version of the Mexican celebration that features mariachi bands, folklorico dance performers, great Latino food, and arts and crafts. Singers and dancers represent most of the countries in Latin and South America. This

INSIDERS' TIP

Over 50,000 people a day are said to attend the Sparks Best in the West Nugget Rib Cook-off every September.

event is one of the most fun in the Reno/Tahoe area and usually draws a crowd in the thousands. It is not as crowded as it used to be when it was held in Victorian Square in Sparks, but the food and entertainment are just as great. Admission and the entertainment is free, but bring money for the great food and drinks.

Fallon Air Show
Naval Air Station, Fallon, Nev.
• **(775) 423-4556**

This late May event is a fairly standard air show, but it's one of the best air shows in the West in the years that the Navy's Blue Angels perform. According to U.S. Navy regulations, the Blue Angels cannot perform at the same air base two years in a row, so check to see if the year you want to go features the best air performance team in the world. Their last performance here was in 1999 so they won't return until the year 2001. Another highlight of the show is the Wall of Fire, a simulated bombing run performed by attack aviators stationed at NAS Fallon. This part of the show has some great pyrotechnics. Several civilian performers are also on hand, as well as one of the best aircraft static displays in the West. The best part about the show is that parking and admission are free. Fallon is 60 miles east of Reno/Sparks. Take Interstate 80 east to Fernley, Nevada, take the second exit and look for signs to Alt. U.S. Highway 50 and Fallon.

June

Celebrate the River
Downtown Reno, Nev. • **(775) 334-2417**

This early June, three-day festival held downtown celebrates the Truckee River which flows through Reno and Sparks on its way to Pyramid Lake. Visitors and locals alike enjoy the food, fun, entertainment, performers and especially the culinary specialties from downtown hotels and casinos. The free event also features arts and crafts, concerts and children's activities.

Reno Rodeo
Reno Livestock Events Center, 1350 N. Wells Ave., Reno, Nev. • **(775) 329-3877, (775) 688-5751**

The Reno Rodeo is considered by some to be the best rodeo in America. World-class cowboys compete for thousands of dollars in prize money in the "wildest, richest, rodeo in the West." The nine-day event in late June includes not only rodeo events every night but also a parade, a carnival and craft booths. This is one of the premier events in the Reno/Tahoe area. Don't miss this one. Tickets start at $10. See also our Spectator Sports chapter.

Sparks Hometowne Farmer's Market
Victorian Sq., Sparks, Nev.
• **(775) 353-2291**

An old-fashioned farmers' market is held every Thursday from 4 PM to 9 PM starting in the middle of June and running until early September. More than 80 vendors offer fresh-picked fruits and vegetables, specialty foods and breads. Every Thursday brings cooking demos, a children's play area, home-grown music and a friendly atmosphere. This farmers' market is a favorite hangout for Insiders. Bring plenty of cash for the great fruits and veggies.

Valhalla Arts and Music Festival
Tallac Historic Site, South Lake Tahoe, Calif. • **(530) 541-4975**

This is a summer-long program that presents Native American fine arts, reggae, folk, Latin, jazz and bluegrass concerts, as well as a classic film series, theatrical performances for children and adults, art gallery tours and a variety of celebrations honoring the Tallac Historic Site. The festival begins in early June and runs through early October. The concerts are usually held both on weeknights and weekends. One of the best events held around the lake, it makes money for the historic site from small admittance fees. The site is located about 3 miles north of South Lake Tahoe on Calif. Highway 89.

Valhalla Renaissance Festival
Camp Richardson Resort, South Lake Tahoe, Calif. • **(530) 541-4166**

Children really love this festival: an event held over one or two weekends that features knights in combat, damsels in distress, jugglers, magicians and anything else associated with Renaissance-era entertainment. There's

The Burning Man

Some call it "weirdness in the desert." Some call it an "abomination." Some call it "naked fun in the sun." But whatever you want to call it, for a week around the Labor Day weekend, thousands of visitors flock to The Burning Man celebration that temporarily converts the barren playa of the Black Rock Desert into a small art-filled town dubbed Black Rock City.

The event originally came out of the Bohemian scene in San Francisco in 1986 when Larry Harvey said to fellow artists: "Let's build a man and burn it in honor of the summer solstice." But some planners have said that Harvey built the man, not to celebrate anything, but in honor of a failed love affair. The man was a symbol of his ex-girlfriend's new love. Whatever the case, that first time he had 20 attendees and the "burning man" stood 8 feet tall. In 1990, the celebration moved to the Black Rock Desert where more than 800 people attended. In 1999, more than 20,000 people participated in the burning of the symbolic man, which stood 50 feet tall.

Labor Day weekend seemed to be a better time of year for the gathering since the trip to the desert site is more than 100 miles from Reno and a three-day weekend would bring more participants and visitors. Now, these visitors and participants come to make art, get naked, help build a temporary city and then help burn it down.

The festival has been called equal parts Mardi Gras, *The Road Warrior* and a pagan

Photo: Bob Ecker (with thanks)

Participants in the 1999 Burning Man admire the 50-foot structure to be burned at the end of the festival.

— continued on next page

fire ritual, which culminates on Saturday night of the Labor Day weekend when organizers burn the towering effigy of a man filled with explosives and decorated with neon lights. "Burn the Man" is the event's rallying cry.

Organizers of the Burning Man call the gathering just outside of Gerlach, Nevada, an experiment in temporary community. Each year they design a city meant to be a model of civilization like a Utopian community. In 1998, the town stretched out into 80 villages over the Black Rock and contained a fire department, a post office, a daily newspaper, medical services and more than 15 radio stations. Just to give you a taste of the scene, here were some of the village and camp names: Now and Zen Camp, La Inglesia Del Santo Pollo, The Jonestown Kool-aid Company, and The Golden Goddess Temple. The entrance to the festival once had an arch which read: "Drano, The Biggest Little Village in the Desert," spoofing the Reno Arch.

The official line on the Burning Man is that it is a temporary art community set up in the desert to be an experiment in radical self-expression. The unofficial line is that it is a weeklong event where you will see just about anything imaginable and can participate in just about everything: painting yourself silver, wearing only a cowboy hat and pearls in 100-degree heat or riding around the playa in a car shaped like a shark's fin playing the theme from *Jaws*. You'll always see Bay Area and local counter-culture people here: ravers, Wiccans, machine artists and other alternative lifestyle enthusiasts.

Organizers call Burning Man a "mind altering experience without the aid of drugs" and tout that no one is a spectator. The major drawback to this unique experience is that the average temperature during the event is usually in the low 100s and that everyone must bring his or her own food, water and shelter. There are no commercial activities allowed except the selling of ice (with the proceeds going to the students of Gerlach). The barter system is used extensively throughout the city. You may be able to trade that bunch of bananas for a handmade hemp shirt. At the gate, tickets to the event run about $100 for the week (less if you purchase in advance).

To get to the Burning Man from Gerlach, take Nev. Highway 34 3 miles to the turn-off to Black Rock City. For more information about the Burning Man, call the Burning Man Hotline, (415) TO-FLAME, or visit the website: www.burningman.com.

also food, music and arts and crafts vendors. Admission prices generally run $5 for both children and adults.

Beer Fest
The Village at Northstar–at–Tahoe, Truckee, Calif. • (530) 562-1010

If you like beer, here's your event. Northern California microbrewers provide tastings of unusual and unique beers at the lodge at Northstar, usually in late June. Cooks are also on hand to whip up some of the best barbecue around the lake and local bands entertain you with down-home blues. This Insider rates it one of the most enjoyable events at Lake Tahoe. Bring along enough money to taste the beer and sample the barbecue.

July

American Century Celebrity Golf Championship
Edgewood Tahoe Golf Course, 180 Lake Pkwy., Stateline, Nev. • (775) 588-3566

This early July golf tournament boasts some of the biggest names in entertainment and sports as its participants. This event has featured players the likes of Dan Marino, John Elway, Michael Jordan, James Woods, Kevin Costner and Randy Quaid. Any golfer with a U.S. Golf Association handicap of 10 or less may compete in this three-day tournament, which is usually televised live on network TV. Spectators can buy tickets for one or more days at the gate. Prices vary, but usually start at $10.

Fourth of July Celebrations

Many different celebrations are scattered around Lake Tahoe to celebrate our Independence Day (see next entry for Reno's celebration). Call the following numbers for locations and starting times:

North Lake Tahoe, (530) 581-6900 or (530) 583-3494
Squaw Valley USA, (530) 583-6985
South Lake Tahoe, (530) 544-5050
Truckee, (530) 587-2757

Skyfire

Rancho San Rafael Park, Reno, Nev.
• (775) 332-3333

Skyfire is the only free Fourth of July fireworks display in the Truckee Meadows. Come and celebrate America's independence with entertainment and food in the park, working up to a spectacular fireworks display. You have to arrive early for this event if you want a parking spot. Insiders flock to the park and the surrounding area for the just-after-dark fireworks show. Admittance to the park is free, but bring money for food and drinks.

Lake Tahoe Summer Music Festival

Various locations, North Shore Lake Tahoe • (530) 583-3101

One of the Lake's most ambitious undertakings and one of the best-organized in the area, this festival consists of a series of outdoor concerts featuring classical, jazz, Broadway and pops. The festival begins in early July and runs until Labor Day.

The concerts are usually free to the public and are always well done. These concerts are always a good way to spend a family outing. See also our chapter on The Arts.

Uptown Downtown ARTown

Various locations, downtown Reno, Nev.
• (775) 329-1324

This monthlong Reno summer arts festival features more than 150 different performers and exhibits at different city-wide locations. Highlights include a touring Broadway musical, music concerts, ballet on the banks of the Truckee River, and film and visual arts dem-

onstrations. Children are welcome and even have their own acting and arts workshops. Most of the events are free. See our chapter on The Arts for more information.

The Big Easy

Downtown Reno, Nev. • (775) 332-3333

In the middle of July, downtown Reno is transformed into a Louisiana street festival. Insiders call this "Mardi Gras with an attitude." The event features two days of partying, straight out of New Orleans, with Louisiana Zydeco music and Cajun cuisine. Admission is free but bring money for food and drinks. Don't miss this fun, eh!

August

Hot August Nights

Various locations throughout Reno and Sparks, Nev. • (775) 829-1955, (800) 367-7366

Hot nights, hot rods, hot times and a great location to enjoy it — this describes the premiere event in the Reno/Tahoe area. It's a celebration of America's love affair with hot cars and rock-n-roll music. For a week in early August, thousands of pre-1970 autos cruise the streets accompanied by good food everywhere and great live music. This is the largest event in northern Nevada. In 1999 more than 175,000 people flocked to the Truckee Meadows to enjoy the nostalgia of this bygone era. Hotels and motels are usually booked a year in advance, so make sure you plan way ahead for this spectacular event.

Reno Basque Festival

Reno and Sparks, Nev.

A great way to learn about the area's Basque heritage is to attend this festival which is held during the North American Basque Organization's annual convention here, usually in the middle of August. It includes traditional food, dancing and games. The public is welcome to all of the events including a barbecue and a Basque Mass. Don't miss the "Irrinitzi" competition where contestants attempt the loudest and longest Basque yell. The events are free but bring money for food and drinks. Call the Reno/Tahoe Visitors In-

Pandemonium reigns when the Camel Races take to the track.

formation Center, (800) 367-7366, for more information.

Great Eldorado BBQ, Brews and Blues Festival
Eldorado Hotel/Casino, Fourth and Virginia sts., Reno, Nev.
• (775) 786-5700, (800) 648-5966.

Come on down for two days of excellent barbecue, outstanding microbrews and some of the best live blues in northern Nevada. The event is held in the middle of August outside of the Eldorado Hotel/Casino in its Special Events Plaza. It's a really good and inexpensive way to spend a couple of days. You pay only for the beer and barbecue.

Greek Festival
St. Anthony's Greek Orthodox Church, 4795 Lakeside Dr., Reno, Nev.
• (775) 825-5365

Greek food lovers cannot miss this annual event, usually put on toward the end of August by the parishioners of St. Anthony's. Everything from baklava to gyros is on the menu plus live Greek music and dances performed by award-winning dance groups. Admission is usually $3 and food tickets begin at $10. Oh, pah, come on by for a great Greek time.

Nevada State Fair
Reno Livestock Events Center, 1350 N. Wells Ave., Reno, Nev. • (775) 688-5767

This is a really fun, old-fashioned state fair usually held on the last weekend in August and featuring livestock exhibits, baking and cooking exhibits, special events, entertainment, rides and midway games. If you ever wanted to visit a down-home country fair, this is the one. There is a daily entrance fee from $3 to $6 and additional charges for rides, games and food.

Lake Tahoe Shakespeare Festival
Sand Harbor Beach, Incline Village, Nev.
• (775) 832-1600, (800) 747-4697

"The Bard Done Lakeside" or "The Bard on the Beach" — that's how Insiders describe this festival. The monthlong event features noted classical theater troupes performing

INSIDERS' TIP

Even in summer be sure to take a sweater or jacket with you in the evening, since temperatures in the Reno/Tahoe area can plummet when the sun goes down.

some of Shakespeare's greatest plays. The magical backdrop of Lake Tahoe adds to the already perfect atmosphere — you'll see why the event is voted Lake Tahoe's best, year after year. You can bring your own beach chair or rent one. Food and drinks are sold at the performances. Tickets usually cost between $18 and $30. Don't miss this event. For more information, see our chapter on The Arts.

Reno/Tahoe Open
Montreux Golf and Country Club, 2500 Spinnaker Dr., Reno, Nev.
• (775) 849-9441

The newest golf tournament on the PGA Tour hopes to attract the world's greatest golfers. It debuted in late August of 1999 and included practice rounds, a Pro-Am tournament, and a 72-hole tournament round with a $2 million purse. The course was designed by Jack Nicklaus; he called it one of his best. Daily entrance fees were charged, but actual prices were not known at press time (they're expected to be in the $15 per day range).

September

September is the Reno/Tahoe area's busiest month for annual events. If you're planning an extended trip here, this is the month to do it. Besides a plethora of things to do, the weather is perfect for outdoor activities.

The Great Reno Balloon Races
Rancho San Rafael Park, Reno, Nev.
• (775) 826-1181

The early morning Reno sky is alive with color when the nation's top 100 balloonists compete in early September for cash and prizes in three events: the Hare and the Hound, Target Drop and the Key Grab. The Dawn Patrol, at 5:30 AM, offers a spectacular light show as the balloonists ascend in their multicolored balloons. Children especially like this event

because of the variety of balloons, some in the shapes of champagne bottles, frogs, panda bears and giant hamburgers. A great way to spend an early morning in September. Both admission and parking are free. See our Spectator Sports chapter for more.

The Best in the West Nugget Rib Cook-off
Victorian Sq., Sparks, Nev.
• (775) 356-3300, (800) 648-1177

In early September 1999, more than 50,000 people a day crowded into Victorian Square in Sparks to savor some of the best ribs in the world. Directors of the event estimated that the crowd ate more than 60,000 pounds of ribs during the four-day event. Even though the cook-off is great fun and has fantastic food for spectators, the participants get down to serious business. The 25 or so barbecue cookers from all over the U.S. and the world compete for the title of "Best in the West" and the $7,500 Grand Prize. Best Sauce and People's Choice Awards are also given. So for some cookers it's not all fun and games. But for those of us who like barbecue, it's a chance to taste a variety of finger-lickin' good ribs. Rib dinners usually start at $3.50 for a sample of three ribs and climb to $15 for a full slab.

Reno National Air Races
Reno Stead Airport, Reno, Nev.
• (775) 972-6663

If you like airplanes, you won't want to miss this, the longest-running air race in the world. It's held in mid-September. Hundreds of planes fill the sky during this four-day event which features six classes of racing.

Besides the air races, military jets are on hand to thrill the crowd, as well as planes doing aerobatics, skywriting and the ever-popular daredevil wingwalkers. Entrance fees vary from $5 to $10, depending on the day. See our Spectator Sports chapter for more.

INSIDERS' TIP

If you sign up early enough, you can participate in the International Camel Races in Virginia City. The organizers are always looking for people willing to be camel jockeys. Call (775) 847-0311 or (775) 329-7469 for details.

A Sparks Hometowne Farmer's Market vendor arranges corn, fresh from the field.

International Camel Races
Virginia City, Nev.
- (775) 847-0311, (775) 329-7469

This wild and crazy time began in 1960 when Hollywood director John Huston won the first race on a borrowed camel. The yearly event held in mid-September turned into an international event when the Australians jumped into the fray in the 1970s. The races are all in fun and even include ostriches and water buffalo sprints. Other humorous events include a parade down C Street with the town's legal prostitutes dressed in 1880s fashions. Virginia City comes alive once again during this unforgettable weekend: a fun time for the entire family. An entrance fee, usually $5, is charged for the actual camel races. See our Daytrips chapter for more on Virginia City and on the origin of the Camel Races.

Street Vibrations
Downtown Reno, Nev.
- (775) 329-7469, (800) 337-7366

Reno is in Hog heaven in late September. This motorcycle extravaganza is for Harleys and custom tour bikes. The three-day festivities include arts and crafts, parades, an auction, nightly entertainment and a motorcycle poker run. These events are free to participants and spectators.

Great Basin Book Festival
Wingfield Park, Reno, Nev.
- (775) 784-6587

This is a late September, weekend celebration of the written word in downtown Reno. Here you can browse through the many bookseller stands, enjoy readings by local and national writers, discuss books and get books signed by authors from around the country. A great way to spend a weekend if you love books. Admittance is free but book prices vary.

October

Great Italian Festival
Eldorado Hotel/Casino, Fourth and Virginia sts., Reno, Nev.
- (775) 786-5700

Celebrated along with Columbus Day, this event includes great Italian food, entertainment, a grape-stomping contest and a parade. The highlight for most spectators is the spaghetti-eating contest. Admittance is free. All you have to do is pay for your food and drinks. Insiders love this festival.

Celtic New Year Celebration
Downtown Reno, Nev. • (775) 332-3333

If you like bagpipes, this late October celebration is made to order. This is the biggest pipe band competition in the United States. Besides the pipes, this weekend event includes Celtic dancing, entertainment, food booths and craft stalls. It's sure to be a "bonnie"weekend, even if you're not Celtic.

Kokanee Salmon Festival
Taylor Creek, South Lake Tahoe, Calif.
• **(530) 573-2600**

This event is held when the bright-red Kokanee salmon make their annual spawning run up Taylor Creek, usually around mid October. The salmon can be viewed from windows below water level at the Lake Tahoe Visitor Center's Stream Profile Chamber. Also included in this fun two-day festival are a Kokanee cook-off, educational displays and programs, nature walks and a children's fishing booth. All events are free to the public

Nevada Day Parade
Carson City, Nev. • (800) NEVADA-1

Nevada joined the Union on October 31—yes, Halloween — in 1864. Every year, we celebrate with an old-fashioned parade in the state capital. The celebration also includes live music, an art show, a best beard contest and a 1860s period fancy ball at the Governor's Mansion (by invitation only). It's definitely an Insiders' event, but visitors also find the day entertaining. All of downtown Carson City is closed off for this celebration.

November

National Senior Pro Rodeo Finals
Reno Livestock Events Center, 1350 N. Wells Ave., Reno, Nev. • (775) 788-4218

If you were wondering whatever happened to your favorite cowboy or cowgirl, odds are he or she is probably competing in this rodeo, usually held in early November. This event includes the nation's top rodeo stars, 40 years old and older. Contestants compete in all of the traditional rodeo events and vie for some pretty hefty prize money. Ticket prices vary but have been as low as $5.

December

Sparks Hometowne Christmas
Victorian Sq., Sparks, Nev.
• **(775) 353-2291**

This is the only Christmas event in Nevada that has a parade complete with all the local political figures and Santa Claus. This annual Christmas celebration is sponsored by the City of Sparks and includes a crafts fair, holiday music, and a spectacular tree-lighting ceremony in the evening followed by group caroling. This is a great way to get into the holiday spirit and is a wonderful time for the entire family. It's usually held in early December.

Buck 'N Ball
Reno Livestock Events Center, 1350 N. Wells Ave., Reno, Nev.
• **(800) FOR-RENO**

You can ring in the New Year Nevada-style with this unique celebration that includes a rodeo, a country western music concert, and dancing. This may be the only New Year's Eve Party where you can dance the night away after rooting for your favorite bull rider. The event costs about $50 for the entire evening and is recommended for adults only.

Since pioneer days, music and drama have been important to people living in this part of the West where the first entertainers wandered from mining camp to mining camp, performing in tents before audiences craving culture and amusement.

The Arts

Most people know the Reno/Tahoe area is absolutely tops for outdoor recreation and nonstop casino action; but they probably don't know that it's also rich in culture, with an appreciation of the arts that's deeply ingrained in its history. Far from a cultural wasteland, Reno was recently dubbed, "the Paris of Northern Nevada," by VIA magazine. And because a national survey of reading habits found Reno to be the most well-read city in the country, it could also be nicknamed "The Biggest Little Literary City in the World."

Since pioneer days, music and drama have been important to people living in this part of the West. The first entertainers wandered from mining camp to mining camp, performing in tents before audiences craving culture and amusement. Banjos, off-color jokes and fleeting appearances by "real" women were the unsophisticated fare of the day (or night). As the mines prospered, the demand for quality live entertainment increased, ushering in a golden age of theater and music by the second half of the nineteenth century.

The first real theater in Nevada, The Howard Theater, was built in 1860 in Virginia City. With millions of dollars pouring out of the Comstock mines, the silver barons had plenty of money to indulge their appetites in cosmopolitan pleasures. Other mining towns followed suit (although not in quite so elaborate a fashion), with theaters springing up in such hamlets as Eureka, Gold Hill and Carson City. While Virginia City was home to a number of theaters and tent shows, the most famous venue is Piper's Opera House, which is listed by the League of Historic Theaters as the most significant vintage theater in the West. This "Grand Dame of the Comstock" is being renovated to its original splendor using a phased-in approach which allows for selected events to take place during the restoration. For details about the theater and upcoming events call (775) 847-9322. Be sure to read our Daytrips chapter to find out about other things to see and do in Virginia City.

As frontier entertainment moved to more elegant surroundings, it became more refined, with leading performers from the East eagerly heading to stages in the wild, wild West. Famous players and singers — such as Enrico Caruso, Edwin Booth, Lillie Langtry and Joe Jefferson — presented Shakespearean drama and popular music to packed houses. A particular favorite was Adah Isaacs Menken, nicknamed "The Menken," who shocked audiences by riding across the stage, while lashed to a horse and wearing only flesh-colored provocative tights. During its heyday Virginia City rivaled San Francisco as the cultural center of this part of the West.

But as the fortunes of the mines petered out, so did the ability to pay for topnotch entertainment. The focus of culture shifted to Reno, where its first playhouse, Dyer's Theater, was built in 1871. It was followed by Smith's Academy of Music, Hammond and Wilson's Theater, Wheelman's Theater, the McKissick Opera House, the Wigwam and the Majestic Theater. By the time the Rialto (later renamed the Granada) opened in 1915, Reno was a major stopover for theater companies en route by train from New York to San Francisco, due to special privileges granted by the railroad. This was somewhat short-lived, however, since World War I put a damper on lavish stage productions and the railroad later rescinded its privileges. By about 1920, Reno's theaters had switched to the latest entertainment craze — movies.

Although films took the place of traveling roadshows, art in its various forms continued to develop in the Reno/Tahoe area. The Latimer Art Club was organized in Reno in 1921 and remained the only organization of its kind in the state until other arts groups joined the scene in 1939. The Reno Municipal Band, founded in 1890, continued to perform (as it does today) and the Reno Little Theater opened to enthusiastic performing arts fans in 1935. Beginning in the 1960s the arts blossomed with the arrival of the Nevada Arts Council in 1967, Nevada Opera and the Pioneer Center for the Performing Arts in 1968, the Reno Philharmonic Association in 1969, the Sierra Arts Foundation in 1971, the Reno Chamber Orchestra in 1974, the Lake Tahoe Shakespeare Festival in 1978, and the Nevada Motion Picture Division and the Nevada Festival Ballet in 1984. The strong support enjoyed by the arts in the Reno/Tahoe area is envied by some other communities since it's remarkable for an area with a relatively small population to have its own opera and symphony.

www.insiders.com

See this and many other **Insiders' Guide®** destinations online.

Visit us today!

Far from an elitist "arts and furs" scene, the arts reach into every area of the community. Outreach is the name of the game, with a comprehensive variety of programs available to everyone regardless of age or income. The direction of the future is to increase this inclusive appeal, by continuing to cultivate new audiences and to develop more arenas for the celebration of the arts. In Reno the focus is directed in part toward developing an arts corridor downtown, extending along the Truckee River from the National Automobile Museum to the McKinley Park School, which was recently renovated into an arts facility. Included in this cultural district are Wingfield Park and the Lear Theater plus the planned OliverMcMillian complex of theaters, restaurants and shops and the rejuvenated artists-in-residence Riverside Hotel.

As the Reno/Tahoe area continues to grow, support for the arts is anticipated to increase. Many new residents who are transplants from larger cities expect sophisticated cultural choices in their new home and have stepped up to the plate in support of existing as well as future artistic endeavors. For many years artists have been attracted to the area because of its beauty and quality of life. This trend will undoubtedly continue, bringing more residents who embrace the arts as a part of their everyday life.

If you're looking for volunteer activities, there's a wealth of opportunities in the myriad of events and groups associated with the arts. Virtually every organization welcomes volunteer help with open arms. The entire arts movement in the Reno/Tahoe area owes its success in part to the thousands of devoted arts boosters who give unselfishly of their time, talent and resources to make the area increasingly artistic and arts-friendly.

In this chapter we organize information about the arts into six categories: support organizations, performing arts (theater, music and dance), visual arts, educational institutions, literary arts and galleries. We've used our regular geographical sequence, except that we've combined Reno and Sparks into one area because most of the arts offerings aren't restricted to either one community or the other. (Though we've divided it geographically, don't let that limit your options since the regions are close enough for day- or afternoon trips. If you're staying in Reno, you might still enjoy some of the offerings in the Tahoe area and vice versa.) We also tell you about some of the ethnic and cultural organizations that celebrate the rich diversity of the area. For performing arts associated with nightclubs and casinos, see our Casino Nightlife and Nightlife chapters.

While our treatment of the arts is designed to show the richness and diversity of offerings available, it's not intended to be exhaustive. Since we can't list everything, we hope our representative sample will whet your appetite to find out more about your particular interests in the arts. For an all-inclusive listing, you can contact Sierra Arts at (775) 329-ARTS. Ask for a copy of their Registry of Arts and Cultural Organizations and also their monthly publication, *Encore*. You can also find updated information about arts events by reading *Artifacts*, a quarterly publication available free in newspaper racks in the Lake Tahoe Basin, and the *Reno News & Review*, a weekly publication distributed free in newspaper racks throughout the Reno/Tahoe area. The *Reno Gazette-Journal* publishes arts news in *Best Bets* on

Thursday and *Calendar* on Friday. Contact the Nevada Arts Council at (775) 687-6680 for copies of its publication, *neon* (see our Media chapter for more details).We don't list all of the Reno/Tahoe art galleries, but instead give you examples which illustrate the richness and variety of artistic works available in the area. You'll find additional galleries listed in local telephone directories.

Reno/Sparks

Support Organizations

City of Reno Arts and Cultural Division
100 Washington St., Reno, Nev.
• **(775) 334-2262**

As part of the City of Reno Parks, Recreation and Community Services department, the Arts and Cultural Division promotes a full agenda of artistic events through the auspices of the city. With a focus on a downtown arts corridor along the Truckee River, the division produces the Festival of Trees and the Celebrate the River special events. It also manages the amphitheater in Wingfield Park where a large number of outdoor artistic performances are held. The division works with the C.I.T.Y. (Culture in the Year) 2000 Commission, which facilitates a gallery in the Reno City Hall at 490 S. Center Street. The parks department also offers a variety of arts, crafts and dance classes for people of all ages. You can pick up a catalogue of specific programs at their office on Washington Street or have one mailed to you.

Nevada Arts Council
602 N. Curry St., Carson City, Nev.
• **(775) 687-6680**

Since its creation as a state agency in 1967, the Nevada Arts Council has instituted a number of programs to enrich the cultural life of the people of Nevada. It supports the work of local artists through the Artists' Services Program. It promotes art in the schools with its Arts in Education Program. And it preserves the traditional arts of Nevada's many cultural groups in the Folk Arts Program.

One of the best ways to experience Reno/Tahoe's varied culture is to attend the Sierra Folklife Festival in Wingfield Park in Reno. Sponsored jointly by the NAC and Sierra Arts, the festival is a celebration of music, dance, crafts and food traditions of the many ethnic groups in the region. It's usually held in September, but call the council for exact dates. You can also learn about Nevada's arts scene by reading *neon,* the art journal published by the Nevada Arts Council.

Nevada State Commission on Economic Development, Motion Picture Division
• **(775) 687-1814**

The history of Nevada and the movies goes back to 1897 when the state's first film, *The Corbett-Fitzsimmons World Champion Fight*, was filmed in Carson City. From then on, hundreds of movies have been shot in the state, using the picturesque desert/mountain landscapes and the miles of open road as realistic backdrops. Favorite locations in Reno include the famous Reno Arch, proclaiming "The Biggest Little City in the World," and the campus at the University of Nevada, Reno, with its wooded Ivy League look. The gorgeous scenery anywhere around Lake Tahoe is a sure winner for any film needing an authentic mountain location. The list of movies filmed in the Reno/Tahoe area parallels the history of film, and the roster of stars reads almost like a who's who in the industry.

In 1983 the State of Nevada acknowledged what moviemakers had known for years: Nevada is an extremely attractive location for shooting and casting films. To facilitate and attract more film ventures in the state, the Motion Picture Division of the Economic Development Commission was established. With the financial impact from films running in the millions of dollars each year, movies continue to be big business in the Reno/Tahoe area.

Sierra Arts
200 Flint St., Reno, Nev.
• **(775) 329-ARTS**

If you want to find out about the local arts scene, your first phone call should be to Sierra Arts. Established in 1971 to assist artists and arts organizations, the foundation maintains a complete up-to-date list of all arts groups. It also keeps a master calendar of upcoming performances, exhibitions and events and publishes a monthly arts magazine titled *Encore*. SA functions in many ways as a large clearinghouse of information for anything that has to do with the arts in the Reno/Tahoe area.

The foundation has an ambitious outreach program that brings the arts and arts appreciation to a wide audience in the community. It places professional artists in school classrooms and helps teach teachers how to use the arts across the curricula. It offers free classical music in its Concerts in the Atrium, celebrates cultural diversity in the Sierra Folklife Festival and manages the C.I.T.Y. 2000 Gallery at Reno City Hall. It also sponsors a variety of special events, such as movie festivals and storytelling presentations. The foundation is headquartered in the Sierra Arts Center, which also provides gallery space and inexpensive office and meeting facilities for a large number of arts organizations.

Sierra Arts takes a leadership role in increasing the presence and vitality of the arts in downtown Reno. It has partnered with Artspace Projects to form Sierra Arts Riverside Lofts, which will renovate the historic Riverside Hotel into artists homes with studios.

The Reno/Sparks Theater Community Coalition
528 W. First St., Reno, Nev.
• **(775) 786-2278**

The Reno/Sparks Theater Community Coalition was founded in 1994 to meet a growing need for more professional performance facilities for the regional arts community. More than 50 performing arts, educational and cultural organizations joined the coalition to purchase the First Church of Christ, Scientist, and renovate it into the Lear Theater (see our description of the theater later in this chapter).

In addition to the theater project, The The-ater Coalition promotes performing arts with its summer "Theater in the Park" series; its weekly TV program, *City Stages*; its monthly newsletter, *City Stages News*; and its multidisciplinary arts workshop, "Journey to the Center of the Arts."

Uptown Downtown ARTown
(775) 322-1538

Awarded the "Outstanding Achievement Award for City Livability" in 1998 by the U.S. Conference of Mayors, Uptown Downtown ARTown celebrates the art and soul of Reno in sizzling style throughout the month of July. At a dozen different indoor and outdoor venues in Reno, a smorgasbord of more than 200 performing and visual arts events is offered up to eager arts buffs.

The *Reno/Tahoe Visitor* dubbed this event "The ultimate in cultural tourism," and we suggest you try an eclectic sampling from this gala since each event is distinct. You can learn about history at the Great Basin Chautauqua in San Rafael Park. You can enjoy world-famous art exhibits at the Nevada Museum of Art. And you can experience fine music and dance along the banks of the Truckee River. The festival is unique not only because of the variety of activities, but because most functions are either free or very low-cost. Uptown Downtown ARTown may very well be the best art bargain in the country. Don't miss it. (See also our Annual Events chapter.)

Very Special Arts Nevada
4598 S. Virginia St., Reno, Nev.
• **(775) 826-6100**

Very Special Arts Nevada brings the arts to children and adults who are under-served because they are disadvantaged, disabled or at-risk. The organization conducts workshops in the visual and theater arts at a variety of events and in conjunction with other community programs.

The group makes its home in the historic

INSIDERS' TIP

Sundance Books, a locally owned bookstore in Reno, hosts a variety of poetry readings, book signings and literary events throughout the year. Call (775) 786-1188 for details.

Lake Mansion, owned at one time by Myron Lake, the founder of Reno. A house museum filled with period furnishings, the mansion is an intriguing example of the Italianate style of Victorian architecture. It's open to the public by reservation and is also available for meetings and special events. Call (775) 829-1868 for information. The home was relocated in 1972 to its present location on the grounds of the Reno–Sparks Convention Center at the corner of S. Virginia Street and Kietzke Lane.

Performing Arts

Theater

Actors Workshop West
200 Flint St., Reno, Nev.
• **(775) 359-9755**
Kids and young adults from 9 to 17 years old can channel their creativity into positive action with workshops at the Actors Workshop West. Taught by veteran Hollywood actors, most workshops are ongoing at the Sierra Arts Center. See also our Close-up in this chapter.

AdRem Theater Group
(775) 358-1827
With three separate divisions, AdRem Theater Group provides intimate inspirational theater in a variety of venues in the Reno/Tahoe area. The Tumbleweed Gang performs melodramas, story theater and singalongs for family-oriented audiences. Theaterweb offers productions for adults and the Teen Wing provides classes and showcases for teenagers.

Brüka Theatre of the Sierra
99 N. Virginia St., Reno, Nev.
• **(775) 323-3221**
For bare-boned theater (minus high-tech bells and whistles), Brüka Theatre of the Sierra offers children's and avant-garde adult theater at its very best. Stripped of elaborate props, the emphasis is on the quality of acting, which local theater fans know is always topnotch.

Its downtown venue is quintessential casual, with cozy couches tucked casually around the intimate stage. Right next to the Truckee River, it's also convenient to downtown casinos and restaurants. In case you're wondering what "Brüka" means, it was the name of a turn-of-the-century German artistic group.

Gothic North Theater
3697A Kings Row, Reno, Nev.
• **(775) 329-7529**
While most nonprofit organizations have lofty mission statements, the Gothic North Theater has a cheerful motto: "If we aren't having fun, what in the world are we doing this for?" The all-volunteer group has a great time putting on about eight different shows with 11 performances each during a typical year. Variety is the name of the game with a mixed bag of comedy, drama and music. The 1998-1999 season, titled "Off the Beaten Path," included such offerings as *Edgar Allen Poe Reader's Theater*, *Perfect Crime*, *Nobody Knows I'm a Dog* and *Closer Than Ever*.

The theater also publishes a newsletter *Strut & Fret* and offers beginning and intermediate acting classes for children as young as 8. Using theater games and improvisational techniques, students work creatively with others to complete a production.

The group boasts about 50 volunteers and can always use more talent. Members stress that community theater involves a wide range of duties besides acting so you don't have to be a performer to get involved.

Reno Little Theater
(775) 331-1877
In 1935 the population of Reno was only 19,000 and live entertainment was sparse, to say the least. But a small group of determined theater aficionados joined together to form the Reno Little Theater, which has played to enthusiastic supporters ever since. The dedicated group of volunteers performed in its own venue until 1996 when their facility was demolished to make room for a parking garage on Sierra Street. The RLT's present home is the Reno Elks Club where it continues to offer a wide variety of high quality productions each season. Call for dates and performance offerings.

Storybook Theatre
(775) 348-8081
Storybook Theatre offers wholesome en-

tertainment for children, with adaptations of fairy tales that have a moral message. The scripts and music are the original works of the theater's founders. With audience participation encouraged, it's great fun for both children and adults. Call for locations, times and specific productions.

The Actory
610 S. Rock Blvd., Ste. 143, Sparks, Nev.
• (775) 331-9228

If you like your theater up-close and personal, you'll love the intimate ambiance of The Actory. At home in a 50-seat studio theater with cushioned seats and full lighting and sound systems, this nonprofit, artist-built company consists of both professional and semi-professional actors, designers and technicians.

The eclectic offerings of The Actory include comedies, serious dramas, classics and modern works, such as I Hate Hamlet, Twelfth Night and In His Words. The company performs about 10 full-scale and seven children's shows each year. If you've always wanted to get involved in the theater, the Actory Academy at The Actory is a great place to start. It offers workshops, acting seminars and production opportunities for both children and adults.

Music

Concerts in the Atrium
1325 Airmotive Wy., Reno, Nev.
• (775) 329-1324

You can make your lunch hour a musical break with the free concerts at noon on Fridays in the Atrium of the Airport Gardens Office Building. Programs vary from jazz to classical to contemporary. You can bring your own lunch or sample goodies from Gimmie's Restaurant and Catering. To special order lunch ahead call (775) 857-2224.

High Sierra Harmony
(775) 331-0634

High Sierra Harmony performs four-part a cappella barbershop music at community events throughout the year. The group is open to women who love to sing and perform. (For the men's counterpart to this group, see the subsequent listing for the Reno Barbershop Society.)

Interfaith Gospel Choir
(775) 828-0401

The Interfaith Gospel Choir was organized in 1972 to bring singers from various religious denominations and ethnic groups together in a celebration of contemporary gospel music. With as many as 130 participants representing 35 different churches in recent years, the choir has more than met its original goal. The group rehearses for several months in the fall and presents its annual concert in the Pioneer Center for the Performing Arts. Musical selections include original works of area songwriters in addition to well-known traditional songs.

Nevada Opera
(775) 786-4046

A nationally recognized regional opera company, Nevada Opera has been called the "grand dame" of Nevada's performing arts groups. It debuted in 1968 in the tiny 260-seat Reno Little Theater (which has since been torn down) with The Barber of Seville and Rigoletto. In just three years it outgrew this small venue and relocated to the Pioneer Center for the Performing Arts, where it's been performing since 1971.

Far from stuffy and boring, Nevada Opera performances are ambitious, exciting affairs. They are always fully staged with elaborate costumes, sets and a full orchestra. And even though they are sung in the original language, opera buffs can easily follow the plot because the English translation is projected above the proscenium stage.

The company has performed a provocative variety of works over the years, ranging from the grand Verdi Requiem and the familiar classic Swan Lake to light operettas, such as Showboat and Mame. With well over 100 mainstage productions to its credit, the opera performs three separate works each season.

The company offers emerging artists opportunities to perform with mature talents by showcasing guest performers from other opera companies in Europe and the United States. Many young talents whose careers began with Nevada Opera have gone on to national and world acclaim, including famous mezzo-soprano Dolora Zajick.

As part of the opera's extensive outreach and education program, the Nevada Opera

Youth Chorus offers professional training and performing experience to school-age talented youngsters. The Nevada Opera Studio brings shortened versions of standard operas to more than 50,000 area students each year.

Reno Barbershop Society
(775) 331-0634

The group is the male counterpart for High Sierra Harmony, previously listed in this section.

Reno Chamber Orchestra
(775) 348-9413

Known as Reno/Tahoe's "intimate orchestra," the 30-some member Reno Chamber Orchestra plays music designed specifically for small orchestras. Performances are classy but cozy affairs at the 615-seat Nightingale Concert Hall on the campus of the University of Nevada, Reno. In spite of some ups and downs weathered over the years, the group has enjoyed a growing audience of enthusiastic supporters since its founding in 1974. An impressive role call of guest soloists and conductors have shared its stage along the way, including Daniel Heifetz, Itzhak Perlman, Scott Yoo, Pepe Romero, Bion Tsang and Emil de Cou.

Part of the mission of the RCO is to assist the area's young musicians in developing their talents. It sends many promising musicians to summer camps each year and offers opportunities to perform with its Youth String Competition, the Reno Youth Symphony and the RCO College Concerto Competition. It also reaches outlying areas in northern Nevada and California, where classical music is a rarity, through broadcasts on radio station KUNR-FM.

Rated Best Performing Arts Group in the *Reno Gazette-Journal's* 1993 "Best of Reno" poll, the Reno Chamber Orchestra makes a distinctive contribution to the local performing arts scene.

Reno Municipal Band
(775) 329-7488

Founded in 1890, the Reno Municipal Band is the oldest performing arts group in the Reno/Tahoe area. It's also one of only three municipal bands in the country that are professional, with funding provided equally by the city and various foundations. With a whopping 150 performances each year, funders don't need to worry about getting their money's worth from this group.

In addition to playing in the principal band, the 50+ players perform in smaller groups, which include the swing bands, the banjo band, the barbershop group, the country band, the brass quintet and the String Beings. Most members are professional musicians or music teachers. Although the bands play at special events throughout the year, the best place to catch a performance is during the band's Summer Concert Series in Wingfield Park in downtown Reno. For details call the City of Reno Parks and Recreation Department at (775) 334-2262.

Reno Philharmonic Association
300 S. Wells Ave., Ste. 5, Reno, Nev.
• (775) 323-6393

Frequently voted Best Performing Arts Group in the *Reno Gazette-Journal's* annual "Best of Reno" contest, the Reno Philharmonic Orchestra is a splendid mainstay to the Reno/Tahoe music scene. A professional symphony comprised of the area's finest musicians, the Phil (as it's affectionately known by locals) has grown steadily in stature and popularity since its founding in 1969. In a typical year the group performs six MasterClassics subscription concerts and six Young People's Concerts for students plus a variety of special performances. A not-to-be-missed gala is Pops on the River, where music fans feast on gourmet picnics and pops music at festively decorated tables along the banks of the Truckee River. Over the years the Phil has also had the honor of performing with a number of well-known guest artists, including Luciano Pavarotti, Ray Charles, Jose Iturbi, George Shearing and Jerry Lewis.

In keeping with its commitment to Reno/

INSIDERS' TIP

John Wayne's last movie, *The Shootist*, was filmed in Carson City.

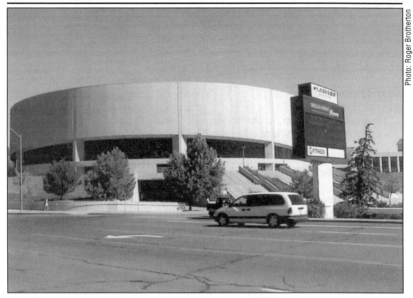

When not hosting ball games and sports events, the UNR Lawlor Center is used for ice shows, concerts and other special events.

Photo: Roger Brotherton

Tahoe's young people, the Reno Philharmonic Association sponsors the Reno Philharmonic Youth Orchestras, consisting of the brightest up-and-coming school-age musicians in the area. The youth orchestras usually perform about 15 concerts each year in various venues around the region. Through the youth and adult orchestras and the in-school Discover Music program of ensemble performances, more than 40,000 students enjoy first rate live concerts every year.

The social and fundraising arms of the association are the Reno Philharmonic Guild for the Reno/Sparks area and the Sierra Philharmonic League for the Carson Valley. Both groups sponsor events during the year that support the Philharmonic's programs while also enhancing the culture of the region.

Reno Pops Orchestra
(775) 673-2276, (775) 673-1234

The love of music and performing motivates the 40+ members of the Reno Pops Orchestra. Composed of players from all walks of life, it's truly a community group. With a mission to make music available to everyone, the group offers its seven annual concerts free as gifts to the general public. The orchestra also brings its performances to area at-risk schools for no cost.

Although you might think all concerts are just "pops" music, the orchestra's repertoire

INSIDERS' TIP

One of the most glorious sounds in the Reno/Tahoe area is the Casavant pipe organ at Trinity Episcopal Church, 200 Island Avenue in Reno. Custom built in Quebec, Canada, the organ has 2,000 pipes and took 85 employees about six months to construct. It made its debut at Trinity in May 1999. To hear this magnificent musical instrument, call the church at (775) 329-4279 for times of services.

is much broader. Beyond the basic criteria that selections have instant audience appeal, programs include overtures, well-known symphonies and concertos.

If you've ever contemplated dusting off your old clarinet from high school band days, now might be the time: the orchestra is always looking for additional players.

Sierra Nevada Master Chorale
(775) 333-9224

With an appearance at Carnegie Hall in its resume, the Sierra Nevada Master Chorale is one of the most outstanding performing arts groups in the Reno/Tahoe area. More than 80 trained and auditioned singers make up this volunteer-based choral group. You can enjoy their diverse repertoire, which includes opera, spirituals, Broadway musicals and classics, in their two annual concerts or in other performances in area communities.

Washoe County Community Concerts
(775) 323-2367

If you're looking for quality entertainment at an affordable price, Washoe County Community Concerts will certainly fill the bill. You can buy an annual membership for as little as $60, which entitles you to five concerts at the Pioneer Center for the Performing Arts. Performances vary from the classics to popular music and include soloists and small groups. The association has sponsored first-rate touring musicians to the Reno/Tahoe area for more than 50 years. Call for specific dates and offerings.

Dance

AREA-51 Dance Theatre
(775) 322-1343

AREA-51 Dance Theatre enriches the Reno/Tahoe performing arts scene by making modern dance an accessible art form for all audiences.

Public performances are given in a variety of venues in northern Nevada. The group also offers instruction in dance arts with residencies, lecture demonstrations, artistic presentations and performance tours.

International Folkloric Ballet Company
(775) 784-1540 ext. 231

The International Folkloric Ballet Company teaches and performs Hispanic dances from Spain, Mexico, Puerto Rico, Cuba and countries in Central and South America. Because of the growing Hispanic population in the Reno/Tahoe area, the company has enjoyed increasing popularity since its founding in 1983. Classes are free and take place several times a week at the YMCA on Foster Drive in Reno. To experience Hispanic culture on a deeper level, small groups of participants also travel periodically to other countries.

Native American Ensemble Theater
(775) 786-8889

For an exciting celebration of Native American dance, nothing beats the full powwow performed by the Native American Ensemble Theater. Complete with vibrant native dress and a verbal interpretation, programs are an eloquent portrayal of the Washoe, Paiute and Shoshone cultures. The contemporary dances are performed in a traditional style. The group appears frequently at community events in the Reno/Tahoe area.

Nevada Festival Ballet
1790 W. Fourth St., Reno, Nev.
• (775) 785-7915

When you attend the Nevada Festival Ballet, you're treated to a full-scale performing arts experience: it's one of the few ballet organizations in the country that uses live orchestra instead of taped music for all its performances. While it may surprise you that ballet flourishes amidst the glittering casino revues, the NFB has thrived since its founding in 1984 by well-known dancer and choreographer, Maggie Banks.

The NFB produces three major, full-length classical programs each season in the Pioneer Center for the Performing Arts. Selections have included *Swan Lake*, *Cinderella*, *Giselle*, *Coppelia, Sleeping Beauty, The Nutcracker* and *Don Quixote*. The company's prestigious reputation attracts internationally acclaimed guest principals for most productions, but the annual performance of *The Nutcracker* boasts one star that's a local, through and through. The horse pulling the sleigh in the first two acts is Bashful Star, a wild mustang captured near the small town of Lovelock, north of Reno. In addition to their in-house productions, NFB also presents an eclectic variety of touring shows, which have included the Diablo Ballet, the Martha Graham Ensemble, Jose Greco I & II, the Joseph Homes Chicago Dance Theatre and the Lakota Sioux Indian Dance Theatre.

Besides presenting topnotch performances, NFB exposes thousands of young people to ballet each season in its impressive outreach program. Through the School Outreach Program, at-risk youth join dance students in working with guest choreographers to present a performance that includes acting, singing and dancing. In the Dance for the Schools program, about 8,000 students from area public and private schools attend free ballet presentations.

The NFB School reaches hundreds of children and adults with its diverse curriculum, offering classes in ballet, jazz, modern and tap dancing as well as aerobics. Located in the Nevada Festival Ballet Center, classes take place in fully equipped dance studios with state-of-the-art floors and high, open ceilings. Because of the fine reputation the school enjoys, it's also a national audition site for major dance companies, such as the Joffrey Ballet School and Disney World.

Reno Folk Dancers
(775) 358-2306

Established for more than 50 years, the Reno Folk Dancers is a true melting pot. You can learn dances from all around the world, such as Greece, Israel or Serbia. Beginners are welcome and many dances are non-partnered. Call for times and meeting places.

Wing & A Prayer Dance Company
(775) 324-1082

With members ranging in age from 6 to 47, Wing & A Prayer Dance Company is one of the few intergenerational dance companies in the country. It was born in 1992 as a choreography project at the University of Nevada, Reno and now, as a mature company, offers lecture presentations, artist-in-residence programs, dance workshops and master classes

as well as a full schedule of exciting contemporary performances. Its Dance-in-Education Series provides free performances for students; its Master Dance Workshops offer classes taught by nationally acclaimed dancers; its Loneliest Roads Tour brings quality dance to rural communities in Nevada and California.

The name of the group reflects the uplifting nature of its performances. To celebrate the joyful aspects of life and movement, we recommend you catch this group in action at any of their appearances in the Reno/Tahoe area.

Venues

Brewery Arts Center
449 W. King St., Carson City, Nev.
• (775) 883-1976

Even though Carson City is covered as a daytrip in this book (see our Daytrips chapter), we'd be remiss in the Arts chapter by not telling you about the Brewery Arts Center. Since its founding more than 20 years ago, it's been a veritable hotbed of artistic activity. The 140-seat black box theater hosts more than 50 dramatic and musical performances every year. Resident companies include the professional Renaissance Players, the BAC Stage Kids, and the Proscenium Players, the second oldest local theater group in northern Nevada.

The visual arts are equally well-represented in the center with a full-service pottery studio, a full array of classes and workshops, receptions, exhibits and the Artisans' Store, which features works from more than 70 local artisans.

Because Carson City is within an hour's drive of most parts of the Reno/Tahoe area, it's easy to attend events at the Brewery Arts Center.

Lawlor Events Center
N. Virginia St., Univ. of Nevada, Reno, Reno, Nev. • (775) 784-4444

Lawlor Events Center is a multipurpose arena that's the home address for many University of Nevada, Reno athletic events. But when it's not busy hosting Wolf Pack basketball, it's available for ice shows, concerts and other special events. With a seating capacity of about 12,000, the center is a large no-frills venue. When attending events here, don't expect luxury since the ambiance is strictly gymnasium.

(We can't give you a physical address for the center because it doesn't have one. Just look for the large circular building perched on N. Virginia Street on the north end of the UNR campus.)

Lear Theater
501 Riverside Dr., Reno, Nev.
• **(775) 786-2278**

Designed by internationally acclaimed architect Paul Revere Williams, the First Church of Christ, Scientist has been an historic landmark in downtown Reno since it was constructed in 1939. Williams achieved fame during the Golden Age of Hollywood with such works as Chasen's and Perino's restaurants, the Fountain Coffee Shop at the Beverly Hills Hotel, and the Los Angeles Airport.

The Reno/Sparks Theater Community Coalition purchased the Reno church in 1998 with plans to convert the building into a state-of-the-art theater facility named after philanthropist Moya Olsen Lear Renovations will preserve the historical integrity of the building while providing a 450-seat auditorium, a studio theater, a rehearsal hall and dressing rooms. The major structural and interior work is scheduled for completion in the summer of 2000. With its picturesque location on the banks of the Truckee River, the Lear Theater is part of a growing arts presence in the heart of downtown Reno.

Pioneer Center for the Performing Arts
100 S. Virginia St., Reno, Nev.
• **(775) 686-6610**

The Pioneer Theater Auditorium was constructed in 1968 to meet the need for more convention and meeting facilities in downtown Reno. Later renamed the Pioneer Center for the Performing Arts, it's become the focal point and premier venue for many topnotch cultural events in the Reno/Tahoe area. Some of the groups who call it home include the Reno Philharmonic, the Nevada Opera, the Nevada Festival Ballet, the Washoe County Community Concert Association and the Sierra Nevada Master Chorale. With about 130 different

cultural productions presented annually, the facility is busy with events approximately 240 days out of the year. In addition to local and regional groups, it hosts a variety of touring performances. As part of the center's Broadway Comes to Reno series, theatergoers have enjoyed world-class presentations of Les Miserables, Cats, 42nd Street, Tommy, Stomp and She Loves Me.

The theater's gold geodesic dome, considered an architectural masterpiece at the time it was constructed, is a standout among the mostly mundane banks and office buildings close by. Its upscale interior is hushed and quiet, almost cathedral-like, which lends an air of expectation to most performances. Since the classy surroundings provide just the right background for formal attire, don't be surprised if you find yourself in a sea of fur coats, especially at the opera or philharmonic concerts.

But even a facility as lovely as this has downsides, mainly its small size and lack of parking. Although its 1,500-seat capacity gives an almost intimate feel to large productions, many shows are sold out early. And with no parking provided by the center, patrons are forced to park on the street or in nearby garages.

We recommend you reserve tickets as early as possible and that you allow plenty of time to park prior to performances. When buying tickets ahead of time, we also recommend that you try to pick them up before coming to the performance or have them mailed to you. The box office is open weekdays from 10 AM to 6 PM. If you wait to get them at "will call" right before the event you could end up standing in a lengthy line and perhaps miss some of the performance. Whatever system is used (or perhaps because of the lack of one), it's often inadequate to process a large crowd, especially if the theater is near capacity.

R. Z. Hawkins Cultural Amphitheater
6000 Bartley Ranch Rd., Reno, Nev.
• **(775) 828-6612**

Tucked into a natural bowl in Bartley Ranch Regional Park, the R. Z. Hawkins Cultural Amphitheater is a 400-seat outdoor facility for drama and music productions. In keeping with the ranch theme of the park, the stage has a country look, with barn doors and a corrugated tin roof. You can picnic in the park and then attend evening performances under the stars when the weather permits. See our Parks chapter for details about the park.

Wingfield Park Amphitheater
2 N. Arlington Ave., Reno, Nev.
• (775) 334-2077

In downtown Reno next to the Truckee River Walk, the Wingfield Park Amphitheater is a venue with a view: you can drink in the beauty of the river with the city lights of downtown Reno as a bedazzling backdrop. The outdoor site of numerous concerts and special affairs, it's a real treat to attend events here when the weather permits (see our description of Wingfield Park in our Parks chapter).

Visual Arts

Brain Productions
(775) 747-4184

If you've always wanted to make a movie, here's your chance. Brain Productions is a small group of independent filmmakers who pursue film as an artistic endeavor. From scripting to casting to producing, all aspects of creating a film are performed by local residents. The group is open to anyone with talent and interest in creative film.

Caughlin Arts Center
4100 Caughlin Pkwy., Reno, Nev.
• (775) 747-6008

Located in the Caughlin Club in the Caughlin Ranch residential area, the Caughlin Arts Center offers a variety of arts classes for children and adults. It also sponsors workshops, special events and seminars as well as providing a small gallery for local art displays.

Connections
(775) 358-5149

An alliance of regional artists representing a variety of disciplines, Connections meets monthly to network and plan group exhibits.

Membership is open to both working and amateur artists.

Great Basin Basketmakers
(775) 747-0895

Baskets are a magical art form when created by artisans in the Great Basin Basketmakers group. Members gather each month to network, attend workshops and sponsor exhibits. The yearly dues of $12 entitles these artists to the group newsletter and access to a large library.

Keystone II Cinema
2500 E. Second St., Reno, Nev.
• (775) 786-4411

With its cozy couches just big enough for two, the Keystone II Cinema is the next best thing to having your own private screening room. Tucked away in the lower level of the Reno Hilton, it shows classics and foreign films not available in traditional theaters, in addition to first-run movies. We recommend a movie followed by dinner in Andiamo, the delightful Italian restaurant upstairs on the casino level. For more information about entertainment at the Reno Hilton, see our Kidstuff, Resorts and Casino Nightlife chapters.

Latimer Art Club
(775) 851-1712

Founded in 1921 by acclaimed landscape artist Lorenzo P. Latimer, the Latimer Art Club is the oldest art group in Nevada. It sponsors workshops and brings well-known artists to the Reno/Tahoe area to teach. Besides painting and studying together, members travel to neighboring states and cities to view exhibits. Latimer is also known as one of the founders of the Nevada Art Gallery, which later became the Sierra Nevada Museum of Art.

Nevada Casting Group, Inc.
100 Washington St., Suite 100, Reno, Nev. • (775) 322-8187

So you wanna be a star? Nevada Casting Group, Inc., gives many newcomers a start in the movies and television. You can pick up

---

INSIDERS' TIP

To see a whimsical display of casino art, check out the lobby of the Hampton Inn at Harrah's at 219 N. Center Street in Reno.

information about how to sign up at their office on Washington Street. Just look in the box next to the office door for printed materials. Don't be surprised if the staff isn't in since they're usually out filming somewhere in the area.

Nevada Museum of Art, E. L. Wiegand Gallery
160 W. Liberty St., Reno, Nev.
• (775) 329-3333

The only accredited fine arts museum in Nevada, the Nevada Museum of Art had humble beginnings as the Nevada Art Gallery in 1931. From its early days as a volunteer-run organization, it has evolved into a major visual arts institution that is professionally administered and staffed by 10 full-time and four part-time employees.

The museum provides a forum for creative ideas through its collections, exhibitions, community outreach and education programs. With about 1,200 works of art, the Permanent Collection centers on the aesthetic articulation of western environment. The exhibitions change every month or so and present the works of the world's finest artists, such as Rodin and Miro. The community outreach program offers lectures, films and speakers in conjunction with the exhibitions as well as workshops for local school students. And the E.L. Cord Museum School presents classes in a variety of media that are taught by professional artists for low tuition. Far from being stuffy and elitist, the NMA strives to be the cultural resource for everyone in the community.

We highly recommend you drop by the museum for a leisurely artistic experience. It's especially convenient if you're walking along the Truckee River Walk since it's just about a block away in the downtown area. Museum hours are 10 AM to 4 PM Tuesday, Wednesday and Friday; 10 AM to 7 PM on Thursday and noon to 4 PM on Saturday and Sunday. It's closed on Monday and national holidays. Admission is $5 for adults, $3 for seniors and students and $1 for children 6 to 12 years old. Be sure to stop by the gift shop for that one-of-a-kind gift you'll never find anywhere else.

Sierra Watercolor Society
(775) 825-8527

The Sierra Watercolor Society was orga-

nized in 1989 to help promote local artists' love of watercolors. With about 100 member artists from around the area, the group sponsors exhibits of members' works, gives demonstrations in the schools and presents workshops by visiting artists. Members network through their bimonthly meetings at the Sierra Arts Center and also keep in touch through a monthly newsletter.

Wine of the Week
(775) 352-4969

Members of the Wine of the Week club (WOW) share their love of fine wine and art at monthly get-togethers at area galleries. There's no cost to join; just bring your favorite wine or bread and cheese and enjoy the friendly hospitality. Call to get your name on the mailing list of events.

Literary Arts

Barnes & Noble
5555 S. Virginia St., Reno, Nev.
• (775) 826-8882

The epitome of a super bookstore, Barnes & Noble is a one-stop cultural emporium. More than just a splendid shopping mart for books, music and videos or a cozy place to enjoy a steaming cup of espresso, it's a vibrant center for special cultural events. Literary-minded Insiders will tell you it's also a great place for culturally inclined singles to meet and greet.

Borders Books
4995 S. Virginia St., Reno, Nev.
• (775) 448-9999

It's not enough for megabookstores to simply sell books, videos and music. They also sponsor special events, such as book signings, poetry readings and concerts. As a mini cultural center with its own gourmet cafe, Borders is a comfortable hangout for literary fans. Check local newspapers or call the store for their upcoming events.

Creative Writing
(775) 345-6153

A group for seniors who love to write, Creative Writing meets once a week at Classic Residence in Reno. It's primarily a support group for both published and unpublished writ-

All the World's a Stage —
Including the Reno/Tahoe Area

"Lights — camera — action."

Who hasn't had the fantasy about how great it would be to hear those words as an actor? Well, thanks to veteran movie stars Michael Moore and Darlanne Fluegal, the husband and wife team who founded Actors Workshop West in Reno, area residents are turning those fantasies into reality.

Thanks to the need to escape the hustle and bustle of New York and Hollywood for their children's sake, Michael and Darlanne are now Reno residents, and they've decided to pass on their more than 20 years' experience in the acting business with their workshops.

Michael's films have included *Cheating Hearts* with James Brolin and Kris Kristofferson. Darlanne was a regular on TV's *Crime Story* and *Hunter*. She has also appeared as Sylvester Stallone's girlfriend in *Lock Up* and acted in more than 20 movies with the likes of Kirk Douglas and Billy Crystal. The couple has also directed several documentaries and music videos so their talents are well-rounded. Now, they are content with passing on their expertise to fledgling actors.

Their teaching style is unique and based on the training they received from acting teachers like Milton Katesalas, Stella Adler and Uta Hagen. They have practical experience in the real world of acting and teach techniques that work well in film, TV and on the stage. They have also worked with singers who want to become entertainers.

"Our philosophy is that real winners are ordinary people with extraordinary determination and drive to do things ordinary people wouldn't let themselves dream of doing," Michael says. "Darlanne and I love being part of that process."

After teaching in New York, they came to Reno to fulfill their dream of running a school for actors and filmmakers. They like to say they're far enough away from Hollywood to be creative but close enough to be accessible.

Their workshops include Introduction to Acting for both adults and children, several other acting classes, an improv class and a performance class. Other than the intro class, which is a two-month course with new sessions beginning every month, all workshops are ongoing and can be started at any time.

"Actors Workshop West is a safe environment where everyday dreamers break the bonds of creative limitation through the art and exploration of acting," Darlanne says. "This is where you can move toward your dreams, increase your self confidence and find and explore your talent. You'll be amazed at the results."

But to show their students that they indeed still practice what they preach, Michael and Darlanne remain active in the world of glitter and lights. Michael has been recruited to be the lead in a proposed New York cop drama for HBO and the couple has received an offer to be in a major motion picture. They also perform in the Reno/Tahoe area and wowed theatergoers in July of 1999 with their adaptation of A.R. Gurney's play *Love Letters*. The couple has recently received funding and are looking forward to building their own theater in Reno to showcase their students' talents.

For more information about the Actors Workshop West or to talk to Michael and Darlanne if you are contemplating fine-tuning your acting skills, telephone them at their workshop at (775) 359-9755.

ers, and meetings are structured with writing exercises and lessons. The group is limited to 15 and there's usually a waiting list, but newcomers are always welcome to sign up.

Great Basin Book Festival
(775) 784-6587

Sponsored by the Nevada Humanities Committee in September, the Great Basin Book Festival celebrates literary arts with a huge outdoor exhibit in Wingfield Park and lectures and discussions in various downtown Reno locations. You can browse the booths along the banks of the Truckee River and buy autographed books from the authors themselves. With just a hint of fall in the air and a touch of gold in the trees, the festival offers a delicious opportunity to expand your mind while enjoying nature at its most irresistible. (For more information, see our Annual Events chapter.)

Nevada Poetry Society
(775) 322-3619

As a member of the National Federation of State Poetry Societies, the Nevada group helps area poets hone their craft. At its monthly meetings, members critique each other's work and study different forms of writing poetry. It's literally a prizewinning group: with the encouragement of their peers, many members have won awards in national and state poetry contests.

Sierra Nevada Chapter of the Society of Children's Book Writers and Illustrators
13484 Rick Cr., Reno, Nev.
• (775) 853-3386

A regional chapter of the international society of childrens' book writers, which was established in 1970, this organization provides both writers and illustrators with information on publishers from around the world, acquiring an agent, and how to submit work. The 100-member regional chapter meets monthly for workshops and seminars and cosponsors

the annual Art of the Children's Book Festival, which is held in the fall. Some members are published, but anybody who is interested in writing or illustrating children's books or magazines can join.

Northern Nevada Romance Writers of America
(775) 358-8679

Writing isn't a solitary business for the area romance writers who network through the Northern Nevada Romance Writers of America. Founded in 1989 as part of the national Romance Writers of America, the group meets every month to discuss writing and to critique each other's work.

Reno, Nevada, Branch of the National League of American PenWomen
(775) 885-0716

A branch of the national organization founded more than 100 years ago in Washington, DC, the group is composed of professional artists, writers and musicians. It encourages creative work through charitable activities and scholarships.

The Reno News & Review Western Lit Book Club
(775) 324-4440

One of the best things about reading a good book is sharing it with others. Members of the Western Lit Book Club meet monthly at Borders Books to discuss selected works by contemporary literary authors who live in the West or who write about the West. Organized by staff at the *Reno News & Review*, the area's alternate weekly newspaper, the group provides a comfortable, kicked-back forum for those who love to read.

Unnamed Writers' Group
(775) 329-4610

Started by three writers in 1995, the Unnamed Writers' Group has about 150 members who are published and unpublished writers. With its mission of "helping writers write better," the group sponsors workshops and seminars on different forms of writing and presents guest speakers at its monthly meetings. Members also critique each other's work and participate in a community writing project that involves charity each year.

Washoe County Library System
301 S. Center St., Reno, Nev.
• (775) 785-4190
• www.washoe.lib.nv.us

When the Washoe County Library System tells you it "offers more than just books," you'd better believe it. Its 13 physical facilities are focal points for community activities as well as storehouses of information for every interest imaginable. The system boasts seven library buildings, six partnership branches, 12 meeting rooms, two art galleries, two theaters and 12 multipurpose rooms. The main branch on Center Street in Reno is a wonderful place for reading and browsing. With loads of leafy green plants and trees, its arboretum atmosphere is a delightful haven from the busy downtown streets outside. The newest library branch on Robb Drive is especially user-friendly, with a latte cart, a drive-up window and a used bookstore operated by the Friends of Washoe County Library.

Although libraries have been synonymous with the printed word for many years, today most of them are also high-tech, with all the bells and whistles needed for high-speed transmittal of electronic information. The Washoe system is no exception since its Internet Branch provides access to more than 1,000 information sources on the Internet.

With about 130 programs for adults and an amazing 1,737 for children and young adults, outreach is alive and well in this library system. The variety of specific events is impressive to say the least and much too long to list in this chapter. You can call the library for

their calendar of events and watch local newspapers for current happenings.

If you love to buy books (and what avid reader doesn't?), you won't want to miss the "Booksale Bonanza," sponsored by the Friends of Washoe County Library the first part of June. It's Northern Nevada's largest community-wide booksale, with more than 25 tons of books up for grabs.

Educational Institutions

Truckee Meadows Community College
7000 Dandini Blvd., Reno, Nev.
• (775) 673-7000

TMCC offers a wide variety of classes in the performing, visual and literary arts. We can't begin to describe them all: consult the college catalogue for a complete listing. The public frequently shares the work and accomplishments of TMCC's arts students and faculty through their theater productions and visual arts exhibits. The college does more than just teach the arts: it brings them to the community as a way of enriching life in the Truckee Meadows. For more information on the school see our Education and Child Care chapter.

University of Nevada, Reno
N. Virginia St., Reno, Nev.
• (775) 784-1110

It's possible to estimate the economic impact of the University of Nevada, Reno on the Reno/Tahoe area, but how do you begin to describe its influence on the local culture and quality of life? Since the answer to that question is quite subjective, we think it's enough to simply understand that a major university permeates every facet of life in a community, injecting intellectual choices and cultural contributions that the area might not have had otherwise.

INSIDERS' TIP

For dinner with a murder thrown in, you can attend the mystery dinner theater in the Odeon Hall above Mia's Swiss Restaurant on Pike Street in historic Dayton, Nevada. It's just an hour's drive from Reno. Call (775) 246-3993 for details.

The Pioneer Theater Auditorium in Reno hosts topnotch cultural events.

Because it offers a wide variety of programs and degrees in various artistic disciplines, UNR has been a focal point for the local arts scene for many years. The university sponsors a veritable kaleidoscope of stimulating events throughout the year, presented by students and faculty as well as members of the community, guest artists and speakers. In the university's Nightingale Concert Hall you can enjoy first-class performances by such talented resident groups as the Argenta Quartet, the UNR Orchestra, the UNR Mastersingers and the Reno Jazz Quintet. In the Redfield Proscenium Theatre and the Redfield Studio Theatre you can delight in exquisite dance and lively theater. And in the Lawlor Events Center (when not used for major athletic events), you can attend large productions, such as ice shows and rock concerts in a typical arena-style venue.

As the only university repertory company in the country, the Nevada Repertory Company gives students, faculty and community members the opportunity to work in a different show each night. With four distinct productions offered each season, the company provides a well-rounded theater experience to both cast and crew. Selections are widely varied, with the 1998-1999 season offering *Into the Woods*, *Angels In America*, *A Clockwork Orange* and *A Grand Night for Singing*. For information call (775) 784-6847 and be sure to ask about weekend dinner/theater options.

Aside from this tantalizing array of performing arts events, UNR is also a dynamic supporter of the visual and literary arts. You can always count on a topnotch exhibit in the Sheppard Art Gallery plus an interesting display of student literary work outside the Kenneth J. Printing Studio in the Getchell Library. The university's Black Rock Press has been a mainstay for local writers for many years, publishing such well-known authors as Robert Laxalt and Gary Snyder.

Although parking on university campuses is often restrictive and challenging for visitors, UNR's parking garage just north of the Church Fine Arts building provides adequate parking for most events. For information call (775) 784-1985.

For updated information on all UNR arts events be sure to call the University Arts Hotline at (775) 334-9696.

Galleries

Addi Galleries Reno
2500 E. Second St., Reno, Nev.
• **(775) 323-1920**

Addi Galleries Reno presents a feast of fine art in its sumptuous location on the casino level of the Reno Hilton. From sculptures to oil paintings, there's something to please everyone's artistic tastes. Hours are 9 AM to 10 PM daily.

Art & Rubbish
250 W. First St., Reno, Nev.
• **(775) 348-8858**

One of the area's newest galleries, Art & Rubbish is Reno's only consigned original art and refurbished furniture gallery. If you're looking for real affordable art, don't miss this store since most everything is very reasonably priced. The focus is on emerging local artists in all types of media, with new exhibits featured every month. Since it's located near Wingfield Park in downtown, you can easily combine a visit to this gallery with a jaunt along the Truckee River. Hours are 10 AM to 5 PM Monday through Saturday and from noon to 4 PM Sunday.

Artists Co-op Gallery
627 Mill St., Reno, Nev. • (775) 322-8896

Situated in an historic brick building at the corner of Wells Avenue and Mill Street, the Artists Co-op Gallery was the first art cooperative in Nevada when it opened in 1966. The 20 award-winning artist members offer original art at reasonable prices and with payment schedules. The works include oils, watercolors, pastels, mixed media, photography and pottery. The gallery is open daily from 11 AM to 4 PM.

Boyce Art Images
4900 Charlotte Wy., Reno, Nev.
• **(775) 857-6136**

Award-winning wildlife artist Fred Boyce is one of the best-known outdoor artists in the Reno/Tahoe area. For those who love "nature" art and Nevada landscapes, his gallery is truly a treasure. He has also published two coffee table books with photos of his work, *The Other Nevada* and *The Other Nevada II*. You can view his originals, limited editions and lithographs prints from 8 AM to 5 PM daily, but we recommend you call ahead.

C.I.T.Y. 2000 Gallery
490 S. Center St., Reno, Nev.
• **(775) 321-8315**

The City of Reno's support for the arts is clearly evident when you walk into city hall: you can enjoy the diverse collection of art that's displayed in the C.I.T.Y. 2000 Gallery just inside. Sponsored by the city's arts commission and managed by the Sierra Arts Foundation, the gallery showcases the works of local artists or works of interest to the local community.

To maintain a standard of excellence in the exhibits, a panel of professionals selects the works to be shown. The gallery is open Monday through Friday from 8 AM to 5 PM.

Gene Speck's Silver State Gallery
719 Plumas St., Reno, Nev.
• **(775) 324-2323**

Housed in a quaint old house built in 1912, Gene Speck's Silver State Gallery features Mr. Speck's western oils in addition to original works by other well-known artists. Media represented usually include watercolors, ceramics, pastels, pottery, baskets and bronze sculptures. The gallery hosts regular shows and receptions which are open to the public. Hours are 11 AM to 6 PM Monday through Saturday and noon to 5 PM on Sunday.

Hermitage Gallery
8155 S. Virginia St., Reno, Nev.
• **(775) 852-2215**

Hermitage Gallery combines a tantalizing selection of fine art with historical collectibles, such as original autographs of famous people, antique posters and prints, rare books and early engravings. It also offers one of the area's finest custom framing services. Hours are 10 AM to 6 PM Monday through Friday and 10 AM to 3 PM on Saturday.

Richardson Gallery of Fine Art
3670 S. Virginia St., Reno, Nev.
• **(775) 828-0888**

Showcasing a delightful variety of inspirational paintings and exquisite sculptures,

INSIDERS' TIP

Check with your hotel concierge for current gallery showings.

Richardson Gallery of Fine Art is a great place for both art browsers and serious buyers. Conveniently located between the Peppermill and Atlantis casinos, you'll find a large variety of works by today's most talented and well-known artists attractively displayed here. The gallery is open Monday through Saturday from 10:30 AM to 6:30 PM and on Sunday from 11 AM to 5 PM.

River Gallery
135 N. Sierra St., Reno, Nev.
• **(775) 329-3698**
You can combine a walk along the Truckee River with a visit to the River Gallery since it's just a stone's throw away. Specializing in ceramics, masks, glass, folk art and fine crafts from all over the world, the gallery offers a unique selection of artistic works for your own home or gifts for friends. Hours are 10 AM to 6 PM Monday through Saturday and noon to 6 PM on Sunday.

Sheppard Gallery
Church Fine Arts Building, Univ. of Nevada, Reno, Reno, Nev.
• **(775) 784-6658**
Sheppard Gallery showcases the wonderfully eclectic works of students and faculty at the University of Nevada, Reno as well as nationally known artists. Exhibits change every month and include all types of media. You can browse or buy from 8 AM to 5 PM on Monday, Wednesday and Friday and from 8 AM to 6 PM on Tuesday and Thursday. To park at the university, pick up a visitors parking pass from the information booth just off Ninth Street.

Sierra Arts Center Gallery
200 Flint St., Reno, Nev.
• **(775) 329-1324**
It's very fitting to walk right into an art gallery when you visit the Sierra Arts Foundation on Flint Street. After all, much of the brainstorming and creative work that goes into artistic events in the area takes place in the offices and meeting rooms in this building. The gallery provides an intimate setting for display of contemporary works that are innovative and challenging. You can enjoy this art weekdays from 8:30 AM to 5 PM.

Stremmel Gallery
1400 S. Virginia St., Reno, Nev.
• **(775) 786-0558**
Founded in 1969, Stremmel Gallery is one of the oldest galleries in the Reno/Tahoe area. Its modern, sleek exterior is a reflection of the contents within, mainly abstract and representative contemporary art. The gallery displays an interesting mix of two- and three-dimensional works, in such media as oils, pastels, bronzes and marbles. It's open from 9 AM to 5 PM Monday through Friday and by appointment only on Saturday.

Valle Art Gallery
213 E. Plumb Ln., Reno, Nev.
• **(775) 323-1887**
Esteban Valle displays his original paintings of Nevada and the Southwest in his gallery on the second floor of Shoppers Square shopping center. His works also include wildlife and florals. Gallery hours are 10 AM to 5 PM Monday through Saturday.

Western & Wildlife Galleries
2500 E. Second St., Reno, Nev.
• **(775) 786-1558**
995 Forest St., Reno, Nev.
• **(775) 826-7022**
If you love animals, this is definitely the place for you. Both locations of the Western & Wildlife Galleries feature captivating representations of wildlife in a variety of media. You can also relive the wild, wild West through provocative collections of Western art. Hours for the Second Street location, on the casino level of the Reno Hilton, are 9 AM to 9 PM daily and for the Forest Street store, 9 AM to 5 PM Monday through Saturday.

North Shore Lake Tahoe

Support Organizations

Arts For The Schools
(530) 546-4602
Arts For The Schools is the only organization that provides year-round artistic multicultural programs in the North Shore Lake

Tahoe area. Although it was founded to expand quality arts experiences in the schools, the group's accomplishments reach the entire community. Programs include arts outreach, cultural events and artistic performances.

Performing Arts

Theater

Lake Tahoe Shakespeare Festival
Sand Harbor, Incline Village, Nev.
• **(800) 747-4697**

Shakespeare might be astonished to see his classic works performed on the shore of North America's largest alpine lake, but somehow the richness of productions like *Romeo and Juliet* and *Twelfth Night* is enhanced by the awesome beauty of the outdoor venue. The Lake Tahoe Shakespeare Festival has enjoyed robust success since its founding in 1978 and in 1999 was named one of the "Top 100 Festivals in North America" by *Destinations* magazine. Although the setting is laid-back and natural, a night at the festival offers much of the pageantry found in a traditional theater, from the call of the trumpets signaling the start of the performance to the colorful Shakespearean banners decorating the entrance.

With a first-class setting and a first-rate performance, only fine wining and dining can complete the picture. You can bring your own gourmet picnic or you can choose from a wide variety of delicacies offered for sale at the park. For maximum comfort we suggest you bring beach chairs (they must be the low-back short-legged type) or consider renting them for $3. And because the temperature drops rapidly after the sun goes down, be sure to bring a sweater or jacket to avoid getting cold.

Performances begin at 7:30 PM, but theatergoers begin arriving at 6 PM to enjoy dining with a world-class view. The festival takes place the last five weeks of the summer before Labor Day, with performances daily except Monday. Prices range from $18 for general admission on Sunday, Tuesday and Wednesday to $28 for early seating on Thurs-day, Friday and Saturday. If you suspect a performance may be cancelled because of rain, be sure to call on the day you plan to attend. (See also our Annual Events chapter.)

The cast for the festival is provided by The Foothill Theatre Company, which also hosts a Shakespeare Camp for children 8 to 16 years old. Students from all over the country learn set and costume design, acting, makeup and character design at the one- and two-week sessions in August. For details call the company at (888) 730-8587.

Music

Incline Village Chamber Music Society
(775) 831-0334

Although we've often heard "there's no free lunch," the Incline Village Chamber Music Society proves that old aphorism wrong with its Sunday Afternoons at the Chateau. For six consecutive Sundays in July and August you can attend live performances by top-quality classical artists — absolutely free. The series is made possible through the generous support of local patrons. Concerts are at 3 PM at the Chateau, 955 Fairway Boulevard in Incline Village. Call for specific dates and program details.

Lake Tahoe Summer Music Festival
(530) 583-3101

The Lake Tahoe Summer Music Festival is a magical marriage of fine classical music and nature at its most exquisite. Founded in 1986 by Edgar Braun, the longtime conductor of the San Francisco Chamber Orchestra, the festival offers an exciting feast of concerts from July through Labor Day. Venues are at Sand Harbor, Granlibakken Resort, Valhalla at the Boathouse, Squaw Valley, Tahoe Donner and the Topol Pavilion at Homewood. Braun conducts the Festival Orchestra in a diverse range of programs from contemporary to classic.

If you enjoy high-quality music and gorgeous scenery (and who doesn't?), you simply can't go wrong in attending any of these events. Call for specific locations, programs and times (see our Annual Events chapter for more information).

Visual Arts

Sierra Artists' Network and North Tahoe Art Center
380 N. Lake Blvd., Tahoe City, Calif.
• **(530) 581-2707**

Since its founding in 1989, the Sierra Artists' Network has been the heartbeat of the arts scene in the North Shore Lake Tahoe area. With a membership of about 200 enthusiastic artists and art appreciators, the group sponsors art shows, receptions, guest speakers and fundraisers. It also publishes a monthly newsletter, *Tahoe ARTour*. SAN's Tahoe ARTour is Lake Tahoe's oldest annual open studio tour and sale which showcases local artists in their own environment.

Since 1994 SAN has been headquartered in the North Tahoe Art Center, one of Tahoe City's historic lakeside buildings. The center serves as a focal point for artists, with its gallery exhibits, gift shop and meeting rooms for workshops and classes.

Tahoe International Film Festival
(530) 583-3378

With all the trappings of a major film fest, the Tahoe International Film Festival showcases an eclectic menu of independent features, documentaries, shorts and animations from filmmakers around the world. It's a fun-filled event, with formal galas in Squaw Valley and Incline Village sprinkled among the film showings. Call for specific dates and events.

Educational Institutions

Sierra Nevada College
800 College Dr., Incline Village, Nev.
• **(775) 831-1314**

Although it's a small school by university standards (see our Education and Child Care chapter for details), Sierra Nevada College offers an interesting variety of classes in the arts, including art history, ceramics, drawing, painting, photography, printmaking, electronic arts, sculpture, music and theater. It offers bachelor's degrees in art and music. For lifelong, non-degree learners it also has a continuing education program that includes creative arts courses. SNC's summer Visiting Arts Workshops present an amazing potpourri of artists that span the spectrum of disciplines, such as high-fire porcelains, wheel-thrown ceramics, raku firing, conceptual sculpture, digital imaging, musical pet therapy and modern poetry.

But if you're not into classroom settings, you can still soak up culture through SNC's Second Sunday Series. Running from September to May each year, the forum showcases locally based artists who share their creativity with the community at large. You can also enjoy performances and exhibits by SNC students and visiting artists in the Croom Theater and the Tahoe Gallery at the Mountain Campus. Call for schedules and details.

Galleries

Art Attack Gallery
868 Tahoe Blvd., Incline Village, Nev.
• **(775) 832-7400**

Browsing is a delight in this roomy gallery in the Christmas Tree Village shopping mall in Incline Village. (We tell you more about the picturesque mall in our Shopping chapter.) Art Attack Gallery hosts many well-advertised special exhibits throughout the year in addition to its ongoing displays of originals and limited edition prints. You can visit the gallery daily from 10 AM to 6 PM.

Artists of Tahoe–Art's Desire
761 Northwood Blvd. #2, Incline Village, Nev. • **(775) 831-3011**

Focusing primarily on local artists, Artists of Tahoe–Art's Desire displays innovative works in a variety of media. The gallery also offers vintage photographs and custom framing service. It's open 10 AM to 5 PM Monday through Friday and from noon to 5 PM on Saturday.

Frames by Ryrie
475 N. Lake Blvd., Tahoe City, Calif.
• **(530) 583-3043**

In the picturesque Cobblestone Mall across the street from Lake Tahoe, Frames by Ryrie offers unique gifts, posters and ready-made frames as well as a beautiful collection of ski prints by Cecile Johnson. The mall is great for browsing (see our Shopping chapter for details). The gallery is open Monday through Saturday from 10 AM to 5:30 PM and Sunday from 11 AM to 5 PM.

Gallery at Squaw Creek
400 Squaw Creek Rd., Olympic Valley, Calif. • **(530) 581-2000**

You can appreciate beauty on the inside as well as on the outside when you visit this lovely gallery in Olympic Valley. Tucked away in the Resort at Squaw Creek Mall, adjacent to beautiful Squaw Valley USA, you can enjoy an extensive collection of fine art originals, sculptures and limited prints along with a boutique of exquisite designer jewelry. Hours are 10 AM to 6 PM Sunday through Thursday and 9 AM to 9 PM Friday and Saturday. Hours may vary during Squaw Valley's off season, which is late spring and fall.

James Harold Galleries
760 N. Lake Blvd., Tahoe City, Calif.
• **(530) 581-5111**

When you're browsing the Boatworks Mall in Tahoe City, be sure to stop by James Harold Galleries on the second level. It features a diverse collection of original paintings, objets d'art, sculptures, glass art, limited reproductions and collectibles. The mall offers an interesting mix of stores and restaurants right on the shore of Lake Tahoe (see our Shopping chapter for details). Winter hours for the gallery are 10 AM to 6 PM Sunday through Thursday and 10 AM to 9 PM Friday and Saturday. Hours are extended to 10 PM during the summer months.

Kilim Hand Woven Rugs
8675 N. Lake Blvd., Kings Beach, Calif.
• **(530) 546-4011**

Although it might seem odd to shop for Oriental rugs along the shore of an alpine lake,

Photo: Brooks Walker/Lake Tahoe Shakespeare Festival

Outdoor performances at Tahoe combine the best of natural beauty and cultural experience.

Photo: Corel Print House

Dance and the performing arts have become an important part of the Reno/Tahoe cultural scene.

you can choose from the largest selection of Kilims in the country at Kilim Hand Woven Rugs. The owner takes pride in offering the finest in exotic carpets from his travels to Pakistan, India and Turkey. Hours are from 10 AM to 5 PM daily, and until 6 PM during the summer.

Lakeside Gallery & Gifts
8636 N. Lake Blvd., Kings Beach, Calif.
• **(530) 546-3135**

Offering art supplies, painting workshops and framing service, Lakeside Gallery & Gifts is a full-service art store as well as gallery. One of the oldest galleries at the lake, it exhibits mostly landscapes, impressionism, prints and watercolors by local artists. Hours are 10 AM to 5 PM Monday through Saturday.

North Tahoe Art Center
280 N. Tahoe Blvd., Tahoe City, Calif.
• **(530) 581-2787**

You can view a new exhibit and meet the artist who created it the first Friday of every month in the North Tahoe Art Center. The gallery features an intriguing mix of artistic works

throughout the year, mostly from artists who live and work in the Lake Tahoe area. You can also buy local artists' work in the gift shop. Hours are 11 AM to 4 PM Wednesday through Sunday and 10 AM to 5 PM daily during the summer.

Pogan Gallery
255 N. Lake Blvd., Tahoe City, Calif.
• **(530) 583-0553**

The only strictly fine arts gallery in the Lake Tahoe area, Pogan Gallery sells only original work. Inspired by the beauty of the Lake Tahoe Basin, well-known artists come from all over the country to paint at the lake and the gallery reaps the rewards with its large collection of landscapes of the region. Hours are 10 AM to 5:30 PM daily.

The Potlatch
930 Tahoe Blvd., Incline Village, Nev.
• **(775) 831-2485**

Visiting The Potlatch is a visual delight: the variety of textures and hues in this vibrant collection of Native-American and Southwestern art is colorful, to say the least. With a large selection of fine crafts and jewelry, it's a great place to purchase gifts at a reasonable price. It's open daily from 10 AM to 5:30 PM.

The Potter's Wheel
8331 N. Lake Blvd., Kings Beach, Calif.
• (530) 546-8400

If you're looking for fine pottery, this store is a must stop. It offers a selection of weavings, watercolors and woodworking. Hours are 10 AM to 6 PM Friday through Tuesday.

Tahoe Gallery
800 College Dr., Incline Village, Nev.
• (775) 831-1314

Sierra Nevada College displays students' work as well as the works of visiting and local professional artists in the Tahoe Gallery in Abernathy Hall at the Mountain Campus. Special exhibits with receptions for the artists are also held every few weeks throughout the school year. Regular gallery hours are 8 AM to 5 PM Monday through Friday.

Vista Gallery
7081 N. Lake Blvd., Tahoe Vista, Calif.
• (530) 546-7794

If you're looking for vintage Lake Tahoe photographs, check this gallery out: it has a collection of more than 600. It also features original antique memorabilia and prints of the lake and the Sierras. Other works displayed include wood sculptures, blown glass, paintings and ceramics by about three dozen different artists. While many galleries don't encourage children to visit (for obvious reasons), this gallery is child-friendly with a play area set aside especially for them. Located above the Old Range Steakhouse with a lovely view of the lake, we recommend feasting on the artwork upstairs and then feasting on a mouthwatering steak downstairs. The gallery is open from 10 AM to 5:30 PM Tuesday through Saturday.

South Shore Lake Tahoe

Support Organizations

South Lake Tahoe Arts Commission
1052 Tata Ln., South Lake Tahoe, Calif.
• (530) 542-7141

Created in 1991 as an advisory group to the South Lake Tahoe City Council, the South Lake Tahoe Arts Commission (SLTAC) promotes visual, literary and performing arts throughout the Lake Tahoe Basin. The commission helps local artists exhibit their work by sponsoring the annual Artists' Studio Tour/South Lake Tahoe. It also sponsors Heritage Murals of Lake Tahoe, a one-of-a-kind self-guided tour of outdoor murals around South Lake Tahoe.

You can start the murals tour at the Lake Tahoe Historical Society with its colorful rendition of John C. Fremont's first view of Lake Tahoe. From there you can go on to seven other outdoor sites that depict the geography and culture of the Lake Tahoe Basin in distinctly artistic ways. Although it's quick and easy to drive the route, it's especially fun on a bike when the weather is nice. You can contact the commission about a tour map or pick one up at the Lake Tahoe Visitors Authority at 1156 Ski Run Boulevard, South Lake Tahoe, California, (530) 544-5050.

Tahoe Arts Project
(530) 542-3632

Because Lake Tahoe is geographically isolated by mountainous terrain, exposure to performing arts is limited. The Tahoe Arts Project was established in 1987 in South Lake Tahoe, California, to bring fine arts to children in the schools and artistic performances to the general public. Since its founding, TAP has pro-

---

INSIDERS' TIP

It is a good idea, during the high season, to double check your tickets for performance times and seating information. Call ahead for parking locations and make your dinner reservations well in advance of the performance.

duced more than 700 lectures, master classes and workshops in the South Shore Lake Tahoe area. TAP helps fill an important void in the educational curriculum since school budgets are often inadequate to provide quality arts-in-education.

Public events are a mixed bag. In 1999 they included such offerings as a mystery dinner, Gamelan music from Indonesia, children's theater, An Evening with the Academy Awards and musical ensembles. Call for the current schedule of events.

Tahoe Tallac Association
(530) 542-4166 (winter),
(530) 541-4975 (summer)

The Tahoe Tallac Association was formed in 1979 to restore the historic estates in the Tallac Historic Site near South Lake Tahoe, California (see our description of the site in our Attractions chapter). The association also produces the annual Valhalla Arts & Music Festival, a wildly diverse celebration of art, music and theater that lasts throughout the year.

Some events include the Valhalla Renaissance Festival, Celtic Sunday, the Brews & Blues Festival, Reggae Sunday and the Classic Film Festival, to name a few. You can also attend plays in the historic Valhalla Boathouse Theatre, view local artists' work in the Dextra Baldwin Art Gallery and the Pope Fine Art Gallery or test your acting or artistic wings in a theater or art workshop.

The festival is truly a feast of the sights and sounds of many cultures — a feast that can be relished in one of the most gorgeous natural settings in the world. Be sure to check the schedule of events if you're in the South Lake Tahoe area, especially in the summer. At almost any event, we guarantee you'll experience some of the unique magic of this extraordinary historical setting. See our Annual Events chapter for more information.

Educational Institutions

Lake Tahoe Community College
1 College Dr., South Lake Tahoe, Calif.
• (530) 541-4660

Colleges and universities bring a wealth of culture to their home communities and Lake Tahoe Community College is no exception. Besides its generous class offerings in the arts, the campus of LTCC is an artistic beehive of activity, promoting an array of cultural events for both students and the general public. You can enjoy performances and exhibitions by students as well as by guest performers and artists from around the region.

Drama, dance, music and films are presented by the Performing Arts League in the LTCC New Theatre. Art shows and receptions are free and are held in the Main Art Gallery in the College Commons and the Foyer Gallery in the Theatre Foyer of the Fine Arts building. Call for a complete schedule of activities throughout the year. See our Education and Child Care chapter for more information about LTCC.

Galleries

A Frame of Mind Gallery
U.S. Hwy. 50, Stateline, Nev.
• (775) 588-8081

Voted the "Best of Tahoe" gallery by the *Tahoe Tribune* for 1996-1998, A Frame of Mind Gallery showcases all natural landscape photography. You can drink in the beauty of Lake Tahoe and its surrounding environs in this luscious collection of local photos. The gallery is easy to find in Harveys Resort Hotel/Casino, but hours vary. It's usually open daily from 11 AM to 3 PM and again from 6 PM to 9 PM. We recommend you call first to make sure.

Addi Galleries
U.S. Hwy. 50, Stateline, Nev
• (775) 588-1505

A sister gallery to Addi Galleries in Las Vegas, Maui, Reno and San Francisco, the Lake Tahoe location is unique in its focus on modern and pop art. All media are represented and most works are original. In the shopping arcade just inside the lobby of Harrah's Lake Tahoe, its hours are 9 AM to 10 PM daily.

Augustine Arts
164 Glen Ct., Stateline, Nev.
• (775) 588-3525

Serious collectors and lovers of art are de-

This audience enjoys a Lake Tahoe Shakespeare Festival performance by the lake.

lighted with the personalized service offered by Augustine Arts. It's not your usual gallery: the owner will guide you through the international art community, providing access to truly distinctive works just right for your home or office. Call for an appointment.

Eagle Valley Frames
2660 Lake Tahoe Blvd., South Lake Tahoe, Calif. • (530) 544-4099

Eagle Valley Frames is your best bet if you're in the market for posters and limited edition prints of local events and locations. The gallery also offers a huge selection of moldings for custom framing.

Hours are 10 AM to 6:30 PM Monday through Friday and 10 AM to 5 PM Saturday. Other locations for Eagle Valley are in Meadowood Mall, (775) 828-1202, and Park Lane Mall, (775) 827-6206, in Reno, and at 560 E. Prater Way in Sparks, (775) 359-1515. Call for specific store hours.

Gallery of Legends
U.S. Hwy. 50, Stateline, Nev.
• **(775) 588-8300**

It may not be considered "fine" art, but the sport and celebrity memorabilia showcased in Gallery of Legends is first-class in every way. Definitely a cut above the usual poster store, it features individual and team-signed art, signed photographs and a large selection of memorabilia. If you're looking for just the right gift for family or friends, we recommend you check out the unique collection on display here. Conveniently located in the shopping arcade in Harrah's Lake Tahoe, the gallery is open daily from 9:30 AM to midnight.

Lake Tahoe Community College
1 College Dr., South Lake Tahoe, Calif.
• **(530) 541-4660**

You can view student, faculty, local and visiting artists' works at the periodic exhibits and receptions in LTCC's Foyer Art Gallery and Main Art Gallery. The Foyer Art Gallery is located in the Theatre Foyer of the Fine Arts building and the Main Art Gallery is in the College Commons. Both galleries are free and open to the public from 7 AM to 10 PM Monday through Friday, from 8 AM to 5 PM Saturday and from noon to 5 PM Sunday.

Sierra Galleries
55 U.S. Hwy. 50, Stateline, Nev.
• **(775) 588-8500**

In the same location since 1983, Sierra Galleries exhibits upscale original paintings, limited edition graphics, glass art and works of world-renowned sculptors. The displays are exceptionally fine so it's a treat to just browse, even if you're not able to buy. In the shopping arcade at Caesars Tahoe, the gallery is open from 10 AM to 9 PM Monday through Thursday, from 10 AM to 10 PM Friday, from 9:30 AM to 10 PM Saturday and from 9:30 AM to 9 PM Sunday.

Ethnic and Cultural Groups

Reflecting Reno/Tahoe's cultural diversity, a variety of area ethnic groups preserve and enhance the language, arts, food and customs of cultures from all over the world. You can globetrot without leaving home through the groups' ethnic celebrations, visual arts exhibits, performing arts performances, classes and workshops. The following is a sampling of groups active in the Reno/Sparks area:

Balalaika and Domra Association of America, (775) 329-1333
Chinese Association of Northern Nevada, (775) 355-2160 Ext. 195
Daughters of Norway, (775) 746-0506
Daughters of Penelope (Greek Orthodox), (775) 825-5365
Filipino Barangay Cultural Group, (775) 356-3601
Gujjarati Samaj of East India, (775) 329-4594
Hellenic Dancers of St. Anthony, (775) 825-5365
Inter-Tribal Council, (775) 355-0600
Japanese American Citizens League, (775) 786-7799
Korean American Citizens Association, (775) 784-6991
NAACP, (775) 322-2992
Nevada Hispanic Services, (775) 786-6003
Nevada Society of Scottish Clans, (775) 825-8233
North American Basque Organization, (775) 329-1476
Northern Nevada Black Cultural Awareness Society, (775) 329-8990
Philoptochas Society (Greek Orthodox), (775) 825-5365
Polynesian Community, (775) 358-9272
Sierra Nevada Celtic Society, (775) 626-6226
Sons and Daughters of Erin, (775) 322-6585
Zenbat Gara Basque Folk Dance Ensemble, (775) 356-3601

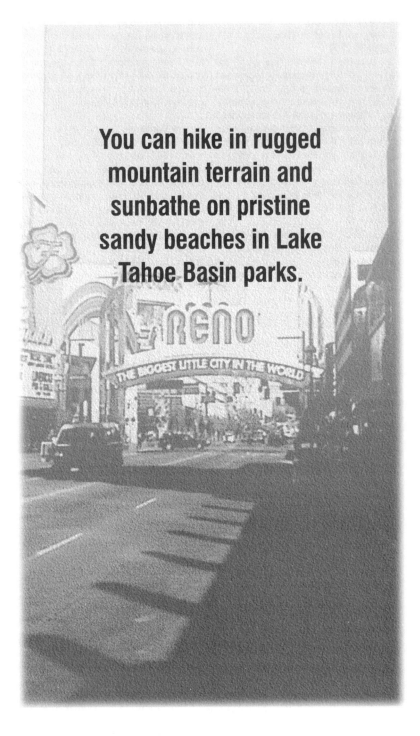

You can hike in rugged mountain terrain and sunbathe on pristine sandy beaches in Lake Tahoe Basin parks.

Parks

With Mother Nature as the chief architect, the Reno/Tahoe area is blessed with all the natural ingredients for awesome parks. Managed by a variety of governmental agencies, the plethora of area parks goes a long way toward preserving the environment and making the great outdoors more accessible for everyone to enjoy. You can hike in rugged mountain terrain and sunbathe on pristine sandy beaches in Lake Tahoe Basin parks. You can bike along the Truckee River and attend cultural events in Reno/Sparks parks. And you can relax with family and friends over a gourmet picnic in any of the dozens of neighborhood parks scattered throughout the Reno/Tahoe area.

Using our four geographical areas, in this chapter we give you a sampling of the kinds of parks just waiting your exploration. Since our descriptions aren't meant to be all-inclusive, we also tell you where to get complete lists of parks from the various parks departments and visitors bureaus. You can also let your fingers do the walking through area telephone directories for maps and parks listings. If you're interested in the myriad programs offered by the parks departments, be sure to request their program booklets. You'll be amazed at the variety of activities offered, from every sports adventure you can possibly imagine, to a tantalizing array of arts, crafts and self-improvement courses.

Many parks, especially the neighborhood variety, are free and accessible year-round. For others we tell you about fees, seasons and hours as of press time. Be aware, however, that these specifics could change. Your visit to most any of the parks will be more enjoyable if you're informed about what's offered there. We strongly recommend getting information from one of the visitor centers or parks departments ahead of time or picking up maps and brochures when they're available at the parks themselves. Although we describe here some of the recreational opportunities you can enjoy in area parks, our Recreation chapter gives more details, such as additional beaches for swimming at Lake Tahoe and specifics of the area's not-to-be-missed hiking trails.

The Incline Village General Improvement District manages a variety of parks and recreational facilities in Incline Village largely for the benefit of local residents. The golf courses and ski resort are open to the public, but the recreation center is not. Access to Ski, Incline and Burnt Cedar beaches is restricted to residents during the summer but is available to the public the rest of the year. If you've booked accommodations in Incline Village, be sure to ask if it includes an IVGID recreation pass.

And last, but by no means least, before you head out to bask in nature's glory, take proper precautions to protect yourself against the elements and the environment. Be sure to use sunscreen and to carry food and water if you're planning to hike or cross-country ski for any distance. Be aware of the weather and wear proper clothing for the occasion. If you're planning to swim in Lake Tahoe, you need to know its frigid waters can be dangerous. Although it's extremely inviting, the lake's 60-degree temperature can cause hypothermia in just minutes: be sure to take precautions (for more outdoor safety tips see our Winter Sports chapter).

Here are some helpful numbers for information on parks:

California State Parks, (530) 525-7232

City of Reno Parks & Recreation & Community Services, (775) 334-2262

City of Sparks Parks & Recreation, (775) 353-2376

Incline Village Parks & Recreation Department, (775) 832-1310

Lake Tahoe Visitors Authority (South Shore Lake Tahoe), (530) 544-5050

Nevada State Parks, (775) 831-0494

North Lake Tahoe Chamber of Commerce, (530) 581-6900

Tahoe-Douglas Chamber of Commerce, (775) 588-4591

U.S. Forest Service, (530) 573-2694

Visitors Bureau (North Shore Lake Tahoe), (530) 583-3494

Washoe County Parks and Recreation Department, (775) 785-4319

Reno

Bartley Ranch Regional Park
6000 Bartley Ranch Rd., Reno, Nev. • (775) 828-6612

On the site of a former working ranch, Bartley Ranch Regional Park gives visitors a snapshot of Nevada's ranching heritage. Tucked in a quiet pastoral setting, the picturesque ranch house and surrounding 2-mile walking trail offer a chunk of quiet solitude on the edge of the city. You can spread a gourmet picnic in the shade, ride horses on the trail or in the arena and attend cultural events in the amphitheater (see our chapter on The Arts for details). If you're curious about the huge white-fenced spread next door, we'll satisfy your curiosity right now: once the home of Bill Harrah (founder of Harrah's Hotels/Casinos), it's the residence of John Harrah, Bill's son.

Bowers Mansion Park
U.S. Hwy. 395, 21 mi. south of Reno, Nev. • (775) 849-1825

The next best thing to a time machine, Bowers Mansion (in its namesake park) allows visitors to step back into the opulence enjoyed by Nevada's mining barons in the 1860s. Built by L.S. Sandy Bowers, the first Comstock Lode millionaire, the 16-room mansion is completely restored and decked out with furnishings from around the world. Daily tours are offered every half hour from 11 AM to 4:30 PM during the summer. Admission is $3 for ages 17 to 61 and $2 for children and seniors.

Surrounded by expansive lawns and huge shade trees, the mansion is a delightful play-

ground for picnics and affords a lovely view of Washoe Valley. The park also has a swimming pool and a snack bar (summer only) along with a children's playground. Daily summer hours are 8 AM to 9 PM and winter hours are 8 AM to 5 PM. No pets are allowed.

Davis Creek Park
U.S. Hwy. 395, 20 mi. south of Reno, Nev. • (775) 849-0684

Tucked in tall Jeffrey pines on the eastern slope of the Sierra Nevada mountains, Davis Creek Park offers hiking, picnicking and overnight camping. You can take easy self-guided nature strolls around the park or head up the Ophir Creek Trail to Price Lake (about 3 miles) and on to Tahoe Meadows (about 6 miles). The campsites have water and showers but no trailer hook-ups. The park is open year-round and camping facilities are on a first-come, first-served basis.

Galena Creek Park
18350 Nev. Hwy. 431, Reno, Nev. • (775) 849-2511

Nestled in the shadow of Mt. Rose, Galena Creek Park boasts a refreshing alpine environment just 25 minutes from downtown Reno. The recreational day-use area offers lovely picnic spots under immense pine trees, a self-guided nature trail and evening campfire programs during the summer. The park is also the trailhead for hikes along Galena, Whites and Jones creeks as well as the strenuous trek to the summit of Mt. Rose. Because it's so close to Reno, it's a favorite with hikers and bikers who want a quick escape from the summer heat. In winter it's often the closest spot for cross-country skiing, sledding and snowshoeing.

Idlewild Park
1900 Idlewild Dr., Reno, Nev. • (775) 334-2262

Stretching along the Truckee River just minutes from downtown casinos, Idlewild Park is a popular oasis for walkers, RollerBladers and picnickers. You'll find a paved path right

Photo: City of Reno Parks and Rec

A concert by the river at Wingfield Park in Reno is something Insiders know will be a special event.

alongside the river, meandering through the 49 acres of lush green grass and tall trees. There's also a large kiddie park with a variety of rides, a swimming pool, skate park, picnic areas and a first-class rose garden sure to delight any horticulturist. If you're strolling west along the Truckee River Walk from downtown, you're sure to wander through Idlewild Park. The park is also home to dozens of Canada geese who find the river and nearby ponds especially welcoming. (See also our Kidstuff chapter.)

Oxbow Nature Study Area
3100 Dickerson Rd., Reno, Nev.
• **(775) 334-2262**

Devastated by the 1997 New Year's flood, Oxbow Nature Study Area is back, bigger and better than ever. Although the park was submerged under water for 21 days and lost boardwalks and viewing areas, reconstruction and expansion (still underway at press time)

have made the popular viewing area available to visitors again. You can see flora and fauna native to riparian upland, pond and river habitats along this stretch of the Truckee River. It's a peaceful spot to commune with nature, whether you're fishing, bird-watching or strolling along the riverbanks.

Rancho San Rafael Park
1502 Washington St., Reno, Nev.
• **(775) 785-4319**

Rancho San Rafael Park is best known as the starting point of The Great Reno Balloon Races and the site of The Wilbur May Center (see our Annual Events and Attractions chapters for details). It's popular with picnickers, walkers, bikers and kite flyers. You'll find lovely expanses of green grass, shaded picnic areas and a 1.5-mile self-guided nature walk. It's open year-round and easily accessible off Sierra Street near the University of Nevada, Reno campus. (See our Kidstuff chapter.)

INSIDERS' TIP

The Lake Tahoe Basin averages 273 days of sunshine every year, each one an opportunity to enjoy the unlimited outdoor activities available in area parks.

This vista of Emerald Bay State Park includes Fannette Island.

Virginia Lake
1980 Lakeside Dr., Reno, Nev.
• (775) 334-2262

With an inviting running path encircling it, Virginia Lake is one of Reno's most popular jogging/walking areas. Come rain or shine it's always a beehive of activity, with kids in strollers and dogs on leashes joining the pack of RollerBladers, walkers and joggers. The course isn't long — about a mile — but nothing will prevent you from going round and round until you get enough exercise. If you're into bird-watching/feeding, bring a sack of bread crumbs: Virginia Lake is also a favorite hangout for hundreds of local birds. (See also our Kidstuff chapter.)

Wingfield Park
2 N. Arlington Ave., Reno, Nev.
• (775) 334-2077

A small oasis in busy downtown Reno, you can't miss Wingfield Park if you're strolling along the Truckee River Walk. Just three acres in the middle of the river, it's a lovely spot to sit and watch the water rush by. The amphitheater is the site of many outdoor cultural events (for details, see our chapter on The Arts).

Sparks

Pah Rah Park
1750 Shadow Ln., Sparks, Nev.
• (775) 353-2376

Some years ago the city fathers in Sparks decided that every neighborhood should have a park. As the city has grown, they've kept up with this goal by building parks along with the new housing developments. The landscape of Sparks is splashed with green from the 25 neighborhood parks that offer inviting spots for play and relaxation. They offer a variety of amenities that include tennis courts, swimming pools, picnic areas and playgrounds.

Typical of parks in Sparks, Pah Rah Park is a great place to bring the family for an outing right in town. Its huge grassy area provides plenty of room for the kids to run and play games. There's also several playground areas with a variety of equipment, a couple of covered picnic spots, tennis courts and bathrooms. A big plus is the great view of downtown Reno and the Sierra Nevada mountains you can enjoy to the west.

To get to the park from Sparks take Interstate 80 east, exit on Vista Boulevard and go north for about 2 miles. You'll see the sign for the park just after crossing Baring Boulevard.

Sparks Marina Park
East end of Nichols Blvd., Sparks, Nev.
• **(775) 353-2376**

Not too long ago, the site of Sparks Marina Park was an ugly eyesore and an embarrassment to the city. As part of an ambitious reclamation project, however, what was once a gaping gravel pit has become an 80-acre lake that's a source of pride and joy for the community. Stocked with trophy-size trout, the sparkling lake is already a favorite fishing hole with Insiders. Soon to come is a jogging path encircling the water, an amphitheater, swimming lagoon and shaded picnic areas.

To get to the park from Reno or Sparks, head east on I-80, exit on McCarran Boulevard and go north to the intersection of Nichols Boulevard. The park is about one block east, just behind the Western Village Inn/Casino.

North Shore Lake Tahoe

Lake Tahoe–Nevada State Park
2005 Nev. Hwy. 28, Incline Village, Nev.
• **(775) 831-0494**

One of the loveliest sections of shoreline and backcountry in the Lake Tahoe Basin is preserved for public use in Lake Tahoe–Nevada State Park. Extending along the east shore of Lake Tahoe south and east of Incline Village, the park encompasses miles of exquisite beach from Sand Harbor to Skunk Harbor, beautiful Spooner Lake at the junction of U.S. Highway 50 and Nev. Highway 28, Cave Rock Marina about 7 miles north of Stateline, Nevada, and more than 13,000 acres of rugged forest in the Marlette/Hobart Backcountry near Spooner. The variety of terrain offers limitless opportunities for outdoor fun.

The crystal white sand beach and vivid turquoise water at Sand Harbor (about 4 miles from Incline Village) make it one of the most popular and picturesque playgrounds at Lake Tahoe. You can swim, sunbathe, picnic, hike, launch your boat or just sit under a spreading Jeffrey pine and drink in one of the most beautiful views on earth. The parking lot fills fast in the summer so if you're spending the day, be sure to arrive early. It's open daily from 8 AM to 9 PM, and the parking fee is $6 during the summer and $2 the rest of the year. Be sure to stop by park headquarters where you can pick up information about the park. Sand Harbor is also the site of the Lake Tahoe Shakespeare Festival (see our chapter on The Arts for details).

About 2 miles north of Sand Harbor you'll find additional beach access at Hidden Beach and at Memorial Point about 1 mile north. About 2.5 miles south of Sand Harbor you can park in the paved parking lot above the lake or along the road and walk into Chimney Beach, Secret Harbor and Whale Beach. Hidden amongst huge boulders and enormous trees, numerous tiny coves offer secluded hideaways perfect for nude sunbathing. About 2.5 miles further south you can park and walk into Prey Meadows (ablaze with wildflowers in late spring and early summer) or to Skunk Harbor. Even with several parking lots, parking is usually a challenge along this section of Nev. 28. You can park along the road, but be sure to pay attention to the stretches with no parking signs to avoid getting a ticket.

Cupped beneath heavily forested peaks, Spooner Lake offers hiking, biking and catch-and-release fishing in the summer. You can take a leisurely 2-mile stroll around the lake or strike out into the Marlette/Hobart Backcountry to Marlette Lake and other wilderness destinations (see our Recreation chapter for hiking and biking details). Parking fees are about $4. In the winter Spooner Lake is a prime cross-country ski resort (see our Winter Sports chapter for details).

North Tahoe Beach Center
7860 N. Lake Blvd., Kings Beach, Calif.
• (530) 546-2566

Hugging the lakeshore in Kings Beach, North Tahoe Beach Center offers a plethora of activities for a reasonable fee all year long. Inside you'll find all the accouterments of a health club, including fitness equipment, sauna and spa. Outside you can enjoy a variety of beach activities, such as volleyball, swimming and boating. Admission is $7 for adults and about $4 for children. Hours vary, so call ahead.

North Tahoe Regional Park
Tahoe Vista, Calif. • (530) 546-5043

You can enjoy periodic glimpses of Lake Tahoe from about 5 miles of multiuse trails that loop through the tall pines at North Tahoe Regional Park. In summer it's popular with hikers, bikers and picnickers (see our Recreation chapter for more information). In winter it's a vision of white, perfect for snowshoeing, cross-country skiing and snowmobiling (see our Winter Sports chapter for details). You'll also find a softball field, playground, restrooms and picnic areas. To get to the park from Incline Village, go west on Nev. 28 to Tahoe Vista (just past Kings Beach), turn right on National Avenue and follow the signs to the park. It's open from 6 AM to 10 PM and the parking fee is $3 in a self-pay box.

South Shore Lake Tahoe

Bijou Community Park
Al Tahoe Blvd., South Lake Tahoe, Calif.
• (530) 542-6056

If you want to escape the crowds at the beaches on Lake Tahoe, you can spread your picnic at Bijou Community Park. You'll find sand volleyball courts, horseshoe pits, a skateboard park, a disc golf course, playground equipment and picnic shelters. The park is located about 1 mile southeast of the intersection of Al Tahoe Boulevard and U.S. 50.

D.L. Bliss State Park
Calif. Hwy. 89, 9 mi. north of South Lake Tahoe, Calif. • (530) 525-7277

Boasting 3.5 miles of shoreline along the west side of Lake Tahoe, D.L. Bliss State Park is paradise found for anyone who loves the outdoors. Two sun-drenched beaches beckon sunbathers to warm sands — Calawee Cove Beach, a protected cove ringed by boulders and trees, and Lester Beach, a wide-open expanse of white sand with maximum exposure to the sun. When you get tired of catching rays on the beach, be sure to take a hike in the area. We highly recommend the spectacular Rubicon Trail which takes you south along the lakeshore to Emerald Point, the entrance to Emerald Bay. We tell you more about this splendid hike in our Recreation chapter.

The park also has one of the best campgrounds in the area (see our Camping and RVing chapter for details), but it fills fast so be sure to reserve ahead. Day parking is around $5, but is very limited: we suggest you arrive at least by 10 AM during July and August.

Bliss is just a few short miles from Emerald Bay State Park (see next entry), Vikingsholm Castle (see our Attractions and Kidstuff chapters) and Sugar Pine Point State Park (see our write-up later in this chapter).

Emerald Bay State Park
Calif. Hwy. 89, 5 mi. from South Lake Tahoe, Calif. • (530) 525-7277,
(530) 573-2600

Emerald Bay in Lake Tahoe is easily the most photographed site in the entire Lake Tahoe Basin. Its emerald green water shimmering against snowcapped granite peaks is

INSIDERS' TIP

A self-appointed protector and advocate of the Truckee River, John Champion walked its banks every day, picking up trash and planting greenery. Following his death in 1997, his work was continued by the volunteer Champions of the Truckee organization, which also spearheaded the construction of John Champion Park on the east side of the *Reno Gazette-Journal* building at 955 Kuenzli Street in Reno.

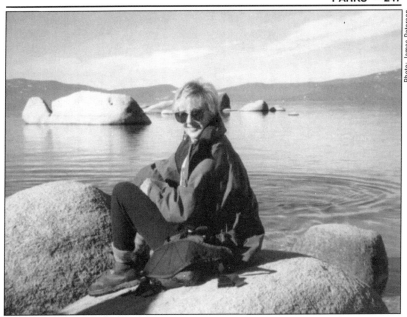

Photo: James Peterson

Granite boulders seem like sleeping whales in the still waters
off Whale Beach at Lake Tahoe–Nevada State Park.

spectacular in anyone's book. Attractions in Emerald Bay State Park include the shoreline around the bay, Vikingsholm Castle and Eagle Falls, a string of waterfalls that tumble out of the Desolation Wilderness into the bay. Created in 1969 to preserve more than 60,000 acres of unique mountain environment, the wilderness is a wonderland of alpine lakes sprinkled amongst velvety meadows and rugged peaks.

You'll find lovely spots to picnic, swim and sunbathe along the shore of Lake Tahoe in the park. You can take a 1.5-mile level hike to Emerald Point where you'll see gorgeous views of the rugged pinnacles framing the end of the bay. From the point you can turn north and follow the Rubicon Trail along the lakeshore toward D.L. Bliss State Park. If you're feeling very ambitious, we recommend following Eagle Creek up to Eagle Lake in the Desolation Wilderness. Although it's somewhat of a steep climb, it's only a mile and affords luscious panoramic views along the way. Once you've made it to Eagle Lake, the grandeur of the Desolation Wilderness unfolds before you,

with more than 100 lakes just waiting to be explored. The Eagle Lake trailhead is in Eagle Falls Picnic Area, across Calif. Highway 89 from the parking lot at Emerald Bay State Park. You'll need a permit to enter the Desolation Wilderness: stop at the Taylor Creek Visitor Center at 870 Emerald Bay Road in South Lake Tahoe to get one.

Because this area of Lake Tahoe is extremely congested during the summer, parking is difficult. Our advice is to get there as early in the day as possible during July and August. For more information about Emerald Bay see our Attractions chapter and for hiking and wilderness outings see our Recreation chapter.

South Lake Tahoe Recreation Area
**U.S. Hwy. 50 and Rufus Allen Blvd.,
South Lake Tahoe, Calif.**
• (530) 542-6056

Close to all the casino action in Stateline, South Lake Tahoe Recreation Area offers access to Lake Tahoe along with picnic areas and facilities for horseshoes, basketball and

Photo: City of Reno Parks and Rec

The Reno park system offers visitors and residents a place to relax in the shade, enjoy a concert, or, like these young girls, dance in the bubbles.

volleyball. Other amenities include a children's playground, jogging trails, swimming pool, fitness center and a boat ramp. The campground (summer only) has 172 sites for tents and RVs and provides piped water, fire rings and flush toilets.

Sugar Pine Point State Park
Calif. Hwy. 89, 1 mi. south of Tahoma, Calif. • (530) 525-7982

You can soak up a chunk of Lake Tahoe's history while enjoying its incredible natural beauty at Sugar Pine Point State Park. With

Idlewild Park sits along the Truckee River and its flock of Canada geese always enjoys a handout.

more than 2,000 acres stretching along 1.75 miles of shoreline, the park offers a lovely swimming beach and choice hiking trails along with the historic Ehrman Mansion, a nature center and a 19th-century log cabin.

Built in 1902, the mansion is an elegant example of Queen Anne Victorian architecture, with about 12,000 square feet of period extravagance. We suggest taking the tour to relive the turn-of-the-century heydays of the wealthy who spent their summers at the lake in the lap of luxury. Tours are held every hour from 11 AM to 4 PM from July to September and cost about $3. Although much less sumptuous than the mansion, be sure to see the log cabin that was built in 1860 by General William Phipps, a trapper believed to be the first permanent settler of record in this area of the Lake Tahoe Basin. If you're interested in the wildlife of the area, stop in at the Edwin L. Z'Berg Natural Preserve and view its bird and animal exhibits.

You'll find hiking trails suitable for almost everyone at Sugar Pine Point, from the easy Dolder Nature Trail, which meanders along the lakeshore, to the moderate General Creek Trail, a 6.5-mile loop to Lily Pond. From there you can continue on to a large variety of alpine lakes and meadows in the Desolation Wilderness. If a laid-back picnic is more your style, the beautifully manicured lawn in front of the Ehrman Mansion is the perfect place. Open all year, the park is a favorite place for cross-country skiing and snowshoeing in the winter. Be sure to pick up a Sno-Park permit for winter parking at the Lake Tahoe Basin Management Unit of the forest service at 870 Emerald Bay Road in South Lake Tahoe. For a description of the General Creek campground at the park, see our Camping and RVing chapter.

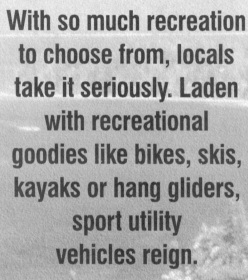

With so much recreation
to choose from, locals
take it seriously. Laden
with recreational
goodies like bikes, skis,
kayaks or hang gliders,
sport utility
vehicles reign.

Recreation

Dubbed by Rand McNally as the "top destination in the United States for outdoor recreation," the Reno/Tahoe area serves up a mind-blowing menu of activities guaranteed to challenge your wildest expectations. The variety is huge — so huge we devote entire chapters to Winter Sports, Golf, and Fishing and Hunting. We describe other recreation in this chapter, organized alphabetically by activity rather than by geographical area.

With so much recreation to choose from, locals take it seriously. Laden with recreational goodies like bikes, skis, kayaks or hang gliders, sport utility vehicles reign. You'll see a higher percentage of them here than in most communities. But unlike sparkling showroom models, local SUVs are more likely to be frosted with snow or coated with mud from recent 4-wheel–drive treks into the mountains.

If gambling's your game, you can enjoy it to your heart's content here. But don't forget that one of the most magnificent destinations on the planet is just outside. You can best see it, feel it, smell it and taste it from a hot air balloon hovering over the tops of tall Jeffrey pines or from a kayak sliding silently through crystal clear waters or from a forest trail meandering through a meadow hip-high with wildflowers.

This chapter is chock full of suggestions to help you make the very most out of your time in the Reno/Tahoe area. But whatever activities you choose, remember the most important thing is to relax and have fun.

Auto Racing

The Reno/Tahoe area is devoid of auto racing facilities but if you're a die-hard enthusiast of the "fastest sport in America," we have listed three oval tracks and a drag strip that are close enough to make the drive worthwhile.

Rattlesnake Raceway
2000 Airport Rd., Fallon, Nev.
- **(775) 423-7483**

This ¼-mile dirt track is located about 60 miles southeast of Reno in the small farming town of Fallon. The track is located on Rattlesnake Hill and provides mud-slinging action every Saturday night and on some Sunday afternoons from May through September. Spectators can expect to pay about $7 for admission to a night of racing that includes five different classes of racers (street stocks, bombers, mini-stockers, compact bombers and super-trucks). The gates open at 4 PM on Saturday with racing beginning at 7 PM. On Sunday, the gates open at noon with the racing action starting at 2 PM. The track offers a pit pass for $15 for any of the racing days.

To get to Fallon from Reno, take Interstate 80 east to Exit 48 (east Fernley). Continue over the railroad overpass and turn left onto Alternate U.S. Highway 50 and follow the signs to Fallon. (For other activities in Fallon, see our Daytrips chapter.)

Reno-Fernley Raceway
Alt. U.S. Hwy. 95, Fernley, Nev.
- **(775) 575-7217**

Reno-Fernley Raceway's ³/₈-mile, clay oval is called the "Racing Field of Dreams" and is located about 36 miles from Reno. This facility has it all: clay oval racing, motor-cross trucks, off-road racing, sand drags, BMX and go-kart racing. Oval track racing is presented every Saturday during the summer months with racing action in four classes (IMCA & Outlaw modifieds, street stocks, bombers and mini-stockers). The gates open at noon with hot laps going from 1 to 4 PM. The racing action begins at 5 PM. Spectators pay just $5 to watch everything. The track also offers a special pit pass for $10. Telephone the track for the schedule of the other racing events. The track usually has one other type of racing offered along with the oval racing. Overnight campers are welcome.

To get to the raceway, take I-80 east from Reno to Exit 46 (west Fernley). Follow Main Street until the intersection of Alternate U.S. Highway 95. Take Alt. U.S. 95 about 6 miles until you see the signs for the raceway on the right-hand side of the highway.

Silver State Raceway
Bigelow St., Carson City, Nev.
• **(775) 885-2079**

The only paved high-speed track in northern Nevada, the Silver State Raceway is home to late model sportsmen, mavericks and the Legend cars. The Legends are $5/8$ replicas of the 1930- and 1940-type cars that started NASCAR racing.

Racing action begins on this $1/3$-mile, high-banked oval every Saturday at 4:30 PM with time trials. The actual races start at 7 PM. Tickets begin at $10. On occasion, SSR presents the World of Outlaws sprint cars and began Crazy-8 racing in 1999. Crazy-8 racing is done on a figure-8 track which makes close-calls and crashes the mode of the day. This is the fastest track of the three ovals.

To get to this raceway from Reno, take U.S. Highway 395 south to Carson City, about 30 miles. Turn left at Snyder Road from U.S. 395. Go east on Snyder for about one mile to Bigelow Street. Turn right on Bigelow and follow it until it dead-ends at the raceway.

Top Gun Motor Sports Complex
U.S. Hwy. 95, Fallon, Nev.
• **(775) 423-0223**

This is the only sanctioned NHRA drag strip in northern Nevada. The 1/4-mile drag strip is located just 10 miles south of Fallon on U.S. Highway 95 and features drag racing in several different classes on Saturdays and Sundays from March through November. For the daytime drags, the gates open at 8 AM, with time trials beginning at 9 AM and the actual races beginning at 1 PM. For the evening drags, the gates open at 11 AM, with time trials beginning at 2 PM and the racing action beginning at 6 PM.

Besides the professional programs, the track also offers junior drag racing for high school students. Telephone the strip for race-day information. Tickets run anywhere from $5 to $25 depending on the type of drags.

To get to Fallon from Reno, take I-80 east to Exit 48 (east Fernley). Continue over the railroad overpass and turn left onto Alternate U.S. Highway 50 and follow the signs to Fallon. Once in Fallon, pick up U.S. 95 south and follow signs to the raceway. (For more things to do in Fallon, see our Daytrips chapter.)

Backpacking

If you can't get enough of nature with a simple day-hike, rest assured that most area hiking destinations are also suitable for overnight camping. With its huge variety of lakes, one of the most popular backpacking areas is the Desolation Wilderness (see the "Hiking" section later in this chapter). Once in the wilderness you can spend days backpacking from lake to lake.

You can split up longer hikes to any destination by overnight stays or you can hike into a single site and stay for a day or two. We suggest stopping at visitor centers (see our Attractions chapter for locations) or the U.S. Forest Service office at 870 Emerald Bay Road in South Lake Tahoe, (530) 573-2674, for more information. Be sure to have maps and proper equipment if you're backpacking and remember you'll need a permit for the Desolation Wilderness. See the "Hiking" section in this chapter for some suggested destinations.

Ballooning

Balloons Over Lake Tahoe
South Lake Tahoe, Calif.
• **(530) 544-7008**

When you book a flight with Balloons Over Lake Tahoe, you can marvel at the majesty of

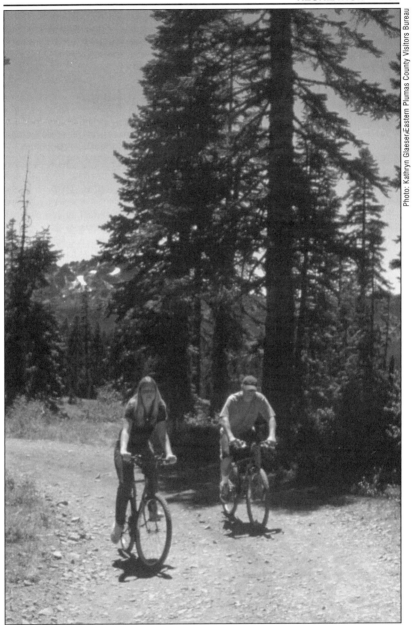

There's something for every kind of rider in the Reno/Tahoe area: roads, trails, rough country and groomed paths can all be found in the mountains and towns.

Photo: Kathryn Glaeser/Eastern Plumas County Visitors Bureau the lake from two vantage points: floating over it in a hot air balloon and floating on it in a 40-foot catamaran. After flying over verdant mountain meadows and hovering above the crystal clear waters of the lake, the balloon lands on the boat where you can indulge in a delicious champagne brunch while cruising back to shore. The cost of the three-hour trip is $175 per adult, $150 for children who weigh 70 pounds or less and $125 for very young children. The company offers free shuttle transportation within the South Lake Tahoe area, and customized wedding services too.

Dream Weavers Hot Air Balloon Co.
1321 Job's Peak, Gardnerville, Nev.
• (775) 265-1271, (800) 386-2563
If you're looking for a nontraditional wedding site, how about tying the knot with an awesome bird's-eye view of the Carson Valley and Lake Tahoe all around you? Dream Weavers Hot Air Balloon Co. will help you plan your special occasion, such as a wedding, anniversary, birthday or engagement. Amenities for flights include champagne, a certificate of ascendancy and touring the inflation and assembly of the balloon. Trips operate year-round out of Gardnerville, Nevada, and cost $145 per person. Children younger than 9 are not encouraged to ride and reservations are required. (See our Daytrips chapter for details on other sights in the Carson Valley area.)

Mountain High Balloons
Truckee, Calif. • (530) 587-6922,
(888) 231-6922
The oldest balloon company in the Reno/Tahoe area, Mountain High Balloons will take you up, up and away on half-hour and one-hour trips in the Truckee area. The balloons lift off from nearby Prosser Reservoir and then drift lazily over the Martis Valley south of downtown Truckee. You can see gorgeous views of Lake Tahoe to the south and pick pinecones from the tops of huge trees. Floating through the peace and quiet as the sun rises to the east is an incredibly special way to greet a summer day.

The cost per person is $85 for a half-hour and $145 for one hour. Kids younger than 10 years old can fly free when accompanied by an adult (limit of one child per adult). Flights are available at 7 AM daily from May through November, but reservations are necessary. (For more to do and see in Truckee, see our Daytrips chapter.)

Biking

With hundreds of miles of dirt roads and paved paths that give ready access to the great outdoors, biking in the Reno/Tahoe area is very popular. You'll see cyclists everywhere, zipping along city streets and huffing up rocky mountain paths. Whether you're an experienced rider or first-time-ever cyclist, you'll find terrain and paths just right for you. You can enjoy biking on paved streets and paths, on dirt roads and trails and in mountain bike parks complete with chairlifts. We can't possibly list all the opportunities and adventures that await you: it's simply too exhaustive. But we will tell you about some of the favorite rides around the area to give you an idea of the variety of biking fun that's available.

Be aware that many of the paths and trails we describe in the walking, running and hiking sections of this chapter are also suitable for biking. For maps and other routes we suggest you stop at area visitor centers (see our Attractions chapter for locations) and also inquire at local bike shops. Also see our Parks chapter for information about walking/biking paths in local parks.

Before heading out, it's important to be aware of a few basic safety rules for biking in the Reno/Tahoe area. Always plan ahead by knowing where you're going and whether the skills of everyone in the group are suited to the expected terrain. Some strenuous routes are not advisable for children, for example. If you're not familiar with a particular trail, find out from appropriate authorities what it's like. Dress for the weather and be prepared for the sudden storms which frequently come up in the mountains. Use sunscreen and carry plenty of water and snacks. And last, but not least, know the courteous rules of the trail and practice them. Since many trails are shared with others — walkers, joggers, hunters, anglers, animals and 4-wheel–drive vehicles — be ready to yield the trail and ride under control at all times.

If you're interested in biking clubs, you can call the **Alta Alpine Cycling Club** in South Lake Tahoe at (775) 265-5412, the **Procrastinating Pedallers** in Reno at (775) 747-1413 or the **Reno Wheelmen** at (775) 747-5649.

Angora Ridge
Fallen Leaf Campground, 2 mi. north of South Lake Tahoe, Calif., off Calif. Hwy. 89

For spectacular views of Fallen Leaf Lake and Mt. Tallac, you can take this moderate 8-mile round-trip jaunt that ends at lovely Angora Lakes. Starting at Fallen Leaf Campground, where you can park your car, pedal along Fallen Leaf Lake Road and take the first left, and continue for about one-half mile to Angora Ridge Road and then turn right. Be prepared for a veritable Kodak moment when you reach the abandoned Angora Lookout — the panoramic view from the saddle of this glacial moraine is stunning, to say the least. Just down the road you'll find a dirt parking lot where you can lock up your bike to follow the last one-half mile of the route on foot. Your reward at the end of the trail is two sparkling alpine lakes, with a rustic resort tucked on the shore of the second lake. Be sure to save time for a refreshing swim and lunch.

General Creek Loop Ride
Sugar Pine Point State Park, Calif. Hwy. 89, 1 mi. south of Tahoma, Calif. • (530) 525-7982

You don't have to have legs of steel for the General Creek Loop Ride. In fact, you can be a first-time mountain biker and get along just fine. Snaking through the forest for about 6 miles, the trail is mostly level and easy to navigate. Look for the trailhead in Sugar Pine Point State Park (see our Parks chapter for more about this lovely park).

Marlette Lake/Flume Trail
Trailhead at Spooner Lake, junction of U.S. Hwy. 50 and Nev. Hwy. 28

A heart-stopping ride for intermediate bikers and above, the Flume Trail will thrill you with challenging terrain and awesome views of Lake Tahoe. The trail follows an old water flume line, climbing about 5 miles to Marlette Lake and then continuing another 7 miles to

Tunnel Creek Road near the Ponderosa Ranch in Incline Village. If you ride the entire 12 miles, you'll need to park a car at Incline Village. We don't recommend a round-trip of 24 miles since the first 12 is rugged enough for most bikers.

The most difficult part of this ride is the 7 miles past Marlette Lake, where the narrow trail hugs a ledge with sheer drop-offs toward Lake Tahoo far below. You should be in good physical shape and not be afraid of heights to ride this trail. It's not for families and not for children. You might want to try a trial run to test your stamina by riding the 10-mile roundtrip to Marlette Lake and back first. For information about the Ponderosa Ranch, see our Attractions chapter.

North Tahoe Regional Park
Tahoe Vista, Calif. • (530) 546-5043

With 5 miles of dirt paths winding through the trees, the trail system at North Tahoe Regional Park offers gentle runs for beginners and steeper terrain for more advanced riders. Never crowded and close to residential areas, it's a favorite with locals year-round. See our Winter Sports and Parks chapters for more details on this fun-filled spot in Tahoe Vista.

Northstar–at–Tahoe
Calif. Hwy. 267, 6 mi. north of Tahoe City, Calif. • (530) 562-1010

With more than 100 miles of forested trails to explore, Northstar–at–Tahoe offers Lake Tahoe's most extensive mountain bike park. You can enjoy everything from gentle leisurely loops to stiff uphill climbs, including jaunts to Watson Lake and Northstar Reservoir. There's something for everyone and best of all, you can conserve your stamina by taking advantage of Northstar chairlifts. We tell you more about this first-class resort in our Resorts and Winter Sports chapters.

Squaw Valley USA
Calif. Hwy. 89, 6 mi. north of Tahoe City, Calif. • (530) 583-6955

Winding past mountain pools and streams, the 25 miles of biking trails at Squaw Valley USA offer scenic and challenging terrain for riders of all abilities. You can take the easy way up the mountain by riding the cable car to High Camp Bath & Tennis Club. From there

Photo: K. Markgraf

Boating Lake Tahoe can mean anything from
the luxury of this beautiful racing boat to fishing in a small rowboat.

you can choose from easy cruiser runs to alpine meadows and steeper climbs to the tops of Squaw and Emigrant peaks. A day at Squaw, whether you're skiing, hiking or biking, is special indeed and we highly recommend it. See our description of tennis and bungee jumping in this chapter for more information about Squaw.

Billiard Parlors

Though you won't be overwhelmed with options for billiards in the Reno/Tahoe area, here are our favorites if 8-ball is your game.

Breaktime Billiards
5890 S. Virginia St., Reno, Nev.
• (775) 828-0616

Breaktime has 13 4½-foot by 9-foot, top-of-the-line Robertson Black Max pool tables. The owner likes to say that his billiard room is the classiest in town and he is right. All the pros who come to Reno for tournaments throughout the year prefer to practice at this establishment. The owner constantly re-felts and re-levels the tables to keep them in tip-top playing shape. Breaktime is open from 10 AM

to 2 AM, Monday through Friday, and noon to 2 AM on the weekend. It also has a full bar and video poker machines. Per-hour rates run from $4.25 an hour for one person to $16 an hour for six people.

Classic Cue
1965 Lake Tahoe Blvd., South Lake Tahoe, Calif. • (530) 541-8704

Classic Cue calls itself the best billiard room and burger joint on the lake. Besides its 10 pool tables, there's also indoor hoops, Foosball and darts. This pool hall also provides patrons with a satellite TV. Mostly frequented by a younger crowd, Classic Cue also repairs and sells pool cues. The hours of operation are from 11 AM to midnight.

Keystone Cue & Cushion
935 W. Fifth St., Reno, Nev.
• (775) 323-2828

The younger crowd likes to congregate here, and Keystone Cue likes to cater to them. It has 11 regulation-sized pool tables and one coin-operated, shorter bar pool table. Keystone serves beer and wine only and has a video arcade. This is a favorite hangout of the university pool shooters. It is open from 10 AM to 2 AM, Monday through Thursday, 10 AM to 6 AM on Friday and Saturday and noon to 2 AM on Sunday. Charges are prorated by the minute but work out to be about $6 per hour for the pool table.

Q's Billiard Club
2295 S. Virginia St., Reno, Nev.
• **(775) 825-2337**

This over-21 club likes to call itself the coolest pool hall in Reno. It has 12 tables and is open from 3 PM to 3 AM, with Happy Hour every day from opening to 7 PM featuring $2.25 microbrews. The going rate for shooting a game of pool is $6 per hour for 10 of the tables, but on two of the newer tables, Q's charges $8 per hour. This pool hall is located in the Orchard Plaza Shopping Center.

Boating

Nowhere is boating more popular than on the sapphire-blue water of Lake Tahoe. Just imagine gliding across the ripple-free water in the morning with the sun's rays glancing off the mirror-like surface and soaking up some of the most spectacular scenery in the United States. On any given day, especially during the warmer months, you can see every type of water craft imaginable navigating the lake from before sunrise to well after sunset. Here, we list the ramps available for launching your private boat, as well as facilities which will rent you just about any type of watercraft to fit your fancy: speedboats, fishing boats, sailboats, pontoon boats, paddle boats, canoes, kayaks, JetSkis, WaveRunners, sailboards and float tubes.

Boat Ramps

All the boat ramps listed charge a fee for launching, except Kings Beach, which is free, but which charges a $5 parking fee. The launch fees range from $5 each way for the little boats to $35 each way for the bigger boats. All the launch facilities listed have paved ramps.

Anchorage Marina, Camp Richardson, California, (530) 541-1777

Cave Rock, near Zephyr Cove, Nevada, (775) 831-0494

El Dorado, South Lake Tahoe, California, (530) 542-6056

High & Dry, near Homewood, California, (530) 525-5966

Kings Beach, Kings Beach, California, (530) 546-7248

Lake Forest Beach, between Tahoe City and Carnelian Bay, California, (530) 583-5544

Lakeside Marina, South Lake Tahoe, California, (530) 541-6626

Meeks Bay Resort, Meeks Bay, California, (530) 525-7242

North Tahoe Marina, Tahoe Vista, California, (530) 546-8248

Obexer's, between Meeks Bay and Homewood, California, (530) 525-7962

Sand Harbor, Incline Village, Nevada, (775) 831-0494

Sierra Boat Company, Carnelian Bay, California, (530) 546-2552

Sunnyside Marina, near Tahoe City, California, (530) 583-7201

Tahoe Boat Company, Tahoe City, California, (530) 583-5567

Tahoe Keys Marina, South Lake Tahoe, California, (530) 541-2155

Zephyr Cove Marina, Zephyr Cove, Nevada, (775) 588-3833

Boat and Watercraft Rentals

No matter what type of watercraft suits your fancy, you can find it floating on Lake Tahoe. At last count, about 25 watersports rental businesses encircle the lake. At these concessions you can rent just about anything that floats.

Sailing the translucent water of Lake Tahoe has been a longtime recreational activity and when the wind kicks up in the afternoon, you'll see why. Sailboarding has also become a popular sport on the lake and every afternoon, brave souls can be seen whipping over the waves, seemingly hanging on for their lives. And if power boats are more to your liking, speedboat rentals are available for the novice to the advanced boater.

Prices for the rentals seem to change every season and are dependent on the size of the watercraft, the time of the year and the time of day. Generally, hourly rental rates are close to these prices: power boats, $75 to $100; sailboats, $40 to $60; paddle boats, $20; fishing and pontoon boats, $35 to $60; canoes and kayaks, $20 to $30; JetSkis and WaveRunners, $80 to $100; and water ski tows, $40 to $50.

Action Watersports of Tahoe
967 Lakeshore Blvd., Incline Village, Nev. • (775) 831-4386
3411 U.S. Hwy. 50, South Lake Tahoe, Calif. • (530) 544-2942

Action Watersports owns two rental businesses at Lake Tahoe. One is located in Incline Village and the other is located in South Lake Tahoe. Both establishments are open from 9 AM to 6 PM during the summer.

The Incline Village shop is located on a private beach used mainly by locals, renters and guests of the Hyatt Regency Lake Tahoe. It offers power boats and JetSkis.

Action Watersports in South Lake Tahoe is located at Timber Cove Marina and rents just about anything that floats. From power boats to floating lounge chairs, this concession rents them out at some of the most reasonable rates around the lake.

Captain Kirk's Beach Club
Zephyr Cove, Nev. • (775) 588-3530

The Captain's is located at Zephyr Cove Marina and offers almost every type of watercraft for rent. It specializes in power boats and JetSkis. It also offers parasailing (see the "Parasailing" section in this chapter). It's open during the summer from 8 AM to 5 PM. You can write to Captain Kirk's at PO Box 481, Zephyr Cove NV 89448.

Camp Richardson Marina
1900 Jameson Beach Rd., South Lake Tahoe, Calif. • (530) 542-6570

This marina is open from May through the end of September from 8 AM to 7 PM and offers the best selection of power boats on the lake. It has Four Winns bowriders, two-person WaveRunners, pontoon boats, kayaks, canoes and paddle boats. Its location at Camp Richardson makes it a popular and sometimes crowded place. This is one of the only rental concessions that accepts reservations.

H₂O Sports
Stateline, Nev. • (775) 588-4155

This shop guarantees the lowest rental prices at the lake. H_2O has a full line of watersports rental equipment. It's located 2 miles north of Stateline at Round Hill Pine Beach. It also provides a daily tour of Emerald Bay by SeaDoos. Write to them, if you like, at PO Box 311, Stateline NV 89449.

Kings Beach Aqua Sports
Tahoe City, Calif. • (530) 546-2782

This is the largest rental operation on the North Shore (and maybe the lake). Located at Kings Beach State Recreation Area, it rents every kind of watercraft imaginable: Hobie Cats, power boats, fishing boats, canoes . . . and the list goes on. It's open from 7 AM to 7 PM during the summer months. The mailing address is PO Box 752, Tahoe City CA 96145.

Tahoe City Marina
700 N. Lake Blvd., Tahoe City, Calif. • (530) 583-1039

Tahoe City Marina specializes in power boat rentals. It has in its inventory 10 SeaSwirl power boats and several 14-foot fishing boats. It's also a full-service marina which offers fuel and docking and is close to two shopping centers. The marina is open from 8 AM to 6 PM during the summer.

Tahoe Sailing Center
700 N. Lake Blvd., Tahoe City, Calif. • (530) 583-6200

If you'd like to set sail on Lake Tahoe, this center has it all — skippered sailing cruises, yacht charters, sailing lessons and regatta racing. Here you can enjoy sailing by yourself or sit back and let someone else do all the work while you enjoy the lake's spectacular scenery. Sailing lessons (from basic to advanced

INSIDERS' TIP

Don't approach any animals in the wild, especially bears, mountain lions, squirrels, coyotes or raccoons.

sailing) begin at $25 for a 2-hour lesson. Sailing cruises at sunset and cruises to Emerald Bay range from $45 for a 2-hour cruise to $350 for a boat that holds up to six people. As an added adventure, you can race as a crew member at the Wednesday regattas for $35 per person. The Tahoe Sailing Center is the ultimate sailing rental business on the lake.

Bowling

The Reno/Tahoe area is usually known around the United States because of its outdoor recreation. But if indoor sports are more to your liking, you have to try the bowling alleys scattered around the area. Remember, too, that if watching professionals hit the lanes is your thing, Reno's National Bowling Stadium has top-ranked tournaments (see our Spectator Sports chapter for more details). If you're relocating here and would like to join a league, contact the Reno/Sparks Men's Bowling Association, (775) 358-2695, or the individual bowling alleys for more details on league play.

Bowl Incline
920 Southwood Blvd., Incline Village, Nev. • (775) 831-1900
This bowling alley bills itself as the North Shore's only complete family recreation center. Bowl Incline has 16 lanes with automatic scoring, bumper bowling, a pool table, a video arcade, video poker machines, darts, a bar, and a full-swing golf simulator. Sundays are designated smoke-free. The alley is open from 11 AM to midnight every day. At least three to seven lanes are open every night for open bowling; the rest are reserved for leagues. Open bowling prices are about $2 per game.

Greenbrae Lanes
670 Greenbrae Dr., Sparks, Nev.
• (775) 358-4477
This bowling alley is the only one in Sparks and is used heavily during the winter months for league play. The owner said the best time

to come down for open bowling is during the summer months and before 6 PM during the winter. Greenbrae has 24 lanes, video poker machines, a bar and a pool table. It charges $2 a game for bowling plus $1.25 to rent shoes. It's open from 9 AM to midnight, 7 days a week.

Reno Hilton
2500 E. Second St., Reno, Nev.
• (775) 789-2295
The Reno Hilton has a 50-lane bowling alley which is the most popular in the Reno/Tahoe area. Even though it's open 24 hours per day, 7 days a week, bowling is on a first-come, first-served basis. The best times to find an open lane are early afternoon or late evening. Rates depend upon the time of day: From midnight to 8 AM, rates are $1.70 per game with shoes costing $1.60 to rent. From 8 AM to 6 PM, bowling a game will cost you $2.30 with shoes renting for $1.85. The most expensive time to bowl is between 6 PM and midnight: rates during this prime time run $2.75 for the game and $1.85 for shoes.

Starlite Bowl
1201 Stardust St., Reno, Nev.
• (775) 747-3522
This bowling alley is the oldest in Reno and a favorite hangout of Insiders. It has 32 lanes, a snack bar and video poker machines. This alley caters to leagues but open bowling is still possible if you come to the alley between noon and 6 PM (before the leagues start) or show up after 9 PM (when most of the leagues finish). Open rates are $2.50 per game until 5 PM, when they go up to $2.75. Shoe rental costs $1.60.

Tahoe Bowl
1030 Fremont Ave., South Lake Tahoe, Calif. • (530) 544-3700
This bowling alley has 16 brand-new synthetic lanes and features new, lighted bumper bowling and a video arcade. It's open from 11 AM to 11 PM daily and caters to leagues during the winter. It's relatively quiet during the sum-

mer months so open bowling is no problem. During the winter, show up before 6 PM to get a lane. Rates are $2.75 per game before 6 PM. After 6 PM, it's $3 per game. Shoe rental any time of day is $1.50.

Bungee Jumping

Bungee Squaw Valley
Top of cable car, Squaw Valley USA, Calif. Hwy. 89, 6 mi. north of Tahoe City, Calif. • (530) 583-4000, (530) 583-6985

Whether you're diving into space from a hot air balloon or the edge of a cliff, bungee jumping is a wild experience. Perched at the top of the world at 8,200 feet in elevation, Bungee Squaw Valley is guaranteed to thrill you with a fantastic 75-foot plunge to earth. If you keep your eyes open as you free-fall to the giant safety mattress below, the view of Lake Tahoe and the surrounding wilderness terrain is majestic, to say the least.

As the country's highest elevation bungee jump, the Squaw facility is part of the resort's High Camp Bath & Tennis Club. You can while away an entire day up here, winter or summer (see our Winter Sports, Attractions and Resorts chapters for more information on Squaw Valley). The bungee is open daily, but since hours vary with the season and the weather, we recommend calling ahead. The cost of the first jump is $45, and if that doesn't excite you enough, you can jump again the same day for just $15. You must be at least 10 years old and weigh between 80 and 250 pounds.

Canoeing

If canoeing is your aquatic preference, Lake Tahoe is the perfect spot to take to the paddle. The scenery is magnificent and the water is crystal clear, making a trip by canoe a tranquil adventure. Most canoers cruise close to the shoreline because once the wind picks up, often times with little or no warning, staying upright can be a big challenge. You don't see canoes on the Truckee River because of its swift current and because of the many hazardous boulders poking out from beneath the water. The Truckee River is preferred by rafting and kayaking enthusiasts. Canoes can

be rented from the many watersport companies around the lake (see the "Boat and Watercraft Rentals" section, under "Boating" earlier in this chapter).

Disc Golf

With the cost of playing a round of golf going up, up, up, it's refreshing to find a course that's absolutely free. But you won't be teeing off with a Big Bertha driver and you won't be chipping out of sand traps. Instead you'll be throwing golf discs (similar to Frisbees) into a series of baskets that are laid out in a golf course format. Played in several area parks, disc golf has been growing in popularity by about 15 percent a year since 1996. It's far less structured than traditional golf and offers a great way for families to get out and have fun in the sun together.

You can try your skill at this up-and-coming sport at **Bijou Community Park** in South Lake Tahoe, where you'll find an interesting 27-hole layout that's been challenging local golfers since 1994. The park is on Al Tahoe Boulevard, about 1 mile southeast of the boulevard's intersection with U.S. 50. For information call (530) 542 6056 (see our Parks chapter for more details about the park).

You can also tee off at **Zephyr Cove Park** in Zephyr Cove. To reach the park drive about 6 miles north of Stateline on U.S. 50, turn right on Warrior Way and follow the drive in the park to the end. For information call (775) 588-0271.

You can buy discs (which run around $10 apiece) at the City of South Lake Tahoe Parks & Recreation Department at 1180 Rufus Allen Boulevard in South Lake Tahoe, (530) 542-6055, or at Big 5 Sporting Goods at 4986 S. Virginia Street in Reno, (775) 825-2322.

Diving

Although you won't see coral reefs and schools of tropical fish, diving in Lake Tahoe is a spectacular experience because the water is so clear. With visibility from 45 to 90 feet in the summer, you'll feel as if you can reach out and touch the native fish swimming by, including rainbow, brown and cutthroat trout. But remember the temperature of the water is

Photo: K. Markgraf

When the wind whips Lake Tahoe, you'll see the windsurfing enthusiasts riding the waves on their colorful boards.

anything but warm: you'll need drysuits to protect yourself against the frigid water. If you're inexperienced in high altitude diving, we suggest you contact a dive school for proper training.

Tropical Penguins Scuba & Water Sports
180 W. Peckham Ln., Reno, Nev.
• **(775) 828-3483**

Whether you're a first-timer or an experienced diver just needing a refresher course, the professional staff at Tropical Penguins Scuba & Water Sports will help you splash into the underwater world of adventure. Classes at this complete dive facility include basic and advanced open water certification, rescue diver, divemaster, instructor development, SCUBA tune-up and specialty courses such as altitude diving. The shop features all levels of PADI and ANDI certification plus equipment sales and rentals.

Before you decide to explore the hidden treasures of Lake Tahoe (or other dive sites included in their travel packages), we suggest you stop by and assess your readiness to dive with their trained staff. Call for schedules and prices on travel and classes.

Sierra Diving Center
104 E. Grove St., Reno, Nev.
• **(775) 825-2147**

With more than 30 years of experience in Lake Tahoe diving, Sierra Diving Center can certainly claim to be experts on the subject. The company offers a full range of dive services, including PADI certified classes, instructor certification, equipment sales and rentals and tours. If you've ever had a yen to SCUBA dive, the professionals here will make it easy for you with short evening and weekend sessions.

To dive safely in Lake Tahoe you can take the one-day Altitude Specialty Course, which includes two open dives in the lake plus training in all the high altitude changes that affect divers. For up-to-date schedules and prices call the number above.

Four-Wheeling/Off-Road Adventures

You'll definitely want to bring your camera or camcorder if you decide to strike out on one of the many off-road tours of the Reno/Tahoe area. One visitor called his 4x4, off-road trip near Lake Tahoe "the best half-day of my life." If off-roading has been something you've always wanted to try, Lake Tahoe has the premier company to hook up with.

Lake Tahoe Adventures
(530) 577-2940

This company has off-road tours ranging from easy to rugged and challenging. Tours include riding the trails in ATVs, Jeeps and Hummers, with off-road rides lasting anywhere from 2 hours to 3 days. The Scenic Tour for example, is three hours by ATV and costs $79.

The Ultimate Challenge is a 3-day trek featuring a two-way excursion on the Rubicon Trail, a trail that naturalists have called one of the most primitive and challenging trails in the United States. This 3-day tour includes camping along the trail and costs about $795.

More tours are available, such as the 5-hour lake and stream fishing excursion, the historic desert tour or the combo package which includes ballooning, off-roading, rafting, hiking and parasailing. This company also specializes in custom packaged tours so if you don't see anything you like, just ask.

Lake Tahoe Adventures has two stations to accommodate you. The Meeks Bay station is located on Calif. Highway 89 just north of Emerald Bay, (530) 541-5875. The tour center is located in South Lake Tahoe, California, on U.S. 50, (530) 577-2940. The mailing address for Lake Tahoe Adventures is PO Box 11521, South Lake Tahoe CA 96155.

Go-Karts

Wild Island
250 Wild Island Ct., Sparks, Nev.
• (775) 359-2927

Wild Island has the only go-kart racetrack in the Reno/Tahoe area. Their Formula K Raceway has two tracks, one for larger children and one for smaller. The big kids get to drive gas-powered Indy cars and the little ones get to drive electric-powered Sprint cars. The cost is about $10 for 10 laps.

Hang Gliding

Adventure Sports
3650-22 Research Wy., Carson City, Nev. • (775) 883-7070

In the summer, hang gliders are a common sight around Mt. Rose, as they launch from the top of Slide Mountain and flirt with the warm currents of air rising from the ground.

If you've ever wanted to "fly," you should consider learning in the Reno/Tahoe area: the Sierra Nevada mountains offer one of the premier soaring sites in the country. You can earn your wings with the professionals at Adventure Sports through either hang gliding or paragliding lessons. The 25-hour course is $750 and a one-day introduction is $100. You'll learn aerodynamics, soaring and the basics of flight in both ground school and on-the-hill training.

(Before taking lessons you should know the difference between a hang glider and a paraglider. A hang glider is a fairly stable contraption with rigid wings spanning about 18 feet. A paraglider is a parachute that can be stowed in a backpack, enabling the flyer to launch from sites inaccessible to hang gliders.)

Hiking

Although you can appreciate the beauty of the Reno/Tahoe area driving through it in your car, the very best way to experience this wonderland is to grab your backpack and hit the trail. Let's smell the fields of wildflowers, hear the rushing mountain streams and feel the crunch of pine needles under our hiking boots as we explore on foot one of the most gorgeous natural habitats in the world. We're not necessarily talking extreme sports: you can choose hikes for any and all abilities. You don't

---

INSIDERS' TIP

Hiking trails that are suitable for wheelchairs include the bike paths around Lake Tahoe, the interpretive path at Sand Harbor in Lake Tahoe–Nevada State Park and trails at Tallac Historic Site.

have to scale Mt. Tallac to be a hiker. You can take a leisurely stroll in Tahoe Meadows (one of our very favorite outings any time of the year) and still sink into nature at her very finest.

In this section we describe some of the not-to-be-missed hikes in the area which we're sure you'll enjoy. But with hundreds of miles of trails, we can't list all the magical destinations awaiting your discovery. We leave those for you to find with the aid of maps you can pick up at visitor centers (see our Attractions chapter for locations). Be sure to check out the large variety of hikes in area parks and historical sites. You can take easy jaunts at Spooner Lake and Sand Harbor (see our Parks chapter) and also at the Taylor Creek Visitor Center and the Tallac Historic Site (see our Attractions chapter).

Because this lovely mountain environment is so very fragile, it's important that every visitor minimize his or her impact on the area. Hikers should be especially careful to leave no trace of their having visited a wilderness destination. To leave no trace you should always pack in, pack out: don't leave any trash behind, even if it's buried, because it can be dug up by animals. Don't pollute streams or lakes and when hiking, stay on the trails. Enjoy the wildflowers, but never pick them. For more information about responsible hiking you can call Leave No Trace, Inc. at (800) 332-4100.

For your safety and comfort, always dress properly and be prepared for sudden changes in the weather. Get a map to find out exactly where you're going and about how long it will take. Be sure to take food, water and first-aid items in your backpack. Don't drink the water in the wild unless you have water purification tablets. Many hikers have learned the hard way that even though the water in mountain streams looks crystal clear it contains *giardia lamblia*, an organism that can cause severe intestinal disease.

Also be aware that no fires are allowed in the wild. If you're hiking with dogs, keep them under control and don't let them wander too far from you. For more tips about dos and don'ts in the backcountry see our Winter Sports chapter.

Desolation Wilderness
Southwest of South Lake Tahoe, Calif.
• (530) 573-2600

Spanning about 100 square miles high above Lake Tahoe, the Desolation Wilderness is a veritable Shangri-la for hikers and backpackers. Tucked into the backcountry are more than 100 shimmering alpine lakes and 20 majestic peaks towering more than 9,000 feet above sea level. Exploring this entire wonderland would take months: we can't possibly describe in detail all of the hikes you'll find here. We suggest you pick up maps from area visitor centers (see our Attractions chapter for directions) or from the U.S. Forest Service office at 870 Emerald Bay Road in South Lake Tahoe. You'll also need a free permit to day-hike in the wilderness and a $5 backcountry permit to spend the night. Permits can be obtained from the Forest Service. Since the number of overnight permits is limited, you should call (530) 644-6048 for reservations.

You can access the wilderness from three major trailheads: Eagle Falls, Glen Alpine and Echo Lakes. Eagle Falls is 5 miles west of South Lake Tahoe on Calif. 89, directly across from the parking lot at Emerald Bay. Glen Alpine is at the south end of Fallen Leaf Lake. To reach the lake from South Lake Tahoe, take Calif. 89 northwest from its junction with U.S. 50 and turn left onto Fallen Leaf Road about 3 miles farther on. To reach Lower Echo Lake take U.S. 50 southwest from South Lake Tahoe past Echo Summit and turn onto Johnson Pass Road. Continue through this residential area to the parking lots at the lake.

One of the most popular hikes in the wilderness is to Eagle Lake, a 1-mile jaunt from the Eagle Falls Trailhead that climbs through huge stands of trees to give stunning views of Lake Tahoe along the way. Eagle Lake is a tiny azure jewel, perfect for swimming and picnicking. If you continue on this trail another 4 or 5 miles you'll reach Middle Velma, Upper Velma and Fontanillis lakes. Be prepared for a trail that's steep and rocky in places. Starting from the Glen Alpine Trailhead, you can take a steady uphill climb of about 6 miles that passes Grass, Suzie and Heather lakes and ends at Lake Aloha, perched in a glacial area on top of the Sierra Crest.

Photo: Greg Gilman/Eastern Plumas County Visitors Bureau

The hiking opportunities in the Reno/Tahoe area are
limited only by your imagination (and, of course, your aching feet!).

An outing perfect for families begins at the marina on Lower Echo Lake. You can take a 15-minute water taxi across the lake and through a channel connecting to Upper Echo Lake. From there you can take a leisurely stroll back to the marina (less than a couple of miles) or continue on to a variety of lakes, including Ralston, Tamarack, Lake of the Woods and Lake Aloha.

Five Lakes
Trailhead 1.5 mi. west of Calif. Hwy. 89 on Alpine Meadows Rd., 6 mi. north of Tahoe City, Calif.

Snuggled in high alpine country on the back side of Squaw Peak, Five Lakes (none of which is named) is a popular destination for hikers, anglers and dogwalkers. The round-trip jaunt is only about 5 miles with an elevation gain of about 1,000 feet. The well-marked trail is rocky in spots, but very easy to follow. From the trailhead on Alpine Meadows Road, the path climbs sharply through forest sprinkled with an eclectic variety of wildflowers (if you're hiking in spring or summer). After about a mile, the trail breaks into the open and you're treated to breathtaking views of the granite peaks around Alpine Meadows ski resort.

Approaching the lakes, you enter the forest again, and if you look up to the north you can see the ski lifts on top of Squaw Peak and KT-22 at Squaw Valley USA. You can wander around from lake to lake and find your own little Eden for swimming and relaxing. Although this area gets heavy use during high season, it's still possible to find a niche of privacy to enjoy the day. But if you're looking for a total wilderness experience, this probably won't fit the bill, unless you hike after Labor Day.

To reach the trailhead from Tahoe City, go north on Calif. 89 about 6 miles to Alpine Meadows Road and follow it for about 1.5 miles. The trailhead is on the right side of the road in a residential area. You'll need to park along the road.

Marlette Lake
Trailhead at Spooner Lake, junction of U.S. Hwy. 50 and Nev. Hwy. 28

With an elevation gain of 1,157 feet, the 5-mile hike to Marlette Lake is a bit of a challenge but well worth the effort. The dirt path is wide and easy to follow but aerobic for most hikers with its steady uphill ascent. As you hike through North Canyon to the lake you'll climb past thick aspen groves, velvety alpine meadows and tumbling mountain creeks. In spring and summer you'll see wildflowers ablaze with color everywhere and in fall you can enjoy the mountain landscape showing off its reds, golds and yellows.

When you arrive at the lake, be sure to pick the perfect spot for a picnic to enjoy this special alpine hideaway. You can look at the large fish in the lake but don't touch, since fishing isn't allowed here. You can continue on the trail toward the Flume Trail, a harrowing 7-mile plunge down the ridge to Incline Village. Drink in the great views of Lake Tahoe from the start of this trail, but don't go farther since it's mainly for hardcore bikers (see our "Biking" section in this chapter for more details). Be sure to be on the lookout for cyclists throughout this hike, particularly those on the downhill run from the lake.

Marlette Lake is not only scenic but historic as well. A system of flumes (including the one along the Flume Trail) used water from the lake to float timber to the silver mines in Virginia City back in its heyday.

Mount Rose (Peak)
Trailhead .5 mi. south of summit on Nev. Hwy. 431

Because so many things have the name "Mt. Rose," we think a brief explanation might head off any confusion you might have. The Mt. Rose Highway (Nev. Highway 431) connects Reno and Incline Village, passing between Mt. Rose peak and Slide Mountain. The highest point of the highway is called the Mt. Rose Summit. Mt. Rose–Ski Tahoe ski resort

Photo: K. Markgraf

JetSkis have become one of the most popular water vehicles of choice on Lake Tahoe.

is on Slide Mountain (not on Mt. Rose) and Mt. Rose peak (the mountain described in this hike) is located northwest of Slide Mountain.

As the third highest peak in the Reno/Tahoe area, Mt. Rose at 10,776 feet is a challenge worth exploring. The view from its barren summit is truly breathtaking, and in spring and summer the trek up offers an explosion of wildflowers hard to beat. With a round-trip of 12 miles and an elevation gain of about 2,000 feet, you should be in good shape to take this hike. Proper clothing is also important: dress in layers to accommodate the winds from exposed ridges and wear comfortable hiking boots suitable for rocky terrain. Be sure to bring plenty of water and snacks and don't forget your camera to commemorate your summiting the peak.

The first several miles of this hike are a steady climb along a dusty closed road, affording views of Lake Tahoe cupped below the peaks of the Desolation Wilderness. The trail passes through radiant fields of wildflowers, including blue lupine, crimson evening primrose and yellow mule ears. At a small snowmelt pond the path forks: the right-hand path takes you to the top of Mt. Rose and the left to a relay station which also has great views. If you're not up to going to the top, consider hiking just to the pond: it's a great 5-mile round-trip outing, with spectacular views and the aforementioned wildflowers. You can also take your time to explore the tiny moun-

tain meadow around the pond and see how many wildflowers you can identify. If you're continuing on to the summit, the path begins a steep rocky ascent from here through a series of switchbacks. Breaking through the trees at the top of the mountain, you enter a special environment indeed — an exhilarating alpine habitat awash in the dazzling colors of hardy wildflowers.

To reach the trailhead from Reno/Sparks, take U.S. 395 southwest to Nev. 431 and follow it south to just past the summit where you'll see an old maintenance building next to a closed dirt road. From Incline Village take Nev. 431 northeast just past Tahoe Meadows and look for the trailhead on the left. You can park along the road or in the pullout just down the road.

Prey Meadows/Skunk Harbor
Trailhead on Nev. Hwy. 28, 2 mi. north of intersection with U.S. Hwy. 50

You can stroll through a lovely sun-washed meadow brimming with wildflowers and swim and sun in private coves tucked deep in the forest on this hike along the east shore of Lake Tahoe. From Nev. Highway 28 the trail descends along a sandy road through stands of Jeffrey pine, white fir and cedar. Along the way you'll see the remains of a railroad grade used in the 1870s as part of a system to supply timber for the mines in Virginia City, Nevada. About .5 mile down the trail it forks, with

Photo: K. Markgraf

Here's a great way to mountain bike the mountains: some ski areas operate during the summer and fall months to allow hikers, sightseers and bikers to get up into the mountains.

the left branch going to Prey Meadows and the right to Skunk Harbor.

If you choose the left branch, be on the lookout for wildflowers in spring and summer all the way down. You'll likely see pink buckwheats, red snowplants, yellow Sierra wallflowers and purplish-brown spotted mountain bells. Once in the meadow you can wander along the creek and marvel at the tiny flowers, clinging to life, along its banks. It's a wonderful place to sit back, relax and enjoy a picnic lunch.

If you choose the right branch of the trail, you'll follow its gradual descent to the shore of Lake Tahoe, enjoying teasing peeks of the lake as you go. The large gray stone structure you'll notice as you get to the lake was built by a prominent San Francisco family in the 1920s as a secluded picnic spot. It's now owned by the U.S. Forest Service. The tiny inlets along this section of the lake are perfect for private sunbathing and swimming. Just wander along the path and find your perfect spot for the day.

You can visit both the harbor and the meadows if you allow enough time. The round-trip hike to the harbor is about 3 miles and the hike to just Prey Meadows is about the same

distance. With an elevation gain of only about 600 feet, the outing is considered moderate and is suitable for most hikers.

To find the trailhead look for a green gate and "closed" sign on the west side of Nev. 28 about 2 miles north of the intersection with U.S. 50. There are several parking pullouts right near the trailhead. See our Parks chapter for more information about Lake Tahoe–Nevada State Park.

Rubicon Trail
**D.L. Bliss State Park, Calif. Hwy. 89,
9 mi. north of South Lake Tahoe, Calif.**
• **(530) 525-7277**

Winding along a heavily wooded rocky section of Lake Tahoe shoreline, the Rubicon Trail is a splendid example of the best Tahoe has to offer. With stunning views of deep turquoise water lapping at huge granite boulders, the trail begins in the campground of D.L. Bliss State Park and ends 4.4 miles later at Vikingsholm Castle on Emerald Bay. You can hike the 9-mile round-trip or leave a car in the parking lot above Emerald Bay, about 1 mile from Vikingsholm.

The only down side to this hike is the difficult parking situation. If you're planning to hike during July or August, it's a good idea to arrive very early in the day. The trailhead is 2.5 miles past the park entrance and parking near it is very limited. If you're hiking after Labor Day, be sure to call ahead to ensure that the park entrance is open so you can drive to the trailhead. Dogs aren't allowed on the trail, but are okay in the park if they're leashed. For more information about Bliss and Emerald Bay see our Parks chapter.

Tahoe Meadows
West of summit on Nev. Hwy. 431

An enchanting carpet spread beneath imposing granite peaks, Tahoe Meadows is an intriguing escape to another world any time of the year (see our Winter Sports chapter for fun in the snow here). But in spring and summer, when the meandering Ophir Creek becomes a series of streams overflowing with snowmelt, the meadow explodes with color from the amazing variety of wildflowers bursting into bloom.

Beginning in late spring, this alpine paradise becomes a sea of gold with masses of buttercups flowering among the verdant grass. As the season progresses, the meadow becomes an ever-changing kaleidoscope of hues — purple from the larkspurs, orange from the giant red paintbrushes, white from the marigolds and blue from the alpine veronicas. The colors are stunning and brilliant, almost seeming to shout at you as you stroll along the bubbling streams. But take the time to look closer: some of the real treasures in this alpine garden are the tiny blooms almost hidden from view. Look for delicate alpine shooting stars, clinging in solitary splashes of pinkish-purple along the banks of the streams, or little elephant head flowers with their miniature pink trunks nodding in the gentle wind.

You can follow the meandering water and variety of paths to the back of the meadow where the trail enters the trees and descends to Price Lake and eventually to Davis Creek Park south of Reno on U.S. 395. If you're planning to go all the way to Davis Creek, we suggest you leave a car there since the round-trip back to Nev. 431 is about 12 miles.

Tahoe Meadows is really not about long distance hiking for most locals, however. It's more of a touchstone with nature, a place to sink into the magic of a mountain meadow all year long. The real joy is taking the time to smell the flowers (literally) and viewing this special environment as it changes with the seasons. Tahoe Meadows is very dog-friendly (just be careful of the occasional coyote), so be sure to bring Fido along. The northeast end of the meadows has a wide, smooth path a little more than a mile long that's suitable for wheelchairs. Look for the parking lot and trail access just west of the summit.

To reach the meadow from Reno/Sparks, take U.S. 395 southwest to Nev. 431 (the Mt. Rose Highway) and follow it south to just past the summit. From Incline Village take Nev. 431 northeast to where it levels out just before the summit. You can park along the road or in the parking lot just west of the summit.

Tahoe Rim Trail
Circling Lake Tahoe along the ridgetops

Ranging from 6,300 to 9,400 feet in elevation, the Tahoe Rim Trail rambles for 150 miles all the way around Lake Tahoe. Along with spectacular views of the lake and nearby mountain ranges, the trail offers a trip into the historical past of the area. You can follow the same routes used by the first Basque sheepherders more than 100 years ago or you can wander through old Washoe hunting grounds and along abandoned game trails. Built entirely by volunteers, the trail passes through six different counties in two separate states.

You can access the trail at six different trailheads — U.S. 50 at Spooner Summit, U.S. 50 at Echo Summit, Tahoe City from Calif. 89, Calif. Highway 267 at Brockway Sum-

---

INSIDERS' TIP

Be aware that Lake Tahoe's winds are often unstable and can come up quickly during the late afternoon. If you see whitecaps forming, head for shore.

mit, Calif. 89 at Big Meadows near Luther Pass and Nev. Highway 207 at Daggett Pass. Information and maps about specific sections of the trail are available at visitor centers around the lake (see our Attractions chapter for locations) or at the Tahoe Rim Trail office at 298 Kingsbury Grade in Stateline, Nevada, (775) 588-0686.

Horseback Riding

High Sierra Stables
3105 Indian Ln., Reno, Nev.
• **(775) 677-1477**

Exploring the back country of Reno on horseback makes most visitors feel like the pioneers who first discovered this wonderful area. High Sierra Stables can provide riders of all skill levels with the right horse to ride through the tall pines. This stable can arrange private rides if you are experienced and they have facilities for barbecues, dinner rides and parties. The stables are open from 9 AM until sunset all year and will pick up and deliver you to your hotel. Prices begin at $25 per hour.

Verdi Trails
1850 W. Old Hwy. 40, Verdi, Nev.
• **(775) 345-7600**

Horseback riding is a tradition in the Reno/Tahoe area and at Verdi Trails, the wranglers help keep this tradition alive. This outfit caters to families but suggests that the younger riders be at least 10 years old unless they are experienced. This stable is located at the foot of the Sierra Nevada mountains and their rides provide outstanding scenery. They specialize in trail rides but will also do hayrides, if that's your preference. They open at 9 AM and go until sunset. Prices for an hour ride start at $25.

North Shore Riding Stables

There are many places to go horseback riding around the North Shore of the lake. All these stables have hourly rides (they start at $20 per hour) and provide guides. All of these stables also offer riding lessons. Some have hayrides during the summer and some have sleigh rides during the winter. Call them for the latest info.

Alpine Meadows Stables, Calif. Highway 89, between Tahoe City and Truckee, California, (530) 583-3905

Cold Stream Corral, Donner Lake exit, I-80, Truckee, California, (530) 587-4121

Northstar Stables, Northstar exit, Calif. Highway 267, Truckee, California, (530) 562-1230

Ponderosa Ranch, Nev. Highway 28, Incline Village, Nevada, (775) 831-2154

Squaw Valley Stables, Squaw Valley exit, Calif. Highway 89, between Tahoe City and Truckee, California, (530) 583-7433

South Shore Riding Stables

Like the North Shore, the south part of the lake has many outfits that rent horses. At most of them, you can have lessons, go riding, go on hayrides and in the winter go on sleigh rides. Check out any of these horseback-riding places. Prices start at $20 per hour.

Camp Richardson, Calif. Highway 89, South Lake Tahoe, California, (530) 541-3113

Cascade Stables, Calif. Highway 89, near Cascade Lake, California, (530) 541-2055

Sunset Stables, U.S. Highway 50, near the airport, South Lake Tahoe, California, (530) 541-9001

Zephyr Cove Stables, U.S. Highway 50, Zephyr Cove, Nevada, (775) 588-5664

Kayaking

If you've never been in a kayak before (but are interested in trying it out), we recommend taking a short guided tour to teach you the basics. Hugging the shoreline of the lake, the tours on Lake Tahoe provide a good introduction to the sport without dealing with the rough water sometimes found in rivers. If you're an experienced paddler, however, you can rent a kayak and do your own thing, either on the lake or in nearby rivers. It's important to follow safety instructions, whichever way you choose, and to remember that the water of Lake Tahoe is beautiful but can become deadly if you're tipped over.

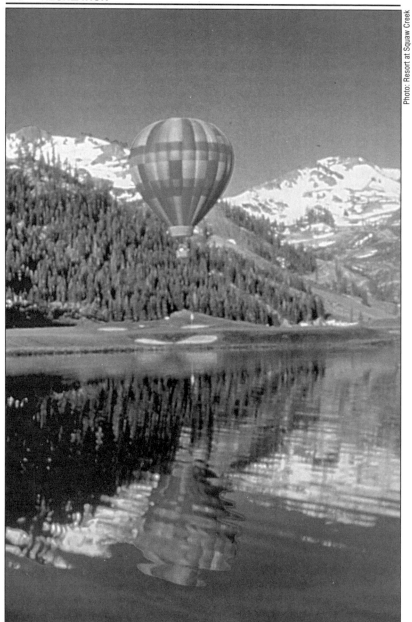

Photo: Resort at Squaw Creek

From horseback riding to hot-air balloon riding, the opportunities for recreation in the area surrounding Reno/Tahoe are outstanding in both variety and ease of access.

Emerald Bay Kayak Tours
Tahoe City, Calif. • (530) 581-2441

It's one thing to view gorgeous Emerald Bay from Calif. 89 as you snake along the road high above it. But it's quite another to experience it from the bay itself as you paddle a kayak through the deep green water. Don't worry if you've never been in one of these sleek craft before: the guides will teach you how to effortlessly steer it and will accompany you on your tour around the shoreline. Along with the most highly photographed spot at Lake Tahoe, you're sure to see eagles, osprey, geese and ducks from your watery vantage point. You'll enjoy lunch on tiny Fannette Island, followed by a paddle to Vikingsholm Castle (see our Attractions and Parks chapters for more details about Emerald Bay and Vikingsholm). The per-person cost of this tour, including lunch, is $95. Moonlight tours along the north shore of Lake Tahoe are also offered.

Kayak Tahoe
3411 U.S. Hwy. 50, South Lake Tahoe, Calif. • (530) 544-2011

For just $30 per person, you can enjoy the splendor of sunset on Lake Tahoe as you paddle your own kayak along the shore. Kayak Tahoe offers sunset trips along with moonlight tours for $35, wildlife tours on the Upper Truckee River for $40 and trips to Emerald Bay for $65. Located at the Timber Cover Marina in South Lake Tahoe, the company also rents kayaks and gives lessons.

Tahoe Paddle & Oar
7860 N. Lake Blvd., Kings Beach, Calif. • (530) 581-3029

You can explore the picturesque boulder fields and hidden coves of Crystal Bay with a guided tour through Tahoe Paddle & Oar. The cost is $50 per person, with a minimum of two people, and reservations are required. For a longer trip you can hop on a pontoon boat to Sand Harbor, where you'll paddle your own kayak along the dramatic granite boulders and turquoise waters between Sand Harbor and Secret Harbor.

A minimum of four people is required and the cost is $95 per person, including lunch. If you're a free spirit and want to go it on your own, you can rent several sizes of kayaks rang-

ing in price from $10 an hour to $100 for a full day. Look for the facility at the North Tahoe Beach Center.

Martial Arts

From young children to retired seniors, the interest in martial arts is growing in the Reno/Tahoe area. When you check local telephone directories, you'll find a somewhat bewildering array of self-defense classes listed under the umbrella of "martial arts." The various types include karate, kodenkan jujitsu, taekwondo, judo and tai chi.

Academies in the Reno/Sparks area include **Bushidokan Martial Arts Temple**, 311 Ninth Street, Sparks, (775) 358-1518; **Family Karate Center**, 960 Matley Lane, Reno, (775) 786-4441; and the **American Martial Arts Academy**, 2999 S. Virginia Street, Reno, (775) 826-4711. In the South Shore Lake Tahoe area you'll find classes offered at **Taekwondo USA**, 2565 Lake Tahoe Boulevard, South Lake Tahoe, California, (530) 542-4373 and in the North Shore Lake Tahoe area at **East West Karate**, 175 Macinaw Road, Tahoe City, California, (530) 583-9447. For a complete listing of locations and types of classes, we suggest you let your fingers do the walking through local telephone directories.

Miniature Golf

Fantasy Kingdom Miniature Golf
U.S. Hwy. 50, South Lake Tahoe, Calif. • (530) 544-3833

This miniature golf course has 23 holes and is open during the summer from 10 AM to 9 PM daily. The course is decorated with sharks, whales, dragons and castles and is a favorite among the younger children. Price per person is $5 for a round of golf.

Horizon Family Magic Carpet Golf
6925 S. Virginia St., Reno, Nev. • (775) 853-8837

This is the only miniature golf course in Reno. Located on Virginia Street, heading out of town toward Carson City, this course has two 19-hole courses and one 28-hole course. It's open daily from 11 AM to 6 PM during the winter, weather permitting, and from 11 AM to

10 PM during the warmer months. Prices start at $4.50 for the 19-hole courses.

Magic Carpet Golf
5167 N. Lake Blvd., Carnelian Bay, Calif. • (530) 546-4279

Magic Carpet Golf was remodeled in 1998 and has a 19-hole course and a 28-hole course. The only miniature golf course on the North Shore, it's open from 10 AM to 7 PM, April through November. It's usually crowded. The cost for the 19-hole course is $4.50 and for 28-holes, it's $6.

Magic Carpet Golf
2455 Lake Tahoe Blvd., South Lake Tahoe, Calif. • (530) 541-3787

The lake's largest miniature golf course consists of three courses: two 19-hole courses and one 28-hole course. Each 19-hole course costs $4.50 to play and the 28-hole course costs $6.50. It's open daily from 10 AM to 11 PM during the summer, from 10 AM to 11 PM on the weekend during spring and fall, and is closed during the winter.

Wild Island
250 Wild Island Ct., Sparks, Nev. • (775) 359-2927

Part of the Wild Island Water Park complex, this miniature golf course has two 18-hole courses, which feature piped-in music on all of the holes. It's open all year from 10 AM to 9 PM on weekdays and 10 AM to midnight on the weekend, except during the winter when it cuts its hours back to 1 to 9 PM. Prices are $4.50 for 18 holes.

Paintball

Playing paintball is an excellent way to test your mettle as a warrior without worrying about dying in battle. The worst that can happen in this game is that your clothes take a hit from the multicolored paintballs splattering all over. The Reno/Tahoe area doesn't have a paintball battlefield but one is located in Fernley, Nevada, only 30 miles from Reno.

Herbie's Paintball Games Inc.
Alt. U.S. Hwy. 95, about 6 mi. outside of Fernley, Nev. • (775) 575-6946

Herbie's catch phase is "just show up and squeeze the trigger." The battlefield is open on Saturdays from 9 AM to 4 PM and during the week by reservation only. Herbie welcomes walk-ons and single players but suggests calling ahead to see if a game is on. The course can be rented for private wars for half-days and full-days during the week. One of the battlefields is a simulated ghost town.

Rates depend on the package you purchase. The standard package at $28 per person includes an entrance fee, a semiautomatic paintball gun, 100 paintballs, goggles and a mask. The VIP package includes all the above plus 300 more paintballs, a camo-suit, lunch, drinks and a videotape of your war. This package runs about $60 per person.

To get to Herbie's from Reno, take I-80 east to the West Fernley exit, No. 46. Turn right from the interstate and follow Main Street through town to Alt. U.S. 95. Take Alt. U.S. 95 for 6 miles. The battlefield is on the right-hand side of the road near the Reno-Fernley Raceway.

Parasailing

If you prefer sailing *over* Lake Tahoe instead of on it, there are several companies which offer parasailing. Imagine flying high over the water under a multicolored parachute being towed by a fast-moving speed boat skippered by U.S. Coast Guard–approved captains. Flying high above the shoreline lets you check out the fabulous scenery and the gorgeous lakefront estates. You'll really appreciate the phrase "bird's-eye view" after a parasailing adventure.

Flights last anywhere from 8 to 20 minutes and cost between $45 and $180, depending

Photo: K. Markgraf

Horseback riding is a great way to see the country around Reno and Lake Tahoe. Few people experience this kind of freedom in such a gorgeous natural setting.

upon number of flyers and height of the parachute over the lake.

Besides renting watersports equipment (see listings under "Boating/Boat and Watercraft Rentals" earlier in this chapter), the following companies also offer parasailing. Their rates are similar and hover around $50 for a short, low altitude ride and $90 for a long, high altitude flight.

Action Watersports of Tahoe, 967 Lakeshore Boulevard, Incline Village, Nevada, (775) 831-4386; 3411 U.S. Highway 50, South Lake Tahoe, California, (530) 544-2942

Captain Kirk's Beach Club, Zephyr Cove, Nevada, (775) 588-3530

Camp Richardson Marina, 1900 Jameson Beach Road, South Lake Tahoe, Calif., (530) 542-6570

Kings Beach Aqua Sports, (530) 546-2782

Lake Tahoe Parasailing
700 N. Lake Blvd., Tahoe City, Calif.
• (530) 583-7245

This center operates from sunrise to sunset and offers three different rides. The rides last anywhere from 8 to 12 minutes. The 8-minute ride flies you at 450 feet and costs $45 for a single and $90 for a tandem ride. The 800-foot flight costs $55 for a single and $110 for a double ride and lasts about 10 minutes. The ultimate flight lifts the flyers to 1,200 feet in altitude and lasts about 12 minutes. The cost for this flight runs between $90 and $180. They'll also dunk you in the water as a part of your ride, if you want.

Lake Tahoe Parasailing boasts the record for number of people flown by parasail. Since 1988, they estimate they have flown more than 30,000 people. (See also our Kidstuff chapter.)

Racquetball

With more than 30 health clubs in the area (many of which have racquetball courts), it's not hard to find a place to get up a game of racquetball. Because the costs and types of memberships vary widely, we recommend you call individual clubs about court availability.

You'll find courts in the Reno/Sparks area at **Sports West Athletic Club**, (775) 348-6666;

the **Reno Athletic Club** at (775) 788-5588; **Double Diamond Athletic Club** at (775) 851-7171 and the **YMCA** at (775) 329-1311. In the North Shore Lake Tahoe area you can play at the **Incline Athletic/Racquetball Club** at (775) 831-4212 and in the South Shore Lake Tahoe area at **Time Out Health Spa & Fitness** at (530) 544-6222. For a complete listing of health and fitness clubs, check local telephone directories.

Rafting

RAM River Adventures and More
Reno, Nev. • (800) 466-7238

Billing themselves as "the best little adventure company in the West," RAM has been offering splash and laugh rafting since 1978. You can choose the quiet solitude of the East Carson River, a more than 20-mile journey from alpine forest to high desert southeast of Lake Tahoe. Or you can run the rapids on the Lower Truckee River, beginning west of Reno and floating right through the heart of downtown.

While neither of these runs challenges class IV and V rivers (such as the Colorado or the American rivers) in terms of difficulty, the trips are guaranteed to be wet and wild adventures for anybody who comes along. Outings vary in length from half-day to two days and nights, with prices ranging from as low as $48 to $268 per person.

Tahoe Whitewater Tours
Tahoe City, Calif. • (530) 581-2441

Trips with Tahoe Whitewater Tours offer fun and excitement for first-time rafters as well as experienced paddlers. In the immediate Reno/Lake Tahoe area, you can choose from two-hour or full-day runs on the Truckee River and half-day and full-day outings on the East Carson River. Both these rivers provide a fair amount of pristine solitude and placid water coupled with sections of exciting whitewater. The company also provides several daytrips on the South Fork of the American River. The 21-mile whitewater section of this river from Chili Bar (near Placerville, California) to Salmon Falls (near Folsom Reservoir) is one of the most popular river runs in the West. Prices range from about $60 to $100 and longer trips include lunch. This same company also offers kayak trips at Emerald Bay (see our listing for Emerald Bay Kayak Tours under "Kayaking").

Truckee River Raft Rentals
Fanny Bridge Raft Rentals
Calif. Hwy. 89 at Fanny Bridge, Tahoe City, Calif. • (530) 581-0123, (530) 583-0123

With a location on each side of Fanny Bridge, you won't have any trouble finding this raft company: just look for their trademark big red bus. The first 5 miles of the Truckee River, as it empties out of Lake Tahoe at Fanny Bridge, to the River Ranch near Alpine Meadows ski resort, is the most popular rafting run in the Reno/Tahoe area. Meandering lazily through the huge trees along Calif. 89, this self-guided float takes most rafters two or three hours to complete. The turquoise water found along this route makes it easily one of the most beautiful sections of the Truckee River. After taking your raft out at River Ranch Pond, be sure to head up to the River Ranch deck for drinks and lunch before catching the free shuttle bus back to your car at Tahoe City.

Although this outing is convenient, safe and scenic, most of the time it's quite crowded. If you're looking for solitude, you probably won't find it here, unless you go after Labor Day. Weather and water permitting, the rafts operate daily from May to October from 8:30 AM to 3:30 PM. The last shuttle from the River Ranch back to Tahoe City runs at 6 PM. Rates are $20 for children 12 and younger and $25 for adults. Group discounts are also available.

Rock Climbing

Insiders who thrive on the excitement of scaling the face of solid rock cliffs will tell you the secret to great rock climbing: find a place with perfect rocks and perfect weather. We've tried to make it even easier for you by listing some of the Reno/Tahoe area's best indoor and outdoor rock-climbing centers with instructors just waiting to help you take that first step. Today the wall, tomorrow Mt. Everest.

Adventure Park
Northstar-at-Tahoe, 129 Basque Dr., Truckee, Calif. • (530) 562-2285

Northstar provides climbers of all ages and abilities a 25-foot, high granite-like, multifaced

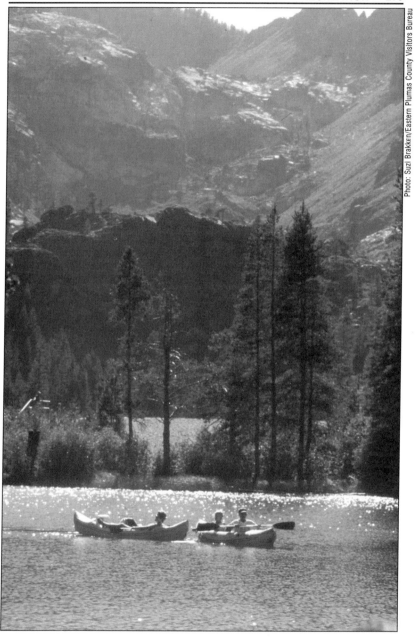

Photo: Suzi Brakken/Eastern Plumas County Visitors Bureau

Paddling is an enjoyable way for the whole family
to get away from the hustle and bustle of modern life.

outdoor climbing wall to practice on. It's located in the Adventure Park behind Northstar Village. The friendly and talented staff teaches belaying and supervises the climbs. The wall is open for climbs from 10 AM to 6 PM, Wednesday to Sunday. All ages may climb but belayers must be at least 14 years old or have staff approval. An hour pass runs about $11 but they do offer discounts for three or more climbers in the group. All-day passes are available for $20.

Camp Richardson Resort
South Lake Tahoe, Calif.
• **(530) 542-6584**

Camp Richardson has a 30-foot high climbing wall known as "The Rock," located behind its sports center. Staff members supervise the climbs, which run about $8 per single climb. Children are welcome and rental shoes are available. The mailing address for Camp Richardson Resort is PO Box 9028, South Lake Tahoe CA 96158.

Headwall
The Cable Car Bldg., Squaw Valley, Calif. • **(530) 583-ROPE**

This climbing center is located in the Cable Car Building at the base of Squaw Valley USA. The wall is 30 feet high and has 25 different routes, ranging in difficulty from beginner to expert. The center supplies harnesses and ropes which must be used when climbing. The fees run about $10 per hour with climbing shoes costing about $5 extra to rent. It's open from noon to 8 PM in the winter and from 10 AM to 8 PM in the summer. It's a low-key, fun climbing facility.

Sierra Mountain Guides
3422 Bowie Rd., Reno, Nev.
• **(775) 747-7478**

If climbing walls is too tame for you, Sierra Mountain Guides can lead you to the real thing — some of the most impressive climbing routes in the Reno/Tahoe area. Its guides offer climbs for all ability levels, from beginner to expert. The company provides all the climbing equipment except for climbing shoes, but these can be rented at the store located in Reno. Cost varies depending upon the area and the climb, but full-day rates start at about $100 and go up. Half-day rates are also available.

Rock Sport Indoor Climbing Center
1901 Silverado Blvd., Sparks, Nev.
• **(775) 352-7673**

Rock Sport's climbing wall is the biggest in the Reno/Tahoe area. It's 32 feet high and spans the entire length of this warehouse's wall. The center offers several workshops during the week, ranging from belaying lessons to kid's climb night. It also offers monthly memberships starting at $40. If you just want to climb, it's open from 10 AM to 10 PM during the week, 10 AM to 8 AM on Saturday, and from 10 AM to 6 PM on Sunday. Rock Sport only offers day passes ($10 for students, $12 for adults). The center provides all the necessary equipment, which you can rent for $5 per day for students or $8 per day for adults.

Shooting

Sage Hill Clay Sports
11500 Mira Loma Rd., Reno, Nev.
• **(775) 851-1123**

This is the only trap and skeet range operating now in the Reno/Tahoe area. Located in south Reno, this facility is very classy. It has 30 trap fields and seven skeet ranges. To blast away at those clay pigeons, expect to pay $5 for 25 targets on both the trap and skeet ranges. Of course, shotgun shells are extra and you have to provide your own weapon. Sage Hill is noted for its sporting clays and has several tournaments throughout the year. If you want to shoot the 50 stations, it's $35 for 100 clays or $17.50 for 50 clays. The club also has several leagues throughout the year.

INSIDERS' TIP

Rattlesnake Raceway in Fallon, Nevada, raffles off the chance to drive a race car at each of its Friday night races. The price of a ticket is $5.

Skateboarding

If you're into skateboarding and don't want the hassle of dodging pedestrians on public sidewalks, the Reno/Tahoe area has two skateboard parks to accommodate you. Both are public facilities so there is no cost associated with their use.

Reno Skateboard Park
Idlewild Park, 1900 Idlewild Dr., Reno, Nev. • (775) 334-2270

This is a 7,000-square foot park located at Idlewild that is open to the public. It doesn't require safety equipment so it's skate-at-your-own-risk. The park is open year-round, weather permitting, during daylight hours.

South Tahoe Skateboard Park
Bijou Park, Al Tahoe Blvd., South Lake Tahoe, Calif. • (530) 542-6055

This city-run park requires helmets and pads. It's located in Bijou Park on Al Tahoe Boulevard, 1 mile from U.S. 50. The park is open from dawn to dusk during the non-snow months.

Skydiving

Some people like the thrill of jumping from perfectly good airplanes, feeling the rush of wind go by and floating to the ground beneath a billowing parachute. If you happen to be one of these people (or want to see if it's indeed exhilarating falling at 32 feet–per-second-squared), check out the area's only skydiving school:

Skydive Lake Tahoe
82335 Calif. Hwy. 70, Beckwourth, Calif. • (530) 583-4084

This skydiving school is the only game in town if you want to leap out of airplanes. A little outside of the Reno/Tahoe area in Beckwourth, California, the school provides a full line of skydiving instruction, offering something for the first-time jumper all the way up to the world champion skydiver. This is a unique way to see the entire Reno/Tahoe area.

For your first time, you can make a tandem jump from 13,000 feet strapped to an instructor licensed through the USPA (United States Parachuting Association). The freefall lasts about 60 seconds, then after pulling your own ripcord, you fly for 4 to 5 minutes in a modern, square parachute, landing near your takeoff point. The entire ride lasts about 1 hour from start to finish and the cost is about $185.

If you find that skydiving is your newfound love, the school also offers a training program which enables you to earn your Class A, Accelerated Freefall license. This 20-jump school runs about $1,900.

The school uses a Beechcraft Super King Air as its jump aircraft and also offers freefall coaching for the most experienced skydivers.

The school is located about 45 minutes from Reno and about 1 hour from the North Shore of Lake Tahoe. To get to the school from Reno, take U.S. 395 north to Hallelujah Junction. Then take Calif. Highway 70 about 15 miles west to Beckwourth. From Lake Tahoe, take Calif. 89 to Calif. 70 and then go east to Beckwourth, about 15 miles.

Soaring

One of the most spectacular and serene ways to view the grandeur of the Reno/Tahoe area is from 10,000 feet in the cockpit of a glider. If you think that the excitement of flying motorless high above the Sierra might be your thing, check out these area companies which provide glider rides and lessons. And don't forget your camera!

High Country Soaring
Douglas County Airport, Minden, Nev. • (775) 782-4944

High Country offers single-passenger rides out of the Douglas County Airport. Even though this airport is outside the Reno/Tahoe area, it is one of only three companies that provide scenic views of Lake Tahoe from sailplanes. Forty-five–minute to one-hour rides run about $100.

To get to the airport from Reno, take U.S. 395 south to Airport Road, just south of Carson City. Follow Airport Road for about 2 miles to the large paved parking area. From Lake Tahoe, take either U.S. 50 or Nev. Highway 207 to U.S. 395, go north (from U.S. 50) or south (from Nev. 207) to Airport Road, then drive down the road to the airport.

Palomino Valley Soaring
15000 Winnemucca Ranch Rd.,
Palomino Valley, Nev. • (775) 475-2440

Located at the Air Sailing Gliderport, 25 miles north of Sparks, this company provides glider rides and lessons. It includes scenic flights by Pyramid Lake and provides first-time flyers with introductory lessons and aerobatic flights. Flight prices start at $60. All flights and lessons are conducted by FAA–certified commercial pilots.

To get to the gliderport from Sparks, go north on the Pyramid Highway (Nev. Highway 445) to Winnemucca Ranch Road (about 15 miles). Turn left at Winnemucca Ranch Road and go about 10 miles to the gliderport.

Soar Minden
Minden, Nev. • (775) 782-7627,
(800) 345-7627

Soar Minden provides year-round glider flights from the Douglas County Airport. It charges $55 to $75 for a one-person ride, $99 to $145 for a two-person flight or $125 for its Top Gun aerobatic flight. The cost depends on the time aloft. This company soars over the Carson Valley but high enough to catch a great view of Lake Tahoe. It also provides private pilot lessons.

Soar Minden is located at the same airport as High Country Soaring. To get to the airport from Reno, take U.S. 395 south to Airport Road, just south of Carson City. Follow Airport Road for about 2 miles to the large paved parking area. From Lake Tahoe, take either U.S. 50 or Nev. 207 to U.S. 395, go north (from U.S. 50) or south (from Nev. 207) to Airport Road, then drive down the road to the airport. The mailing address is PO Box 1764, Minden NV 89423.

Soar Truckee
40100 Truckee Airport Rd., Truckee,
Calif. • (530) 587-6702

Soar Truckee is located at the Truckee–Tahoe Airport just a few miles north of Lake Tahoe on Calif. 267 (see our Getting Here, Getting Around chapter for details on the airport). This soaring center has everything to keep you entertained — lessons, scenic rides, towing services, rental gliders and a campground for pilots and passengers. A half-hour flight costs about $95 and lessons run $35 per

hour for the instructor, $30 per hour for the plane and $40 for a high-elevation tow. The sightseeing flights are usually flown a little north of the airport, but Lake Tahoe is still visible. (See our Daytrips chapter for more to see and do in Truckee.)

Softball

No one in Nevada or California will dispute the fact that softball is the "King of Sports" in the Reno/Tahoe area. The cities of Reno and Sparks are home to most of the teams because of the cooperative weather, but leagues do exist around the lake as soon as the snow melts. In Sparks alone, parks and recreation figures estimate that about 7,000 people (out of a population of 61,000) play softball. Between Reno, Sparks and Lake Tahoe, you can hook up with one of about 500 teams in a number of different leagues depending upon your age, skill level and gender. The leagues consist of 18 and older fastpitch, modified pitch, church co-ed, adult slowpitch, senior, 65+ senior, youth slowpitch, youth fastpitch, ponytail, and American Girl. So you can see that there's a league and an ability level for anyone who wants to "chuck that white pill around."

For more information on softball leagues near you, contact the following organizations:
Reno Recreation Department, (775) 321-8333
City of Sparks Parks and Recreation, (775) 353-2376
Tahoe City's Pomin Park, (530) 583-3796
Kings Beach Neighborhood Park, (530) 546-7248
Incline Village Parks and Recreation, (775) 832-1310
South Tahoe Parks and Recreation, (530) 542-6055

Swimming

If your accommodations in the Reno/Tahoe area offer a swimming pool, you won't have far to go to beat the heat or to get some exercise. You can also head to one of the glorious beaches at Lake Tahoe or to one of the area's public swimming pools to swim your laps. Remember, however, to take precautions in the frigid waters of the lake: you might consider wearing a wetsuit if you're a serious swimmer.

We describe several popular swimming beaches here and also tell you where to find some local swimming pools (see our Parks chapter for additional swimming holes). For exotic dips we suggest you try the soothing waters at **Steamboat Villa Hot Springs Spa** at 16010 S. Virginia Street in Reno, (775) 853-6600; or **Walley's Hot Springs Resort** in Genoa, Nevada, (775) 782-8155 (see our Daytrips chapter for more about Genoa). You'll also find swimming pools and spas at area health and fitness clubs. Weather permitting, we highly recommend a leisurely day at the spa and swimming lagoon at **High Camp Bath & Tennis Club** at Squaw Valley USA (see our description under "Tennis" in this chapter).

Swimming Pools

Alf Sorenson Community Center, 1400 Baring Boulevard, Sparks, Nevada, (775) 353-2385 (indoor)

City of South Lake Tahoe Pool, 1180 Rufus Allen Boulevard, South Lake Tahoe, California, (530) 542-6056 (indoor/outdoor)

Deer Park Pool, 1700 Prater Way, Sparks, Nevada, (775) 353-2385 (outdoor)

Idlewild Pool, 1805 Idlewild Drive, Reno, Nevada, (775) 334-2267 (outdoor)

Moana Pool, 240 W. Moana Lane, Reno, Nevada, (775) 689-2964 (indoor)

Northeast Pool, 1401 Valley Road, Reno, Nevada, (775) 321-8333 (outdoor)

Northwest Pool, 2925 Apollo Way, Reno, Nevada, (775) 334-2203 (indoor)

Oppio Park Pool, 2355 18th Street, Sparks, Nevada, (775) 353-2385 (outdoor)

Traner Pool, 1600 Carville Drive, Reno, Nevada, (775) 334-2269 (outdoor)

Beaches

Baldwin Beach
Calif. Hwy. 89, 4 mi. north of the "Y," South Lake Tahoe, Calif.
• **(530) 573-2674**

This lovely stretch of white sand is tucked along the lakeshore near the Tallac Historic Site. After swimming and enjoying a picnic near the lake, you can take in the cultural events at Tallac (see our chapters on The Arts and Attractions for details). No dogs are allowed.

Kings Beach State Recreation Area
N. Lake Blvd., Kings Beach, Calif.
• **(530) 546-7248**

If you like lots of activity while you swim and sunbathe, this just might be the spot for you. You'll find all the usual water sports at Kings Beach State Recreation Area, along with a day-use park. It's a very busy place with easy access to shops and restaurants in Kings Beach.

Nevada Beach
Elk Pt. Rd. near Zephyr Cove, Nev.
• **(775) 588-6644**

Next to a popular campground, Nevada Beach offers a large expanse of sand along with amenities, such as picnic facilities and restrooms. It's close to the action at Stateline, but worlds away when you're lazing on the beach. Come early in the day: the parking lot and picnic spots fill up fast during high season. No dogs are allowed.

Pope Beach
Calif. Hwy. 89, 2 mi. north of the "Y," South Lake Tahoe, Calif.
• **(530) 573-2674**

Pope Beach offers a picturesque oasis of sun and sand close to all the action in South Lake Tahoe. The unobstructed access to the water is great for families, but leave the family pet at home since they're not allowed here. You'll also find picnic facilities and restrooms on the beach.

Sand Harbor
Nev. Hwy. 28, 4 mi. south of Incline Village, Nev. • **(775) 831-0494**

With sparkling turquoise water lapping at a mile of white sand beach, Sand Harbor is considered by many Insiders to be the most beautiful beach at Lake Tahoe. We recommend you judge for yourself: we're sure you won't be disappointed. You can take nature walks, launch your boat, swim or just laze on the sand. In the evening, stick around for culture since Sand Harbor is the site of the Lake Tahoe Shakespeare Festival. For more information on Sand Harbor see our chapter on The Arts and our description of Lake Tahoe–Nevada State Park in our Parks chapter.

Secret Harbor
Nev. Hwy. 28, 2.5 mi. south of Sand Harbor, Nev. • (775) 573-2674

Although Secret Harbor is no secret to Insiders, its tiny beaches are completely hidden from sightseers on Nev. 28. Known locally as the Nude Beaches, clothing is optional. You won't find groups of naked people standing along stretches of sand staring at each other, however. Access to the water is found in a series of coves, each secluded from the next. To reach the lake from the parking lot above requires a walk of between a half-mile and a mile, but the beauty and seclusion at the end of it is well worth every step. Be sure to bring Rover: this lovely natural setting is very welcoming for dogs. For more information on Secret Harbor and nearby beaches, see our description of Lake Tahoe–Nevada State Park in our Parks chapter.

Tennis

You'll find tennis courts in public parks, on school grounds and at resorts and hotels in the Reno/Tahoe area. If you're used to playing at or near sea level, don't be surprised if you're gasping in the thin mountain air after just a few games. You can take heart knowing your stamina and game should return to normal after a few days of getting used to the higher elevation, however.

We can't list all of the tennis facilities available in the area; they're just too numerous. As Insiders we suggest several places guaranteed to be winners if tennis is part of your vacation. We also direct you to some public courts sprinkled around the area. For more locations you can call parks departments (see our Parks chapter) or inquire about tennis facilities when booking your accommodations.

Incline Village Tennis Complex
**964 Incline Wy., Incline Village, Nev.
• (775) 832-1235**

In a lovely mountain setting, the Incline Village Tennis Complex is sure to meet all of your tennis needs and expectations. The facility includes a pro shop, viewing deck, backboard and snack bar along with seven courts. You can participate in tournaments, take lessons and clinics, and just play for enjoyment. Fees are lower for Incline Village residents and their guests or for those staying in accommodations that include IVGID recreation passes. Because of heavy demand, we strongly suggest you call ahead to reserve your court.

Lakeridge Tennis Club
**6000 Plumas St., Reno, Nev.
• (775) 827-3300**

A members' only club, Lakeridge Tennis Club has 14 outdoor and four indoor courts. Along with playing tennis year-round, you can also enjoy all the amenities of a full-service health club. For dedicated players living in the Reno area, it's the best place to immerse yourself in the game.

Lakeside Tennis and Ski Resort
**955 Tahoe Blvd., Incline Village, Nev.
• (800) 821-4912**

With comfortable apartments and a focus on perfecting your tennis game, Lakeside Tennis and Ski Resort offers just the right environment for a great tennis vacation. Nestled deep in the pines in Incline Village, it's close to golf, hiking and boating as well as the Ponderosa Ranch (see our Vacation Rentals chapter for more information about Lakeside).

North Tahoe Regional Park
Tahoe Vista, Calif. • (530) 546-5043

You can volley long after the sun goes down on the five lighted tennis courts at North Tahoe Regional Park. It's first come, first served so pack a picnic lunch or enjoy a short hike in the park if you need to wait for a court (see our Parks chapter for more information on the park).

Northstar–at–Tahoe
Calif. Hwy. 267, 6 mi. north of Kings Beach, Calif. • (530) 562-1010

Northstar–at–Tahoe offers tennis lessons, camps and leisure play for residents and guests only. If you're looking for an all-inclusive resort experience that includes tennis, Northstar is a great choice. Ask about specific packages when booking accommodations. See our Winter Sports and Resorts chapters for more details about this fun-filled family resort.

Reno Tennis Center
2601 Plumas St., Reno, Nev.
- **(775) 334-2262**

Owned and managed by the City of Reno, the 16 outdoor courts at the Reno Tennis Center are busy all year long. Leisure play is free and on a first-come, first-served basis. It's a popular site for tournaments and group events, which can be arranged for reasonable fees. The city also sponsors a variety of tennis events here, including junior clinics and lessons.

Squaw Valley USA
Calif. Hwy. 89, 6 mi. north of Tahoe City, Calif. • (530) 583-6955

It might be hard to keep your eye on the ball when playing at Squaw Valley USA: the scenery is absolutely first-rate, even if your game isn't. You can play at elevation 6,200 feet at the Resort at Squaw Creek or huff and puff your way through a set at High Camp Bath & Tennis Club at 8,200 feet. A variety of packages, lessons, clinics and leisure play options are available so we suggest you call to find what suits you best.

Indisputably a world-class resort, Squaw is a winner year-round, with activities galore and a natural setting guaranteed to take your breath away. We tell you more about this very special resort in our Attractions, Winter Sports, Resorts and Golf chapters.

Walking/Running

You can run and walk almost anywhere, but let's face it, some terrain is more scenic and suitable for outings than others. We assume most walkers and runners prefer fairly level courses that are well-defined (even though a few super jocks sprint up steep mountain trails designed for hiking). So keeping in mind this average walker/runner, we tell you about some paved and some dirt paths that are free of obstacles and easy to navigate in running or walking shoes.

Incline Village/Lake Shore Drive
Incline Village, Nev.

For scenic Lake Tahoe views and peeks at luxurious gated estates, you can run, walk, or bike the 2.5-mile paved path along Lake Shore Drive in Incline Village. For your first visit to Lake Tahoe, it's a great way to get oriented and to ease into the laid-back tempo of mountain life. The level course parallels the shore of

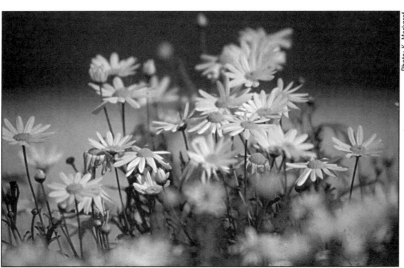

Photo: K. Markgraf

Don't forget to stop and smell the daisies!

the lake, winding through huge trees and past gorgeous beaches. You can access the path easily all along the way, but it's convenient to park at the Hyatt Regency Lake Tahoe and begin your outing there. Don't forget the family dog (leashed): the route is a veritable dog show, with every breed imaginable on display by proud owners. At the end of your walk, we suggest enjoying your favorite drink by the firepit on the beach in front of the Hyatt (see our Resorts chapter for details).

Pope-Baldwin Bike Path
Calif. Hwy. 89, from .5 mi. north of the "Y" to Camp Richardson

Drinking in the gorgeous South Shore Lake Tahoe landscape from this 3.4-mile paved path is entertainment in itself. But you can also take in cultural events at Tallac Historic Site, enjoy a wide variety of outdoor sports at Camp Richardson and stop for refreshments at picnic spots and restaurants along the way (see our Attractions and Vacation Rentals chapters for more details).

Steamboat Ditch Trail
Reno, Nev.

Beginning at the California–Nevada border near Verdi, Steamboat Ditch carries irrigation water for 48 miles through ranches and housing developments to its endpoint near Rhodes Road south of Reno. Although its main purpose for many years has been to water thirsty ranch and farm lands, the trail used for maintaining the ditch has become one of the most popular walking, running and biking routes in Reno.

The ecosystem supported along the banks of the ditch is a kaleidoscope of nature, changing with the seasons to offer up delightful surprises for the unsuspecting outdoor enthusiast. In spring and summer you see an amazing array of flowers bursting with color against the beige desert landscape — the regal purple of hardy thistles, the brilliant pink of dainty wild roses and the soft gray of fuzzy pussy willows. In fall you enjoy the bright oranges and golds of leaves as they drop lazily into the flowing water. And in winter you see the delicate white patterns of crusty snow and ice as they freeze along the ditch banks and the trail.

You can access the trail from a variety of spots as it wanders through Reno, but we suggest trying Horsemans Park at the corner of Skyline and Pioneer drives or off Mountaingate Drive in the Caughlin Ranch area. To get to Mountaingate, go west on Mayberry Drive to Plateau Road and turn left, follow Plateau until it intersects with Mountaingate and then turn right. Follow Mountaingate until you come to a dirt parking area right next to the ditch.

One of the most scenic sections of the trail is west of Mountaingate as it follows Hunter Creek tumbling down from the Mt. Rose Wilderness area and finally emptying into the Truckee River. If you're wearing sturdy shoes, you can hike up the creek for several miles, but keep in mind this is definitely a hike (and not a walk): the going gets rough and hiking boots are definitely in order. If you stick to the main trail along the ditch, you'll see great panoramic views of both the city and the Truckee River along with the mountains and rural areas to the west.

The trail is bisected by roads as it courses through Reno so occasionally you need to cross streets and pick up the trail on the other side. It's also an easement through private land so remember to respect the property rights and privacy of those living along the trail. The trail is one of the most popular areas for exercising dogs since you can let them run free if they're well behaved. One last note — don't be surprised if the ditch is dry in the winter: the water runs only from April to October.

Truckee River Recreation Trail
Along Calif. Hwy. 89, from Tahoe City, Calif. to 1.5 miles north of the River Ranch

Hugging the banks of the Truckee River as it flows from its source at Fanny Bridge, the Truckee River Recreation Trail is a relatively flat, paved path that meanders for about 4.5 miles next to Calif. 89. Along the trail you'll meet lots of joggers, walkers and bikers and in the river you'll see rafters, tubers and anglers. It's a strikingly beautiful section of the river, with enormous trees shading the crystal clear water. We suggest stopping at the River Ranch for people-watching and refreshments as part of your outing (see our description of the River Ranch in the "Rafting" section of this chapter and in our Winter Sports chapter).

Truckee River Walk
Arlington and Island aves., Reno, Nev.

Strolling along the Truckee River Walk, you can trace the route of the river as it flows from west to east through various neighborhoods in Reno. For details about what you'll see along this paved path, see our Attractions chapter. Be sure to bring Fido's leash for this outing.

Virginia Lake
1980 Lakeside Dr., Reno, Nev.
• (775) 334-2262

In a busy urban neighborhood, Virginia Lake is a mecca for runners and walkers. It's a great people-watching and bird-feeding spot, but won't offer much in the way of solitude (see our Parks chapter for more details).

West Shore Bike Path
Along Calif. Hwy. 89, between Tahoe City, Calif. and Sugar Pine Point State Park

The West Shore Bike Path winds for about 9 miles between Tahoe City and Sugar Pine Point State Park, passing beaches, picnic areas and the small towns of Tahoma and Homewood. You can walk or run any section along the way, stopping for sightseeing and meals. The paved route crosses Calif. 89 several times so you need to be alert to traffic. If you're looking for a quiet walk, this popular path may be too busy for you, especially during high season. You can access the path in Tahoe City or farther along the way by parking at Kaspian Campground, about 4 miles south of Tahoe City on Calif. 89, or at Sugar Pine Point State Park.

Watercraft Rental

See "Boat and Watercraft Rentals" under "Boating" earlier in this chapter.

Water-skiing

Only water-skiers truly understand that special thrill of skimming effortlessly across the surface of a sparkling body of water. With a number of lakes nearby, you can indulge in this sport to your heart's content in the Reno/Tahoe area.

If you have your own boat and equipment, you can launch at a number of sites on Lake Tahoe, such as Cave Rock Marina, about 7 miles north of Stateline on U.S. 50; Sand Harbor, about 4 miles south of Incline Village on Nev. 28; and Captain Jon's at 7220 N. Lake Boulevard in Tahoe Vista (see our "Boating" section in this chapter). You can also head out to neighboring lakes, such as Pyramid and Lahontan or Donner Lake, on I-80 near Truckee, California, and Boca Reservoir, about 9 miles east of Truckee on I-80.

If you're looking for lessons or a tow, you can try one of the water-ski schools at Lake Tahoe: they'll furnish everything you need (including the all-important wetsuit) to guarantee a great time on the water.

Action Watersports of Tahoe
3411 U.S. Hwy. 50, South Lake Tahoe, Calif. • (530) 544-2942
Ski Beach, Incline Village, Nev.
• (775) 831-4386

Covering both the North Shore and the South Shore of Lake Tahoe, Action Watersports of Tahoe can outfit you with almost any equipment you could want for fun on the water. You can rent Jet Skis, Seadoos, WaveRunners and a variety of boats. They offer water-ski lessons for $110 an hour and tows for $40. If all this isn't enough excitement for you, ask them to hook you into a parachute for an aerial view of the shoreline from their parasailing rig. (See also our previous listing under "Boating" in this chapter.)

Goldcrest Water Ski School Inc.
8194 N. Lake Blvd., Kings Beach, Calif.
• (530) 546-7412

With a water-ski school right on the premises, the Gold Crest Resort Motel Inc. offers water-ski-in/water-ski-out accommodations. You can learn to ski for just $90 per hour, including all equipment, instructor and experienced boat driver. After an exhilarating ride on skis, you can relax on the lovely sand beach, complete with hot tub and swimming

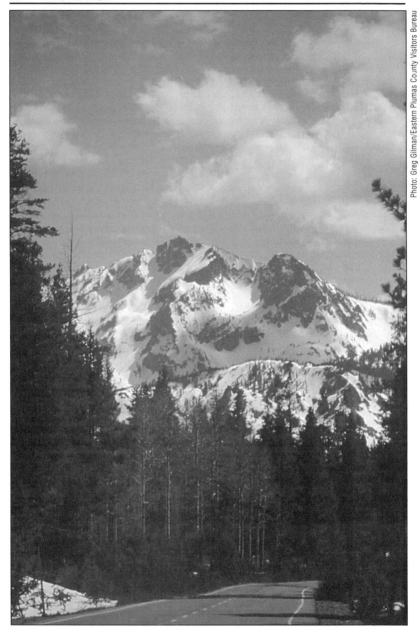

Photo: Greg Gilman/Eastern Plumas County Visitors Bureau

The Sierra Nevada mountain range is the centerpiece of the area, described by
Rand McNally as "the top destination for outdoor recreation" in the U.S.

pool. For information about the accommodations call (530) 546-3301.

Lahontan State Recreation Area
Alt. U.S. Hwy. 95, 50 mi. southeast of Reno, Nev., • (775) 687-4384, (775) 867-3500

If you're looking for smooth, warm water (and what water-skier isn't?), try Lahontan Reservoir in the Lahontan State Recreation Area. Less windy and warmer than Lake Tahoe or Pyramid Lake, Lahontan has been a favorite almost since the first skiers strapped wooden boards onto their feet and yelled "Hit it!" some years ago. The best months to ski here are June and July since algae sometimes causes the lake to turn greenish in August.

You can launch your boat for $5 at the Silver Springs entrance to the park (just past the tiny town of Silver Springs) and at the Cove Marina just a few miles east of Silver Springs on U.S. 50. The lake boasts about 70 miles of predominantly sandy shoreline interspersed with clumps of hardy trees, but for dependable shade we recommend bringing along a tarp or umbrellas. To reach Lahontan from Reno take I-80 west 33 miles to Fernley and then Alt. U.S. 95 south to Silver Springs. See the description of Fallon in our Daytrips chapter for more information on the reservoir.

Lake Tahoe Water-Ski School
Camp Richardson Resort, 1900 Jameson Beach Rd., South Lake Tahoe, Calif. • (530) 544-7747

For a great time on water skis, at Camp Richardson Resort all you need is to show up with a camera and a smile. For $125 an hour Lake Tahoe Water-Ski School provides everything you need — wetsuits and skis plus a boat with an experienced driver. The company also offers 2-mile tows for $35. A full-service resort on a gorgeous stretch of Lake Tahoe frontage, Camp Richardson has all the amenities needed to keep you entertained all day long (for details, see our chapters on Camping and RVing and Vacation Rentals).

Pyramid Lake
Nev. Hwy. 445, 33 mi. northeast of Reno, Nev. • (775) 476-0500, (775) 574-1000.

On a calm sunny day, Pyramid Lake is an absolutely prime choice for water-skiing. Its huge expanse of pristine water and miles of isolated beaches ensure quality fun in the sun without being on top of other outdoor enthusiasts. You need to be mindful of the wind, however: skiing on this placid playground can quickly become a risky venture when the wind churns the surface into a sea of dangerous whitecaps. See our Daytrips chapter for a detailed description of this lovely desert oasis.

Yoga

In their pursuit of good health and fitness, an increasing number of people in the Reno/Tahoe area are looking to the ancient art of yoga for exercise and healing. For some aficionados it offers another health practice in addition to other exercise forms. For others it becomes a total conditioning program and even a way of life. Space doesn't permit us to discuss all the various forms of yoga, but classes on all levels are available in the area.

First Class at **The Yoga Center**, 529 Forest Street in Reno, (775) 881-7848, is designed to demystify yoga and inform first-timers of the many benefits of this form of discipline. The center also has a full schedule of classes for varying abilities and includes prenatal and children's sessions. Many health and fitness clubs include yoga in their class schedules. You can find classes in Reno at **Sports West Athletic Club**, 1575 S. Virginia Street, (775) 348-6666, and **Reno Athletic Club**, 920 Matley Lane, (775) 788-5588; in South Shore Lake Tahoe at **Time Out Health Spa & Fitness**, 2465 Lake Tahoe Boulevard, South Lake Tahoe, California, (530) 544-6222; and **Kingsbury Athletic Center**, 128 Market Street, Stateline, Nevada, (775) 588-7600; and in the North Shore Lake Tahoe area at **Incline Athletic/Racquetball Club**, 800 Northwood Boulevard, Incline Village, Nevada, (775) 831-4212.

INSIDERS' TIP
You can book guided adventure tours around the Lake Tahoe Basin by calling (800) 581-HIKE.

We have top-notch courses designed by such pro players as Jack Nicklaus, Arnold Palmer and Fuzzy Zoeller, and of course we have our share of Robert Trent Jones Jr.–designed masterpieces, too.

Golf

If you love golf, you'll love the Reno/Tahoe area. Insiders have been golfing here in the high desert and the mountains since the beginning of the century and the courses have never been in better shape than right now. We have top-notch courses designed by such pro players as Jack Nicklaus, Arnold Palmer and Fuzzy Zoeller, and of course we have our share of Robert Trent Jones Jr.–designed masterpieces, too.

We guarantee that you won't hear any golfers complaining about the lack of quality courses. We have 33. And golfers here don't complain about the variety in the types of courses either, because we have some courses that are wide-open and a few courses squeezed in so tight among the pine trees that you'll need a laser-sight to get a ball through. The greens fees are varied to fit most golfers' budgets, too. We have them ranging from $30 to $150. And the influx of new courses in the area (more than a dozen in the last five years) is making the Reno/Tahoe area a definite golfing destination.

We like to think that Reno/Tahoe is turning into a golf mecca, at least during the warmer months. Most of the courses at the higher elevations are closed during the winter (it's tough trying to find that white ball in the snow). And most of the courses on the valley floor exchange their green, luscious look during the winter for the more familiar Nevada brown. But during the warmer months, our courses are loaded with variety and personality.

We have one intertwined with a protected wetlands. We have another filled with rolling hills and nicknamed "The Wild Bounce." And we have one course which is so flat and wide open, the big hitters can't resist the temptation to just "grip it and rip it." We often brag about our golf courses because we have one to fit almost any game. And if one is too crowded for your liking, we have 32 others waiting for you.

This chapter will acquaint you with the Reno/Tahoe golf courses open to public play. We have included the kinds of information that'll help you choose the one to fit your game and style: the yardage (from the men's white tees), pars, United States Golfing Association (USGA) ratings, greens fees with cart included, reservation policy and a brief description of each course. Unless stated otherwise, each course has a driving range, putting green, pro shop and restaurant and is open all year.

To help orient you to the location of the courses, we have divided the chapter into our four standard geographical areas — Reno, Sparks, North Shore Lake Tahoe and South Shore Lake Tahoe.

Some of the courses we mention fall outside of these areas, but we think they are close enough and worthwhile to play. So we have designated these courses "Worth the Drive" (big pun intended) and we have included these courses at the end of the geographical section closest to the course.

The Reno/Tahoe Open is the newest tournament on the PGA Tour. At its debut on August 26 to 29, 1999, the Open included practice rounds, a Pro/Am tournament and a 72-hole tournament round with a $2 million purse. The new event is played on one of the area's newest golf courses — Montreux. This private course is built amidst a Ponderosa pine forest at the foot of Mt. Rose. Jack Nicklaus, who designed the course, called it one of his top four designs. The top 125 money winners from 1998 and tournament winners over the past two years took part in this new PGA event.

So let's tee it up and get started. But remember one other thing: the views from all of the golf courses in the area are so magnificent that you won't mind hooking the occasional ball into the sagebrush or slicing one into that sapphire-blue lake crowned with Canada geese. Honest.

Reno

Arrowcreek Golf Club
2905 Arrowcreek Pkwy., Reno, Nev.
• **(775) 850-4653**

The newest addition to the public courses in the Reno/Tahoe area, Arrowcreek sits in the foothills of southwest Reno. The club has two 18-hole courses, one designed by gold legend Arnold Palmer and one designed by PGA pro Fuzzy Zoeller and golf architect John Harbottle. This 36-hole private and semi-private club should provide some of Nevada's best golf.

The Zoeller/Harbottle course, **The Challenge**, opened in the late summer of 1999 but is a members-only course.

The 18-hole course called **The Legend** was designed by Palmer and is open for public play. It's 7230 yards and was rated by the Northern Nevada Golf Association as a 75, which means that a scratch golfer would most likely shoot a 75 here. The course's professional, Mark Range, called the course "pretty tough." Range has not yet determined the course's signature hole but he said it might be the par 3 No. 15, which is 212 yards long with about 80 percent carry to the green over Thomas Creek.

Yardage	7230
Par	72
NNGA	75
Greens Fees	$80, Monday through Thursday; $90 weekend
Reservations	7 days in advance

Lakeridge Golf Course
1200 Razorback Rd., Reno, Nev.
• **(775) 825-2200**

Insider golfers voted Lakeridge the best course in Reno from 1990 to 1994. This Robert Trent Jones Jr.–designed course built in 1969 has large greens, large tee boxes, large bunkers and lots of water. Most visitors know the course because of its signature hole — the 15th, a 230-yard par 3, which features a tee box 360 feet above Lake Stanley, requiring a tee shot to an island green. This is prob-

ably the most-talked-about and most-photographed hole in the Reno/Tahoe area. Access to the green is by a footbridge. During the winter, you are only allowed to walk on this course. The course is located in a prestigious neighborhood and sports a country-club atmosphere with upscale homes lining the fairways. It's closed for several months during the winter. Reservations for a group of 20 or more may be made a year in advance.

Yardage	6140
Par	71
USGA rating	68.3
Greens fees	$60 Monday through Thursday; $70 weekend
Reservations	7 days in advance

Northgate Golf Club
1111 Club House Dr., Reno, Nev.
• **(775) 747-7577**

Northgate is a desert links-style course with fast, undulating greens surrounded by grass and sand bunkers. The fairways are hilly and open — if you manage to hit one. The course is one of the most challenging in the area because of the potential to miss the landing zones and hit into the sagebrush and sand of the high desert. Don't come here unless you are sure of your game: the course has crushed the egos of some good golfers. Many holes have the desert coming into play, meaning that shots have to be made over this natural hazard. This course will require you to use every club in your bag. Designed by Brad Benz and Mile Poellot and built in 1988, Northgate played host to the Ben Hogan Tour in 1990 and 1991 and the U.S. Open Qualifying Tournament in 1988 and 1989. The only hang-up to this course is its slow play. The last time we played it, the round took 6 hours.

Yardage	5920
Par	72
USGA rating	67.5
Greens fees	$48
Reservations	7 days in advance

Rosewood Lakes Golf Course
6800 Pembroke Ln., Reno, Nev.
• **(775) 857-2892**

This is not a long course but it is difficult

because it plays like a links-style course. Rosewood was built around a protected wetlands preserve and if you don't hit the ball straight, it will end up in the tules. Once the ball enters the wetlands, you are not allowed to retrieve it. So the Insiders' tip is bring plenty of balls when you play this course. The fairways are flat and open and the greens are medium sized and on the slow side. Water comes into play on every hole, making this a challenging course. The greens fees are some of the cheapest in the area, and it's popular with Insiders. The signature 17th hole is a treacherous par 4 with a bunker and lake lining the entire right side and a lake lining the left. An accurate drive is a must, making the second shot to the large, elevated green easy. One par 3 is a blind tee shot because the tules have grown so tall that they completely block the view to the green. This course, designed by Brad Benz and built in 1991, is one of top conditioned municipal courses in the West because of its easy access to year-round water.

Yardage	6104
Par	72
USGA rating	68.5
Greens fees	$35
Reservations	7 days in advance

Sierra Sage Golf Course
6355 Silver Lake Blvd., Reno, Nev.
• **(775) 972-1564**

This course is located in Stead, a bedroom community north of Reno located in the sagebrush of the high desert. The U.S. Air Force built the front nine in 1960 and the back nine was added in 1970. Sagebrush lines almost all of its large, rolling fairways and big hitters have a tendency to go for the long ball here. Accuracy is a must if you go for it or you will be off into the sagebrush with the quail and the jackrabbits. Water comes into play on six holes and four holes are built around a lake. The greens are small and fast with bunkers protecting most. A Senior Tour event was played here in 1970. This course is played heavily by locals because we get a break on the greens fees. But visitors seem to forget it's here, which is a shame because it is fun to play and one of the cheapest around.

Yardage	6207
Par	71
USGA rating	67.9
Greens fees	$35.75
Reservations	7 days in advance

Washoe County Golf Course
2601 S. Arlington Ave., Reno, Nev.
• **(775) 828-6640**

Washoe County is the oldest golf course in Reno. Built in 1936, this course is well established and popular among Insiders, especially the seniors (greens fees are cheap for residents in comparison to other courses around the area). The first hole has a great view from an elevated tee box, overlooking a dogleg left par 4. A good drive here sets you up for an easy shot to the green, but trees lining both sides of the fairway can intimidate the best hitters. In fact, trees line the fairways on the entire front 9. Don't let the flat and wide fairways on the front fool you into thinking the entire course is flat: the back 9 is extremely hilly and tight and you still have to contend with some trees. The course has small bentgrass greens, well protected by sand bunkers. The course is always in good shape now that it has its own water supply. Try to do your best scoring on the relatively easy front nine because you'll need all the strokes you can get for the back.

Yardage	6468
Par	72
USGA rating	68.8
Greens fees	$34
Reservations	7 days in advance

Wolf Run Golf Club
1400 Wolf Run Rd., Reno, Nev.
• **(775) 851-3301**

This semiprivate course opened in the summer of 1998 and is owned by the University of Nevada, Reno; it's home to the university's men's and women's golf teams for practice and matches. The public is invited to play 7 days per week on the state's first golf course built especially for a university. The course winds its way through rolling desert terrain southwest of Reno and offers great views of the valley, downtown and Mt. Rose. The course was designed by John Fleming, Steve Van Meter and Lou Eiguren and the three made sure that the high desert and loads of sagebrush come into play on almost every hole. Eiguren, who is also the course's director of golf, has worked at such legendary courses as the Olympic Club in San Francisco and Edgewood at Lake Tahoe. The signature hole, No. 15, is a long par 5 with a large green surrounded by Thomas Creek, creating an island-green effect and making it a great three-shot hole. The Wolf Pack (UNR's team name and mascot) is featured throughout the course and this golf club has a no-kidding 19th hole. This short hole is designed in the shape of a wolf's paw and can be used to settle any carry-over bets or can be used as a playoff hole. The university's logo can also be found in two large rock display areas. The course is extremely enjoyable and very playable.

Yardage	6086
Par	71
USGA rating	67.9
Greens Fees	$55
Reservations	7 days in advance

Sparks

Red Hawk Golf Club
7755 Spanish Springs Rd., Sparks, Nev.
• (775) 626-6000

The newest golf course in Sparks, Red Hawk will eventually have 36 holes — 18 designed by Robert Trent Jones Jr., and 18 designed by Hale Irwin. Jones's 18 are open for play now and offer magnificent views of the Truckee Meadows and the surrounding mountains. Jones designed this course around the marshlands and lakes of an old hunting club so water comes into play on several holes. The fairways are so plush that you almost hate taking a divot and the bentgrass greens are extremely well manicured and fast. The course is lengthy with wide-open fairways but beware when the wind kicks up. This is one of the examples of the scenic backdrop being so magnificent that you really don't mind playing a lousy game of golf. The golf carts are equipped with state-of-the-art measuring devices. Red Hawk features northern Nevada's only Golf Learning Center, a program designed

to teach every part of the game for every level of play.

Yardage	6138
Par	72
USGA rating	68.4
Greens fees	$60 Monday through Thursday; $75 weekends and holidays
Reservations	7 days in advance

Wildcreek Golf Course
3500 Sullivan Ln., Sparks, Nev.
• (775) 673-3100

This club has two courses — an 18-hole regulation course and a 9-hole executive par 3 course.

Course One — The 18-hole design features rolling fairways, lots of water, bunkers and sagebrush. The course was carved from a hillside, making the fairways uneven and leading Insiders to nickname the course "Wild Bounce." Besides the undulating fairways, the course has six lakes and a creek running through it to make your game even more challenging. The bentgrass greens are big and well protected by lots of sand. Some of the holes feature elevated tees and terraced greens, making the course one of the toughest to play in the area. It was home to two Senior Tour events in 1982 and 1983 and the Gatlin Brothers Open in 1985, 1986 and 1987.

Yardage	6244
Par	72
USGA rating	69.1
Greens fees	$50
Reservations	7 days in advance

Course Two — The 9-hole executive par 3 features tiny greens and tight fairways. Several water hazards are sprinkled in among the holes, making shot placement a priority. The course is always crowded but it is an excellent place to come to hone your short-game skills or to teach a new golfer.

Yardage	1300
Par	27
USGA rating	N/A

INSIDERS' TIP

Four more golf courses are scheduled to open in 2000 in the Reno/Tahoe area.

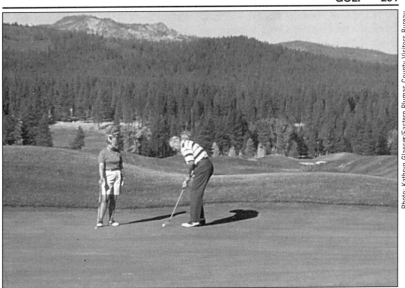

Photo: Kathryn Glaser/Eastern Plumas County Visitors Bureau

Scenic surroundings are an added benefit to playing the Whitehawk Ranch Golf Course.

Greens fees $12
Reservations   7 days in advance

Worth the Drive

Desert Lakes Golf Course
4000 Farm District Rd., Fernley, Nev.
• **(775) 575-4653**

This 18-hole bentgrass course, opened in 1996, is located in Fernley, Nevada, about 35 miles east of Sparks. As the name suggests, the course was built among the sagebrush of the high desert but just to add a little more of a challenge, designer Bob Bingham laced 30 lakes around the 18 holes. The course plays easily, though, if you can control your shots. It's almost a guarantee that errant shots will find water or the sagebrush. Most greens are moderately fast and protected by white sand bunkers. The course plays fast and is never crowded during the week. Insiders love this course because it has the best twilight rates around. After 1 PM in the summer, you can play the course with a cart for half price. The only drawback is the fact that during the summer, temperatures in Fernley can reach or even exceed the 100-degree mark. The course fea-tures a 605-yard par 5 that doglegs around the sagebrush and a lake. The signature hole is a short par 3 called The Hanging Tree which features water in the front and the back and a 100-year-old cottonwood tree looming next to the green. The course is wide open with only a few trees so when the wind kicks up, usually during the afternoon, it can wreak havoc with your game.

Yardage   6085
Par   71
USGA rating   68
Greens fees $30
Reservations   7 days in advance

North Shore Lake Tahoe

Incline Village Golf Resort
955 Fairway Blvd., Incline Village, Nev.
• **(775) 832-1146**

This club has an 18-hole championship course and an 18-hole executive course. Both courses are tucked in among the Sierra Nevada mountain pines of Incline Village overlooking Lake Tahoe. The courses are usually open from May through October, but always check with the pro shop for the exact dates.

The Championship Course — This course has tight, rolling fairways bordered by towering pines. A mountain creek snakes its way through the course and provides for strategically placed water hazards on 13 of the 18 holes. Robert Trent Jones Sr. called this course "an example of an ideal mountain course," and he should know because he designed it. His layout demands accuracy as well as distance. Golfers are faced with heavily bunkered greens on almost every hole (more than 50 sand traps are scattered around the course). The greens are large, undulating and fast. Almost every shot here poses a challenge to the most experienced golfer. The signature hole, No. 16, is a 406-yard par 4 with a dogleg-right fairway and a spectacular view of Lake Tahoe in the distance. The second shot on this magnificent hole requires you to hit over a ravine to an isolated green. *Golf Digest* magazine always rates this course as one of the best in the West. It lives up to Jones's philosophy that every hole should be a tough par but an easy bogey.

Yardage	6447
Par	72
USGA rating	70.2
Greens fees	$115
Reservations	7 days in advance

The Mountain Course — This par 58, 3500-yard course was designed by Robert Trent Jones Jr. and is rated as one of the top five executive courses in the United States. It is also cut out of the gigantic pines and has outstanding views of Lake Tahoe. The course is hilly and has all of the hazards of the Championship Course with the exception of length. The Mountain Course features 14 par 3 holes, averaging more than 170 yards in length. This course has played host to the National Executive Course Championship.

Yardage	3500
Par	58
USGA rating	56.6
Greens fees	$50
Reservations	7 days in advance

Northstar–at–Tahoe Golf Course
129 Basque Dr. at Northstar–at–Tahoe, Truckee, Calif. • (530) 562-2490

Spectacular scenery of the mountains near Lake Tahoe add to this course's appeal. Its 18 holes are intertwined among woods and fields and golfers like to call this kind of course "two-faced," because the front and back 9 are totally different. The front 9 is played through a valley with rolling, wide-open fairways, and the back 9 changes looks as it climbs into the tall pines. These holes have skinny fairways, numerous doglegs and require tricky, target golf shots. The course has plenty of water, sand bunkers and its par 3s are gorgeous. The greens are medium-sized and fast. The course has a habit of eating golf balls so bring plenty. The course usually opens in May and closes sometime in October. The course is located in the Northstar–at–Tahoe resort (see our Resorts chapter).

Yardage	6015
Par	72
USGA rating	67.5
Greens fees	$67
Reservations	7 days in advance

Old Brockway Golf Club
7900 N. Lake Blvd., Kings Beach, Calif. • (530) 546-9909

This 9-hole course is located a block from Lake Tahoe and features rolling hills, a meandering creek, tall pines and excellent views. This is one of the oldest golf courses at Lake Tahoe. It was built is 1924 and was home to the first Bing Crosby Tournament before the tourney moved to Pebble Beach. The course was also a favorite of the Rat Pack (Frank Sinatra, Dean Martin, Sammy Davis Jr. and crew). This course is extremely challenging because of its narrow fairways and wooded roughs. It is usually the first to open and the last to close at the lake. The following information is based on 18 holes of play.

Yardage	6414
Par	72
USGA rating	67.6

INSIDERS' TIP

Generally speaking, tee times are usually easy to get during the week, even during the height of the golfing season.

Photo: Hank Faglian>/Eastern Plumas County Visitors Bureau

Snowcapped mountains form a spectacular backdrop for Graegle Meadows Golf Course.

| Greens fees | $45 |
| Reservations | 7 days in advance |

Ponderosa Golf Course
10040 Reynold Wy., Truckee, Calif.
• (530) 587-3504

This is the easiest course at Lake Tahoe and is suited for the beginning golfer and the weekend duffer. The 9-hole course is mostly flat and nestled beneath towering pines, but it is forgiving. The course has no water hazards and the greens are in excellent condition. Don't play this course unless you like to wait while playing. The course is open from May through October. The following information is based on 18 holes of play.

Yardage	5800
Par	72
USGA rating	66.6
Greens fees	$50
Reservations	7 days in advance

Resort at Squaw Creek
400 Squaw Creek Rd., Olympic Valley, Calif. • (530) 583-6300

This Robert Trent Jones Jr.–designed course is everything you would expect from both the prolific designer and a Lake Tahoe resort course: beautiful mountain and meadow views and a challenging course set among existing wetlands and forested hills. The course is lush and plays like a links course, with tees, landing areas and greens strategically placed to take advantage of the natural hazards. The front 9 has narrow fairways and rows and rows of towering pines. The back 9 has elevated wooden cart paths built over the wetlands and has a propensity for eating golf balls, so bring an extra supply. The signature hole is the par 5 13th that is 500 yards long and requires at least a 200-yard drive off the tee to carry the wetlands. The entire Olympic Valley is surrounded by the mountains of Squaw Valley USA, home to the 1960 Winter Olympics. (See our Winter Sports, Recreation and Resorts chapters for more information on Squaw Valley). The course is usually open from April through October.

Yardage	6010
Par	71
USGA rating	69.1
Greens fees	$110
Reservations	7 days in advance

Tahoe City Golf Course
251 N. Lake Blvd., Tahoe City, Calif.
• (530) 583-1516

Located behind a commercial block off the

main thoroughfare in Tahoe City and easily spotted from Fanny Bridge, this 9-hole course is hilly, wooded and well bunkered. Built in 1917, it is the oldest course in the Tahoe Basin and has some spectacular views of Lake Tahoe, which is right across the street. Its claim to fame is that it drew Hollywood stars like Frank Sinatra, Bing Crosby and Bob Hope regularly during the 1940s and 1950s and it has remained an Insiders' hangout to this day. It is the shortest course at the lake and is open from April through October. The following information is based on 18 holes of play.

Yardage	5261
Par	66
USGA rating	65.1
Greens fees	$52
Reservations	7 days in advance

Tahoe Donner Golf Club
12850 Northwoods Blvd., Truckee, Calif.
• **(530) 587-9440**

This course is located in a residential/resort development and features narrow, tight fairways through the pines. Here, accuracy is more important than power. The first hole is an example of the kind of play needed on the entire course. The hole is a straight-ahead 450-yard par 5 lined with pines requiring straight hitting. A slice or a hook here is real trouble. A creek comes into play on eight holes and the course is hilly with many drops from tee to fairway to green. This course is extemely well maintained and difficult to play. But it may be even more difficult to get a tee time since the residents get first pick during the season that lasts from May through October.

Yardage	6587
Par	72
USGA ratings	71.2
Greens fees	$100
Reservations	7 days in advance
	(good luck!)

Worth the Drive

The following golf courses are located in and around the Graeagle area of California adjacent to Calif. highways 89 and 70. (See our Daytrips chapter for more information about Graeagle.) This section of the Sierra has been dubbed "The Pebble Beach of the North" because of the many excellent and scenic golf courses in the area that are open for seasonal play. The driving time is about 40 minutes from the north shore of Lake Tahoe and one hour from Reno.

Feather River Inn
Golf Course and Resort
At the junction of Calif. Hwy. 89 and Calif. Hwy. 70, Blairsden, Calif.
• **(530) 836-2722**

This 9-hole course has an extremely challenging layout. Like most of the courses in the Sierra, its fairways are tight and lined with trees and the greens are fast. One thing that favors golfers here is the terrain: at least it's mostly flat. Here again, like the other mountain courses, accuracy is rewarded over distance. The 9th hole is probably the prettiest hole of all the courses in the area. It is uphill to a green surrounded by the resort, which features a rustic-looking lodge. This course has no driving range. The following information is based on 18 holes of play.

Yardage	5758
Par	70
USGA rating	64.8
Greens fees	$30
Reservations	7 days in advance

Feather River Park Resort
8339 Calif. Hwy. 89, Blairsden, Calif.
• **(530) 836-2328**

Because the holes are short and not intimidating, this course is ideal for senior and

---

INSIDERS' TIP

It can be tough to get a tee time at a number of our most popular mountain courses, in part because of the short golf season. If you know ahead of time when you're going to want to play, you might try making a reservation before you even leave home. If you get here and still need a tee time, starting times are easier to come by on weekdays.

Photo: Suzi Brakken/Eastern Plumas County Visitors Bureau

Golf courses in the Reno/Tahoe area make use of both mountain and high desert natural hazards.

junior golfers. Located along the Feather River, this 9-hole course is flat and relatively open. A few pine trees are sprinkled around the course but they pose little problem and mostly just add to the great scenery. The two par 5 holes on the course are less than 450 yards, making them reachable in two. This course is part of a resort with small cabins and other recreational activities. It has no driving range. The following information is based on 18 holes of play.

Yardage	5164
Par	70
USGA rating	N/A
Greens fees	$33
Reservations	7 days in advance

Graeagle Meadows Golf Course
18 Calif. Hwy. 89, Graeagle, Calif.
• **(530) 836-2323**

Graeagle Meadows weaves its way through the Mohawk Valley, straddles the Feather River and makes good use of the towering pines. This course is always in excellent shape and, like so many others in the Sierra, it has spectacular scenery. The most renowned landmark is Chief Graeagle, a rock formation to the west of the 6th tee. Ask any Insider to point out his headdress and moccasins at either end of the 2-mile–long formation. Great scenes like this can almost make you forget about the flat, narrow fairways and well-pro-

tected greens. The most intimidating hole is the short par 3 16th, with a pine tree blocking the center of the green. The course is usually open from late March through October and is one of the best in the area and one of the cheapest to play.

Yardage	6680
Par	72
USGA rating	70.7
Greens fees	$50
Reservations	7 days in advance

Plumas Pines Country Club
402 Poplar Valley Rd., Blairsden, Calif.
• **(530) 836-1420**

This country club is open to the public and is one of the most popular around if you are a low-handicap player. Another "two-faced" course (distinctively different front and back 9s), it has a front 9 which lies in a valley surrounded by lots of water and a narrow, hilly back 9 which climbs into the pines. One of the best-manicured courses in the Sierra, it demands a high level of play. Water exists on 11 holes and it has several blind doglegs. The greens are heavily bunkered and houses parallel many of the holes, making accuracy your prime objective. The signature hole is the 395-yard par 4 No. 9 with its view across a small lake to the clubhouse, which sits on a hill overlooking the course. The most difficult hole may be the 18th with a double dogleg, an uphill approach and a tiered green. Some of the holes on this course are the most difficult of all the courses in the area. This golf club is usually open from May through October.

Yardage	5894
Par	72
USGA rating	69
Greens fees	$50
Reservations	7 days in advance

Whitehawk Ranch
1137 Calif. Hwy. 89, Clio, Calif.
• **(530) 836-0394**

Resting against the eastern slope of the Sierra in the Mohawk Valley, this championship course is located in the middle of a housing development. But don't panic: the development only has 450 homes, each on one-third of an acre and the developers have maintained the rustic, rural charm of the mountain atmosphere. They hired Dick Bailey to design the course (a first for this architect) and he did such a good job that the California Golf Writers' Association awarded Whitehawk its 1997 Environmental Award for protecting the environment while furthering the game of golf. The course was built in 1996 and includes plenty of pines, water and 45 acres of native grasses and wildflowers bordering the fairways. Some Insiders think this course is on even par with the prestigious Edgewood at South Shore Lake Tahoe. The course has four signature holes, but the prettiest may be the 16th, which has a magnificent view of the Mohawk Valley. Most of the holes have streamlined fairways and multitiered greens. The course is well maintained and once again the views will almost make you forget your golf game. Don't come here unless you like a challenge. The Northern California Golf Association added Whitehawk to its championship rotation that includes such renowned courses as Pebble Beach, Spyglass and the Olympic Club.

Yardage	6420

Par	71
USGA rating	69.8
Greens fees	$80
Reservations	6 months in advance

South Shore Lake Tahoe

Bijou Golf Course
3464 Fairway Blvd. at Johnson Blvd., South Lake Tahoe, Calif.
• **(530) 542-6097**

A historic 9-hole executive course built in 1920 in the center of South Lake Tahoe, this course is perfect for all level of players. Bijou Creek winds through the course providing water hazards, and of course pine trees add to golfers' frustration. It has a great view of Heavenly Ski Resort and Freal Peak. The course allows only pull carts and doesn't take advance reservations, but it is usually easy to get on. The following information is based on 18 holes of play.

Yardage	4056
Par	64
USGA rating	N/A
Greens fees	$22
Reservations	None taken in advance

Edgewood Tahoe Golf Course
180 Lake Pkwy., Stateline, Nev.
• **(775) 588-3566**

This course is IT — *the* premier golfing experience in the Reno/Tahoe area. Built along the lush shoreline of Lake Tahoe, Edgewood features both wide-open fairways and narrow ones laced through the pines with both rolling and flat terrain. It is rated by *Golf Digest* as one of the Top 25 courses in the country. Edgewood has more than 80 sand traps, many of which protect the large, undulating and terraced greens that are pro-caliber and superfast. Many strategically placed trees come into play; water is a factor on 11 holes. This course is the most difficult to score well on in Nevada.

INSIDERS' TIP

Golf course elevations in the Reno/Tahoe area range from 4,500 feet to 6,500 feet — so golf shots will carry farther here in the thinner air!

The Crown Jewel of the Sierra, Edgewood has the distinction of having the only holes on the shore of Lake Tahoe: the signature 17th, a 207-yard par 3, and the 574-yard par 5 18th.

This course is a must-play for the true golf aficionado but its popularity makes it difficult to get a tee time. Take it from us, though, the course is well worth the hassle of acquiring a start time (no more than 160 golfers are allowed to play each day). The course has played host to many professional events and is presently home to the American Century Golf Championship every July (see our Spectator Sports and Annual Events chapters). Do yourself a big golfing favor, and don't leave the area without playing this George Fazio–designed masterpiece.

Yardage	6505
Par	72
USGA rating	70.2
Greens fees	$150
Reservations	2 weeks in advance

Lake Tahoe Golf Course
2500 Emerald Bay Rd., South Lake Tahoe, Calif. • (530) 577-0788

This course used to be called the Lake Tahoe Country Club, to give you an idea of the quality of play here. But it remains an underplayed course when compared to the premier courses around the lake. Golfers just seem to forget that it's here, even though it's conveniently located in an alpine meadow surrounded by tall Sierra peaks just minutes from the glitter of Stateline, Nevada. The course is flat to slightly rolling, with the Upper Truckee River and artificial lakes coming into play on 16 holes. The greens are in excellent condition. This course isn't long but it is treacherous, making good ball placement a top priority. Over the last 10 years, the course has gone through extensive renovations. It used to be considered one of the lake's best bargains but its greens fees have climbed in the last couple years. Tee times are usually easy to get here.

Yardage	6160
Par	71
USGA rating	68.8
Greens fees	$60
Reservations	7 days in advance

Tahoe Paradise Golf Course
3021 Emerald Bay Rd., South Lake Tahoe, Calif. • (530) 577-2121

Located just down the highway from the Lake Tahoe Golf Course, this executive course was South Lake Tahoe's first 18-holer. The course is short but once again has all the nasty quirks of a mountain course — narrow fairways, tree-lined roughs and small greens. But thankfully, water comes into play on only two holes. The most difficult hole is a 377-yard par 4 that requires a tee shot through a gap only 50 yards across. The signature hole is the 14th, a 110-yard par 3 with a lake in front and a view of the surrounding mountain peaks.

Yardage	4028
Par	66
USGA rating	59.9
Greens fees	$43
Reservations	7 days in advance

Worth the Drive

Carson City, Nevada's capital, and the surrounding Carson Valley sit just over the mountain from Lake Tahoe and 30 miles down U.S. Highway 395 from Reno. Here, nine excellent golf courses wait for you to tee one up. All of these courses are definitely Worth the Drive because they are some of the best-maintained in Nevada and fun to play. Insiders like to call them the "Divine Nine."

Carson Valley Golf Course
1027 Riverview Dr., Gardnerville, Nev. • (775) 265-3181

Just by the address, you can guess the biggest hazard on this course: water. The East Fork of the Carson River snakes its way through this 18-hole course creating a natural water hazard on all but two holes, so bring plenty of extra golf balls. This course is always in good shape because of its easy access to plenty of water but in 1996 and 1997, it got too much of the wet stuff when the river overflowed its banks and flooded some of the holes. Even though this course is not in the mountains, its fairways are still narrow with a lot of rough and out of bounds but at least you won't have to worry about pine trees — here, it's towering cottonwoods that line the fairways. This course is always a joy to play but quite frustrating if you can't hit a straight shot. Carson Valley has a real rustic feel to it and is located on the outskirts of one of the prettiest small towns in Nevada. (Check out our Daytrips chapter for more to see and do in Gardnerville.)

Yardage	5760
Par	71
USGA rating	66.5
Greens fees	$32
Reservations	7 days in advance

Dayton Valley Country Club
51 Palmer Dr., Dayton, Nev.
• (775) 246-7888

This is a magnificent Arnold Palmer–designed course located 11 miles east of Carson City in the high desert. Even though this course has country club in the title, it is open to public play. The course has only been open since 1991 and it already ranks sixth on *Golf Today*'s list of Top 20 daily fee courses in Northern California and Nevada, which means it is in the same company as Pebble Beach, Spyglass and Spanish Bay. The other delightful thing about Dayton Valley is that it offers the lowest greens fees of the Top 12 courses of the *Golf Today* list. This course is our favorite to play of all the courses in the area including Edgewood and the new Sierra Nevada Golf Club and it's cheaper to play.

Palmer designed a beautiful course which combines the natural beauty of the high desert with rolling fairways sculpted in a links-style, rolling hills dotted with sand traps surrounding the fairways and huge, sloping greens. The course has few trees but strategically placed water hazards come into play on 12 holes. The course is superbly maintained and is known for its plush, velvet-like fairways and immaculate greens. The first par 3 on the front 9 is dubbed the "Moon Crater" because the green sits below the tee box in a small glade surrounded by steep hills and sand traps, giving the hole a surreal feel.

Everyone who has played this course has his or her favorite hole but for us it has to be the par 3 No. 6. This intimidating hole is only 135 yards long but it is all over water to an island green surrounded not only by a lake but by sand traps, too. A par on this hole is good golf. The No. 1 handicapped hole is the par 4 No. 9, which requires you to hit over and around two water hazards. After a good tee shot (more than 230 yards), you still have at least 160 yards all over water to carry the green. As with the No. 6, a par on this hole is an accomplishment. This course looks and feels like a country club and it even provides you with a course manager booklet which has the holes listed and diagrammed to aid you in club selection and course management.

Yardage	5897
Par	72
USGA rating	68.2
Greens fees	$53 Monday through Thursday; $70 weekend
Reservations	2 weeks in advance

Eagle Valley Golf Courses
3999 Centennial Park Dr., Carson City, Nev. • (775) 887-2380

This golf facility has two regulation 18-hole courses — The West and The East. These two courses offer two distinctively different modes of play. The West Course has lots of water, trees, sand bunkers and sagebrush. The East Course is wide open.

The West — This links-style course is hilly and requires you to hit the ball straight since almost every hole is lined with water or sagebrush. It was designed by Jack Snyder in 1977 to challenge you on every hole and it does that and more. The course demands correct club selection and good course management. This course has great views of Carson City as it winds its way up, down and around the foothills on the northeastern side of town. The 14th tee offers spectacular views of the eastern side of the Sierra. Changes in course elevation and strategically located water and

---

INSIDERS' TIP

Some of the courses in the area are now requiring soft spikes. Check with the pro shop when you call for a tee time.

bunkers add to its challenging layout. This course is not for the faint-hearted golfer. If your game isn't top drawer, this course can be frustrating.

Yardage	6245
Par	72
USGA rating	71.5
Greens fees	$37.50
Reservations	3 days in advance

The East Course — This 18 is wide open and offers a good game for all styles of play. A great course for couples, seniors, juniors and beginning to intermediate golfers, this course features manicured fairways and quick greens. The course rambles throughout the flat valley beneath the foothills and was made for the big hitters who like to go for broke. A wayward shot on this course will usually find another fairway so trouble is at a minimum here. The East Course is great for walking a quick nine or riding a leisurely 18.

Yardage	6314
Par	72
USGA rating	67.3
Greens fees	$30
Reservation	3 days in advance

Empire Ranch Golf Course
1875 Fair Way Dr., Carson City, Nev.
• **(775) 885-2100**

This course opened in 1997 and is set among the wetlands overlooking the Carson River. Its 27 holes are squeezed between high bluffs and include 46 acres of wetlands and six lakes. You can see that water hazards are plentiful so bring a lot of golf balls. You can start on any nine holes so you really have a choice of playing three courses here. Once again several shots must carry the wetlands, but course designer Cary Beckler was thoughtful of the high handicappers. He designed in a bailout option on almost every hole for those who need the help. Empire Ranch is rapidly becoming an Insiders' hangout because of its reasonable greens fees.

Yardage	6207
Par	72
USGA rating	67.9
Greens Fees	$30
Reservations	7 days in advance

The Golf Club at Genoa Lakes
1 Genoa Lakes Dr., Genoa, Nev.
• **(775) 782-4653**

One of the prettiest golf courses in the Carson City area, Genoa Lakes is located in Nevada's oldest town. This Peter Jacobson/ John Harbottle–designed course is spectacular and rests against the slopes of the eastern Sierra with miles and miles of valley and mountain views. The course was built around a large wetlands that attracts all kinds of waterfowl. This links-style course is long and extremely challenging. Water comes into play on 13 holes and its huge sand traps have a propensity for reaching out and grabbing even the best golf shots. *Golf Digest* voted Genoa Lakes the "4th Best Public Course" in 1994 and the "3rd Best Course in Nevada" in 1995. This course will definitely test every part of your game but again, the views are so magnificent you won't mind shooting a mediocre game of golf. The signature hole is the 13th, a 652-yard par 5, the longest in Nevada. The trick to this course is a well-placed tee shot. Any other type of tee shot is trouble with a big "T."

Yardage	6057
Par	72
USGA rating	68.2
Greens fees	$70 Monday through Thursday; $90 weekend
Reservations	7 days in advance

Sierra Nevada Golf Club
2901 Jacks Valley Rd., Genoa, Nev.
• **(775) 782-7700**

The newest course to the area, Sierra Nevada opened in August 1998 to rave reviews and sits just up the road from Genoa Lakes. This course has a western theme and was built on a former hunting club. Each hole has a name such as Pony Express, Stagecoach, or Tombstone, in keeping with the Western motif. The course manager also says that the course marshals will ride horses from time to time.

Johnny Miller and John Harbottle designed this course with 360-degree views of the Savannah Desert and the rugged Sierra. It was designed in what golf architects call a non-parallel format, meaning holes don't run next to one another. This gives the effect that you

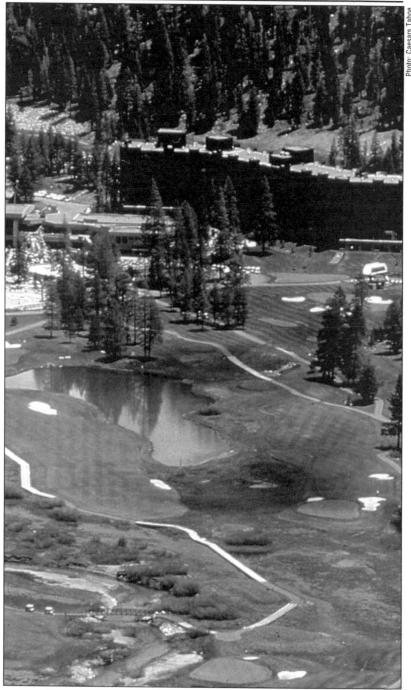

Resort golf courses offer some of the finest golf right outside your room.

and your foursome are the only golfers on the course because you can't peek over onto the next fairway to see anyone else. The holes are laid out with a sense of solitude in mind.

The front 9 begins on the valley floor and climbs 300 feet up the eastern slope of the Sierra. The back 9 snakes its way through desert torrain. Water comes into play on four holes, including a spectacular waterfall on No. 17. The course also has 114 sand bunkers and several grass ones lining the greens and fairways. The 10th hole is one of the prettiest, with the entire right side framed by a cascading creek. The signature hole is No. 17, a 165-yard par 3 with a huge island green surrounded on three sides by a lake with a waterfall located in back. The hole with the best view from the tee is the 478-yard 6th. The green on this hole seems to float above the purple-hued valley with the Sierra looming in the background. This is also the No. 1 handicapped hole so don't let the wonderful view distract you.

The facility offers 10 acres of practice area, which the club calls "The Shooting Range" instead of the driving range. It also has the largest clubhouse in Nevada, a 20,000-square-foot wood and stone building which used to be a hunting lodge. The course is well worth the expensive greens fees.

Yardage	6207
Par	72
USGA rating	69.5
Greens fees	$115
Reservations	2 weeks in advance

Silver Oak Golf Course
3075 College Dr., Carson City, Nev.
• (775) 841-7000

Silver Oak is the newest golf course in Carson City and rounds out the "Divine Nine." It opened in the summer of 1999 and provides middle- to high-handicappers a great course that is quite forgiving. It's located behind the Kmart store in northwest Carson City and winds its way through the Silver Oak development and the Sierra foothills. The course is relatively short, even from the tournament tees (6564 yards long) and it offers five tee boxes

on every hole (tournament, championship, regular, senior and ladies).

Designed by Tom Duncan and Sid Salomon, Silver Oak is a fun but challenging golf experience. The golf pro here won't say what the signature hole is because, according to him, all of them are unique and wonderfully laid out. But most golfers who have tested the course say they like the middle-lengthed par 5s, especially No. 12, except when the wind picks up. The 18-hole course stretches over 150 acres and it has a beautiful practice facility with a driving range, a bunker and a putting green.

Yardage	5716
Par	71
USGA rating	66.6
Greens fees	$40
Reservations	1 month in advance

Sunridge Golf Course
1000 Long Dr., Carson City, Nev.
• (775) 267-4448

Sunridge was carved from the steep hills on the southern edge of Carson City. Its entrance is through a development just off U.S. 395 and after rounding the last corner of the development, you can see the course cut from the hills and nestled on the valley floor. The front 9 opens with a tough par 5 that is almost impossible to reach in two. The rest of the holes require good club selection and course management. The uphill No.7 is a par 3 that will scare the daylights out of you. You have to hit a 150-yard shot over a gully to an elevated green surrounded by sand traps. Once there, you have to contend with a big swale that cuts through the huge green. This course is not for the high handicapper because water is everywhere and the up- and downhill lies will drive them crazy. Sunridge could become one of the most challenging in the area.

Yardage	6061
Par	72
USGA rating	68.1
Greens fees	$55 Monday through Thursday; $75 weekend
Reservations	7 days in advance

Around here, snow is often measured in feet, not inches, and a normal winter will see accumulations of 30 to 40 feet in the higher elevations.

Winter Sports

When you ask winter sports enthusiasts to describe winter in the Reno/Tahoe area, one word comes up over and over again — *awesome*! In some years the heavy storm fronts begin arriving from the Pacific Ocean as early as October, dumping huge amounts of that wonderful white stuff that turns the Sierra Nevada mountains into a winter wonderland. Snow is often measured in feet, not inches, and a normal winter will see accumulations of 30 to 40 feet in the higher elevations. Winter can last up to six months in the mountains so there's plenty of time to indulge in your favorite outdoor activity. But in spite of massive amounts of snow, the temperatures stay relatively mild, usually above freezing during the day and dipping into the 20s at night. When it's not snowing you can count on plenty of sunshine, making most days absolutely glorious for outdoor recreation.

Since Reno and Sparks get much less snow than the Lake Tahoe Basin (usually not more than a total of 2 feet), you can live in the banana belt but be on the ski slope in less than an hour. It's not unusual to play golf in Reno or Sparks and ski in the nearby mountains in the same day.

During normal snow years, many ski resorts are open by Thanksgiving and often the diehards, like Squaw Valley USA and Alpine Meadows, operate through July 4. For an especially invigorating day, you can combine skiing in the morning with river rafting in the afternoon when the ski season extends into the summer months. But when Mother Nature doesn't cooperate, ski resorts compensate by making snow. Occasional droughts have caused most resorts to install sophisticated snowmaking equipment on a large percentage of their terrain.

The first skiers in the Reno/Tahoe area were gold miners from Scandinavia who introduced the long wooden boards as a means of transportation in the mid 1800s. With deep snow blocking roads and trails during the winter, even the mail was carried on skis in those early pioneer days. Between 1856 and 1876 the legendary Snowshoe Thompson made the trip from Placerville, California, to Genoa, Nevada, twice a month, lugging about 100 pounds of mail. During the winter months, Thompson was able to get through the rugged mountainous terrain by strapping on hefty 10-foot long skis that weighed about 25 pounds. Although skiing was simply utilitarian in the beginning, it wasn't long before it evolved into a recreational sport with lifts, competitions and established resorts. To find out more about the history of skiing in the West, you can visit the Western SkiSport Museum at Boreal Ski Resort near Truckee, California. See the description of Truckee in our Daytrips chapter.

Today the Reno/Tahoe area has the largest concentration of ski resorts in North America, with 15 alpine resorts and 12 cross-country resorts. Because they offer such a diverse variety of terrain and amenities, it's a good idea to acquaint yourself with the resorts before you decide where to ski or snowboard. For the ultimate in vertical, you can dive off the heart-stopping chutes at Squaw Valley. For all-out challenging cruising, you can burn down the meticulously groomed slopes at Northstar–at–Tahoe. For a fun first time on skis you can snowplow without fear on the gentle runs at Tahoe Donner.

To help you decide where it's best for you to ski or board, we give you vital statistics about area alpine and cross-country ski resorts in this chapter. We also give you Insiders' tips, such as where you can find the deepest ungroomed powder, which resorts have the most exciting snowboard terrain, what mountains offer the greatest views, which trail systems are the most interesting and much more.

Since the weather influences the quality of your ski experience, you need to consider it when choosing where to go. To avoid the wind on stormy days, one of the best places to go is Northstar since its tree-lined runs will shield you from the gusts. Resorts with high wind exposure include Rose, Squaw, Alpine and Sugar Bowl, where it's not unusual to have upper lifts on wind-hold on windy days. If it's raining and you still want to ski, try resorts at the higher elevations, such as Rose or Boreal, since it may be snowing rather than raining there. For maximum sun exposure, you can ski the open bowls at Squaw and Alpine and the upper runs at Diamond Peak Ski Resort and Heavenly Ski Resort, where you're sure to get a winter tan (or burn) after just a few trips down the mountain.

If you're a first time or novice skier or snowboarder, we strongly recommend you take lessons at one of the resorts. Although your friends may be well-meaning in volunteering to teach you, learning the basics from a professional instructor is the fastest way to

go. All the resorts offer packages which include rental equipment, lift tickets or trail passes along with lessons. You can choose from individual or group instruction. If you plan to be at the resort for a full day, try to get a lesson first thing so you can use the rest of the day to practice your new skills.

When you're unfamiliar with a resort, be sure to carry the trail map with you all the time. It's very easy to become disoriented on the mountain, especially if the weather turns stormy. To help avoid injuries it's a good idea to stretch before hopping on the lift and to make your first runs easy warmups to get the feel of the snow. Also be sure to follow the Skier Responsibility Code which is printed on most trail maps and lift tickets.

To beat the crowds, Insiders ski the major alpine resorts like Squaw, Alpine, Heavenly, Northstar, Diamond Peak and Kirkwood during the week rather than on weekends. You can try smaller alpine resorts and cross-country locations on the weekends. Some of the best uncrowded skiing is between Thanksgiving and Christmas Day since the season doesn't seem to kick into high gear until after those holidays. Four days almost guaranteed to have few people on the slopes are Thanksgiving Day, Christmas Day, New Year's Day and Super Bowl Sunday.

Be sure to ask about special deals when buying your lift ticket or trail pass since every resort has packages that may save you significant amounts of money. If you're also booking accommodations, find out if tickets and passes are included in your rental rate.

But winter isn't just about skiing and snowboarding; it's also the jingle of sleigh bells on horse-drawn sleighs, the swoosh of skates skimming on ice, the purring of snowmobiles zigzagging through the forest, the plopping of snowshoes in deep powder snow and the barking of dogs pulling fur-laden sleds. In this chapter we tell you where and how you can enjoy these other winter activities as well.

Now let's get back to skiing and boarding and take a look at the eclectic variety of resorts you can choose from. The ski resorts in the Reno/Tahoe area are scattered in and around the Lake Tahoe Basin so we list them by the two geographic areas at the lake. We quote prices as of press time for all-day adult lift tickets and trail passes, but keep in mind that they could be slightly higher since resorts raise them periodically.

Alpine Skiing and Snowboarding

North Shore Lake Tahoe

Alpine Meadows
2600 Alpine Meadows Rd., Tahoe City, Calif. • (530) 583-4232, (800) 441-4423
Base elevation: 6,835 feet
Top elevation: 8,637 feet
Vertical drop: 1,802 feet
Number of runs: 100
Capacity: 16,500 skiers per hour
Terrain: 25 percent beginner, 40 percent intermediate, 35 percent advanced
Skiable acres: 2,000
Longest run: 2.5 miles
Number of lifts: 11
Average snowfall: 340 to 510 inches
Lift tickets: $48
Snowphone: (530) 581-8374
    Getting there: To get to Alpine Meadows, take Calif. Highway 89 north 6 miles from Tahoe City or Calif. 89 south 13 miles from Interstate 80 in Truckee to Alpine Meadows Road.

From plunging chutes to gentle trails and from open bowls to tree-lined runs, Alpine Meadows has it all. Because of the diversity of terrain for all levels of skiers and boarders, it's a great favorite with locals. The resort includes both sides of Ward and Scott peaks, with ungroomed advanced territory sprinkled amongst the groomed beginner and intermediate runs. Novice skiers can feel comfortable with two chairlifts servicing several gentle runs that are out of the way of more advanced skiing terrain. Fearless young boarders and skiers especially like Alpine's adventure zones, which are similar to backcountry areas, along with its terrain parks that feature jumps, spines, halfpipes and table tops.

The resort has several restaurants on the mountain as well as the usual bars and cafes in the lodge at the base. For the best après-ski action, be sure to stop at the River Ranch at the intersection of Calif. 89 and Alpine Meadows Road. Jutting out over the Truckee River, this old lodge, with its huge rock fireplace, is warm and cozy after an invigorating day on the mountain. Check out the trout swimming by while you enjoy your favorite drink and then stay for a lovely continental dinner in the inviting dining room. During the summer the outdoor patio is a great people-watching hangout since it's the termination point for rafters coming down the Truckee River.

Because it's so popular, Alpine can be very crowded. The parking lot fills up fast so try to arrive early to minimize your walk from the car to the base of the mountain.

Boreal Ski Resort
I-80 45 mi. west of Reno, Nev.
• (530) 426-3666
Base elevation: 7,200 feet
Top elevation: 7,800 feet
Vertical drop: 600 feet
Number of runs: 41
Capacity: 8,000 skiers per hour
Terrain: 30 percent beginner, 55 percent intermediate, 15 percent advanced
Skiable acres: 380
Longest run: I mile
Number of lifts: 9
Average snowfall: 350 inches
Lift tickets: $28
Snowphone: (530) 426-3666

Getting there: Boreal Ski Resort has easy access from Interstate 80, 45 miles west of Reno off the Castle Peak Exit.

With short runs on mostly beginner to intermediate terrain, Boreal appeals to those who are learning to ski. You don't have to spend a fortune to learn at Boreal since lift tickets and lessons are cheaper than at most other resorts. It boasts a variety of children's programs and because of the resort's small size, it's easy for parents to observe their children's learning progress. Boreal's Jibassic Park, designed for big air enthusiasts, makes the resort a favorite hangout for snowboarders. The Children's Park features adventure opportunities on a smaller scale with mini spines and rollers for less advanced skiers and boarders.

Boreal's high elevation and comprehensive snowmaking allow it to be one of the first resorts to open every year. It offers night skiing until 9 PM and bar and restaurant service in its base lodge. Rooms are also available in the Boreal Inn, just steps from the lifts. While at Boreal be sure to visit the Western SkiSport Museum (for more information, see our Daytrips chapter).

Diamond Peak Ski Resort

1210 Ski Way Dr., Incline Village, Nev.
• (775) 832-1177, (800) 468-2463
Base elevation: 6,700 feet
Top elevation: 8,540 feet
Vertical drop: 1,840
Number of runs: 30
Capacity: 7,700 skiers per hour
Terrain: 18 percent beginner, 49 percent intermediate, 33 percent advanced
Skiable acres: 655
Longest run: 2.5 miles
Number of lifts: 6
Average snowfall: 300 inches
Lift tickets: $38
Snowphone: (775) 831-3211

Getting there: To reach Diamond Peak from Reno/Sparks, take Nev. Highway 431 to Incline Village, turn left on Country Club Drive and then look for Ski Way Drive and follow it to the top. From Incline Village take Nev. Highway 28 to Country Club Drive and then turn onto Ski Way Drive and continue to the top. For information on free local ski shuttles call (775) 832-1177. The Hyatt Regency Lake Tahoe Resort & Casino also provides free transportation for its guests.

Not very many communities own and manage their very own ski resorts, but Incline Village isn't your average town. Operated by the Incline Village General Improvement District (IVGID), the governing body of the town, Diamond Peak Ski Resort emphasizes family fun. The resort offers a variety of passes that make family skiing a little more affordable, such as teen tickets and interchangeable parent passes. Residents of Incline Village are also eligible for special discounts. You don't have to worry about keeping track of your children at Diamond Peak since all of the runs funnel into one base area, making it a very secure environment for families.

Along with its intimate atmosphere and short lift lines, Diamond Peak offers some of the most spectacular views of any ski resort in the area. For a stunning panorama of Lake Tahoe, ride the Crystal Quad chair to the top and take a leisurely run down the ridge. With an unobstructed all-around view, it will seem as though the lake engulfs you as you cruise to the base. For lunch with a view, nothing beats a big juicy hamburger at the Snowflake Lodge perched high above the lake at the top of the Lakeview Quad chair.

Because many of the upper runs here are exposed to the wind and sun, you have to be careful about icy conditions, especially if no new snow has fallen recently. Also the parking lot at Diamond Peak fills up fast on weekends so try to arrive early if you plan on skiing a full day. At the end of your ski day we highly recommend an après-ski drink at the Big Water Grille which is just across the lower end of

Great cross-country skiing is plentiful around the Reno/Tahoe area.

the resort parking lot. The sunset view of Lake Tahoe from this tasteful bar/restaurant is absolutely stunning (see our review in the Restaurants chapter).

Donner Ski Ranch

**19320 Donner Pass Rd., off I-80,
Norden, Calif. • (530) 426-3635**
Base elevation: 7,031 feet
Top elevation: 7,781 feet
Vertical drop: 750 feet
Number of runs: 45
Capacity: 7,200 skiers per hour
Terrain: 25 percent beginner, 50 percent intermediate, 25 percent advanced
Skiable acres: 400
Longest run: 1.2 miles
Number of lifts: 6
Average snowfall: 396 inches
Lift tickets: $23
Snowphone: (530) 426-3635

    Getting there: To get to Donner Ski Ranch, take I-80 west about 45 miles from Reno and exit at the Soda Springs/Norden exit onto Donner Pass Road. The resort is 3.5 miles east.

    Tucked away at the top of Donner Summit, Donner Ski Ranch is one of Reno/Tahoe's best-kept ski and snowboard secrets. It's not the Ritz, but it offers a back-to-basics mountain experience for half the price of major resorts. One of the oldest ski resorts in the West, its setting is simply spectacular, with gorgeous views of Donner Lake and the surrounding Sierra Nevada mountains. Since the runs are wide open, you can enjoy the panorama all the way from the top to the bottom.

    Donner Ski Ranch can provide welcome relief from the hassles found at major ski resorts. If you don't need dozens of watering holes, world-class cornices and multimile runs, you can kick back here and just commune with the unspoiled mountain environment. Insiders know it's a great place for beginners since the small size and uncrowded slopes give novice skiers and snowboarders a feeling of comfort and security. Donner Ski Ranch offers the essential amenities found at most resorts, including a ski school, a base lodge with bar and restaurant and a ski shop. Package rates are available with accommodations at the Summit House on the mountain. Call (530) 426-3622 for information and reservations.

You can learn about the history of the area along with mountain safety with the resort's free guided tours given daily at 9 AM, 10:30 AM and noon. Our only word of caution about this resort is to be aware that it can get very windy when winter storms are coming into the area.

Granlibakken Ski Resort

625 Granlibakken Rd., Tahoe City, Calif.
• (530) 581-7333
Base elevation: 6,310 feet
Top elevation: 6,610 feet
Vertical drop: 300 feet
Number of runs: 1
Capacity: N/A
Terrain: 25 percent beginner, 75 percent intermediate
Skiable acres: 10
Longest run: N/A
Number of lifts: 2
Average snowfall: 325 inches
Lift tickets: $15

Getting there: Granlibakken is about one-half mile south of Tahoe City, just off Calif. 89.

Tiny Granlibakken has three claims to fame: it's the oldest, the smallest and the least expensive ski resort at Lake Tahoe. Built in 1927 by Tahoe Tavern Resort and the South-

ern Pacific Railroad, Granlibakken was founded primarily as a training hill for Olympic ski jumpers. While much of the early history of Lake Tahoe skiing took place here, the resort has been eclipsed for many years by the larger, more comprehensive resorts in the Reno/Tahoe area.

The nearby Granlibakken Resort is an upscale conference center with modern condominium accommodations, seminar rooms and restaurant. Resort guests can use the ski hill at half price.

If you're a total novice skier, Granlibakken (which means "hill sheltered by fir trees" in Norwegian) might provide enough challenge for you. Amenities include equipment rentals, lessons, a snack bar in the warming hut, lodging packages, a snow play area and children's programs. The resort is open Friday, weekends and holidays.

Mt. Rose–Ski Tahoe

22222 Mt. Rose Hwy. (Nev. Hwy. 431),
Reno, Nev. • (775) 849-0704
Base elevation: 8,260 feet
Top elevation: 9,700 feet
Vertical drop: 1,440 feet
Number of runs: 41

Combine a snowmobile and a sunny day and you have the ingredients for a mountain-top vista that is incredible.

Capacity: 10,200 skiers per hour
Terrain: 30 percent beginner, 35 percent intermediate, 35 percent advanced
Skiable acres: 900
Longest run: 2.5 miles
Number of lifts: 5
Average snowfall: 400 inches
Lift tickets: $42
Snowphone: (775) 849-0704

Getting there: To get to Mt. Rose take Nev. 431 east for about 11 miles from Incline Village and west for 22 miles from Reno.

With the highest base in the Reno/Tahoe area, Mt. Rose often enjoys snow while resorts lower in elevation are drenched with rain. And when spring has sprung at other resorts, Rose's high altitude keeps the snow longer, blessing the resort with some of the best late season skiing in the area. Although Rose is the major ski resort closest to an international airport in the world (25 minutes from Reno/Tahoe International Airport), it's always been a locals' resort rather than a tourist destination. When you ski here you run into all your neighbors and friends. If your attorney wasn't in his office that morning, don't be surprised if you see him whizzing by you on Northwest Passage.

Until several years ago the terrain was operated as two separate ski areas, with the east bowl area known as Slide Mountain. Now one lift ticket gives access to both the open bowls on the east or Slide side and the tree-lined runs on the Rose side. You can ski either side from the top, but we recommend skiing the Slide side in the morning when it's the sunniest and working your way over to the runs on Rose in the afternoon. The terrain here is varied enough to challenge skiers and boarders of all abilities. And when Mother Nature dumps a foot or so of new snow on this peak, the powderhounds rejoice since it's one of the best spots for ungroomed powder in the area.

Both sides of the mountain have parking, ticket sales, food service and restrooms, but the Rose side has a ski school, equipment rentals and a ski shop. The restaurant on the Rose side is much larger with a lovely deck for outdoor eating and a bar that really hops when the lifts close down. For other après-ski activity, check out the Christmas Tree several miles down the road if you're returning on Nev. 431

to Reno. You can unwind at the bar by a roaring fire and take in a splendid view of the valley below. For really affordable skiing, Rose offers a variety of weekday specials, such as Two-fer Tuesdays, Student Wednesdays and Ladies Day Thursdays.

From the summit of this resort, you can see forever, with Reno and Sparks glinting like tiny toy towns far in the distance. But this mountain catches the wind and the weather in a pretty brutal way so don't be surprised if the resort is closed due to high winds or if the road is impassable because of heavy snow. If the weather looks dicey at all, call ahead first to avoid having to turn around.

Northstar–at–Tahoe

Calif. Hwy. 267 N., 6 mi. from Kings Beach, Calif. • (530) 562-1010
Base elevation: 6,400 feet
Top elevation: 8,600 feet
Vertical drop: 2,200 feet
Number of runs: 63
Capacity: 19,400 skiers per hour
Terrain: 25 percent beginner, 50 percent intermediate, 25 percent advanced
Skiable acres: 2,420
Longest run: 2.9 miles
Number of lifts: 12
Average snowfall: 350 inches
Lift tickets: $48
Snowphone: (530) 562-1330

Getting there: To get to Northstar take I-80 west from Reno to Truckee about 30 miles and then Calif. Highway 267 south for 6 miles. From Kings Beach, California, take Calif. 267 north about 6 miles. For information about shuttle transportation to Northstar from the Lake Tahoe area call (530) 581-6365 or from Truckee call (530) 562-2257.

Northstar–at–Tahoe calls itself the "Mountain of Fun," and as a major year-round destination resort, it's definitely a toss-up whether it's more fun in winter or in summer. We tell you more about Northstar, including warm weather activities, in our Vacation Rentals, Resorts and Recreation chapters. But for now, let's talk skiing and snowboarding.

Because Northstar is one of the most comprehensive and best-maintained resorts in the Reno/Tahoe area, you can always have a great time here. The northfacing slope of Mt. Pluto is sheltered and tree-lined, providing ample protection from wintry weather. Many runs on this side of the mountain are long intermediate cruisers, impeccably groomed for maximum running speed. But powder seekers and extreme skiers can also find their share of steep chutes and ungroomed tree skiing scattered among the more gentle slopes.

The back side of Pluto is for advanced skiers, with 1,860 vertical feet of groomed, ungroomed and mogul skiing and boarding. Because this side of the mountain faces west (you get a gorgeous view of nearby Squaw Valley when riding the lift), it catches the brunt of storms as they approach from that direction. If the wind kicks up when you're skiing back here, you can find plenty of protected runs on the other side of the hill. Northstar also offers 200 acres of off-piste advanced terrain on Lookout Mountain plus several areas groomed especially for snowboarders. When it's time for the last run of the day, we recommend a leisurely looping run of about 3 miles starting at the top of Mt. Pluto and heading down East Ridge, Loggers Loop and The Woods. As you glide on down to the village below, enjoy the spectacular view as the sinking sun paints the surrounding mountains and Martis Valley an intense golden hue. For a meaningful experience with the great outdoors, nothing beats this run for the gold.

As a major destination resort, Northstar is lacking in nothing when it comes to services that enhance your overall mountain experience. The charming Village Mall has a gourmet grocery, child care facility, equipment rental and upscale sports shop plus several bars and restaurants. When hunger pangs hit you can head into the Big Springs Day Lodge which is mid-mountain and enjoy hearty skier food while you people-watch from the expansive outdoor deck. Or if you'd rather have lunch with a gorgeous Lake Tahoe view, you can indulge your appetite at the Summit Deck & Grille perched at the very top of Mt. Pluto.

To minimize hassles and maximize the time

skiers and boarders have on the snow, Northstar has a large electronic board at the top of Mt. Pluto showing the exact wait times for all lifts and restaurants on the mountain. It also runs a trolley from the parking lot and a free shuttle from all its resort accommodations to get you to the base of the mountain quicker and easier. For details on accommodations, see our Vacation Rentals and Resorts chapters.

Frequent skiers and boarders at Northstar can save money plus keep track of the number of vertical feet they rack up by joining the Vertical Plus program. For $49 you can buy a personal electronic bracelet that logs in your vertical feet each time you board a lift. Vertical Plus members have their own lift access plus they can receive discounts and rewards based upon the number of vertical feet they ski. For additional details call (530) 562-2267.

You simply can't go wrong spending a day (or days) at Northstar since this resort has been delivering quality mountain adventures to outdoor enthusiasts for years. Because the number of skiers and boarders allowed on the mountain is cut off once the parking facilities are full, be sure to arrive early on weekends and holidays.

Soda Springs

I-80 at Donner Summit, Norden, Calif.
• (530) 426-3901
Base elevation: 6,700 feet
Top elevation: 7,352 feet
Vertical drop: 652 feet
Number of runs: 16
Capacity: N/A
Terrain: 30 percent beginner, 50 percent intermediate, 20 percent advanced
Skiable acres: 200
Longest run: 1 mile
Number of lifts: 2
Average snowfall: 350 inches
Lift tickets: $16
Snowphone: (530) 426-1010
   Getting there: To get to Soda Springs take

INSIDERS' TIP

The beginning of winter is heralded by the annual Native American Snow Dance in Incline Village. In this event, area tribes dance and pray for snow to fall.

Photo: Northstar–at–Tahoe

The finest lifts and mountain facilities promise skiers a great day on the slopes.

I-80 west from Reno about 45 miles to the Soda Springs/Norden exit and follow the signs to Soda (about 1 mile). From Tahoe City, take Calif. 89 north to Truckee and then I-80 west to the Soda Springs/Norden Exit.

One of the oldest ski resorts in the Lake Tahoe area, Soda Springs is a great beginner hill. You can count on uncrowded runs, even on weekends and holidays, and the prices can't be beat. It's easy for novice skiers to feel comfortable here since the runs are comparatively gentle and wide open. Soda's location at the top of Donner Summit affords breathtaking views of the surrounding mountains on clear days. Amenities include a full-service rental shop, lessons and a cafeteria.

Squaw Valley USA

1960 Squaw Valley Rd., Olympic Valley, Calif. • (530) 583-6985
Base elevation: 6,200 feet
Top elevation: 9,050 feet
Vertical drop: 2,850 feet
Number of runs: 150
Capacity: 50,000 skiers per hour
Terrain: 25 percent beginner, 45 percent intermediate, 30 percent advanced
Skiable acres: 4,200
Longest run: 3 miles
Number of lifts: 30
Average snowfall: 450 inches
Lift tickets: $49
Snowphone: (530) 583-6955

Getting there: To get to Squaw Valley USA take Calif. 89 north 6 miles from Tahoe City. From Reno head west on I-80 about 30 miles to Truckee and then south for about 13 miles on Calif. 89. Shuttle service is available from Reno, Sparks and South Shore Lake Tahoe by calling (800) 822-6009; from North Shore Lake Tahoe call (530) 581-7181. Reservations are required 12 hours in advance.

In February 1960 the greatest winter athletes in the world, representing 34 different nations, gathered in Squaw Valley to compete in the VIII Winter Olympics. A relatively unknown ski resort with four double chair lifts and one rope tow, Squaw Valley USA was catapulted into the world limelight by the resulting media coverage. Since that time Squaw has blossomed expansively, along with the growing popularity of winter sports in general. Big, bold and beautiful, today it's a world-class resort in every way. The aura of the Olympics still abounds at Squaw as you'll notice the Olympic Flame still burning brightly in front of The Tower of Nations at the entrance to the resort. Sporting the five Olympic rings that represent the continents that compete, the tower stands 79 feet high and 29 feet wide.

Spread out over six spectacular peaks, the amount of skiable terrain is absolutely daunting. It's divided into three sections: the base level at 6,200 feet, the upper level at 8,200 feet and the Snow King area on the resort's eastern side. Some of the best beginner runs are on the upper elevation, which gives novices the same full mountain experience as more advanced skiers and snowboarders. Intermediates find comfortable runs in all sections and advanced skiers are challenged by the spine-tingling chutes off Squaw Peak and KT-22, so named for the 22 kick-turns needed by most skiers to get to the bottom. Snowboarders are not forgotten: Squaw also has a Snowboard Park designed especially for them.

Because of its size, it's important to study the trail map to find your way around. Most of the skiable terrain is open and treeless, a disadvantage during windy weather. The new state-of-the-art funitel transport system reduces upper mountain wind closures during high winds, but doesn't diminish the wind on you once you get up to the higher elevation. But even if you decide to confine your skiing and boarding to the lower elevations, be sure to go to the top to enjoy the view. You can literally see for miles in every direction, with gorgeous Lake Tahoe shimmering to the south and magnificent snow-dusted mountains all around you.

Because Squaw is a major destination resort by anyone's standards, the list of its amenities goes on and on. See our Resorts, Vacation Rentals and Recreation chapters for information about accommodations and warm-weather activities. You can find dining and entertainment mid-mountain at High Camp and Gold Coast, with 10 eating and watering holes to choose from. In the base village you'll find an eclectic variety of more than 20 pubs and restaurants sprinkled among the upscale boutiques and sports shops. You can learn about the 1960 Winter Olympics at the Olympic Winter Games Museum or take in a movie in the Opera House Theater or just continue skiing and boarding until 9 PM since Squaw also offers night skiing.

For a total mountain experience, with all the glitz and glamour you read about in ski magazines, you can't go wrong at Squaw. It has everything any skier or snowboarder could conceivably imagine. But because it has so much to offer, it's usually extremely crowded. Even though its highly sophisticated lift system has been successful in eliminating long lift lines (you get your money back if you wait more than 10 minutes), you still have to contend with crowds at the base. The word to the wise is to arrive early to find a place to park your car. Then with so many restaurants to

---

INSIDERS' TIP

You can spend the night in isolated splendor in a cozy Scandinavian cabin accessible only by skis or snowshoes at Spooner Lake Cross-Country Ski Area. Call (775) 721-1014 for information.

choose from mid-mountain, consider having breakfast with a view before you start your skiing day.

Sugar Bowl

I-80 at Donner Summit, Norden, Calif.
• (530) 426-9000
Base elevation: 6,883 feet
Top elevation: 8,383 feet
Vertical drop: 1,500 feet
Number of runs: 58
Capacity: 11,300 skiers per hour
Terrain: 15 percent beginner, 40 percent
intermediate, 45 percent advanced
Skiable acres: 1,110
Longest run: 3 miles
Number of lifts: 11
Average snowfall: 500 inches
Lift tickets: $45
Snowphone: (530) 426-3847

Getting there: To get to Sugar Bowl take I-80 west about 45 miles from Reno and exit at the Soda Springs/Norden exit onto Donner Pass Road. The resort is about 3 miles east. From Tahoe City take Calif. 89 north to Truckee and then I-80 west about 10 miles to the Soda Springs/Norden exit.

If you've always wanted to ski in Europe but never quite made it, come to Sugar Bowl since the ambiance is decidedly Old World Austrian. Built in 1939 by wealthy families from San Francisco (who continue to own and operate it), Sugar Bowl has a colorful history that includes the rich and famous. It was the winter playground for celebrities like Walt Disney (he even had a mountain named for him), Errol Flynn and Janet Leigh, who would arrive on the train and cozy up in the charming Sugar Bowl Lodge or in the picturesque cabins scattered amongst the pine trees. Home to the first chairlift in northern California and the first gondola in the country, Sugar Bowl offers a peek into the past with a dash of high-tech. Today it maintains its quintessential classic flavor amidst the sophisticated technology of a modern-day ski resort.

Skiing here is on three mountains: 8,238-foot Mt. Judah, 8,683-foot Mt. Lincoln and 7,953-foot Mt. Disney. Most of the beginner terrain is at the bases of Mt. Lincoln and Mt. Disney and intermediate terrain is found on the west side of Disney, the east side of Lincoln and also on Judah. Because Sugar Bowl is often the snowiest of all Reno/Tahoe resorts, expert skiers absolutely revel in its deep ungroomed powder. Insider shredheads (ardent snowboarders) know that Sugar Bowl is one of the best boarding resorts in the area: it offers an abundance of natural chutes along with a large state-of-the-art snow park, with halfpipes perfectly carved each time by a Scorpion pipe groomer. With magnificent views from almost any run, Sugar Bowl delivers a quality mountain high for skiers and boarders of all abilities.

Parking is somewhat limited at the Magic Carpet gondola, which you reach first on Donner Pass Road, but if you arrive early enough, we recommend taking the gondola since it's a very picturesque way of getting to the base of the mountain. Other parking and base facilities are found just a short ways down the road at Mt. Judah. Amenities include bars and restaurants mid-mountain and at both bases, but the most colorful is the original Sugar Bowl Lodge near the gondola. For a truly romantic ski getaway, the lodge offers a classic alpine experience, with comfortable rooms and gourmet dining.

Tahoe Donner

11509 Northwoods Blvd., Truckee, Calif.
• (530) 587-9444
Base elevation: 6,750 feet
Top elevation: 7,350 feet
Vertical drop: 600 feet
Number of runs: 14
Capacity: 1,000 skiers per hour
Terrain: 40 percent beginner, 60 percent
intermediate
Skiable acres: 120
Longest run: 1 mile
Number of lifts: 3
Lift tickets: $26
Snowphone: (530) 587-9444

Getting there: To get to Tahoe Donner from Reno, take I-80 west about 30 miles to Truckee and exit at the Central Truckee exit, which puts you on Donner Pass Road. About one-half mile down the road, turn right onto Northwoods Boulevard and follow the signs for about 5 miles to the ski area. From Tahoe City head north on Calif. 89 to Truckee and turn left onto Donner Pass Road. Several blocks further on, turn right onto Northwoods Boulevard and follow the signs to Tahoe Donner.

Tucked away in the Tahoe Donner residential area in Truckee, this resort is a great learn-to-ski hill. The terrain is a relatively gentle open bowl with few obstacles for beginners to worry about. Meticulous grooming makes the snow very forgiving, even for the very novice skiers and snowboarders. And since there are no crowds and no lift lines, you can ski 'til you drop. Amenities include a full-service ski shop and a comfortable alpine ski lodge at the base of the hill. Strong intermediates and expert skiers and boarders won't be challenged here, but we strongly recommend that beginners give it a try since the price is right and it offers a quality mountain experience with none of the hassles encountered at larger resorts. There's also a rollercoaster terrain park with table tops and a children's snowplay area.

South Shore Lake Tahoe

Heavenly Ski Resort

End of Ski Run Blvd., off U.S. Hwy. 50, South Lake Tahoe, Calif.
• (530) 541-1330, (775) 586-7000
Base elevation: 6,540 feet
Top elevation: 10,040 feet
Vertical drop: 3,500 feet
Number of runs: 82
Capacity: 29,000 skiers per hour
Terrain: 20 percent beginner, 45 percent intermediate, 35 percent advanced
Skiable acres: 4,800
Longest run: 5.5 miles
Number of lifts: 26
Average snowfall: 336 inches
Lift tickets: $52
Snowphone: (530) 541-7544

Getting there: Because this resort is often very congested at the base, it's a good idea to take advantage of the free shuttle transportation that's available on both sides of the mountain. For information call (775) 586-7000. To reach the California side of Heavenly from the Reno/Sparks area, head south on U.S. Highway 395 through Carson City and then take U.S. Highway 50 west to South Lake Tahoe. The base of the mountain is at the east

end of Ski Run Boulevard. To get to the Nevada side from Reno/Sparks, continue south on U.S. 395 past Carson City to Jacks Valley Road where you turn west and then south through the tiny town of Genoa. Just past Genoa, turn west on Nev. Highway 207 (Kingsbury Grade) and follow the signs for the resort at the top of the summit.

From Incline Village, take Nev. 28 south to the intersection with U.S. 50. Continue south on U.S. 50 to Nev. Highway 207, turn east and follow the signs at the summit to the Nevada side of the resort. To reach the California side, continue south on U.S. 50 to Ski Run Boulevard in South Lake Tahoe and follow the signs to the east end.

With a name like "Heavenly," how can your ski experience here be anything but out of this world? Sprawling across the California–Nevada border, Heavenly Ski Resort has more skiable acres than any other Reno/Tahoe ski resort. The variety of terrain is awesome to say the least, from the hip-high knee-burning moguls on Gunbarrel to the immaculately groomed cruiser snow on Orion to the deep and steep untracked powder in Mott Canyon. Although there's a smattering of beginner runs sprinkled around the mountain, Heavenly appeals largely to intermediate and expert skiers and snowboarders. Because of its daunting size, it's hard to sample it all in one day. With the highest elevation at Lake Tahoe and the most comprehensive snowmaking capacity, Heavenly is usually able to open early in the season and to maintain quality snow until its late closure.

Along with the mind-boggling variety of runs to choose from, Heavenly offers spectacular views of Lake Tahoe to the west and the Carson Valley to the east. True to its name, the mountain experience here is divine, giving you a feeling you are skiing at the top of the world. Amenities include seven on-mountain lodges, the most dramatic of which is the Top of the Tram, perched on the edge of the mountain on the California side. The sit-down restaurant and bar here are delightful and when the weather is warm you can enjoy the gorgeous view from the expansive outdoor deck. You can start your skiing day from the two lifts on the Nevada side of the resort or at the base on the California side. Because the Nevada side of the mountain is usually less crowded than the California side, we suggest you try to escape the crowds by parking there if you're driving.

Heavenly is the closest ski resort to all the casino nightlife at South Lake Tahoe. You can book packages that include lodging, skiing, shows, meals and tours to local sights by calling (800) 243-2836.

Kirkwood

Off Calif. Hwy. 88 at Carson Pass, Kirkwood, Calif. • (209) 258-6000, (800) 967-7500
Base elevation: 7,800 feet
Top elevation: 9,800 feet
Vertical drop: 2,000 feet
Number of runs: 65
Capacity: 16,200 skiers per hour
Terrain: 15 percent beginner, 50 percent intermediate and 35 percent advanced
Skiable acres: 2,300
Longest run: 2.5 miles
Number of lifts: 12
Average snowfall: 425 inches
Lift tickets: $45
Snowphone: (209) 258-3000

Getting there: To reach Kirkwood from the Reno/Sparks area, take U.S. 395 south to Minden and then Calif. Highway 88 west. It's about a 90-minute drive when the roads are clear. From South Shore Lake Tahoe take U.S. 50 west to Myers and then turn left onto Calif. 89 south for about 12 miles; then turn onto Calif. 88 west for another 14 miles.

Nestled in a box canyon ringed by jagged pinnacles at the end of gorgeous Hope Valley, Kirkwood is an impressive sight, even for the nonskier. Although it's tricky to get to (over winding hairpin mountain passes), it's well worth the effort since this resort is a skier's and snowboarder's joy. The diverse terrain presents challenges for all abilities, with heart-stopping chutes and cornices for advanced skiers and boarders, wide sweeping bowls for intermediates and easy gentle slopes for beginners. Kirkwood frequently has the distinc-

tion of having America's deepest snow, with 20 feet at the base and 35 feet at the top of the mountain. With such awesome snow and scenery, you can't go wrong at Kirkwood. You can even earn free lift tickets by signing up for the free Avid Skier Card, which rewards skiers and snowboarders based upon the number of days they ski.

One of the most appealing aspects of this resort is its isolation from crowds and traffic. Tucked away in a world of its own, it offers a total mountain experience, remote from the hustle and bustle of everyday life. Even though the après-ski activities are sedate compared to some other resorts, the recently renovated Kirkwood Village has an interesting mix of watering holes, eateries, shops and accommodations. Its picturesque alpine style is absolutely perfect in this pristine mountain setting. If you're planning to settle down and stay for a few days in one resort, we highly recommend Kirkwood since it's the ideal escape for any skier or snowboarder.

Sierra–at–Tahoe

1111 Sierra–at–Tahoe Rd., Twin Bridges, Calif. • (530) 659-7453
Base elevation: 6,640 feet
Top elevation: 8,852 feet
Vertical drop: 2,212 feet
Number of runs: 44
Capacity: 14,870 skiers per hour
Terrain: 25 percent beginner, 50 percent intermediate, 25 percent advanced
Skiable acres: 2,000
Longest run: 2.5 miles
Number of lifts: 10
Average snowfall: 450 inches
Lift tickets: $45
Snowphone: (530) 659-7475

Getting there: To reach Sierra–at–Tahoe from South Shore Lake Tahoe, take U.S. 50 west for about 12 miles and turn onto Sierra–at–Tahoe Road. From North Shore Lake Tahoe take Calif. 89 south from Tahoe City to U.S. 50 and continue west for about 12 miles. From the Reno/Sparks area take U.S. 395 south to

INSIDERS' TIP

The Reno/Tahoe area has more ski lifts than the entire state of Colorado.

Carson City and then follow U.S. 50 through South Lake Tahoe to Sierra–at–Tahoe Road, about 12 miles farther on. For information on the free shuttle from South Shore Lake Tahoe call (530) 541-7548.

Although Sierra–at–Tahoe provides great terrain for skiers and boarders of all abilities, beginners especially love it because it has such a wide variety of slopes they can feel perfectly comfortable on. You won't find sharp cornices and steep chutes here, but there's plenty of thrilling cruiser runs cutting through the tall timber. Snowboarders head immediately to one of the area's best snowboard parks on the back side of the mountain.

A sister resort to Northstar–at–Tahoe, Sierra offers the Vertical Plus frequent skier program also available at Northstar (see our previous description of Northstar for details). Listed in *Snow Country* magazine as the best resort in the far west for on-mountain food, the seven eateries at this resort are certainly a cut above the average. For a tasty lunch with a world-class view of Lake Tahoe, drop into the Grand View Bar & Grill at the top of the mountain.

Ski Homewood

Calif. Hwy. 89, Homewood, Calif.
• (530) 525-2992
Base elevation: 6,320 feet
Top elevation: 7,880 feet
Vertical drop: 1,650 feet
Number of runs: 56
Capacity: 8,500 skiers per hour
Terrain: 15 percent beginner, 50 percent intermediate, 35 percent advanced
Skiable acres: 1,260
Longest run: 2 miles
Number of lifts: 8
Average snowfall: 350 inches
Lift tickets: $36
Snowphone: (530) 525-2900

Getting there: To reach Homewood from the Reno/Sparks area, take I-80 west about 30 miles to Truckee and then Calif. 89 south to about 6 miles past Tahoe City. From South Lake Tahoe it's about 19 miles west on Calif. 89. You can also ride Tahoe Area Regional Transit (TART) in the North Shore Lake Tahoe region. For the schedule and fares, call (530) 581-6365.

Far from the madding crowds, but with magnificent lake views, Ski Homewood is very popular with locals. Spread over two slopes, the terrain is diverse and challenging enough to keep skiers and boarders of all abilities busy for the entire day. With two separate bases, skiers can start their day at either the South Lodge or the North Lodge. Parking is readily available on both sides. On windy days Homewood is especially attractive because many of its runs are protected; but be careful during spring skiing since its relatively low elevation causes the snow to melt early. If you're looking for glitz, this probably isn't the place for you since this resort offers just the essential amenities in a back-to-basics style. But if maximum time on the snow, spectacular views and hassle-free skiing and boarding interest you at all, give Homewood a try. It's a great place to kick back and sink into a quality mountain experience.

Cross-Country Skiing

North Shore Lake Tahoe

Clair Tappaan Lodge

Donner Pass Rd., off I-80, Norden, Calif.
• (530) 426-3632

Tucked deep into the forest on top of Donner Summit, this rustic old lodge is owned by the Sierra Club. It operates its own track system consisting of 10 kilometers of machine-groomed trails, with about 60 percent beginner and 40 percent intermediate terrain. Wandering through stands of magnificent pines, the striding and skating lanes provide a great workout along with spectacular scenery. Instruction and rental equipment are available and trail passes are $5. Accommodations in the lodge are open to both members and nonmembers of the Sierra Club, but since it's a very popular place we recommend you reserve as far in advance as possible.

To reach Clair Tappaan from the Reno/Sparks area, take I-80 west about 45 miles to the Norden/Soda Springs Exit and then travel east for several miles on Donner Pass Road. From Tahoe City take Calif. 89 north to Truckee and then I-80 west about 10 miles to the Soda

Springs/Norden Exit. The lodge is on the left, partially hidden in the trees above the road so you need to look carefully so as not to miss it.

Diamond Peak Cross-Country
Nev. Hwy. 431, 6 mi. north of Incline Village, Nev. • (775) 832-1177, (775) 742-7957

With the highest elevation of any cross-country resort in the Lake Tahoe Basin, Diamond Peak is often blessed with snow when other resorts have nothing but bare ground. Diamond Peak also has spectacular lake views from a number of its trails. The 35 kilometers of groomed track offer skating, gliding and snowshoe lanes, with about 20 percent beginner, 50 percent intermediate and 30 percent advanced terrain. Although most cross-country resorts with groomed tracks don't allow dogs, Diamond Peak welcomes them every day from 12:30 to 4 PM. A pet trail pass is $3 and an adult pass is $14. Lessons and rentals are available and the tiny day lodge serves lunch and snacks.

For the schedule of the free shuttle to the resort from Incline Village, call the numbers above. To reach Diamond Peak from the Reno/Sparks area, take U.S. 395 south to Nev. 431 (the Mt. Rose Highway) and head west over the summit toward Incline Village. Shortly past Tahoe Meadows look for the parking lot and short uphill trail to the day lodge on the left. From Lake Tahoe take Nev. 431 from Incline Village toward Reno for about 6 miles.

Granlibakken Ski Resort
625 Granlibakken Rd., Tahoe City, Calif. • (530) 581-7333

You can ski free here, but you're pretty much on your own since most of the 7-kilometer trail is not maintained or machine set. For a lovely view of Lake Tahoe, ride the poma lift up and then follow the road to Lookout Point. If you're really ambitious, keep going for about 2 miles and you'll reach Page Meadows. Rental equipment is available, but there are no other amenities.

To get to Granlibakken from the Reno/Tahoe area head west on I-80 about 30 miles to Truckee and then south on Calif. 89 to Tahoe City. The resort is about one-half mile south of Tahoe City on Calif. 89.

Lakeview Cross-Country Ski Area
Country Club Dr., Tahoe City, Calif. • (530) 583-9353

With 65 kilometers of set skating and striding track, Lakeview has something for every skier. Beginners can enjoy the lower trails that wander through the pristine forest. Intermediates can climb higher for peeks at Lake Tahoe. And experts can test their stamina by skiing all the way to Truckee if they wish. The facility is meticulously maintained and offers instruction, equipment rental, moonlight tours and two restaurants. Trail passes are $15.

To reach Lakeview from Tahoe City, head east on Calif. 28 for about 2 miles to the Shell service station at Dollar Hill. Turn left onto Fabian Way, then right onto Village Drive and go up and around the corner to Country Club Drive and turn left. From the Reno/Sparks area take I-80 west about 30 miles to Truckee and then head south on Calif. 89 to Tahoe City and follow the directions above.

Northstar–at–Tahoe
Calif. Hwy. 267 N., 6 mi. from Kings Beach, Calif. • (530) 562-2475

Because the 65 kilometers of machine-groomed track at this major destination resort are near the alpine ski runs, you can enjoy many of the amenities offered to alpine skiers and snowboarders. Scenic trails that wind through the trees are groomed for striding and skating. Northstar is also a great telemark and snowshoe area. Rental equipment and lessons are available and warming huts and picnic tables are scattered throughout the trail system. You can purchase trail passes at the cross-country ticket booth in the Village and then ride the gondola to the Cross-Country Center mid-mountain for equipment and lessons. Trail passes are $17.

If you cross-country ski to escape the hassles found at many alpine resorts, this may not be the place for you. Although the trail system provides the quiet solitude of a backcountry outing, you're integrated with the alpine skiers in the base area and on the gondola. For more details about Northstar, see our previous description under "Alpine Skiing and Snowboarding" and read our Resorts chapter listing.

To get to Northstar take I-80 west from

Reno to Truckee about 30 miles and then Calif. 267 south for 6 miles. From Kings Beach, California, take Calif. 267 north about 6 miles. For information about shuttle transportation to Northstar from the Lake Tahoe area call (530) 581-6365 or from Truckee call (530) 562-2257.

Resort at Squaw Creek Cross-Country Ski Center
400 Squaw Creek Rd., Olympic Valley, Calif. • (530) 583-6300

Tucked in gorgeous Olympic Valley with the towering peaks of Squaw Valley as a backdrop, the 18 kilometers of trail at the Resort at Squaw Creek are scenic to say the very least. Although it's one of the smaller cross-county resorts in the area, it gives you a chance to soak in the awesome beauty of this very special place without the hassles of alpine skiing at Squaw Valley USA. The trails are groomed for striding and skating and you can also try snowshoeing. Since much of the terrain is open and relatively level, it's perfect for novices. But more advanced skiers can also find some ups and downs, including several trails that wind up the mountain behind the hotel. Amenities include rentals, instruction, a ski shop and twilight skiing. The trail pass is $13. Since the Resort at Squaw Creek is easily one of the most exquisite resorts in the Reno/Tahoe area, we suggest you have dinner or an après-ski drink in the hotel after your day on the snow. For more details about this resort see our Resorts chapter. For more information on Squaw Valley see our description of Squaw Valley USA in this chapter.

To reach the resort from Reno/Sparks, take I-80 west for about 30 miles to Truckee and then Calif. 89 south about 13 miles. After turning into Squaw Valley at the main entrance, look for Squaw Creek Road and turn left. You can either valet your car at the resort or use their parking lot. From Tahoe City take Calif. 89 north about 6 miles. For information on shuttle service to Squaw Valley USA from Reno, Sparks and South Shore Lake Tahoe call (800) 822-6009 and from North Shore Lake Tahoe, (530) 581-7181. Reservations are required 12 hours in advance.

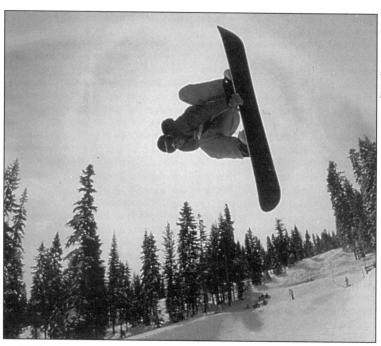

Photo: Northstar-at-Tahoe

This snowboarder takes a high fly from the half-pipe wall.

Royal Gorge
I-80 at Donner Pass, Soda Springs, Calif. • (530) 426-3871, (800) 500-3871

Ranked the number one cross-country ski resort in North America by *Snow Country* magazine, Royal Gorge has absolutely everything you could want for a perfect Nordic ski vacation. With 328 kilometers of groomed track and more than 9,000 acres of skiing terrain, it's also the largest cross-country ski resort in North America. The 88 trails range in elevation from 5,800 feet to 7,538 feet and are ranked 28 for beginners, 44 for intermediates and 16 for experts. The resort also has four surface lifts for telemark skiing. Because of its immense size and diversity, Royal Gorge is almost a world in and of itself. You could ski here for a week and still not explore it all. Beginners especially enjoy the Van Norden Track System, a large open meadow ringed by magnificent jagged peaks. Intermediates have a mind-boggling array of trails to choose from, including the Palisade Peak and Devil's Peak systems for awesome views of the surrounding country. Experts have more than their share of challenging terrain, including the 22-kilometer track to the edge of the Royal Gorge of the American River.

The resort has ten warming huts, four trailside cafes and two overnight lodges. For a total mountain experience, we highly recommend the package that includes a stay at the Wilderness Lodge along with lessons and equipment rental. Imagine wrapping yourself in fur robes and snuggling down in a sleigh that carries you to this century-old lodge hidden deep in the wilderness. The rooms are rustic and not very private, but the food is gourmet and the scenery out of this world. For a more traditionally elegant stay you can choose Rainbow Lodge which is also owned by Royal Gorge. An old stagecoach stop along the Mormon-Emigrant Trail, Western history just seems to ooze out of its heavy rock walls. Insiders have long known that a continental dinner at the lodge's Engadine Cafe, served with just the right wine, is the ideal ending to a day of skiing at Royal Gorge.

With trail pass fees of $21.50 on weekends and holidays and $17.50 during the week, Royal Gorge is more expensive than other cross-country ski resorts. But we can honestly say you get what you pay for here since Royal Gorge offers the penultimate cross-country ski experience.

To reach Royal Gorge from Reno/Sparks head west on I-80 about 45 miles to the Norden/Soda Springs Exit and follow the signs to Summit Station. From Tahoe City take Calif. 89 north to Truckee and then I-80 west about 10 miles to the Soda Springs/Norden Exit.

Spooner Lake Cross-Country Ski Area
Nev. Hwy. 28, near the junction with U.S. Hwy. 50 • (775) 749-5349, (775) 887-8844

With 91 kilometers of groomed track, Spooner Lake is best known for the marvelous lake and mountain views skiers can enjoy from the intermediate and expert trails. The terrain is divided between the high country trails and the meadow trails, with beginners enjoying scenic loops around frozen Spooner Lake and Spooner Meadow and more advanced skiers climbing the surrounding slopes toward Marlette Lake, Snow Valley Peak and Hobart Reservoir. Amenities include lessons, equipment rental, a day lodge, a warming hut and full moon guided ski tours. The carefully groomed tracks have both striding and skating lanes and snowshoeing is also allowed. The trail pass is $15.

To get to Spooner Lake from the Reno/Sparks area, head south on U.S. 395 through Carson City and then take U.S. 50 west for about 15 miles toward South Lake Tahoe. The parking lot is just north of the intersection of U.S. 50 and Nev. 28. From South Shore Lake Tahoe take U.S. 50 east for about 15 miles toward Carson City. From Incline Village take Nev. 28 south for about 12 miles. For information on bus transportation call (530) 542-5900.

Tahoe Donner Cross-Country
Alder Creek Rd., Truckee, Calif. • 530) 587-9484

Stretching over 4,800 acres of terrain, Tahoe Donner Cross-Country offers 85 kilometers of machine-groomed trails over three scenic track systems. Of the 35 trails, 13 are rated beginner, 13 intermediate, 7 advanced and 2 expert. The diversity of terrain includes open meadows, gentle bowls and tree-lined

Winter Safety

In winter the Sierra Nevada Mountains offer a glorious playground with unlimited opportunities to enjoy the great outdoors. But without proper precautions, this winter wonderland can be unpleasant, and sometimes downright deadly. Extreme weather conditions and high altitude present challenges and dangers if you're not adequately prepared. Being "winter aware" and following recommended mountain safety practices will help make your outings safer and more enjoyable.

Mountain health hazards you should know about include altitude sickness, frostbite, hypothermia and sunburn. But with proper precautions they shouldn't present problems for most people. If you have health conditions that could be more hazardous in the mountains, especially heart disease or high blood pressure, you should check with your doctor before planning trips to high elevations.

Since most winter sports in the Reno/Tahoe area are enjoyed at altitudes between 6,000 and 9,000 feet, you are breathing air with less oxygen in it than the air at sea level. This lack of oxygen causes what's known as **altitude sickness** — chemical changes in the bloodstream that can cause headaches, fatigue, decreased appetite, nausea, shortness of breath and restless sleep in some people. Although the body will usually adjust within a couple of days, you should avoid overexertion, get plenty of rest, drink lots of fluids, eat lightly and avoid alcohol, particularly if you experience any of these symptoms.

Frostbite occurs when the water in cells freezes and is indicated by a burning, tingling, numbness or whitish discoloration of the skin. Fingertips, toes, ears, cheeks and the nose are especially vulnerable. To prevent frostbite it's important to cover all areas of your body, especially on cold windy days. Although hats and masks mess up your hair and are sometimes not flattering to wear, they're essential for warmth because a large percentage of body heat is lost through the head. You should dress in layers and even overdress since you can always peel off a jacket or vest if you get too warm. If your toes or fingers start to get cold, keep wiggling them until you can get out of the cold. If you start to feel chilled, keep moving and get inside where it's warm as soon as possible.

When your body is not able to generate enough heat to keep its core temperature at its normal 98.6 degrees, **hypothermia** can occur. Your organs will malfunction with this loss of heat, causing shivering, fatigue, distorted thinking, impaired motor skills and changes in mood. One of the most dangerous aspects of hypothermia is that often those affected don't realize they have it because they are unable to think clearly. It's important that everyone on an outing together monitor each other for any symptoms and help any affected persons get dry and out of the cold right away. To protect yourself against hypothermia you should wear warm, layered clothing, take periodic indoor breaks on cold days, stay dry and refrain from drinking alcoholic beverages.

Sunburn is a risk anytime you're outdoors. But in the mountains it's an even greater risk because in the thin air at high elevations you receive five times the amount of ultraviolet rays that you would receive at sea level. It's pretty easy to protect yourself by using a sunscreen with a minimum of SPF 15 on any exposed areas of your body. Also, because ultraviolet rays are very harmful to your eyes, it's important to wear sunglasses or goggles to protect them. Eyewear also protects your eyes from tree branches when you're skiing or snowshoeing in wooded terrain.

While you should follow these health tips wherever you are in the mountains, we recommend **additional safety precautions for venturing into the backcountry**: Don't even pack the car until you've checked the weather forecast. If it's snowing or if a storm

Photo: Jeanne Lauf Walpole

Sharing the backcountry with man's best friends is both good exercise
and quality time together.

is on the way, it's wise to play it safe and wait for clear weather. Because blowing snow
can greatly reduce your visibility, it's easy to become disoriented in a storm, even in
terrain you're familiar with. If you decide it's okay to go, check your equipment to make
sure everything is in working order. If you have a problem with your skis or snowmobile,
it's better to fix it before you go when you're in a safe environment. Besides your sporting
gear, you should also bring along a backpack or fanny pack containing basic survival
items, including waterproof matches, water, dried fruit or granola bars, a whistle, a
candle, a metal cup for melting snow, a cellular phone or change for emergency phone
calls, two large plastic bags for emergency shelter, a map, a compass and a first aid kit.
Make sure you're well fed and watered and not overly tired before setting out. And also
practice the buddy system by going with at least one other person. It's not only safer but
also more fun to share your outdoor experience with a friend. Last, but not least, tell a
friend or family member where you're going and when you expect to be back.

When you get to your destination, leave a note on the dashboard in your car
detailing where you're going, when you'll return and who is in the group. As you strike
out into the backcountry, pay attention to weather and snow conditions, especially to
areas that may be avalanche prone. Because these deadly slides are more likely to be
triggered on slopes 30 degrees or steeper, stay away from steep-sided ravines and the
bottoms of narrow gullies, particularly just after a heavy snowfall. Also avoid terrain
where vegetation has obviously been cleared away by avalanches in the past. For
updated information about local avalanche danger you can call the Tahoe National
Forest Avalanche Hotline at (530) 587-2158 or access their web site at
www.avalanche.org.

Be sure to **drink water** often to remain hydrated and snack to keep your energy level
up. If you're a newcomer to the backcountry, it's wise to experience it at a leisurely pace
that won't exhaust anyone in your group. Leave the macho spirit at home and be willing
to finish the outing when others are ready to.

But you won't need these winter awareness tips unless you can first get to your
mountain destination. **Winter driving** in the mountains can be a fun-filled adventure or

— continued on next page

a frustrating and hazardous challenge, depending upon how well prepared you are. Before heading into snow country, make sure your car is in good running condition and that you have the proper sized chains. You should also start with a full tank of gas and carry basic survival items, such as a windshield scraper or de-icer, a broom, a shovel, sand, food, water, blankets and warm clothing. Because traffic delays are not uncommon, allow plenty of time to get where you're going. If you encounter ice or snow on the road, slow down and give other cars around you plenty of room. Since your car needs at least three times more distance to stop on slick roads, remember to maintain a minimum distance of four to eight seconds between your vehicle and the one in front of you. If you need to pull off the road to brush off the windshield or put on chains, be sure to get completely off the pavement and to turn on your hazard lights. When you see the "Chains Required" signs, you'll have about a mile to install them before the checkpoint. Be sure to comply because you can be cited and fined if you don't. If you have a four-wheel drive vehicle you can usually proceed right to the checkpoint because chains are usually not required for them.

If you're properly prepared for your mountain experience, it will be safer and more comfortable. Although you can't anticipate absolutely everything that can happen, you can reduce the potential danger by using common sense and being "winter aware."

trails. One of the most pristine track systems in the Reno/Tahoe area is the delightful Euer Valley, where the trails meander along picturesque Prosser Creek. Just 4 kilometers from the day lodge, much of this track system is rated for beginners. You can spend the whole day here, stopping just to enjoy the views and to refuel in the Euer Valley Cookhouse.

Amenities at this resort include snowshoeing, equipment rental, instruction, a retail shop and four warming huts. Tahoe Donner is also the only cross-country ski area to offer night skiing. The trail pass is $15.

To reach Tahoe Donner from Reno/Sparks, take I-80 west for 30 miles to Truckee and then Calif. 89 north for 2.2 miles. Turn left onto Alder Creek Road and travel about another 7 miles. Coming from Tahoe City take Calif. 89 north to Truckee and turn right onto Donner Pass Road and then left onto Northwoods Boulevard. Follow the signs to the ski area, about 5 miles further on.

South Shore Lake Tahoe

Camp Richardson Cross-Country Ski Center
1900 Jameson Rd., South Lake Tahoe, Calif. • (530) 541-1801, (800) 544-1801

For drop-dead gorgeous views along the shore of Lake Tahoe, Camp Richardson has 18 kilometers of groomed track with additional routes to nearby Fallen Leaf Lake Road and Taylor Creek. Amenities include lodging, rentals and a restaurant. Most of the groomed trail is geared to beginners since it's fairly level, but skiers of all abilities can certainly appreciate the gorgeous environment. Since most of the skiing is at lake level, the snowpack is lower than at higher elevations. It's wise to call ahead to check on snow conditions to make sure there's enough for skiing. The trail pass costs $10.

To get to the resort from South Lake Tahoe,

INSIDERS' TIP

The small ski resort just west of Mt. Rose–Ski Tahoe on Nev. 431 (the Mt. Rose Highway) is Sky Tavern. Owned and managed by the City of Reno, it's not open to the general public; it's used exclusively for the city's junior ski program.

take U.S. 50 west to the "Y" (the intersection of U.S. 50 and Calif. 89 in South Lake Tahoe) and then turn right and follow Calif. 89 north for about 2 miles. For more information about Camp Richardson see our Vacation Rentals chapter.

Hope Valley Cross-Country
14225 Calif. Hwy. 08, Hope Valley, Calif.
• (800) 423-9949, (530) 694-2266

If you've got your own equipment, you can ski and snowshoe free on 60 kilometers of gorgeous trail at Hope Valley Cross-Country ski area. Nestled in exquisite Hope Valley, this ski area offers an unspoiled mountain experience that's hard to beat. Environmentalists, including the folks at Sorensen's resort just down the road, have worked successfully for years to preserve the pristine nature of this valley. It's also blessedly tranquil since snowmobiles and other vehicles are prohibited. There's very little set track, but that's part of the charm since you can just head out on your own to explore the marked terrain. Trailside amenities include rental equipment, instruction and guided tours, such as tracing part of Snowshoe Thompson's famous route delivering mail to snowbound residents in the 1800s.

Sorensen's offers cozy overnight lodging in unique alpine cabins with names like Dancehall, Tanglewood and Saint Nick's. You can even bring the family dog along: pets are welcome in some of the units. A hearty meal near the fire in the country cafe here is a delight after an invigorating day on skis or snowshoes. The resort also sponsors periodic cultural events that showcase the history and natural beauty of the area. Since Kirkwood alpine and Nordic ski centers are just 20 minutes away, you can also take advantage of all the amenities they offer. See our descriptions of these resorts in this chapter.

To reach Hope Valley Cross-Country from the Reno/Sparks area, take U.S. 395 south to Minden and then Calif. 88 west. It's about a 90-minute drive when the roads are clear. From South Shore Lake Tahoe take U.S. 50 west to Myers and then turn left onto Calif. 89 south for about 12 miles and left again onto Calif. 88. The cross-country facility is about one-quarter mile past Sorensen's resort.

Kirkwood Cross-Country Center
Calif. Hwy. 88, Kirkwood, Calif.
• (209) 258-7248, (800) 967-7500

Kirkwood Cross-Country is the largest, most comprehensive cross-country ski area in the South Shore Lake Tahoe area, with more than 4,000 acres of exceptional terrain. The 80 kilometers of groomed track are rated 20 percent beginner, 60 percent intermediate and 20 percent advanced. Kirkwood is easily one of the most picturesque regions outside the Lake Tahoe Basin, where you can ski through lovely meadows and along scenic ridgelines in the shadow of jagged volcanic peaks. Because Kirkwood is higher in elevation than many other cross-country ski areas, the snow here is deeper and drier and the season is longer. A trail pass costs $15.

The resort offers a full array of amenities, including equipment rental, lessons, a retail shop, three warming huts, a restaurant and track-side lodging. Kirkwood's alpine ski resort is just down the road so you can also take advantage of all the activities in Kirkwood Village at the base of the ski mountain. See our description under alpine ski resorts in this chapter.

To reach Kirkwood from the Reno/Sparks area, take U.S. 395 south to Minden and then Calif. 88 west. It's about a 90-minute drive when the roads are clear. From South Shore Lake Tahoe take U.S. 50 west to Myers and then turn left onto Calif. 89 south for about 12 miles. Then turn right onto Calif. 88 west for another 14 miles.

Backcountry and Public Cross-Country Ski Areas

You don't have to go to a ski resort to enjoy the great outdoors: there's a large variety of backcountry and public areas where you can play in the snow. You're pretty much on your own, however, since most don't have any facilities. But if you're on a budget, the price is right because many are free and some only require a few dollars for a Sno-Park permit. If there's no set track for skiers, it's usually okay to bring your dog, but consider the depth of the snow before you do since smaller

Photo: Northstar–at–Tahoe

If you would like to take your snow adventure beyond cross country or alpine skiing, think about a trip down the hill in the newest winter thrill – The Zorb.

animals have a difficult time in very deep snow. When snowmobilers are in the area it's also necessary to keep a close watch on your pets. In any of these areas you'll find people enjoying the great outdoors in a variety of ways — tubing, sledding, snowshoeing, skiing and snowmobiling. But however you choose to play in the snow, the main thing is have a good time.

We describe a few of our favorite spots below, but you can find out about others by picking up information at the Tahoe-Douglas Visitor Center at 195 U.S. 50 in Stateline, Nevada. Trail maps and Sno-Park permits are available during business hours at the Lake Tahoe Basin Management Unit of the forest service at 870 Emerald Bay Road in South Lake Tahoe, California. You can call for information at (530) 573-2600 or (916) 324-1222.

On weekends and evenings, permits can be purchased at the Shell station at the "Y" in South Lake Tahoe (the intersection of U.S. 50 and Calif. 89) and the Shell station in Meyers, California. Many retail businesses near Sno-Parks sell permits, including Alpenglow Sports in Tahoe City, California; Mountain Hardware in Truckee, California; and Homewood Hardware in Homewood, California.

Donner Memorial State Park
Donner Pass Rd., Truckee, Calif.
• **(530) 582-7892**

Operated by the California Department of Parks and Recreation, Donner Memorial State Park has a very scenic 2.5-mile set track that meanders through the trees and along the shore of Donner Lake. The terrain is relatively level and perfect for beginner skiers. You'll

---

INSIDERS' TIP

You can ski for just $10 a day with the Gold Ticket, a sampler ski package offering 35 days of mid-week alpine and cross-country skiing at every ski resort in the North Shore Lake Tahoe area for $350. A limited number of passes are sold in September. For details call (775) 832-7625.

need to buy a Sno-Park permit at the park museum for $5. It's a great area for skiing and snowshoeing, but snowmobiling and sledding are not allowed.

To get there from Reno/Sparks take I-80 west for about 30 miles to Truckee, take the Squaw Valley Exit and turn right. At the stoplight turn left at Donner Pass Road and follow it for one half mile. From Tahoe City take Calif. 89 north to Truckee and turn left onto Donner Pass Road at the second stoplight.

Martis Lookout Trail
Just north of Brockway Summit, Calif. Hwy. 267

Like many forest service roads that aren't plowed in the winter, Martis Lookout Road becomes a popular access route to the backcountry when it's covered with snow. If you're really ambitious you can take the whole 8-mile loop that climbs about 1,400 feet to the top of Martis Peak. Once on the summit, you're rewarded with top-of-the-world vistas, since both Lake Tahoe and the Martis Valley spread out in all their splendor directly below. The trek going up is something of a challenge, but the exciting run back down makes it all worthwhile. You'll find cross-country skiers, snowshoers and snowmobilers, with pets, kids and the whole family enjoying the day in this area. Parking is limited to a small area at the turnoff and along the road so it's best to go

early or late in the day to be able to find a spot. When snowplows are working to clear Calif. 267, access may be even further limited.

To get to Martis Lookout Road from Kings Beach, take Calif. 267 north to about one-quarter mile past Brockway Summit and look for the pullout on the right. From the Reno/Sparks area head west on I-80 about 30 miles to Truckee and then south for about 10 miles on Calif. 267.

Mt. Watson Rd.
Brockway Summit, Calif. Hwy. 267

At more than 7,000 feet in elevation, Mt. Watson Road is often covered with snow when areas lower down are completely bare. The road winds through deep forest for more than 20 miles, giving periodic peeks at Lake Tahoe along the way. If you keep to the right when the road forks, the climb is gradual and suitable for most levels of skiers. Going to the left puts you on a narrower, steeper path more adapted to intermediate skiers. This is also a wonderful area for snowshoeing since you can stick to the beaten path or head off into the trees to enjoy a first-rate day in the forest. You need to watch out for snowmobiles, however, since snowmobile tour operators frequently bring groups into the area.

To get to Mt. Watson Road, take Calif. 267 north to Brockway Summit from Kings Beach and either park along the road or use the park-

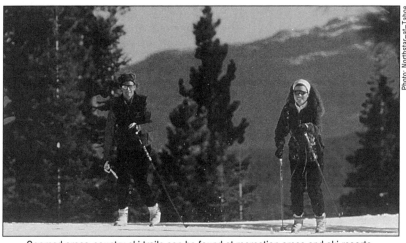

Groomed cross-country ski trails can be found at recreation areas and ski resorts.

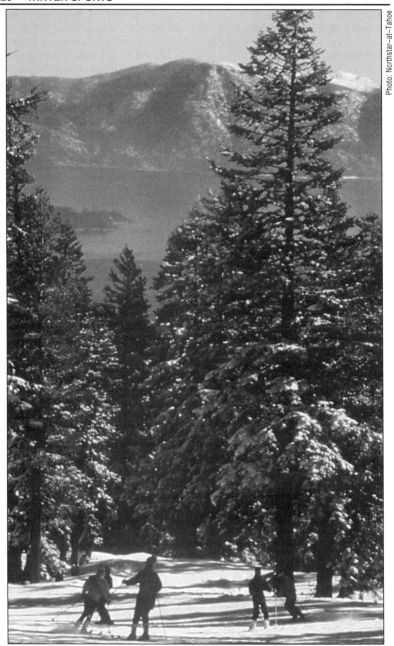

Photo: Northstar–at–Tahoe

Sunshine and the dry Sierra powder snow plus the view of Lake Tahoe below make what most skiers would call a "perfect" day.

ing lot at the top. From the Reno/Sparks area, take I-80 west about 30 miles to Truckee and then Calif. 267 south for about 10 miles to Brockway Summit.

Nev. Hwy. 431
Across from Mt. Rose–Ski Tahoe

You can ski, snowshoe, sled and tube on a little-used tract of heavily wooded land directly across Nev. 431 from the entrance to Mt. Rose–Ski Tahoe ski resort. A forest service road winds through the trees, providing a packed surface with a gentle incline. But for more up and down, especially for tubes and sleds, try the slopes alongside the more level surface of the road. There's room to park just off the highway near a frame building that served as a warming hut some years ago when the area was a ski resort with groomed trails. We don't recommend snowmobiling here, however.

To reach the area take Nev. 431 east for about 11 miles from Incline Village or west for 22 miles from Reno.

North Tahoe Regional Park
Tahoe Vista, Calif. • (530) 546-5043

Insiders know if the wind is gusting over the upper mountain elevations, you can still have a great day in the snow sheltered by the dense forest at North Tahoe Regional Park. With approximately 5 miles of meandering trails, the park offers enough variety of terrain to entertain beginners as well as more advanced skiers. But don't expect impeccable tracks since grooming is best described as sporadic. You can rent sleds and snowmobiles, but you're on your own for any other sporting equipment. It's a great place to bring dogs and also a bargain, since a trail pass is only $3 at the self-pay system near the restrooms at the entrance to the park. Be aware, however, that the park is at relatively low elevation (around 6,000 feet) so be sure the snow level is at least that low before heading out to ski here.

To get to the park from Incline Village, go

west on Nev. 28, just past Kings Beach to Tahoe Vista, turn right on National Avenue and follow the signs to the park.

Tahoe Meadows
West of Summit on Nev. Hwy. 431

An exquisite alpine meadow cupped below Mt. Rose and Slide Mountain, Tahoe Meadows is one of the most popular backcountry playgrounds in the Reno/Tahoe area. You can stick to the flats by staying in the meadow proper or you can find plenty of up and down by venturing through the trees on the surrounding mountains. Climbing up the ridges on the southwest side of the meadow affords gorgeous views of Lake Tahoe and lovely spots to stop for a snowy picnic. If you venture to the end of the main meadow you also get views of Washoe Lake and Washoe Valley. Nev. 431 bisects the meadow with the largest part on the left as you approach from Reno. The smaller area on the other side of the road has less level terrain, but when you climb the ridges you can see Lake Tahoe and tiny Incline Lake just below.

Tahoe Meadows is great for family outings (including the family dog) and you'll find people doing just about everything you can do on the snow — skiing, snowmobiling, snowshoeing, tubing and sledding. There are no facilities so you need to bring your own food and drinks. Because of its high elevation the meadow gets snow early in the year and keeps it well into late spring. When other mountain areas are devoid of the white stuff, you can usually find enough to ski on here. But the high elevation means that the weather can get pretty wild, so check on the forecast before you head up the mountain. The snow really piles up here so don't be surprised if it's over the top of your car when you park along the road. But look for cuts in the snowbanks that you can use to get access to the meadow. Those tall poles with reflectors you see along the road will give you an idea of how high the snow gets; they're used as guides for the snowplows that clear the road.

INSIDERS' TIP

The record snowfall on Donner Summit is 826 inches (69 feet) which fell in 1936. That's ten telephone booths stacked on top of each other!

For a convenient place to get on the snow (it's just minutes from either Reno or North Shore Lake Tahoe), we highly recommend Tahoe Meadows. If you're there at sundown, listening to the swish of your skis on the snow as it turns golden, you'll agree with us that it's a very special place to be.

To reach the meadow from Reno/Sparks, take U.S. 395 south to Nev. 431 (the Mt. Rose Highway) and follow it to just past the summit. From Incline Village take Nev. 431 to where it levels out just before the summit.

Tallac Historic Site Trail
Calif. Hwy. 89, South Lake Tahoe, Calif.

When the snow level drops to the shores of Lake Tahoe, the 2-mile loop that winds through the Tallac Historic Site is perfect for novice cross-country skiers. You're treated to scenic views of Lake Tahoe, Mt. Tallac and some grand old estates dating from the 1800s. See our Attractions chapter for a complete description of this area.

The site is about 3 miles south of the "Y" (the intersection of U.S. 50 and Calif. 89 in South Lake Tahoe) on Calif. 89. Be sure to pick up a Sno-Park permit before you go and get directions to the parking area. Snowmobiles are not allowed here.

Ice Skating

Resort at Squaw Creek
400 Squaw Creek Rd., Olympic Valley, Calif. • (530) 581-6624

The outdoor skating rink at this elegant luxury resort has a classic Christmas card view of Olympic Valley and the surrounding snowclad peaks. You don't have to be a guest to enjoy all the top-of-the-line amenities here so lace up those skates and luxuriate in the ambiance of one of the country's top winter resorts. For a detailed description of Squaw Valley USA and the Resort at Squaw Creek, see previous sections of this chapter along with our Resorts chapter. The skating rink is open for two-hour sessions from 9 AM to 9 PM daily during the winter. The cost per session for an adult is $15; skate rental and instruction are extra.

To reach the resort from Reno/Sparks, take

I-80 west for about 30 miles to Truckee and then Calif. 89 south about 13 miles. From Tahoe City take Calif. 89 north about 6 miles. After turning into Squaw Valley at the main entrance, look for Squaw Creek Road and turn left. You can either valet your car at the resort or use their parking lot. For information on shuttle service to Squaw Valley USA from Reno, Sparks and South Shore Lake Tahoe call (800) 822-6009; from North Shore Lake Tahoe call (530) 581-7181. Reservations are required 12 hours in advance.

Rink on the River
Barbara Bennett Park, 400 Island Ave., Reno, Nev. • (775) 334-2413

Tucked in the trees near the Truckee River in downtown Reno, the Rink on the River is scenic as well as economical. You can glide and spin here in a naturally beautiful environment, just a stone's throw from the bright neon lights of the major casinos. Skating sessions are just $5 for adults and $3 for kids and seniors. You can rent skates, take lessons and also enjoy snacks and drinks at the rink. It's open daily from 8 AM to 11 PM during fall and winter. The rink has been moved from park to park over the years, so we recommend you call first to verify its location.

Squaw Valley USA
1960 Squaw Valley Rd., Olympic Valley, Calif. • (530) 583-6985

Perched mid-mountain, high above exquisite Olympic Valley, the outdoor Olympic Ice Pavilion at Squaw Valley USA gives you a one-of-a-kind skating experience with a breathtaking view. You can buy a transport/skate ticket year-round (which includes two hours of skate rental) for $19 from 10 AM to 5 PM and for $11 from 5 to 9 PM. Once on the mountain you can enjoy all the restaurants, shops and watering holes provided at High Camp. For more details about all the amenities offered at this world-class resort, see our description earlier in this chapter under "Alpine Skiing." Because this part of Squaw Valley can get very windy at times, it's wise to call ahead and get a weather report for the mountain. Also be sure to dress warmly since you'll be skating outside at 8,200 feet in elevation.

To get to Squaw, take Calif. 89 north from

Tahoe City about 6 miles. From Reno, head west on I-80 about 30 miles to Truckee and then south for about 13 miles on Calif. 89. Shuttle service is available from Reno, Sparks and South Shore Lake Tahoe by calling (800) 822-6009 and from North Shore Lake Tahoe at (530) 581-7181. Reservations are required 12 hours in advance.

Wingfield Springs Ice Rink
7755 Spanish Springs Rd., Sparks, Nev.
• (775) 626-1000

Ice skating and golf don't usually share the same venue, but at Wingfield Springs skaters spin and golfers putt right next to each other (see our Golf chapter for details about the course). Unfortunately, however, the skaters miss the lovely views at this first-class planned community since the rink is inside the Special Events Promenade adjacent to Red Hawk Golf Club. Skating sessions are $6 for adults and $4 for children (see also our Kidstuff chapter). You can buy snacks rinkside or enjoy scrumptious meals at Freddie's Roost right next door (see the detailed description of Freddie's in our Restaurant chapter). Hours vary from day to day so call first.

To reach Wingfield Springs from Sparks take I-80 east, exit at Vista Boulevard and travel north for about 7 miles where you'll see signs directing you to Wingfield Springs.

Dog Sled Rides

Sierra Ski Touring
Gardnerville, Nev. • (775) 782-3047

It's the only way to get around in a few spots in the world, but in Hope Valley, just 30 minutes from South Shore Lake Tahoe, riding in a dog sled is a winter experience that's uniquely entertaining. You can drive through this beautiful valley and you can cross-country ski and snowshoe in it. But skimming across the snow, bundled in blankets behind eight highly trained dogs, offers a different perspective altogether. A one-hour ride is $50 for adults and $20 for children. The sled can accommo-

date up to 375 pounds. Moonlight, picnic and special event rides are also offered, but you need to reserve in advance.

Sleigh Rides

What's more in keeping with a winter wonderland vacation than dashing through the snow in a one-horse open sleigh? For details and reservations in the South Shore Lake Tahoe area call **Borges Sleigh Rides** at (530) 541-2953, **Kirkwood Ski Resort** at (209) 258-7433 or **Camp Richardson Corral** at (530) 541-3113. In the North Shore Lake Tahoe area call **Northstar–at–Tahoe** at (530) 562-1010 or **Borges Sleigh Rides** at (800) 726-7433.

Snowmobile Tours

When the mountains and backcountry roads around Lake Tahoe are covered with a deep blanket of snow, one of the most thrilling ways to experience the great outdoors is on a snowmobile. Don't worry if you've never ridden or driven one before: it's easy to learn and the tour operators make sure you know the basics before heading out.

You can take guided tours out to wilderness areas for gorgeous views or you can race around groomed tracks in open meadows and golf courses. Eagle Ridge Snowmobile Outfitters also offers all-day outings and overnight trips which include stays in cozy mountain lodges. If you don't have proper clothing, don't spend a fortune on buying it because most operators will also rent you whatever gear you might need.

For details and reservations in the North Shore Lake Tahoe area, call **Eagle Ridge Snowmobile Outfitters** at (530) 546-8667, **TC Sno Mo's** at (530) 581-3906, **Northstar–at–Tahoe** at (530) 562-1010, **Snowmobiling Unlimited** at (530) 583-5858, or **High Sierra Snowmobiling** at (530) 546-9909. In the South Shore Lake Tahoe area, call **Lake Tahoe Winter Sports Center** at (530) 577-2940, **Sunset Ranch** at (530) 544-8594, or **Zephyr Cove Snowmobile Center** at (775) 588-3833.

Hang around any of the sports bars and you can't help but overhear us talking about the 4-pound trout that got away or about that humongous mule deer we saw bounding over that far-away hill before we could fire a shot.

Fishing and Hunting

Fishing and hunting reach almost religious proportions among Insiders here in the Reno/Tahoe area. Hang around any of the sports bars and you can't help but overhear us talking about the 4-pound trout that got away or about that humongous mule deer we saw bounding over that far-away hill before we could fire a shot.

In this chapter, we'll give you a quick overview of the fishing and hunting scenes in the Reno/Tahoe area. We're not going to make you experts, but we will give you a few tips and hints to help you get started and to have an enjoyable time. Besides everything else the area offers, it is still a rare paradise which includes many opportunities for you anglers and hunters.

Fishing

We're going to share a fishing secret with you.

Now, if you know anything about fishing, you know that sharing secrets is not normal for anglers. In fact, anglers are the most closed-mouth of any sports persons. Just try finding out their favorite fishing hole sometime or what the fish are biting on. . . . But we feel we owe it to you because this is the Insiders' Guide and we are the Insiders. So here goes:

The Reno/Tahoe area is the best location to go trout fishing, far better than any other spot in the contiguous 48 states.

And no, we are not just writing this to help hook (pun intended) you readers who are avid anglers. We mean it and we can prove it.

Within 60 miles of Lake Tahoe, anglers have more than 400 lakes, reservoirs, rivers, creeks and streams to fish for trout. In the rivers, lakes and streams on the Nevada side of the Reno/Tahoe area, the Nevada Department of Wildlife plants about 286,000 catchable-size rainbows each year, along with 32,000 catchable-size brown trout, 11,000 catchable-size cuttbows (a hybrid rainbow and cutthroat trout), and 111,000 catchable-size cutthroats. Another 300,000 fingerling trout are planted each year in addition to the 9+ inch, catchable fish.

In Lake Tahoe, you can fish year-round because the lake never freezes over. In addition to the estimated 500,000 game fish that naturally inhabit the lake, the California Department of Fish and Game and the Nevada Department of Wildlife stock more than 75,000 catchable-size rainbows here each year.

In the Desolation Wilderness (see our Area Overview and Recreation chapters for a description), some 130 lakes wait for the trout angler and all of these lakes are teeming with fish, including the elusive and delicate golden trout, which are scarce and found only in the highest elevated lakes. But an annual survey of the hikers (vehicles are prohibited) who used the area in 1998 said that only 5 percent of them enter the wilderness with the specific purpose of fishing.

Pyramid Lake, a high-desert lake just 35 miles north of Reno, is home to the legendary cutthroat trout, which fascinated Fremont and his group (see our History section for a brief description of Fremont's expedition and our Daytrips chapter for more about Pyramid Lake). The average size cutthroat caught in 1998 was 2 feet long and weighed just over 5 pounds. This lake sits on an Indian Reservation so you don't need a Nevada fishing license.

So you can see that the Reno/Tahoe area is a trout angler's mecca, a year-round fishing paradise. But we would be remiss if we didn't tell you that we can't possibly cover every creek, stream and lake within the 60-mile radius. Heck, we can think of at least three books that try to accomplish that feat and all of them are more than 400 pages long. Instead, we're going to concentrate on the Lake Tahoe–Truckee River–Pyramid Lake water system that sits smack-dab in the middle of the Reno/Tahoe area. It's easily accessible and will provide you with all the fishing action you can handle. (If you're itching for more, you might also want to check out *Dave Stanley's No Nonsense Guide to Fly Fishing in Nevada* by Dave Stanley and *The Nevada Angler's Guide* by Richard Dickerson.)

Lake Tahoe and Pyramid Lake are connected by the Truckee River and together they make up a closed water system. In other words, their waters never reach the ocean. Before the interference of the white man, these two lakes interacted more because at one time fish could swim from one to the other by way of the Truckee River. But today that's not so, and the system is treated as three different fisheries, each with its own techniques for landing the skittish and elusive trout.

We hope this chapter will help you to learn more about the three exceptional fisheries, to catch more trout and to have more fun while you are doing it. But remember, trout fishing, especially in the Reno/Tahoe area, is not only a recreational sport, it's also an art. Trout around here have grown fat and wily and they got that way because most anglers underestimate them. Our advice is: don't. They're smart but we hope to make you smarter.

We will show you a few Insiders' tricks that will help you fill your creel. But also remember, the most remarkable thing about fishing is that you don't always have to catch fish to have fun, especially in this area. Just being out in the fresh air, enjoying the scenery away from the worries and cares of crowded city life is really reward enough. So give your mind a chance to relax and come fishing with us.

And remember the anglers' adage: "A day fishing doesn't count against your life."

Lake Tahoe

When anglers first get a look at Lake Tahoe, they usually scratch their heads and ask, "Where do I begin?" After all, the lake is 22 miles long and 12 miles wide and most experienced Lake Tahoe guides will tell you that successfully fishing this lake takes more skill and finesse than any other American lake. It ranks fifth in the world in mean depth (1,027 feet) and 10th in the world in maximum depth (1,645 feet) and its mirror-like conditions make for some real spooky trout.

Most first-time anglers have a difficult time landing game fish in Lake Tahoe. In fact, we know one experienced angler who fished the lake for five years and only netted two lake trout, called Mackinaw around here. But then he was a stubborn fellow who wouldn't ask the experts for help; thus our first bit of advice for new anglers on Lake Tahoe: hire a guide. We understand that to some this is almost as bad as stopping your car at a gas station to ask for directions . . . but you'll have more fun if you heed our advice.

More than 25 guides make their living on Lake Tahoe (see the end of the chapter for some of our favorites) and hiring one to show you the ins and outs of Tahoe's fishing scene is money well spent. They can show you the techniques needed to land the "big one," then once you've learned from a professional,

---

INSIDERS' TIP

The original race of Pyramid Lake cutthroat trout became extinct in the 1940s.

catching fish on your own should be a lot easier.

Since Lake Tahoe is located both in California and Nevada, the states have agreed to honor a fishing license from either state when fishing the lake. Any person 16 years of age or older must have a license to fish (see the gray box in this section for license fees). Limits are five game fish, of which no more than two may be Mackinaw.

Lake Tahoe is open year-round, 1 hour before sunrise to 2 hours after sunset. The following exceptions apply:

• within 300 feet of its tributaries and upstream to the first lake from October 1 to June 30 on the California side;
• within a 200-yard radius of the mouths of Third, Incline and Wood creeks on the Nevada side;
• within a 500-yard radius of Sand Harbor boat ramp; and
• within the boat-launch area in the jetty at Cave Rock.

Boat Fishing

The first thing to remember about fishing Lake Tahoe is that a boat with a fish-finder is mandatory if you expect to catch The Big One. Lake Tahoe has a lot of water and seven species of game fish (Chinook and Kokanee salmon; brook, brown, rainbow, cutthroat and Mackinaw trout), making trolling the most popular method used by anglers on this lake.

The theory behind trolling is to cover a lot of territory in a short amount of time and to bring the bait to the fish rather than waiting for the fish to come to the bait. On Lake Tahoe, anglers usually use two trolling methods for the prized Mackinaw — downrigging and lead lining.

Downriggers are fishing devices fastened to the boat that let you use heavy weights on a separate reel attached to your fishing line by clips. Once the fish strikes, the weights are released and reeled in and it's just you and

the monster Mackinaw on the other end of the line. The weights help you troll with lures and live bait at varying depths, depending on where the fish are. The fish-finders help determine the depth of the fish, too.

Lead lining is a technique used to go deep, sometimes as much as 200 feet, for the big Macks. The technique is to use a flashy lure like wobbling spoons, Rebels and Rapalas behind a lead-core nylon line or metal line. You run the line out — sometimes as far as 300 yards, depending on how deep the fish are — and wait for a strike.

Jigging is another method anglers use on the lake for Mackinaws. This usually consists of using a live minnow on a treble hook combined with a jig. Jigging lures resemble wounded fish. The idea is to work the rod with small tugs to give the presentation that the minnow is wounded to draw the Mack in for the strike.

To go for the feisty rainbows in Lake Tahoe, the preferred method is to top line, trolling a lure just below the surface. Some anglers find fighting a rainbow on light line a lot more fun than dragging in a half-drowned Mackinaw and 300 yards of lead line. The rainbows fight like crazy, leaping out of the water and making long runs trying to spit the hook. The best place to top-line troll for rainbows is along the rocky shoal areas using Flatfish and Hot Shot plugs or Rebel and Rapala lures.

Pier and Shore Fishing

Don't fret if you don't have access to a boat because pier and shore fishing around Lake Tahoe can be fun and productive, too. You just have to remember a few things — avoid fishing during mirror-like calm on the lake and try to make long casts from piers and the shore so the fish won't see you. Remember, the fish in this lake are already spooky.

The best time to fish from piers and the shore is when there is a healthy breeze over the lake and waves on the water. Large trout will cruise into shore looking for minnows, crawfish or any other food kicked up by the rough water. Spinners and lures work best, but bait anglers using worms, salmon eggs and Power Bait have been known to pull in a few lunkers. Always use light monofilament line to hide the leaders. You can find trout close to shore at Rubicon Point, Dollar Point, Crystal Bay Point, Sand Harbor, Cave Rock and south of Tahoe City.

The Truckee River

The Truckee River, Lake Tahoe's only outlet, begins its trek from the dam at Tahoe City, California, and continues along Calif. Highway 89 through the town of Truckee, California, then along Interstate 80 through Reno and Sparks, eventually emptying into Pyramid Lake. This 115 miles of river used to be the breeding grounds of the monstrous Lahontan cutthroat trout. In autumns of old, these fish would make spawning runs from Pyramid Lake almost back to Lake Tahoe. The days of seeing fish "you can almost walk on" in the Truckee River are gone, but thanks to three consecutive wet years after a seven-year drought, trout fishing in the river is perking up again.

The Truckee River is split into thirds when it comes to fishing. You have the upper section from Lake Tahoe to the town of Truckee, California, the middle section from Truckee to the Nevada state line, and the lower section from the Nevada state line to Pyramid Lake.

The **upper section** of the Truckee River is heavily fished because Calif. 89 runs parallel to the river and several public campgrounds dot its banks, making access to great fishing easy. The flood of 1997 altered some of the characteristics of this upper section but big pools of slow-moving water still exist, hiding some monstrous trout. During the summer, many people enjoy rafting and tubing this section of the river so the best times to fish are usually early morning or late evening. Normally, the river has slowed from late June to early September, making these the best months to fish.

The season lasts from the last Saturday in April to November 15 but no fishing is allowed anytime from Fanny Bridge at Lake Tahoe to

1,000 feet downstream. Just about any trout fishing technique will work on this section of the river — lures, especially Mepps and Panther Martins; salmon eggs and worms bounced along the bottom; and for the fly-fishing enthusiast, caddisflies and nymphs presented just before dark. The limit is five trout per day.

The **middle section** of the Truckee River is wild trout country and legal restrictions vary depending on where you fish. A copy of the California Department of Fish and Game regulations is mandatory to stay out of legal trouble with the game wardens and to enjoy fishing this section. From Trout Creek to Glenshire Bridge, only artificial lures with barbless hooks are allowed. From Glenshire Bridge to Prosser Creek, only artificial flies with barbless hooks are allowed. From Prosser Creek to Boca Bridge, only artificial lures with barbless hooks are allowed. Beyond the bridge to the state line, any type of fishing gear is permissible. Also, a 2-mile stretch of the river is private property and is off-limits. Obviously, close attention to the regulations is mandatory — but the rewards are sweet here.

This section is inhabited by rainbows, browns and the ever-elusive wild trout. Here you'll find some of the most challenging fishing on the river. But watch out near the state line: if you fish on it or cross it, you will need a license from both California and Nevada.

The season on this section is open from the last Saturday in April to November 15. The catch limit varies on this stretch, so consult the regulations.

The **lower section** of the Truckee River, which is entirely in Nevada, has had three good water years and will offer opportunities for some trophy trout. And for the first time in many, many years, Lahontan cutthroat trout will provide for 50 percent of the catchable trout on this section of the Truckee. The best fishing here will be associated with lower-flow conditions following the winter runoff — usually July through October.

From the California border downstream to the I-80 bridge near Crystal Peak Park in Verdi is the trophy section of the river in Nevada, where the trout grow big and smart. Only artificial lures with single, barbless hooks may be used and the limit is two trout and 10 moun-

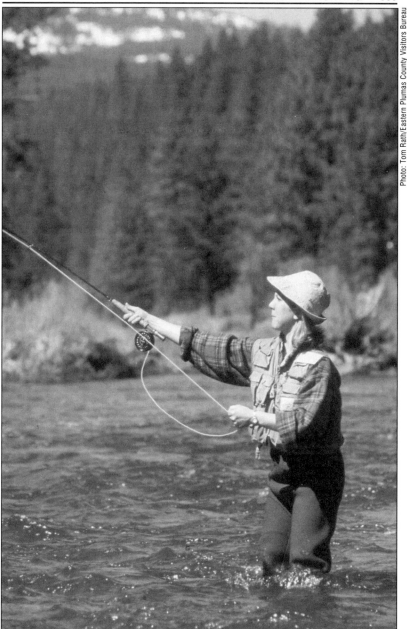

Photo: Tom Rath/Eastern Plumas County Visitors Bureau

Great fly-fishing streams can be found close to town or in the high places
if you want to get your rod out in the Reno/Tahoe area.

Before making that first cast on the beautiful waters around Reno/Tahoe,
make sure you know the local regulations and have a license in your pocket.

Photo: Tom Rath/Eastern Plumas County Visitors Bureau

tain whitefish, with the minimum size for the trout set at 14 inches. The rest of the 75 miles of the river in Nevada has no gear limitations. The river in this section is easily accessed from Crystal Peak Park, Dog Valley Road bridge and both bridges on Third Street.

The one aspect of fishing this section of river that often boggles experienced anglers' minds is the fact that only a few hundred yards from the glitter of Reno's downtown casinos, you can enjoy some of the best trout fishing in the state. Another aspect is that fly fishing on this little river rivals many of the rivers in neighboring states because the Truckee is home to most of the insects fly anglers like to imitate — stoneflies, mayflies, caddisflies. In other words, the trout fishing is just darned good all along this section.

Bouncing salmon eggs and worms along the bottom is always a good technique in this section of the river and using lures like Mepps, Panther Martins, Rapalas and Rebels always works, too. Some of the more popular areas in Reno to fish the Truckee are Mayberry Park, Idlewild Park and any of the three Fisherman's parks.

You can fish this section year-round, any hour of the day or night except within 1,000 feet downstream of Derby Dam which is closed to all fishing. The limit is five trout and 10 mountain whitefish.

Pyramid Lake

Pyramid Lake is located 35 miles north of Reno by way of Nev. Highway 445 (the Pyramid Highway). It is located on the Pyramid Lake Paiute Indian Reservation so a Nevada fishing license is not required. However, you must purchase a permit to fish on the reservation. Permits are available from the reservation store and the ranger station at the lake, as well as from most bait and tackle shops in Reno and Sparks.

The lake received its name from a pyramid-shaped tufa mound (calcium deposits) rising out of the water. It is a starkly beautiful lake flanked by rugged mountains to the east and west but no trees. The one thing it does have though is monstrous cutthroat trout. The average trout pulled from the lake in 1998 was 2 feet long and weighed 5 pounds.

Fishing Pyramid can be great either on shore or from a boat. The cutthroat trout is very active in its search for food and often swims into shallow water. Trolling is the preferred method of catching fish at Pyramid, using lures that imitate minnows and downriggers to get the lures at the correct depth. Boat anglers use Tor-p-Dos, Apex lures, U20 Flatfish, Pink Ladies and flashers. Shore anglers stick to using Tor-p-Dos, Rapalas, Daredevils and Maribu jigs.

Fly fishing is also popular at Pyramid Lake and probably the most exciting method. Cutthroats strike flies with a vengeance. Anglers fly fishing use 6- to 9-pound leaders with fast-sinking fly line (shooting heads) when fishing the drop-offs and a slow-sinking line at the shallow beaches. Black and purple woolly worms and woolly buggers are their favorite flies. And anglers will usually use two sizes of flies, one as a dropper, to find out what the fish are biting on. One of the most peculiar things you'll see at the lake is the many anglers who use small stepladders to stand on in the waist-deep water while casting. The added height makes for increased casting distances but it makes for a weird sight.

The fishing season at Pyramid Lake runs from October 1 through June 30. The keeper size for the cutthroat is 16 to 19 inches and any cutthroat more than 24 inches. The daily limit is two, with only one that is more than 24 inches. One rod and two hooks per angler are allowed and only artificial lures.

Fishing Licenses

California

Everyone 16 years of age and older must have a valid fishing license.
Resident:
>   16 years and older: $26.50
>   Less than 16 years old: Free

Nonresident:
> $73.50 for the year
> $27.05 for 10 days
> $9.70 for 1 day

Nevada

Everyone 12 years of age and older must have a valid fishing license.
Resident:
>   16 years of age and older: $21
>   12 to 15 years of age: $5
>   Less than 12 years old: Free

Nonresident:
>   16 years of age and older: $51
>   12 to 15 years of age: $9
>   One day license: $12

Pyramid Lake

Everyone must have a valid fishing permit to fish Pyramid Lake.
One-day permit: $6
Season permit: $32

Fishing Guides

Lake Tahoe

First Strike
Zephyr Cove, Nev. • (775) 588-4665

These folks specialize in year-round charters for trout and salmon using the latest in electronic equipment and lightweight tackle. They have a morning and afternoon charter. The charter includes bait and tackle, snacks — and they'll even clean your fish. Write to them at PO Box 11268, Zephyr Cove NV 89448.

Kingfish
Tahoe City, Calif. • (530) 525-5360

This outfit runs charters year-round on the lake from a 43-foot boat named the *Kingfish*. All equipment — tackle, rods and reels — is included. Trips leave early in the morning and coffee, soft drinks and snacks are included. Their mailing address is PO Box 5955, Tahoe City CA 96145.

Mac-A-Tac Fishing Charters
North Lake Tahoe Marina, Tahoe Vista, Calif. • (530) 546-2500

Mac-A-Tac specializes in the morning bite and likes to see at least three anglers per trip. Anglers can expect to be out on the lake for about 5 hours.

Mickey's Big Mack Charters
Carnelian Bay, Calif. • (530) 546-4444

Fish year-round with master guide Mickey Daniels. He has been fishing Lake Tahoe for 30 years and guarantees he will find you fish. Call the number above or write for more information: PO Box 488, Carnelian Bay CA 96140.

Tahoe Sportsfishing
900 Ski Run Blvd., South Lake Tahoe, Calif. • (530) 541-5448

Tahoe Sportsfishing trips include all gear, tackle and bait. They have 4-, 5-, and 7-hour trips in the morning and the afternoon. They also clean and wrap your catch.

Pyramid Lake

Cutthroat Charters
29555 Pyramid Hwy., Sutcliff, Nev. • (775) 476-0555

This is a family-owned and -operated business that guarantees you cutthroat trout. Only 30 minutes from Reno and Sparks, George Molino runs the charters 7 days a week during the season.

Fly Fishing

The following establishments will supply you with all your fly-fishing needs including licenses, lessons, fly-tying classes, equipment and local knowledge.

The Gilly, 1111 N. Rock Boulevard, Sparks, Nevada, (775) 358-6113

Mark Fore and Strike, 490 Kietzke Lane, Reno, Nevada, (775) 322-9559

Reno Fly Shop, 294 E. Moana Lane, Reno, Nevada, (775) 825-3474

Trout Creek Flies, PO Box 11528, Zephyr Cove, Nevada, 89448, (775) 588-3310

Hunting

Everything you've heard about the top quality of hunting in California and Nevada is true. Game abounds in these two states. Big animals like deer, bear, mountain lion, Big-

---

INSIDERS' TIP

Showcasing the world-class waterfowl hunting around Fallon, the Wings Over The Valley hunting festival held in September will show you exactly where to go to limit out. With activities for the whole family, the festival offers a wildlife carving show, tours of the Lahontan Valley wetlands, gun-dog demonstrations and duck and goose calling contests. For details, call (800) 874-9093.

Photo: K. Markgraf

The crystal clear waters of Lake Tahoe offer fisherman some trophy-size sport fishing.

horn sheep, elk, antelope and mountain goat can all be found here, along with migratory fowl, quail, grouse, dove, chukar, pheasant, rabbits, squirrels and turkey. The list goes on and most species have a hunting season.

For the purposes of this guide, we have limited the hunting section to just a few paragraphs to inform you about where to go to find out more detailed information on hunting in the area. Yes, the Reno/Tahoe area has some hunting but the regulations are stringent and many, especially around Lake Tahoe, so we thought it best not to delve too deeply into the hunting aspects of both states because they are confusing and detailed.

In the Reno/Tahoe area, places to hunt small game and birds can be found outside of the cities of Reno and Sparks. One section in the Toiyabe National Forest northeast of Lake Tahoe allows 78 tags a year for mule deer. On the California side of Lake Tahoe, hunting is allowed in some parts of the El Dorado National Forest and in the Desolation Wilderness but, again, the regulations are many and varied.

Both states require a hunting license and an application process for obtaining big game hunting tags. In other words, you must know the area you wish to hunt and apply for a tag specifically for that area (sometimes well in advance of the first day of the season). For this process, a copy of the California or Nevada hunting regulations is mandatory. Each edition has a detailed map of their respective states and reference numbers denoting specific hunting areas to be used on the application.

If you do decide to go hunting in either state, contact the following government agencies for a copy of their hunting regulations.

INSIDERS' TIP

Dial (800) ASK-FISH in Nevada to receive the latest fishing report, to find out where to buy fishing licenses and to locate a place to fish.

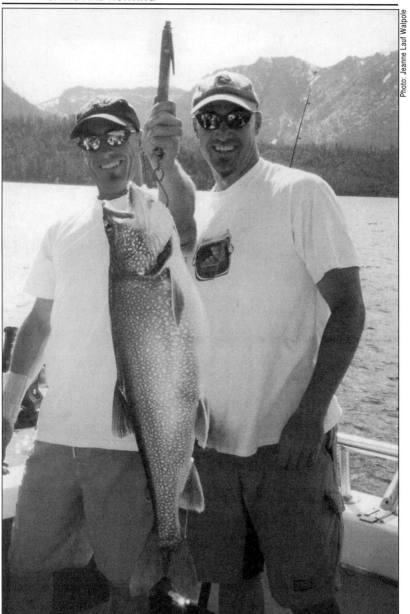

Photo: Jeanne Lauf Walpole

A 14-pound Mackinaw is all in a day's work for Reno/Tahoe area fishing guides.

For **Nevada** hunting regulations or for answers to any hunting-related questions, write or call:

Nevada Division of Wildlife
PO Box 10678
Reno NV 89520-0022
(775) 688-1500

For **California** hunting regulations or for answers to any hunting-related questions, write or call:

California Department of Fish and Game
PO Box 944209
Sacramento CA 94244-2090
(916) 653-7664

Guides

Sometimes the best plan of action is to hire a hunting guide, an Insider who knows the regulations, the game and the lay of the land.

Black Rock Outfitters
Winnemucca, Nev. • (775) 623-5926

A lifelong resident of Winnemucca, Mike Hornbarger of Black Rock Outfitters knows the backcountry of northern Nevada like the back of his hand. Since learning to trap as a child, he's explored every inch of this wild land, guiding friends and clients on hunting and photo trips for years. He'll personalize a tour or hunt just for you, whether you're out to bag a mountain lion or to capture the wonder of the desert in the lens of your camera.

Nevada Trophy Hunts
Gerlach, Nev. • (775) 557-2238

A former wildlife photographer for *National Geographic* magazine, Tony Diebold of Nevada Trophy Hunts is the consummate outdoorsman. His personalized trophy hunts for mule deer, desert sheep, antelope and elk are well known throughout Nevada. If you shoot a camera and not a gun, you can also take wildlife photo trips with him to some of the most unspoiled animal habitats in the area. The mailing address for Nevada Trophy Hunts is PO Box 10, Dept. G, Gerlach NV 89412.

Hunting Licenses
Nevada

Resident:
    16 years and older: $24
    12 to 15 years old: $5

Nonresident:
    General: $111

California

Resident:
    General: $27.05
    Junior, 16 years or younger: $6.85

Nonresident:
    General: $94.75

Every September, Reno National Air Race participants gather from all corners of the United States to compete in the fastest motor sport in the world.

Spectator Sports

Semiprofessional sports teams seem to have a hard time making a go of it in the Reno/Tahoe area. That's not to say that we don't like our spectator sports here. All you have to do is visit the sports book at any casino on any weekend and you'll be standing elbow to elbow with sports fans trying to catch a glimpse of their favorite teams on one of the many big-screen TVs lining the walls. But we do have a university here with a solid sports program that offers year-round sports excitement.

The University of Nevada, Reno's Division I football team has captured the Big West crown five times in the last six years and its up-and-coming volleyball squad is garnering a reputation as a topnotch Division I program.

The Reno/Tahoe area is also home to two unique sporting events that you can't see in other parts of the country —the annual Reno National Air Races and the Great Reno Balloon Races.

Furthermore, Reno's National Bowling Stadium is one of the largest and best in the country and is host to numerous bowling tournaments throughout the year. And there's always that favorite Western sports event, the rodeo.

Read on to see what the Reno/Tahoe area has to offer for those of you who like to be knee-deep in the sports action. We have not used our usual geographical organization in this chapter since most of the sports action happens in the Truckee Meadows — but don't let the drive from Lake Tahoe deter you from enjoying some great sports options.

Air Races

Reno National Air Races
Reno Stead Airport
4895 Texas Ave., Reno, Nev.
• **(775) 972-6663**

Bill Stead was a World War II ace, a Nevada rancher and a dreamer. In 1964, he realized his biggest dream when he convinced local businessmen to bring midwestern style air racing to the Reno/Tahoe area. Today the Reno National Air Races are the biggest in the United States, with more than 150,000 spectators watching six different classes of racing aircraft battling around pylon courses with speeds in excess of 400 m.p.h.

Every September, racers gather from all corners of the United States to participate in the fastest motor sport in the world. In addition to the on-hand, modern military aircraft, P-51 Mustangs, AT-6s, biplanes, Formula Ones, T-28s and sport-class kit aircraft swarm to the Stead Airport to race against the forces of nature, gravity and one another. This spectacle is so amazing and so unbelievable, Insiders say, that "the show needs the heavens as its stage." And every year it seems to get bigger and more electrifying. (See also our Annual Events chapter.)

Tickets for the Thursday through Sunday event range from $12 to $26 and may be purchased over the phone by calling BASS at (800) 225-2277 or at any BASS outlet. Com-

---

INSIDERS' TIP

A pair of binoculars are handy when watching the air races.

plete air race travel packages are available through Western Discovery Travel, 507 Casazza Drive, Reno, (775) 329-9933 or (800) 843-5061.

Balloon Races

The Great Reno Balloon Race
Rancho San Rafael Park
1502 Washington St., Reno, Nev.
• **(775) 826-1181**

For the past 16 years, more than 100 hot-air balloons in all shapes and sizes, including Panda bears, whiskey bottles, D-cell batteries and Burger King Whoppers, have been filling the predawn skies over Reno's San Rafael Park. The event, usually held in September, draws a crowd of more than 125,000 over its four days. This free (both admission and parking) spectacular includes two types of balloon flying competition — a Hare and Hound race and a target drop.

In the Hare and Hound race, with a purse of $15,000, one balloon launches early (the hare) and the other balloons (the hounds) try to follow the path of the first balloon. The hare lands in a safe area and plants a target. The hounds try to drop a marker closest to the center of the target from the air.

The target drop-style of race has the pilots launching their balloons from a 1-mile radius outside the park. The balloonists navigate into the park where a target has been placed on the ground and attempt to place their markers closest to the center of the target from the air. The prize is $5,000.

On Saturday and Sunday of the event, balloonists launch the Dawn Patrol, a pre-sunrise liftoff. The balloons' ascensions are usually choreographed to music and it is a spectacular sight, with the balloons lighting up the dark sky. Only a few pilots worldwide are qualified to fly a Dawn Patrol, making the feat extra-special for spectators.

During the events, spectators are welcome to walk through the park and to talk with flight crews and pilots as they fill their balloons with air. Most spectators bring picnic breakfasts, but an extensive concession area is always set up ready to cater to everyone's needs.

Baseball

UNR Baseball
William Peccole Park, Univ. of Nevada,
Reno, Reno, Nev.
• **(775) 784-6900**

The Wolf Pack's baseball schedule begins in late January and ends in May. UNR plays in the Big West Conference of the NCAA Division I and has a very loyal following. The team's attendance records have placed it in the nation's Top 30 and no wonder, since the team boasts a 185-78 (.703 winning percentage) record at home since 1998. Since 1990, 33 UNR players have been drafted by the big leagues.

Basketball

UNR Basketball
Lawlor Events Center, Univ. of Nevada,
Reno, Reno, Nev.
• **(775) 784-6068**

Lawlor Events Center, an 11,500-seat arena, is home to both the men's and women's basketball teams at UNR. Both programs are up and coming and provide the Reno/Tahoe area with its only hoops entertainment. The men's team posted a 21-10 record in 1996-97, finished second in the Big West Tournament and went on to the second round of the NIT Tournament.

The women won the Eastern Division title of the Big West in 1996-97 and boasted a 13-12 overall record. Both seasons begin in November and end in March. Lawlor Events Center will be the site of the men's and women's Big West Tournament until the 1999 season.

INSIDERS' TIP

You cannot bet on any University of Nevada sporting event or presidential election in Nevada.

Photo: Broderbund

The Great Reno Balloon Race in September is a spectacle worth the trip.

Bowling

National Bowling Stadium
300 N. Center St., Reno, Nev.
• **(775) 334-2600**

This bowling stadium is the world's largest and most advanced. Built in 1995, this block-long masterpiece has 80 championship lanes, a circular theater and a 450-foot–long video scoring system. The facility cost the Reno-Sparks Convention and Visitor's Authority about $45 million to complete.

Only professional tournaments are held in the stadium. Visitors are welcome to tour the stadium as well as watch the pros. Seating is

Mills Lane: From Boxing to the Bench to the Boob-tube

Reno/Tahoe residents know Insider Mills Lane as a "Hang-em High" district attorney and as "Maximum Mills," the district court judge. The rest of the United States recognizes him as a boxing referee of many world championship fights and as a TV court judge.

What boxing aficionado doesn't recognize his catch phase, "Let's get it on," barked in his high-pitched voice to his boxers before each bout he referees? And what TV addict wouldn't recognize his close-cropped look and feisty demeanor from his hit TV show, *Judge Mills Lane*, modeled after other TV courtroom programs, like *Judge Judy* and *The People's Court*?

Lane says he respects his TV adversaries but still thinks his show is more realistic.

"Judge Judy is tough," Lane says. "But at times she's too tough. And Mr. Koch (of *The People's Court*) lets the litigants argue too much and run the show. I run my show like a courtroom."

During his half-hour syndicated program, Lane hears cases ranging from small claims to family disputes. And he always does it with his bulldog style — chastising those who get out of control with his acerbic wit and demeanor. For example:

Judge Mills applies his trademark bulldog style and no-nonsense approach in each case that comes before him.

Defendant: "Judge Lane, I'll be honest with you."

Judge Mills Lane: "Honest? What were you before?"

Lane lays down the law every week in this no-nonsense style and the viewers love him for it. *Esquire Magazine* called him one of the "100 Best People in the World."

Lane has always been a colorful addition to the Reno/Tahoe scene, coming here in 1960 after a stint in the U.S. Marine Corps where he learned to box. Now, he's a national household name.

He is definitely an Insiders' hero who gained international fame on June 28, 1997 when he disqualified Mike Tyson for biting off a chunk of Evander Holyfield's ear in the third round of their heavyweight championship fight in Las Vegas. This one incident propelled Lane into the international spotlight. Afterward, Lane appeared on the *Tonight Show* with Jay Leno, had a multipage spread in *Sports Illustrated* and was offered his own TV program. He decided to retire from his district court judgeship and took the job as a TV courtroom judge. Reno/Tahoe hated to see him leave the bench but knew he would be a success. He didn't prove us wrong. His TV program debuted with a 93-percent approval rating.

After graduating form the University of Nevada, Reno, where he won an NCAA welterweight title, Lane trled his hand at professional boxing but retired with a 15-1 record after he realized that he would never be good enough to be a champion. He then turned to law and to refereeing. He joined the Washoe County District Attorney's office in 1971 and refereed his first championship bout the same year.

In 1982, he was elected district attorney and ran unopposed in 1986. In 1990, he won a seat on the bench as District Court Judge of Department 9 and was reelected in 1994, all the while refereeing world championship bouts like the Sugar Ray Leonard/Bruce Finch fight in 1982 and the infamous Holyfield/Tyson fight in 1997.

And as if this wasn't enough to fill his plate, Lane also wrote a book, *Let's Get It On*, in 1998. Lane's only request to his publisher was to tone down some of his colorful language in the original manuscript. "My mother's going to read this," Lane told them. But the rest of the book is pure Lane, uncensored and uncut.

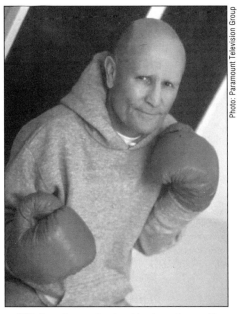

Mills Lane is a professional boxing referee with more than one hundred championship fights under his belt.

Photo: Paramount Television Group

In his memoirs, he writes about his early days on the bench in his down-home style and colorful language. And he writes about the fights he refereed. The book has done well, especially here in "Mills Country." Some readers complained because it was too personal and at times slow moving, but others liked it and raved that it was pure Mills.

"What I said was the truth," Lane says about his book. "If (some people) don't like it, that's too bad."

Lane, who is in his early 60s, still manages to wake up at 5 AM four times per week to run three miles, a habit he picked up in the Marine Corps. He prefers jeans and T-shirts to coats and ties. In fact, he still owns only one suit and two sports coats. He may be colorful and bullheaded, but don't say anything bad about him in the Reno/Tahoe area because he is one of the most respected and well-liked people here.

Photo: Broderbund

The Reno National Air Races are the biggest in the United States.

available for 1,200 spectators. Most of the tournaments charge a small admission price. Contact the stadium for dates and times of the tournaments. (See our Attractions chapter for more information.)

Football

UNR Football
Mackay Stadium, Univ. of Nevada, Reno, Reno, Nev. • (775) 784-6900

The Wolf Pack plays about six home games a season to a SRO crowd at Mackay Stadium, and with good reason — for the past six years, since UNR began playing Division I football, it has generated the most total offense yardage and passing yardage in the country. And to add just a little more excitement to its already prolific offense, for each of the past 14 years a Wolf Pack quarterback has thrown for more

than 2,000 yards. The season lasts from September to November and tickets begin at $12.

Golf

American Century Celebrity Golf Championship
Edgewood Tahoe Golf Course, 180 Lake Pkwy., Stateline, Nev. • (775) 588-3566

See more than 70 sports and entertainment stars including the likes of Michael Jordan, Charles Barkley, Dan Marino, Jerry Rice, John Elway, Oscar De La Hoya and many, many more compete for a $500,000 purse. Not only do these sports legends and movie stars provide a fun-filled week for spectators, they actually play three rounds of some intense golf.

The six-day event includes two days of practice rounds, a one-day celebrity/amateur

INISIDERS' TIP
The south end zone at all of UNR's home football games is inhabited by "The Zonies," a wild bunch of crazed football fans. Seating there is at your own risk.

tournament where Insiders get to play alongside their favorite stars, and the 72-hole tournament. The weeklong event has plenty of opportunities built in for spectators to hob-nob with the stars at one of the most beautiful golf courses in the United States (see our Golf chapter for details on the Edgewood Tahoe Golf Course). The event is usually scheduled in early July with tickets ranging from $10 to $15. Tickets and lodging information are available at (800) AT-TAHOE.

Reno/Tahoe Open
**Montreux Golf and
Country Club,
2500 Spinnaker Dr.,
Reno. Nev.**
• (775) 322-3900

The Reno/Tahoe Open is the newest tournament on the PGA Tour. At its debut on August 26-29, 1999, the Open drew the top money winners of 1998. This Tour event included practice rounds, a Pro/Am tournament, as well as a 72-hole tournament round with a $2 million purse.

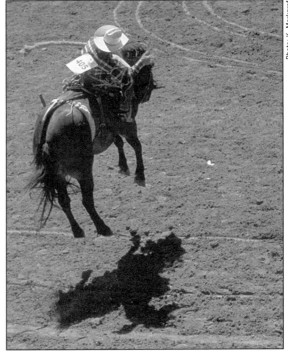

Photo: K. Markgraf

"Ride 'em cowboy" is a familiar scene at rodeo performances.

who designed the course, called it one of his top four designs. (See our Golf chapter for more information about Montreux.)

Rodeo

Photo: K. Markgraf

Here's a "chute's-eye" view of the rodeo as this cowboy gets ready for another ride.

The new event is played on one of the area's newest golf courses — Montreux. This private course is built among a Ponderosa pine forest at the foot of Mt. Rose. Jack Nicklaus,

Reno Rodeo
(775) 329-3877

This rodeo is billed as "The Wildest, Richest Rodeo in the West" and it's not hard to see why. The nine-day event has more than $41 million in prize money waiting for the top cowboys and cowgirls. The event usually kicks off on a Friday in mid-June with a party and a concert featuring a big name in country and western music. From Saturday through the next Sunday, cowboys and cowgirls compete for the million dollars in prize money by team roping, barrel racing, bareback riding, bull riding, steer wrestling, saddle bronc riding and calf roping. The event culminates at 1 PM Sun-

After a wild ride, this cowboy leaves the arena to the cheers and applause of the spectators.

day with the championship rodeo performance.

Other attractions at the rodeo include a carnival, cowboy country shops and a Western exhibit hall, and a behind-the-scenes chute tour. Ticket prices range from $8 to $15 depending on performance, day and seating. Tickets may be purchased by calling (775) 334-3799 or (800) TIC-RODEO or from several ticket centers around the Reno/Tahoe area. Write for more information to PO Box 12335, Reno NV 89510.

Snaffle Bit Futurity
Reno Livestock Events Center
1350 N. Wells Ave., Reno, Nev.
• (775) 688-5750

Though not exactly a rodeo in the classic sense, the National Reined Cow Horse Association's Snaffle Bit Futurity matches 3-year-old horses from around the world against one another in contests of steer cutting. Riders and horses are judged on how well they can cut a steer from a herd, and control the steer's movement along the fence and then into the center of the arena. Points are awarded for how well the horses respond to commands to turn and maneuver. The event is held in Reno during the last week in September and is expected to bring more than 600 horses and 2,000 riders to the area. The participants will be competing for more than $700,000 in prize money.

Soccer

Reno Zephyrs
(775) 832-2283 (in-season only)

Once northern Nevada's only professional soccer team, the Reno Rattlers were reborn in 1999 as the Reno Zephyrs. The new club moved down from the semiprofessional United States Soccer League to the amateur Premier Development League. The club's new owner says he expects between 600 and 700 people to attend when the team plays its home games on Wooster High School's football field. Although the Reno Zephyrs are an amateur club, five of the 19 games in 1999 were played against USL Division III professional clubs. Tickets are $3 each, and the club offers a 10-tickets-for-$20 deal; tickets may be used at any home game. Note that the phone number is operative only during the club's season (May through August), but you can write for information year-round to PO Box 51926, Sparks NV 89435.

Volleyball

UNR Volleyball
The Old Gym, Univ. of Nevada, Reno, Reno, Nev. • (775) 784-6154

The University of Nevada, Reno's volleyball team gained national prominence in 1998 by receiving votes as one of the top 25 teams in the nation. In 1998, under second-year coach Devin Scruggs, the team set a school record by surpassing 20 wins for the season and made it to the first round of the NCAA Championship for the first time. Their home matches are played in UNR's Old Gym and number about 15 for the season. Nevada plays in the Big West Conference which for the past few years has had the No. 1 and No. 3 teams in the United States. The action is fast-paced and the play intense. Tickets are available at the door and are reasonably priced.

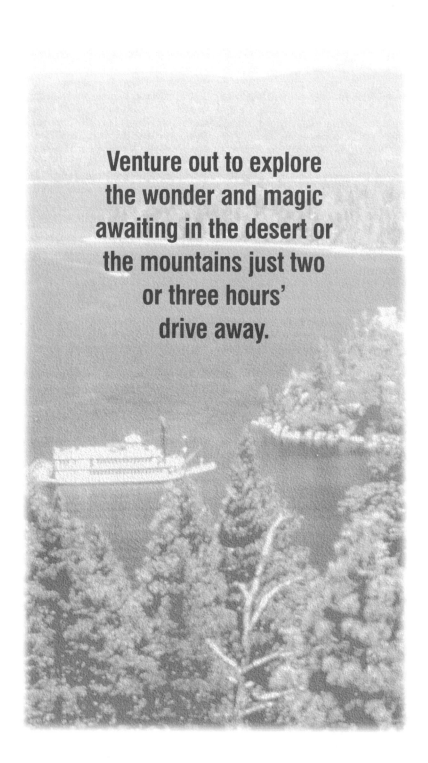

Venture out to explore
the wonder and magic
awaiting in the desert or
the mountains just two
or three hours'
drive away.

Daytrips

When you're surrounded by majestic mountains, dramatic deserts and verdant valleys, it's impossible not to wonder what's just down the road or over the next hill. Although the Reno/Tahoe area itself is certainly captivating enough for even the most discriminating visitor, when it comes to nearby daytrips, the immediate area is most assuredly not "all she wrote."

Come with us in this chapter as we venture out to explore the wonder and magic awaiting us just two or three hours' drive away. We'll drift lazily in a hot air balloon over crimson cattle knee-deep in velvety green grass in the Carson Valley. We'll sink blissfully into the same soothing hot springs once enjoyed by Clark Gable and Mark Twain at Walley's Hot Springs Resort. We'll visit the site of the most highly publicized acts of cannibalism in America in the historic town of Truckee. We'll immerse ourselves in the rowdy routine of a Victorian-era mining settlement in colorful Virginia City. And we'll drink in the primal beauty of an enormous mosaic of moving sand at Churchill County's Sand Mountain. These experiences and more are guaranteed to pique your intellectual curiosity, overwhelm your physical senses and, at the very least, keep you fully entertained for the better part of a day.

But before we head down the road, a word to the wise about the weather in this part of the world. If you're traveling into the desert during the summer months, you should be aware that temperatures during daylight hours often exceed 100 degrees. And to beat the heat once you get where you're going, you can't always count on cooling off in the shade of a tree, since some desert regions are completely devoid of large vegetation. If you're expecting to picnic or to set up a day camp, you'll need an umbrella or tarp to provide shade. To be on the safe side, carry plenty of water and be sure to drink frequently to avoid dehydration, even if you're in the car. If you're tramping around in the desert, you should wear comfortable shoes, loose clothing, a sun hat and sun block. Since temperatures can plummet 60 or more degrees in the desert when the sun goes down, it's also a good idea to have a jacket or light sweater handy if you're out there after dark.

In the winter months, the enemy is not the sun, but winter storms which can create blizzard conditions and make driving hazardous, especially in mountain areas. Insiders know the best rig for winter driving is a four-wheel-drive car, sport utility vehicle or truck. But in the absence of these, you can usually get around pretty well with chains or snow tires when conditions demand it. It's a good idea to keep some warm clothing, water, dehydrated food and other emergency supplies in the car during winter months since it's not unusual to get delayed, even on heavily trafficked roads, during winter storms. We don't want to discourage you from venturing out, but you should know that sometimes hazardous conditions do exist. The best advice we can give you is to make sure you check the weather report and fill your tank with gas before heading into the mountains or out into the desert. For updated road information in Nevada call (775) 793-1313 and in California, (530) 445-7623.

The Black Rock Desert and Gerlach, Nevada

The magnificent, barren playa called the Black Rock Desert lies about 105 miles northeast of the Truckee Meadows. Once the bed of ancient Lake Lahontan, it rested some 500 feet underwater. The desert now stretches more than 100 miles through three counties (Washoe, Pershing and Humboldt) surrounded by jagged peaks of rugged mountains. A dark rock about 400 feet tall, which served as a landmark for pioneers and rises above the paler background of the mountains, gave the desert its name. It sits almost in the middle of the stark plain.

Thousands of pioneers passed through this desert on their way to California via the Lassen–Applegate Trail, which branched off the California Emigrant Trail at Lassen Meadows in Nevada. The Lassen–Applegate Trail cut through the heart of the Black Rock Desert, followed High Rock Canyon and popped the travelers out into Northern California. This section of the trail became known as "The Death Route" for obvious reasons. John Fremont and Kit Carson (see our History chapter for a look at these trailblazers) navigated straight down the desert on their expedition through Nevada, eventually running into Pyramid Lake and the Truckee Meadows. Not much has changed in the desert, and today a trip to the gateway to this historical place, one of the 47 major deserts in the world, is well worth the drive.

The daytrip should begin in Sparks where you pick up Nev. Highway 445, called the Pyramid Highway by Insiders, and drive north (about 30 miles) until you come to an intersection where it connects with Nev. Highway 446 on the Indian Reservation at Pyramid Lake (see the daytrip to Pyramid Lake later in this chapter). Follow Nev. 446 until the intersection with Nev. Highway 447, then turn left and head north on Nev. 447 to the town of Gerlach. Between Pyramid Lake and Gerlach, you will see some of the most beautiful desert scenery in Nevada, but you will not find any place to get gas or pick up food or cold drinks except in the little town of Empire, which is about 5 miles from Gerlach, so stock up and fill up before you leave the Truckee Meadows.

The drive between Nixon and Gerlach is about 60 miles, and for 30 miles you will be traveling through the Indian Reservation. On the way, you will pass through the little town of **Empire**, noted for its garlic fields and owned by a mining company. One of the most interesting sights in Empire is the Burning Sands Golf Course. This course was built over the years by mining company employees and it winds through town and crosses several streets. It's free to play, but a donation is requested. No one takes credit for designing the course; locals just say it happened. If you're dying to play one of the most unique golf courses in the United States, the town's post office has score cards.

Gerlach, a little town of 700 people 5 miles north of Empire, is considered the gateway to the Black Rock Desert. The town originally served as a depot stop for the Western Pacific Railroad; now it provides a jumping-off point to the desert and to Northern California. While in Gerlach, stop by Bruno's Country Club (really a coffee shop) for lunch or dinner, (775) 557-2220. The house specialty is the overstuffed ravioli, which are renowned all over Northern Nevada, or take a leisurely soak in the local hot springs (about $4 per person) discovered by John C. Fremont and his group.

Also, if pottery interests you, visit John and Rachel Bogard's Planet X. This is a solar-powered pottery studio outside of Gerlach. The Bogards produce some of the West's best pottery vases, pots and dishes. Take Nev. 447 north, the left fork, out of Gerlach for about 8 miles or ask directions in Gerlach after you stuff yourself with ravioli.

We must give you a word of warning here about the Black Rock Desert. If you get the urge to take a drive out into the desert, don't. It is an extremely hazardous place unless you know what you are doing and where you are going, have the correct mode of transportation and the right gear, or ride with an Insider

---

www.insiders.com

See this and many other **Insiders' Guide®** destinations online.

Visit us today!

INSIDERS' TIP:

Churchill County Telephone Company in Fallon is the only publicly owned telephone company in the country.

who does. (See our Close-up in this chapter on Desert Safety Tips). So please heed our warning here.

Besides its obvious historical and natural wonders, the Black Rock Desert has several other claims to fame. In 1992, scientists uncovered America's largest complete skeleton of an Imperial mammoth in this desert. The skeleton is on display in the Nevada State Museum in Carson City (see the daytrip to Carson City later in this chapter).

On October 15, 1997, Royal Air Force fighter pilot Andy Green made the record books as the first person to drive a car past the speed of sound. He did it in the *Thrust SSC* on the Black Rock Desert; his speed: 763 m.p.h.

But recently, the Black Rock Desert's No. 1 attraction has been the free-spirited romp called The Burning Man. Some people call it naked fun in the sun. Others call it an abomination. Whatever it may be, the event draws more than 20,000 participants who flock to the desert for this weeklong party over the Labor Day weekend and momentarily convert the barren place into a small town dubbed Black Rock City. (See our Close-up on The Burning Man in the Annual Events chapter).

Whatever your motivation, the Black Rock Desert and Gerlach make a magnificent daytrip. Buck Wheeler described it best in his book *The Black Rock Desert* when he wrote: "It is a land of mystery where ancient man left evidence of his visits thousands of years ago. It is a place of history where Indian warriors fought for their way of life and where legends of the Old West were born."

For a faster return trip to the Truckee Meadows, once you leave Gerlach, heading south on Nev. 447, take the highway all the way to Wadsworth and pick up Interstate 80 west and follow the signs to Reno/Sparks. The total trip length is about 210 miles. For more information on the desert, contact the Bureau of Land Management, (775) 623-1500.

Carson City, Nevada

A daytrip to Carson City, Nevada's state capital, should have history buffs tingling with anticipation: visiting Nevada's historic capital is like sliding back in time. The city sits just 30 minutes down U.S. Highway 395 from Reno and 14 miles over the mountain from Lake Tahoe via U.S. Highway 50 and is teeming with historic buildings, museums, Victorian-style mansions and even a landmark brewery.

Settled as a trading post in 1851 on Indian land, Carson City came to life after silver was discovered on the Comstock. This quaint city became the capital of the Nevada Territory in 1861 and remained the state capital when Nevada entered the Union in 1864. Most people think the city was named for legendary frontiersman Kit Carson, who accompanied John Fremont on his expedition through Nevada (see our History chapter), and in a round-about way, they're right. The city was actually named after the Carson River, which Fremont named in honor of his good friend and scout — so indirectly, the town is a tribute to Kit Carson.

Carson City gained fame around the United States as a town built by the silver barons who owned the Comstock mines. Among their many accomplishments, these men managed to build the Virginia & Truckee Railroad, one of the most productive small railroads in the United States, to supply their mines with goods from Carson City. These entrepreneurs also had mills constructed along the Carson River to process the silver ore, and they convinced the Federal government to erect a U.S. Mint in Carson City to pound out silver coins right in their own backyards. They also erected some of the most magnificent mansions west of the Mississippi, and this residential area west of the State Capitol on N. Carson Street is one of the largest historical districts in the state and one of the best self-guided tours in Nevada.

If you visit Carson City, whether you are a history buff or not, you must explore this resi-

Historical districts, like this one in Virginia City, are a great way for anyone coming to the Reno/Tahoe area to relive the wild, wild West.

dential district. The best way to do that is to walk the blue-lined **Kit Carson Trail**. The trail, with blue lines painted on the sidewalks to point the way, is really a 2.5 mile walking tour of Carson City which encompasses some 60 points of interest. Maps for this tour are available at the **Visitors Center**, (775) 687-7410, at 1900 S. Carson Street, which is open from 8 AM to 5 PM. This is usually an unguided tour, but on summer Saturdays at 10 AM, volunteers lead visitors around the neighborhood. These guided tours start from the **Nevada State Museum**, formerly the U.S. Mint, at 600 N. Carson Street, (775) 687-4810, which is open year-round from 8:30 AM to 4:30 PM and features a look at Nevada's silver-rich history. Considered by some visitors and historians to be one of the best museums in the West, the Nevada State Museum houses a full-scale model of a silver mine and a reconstructed ghost town along with numerous other displays. A visit here costs $3.

On the blue-line trail, you will also find 24 talking homes that broadcast their histories on special radio frequencies. Their locations are listed in a booklet with a map for two self-guided tours. This booklet can be picked up at the Visitors Center. Included on the tour is the **Krebs-Peterson House**, the home featured in John Wayne's last movie, *The Shootist*. For more information on this walking tour, telephone (800) NEVADA-1.

Other points of interest to while away the day in this charming city include the **State Capitol** at 101 N. Carson Street. It's the second oldest capitol building west of the Mississippi and its Alaskan marble and polished wood hallways are magnificent. **The Governor's Mansion** at 606 N. Mountain Street is another must-stop on the tour. This colonial home was built in 1908 and is still used by Nevada's top government official.

Another must-see exhibit is the **Carson Nugget Casino's gold display**. Located at 507 N. Carson Street, this collection is valued at $1 million and contains examples of raw

INSIDERS TIP

When playing keno in a casino, ask for a free drink coupon.

gold in leaf, ribbon, wire, thread and crystallized forms — just as they were taken from the ground.

For train aficionados, Carson City has a wonderful railroad museum located south of town on U.S. 395. The **Nevada State Railroad Museum**, (775) 687-6953, is home to tons of railroad equipment mostly acquired from the Virginia & Truckee Railroad, one of the most famous short lines in the United States. Volunteers offer guided tours of the various pieces of equipment, including steam engines, coaches and freight cars. Don't forget to ask them for a look at the storage warehouse in back, where you'll find more equipment waiting to be refurbished. The hours of this museum are Wednesday through Saturday from 8:30 AM to 4:30 PM. The admission is $2 for adults. Admission is free for children 18 years old and younger.

Other points of interest, depending on your tastes, include: the **Stewart Indian Museum** at 5366 Snyder Avenue, (775) 882-1808, the site of the former Stewart Indian Boarding School closed in 1980 by the Bureau of Indian Affairs; the **Brewery Arts Center** at 449 W. King Street, (775) 883-1976, an old brewery that features art exhibits and concerts and offers arts and craft classes; and the **Roberts House** at 1207 Carson Street, the oldest Victorian home in Carson City with tours offered May through October — telephone (775) 882-4133 for information.

Of course Carson City's main drag is also crammed with several restaurants, bars, markets and shopping centers, as well as the state's Supreme Court and Legislature buildings. Ask for a Calendar of Events at the Visitors Center and if you can, visit during some of the more popular events, like the old-fashioned Nevada Day Parade on October 31 or the Fourth of July picnic and fireworks display. Allow at least a full day to explore this historic city and enjoy at least a leisurely lunch

or dinner from one of the many excellent restaurants around town. We suggest you try one of the following: Heiss Steak and Seafood, 107 E. Telegraph Street, (775) 882-9012; Adele's in Carson City, at 1112 N. Carson Street, (775) 333-6503; or The Buffalo Club, 2729 N. Carson Street, (775) 883-8488.

Carson Valley, Nevada

Tucked between the Sierra Nevada mountains to the west and the Pine Nut Mountains to the east, the Carson Valley spreads out like a giant carpet of fertile farms and rich ranchlands surrounding the small towns of Genoa, Minden and Gardnerville. In spring and summer it's verdant green with fields of thick alfalfa bisected by the meandering Carson River. In fall it's a profusion of color as poplars and aspens dress in their vivid autumn hues. And in winter it's a vintage Christmas card scene, with snow sometimes reaching from the nearby jagged peaks down to the valley floor.

You can get to the valley from Reno by taking U.S. 395 south to about 14 miles south of Carson City. (See our previous description of Carson City.) We recommend starting your tour of the valley in **Genoa**, so turn right onto Jacks Valley Road just after you enter the valley on U.S. 395.

From Lake Tahoe you can take Nev. Highway 207 (Kingsbury Grade) east from Stateline to where it intersects with Foothill Road just south of Genoa. Nev. 207 was part of the historic Pony Express and Overland Stage routes during pioneer days. Turn left and go north on Foothill Road. You'll reach **Walley's Hot Springs Resort** just before getting to Genoa.

Built as an elegant spa in 1862, Walley's has been a welcome retreat for the rich and famous for many years. (Coming from Reno, you can visit Walley's Hot Springs resort after touring downtown Genoa.) Historic personalities such as Clark Gable, Mark Twain and Ida

Lupino have soothed their souls and bodies in these hot mineral baths. Renovated periodically to keep up with the times, today the resort is a sparkling oasis with a swimming pool, fitness center and tennis facility in addition to the mineral spas. There's also a coffee bar where you can buy snacks and beverages plus historic cottages that can be rented overnight. The resort is open daily from 7 AM to 10 PM and you can bask in its pleasures all day for just $12. Children younger than 12 are welcome only on Sundays. The optimum time to sink into Walley's might be after an invigorating day of sightseeing, golfing or skiing in the Carson Valley and its nearby mountains. For more information on Walley's call (775) 782-8155.

Settled by Mormons in 1851 as a trading station for early pioneers, Genoa is the oldest town in Nevada. Known first as Mormon Station, it was later renamed Genoa for the Italian birthplace of Christopher Columbus. If you like history, you'll love Genoa since this tiny town still has the look and feel of early frontier days. The best way to experience it is to park your car and just wander through the many well-preserved historic buildings.

For an introduction to the area, stop at the **Genoa Courthouse Museum** on Main Street where eclectic exhibits showcase every facet of pioneer life. The museum is open daily May to October from 10 AM to 4:30 PM. For details call (775) 782-4325. Just across the road you can visit another museum at **Mormon Station State Park** and also view a replica of an early stockade used by pioneers to enclose their livestock. This museum is open daily from May to September from 9 AM to 5 PM. For details call (775) 782-2590.

Continuing down Main Street, you can quench your thirst at the same saloon frequented by early settlers, the **Genoa Bar**, well known as Nevada's Oldest Thirst Parlor. Other historic buildings along the street include the **Masonic Hall**, built in 1862; the **Genoa Country Store**, dating from 1879; and the **Genoa Town Hall**, dedicated in 1886.

The most famous event in Genoa is the annual **Candy Dance**, held the last full weekend of September. Started in 1919 to raise funds for downtown streetlights, the fair is so successful today that it raises enough money to pay for all the town's basic services. It's a candy lover's dream since local residents sell about 3,000 pounds of their prized homemade fudge, divinity, almond roca and turtles to eager buyers every year. About 30,000 people pack the town during this two-day event to enjoy the dinner dance, arts and crafts show and musical events that are also included. If you'd like to try the prizewinning recipes yourself, you can buy a copy of the Genoa Candy Book at the fair or send a check for $15.50 to PO Box 14, Genoa NV 89411.

From Genoa you can continue your tour of the Carson Valley by heading east on Genoa Lane to U.S. 395 where a right turn heading south will bring you to **Minden**. When the Virginia & Truckee Railroad extended its service to the Carson Valley in 1905, the town of Minden was founded around the train depot. Named for the Prussian birthplace of early pioneer Henry Fredrick Dangberg, Minden is an orderly little town of quiet streets and historic brick buildings. As you enter town you pass the Carson Valley Inn, a full-service casino where you can enjoy fine dining and Nevada-style entertainment 24 hours a day. Further down the street you can see the old **Minden Creamery** buildings, now the site of Bently Nevada Corporation, an international producer of vibration monitoring equipment. Past the creamery on Esmeralda Street is the **C.O.D. Garage**, the oldest continually operating car dealership in the state, founded in 1910 to sell Model Ts. Further north on this street you can see **Minden Park** and the **courthouse**.

Back on U.S. 395 continue south to **Gardnerville**, which blends almost unnoticed into Minden. While Minden's roots are traced to the railroad, Gardnerville's beginnings are linked with agriculture. Founded in the 1860s as a convenient settlement for valley farmers, Gardnerville has also been the center of ranching since Basque sheepherders from the Pyrenees mountains of Europe arrived in the area in the 1890s. To get a taste of valley history and a sample of its art, stop off at the **Carson Valley Museum and Cultural Center** which is right on U.S. 395 as you go through town. Located in the old renovated high school which dates from 1915, the museum is open daily from 10 AM to 5 PM. For more information call (775) 782-2555.

For a different approach to area memorabilia, drop into **Sharkey's Nugget**, also on U.S. 395. Although at first glance you might think it's just another small-town Nevada casino, don't be fooled: it's a chunk of local color not to be missed. A time-honored hangout for locals from all walks of life, Sharkey's is chock full of unusual collectibles and antiques since it functions as the personal museum of its colorful owner, Sharkey Begovich.

If you continue on U.S. 395 south of Gardnerville for about 5 miles, you can visit the **Lahontan National Fish Hatchery**, which raises Lahontan cutthroat trout for stocking Pyramid Lake. Visiting hours are from 7:30 AM to 3 PM and you can call (775) 265-2425 for more information.

About 13 more miles down the road you come to lovely **Topaz Lake**. Like Lake Tahoe, it's ringed by mountains and bisected by the California–Nevada state line. But unlike Tahoe, it's an artificial lake created by storage from the West Walker River. Although Topaz is much smaller and less dramatic than Tahoe, its appeal lies in its natural beauty, relatively uncluttered by homes and businesses. It's a pleasant place to fish, swim and go boating away from the crowds found at more populated lakes. For picnicking and camping, try **Topaz Lake Park**, which has a mile of beach front with 140 campsites and picnic spots. To reach the park, look for its sign on U.S. 395 and follow the road about a mile down to the park on the lake. For information call (775) 266-3343. **Topaz Lake Lodge and RV Park** on the north end of the lake also has camping facilities plus lodge accommodations, a 24-hour casino and a restaurant with a beautiful view of the lake. For details call (775) 266-3338.

While visiting the Carson Valley, you may want to try a round of golf at the Carson Valley Golf Course just off U.S. 395 in Gardnerville, (775) 265-3181, or at the Sierra Nevada Golf Ranch just north of Genoa on Jacks Valley Road, (775) 782-7700. With the Carson River carving a picturesque ribbon through their fairways, both courses are extremely scenic as well as challenging. For details see our Golf chapter.

If you want a bird's-eye perspective of the valley, nothing beats the 360-degree panorama displayed from a hot air balloon. You can contact Dream Weavers Hot Air Balloon Company at (775) 265-1271 for reservations. And for a faster paced all-around view, Soar Minden at (775) 782-7627 will give you a breathtaking, memorable vista from a glider soaring high above the valley floor. (See our Recreation chapter for more information on those activities.)

When it's time to eat, Insiders know nothing beats the legendary prime rib dinners at Sharkey's Nugget. If you want to sample Basque cuisine, try the Overland Hotel at 691 Main Street in Minden, (775) 782-2138; J&T Bar and Restaurant just down the street at 760 S. Main Street, (775) 782 2074; or the restaurant at the Carson Valley Golf Course, 2 miles south of Gardnerville on U.S. 395, (775) 265-3181. For steaks and seafood, Fiona's next to the Carson Valley Inn in Minden, (775) 782-4347, is a good choice. At Topaz Lake the Lakeview Restaurant in the Topaz Lake Lodge and RV Park has reasonable prices plus a great view of the water. Weather permitting, you might want to picnic at Topaz Lake or Mormon Station State Park.

For more information about the Carson Valley, you can stop by the Carson Valley Chamber of Commerce and Visitors Authority at 1512 U.S. 395, Suite 1 in Gardnerville or call them at (800) 727-7677.

Fallon, Nevada

If you spend any time at all in the Reno/Tahoe area, you're sure to hear about "the other side of Nevada." An expression coined by the Nevada Commission on Tourism some years ago to increase overall knowledge about the state, "the other side" encompasses almost everything not directly related to gaming. Most visitors know you can drink, gamble and enjoy live entertainment 24 hours a day in Nevada, but few are acquainted with the state's colorful wild West history, the laid-back lifestyle in its rural ranch communities or the breathtaking beauty of its unspoiled landscape. If you're curious about what real Nevada is like — outside the bright lights of the casinos — head east from Reno on I-80 out to Fallon, the seat of Churchill County, just an hour's drive away.

Desert Safety Tips

More than 85 percent of the land in Nevada is owned by the federal government and most of it's undeveloped desert, spotted with sagebrush and controlled by the BLM (Bureau of Land Management). Whether it be a driving trip to the Black Rock Desert, a hunting trip to northern Washoe County or a daytrip to one of the many ghost towns scattered around Nevada, Insiders are experienced in living and playing in this harsh desert environment. But over the years, many newcomers and visitors have unwisely ventured off into this no-man's land and have paid a heavy toll for it.

So we'd like to offer some desert safety tips here, should you happen to find yourself off the beaten path in God's country. The best overall advice we can give at this point is don't drive off into the desert alone.

Take heed of what Sessions S. (Buck) Wheeler has to say about desert safety. Wheeler, a well-known Nevada author and expert on the Black Rock Desert, cautions that first-timers to Nevada's deserts should be aware of several things before venturing out into the sand and sagebrush.

A first-time trip should always be made with an Insider who knows the desert and its pitfalls. He suggests traveling in a caravan of two or more vehicles, all equipped with four-wheel drive. Roads should not be used, especially in the winter and early spring, without reliable information about their condition.

Also note that many people have misplaced their cars after returning from a hiking expedition. As funny as it sounds, it's easy to miss an automobile parked in the desert, especially if the car is light in color and blends in with the pale terrain. Wheeler suggests tying a bright-colored piece of cloth around the vehicle's antenna to make it more easily visible.

Photo: Roger Brotherton

The Virginia Truckee Railroad is one of the many ways our ancestors used to traverse the desert.

Wear sunscreen, a hat and light-colored clothing with long sleeves and long pants. Always carry lots of water with you. And take along the following equipment for any trek into the desert:

- extra engine oil
- plenty of drinking water
- water for the radiator
- a jack
- several wooden blocks
- a set of tools
- a shovel

Wheeler also cautions those venturing into the desert to beware of the flash flooding that can result from the thunderstorms that occasionally build up quickly over the desert floor. These storms are visual and auditory masterpieces with claps of thunder heralding their approach, sheets of solid rain marching across the desert playas kicking up dust, and bolts of lightning shooting from their swollen black clouds.

But within minutes after these storms pass, that solid desert floor becomes a quagmire and that dry creek bed where you parked your car becomes a raging torrent of water. So don't park in a dry creek bed for precisely this reason. And if you can't get back to your car before the storm hits, stay put on high ground away from any large shrubs or trees until it passes. Then hope your car isn't two miles downstream or up to its axles in mud.

To avoid all this unpleasantness, at the first sign of rain clouds, hightail it out of the desert and head for that asphalted highway you left.

Now you know the basics.

As you leave Reno, you follow the Truckee River as it meanders through the scenic Truckee River Canyon, through ranches and farms, and eventually to the small town of Fernley. Follow the signs to Fallon and exit at Exit 48 to connect with Alternate U.S. Highway 50, heading east again. For an affordable game of golf along the way, you can stop at Desert Lakes Golf Club several miles down the road. Winding through the sand and sagebrush, the emerald green fairways are almost startling to the eye, like an artist's brilliant brush strokes splashed on an enormous beige canvas. The course is open year-round and green fees are $25 to $35 for 18 holes, including cart. For tee times, call (775) 575-4653. (You can also read our Golf chapter for more information about the course.)

From here you continue down Alt. U.S. 50 to Leeteville Junction where the road joins U.S. Highway 50 about 8 miles from Fallon. The junction was also known as Ragtown by early pioneers because they dumped their nonessential household items here to lighten their loads before heading over the Sierra Nevada mountains to the west. From Leeteville you travel on the highway dubbed by *Life* magazine as "**The Loneliest Road in America**," or U.S. 50 as it crosses the state of Nevada. But far from being just a lonely road, you'll discover this ribbon of road bisects a fascinating land of awesome scenery and intriguing history.

With the pinkish Stillwater Mountains as a backdrop, you pass through lush fields of alfalfa as you approach Fallon, which you can see is so aptly named "The Oasis of Nevada." Although the citizens of Churchill County voted to legalize prostitution back in the 1970s, the overused term "family values" is what makes the world go round in this rural farming town. Spectator sports are Little League baseball or Greenwave high school football and the social events of the year are fundraisers for the Churchill Arts Council or the Ducks Unlimited waterfowl habitats in the Pacific Flyway. Small businesses are still passed down from parent to child and local politicians know everyone by their first names. Boring and mundane? Not at all: Churchill County is an interesting

Photo: Plumas County Musuem

Look closely and you'll see that the supposedly barren high desert is actually teeming with life.

mixture of past and present, where supersonic Navy jets zoom over remnants of the Pony Express route and a state-of-the-art electronic warfare range shares the desert with ancient petroglyphs.

As an introduction to the rich history of the area, a must stop is the **Churchill County Museum** at 1050 S. Maine Street. Bursting with artfully designed exhibits and displays, this free facility immerses you in the heritage of the area from the prehistoric to the pioneer days. It's open daily all year except Thursday during the winter. For specific hours call (775) 423-3677. At the museum be sure to look for information about **Hidden Cave**, an archaeological dig east of town, where ancient civilizations lived more than 8,000 years ago. Although you can find the cave on your own by continuing east on U.S. 50 for about 10 miles, the best way to see it is with a group from the museum. Guided tours leave the museum the second and fourth Saturdays of the month at 9:30 AM. Close to the cave is **Grimes Point** where you can stroll along the mile-long path amongst petroglyphs considered to be thousands of years old.

About 15 miles farther down the road is **Sand Mountain**, a 600-foot high sand dune more than 2 miles long. Formed by windblown sand from an ancient prehistoric sea, the mountain booms and moans as the ever-present wind continues to move the fine particles. If you want to enjoy this geological phenomenon in quiet solitude it's best to visit during the week, since it becomes a lively playground for dune buggies and sand skiers on weekends and holidays. The trek to the top can be treacherous, especially in the summer, since the surface is hot and the deep sand makes the going very difficult. At the base of the mountain you can learn about the geology and history of the area by walking the short trail through the **Sand Springs Desert Study Area**. And at the nearby **Sand Springs Station** you can visit a well-preserved Pony Express station that formed part of the legendary route that passed through the area in 1860.

Other sights around Fallon include the **Stillwater National Wildlife Refuge**, the nesting ground of about 80,000 swans, ducks, ibises and other species of birds. To view this relatively unspoiled natural habitat, follow U.S. 50 east of town for several miles and turn left onto Stillwater Road. Past the tiny hamlet of Stillwater you'll hit a gravel road, and after taking a right onto Nutgrass Road you'll see a large serene marsh stretching toward the Stillwater Mountains. Be sure to take insect repellent since it's a rich breeding ground for bugs as well as birds. For more information on the refuge you can call (775) 423-5128.

In the opposite direction out of Fallon, you can visit the **Lahontan State Recreation Area**, a popular playground for camping, fishing, boating and water skiing. **Lahontan Reservoir** is a 23-mile long lake completed in 1915 as part of the Newlands Irrigation Project. Water from the Truckee and Carson rivers is held in the lake behind Lahontan Dam and then used to flood irrigate the fields of alfalfa, corn, sugar beets and Heart O' Gold cantaloupes around Fallon. To reach Lahontan go west on U.S. 50 from Fallon for about 16 miles.

With more than 300 days of clear flying weather a year, the U.S. Navy can't find a more ideal training ground for its pilots than **Naval Air Station (NAS) Fallon**. Home of the Naval Strike and Air Warfare Center (NSAWC) with its prestigious TOPGUN division (remember the movie *Top Gun* with Tom Cruise?), NAS Fallon is the only naval facility that can train an entire carrier air wing in the strike tactics used in combat. The F-18 Hornets and F-14 Tomcats scream off the Navy's longest runway (14,000 feet) and engage in mock dogfights and electronic warfare over the training area east of the Stillwater Mountains. If you want an up-close and personal view of these supersonic flying machines, you can watch them land and take off through a security fence at the base. To get to the base, take U.S. Highway 95 south for about 5 miles until you see the sign for the facility at Union Lane. Follow Union Lane to Pasture Road where a left turn will give you a view of the runway. The Navy opens its gates to thousands of visitors each spring during the Fallon Air Show when you can see free flying demonstrations and static displays of aircraft (see our Annual Events chapter for details).

Aside from the naval air show, Fallon plays host to a large variety of special events and ongoing entertainment throughout the year. You can see professional and amateur race car drivers speed around the track at the new state-of-the-art Top Gun Motor Sports Complex about 15 miles south of town on U.S. 95. See our Recreation chapter for more information or call (775) 423-0223 for race times and dates. You can watch barrel racers and bull riders from all over the country compete in wild West action at the Silver State International Rodeo. You can enjoy the sweet, juicy taste of local Heart O' Gold cantaloupes at the Heart O' Gold Cantaloupe Festival. You can experience local Native American culture at the All-Indian Stampede & Pioneer Days. And for a taste of the arts and music, you can choose from a large variety of events sponsored by the Churchill Arts Council all during the year. For details call (775) 423-1440. The Fallon Convention/Visitors Center at 100 Campus Way (just off U.S. 50 as you enter town from the west) is a good source of information about events in Churchill County. You can call them at (775) 423-4556.

If all this activity gives you an appetite, you don't need to leave town on an empty stomach. For good food at reasonable prices try the Nugget at 70 S. Maine Street in downtown or the Bonanza Inn, Stockman's Casino or the Depot Diner on the Reno Highway (U.S. 50) on the west side of town.

Ghost Towns, Nevada

Old-timers here will tell you that 10 ghost towns exist for every living town in Nevada. Most of the ruins are difficult to find, however, because they remain hidden in the hills and tucked away in the gullies overgrown with sagebrush and tumbleweed. Their only inhabitants now are desert creatures and the memories of past glory days. But they're out there, ready for those who wish to explore them. Rummaging through these ruins is more exciting than reading about them in a dusty, old

INSIDERS' TIP:

The first legal prize fight in the United States was held in Carson City.

Downtown Graeagle overflows with historic wild, wild Western charm.

Photo: Kathryn Glaeser/Eastern Plumas County Visitors Bureau

history book and they make for a worthwhile daytrip if you wish to step way off the beaten path of the Reno/Tahoe area.

Most of these towns sprang up during Nevada's two great mining periods before World War I and most lasted only as long as the silver and gold in their mines. These towns are sprinkled all over the state, but our suggestion is to explore the ghost towns nestled near the foot of the Shoshone Mountain Range in the Toiyabe National Forest just east of **Gabbs**, Nevada, a 2½-hour drive from Reno. To get to Gabbs from Reno, take I-80 east to the east Fernley exit. Pick up Alt. U.S. 50 to Fallon. After Fallon, follow U.S. 50, The Loneliest Road in America, to Middlegate, about 47 miles. Turn right on Nev. Highway 361 to Gabbs. Most of the ghost towns suggested here are located off Nev. Highway 844, 2 miles north of Gabbs.

The ghost town of **Ione** sits 24 miles east of Gabbs at the end of State Route (SR) 91. This town prospered in 1863 after the discovery of a vein of silver. Ione became the seat of Nye County in 1864, but by 1880 only a few hard-core prospectors remained. Several col-

lapsed and dilapidated buildings can be found at the site.

Ellsworth rests about 10 miles west of Ione via an unmarked graded road (the only one there). In 1871, at its peak, this town pumped out silver from its mines and boasted about 200 citizens and several businesses and homes made from rocks. Some rock walls and a cemetery remain.

Berlin, perhaps the most renowned ghost town in Nevada, owes much of its fame to dinosaurs and the Ichthyosaur State Park. This park is home to significant fossil finds of gigantic Ichthyosaurs, marine reptiles that inhabited the state more than 200 million years ago. The word Ichthyosaur means "lizard fish," but these dinosaurs are more closely related to the modern-day whale. The tumbled-down mining town sits close to the park and was abandoned about 100 years ago. Several buildings still stand in what preservationists call "arrested decay." In other words, the buildings aren't restored but they are not allowed to decay any further, either. Berlin and the state park are located 19 miles east of Gabbs, about 2 miles south of SR 91.

About 1¼ miles southeast of Berlin is **Union**. This town sprang up in 1863 about the same time as Ione. Several stone buildings remain in Union. In **Grantsville** (located about 5 miles southeast of SR 91, 18 miles east of Gabbs), which also came into being in 1863, you can see a few building foundations, as well as a small cemetery. But Grantsville's magnificent setting in the mountains and its incredible view are its high points.

On the way back to Reno, stop by **Quartz Mountain**, about 13 miles north of Gabbs just off Nev. 361. This town sprang up in 1920 and withered by 1926. The remains of several wooden buildings still lie scattered about.

We suggest a picnic lunch for this daytrip. Be aware that after Fallon, gas stations and restaurants are scarce, so it's a good idea to fill up your gas tank and cooler before you leave Fallon.

If you wish to learn more about Nevada ghost towns, find a copy of *Nevada Ghost Towns* by Lambert Florin or *Nevada Ghost Towns and Mining Camps* by Stanley W. Paher.

Graeagle, California

If you already live in a mountain paradise, where do you go to "get away from it all?" Insiders escape to the tiny hamlet of Graeagle (pronounced "gray eagle"), the ultimate getaway, tucked deep in the towering pines of the Plumas National Forest about 60 miles northwest of Reno. Named for Gray Eagle Creek that runs nearby, this quaint little community began as a lumber town in 1916. The historic red and white frame buildings that line the main drag were brought in by rail and used as housing for workers in the mill. Today these structures are retail establishments that form the picturesque core of the downtown area. After the mill shut down in 1956, Graeagle was purchased in 1958 for $450,000 by a developer who saw its potential as a planned vacation community. Since then it has thrived primarily as a summer/fall retreat for hikers, golf-

ers and anglers. But in spite of modern development, it retains its historic charm. Quiet and peaceful, Graeagle is worlds apart from the hustle and bustle of many resort communities. And best of all, it's smack in the middle of some of the most gorgeous mountain scenery you'll find anywhere else on the planet.

To get to Graeagle from Reno, take U.S. 395 north about 24 miles to Hallelujah Junction and then take Calif. Highway 70 west to Blairsden; finally, turn south on Calif. Highway 89. About 8 miles from Graeagle you'll go through the lumber town of **Portola** where you can climb on train cars and locomotives at the **Portola Railroad Museum**. Just follow the white and blue tracks painted on the road in downtown that lead you to the museum or look for it at 700 Western Pacific Way. It's open daily March to November from 10 AM to 5 PM. For details call (530) 832-4131.

Coming from Lake Tahoe to Graeagle, take Calif. Highway 267 north from Kings Beach or Calif. 89 north from Tahoe City to Truckee and then continue north on Calif. 89 for about 50 miles. This route takes you through some of the loveliest, most unspoiled forest in the Reno/Tahoe area.

With six golf courses in the area, Graeagle has been called the "Pebble Beach of the Sierra." But even if your game isn't up to par, you can't go wrong on any of these layouts since just enjoying the magnificent scenery can make your round worthwhile. About 5 miles south of Graeagle on Calif. 89 you can test your skills at Whitehawk Ranch; call (530) 836-0394 for tee times. About 7 miles east of Graeagle on Highway A-15 you can play Gold Mountain, the newest course in the area. Call (530) 832-0883 for details. Other championship 18-hole courses include Graeagle Meadows, which is right downtown off Calif. 89, (530) 836-2323, and Plumas Pines Golf Resort, at 402 Poplar Valley Road in Blairsden, (530) 836-1420. The Feather River Park Resort on Calif. 89, (530) 836-2328, and the Feather River Inn on Calif. 70 in Blairsden,

---

INSIDERS' TIP:

Virginia City was the first city in Nevada to have a gas plant and gas lights in 1862.

(530) 836-2623, both offer challenging rounds on beautiful 9-hole layouts. For a more detailed description of these courses, see our Golf chapter.

Bisected by the pristine Middle Fork of the Feather River and dotted with a multitude of crystal clear alpine lakes, the mountainous terrain around Graeagle is a hiker's dream come true. With literally hundreds of trails to choose from, you'll probably want to get a map by calling the **Plumas County Visitors Bureau** at (800) 326-2247 or the **Plumas National Forest** at (800) 283-2050.

Our favorite hike, which takes you to six different lakes, is the **Round Lake Loop Trail** in the Lakes Basin Recreation Area. With spectacular views and a modest elevation gain, this approximately 4-mile outing offers a fantastic diversity of scenery compressed in a relatively small geographic area. It's best done at a leisurely pace so you can enjoy the landscape as it spreads out before you. You can swim, fish and picnic along the way — just pick your favorite lake. To get to the trailhead, look for the sign directing you to the Lakes Basin Recreation area on the Gold Lake Highway just south of Graeagle and travel west for about 7 miles. Then look for the sign for Gold Lake Lodge and the Round Lake Trail at the crest of a hill and park in the lodge parking lot. The Round Lake Loop Trail begins at the end of this lot.

About ¼ mile down the trail, it forks, with the trail to the right reaching Big Bear Lake in about ½ mile and taking you counterclockwise around the loop. We recommend going in this direction since you arrive at the first lake sooner and because the overall climb is more gentle. As the trail meanders through granite boulders and stately pines, it takes you from Big Bear Lake to Little Bear, Cub, Silver, Long and Round lakes. In the shadow of rocky Mt. Elwell, the hike is verdant green with splotches of wildflower color in summer and in fall an explosion of reds, oranges and golds.

At Round Lake be sure to take a look at the abandoned gold mine at the southern end where miners hoped to strike it rich more than 100 years ago. This hike is an absolute jewel, not to be missed by anyone who enjoys the solitude and beauty of the mountains.

If you're curious what life was like for early gold seekers, you can find out at the mining museum in **Plumas Eureka State Park**. Steeped in history and surrounded by gorgeous scenery, this 2,000-acre park encompasses the old mining settlement of Johnsville just 6 miles west of Graeagle on Johnsville Road. The indoor-outdoor museum features a restored miner's home, a blacksmith shop and exhibits of early mining equipment. On **Living History Day**, once a month during the summer, costumed docents recreate the daily life of a miner searching for the big bonanza. For details call (530) 836-2380. You can also try your own luck at gold panning in nearby Jamison Creek. Crisscrossed by a myriad of trails leading to a number of lakes, Plumas Eureka State Park is also popular with hikers.

The more than 100 lakes of the **Feather River** watershed offer a large variety of fishing spots for anglers. In addition, dozens of small streams and the Middle Fork of the Feather River provide rich habitats for rainbow, brown and brook trout. For details on seasons and regulations contact the Plumas National Forest at (800) 283-2050.

For a picture-perfect ending to your day in the mountains, we suggest stopping at the Plumas Pines Golf Resort for a drink or dinner. You can sit on the deck, high above the eighteenth fairway, and watch the last golfers play in as the sun sinks golden behind the emerald green mountains. Other good dinner spots include the Grizzly Grill at 250 Banta Street in Blairsden, (530) 836-1300; Olsen's Cabin on Johnsville Road, (530) 836 2801; and the Coyote Bar & Grill at 8296 Calif. 89, (530) 836-2552 in Graeagle. Reservations are recommended. If you're driving back through

INSIDERS' TIP:

U.S. Highway 50 in Nevada was a part of the first transcontinental road called the Lincoln Highway.

Photo: Roger Brotherton

The Mackay Mansion is but one of the many attractions in Virginia City.

Portola at dinner time, we suggest stopping at the Log Cabin right on the main drag for outstanding German cuisine.

Pyramid Lake, Nevada

In 1844 explorer John C. Fremont was searching for a legendary river that supposedly emptied into the San Francisco Bay. But instead he was astonished to discover one of the most beautiful desert lakes in the world. Shimmering turquoise green against a pinkish beige desert background, the lake seemed out of place, like a magical mirage in a harsh barren environment. Fremont named this large landlocked body of water Pyramid Lake for the giant pyramid-shaped rock that juts 475 feet from the level of the lake near its southern end. (See our History chapter for more about Fremont's explorations.)

The Paiute Indians have made their home at Pyramid Lake since well before Fremont arrived in the area. Because fish from the lake was an important staple in their diet, the tribe became known as "Cui-ui Ticutta" or Cui-ui Eaters. Since 1874 the lake and its environs have been owned and managed by the tribe

as the Pyramid Lake Paiute Indian Reservation.

As a remnant of a large inland sea that used to cover most of northwestern Nevada, the lake is the terminal point for the Truckee River's 105-mile journey from Lake Tahoe. Stretching for 27 miles against the changing desert hues of the nearby mountains, the lake has a beauty and mystery unique in the world. Adding an intriguing contrast to the sparkling water and naked rocks are the odd-shaped tufa formations, which are white calcium carbonate deposits piled up all along the shoreline. Next to the signature pyramid is one of the most prominent tufas, which is aptly named, "Stone Mother and her Basket." But aside from its beauty, the history and geology of Pyramid Lake provide a fascinating lesson about the relationship between humans and their environment.

Two roads lead to Pyramid Lake from I-80: Nev. 445 from Sparks to Sutcliffe and Nev. 447 from Wadsworth (about 30 miles east of Reno) to Nixon. Nev. 446 runs between these two roads along the south shore of the lake. You can make a loop of this route going either way, but we recommend starting on Nev. 445

INSIDERS' TIP:

The first dude ranch built in Nevada (in 1929) was at Pyramid Lake.

since it's a quicker route to the lake and you will need to stop at the ranger station in Sutcliffe to buy a $5-permit for day use.

Traveling east on I-80 in Reno, exit onto Pyramid Way in Sparks, which becomes Nev. 445 as it travels north about 33 miles to the lake. About 20 miles north of Sparks, you'll pass the Wild Horse and Burro Placement Center operated by the Bureau of Land Management. The animals are captured from large herds that roam free in Nevada and are cared for and then adopted out from this facility to qualified people all over the country.

After continuing north to the lake, you can keep to the left on Nev. 445 or turn right onto Nev. 446. If you stay on Nev. 445 you'll travel past several beaches on the way to Sutcliffe before the paved road turns to gravel a few miles further on. Turning right onto Nev. 446 will take you around the southern end of the lake to the intersection with Nev. 447, which travels north to Nixon and the tribal headquarters. The Truckee River empties into the lake here. To get a better idea of the lay of the land around the lake, it's a good idea to pick up a map, preferably in Sutcliffe when you first arrive at the lake.

The waters of the lake provide a rich habitat for Lahontan cutthroat trout and the endangered cui-ui fish. The lake is one of the best trophy trout fisheries in the world, with the average keeper weighing between five and 16 pounds. The prime time to fish is between October and May when cooler surface temperatures lure the fish up from the 300-foot depths of the lake. (See also our Fishing and Hunting chapter.)

The lake also provides one of only eight nesting grounds for white pelicans in North America. Each spring rocky Anaho Island, just southwest of the pyramid, swarms with thousands of pelicans, double crested cormorants, California gulls, great blue herons and Caspian terns as they set up housekeeping and raise their young. And while the surrounding landscape may seem harsh and sterile, it's anything but, in terms of the wildlife it supports. It's not unusual to see herds of deer, antelope and bighorn sheep quietly grazing on the steep hillsides around the water.

When you visit the lake, you'll find ample opportunities to learn about the area's culture and heritage by visiting its museums and visitor centers. Just off Nev. 447 between the towns of Wadsworth and Nixon, there's the **Numana Hatchery and Visitors Center** with its wetlands nature trail; on Nev. 446 near Nixon you can visit the **Scenic Byway Visitors Center and Tribal Museum**, and in Sutcliffe, on Nev. 445, you can stop by the visitors center and museum near the **Pyramid Lake Marina**.

For a fascinating look at one of the most efficient and innovative fishery restoration programs in the country, be sure to stop in at the **Nunn Hatchery** just south of the marina in Sutcliffe. Since its establishment in 1974, the program has planted about 2.8 million cutthroat and 10 to 18 million cui-ui fish every year. Overcoming the problem of raising cold water fish in a desert lake, the hatchery program has helped guarantee the continued propagation of these species of fish. For hours and more information on these points of interest, call the Pyramid Lake Fisheries at (775) 476-0500, the Pyramid Lake Marina at (775) 476-1156 or the Pyramid Lake Paiute Tribal Offices at (775) 574-1000.

Pyramid Lake is a prime spot to enjoy everything the great outdoors has to offer without the crowds found at some other area lakes. As you drive along the shore of the lake, you can choose from a large variety of sandy beaches for swimming and picnicking. You'll need an umbrella or tarp for shade, however, since the shoreline doesn't have trees or shrubs.

On windless summer days, the tepid waters of the lake are a water skier's dream come true, silky smooth and uncrowded by large numbers of boats. For the optimum skiing experience, try it at sundown, when you can skim across the glassy surface as the sinking sun turns the water a gorgeous pink and gold underneath your skis. You can launch your own boat or rent one for the day at the Pyramid Lake Marina in Sutcliffe. But if you're out on the lake when the wind comes up, be sure to head for shore right away since dangerous whitecaps can appear almost in minutes.

Because the facilities all around the lake are pretty sparse, we don't have a list of recommended restaurants and watering holes you simply must try. The best dining experience in this natural wonderland is the picnic lunch or barbecue you bring yourself. Head down to one of the beaches and enjoy your own gourmet cuisine along with an unobstructed view of this prehistoric phenomenon.

Sacramento, California

Over the majestic and scenic Sierra Nevada mountains, Sacramento is the first "big city" you come to as you go west from the Reno/Tahoe area. Most visitors know it as the area responsible for the greatest gold rush in American history. Not many know that it was also the last stop on the Pony Express and the nation's telegraph system and the beginning of the Transcontinental Railroad. About 2 hours from Reno along I-80, California's state capital sits nestled in a valley on the banks of two of the state's biggest rivers and is often described as the "Historic Capital of the West."

John Sutter, a German-Swiss immigrant, founded the first white settlement in Sacramento in 1839 after the Mexican government granted him 50,000 acres of land. He built an outpost known as Sutter's Fort and began ranching. His ranch prospered until an employee discovered gold at Sutter's Mill in Coloma, California, east of the outpost. The find put Sacramento on the map and decimated Sutter's ranch: within the next five years, 500,000 people flooded into the Sacramento area.

The city became California's capital in 1854 and over the years grew in importance as an agricultural center; during World War II it grew as a technology center when the federal government built several defense plants and two airbases here. Today Sacramento is crammed with attractions like the state capitol building, Old Sacramento, Sutter's Fort, the Railroad Museum and the governor's mansion. It also has its share of historic buildings, art galleries, serene parks, rivers and the 23-mile-long American River Parkway.

Like the entire town of Virginia City, Nevada (see the description of the daytrip to Virginia City later in this chapter), **Old Sacramento** is designated a state historic park and national landmark. Located off Interstate 5 and bordering the Sacramento River, the old part of the city was the main riverboat landing for Sutter's Fort. Today, the 28-acre area has more than 60 buildings that have been restored to the 1850–1870 period. This section has been referred to as "The Williamsburg of the West." Of course, specialty shops, restaurants, bars and other businesses share this 19th century part of the city with the historical buildings. Don't miss the **California State Railroad Museum**, 125 I Street, (916) 445-6645, which includes the Central Pacific Depot and the "Big Four" Building. This museum houses one of the world's largest railroad locomotive and relics collections and costs about $6 to enter. While exploring this section of the city, don't forget to jump onboard one of the sightseeing boats and cruise the Sacramento River alongside Old Sacramento. Contact the **Visitors' Information Center**, Second and K streets, (916) 442-7644, for more details on the sightseeing boats.

Capitol Park sits about one mile east of Old Sacramento. This park contains more than 40,000 trees and flowers in an area stretching from L to N streets and Ninth to 15th streets. **The California State Capitol** building, (916) 324-0333, is the main attraction in this park with its golden dome providing an unforgettable landmark. Construction of this capitol building began in 1860 and lingered over a 14-year period finally being completed in 1874. The California Legislature voted to renovate the building in 1982 at the cost of $70 million and the tour of this well-preserved building is well worth the time and the small entrance fee of $2. It is open from 8 AM to 5 PM daily.

The Vietnam Veteran's Memorial, located at the east end of the park, provides a sober reminder of California's military personnel who sacrificed their lives during the war. This memorial is one of the finest examples of bronze statuary in the West and contains the names

INSIDERS' TIP:

Mark Twain began his career as a writer in Virginia City on the staff of the *Territorial Enterprise*.

of the war dead etched on granite panels arranged by home town.

The 1877 **governor's mansion** at 16th and H streets, (916) 323-3047, sits close to the park and provides another enjoyable guided tour. Tours are $2 and run daily from 10 AM to 4 PM.

Sutter's Fort, (916) 445-4422, shares its buildings with the **State Indian Museum**, (916) 324-0971, on 27th and L streets and gives visitors a look at history provided by volunteers dressed in period costumes who demonstrate examples of pioneer and Indian living and skills. Self-guided tours with audio wands of Sutter's Fort are available to explain the exhibits, which include a blacksmith shop, bakery, prison, living quarters and a livestock area. The fort is open from 10 AM to 5 PM with a $2 entrance fee. The Indian Museum displays arts and crafts made by California Indians. It's open from 10 AM to 5 PM and charges a $2 admission.

Just south of downtown on S. Land Park Drive between 13th Avenue and Sutter Road, **William Land Park** spreads out over 161 acres. The park has more than 3,000 trees of 50 different varieties but its main attraction is the **Sacramento Zoo**. This enclosure is considered to be one of the best small zoos in the country with more than 150 exhibits, 167 animal species and more than 500 animals. The park also features a children's theme park, a fishing pond, a wading pool, amusement rides and a nine-hole golf course. A family can make a day of just visiting this park and all of its amenities like picnic tables, barbecues and an amphitheater. The park also has a 2-mile jogging and walking path with sit-up and push-up stands. Free maps of the path are available from the Community Service Department, (916) 449-5200.

But if real outdoor fun is your family's wish, the 5,000-acre **American River Parkway** should be your destination when visiting Sacramento. This magnificent park winds its way about 23 miles through the center of the city from the confluence of the Sacramento and

American rivers at Discovery Park to just below Folsom Lake. It has more than 20 major recreation areas including a scenic, two-lane bike path; miles of equestrian trails; hundreds of fishing spots along the river; and several put-in spots to launch a craft for some exciting white-water rafting.

Sacramento has plenty to do and to see. The difficult task is deciding just what your game plan will be. We recommend that you spend the night in the city to break up the excursion into two leisurely days instead of a hectic one. The **Visitors' Bureau**, 1421 K Street, (916) 264-7777, publishes brochures listing many of the attractions, restaurants, accommodations, and tour information. Such a brochure is a handy guide for planning your trip.

Truckee, California

Sitting astride the original trail used by pioneers who traveled overland from Missouri to California in the 1840s, the bustling tourist town of Truckee, about 30 miles west of Reno, stands as a modern day reminder of just how formidable those trips were. After crossing hundreds of miles of blistering deserts and tortuous mountains, the final test for early emigrants came just west of Truckee, where the rugged pass through the Sierra Nevada mountains presented a formidable obstacle to the fertile valleys of California on the other side. Because heavy snow made the route impassable once winter set in, travelers had to cross before the storms arrived, and cutting it close could mean getting trapped either in between or on the eastern side of the mountains. Even today this section of I-80 is frequently closed because of blizzard conditions during winter months.

In the winter of 1846–47, the dreaded storms not only showed up early but they blew in with a vengeance, dumping record amounts of heavy snow on a group of 91 emigrants who had arrived late in October to cross the pass. These hardy pioneers had taken what

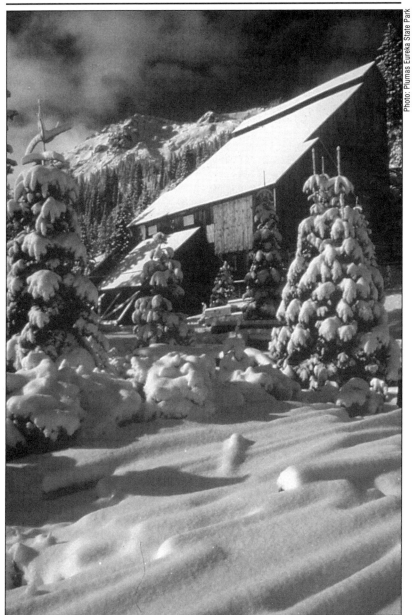

Photo: Plumas Eureka State Park

Mohawk Stamp Mill, part of Plumas Eureka State Park Museum, becomes a Christmas card picture under the heavy blanket of snow that so often covers these mountains.

they believed would be a shortcut across the Utah desert. But instead, the route took them longer, causing them to arrive at the mountain pass several weeks later than what was considered safe for crossing. Named the Donner Party for their leader, George Donner, this group of families became stranded at a small lake near present-day Truckee. As the snow piled up to more than 20 feet, their food supplies dwindled and disappeared. The 49 who survived were forced to subsist off the bodies of those who died of starvation during the long arduous winter. The lake and mountain pass were later named Donner Lake and Donner Pass for these ill-fated settlers. You can visit the site of the Donner Party's ordeal by hunger at the **Donner Memorial State Park**, on the east end of Donner Lake, just west of downtown Truckee.

To get to Truckee from Reno, follow I-80 west and exit at any of the three exits for Truckee. Coming from Lake Tahoe, you can take Calif. 267 north from Kings Beach or Calif. 89 north from Tahoe City for about 12 miles. If you're traveling on Calif. 89, you'll pass Alpine Meadows Ski Resort and Squaw Valley USA and on Calif. 267 you'll go past Northstar-at-Tahoe. For a description of activities at these resorts see our Winter Sports and Vacation Resorts chapters.

When you arrive in Truckee, Donner Memorial State Park is at the west end of town just off I-80 on Donner Pass Road. To learn more about the Donner tragedy and the area's natural history, you can visit the **Emigrant Trail Museum** in the park. The large bronze **Pioneer Monument** behind the museum depicts a typical emigrant family and honors all those who made the difficult trek to the West. On the lighter side of things, the park has several miles of hiking trails, sites for camping and picnicking and lovely beaches for swimming. It's also a popular area for cross-country skiing in the winter.

Just as it was in the 1800s, Truckee's geographical location continues to be the root of its prosperity today. Nestled along the banks of the Truckee River in the heavily wooded mountains, it profits from the many tourists who arrive on I-80 or on Amtrak. Its historic downtown is crowded with colorful shops and funky restaurants, most within easy walking distance along **Commercial Row**. You can browse the boutiques for several hours and then enjoy gourmet dining at a variety of eateries right downtown. You can sample California classic cooking with a view of the main drag at Cafe Meridian, (530) 587-0557. Or you can enjoy California cuisine in a historic setting at The Passage, (530) 587-7619. For a panoramic view of the river and the downtown area, try the Cottonwood on the edge of town on Calif. 267, (530) 587-5711. While wandering around downtown, be sure to take a look at the historic bronze eagle in front of the train station. Mounted on a granite base and with a 7-foot wing span, the **Victory Monument** commemorates U.S. Soldiers killed in World War I.

At 6,000-plus feet in elevation, the golf courses around Truckee are a great place to find out if your drive really does go farther at high altitude. You can tee it up at Tahoe Donner, with its daunting array of undulating fairways carved out of rugged mountain terrain, north of town at 12850 Northwoods Boulevard. Call (530) 587-9440 for rates and tee times. Or 6 miles south of town, just off Calif. 267, the narrow fairways and winding creek at Northstar-at-Tahoe will challenge even the best players' games. Call (530) 562-2490 for details. And for a quick 9 holes right in town, the Ponderosa Golf Course, just off Calif. 267, is an absolute delight at a reasonable price. Call (530) 587-3501 for information. See our Golf chapter for more details on area courses.

If you visit Truckee during the summer you can't miss the gliders, soaring and swooping like enormous birds high over the mountainous terrain. Hang onto your hat (and your stomach): Soar Truckee will give you the ride and the view of your life for just $95. The natural geography of the area creates thermal lifts that are absolutely ideal for soaring. Needless to say, the aerial view of Lake Tahoe and the

INSIDERS' TIP:

The Gold Hill Hotel just outside Virginia City has been operating since 1859.

surrounding Sierra Nevada mountains from one of these big birds is simply breathtaking. Rides can be booked daily May to October from 9 AM to 5 PM by calling (530) 587-6702. The airport is just several miles south of town off Calif. 267. (See our Recreation chapter for more information.)

The lakes and streams around Truckee are especially inviting to those who like to fish since they provide a challenging variety of natural conditions as well as species of fish. **Martis Creek Lake**, just south of town off Calif. 267, is a premier habitat for brown and rainbow trout. But don't bring your frying pan since it's catch-and-release only with barbless hooks. You can also try your luck in **Donner Lake**, known for its large Mackinaws, or in the **Truckee River** on either side of town.

If your idea of a mountain experience is hiking through a pristine forest to appreciate its natural beauty, the **Pacific Crest Trail** will more than satisfy this need. To get to the trailhead, go west on I-80 from Truckee about 8 miles to the rest stops at the summit where you'll see a sign directing you to the trailhead. Hiking north on the PCT for about 3 miles will take you through dense forest toward Castle Peak, where you can enjoy splendid views of Donner Lake and the surrounding mountains. Going south for several miles will also give

you marvelous views of the lake, but from a closer perspective.

For a unique view of area history from the perspective of snow skiing, the **Western SkiSport Museum** is a must stop, for both skiers and nonskiers. Take I-80 west from Truckee about 8 miles and exit on the Castle Peak Exit at Boreal Ski Resort. This one-of-a-kind history of the area's most popular sport is well worth the extra drive out of Truckee. While we think of skiing as merely a recreational activity today, it was introduced by the early gold seekers as the only way to get around in heavy winter snow. The fascinating exhibits show early, antiquated equipment, such as the 10 foot, 25-pound skis used by the legendary Showshoe Thompson when he delivered mail to snowbound settlers from 1856 to 1876. You can also see the Western Ski Hall of Fame honoring individuals who contributed to the development of the sport in the West along with numerous displays of Olympic medals, clothing and vintage pictures. The museum is free and open from 10 AM to 4 PM Wednesday through Sunday during the ski season and summer months. For more information call (530) 426-3313.

If you arrived in Reno by air and don't have a car, you can easily get to Truckee by bus or train. Greyhound has a number of departures

The past comes alive for visitors to Virginia City.

Photo: Roger Brohterton

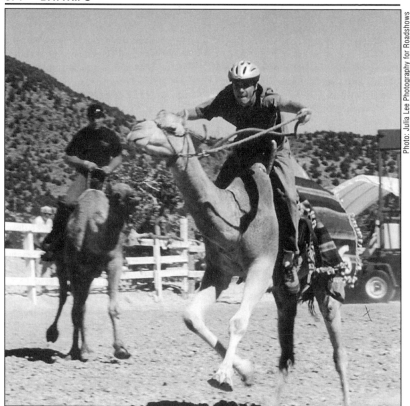

Photo: Julia Lee Photography for Roadshows

Look like fun? Camels can be unpredictable and this gives the Camel Race audience plenty to laugh about.

daily; call (800) 231-2222 for exact times. For details about Amtrak trains which will drop you right downtown at the restored railroad depot, call (800) 872-7245 (see also our Getting Here, Getting Around chapter). You can pick up a walking tour brochure and other information about Truckee at the **Visitor Center** at 12036 Donner Pass Road or call (530) 587-2757.

Virginia City, Nevada

At the height of its glory, Virginia City, the "Queen of the Comstock," was the hell-raisingest town in the United States with something happening almost every hour of the day. Touring actors put on Shakespearean plays, prostitutes plied their trade in a thriving red-light district and the town had its share of gun-fights, murders, opium dens, rival newspapers, and competing fire companies — all of this courtesy of two drunken Irish prospectors and a con man named Henry Comstock (see our History chapter). Today, most people remember it as the city that Ben, Adam, Hoss and Little Joe Cartwright visited when they needed supplies or a night on the town in the old hit TV show, *Bonanza*.

Miners squeezed out more than $300 million in silver during Virginia City's heyday which ended in 1898 with the virtual abandonment of the mines. Today, the entire city stands as a national landmark and the largest federally designated historical district in America maintained in its original condition. Boardwalks still line the streets and the shops and museums are located in original buildings dating back to the 1860s and 1870s. The city, once called the "Richest Place on Earth," offers you a great daytrip and a glimpse at the town's glorious past.

And, even though the drive to Virginia City is only 20 minutes from Reno via U. S. 395 and Nev. Highway 341 and 40 minutes from Lake Tahoe, via Nev. Highway 431 (The Mt. Rose Highway) and Nev. 341, you need to set aside the entire day to get a sufficient taste of the city that's been "Live & Kick'n Since 1859."

Virginia City offers visitors a rare peek into American history. Most of us learn about our past through books. In Virginia City, you can relive it. The city features underground tours of its mines, tours of its churches and cemeteries and a look at some of the most opulent mansions in the West. It still has bawdy saloons where you can get "two fingers of redeye" and you can buy keepsakes and souvenirs from the gift and specialty shops that dot every block. You can take a walking tour of the liveliest ghost town in the West or ride the trolley with a guide narrating the history of the buildings it passes.

Not much has changed since the bonanza days of the silver mines except that now, instead of catering to miners, the city takes care of tourists. The city is open all year with several events, celebrations and attractions for your enjoyment. A few of the attractions include: **A&M Horse-Drawn Carriage Rides**, (775) 246-0322, which offers carriage tours of Virginia City from 10 AM to 5 PM; the **Castle Mansion** tour, (775) 847-0275, 10 AM to 5 PM, which gives you an opportunity to visit a mansion built in 1868 still in its original state and not restored; the **Chollar Mine** tour, (775) 847-1055, open 10 AM to 5 PM, which gives you a glimpse of original square-set lumbering, tools and equipment from the fifth largest producing mine on the Comstock; the **Julia Bulette Red Light Museum**, (775) 847-9394, open 10 AM to 5 PM, which includes displays of contraceptives, medical instruments and medical cure-alls (Julia Bulette was the most famous of the Virginia City prostitutes and was murdered by one of her customers); and the **Mackay Mansion**, (775) 847-0173, open daily from 10 AM to 6 PM, which was built in 1860 as the mining office and superintendent's residence by the Gould & Curry Mining Company

and is completely furnished with period pieces. And don't forget to pop in and look around the *Territorial Enterprise* to see the original 1876 building where **Mark Twain** began his literary career.

From May through November, there is a narrated, 35-minute ride from Virginia City to Gold Hill on the historic **Virginia & Truckee Railroad**. This ride lets you view the mining district from the original 120 year old train. Tickets can be purchased at the train depot in the middle of Virginia City near the train tracks. The depot has no phone.

Also, don't forget to visit the **Comstock Fireman's Museum**, **Piper's Opera House**, the **Fourth Ward School**, the **First Presbyterian Church, St. Mary's in the Mountains Catholic Church**, the **Bucket of Blood** and **The Delta saloons**, the **Marshall Mint and Museum** and ask where you can view the **100-mile canyon**. One of our favorite stores is **Kiefer & Bateson, Ltd.,** an authentic 1880's style mercantile store located on C Street.

Come to think about it, you may need two days to totally enjoy Virginia City. For a schedule of Virginia City events, telephone Roadshows in Reno, (800) 200-4557. If you wish to overnight in Virginia City, we suggest The Gold Hill Hotel, (775) 847-0111, which has been operating since 1859. It is located 1 mile south of Virginia City on Nev. Highway 342. Virginia City has numerous cafes and restaurants and all are about equal in price and value.

The International Camel Races

If we Insiders had to suggest a time of year to visit Virginia City, it would be in September when the hilarious and raucous International Camel Races are held. Traditionally run on the weekend following Labor Day, these races began because of a humorous editor and a slow news week at the *Territorial Enterprise* in 1957.

Originally, the U.S. Army introduced camels into the West in 1856, reasoning that the animals would fare well in the desert here. In 1861, camel-train operators used the animals to carry salt from Nevada's marshes to miners on the Comstock. Prospectors used salt in a

Photo: Kathryn Glaeser/Estern Plumas County Visitors Bureau

Living History Day at Plumas Eureka State Park is an experience that a history-seeking traveller will not soon forget.

process called amalgamation which reclaims gold and silver ore. These pack camels also hauled supplies and firewood to Virginia City residents. But in the mid-1870s, with mining declining, most camel-train operators went bankrupt and most released their animals to roam the high desert. The last wild camel in Nevada was spotted in 1936.

In 1957, in order to fill space in his newspaper, the editor of the *Territorial Enterprise* invented the fictitious camel race. The race never occurred, supposedly due to the camels becoming ill. For the next two years, the editor made up more phony excuses and continually postponed the races. In 1960, however, Clark Gable, Marilyn Monroe and director John Houston were in Virginia City filming *The Misfits* during camel race time. John Houston had heard about the fictitious event and decided to make it a reality. Riding camels from the San Francisco Zoo, he and other Hollywood celebrities began the yearly tradition for real. Now the camel races are the most popular event in Virginia City — and since 1962 they also include ostrich races. City fathers added "International" to the title in 1987 when they challenged officials from Alice Springs, Australia, to come over and join in the races. (Australia's West also used camels as pack animals during its expansion and exploration.)

According to the Nevada Association of Realtors, plenty of older, established homes are on the market and new housing developments are springing up in Reno and Sparks like mushrooms in a warm rain.

Neighborhoods and Real Estate

Thinking about relocating to the Reno/ Tahoe area? Well, now is a perfect time because the housing market is what the real estate agents like to call "healthy," which (they tell us) is one step below "booming." Here you will find a wide variety of home styles, sizes, prices and locations to suit your pocketbook including houses on the edges of golf courses, luxurious mansions around Lake Tahoe, detached homes in family neighborhoods, out-of-town horse properties, town homes, condominiums, mobile homes and apartments. According to the Nevada Association of Realtors, plenty of older, established homes are on the market and new housing developments are springing up in Reno and Sparks like mushrooms in a warm rain. More than 85 new-home developments dot Reno and Sparks with prices varied to accommodate any budget. In Reno and Sparks, the market is definitely in the buyers' favor. Around Lake Tahoe, new developments are scarce because most of the land has already been purchased. In fact, Realtors at the lake say that by the year 2008 no land will be available for any substantial new housing developments — but older homes drop on the market from time to time, making lake property a definite sellers' market.

Don't make the mistake of comparing us to Las Vegas, though. The real estate market down south is nothing less than amazing. They average about 20,000 home sales per year, which makes their market No.1 in the United States. In Reno/Tahoe, we average about 3,400 homes sold per year.

This chapter will help explain to you the different neighborhoods and price ranges available for your move here. We will take you on a whirlwind tour through the housing market in the Reno/Tahoe area broken down into neighborhoods, and we will give you our Insider choices for some of the real estate companies.

The first question most newcomers want answered is: what is the average cost of a house in the Reno/Tahoe area? Well, that question is one of the most difficult to answer because the neighborhoods are so different. For instance, an average house in Reno in 1998 sold for $136,000. An average house in Incline Village, Nevada, on North Shore Lake Tahoe in 1998 sold for $577,500. And the average lakeside home on North Shore Lake Tahoe near Tahoe City, California, in 1998 sold for $1 million. So you can see that the prices are as diverse as the neighborhoods.

Don't panic though: we guarantee you that houses exist here to fit every lifestyle and every budget. Many buyers emigrating from Southern California are amazed at how reasonable housing costs are. Some Montana buyers wonder why housing is so expensive. Basically, it all depends on where you are moving from, what you are looking for and where you want to live.

Two things to always ask Realtors before buying a house in any neighborhood are the quality and cost of the existing infrastructure and the prevailing property tax rates. Here in the Reno/Tahoe area, the infrastructure in place is outstanding. In fact, utility prices on the Nevada side of the Reno/Tahoe area are frozen until the year 2000.

As far as property taxes go in Nevada, all property is assessed at 35 percent of its appraised or market value. The state capped its property tax rate at $3.64 for each $100 of assessed value. In other words, according to state law, the most property tax you would pay on a $100,000 home in Nevada is $1,274. But the unincorporated areas of Washoe County and the cities of Reno and Sparks have set their tax rates below the cap so their tax rates are lower. On the California side of Lake Tahoe, the tax rate is accessed according to Proposition 13, which states that property tax will be set at 1 percent of the home's market price at time of purchase so the property tax on a $100,000 home would be $1,000.

The old real estate saying goes that buyers should watch out for three things when purchasing a home: location, location, location. To help orient you to such a large area, we have divided our four geographic areas — Reno, Sparks, North Shore Lake Tahoe and South Shore Lake Tahoe — into neighborhoods. These neighborhoods are a composite of the neighborhoods used by local Realtors in their multiple listings guide. This chapter concentrates on the characteristics that define the different neighborhoods and the average price of homes in each neighborhood.

Since the housing market constantly changes here, we recommend that after reading this chapter and after arriving here, you pick up a copy of the Reno Gazette-Journal's weekly tabloid — HomeFinder — for a current update about new home sales and communities. Also, free home-buying and rental guides are available at all local grocery stores. A brief description of the guides follows at the end of this chapter. A list of local realtors appears at the end of the chapter, too, along with a brief run-down of Reno/Tahoe apartment living.

Neighborhoods

Reno

We have divided the Reno area into five neighborhoods: North Reno, Verdi/Mogul, the North Valleys, Southwest Reno and Southeast Reno. Some of the neighborhoods are part of the incorporated city of Reno and some are in unincorporated Washoe County but, because the services and atmosphere are generally the same, this chapter does not separate the two.

North Reno

We have dubbed the area north of the Truckee River within the city limits "North Reno." This part of town contains just about everything that makes a city like Reno tick. Here you have hospitals, casinos, churches, stores, businesses, condos, apartments and houses dating from the 1940s to the 1990s. There are three basic sections to this area: the Northeastern, the Northwestern and the Northwest Suburban.

The **Northeastern** section contains the University of Nevada, Reno; Truckee Meadows Community College; and a plethora of housing ranging from low-income to upper-middle class. Most of the older homes border Interstate 80 with the newer models built farther north.

The **Northwestern** section of this neighborhood stretches from the university (N. Virginia Street) to N. McCarran Boulevard. This area is crowded with private homes, apartments, duplexes and multifamily complexes and it contains most of the university's fraternity and sorority houses. This section is about

---

Photo: K. Markgraf

Views of the city from surrounding hillsides are as popular as lakeview property.

60 years old with most of the dwellings rented out to students and university personnel. Some of the old homes are in fantastic shape. Others show the wear of being rentals.

The **Northwest Suburban** section of this neighborhood begins at N. McCarran Boulevard and continues west to Northgate Golf Course. This area is mostly residential with established commercial properties along N. McCarran Boulevard. Realtors warn new buyers in this area, which sits on the slopes of Peavine Peak, that mature trees are a rare commodity and the area is extremely windy. From east to west, the different developments represent the decades of growth in the northwest. The older homes, circa 1940, are closer in toward the university and the newer 1990 models border the golf course. From east to west, you will pass through developments built in the 60s, 70s and 80s.

Realtors call North Reno an "area in transition" where first-time buyers can find older homes ranging from $80,000 to $100,000 and the more ambitious buyer can find new, upscale developments with starting home prices of $300,000. The average time on the market varies with the neighborhoods. The median income here is $36,000 per year.

Verdi/Mogul

These two rural communities sit just northwest of Reno along I-80. The Truckee River winds its way through these two towns and the Toiyabe National Forest butts up against their southern borders.

The splendor of the wide-open spaces dotted with trees and the rural feel make up **Verdi**'s personality. Residents say they like the country atmosphere of the area and also like the idea that Reno and its amenities are only 10 miles away.

Some of the bigger, one-of-a-kind houses are situated in the west Verdi area in neighborhoods surrounding Crystal Peak Park and Dog Valley Road. The most popular areas to live include Lakeview Estates, Belli Ranch subdivision and Donner Trail Ranch. Most of the homes are custom built and prices range from $150,000 to $2 million.

Mogul, although rural like Verdi but without the trees, sports a different feel. Closer in toward Reno (only about 5 miles out), Mogul is a large development with similar-looking houses. The area remains popular because, like Verdi, it appears remote but is close enough to Reno to enjoy all the big city has to offer.

The average income of Verdi/Mogul residents is $43,000 and the average cost of a home in this area is $229,000. Houses usually remain on the market about four months before being sold.

The North Valleys

The North Valley communities include Stead, Lemmon Valley, Golden Valley and Sun Valley. They are located just north of Reno along U.S. Highway 395. Generally, these communities are perfect for people who like the wide-open spaces and want to live away from the busy city but close enough to commute.

Stead evolved during World War II when the government built a training base for the U.S Army/Air Force. Now it is considered a bedroom community of Reno with an ever-expanding manufacturing and warehouse sector. Most people come here to work in the warehouses or industrial centers and to live close to work. Stead remains a manufacturing community, and its airport is home to the annual Reno National Air Races (see our Annual Events chapter).

Lemmon Valley and Golden Valley are ideal for people who want a large block of land but who also want to live close to Reno. Like Stead, these neighborhoods are north of Reno and border U.S 395. **Lemmon Valley** is the farthest out and offers the cheapest, easily accessible property. **Golden Valley** is closer in, is a little more expensive and affords easy access to Reno and Sparks. Both of these neighborhoods offer large horse properties. Closer in toward U.S. 395, mobile (manufactured) homes and older houses dominate the landscape. These valleys have a rural flavor but are only 10 to 20 minutes from downtown Reno.

Sun Valley sits on top of the northern border between Reno and Sparks, with mobile homes making up most of this neighborhood. Even though a few single-family homes dot the area and one new housing development sits in the northeastern corner, the neighborhood is still considered to be a manufactured-home haven. Citizen volunteers have been trying to combat the underdeveloped stigma attached to the neighborhood but it still lacks the amenities of other Reno locations. Sun Valley has few streetlights, even fewer side-walks and a large portion of the streets remain unpaved dirt and gravel.

The average income for North Valley residents is $39,000 with an average home sales price of $115,000 and an average condominium cost of $51,000. The average time for a home to be on the market is three months.

Southwest Reno

The Southwest area of Reno has it all — businesses, older neighborhoods, newer housing developments, several upper-class custom home sites and large country plots of land. This neighborhood gives any buyer a wide variety of locations and home styles from sprawling country living to downtown togetherness. Realtors break the expansive Southwest down into three real estate sections: the Old Southwest, the Southwest and Southwest Suburban.

The **Old Southwest** is bordered by the Truckee River to the north, Plumb Lane to the south, S. Virginia Street to the east and S. McCarran Boulevard to the west. This section is smack in the middle of downtown Reno and contains two city-maintained parks. The architecture here is the oldest in Reno and brick is the dominant building material. Mature trees envelop the area, which has housing ranging from modest single-story homes to gigantic mansions.

The median income of residents in the Old Southwest is $44,000 and the average price for a home is $195,000; condos average $120,000.

The **Southwest** section of Reno sits directly underneath the Old Southwest bordered by Plumb Lane to the north, S. McCarran Boulevard to the south and west and S. Virginia Street to the east. This area has dozens of housing developments both old and new, four city parks, two golf courses and a lake. Some of the more grandiose and older homes are situated around Washoe County Golf Course in the middle of the Southwest section and many lower-priced homes and apartments sit south of Virginia Lake just 3 blocks east of the golf course. This area began its growth spurt in the 1980s when Reno expanded southward.

Lakeridge, one of the most upscale developments in Reno, sits in this Southwest section. Lakeridge community is on the golf course with a montage of houses, condos and apartments built around it and a tennis center. Insiders recognize the area as one of the most highbrow in the city.

But perhaps the most popular and luxurious development in the Southwest is Caughlin Ranch (pronounced like "Collin," without the "gh" sound). This development is one of the first planned communities in Reno; it contains luxury houses and condos but no apartments. The first development began in 1984 and, according to Realtors, it has added a development a year since then. Prices in the 22 developments of Caughlin Ranch range from $140,000 for a condo to $3.7 million for the most luxurious home. The developments all use a wide-open space design with plenty of winding trails for jogging and hiking.

As in the Old Southwest area, home prices in the Southwest section average about $195,000, condos $120,000, and the median income is $44,000.

The **Southwest Suburban** section is the largest area of any real estate section in Reno and Sparks. This area stretches from S. McCarran Boulevard south along U.S. 395 to Nev. Highway 431 (the Mt. Rose Highway), up the highway to the Mt. Rose–Ski Tahoe ski resort. Most of this section is in unincorporated Washoe County and, like Verdi and Mogul, the expansive space gives the feel of country living.

Huffaker development sits at the extreme north of this section and includes a subdivision of larger, upscale houses with its own park, lake and tennis courts. Working southward, most of the developments in the area feature the more expensive custom-built homes, but the dedicated buyer can find a subdivision to fit any lifestyle with varied price ranges. This area has four new golf courses and plenty of wide-open spaces.

Among the most popular of the newer subdivisions is Saddlehorn just northwest of the Mt. Rose Highway. These custom homes have a southwestern ranch-style look with an average price tag of $460,000. People buying here like the idea that their homes are unique and located equidistant between Reno and Lake Tahoe.

Along the Mt. Rose Highway, several subdivisions dot the landscape. New buyers looking here have several price ranges and styles to chose from. For the more discriminating buyer, two new gated communities have sprung up around the area's three newest golf courses. Old European-style houses surround the Jack Nicklaus–designed Montreux Golf Course. Realtors like to say that these houses give homeowners a feeling of "private country-club living in an alpine setting."

Arrowcreek's two golf courses, designed by Arnold Palmer and Fuzzy Zoeller, are neighbors to Montreux. The gated community surrounding these two golf courses provides 1,500 acres of open land, large custom homes, semicustom homes and a 12-acre swim and tennis center. A little further up the highway Galena Forest Estates and St. James's Village offer luxurious custom homes tucked deep into the forest.

In the Southwest Suburban area, the median income is $50,000 and the median price for a home is $250,000, with some of the custom-built homes slipping into the millions.

Southeast Reno

For this guide, we include the neighborhoods of Hidden Valley, Donner Springs, Virginia Foothills, Steamboat and the Virginia City Highlands in the area we call Reno's Southeast. This section stretches from the Truckee River southeast along U.S. 395 to Tahoe Junction (the intersection of U.S. 395 and the Mt. Rose Highway). This large area contains the Reno/Tahoe International Airport, Meadowood Mall (Reno's biggest shopping center) and an extensive commercial sector along U.S. 395.

Hidden Valley and Donner Springs housing developments lie to the east and southeast of the airport and provide quality homes for the more upscale buyer. Homes in the older, more established **Hidden Valley** area range from $200,00 to $400,000 and are sprinkled in and around the Hidden Valley Country Club. This neighborhood also has a large country park and includes Rosewood Lakes Golf Course, just east of the country club.

The newer **Donner Springs** neighborhood southeast of S. McCarran Boulevard has more moderately priced homes ranging from $120,000 to $170,000 with less expensive homes (in the $120,000 to $130,000 range) in the neighborhoods east of Longley Lane.

Buyers can find houses from $120,000 to $160,000 in Huffaker Hills development on E. Huffaker Lane. The new Double Diamond Ranch development along S. Meadows Parkway off U.S. 395 will cover about 1,000 acres with homes selling from $130,000 to $240,000.

Just east of Tahoe Junction on either side of Nev. Highway 341 (the Comstock Highway), which winds its way up to Virginia City, sit the communities of **Virginia Foothills** (north of Nev. 341) and **Steamboat** (south of Nev. 341). Houses here are priced from $160,000 to $390,000. Some of the older homes were built in the 1960s but full-scale development here began in the 1970s. This area is more rural than the rest of the Southeast.

The last neighborhood in the Southeast is the **Virginia City Highlands** located up the Comstock Highway just off Geiger Grade, which snakes its way to Virginia City. Houses here are scattered along the mountainside with an outdoorsy feel and spectacular valley and mountain views. These properties usually have a large plot of land included and range from $180,000 to $250,000. A big problem in this neighborhood is the fact that the Comstock Highway is a two-lane road which gets lots of snow during the winter months.

One of the drawbacks to living in the Southeast is that during the New Year's Day flood of 1997 parts of this area found themselves underwater, including the airport, and the city is

still struggling with a comprehensive flood plan. Other drawbacks include the airport's plan to expand to the west, which could entail some homes being demolished or moved to make room for the expansion. One area to be wary of is the neighborhood surrounding Neil Road just north of Meadowood Mall. This neighborhood has a high crime rate.

For the entire Southeast, residents' median income is $37,000 with the median home price at $132,000 and the median price of a condo at $71,000.

Sparks

We have divided Sparks into four neighborhoods: Old Sparks, East Sparks, Sparks Suburban and Spanish Springs. Once again some of the neighborhoods fall within the city limits and some are within the unincorporated confines of Washoe County. We do not make a distinction between the two.

Generally, Sparks is considered by most residents to be a family-friendly area with a high concentration of single-family homes. Residents of Sparks say they feel that life is laid back and the Sparks City Council has made sure that the warehouse areas of the city stay separated from the residential neighborhoods.

The average income for Sparks residents is $44,000, with the median home going for $137,000 and the average condo costing $80,000.

Old Sparks

This is the oldest section of the city, and it lies north of I-80 between El Rancho Drive and N. McCarran Boulevard. This is the original railroad settlement and contains City Hall, the casino area and Victorian Square, Sparks's redevelopment project (see our Area Overview and Attractions chapters). The area is clustered with older, single-family homes ranging from $80,000 to $140,000. The housing has the late 1940s, early 1950s look and feel with small, crackerbox designs and mostly single-story homes. Even though this section is old, the Sparks Police Department says the neighborhoods are safe.

East Sparks

East Sparks is bordered by I-80 to the south, Pah Rah Park to the north, N. McCarran Boulevard to the west and Vista Boulevard to the east. Most of Sparks's industrial sector is south of I-80 and along the first few miles of Vista Boulevard. The rest of east Sparks is made up of newer homes; a 2,400 home development is going in along the northen part of Vista Boulevard. This area of Sparks houses the largest concentration of single-family residences in the city. The development began in the 1970s and continues today. Most homes are in the $120,000 to $220,000 range with styles and sizes to fit most any buyer's requirements. East Sparks is also the home to Sparks Marina Park, a recreational area built around an artificial lake that was once a gravel pit (see our Parks chapter).

Sparks Suburban

The Sparks Suburban area is bordered by Nev. Highway 445 (the Pyramid Highway) to the west, Red Hawk Golf Course to the north, and Pah Rah Park to the south. The east is wide-open, hilly space with tons of room for growth. This area is home to the newest housing developments, including Wingfield Springs, a community surrounding Red Hawk Golf Course. The enormous growth in this area required developers to construct a shopping center at the intersection of Disc Drive and Vista Boulevard to accommodate the suburban residents. Houses in the many developments here range from $150,000 to the low $200,000s, though the prices do top $1 million for some homes.

Spanish Springs

This area stretches north along the eastern side of the Pyramid Highway and is an area where most of the new construction is happening. The feel in this section is definitely rural, with houses built among the sagebrush of northern Nevada's high desert. Housing projects are constantly springing up all over the Spanish Springs Valley with homes ranging from $150,000 to $220,000. Most of the residents here say they like the country feel and the fact that the city is only 8 to 10 miles away.

Lake Tahoe

The 72 miles around Lake Tahoe take you on an inspirational tour of some of the most magnificent homes in the United States, from those resting on the shore of this pristine lake to those tucked away in the pine trees. Less expensive homes are available for the motivated buyer but let's face the facts: property around Lake Tahoe is expensive and it's a sellers' market. According to real estate agents around the lake, there are more prospective buyers than property available. The real estate around the lake is mostly upscale with the least expensive property located in South Lake Tahoe, California, and the most expensive in Tahoe City, California, and Incline Village, Nevada. Most of the homes are custom built, what Realtors call "one-of-a-kind properties." Even in the few housing developments around the lake the homes are unique and average about $480,000.

Here we will give a brief description and average price of the homes available around the lake; for a more detailed description of the different areas, read our Area Overview chapter.

North Shore Lake Tahoe

From Meeks Bay, California, on the western side of North Shore to Incline Village, Nevada, on the eastern border of the area, the houses and condos are upscale residences. Several communities line the lake as you travel clockwise around the North Shore and most of the properties for sale range in price from very affordable ($99,000) condos near Tahoe City, California, to the million-dollar plus properties in Incline Village, Nevada. The architecture of most of the homes fits into the Old Tahoe look — wood exteriors and interiors, rock fireplaces, some houses tucked away beneath majestic ponderosa pine trees and some with lake frontage amid natural boulders and glistening, white sand.

No less than 50 neighborhoods line the

lake on the North Shore where prospective buyers can search for their one-of-a-kind homes, but one of the most populated is **Incline Village**. This unique village once attracted retired people and those looking for second homes. Now, more than 70 percent of the 9,000 citizens are permanent residents less than 50 years old. Lake Shore Boulevard and the steep slopes overlooking the lake showcase the luxurious estates of many of the country's rich and famous. Incline Village is also home to Sierra Nevada College, a four-year liberal arts school.

The average income on the North Shore ranges from $44,000 in Tahoe City to $59,000 in Incline Village. The average price of a two- to five-bedroom home in Tahoe City is $281,000. The same house with lake-front property would cost about $1 million. In Incline Village, the average home goes for $577,500 and the average cost of a condo is $267,000. The homes along Lake Shore Boulevard cost in the millions.

South Shore Lake Tahoe

Real estate doesn't get any cheaper as you travel south around the lake from Incline Village. The first community in the northeastern corner of the area we call South Shore is **Glenbrook**, an upscale neighborhood nestled in and around Glenbrook Golf Course. The average cost of these unique homes is $500,000. And just down the road from Glenbrook is the most expensive piece of property for sale on Lake Tahoe.

Chase International Real Estate Company of Lake Tahoe, Nevada, is offering Paradise Cove for $12.5 million. This 15.5-acre estate sits on its own private cove near South Point surrounded by Ponderosa pines. The home boasts 21 rooms, a caretaker's house, a seven-car garage and a warehouse.

Between Glenbrook and Stateline, Nevada, about 12 residential areas line the lake. From Uppaway, Logan Creek and Lakeridge in the northern part to Zephyr Heights, Roundhill and

Lake Village in the southern part of the area, buyers can find a variety of unique mountain and lake homes with the average home costing about $250,000.

Perhaps the best buys around the lake are located in **South Lake Tahoe**, California This city is the most populated around Lake Tahoe and contains all the amenities expected of a larger city — shopping centers, fast-food restaurants, an airport and three golf courses. Here a buyer can find almost any type of residential property offered at prices lower than any other locale around the lake. South Lake Tahoe has single-family residences, condos, townhomes and apartments, with prices ranging from $80,000 to $250,000. Once again the architecture is unique, with lots of wood, rock and brick. The average cost of a home in South Lake Tahoe is $170,000.

Apartment Living

Many new residents to the Reno/Tahoe area prefer apartment living, which is affordable living at its best. This type of lifestyle gives the newcomer a chance to get out and explore the different neighborhoods before committing to investing in a new home. The area is loaded with apartment complexes (about 300) that have rents ranging from $425 per month for a studio apartment to $900 per month for a three-bedroom/two-bath unit. The average is about $600 per month.

Most of the newer complexes (about 80) have more up-to-date amenities like built-in washer/dryers, swimming pools, tennis courts and covered parking. According to one rental agency, the vacancy rate for 1998 was about 6 percent, but the vacancy rate was expected to go down to 2 percent by 1999.

Real Estate Companies

Five associations of Realtors in the Reno/Tahoe area maintain lists of more than 350 real estate firms with more than 2,000 regis-

INSIDERS' TIP

Buyers need Realtors as much as sellers do. Find one to help you look for your new home. Their commissions are paid for out of the sellers' profits.

Photo: K. Markgraf

The variety of real estate around the Reno/Tahoe area is astounding to the new arrival home-buyer.

tered Realtors. The lists are free and can be obtained by calling one of these five associations:

Reno/Sparks Association of Realtors, (775) 823-8800
Incline Village Association of Realtors, (775) 831-3777
Tahoe City Association of Realtors, (530) 583-0275
South Lake Tahoe Association of Realtors, (530) 541-7007
Carson/Douglas/Lyon/Tahoe Association of Realtors, (775) 885-7200

These associations will answer most of your questions about the real estate market in their particular areas but they will not specifically recommend one of their member Realtors over another. One way to obtain a Realtor is to choose the area you would most like to live in and see which realty firm is most active there; another is to solicit referrals from friends or coworkers.

Our list of Realtors, broken down into two general areas (Reno/Sparks and Lake Tahoe), just touches on a cross-section of the many real estate firms in the Reno/Tahoe area. All of our choices have access to the MLS (Multiple

Listing Service). Some of the firms are affiliated with nationwide chains and some are smaller firms with good local references and reputations. The following list is by no means exhaustive.

Reno/Sparks

Assist-2-Sell USA
535 Plumb Ln., Reno, Nev.
• (775) 688-6060
This independently owned franchise is one of more than 50 offices around the United States that help in relocating buyers. This office began in 1987 and specializes in single-family residences. Their unique way of doing business is to charge a flat fee of $1,995 for selling a residence. The owner says that this low fee has saved customers more than $1 million each year. The firm has 13 Realtors to assist you.

Century 21 — A Touch of Class, Inc.
5890 S. Virginia St., Reno, Nev.
• (775) 828-3333
Century 21 is the nation's largest network of real estate firms. In the Reno/Tahoe area,

12 independently owned and -operated offices are ready to serve your real estate needs. Century 21 uses a computerized list of homes across the country to help relocating buyers. With 35 Realtors, A Touch of Class, Inc., is the largest Century 21 office in Reno.

Coldwell Banker — Plummer & Associates
290 E. Moana Ln., Reno, Nev.
- **(775) 689-8228**

One of the largest real estate firms in the area with more than 70 Realtors, this locally owned franchise specializes in relocation. It has a team of Realtors who specialize in making moving into the area easy. Realtors for this firm work in all aspects of real estate from residential to commercial and there is a special section which premieres homes with price tags in excess of $350,000. It also handles land and lot sales. This firm has been in business since 1978.

Dickson Realty
1030 Caughlin Crossing, Reno, Nev.
- **(775) 831-1515**

For more than 25 years, this real estate firm has been helping buyers relocate to the Reno/Tahoe area. It is a member of Reliance Relocation Network and has a full-time staffed relocation department. This firm is the largest independently owned real estate firm in Reno with more than 90 Realtors. Dickson Realty has exclusive rights to Property Source, an interactive phone system that lists properties 24 hours a day, 7 days a week. The company only hires Realtors with proven track records.

Ferrari-Lund Real Estate
325 W. Liberty St., Reno, Nev.
- **(775) 688-4000**

Ferrari-Lund Real Estate firm has been operating in Reno since 1988 and specializes in relocation. It handles mostly residential listings but also has a good supply of commercial properties. The firm is one of the 50 top producers in the United States and hires only veteran Realtors. The firm has a relocation division and has more than 50 Realtors to attend to your needs.

Help-U-Sell Drakulich Realty
2205 N. McCarran Blvd., Sparks, Nev.
- **(775) 685-8585**

Drakulich Realty specializes in residential properties and charges a flat fee of $2,950 instead of the normal 6 percent of the sale price. Its 11 Realtors sold more than 300 homes in 1998 and do not charge any upfront fees. The firm is a member of International Relocation Services and has a money-back guarantee. It offers a free, weekly list of properties complete with prices, descriptions and addresses. Drakulich is a full-service firm which shows both its listings and listings of other brokers.

Keystone Realty
652 Forest St., Reno, Nev.
- **(775) 688-4000**

For more than 20 years, this firm with its 50 Realtors has been specializing in the sale of residential property in the Reno/Tahoe area. Although it does handle a small number of commercial listings, it is a top producer in the home buying and selling market. It bills itself as a full-service company with highly experienced Realtors. The firm also has a satellite office in Fernley, Nevada, 30 miles east of Reno.

Landfinder
1010 12th St., Sparks, Nev.
- **(775) 358-0555**

A small firm which specializes in out-of-town properties, this three-Realtor office concentrates on horse properties, ranches and land away from the hustle and bustle of city life. Landfinder has been selling ranches for 12 years and has a good selection of rural properties for sale. Its Realtors are licensed in both Nevada and California. The owner says she is not a "city girl" and points out that she lives on a ranch 20 miles north of Reno.

INSIDERS' TIP

Shop around for the best deal when looking for a mortgage company. Loan rates can differ greatly from one to another.

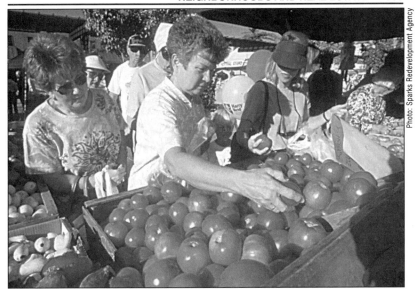

Photo: Sparks Redevelopment Agency

One of the high points of living in or near Sparks
is the Hometowne Farmer's Market in Victorian Square.

Prudential Clement Realty, Inc.
630 E. Plumb Ln., Reno, Nev.
• **(775) 829-3131**

Prudential Clement Realty has more than 37,000 Realtors and 1,300 offices around the nation to link to for relocation services. That's one of the reasons its owner says, "Relocating is our forte." Residential property sales make up the majority of the firm's business and it boasts about its 88 percent success rate in sales of all its listings. The firm also provides each of its Realtors with 12 weeks of intensive training. The 18-year-old office has more than 40 Realtors working for it.

Realty 500, Myers Realty
4990 S. Virginia St., Reno, Nev.
• **(775) 827-6644**

This is the largest real estate firm in the area, with five offices and more than 200 Realtors. The company has been in business for 33 years and has one of the best reputations around. It is a member of CENDANT, the largest relocation company in the country and has its own in-house relocation packages available upon request. This firm can provide you with any type of property from rentals to large estates.

RE/MAX Realty Professionals
6121 Lakeside Dr., Reno, Nev.
• **(775) 828-3200**

The owner of this independent firm only hires full-time, experienced, professional Realtors. "We have no part-timers here," he says. The firm handles both residential and commercial properties and has a relocation division among its 50 Realtors. The firm also uses a worldwide network for relocating. The office has only been open since 1990, but the owner has been in business in Nevada for 20 years. He claims that no other real estate firm in the area outproduces his.

Lake Tahoe

Ann Nichols and Company
201 Stateline Rd., Crystal Bay, Nev.
• **(775) 831-0625**

This small, independently owned office specializes in luxury second homes on the North Shore of Lake Tahoe. Its six Realtors are licensed in both California and Nevada and they handle properties from Tahoma, California, to Incline Village, Nevada. The firm likes to boast that it has Realtors who specialize in personalized service and who really know the area. The office has been selling property since 1956.

Better Homes Realty
3000 N. Lake Blvd., Tahoe City, Calif.
• **(530) 583-0199**
Better Homes is a small office with a great reputation around Lake Tahoe. This firm handles single-family homes, condos and townhomes all over the California side of the North Shore. It has five Realtors spread out in Tahoe City, Soda Springs, Truckee and North Lake Tahoe.

Fred Sands Distinctive Homes
292 Kingsbury Gr., South Lake Tahoe, Nev. • **(775) 588-7710, (800) 878-1066**
This is an upscale firm which specializes in high-end private residential properties. Its target buyers are those who can afford homes priced at more than $500,000. The Realtors do not rely on volume sales but rather offer very personalized service. The office is the only branch in Nevada and the six Realtors are what the owner calls "a bunch of old-timers" in the business.

Hauserman Real Estate
475 N. Lake Blvd., Tahoe City, Calif.
• **(530) 583-5581**
This office has been dealing with buyers and sellers on the North Shore of Lake Tahoe since 1966. The 20 full-time and five part-time Realtors specialize in residential sales from Tahoe City to Incline Village. The firm has a branch office in Tahoe Vista, California, and sells properties ranging from cozy cabins to lakefront estates.

RE/MAX
8611 N. Lake Tahoe Blvd., Kings Beach, Calif. • **(530) 546-3356**
This RE/MAX location is a four-person office that handles residential properties, con-

dos and lots on the extreme northern shore of Lake Tahoe. The bistate office has a solid reputation among Insiders and offers very specialized services. It is almost impossible to find any of the Realtors in the office because of the demand for their services. The four have a lot of local experience selling property at the lake.

Home Buying and Rental Guides

Several real estate guides are available for the new-home buyer or renter in the Reno/Tahoe area. Almost every grocery and convenience store carries these free publications. Reno's daily newspaper, the *Reno Gazette-Journal,* also prints a weekly tabloid dealing with home sales.

The following are what we consider some of the best:

For Rent Magazinze
3550 Barron Wy., Reno, Nev.
• **(775) 829-7368**
This free magazine is published every two weeks and contains about 100 pages of the area's rental properties. The guide includes university and student housing, senior living and apartment complexes all over Reno and Sparks. The magazine includes a map of the area's apartment complexes, a quick-check guide of all properties listed with amenities, a reader's inquiry service to mail in for more information on individual apartments, and a national relocation service.

Greater Reno Apartment Guide
102 Vine St., Reno, Nev.
• **(775) 329-1442**
A monthly publication which features about 150 pages of apartments for rent throughout the Reno and Sparks areas, this magazine groups the apartment complexes by neighborhoods and contains a detailed list of prices plus the amenities associated with each com-

---

INSIDERS' TIP

If you're moving your family to the Reno/Tahoe area, refer to our Education and Child Care chapter for an overview of the local school systems.

plex. This publication can be picked up at most grocery stores and is free.

HomeFinder
Reno Gazette-Journal, **955 Kuenzli St., Reno, Nev. • (775) 788-6200**

HomeFinder is a weekly tabloid insert to the *Reno Gazette-Journal* which is billed as "Your weekly real estate guide." The tab is paid for by advertising from local real estate companies and is chock-a-block full of properties for sale, rentals, mobile homes, land and information on real estate loans and mortgage rates. The tabloid averages about 40 pages and is an excellent reference guide to the Reno/Tahoe area. The tab is loaded with articles on how to obtain loans, relocation tips, local mortgage company rates and how-to tips. It has a special section that focuses on one local neighborhood and one apartment complex each week. It is probably the most comprehensive real estate guide in the area.

Homes & Land
(775) 851-1141

This free weekly magazine is a nationwide realty guide with zoned editions for Reno, Sparks, North Shore and South Shore of Lake Tahoe. *Homes & Land* averages about 65 pages and is loaded with properties offered by local real estate companies. It has no nar-

rative but lists about 250 residences per issue with a brief description and price. Real estate companies pay to advertise in this guide.

Premier Properties
(775) 833-3333, (800) 336-7773

A small publication that features properties on the North Shore of Lake Tahoe and is paid for by real estate companies advertising their listings, this once-a-month magazine averages about 25 pages per issue and has zoned editions for the Nevada and California sides of the North Shore. The magazine can be found at most grocery and convenience stores along the North Shore. Write them at PO Box 5057, Incline Village NV 89451.

Realtors Real Estate Directory
5650 Riggins Ct., Reno, Nev.
• (775) 823-8800

Printed every other week by the Reno/Sparks Association of Realtors, this magazine averages about 85 pages and is bursting with properties for sale. It is a scaled-down version of the Multiple Listings Guide. This publication offers one to two pages of narrative; the rest of the pages are devoted to homes for sale. The write-ups include price, house and lot dimensions, and photographs. This magazine is free and can be found at all grocery and convenience stores.

After spending their working years fighting traffic and breathing smog, retirees in the Reno/Tahoe area think they've died and gone to heaven in this natural mountain/desert environment.

Retirement

Silver is once again playing a hand in the economy and lifestyle of the Reno/Tahoe area. But instead of coming from the mines in Virginia City, it's arriving as a silver wave of retirees who've discovered that the area is the perfect place for their retirement. After spending their working years fighting traffic and breathing smog, they think they've died and gone to heaven in this natural mountain/desert environment. Washoe County, which includes Reno, Sparks and Incline Village, has seen more than 23 percent growth in seniors in recent years. And as more baby boomers retire in the near future, demographers say Reno/Tahoe can expect an even greater number of retirees to make their homes here.

It's not hard to understand why so many people choose to relocate here. If they've visited before (which most have), they've probably fallen in love with the gorgeous scenery and the unlimited opportunities for recreation. And then there's the weather: four distinct seasons, all of which are relatively mild. The sky is a deep azure blue most days, with smog infrequent in Reno/Sparks and unheard of at Lake Tahoe. Many retirees are attracted to Nevada for financial reasons because the state has no income tax and no inheritance tax. They also find they can buy more house for their money in Nevada than in some other states, such as California. Washoe County is the fifth-most affordable new housing market in the Western United States, with a record number of new homes being built by contractors who are conscious of keeping prices competitive. And last but not least, Reno/Tahoe is senior-friendly and welcomes newcomers with open arms.

Because they lead such busy lives, the word "retirement" is a misnomer to most Reno/Tahoe retirees. They've traded their three-piece suits for jogging outfits and are just as likely to leave home each morning with a pair of skis as a briefcase. When they're not pursuing their favorite outdoor sports or hobbies, you can find them volunteering, taking classes or even developing new careers. They live life with gusto and seem bent on making the most of their golden years. If retirement to you means a life full of new challenges and adventures, Reno/Tahoe offers a plethora of options. In this chapter we tell you about the enriching opportunities you'll find for education, employment, entertainment and volunteering.

If you're considering retiring in the Reno/Tahoe area, it's important to know the differences between living in the small mountain towns at Lake Tahoe and living in urban Reno or Sparks. While the small communities at the lake offer a comfortable laid-back lifestyle, they aren't large enough to provide the variety of services that are found in the Reno/Sparks area. But even if you live at the lake, you can take advantage of some of the senior services in Reno/Sparks since it's less than an hour's drive away. Your best sources of information about what's offered at the lake are the senior centers we tell you about in this chapter.

In addition to having fewer services, full-time residence at Lake Tahoe can present problems in the winter because of snow removal. You should also know that some financial advantages available in Nevada are not offered by California and that housing at Lake Tahoe is usually more expensive than in Reno or Sparks. In general the people who retire successfully at Lake Tahoe tend to be self-reliant and financially independent individuals.

To find out about senior issues and events, you can read the *Senior Spectrum* and *Senior Advocate* newspapers, which are available free at newsracks in the area. The *Reno-Gazette Journal* covers senior news in its Tuesday edition. You can also tune in to radio station KSRN at 92.1 Saturdays at 8:05 AM for the program, *Sanford Center's Salute to Seniors*. (See our Media chapter for more on all of these.)

Senior Centers

Aging ultimately means significant life changes for most people. When they move or retire or suffer the loss of a spouse, they are often faced with having to build new lives and to make new social connections. Senior centers provide a touchstone for many by offering opportunities to socialize and to learn with people their own age. You can enjoy a nutritious meal with newfound friends, stretch your intellectual awareness in a class or seminar, get in touch with your emotional side in a support group, find out about services designed with seniors in mind and forget all your worries and woes with musical entertainment at Reno/Tahoe senior centers. Most businesses or organizations say they can't be all things to all people, but senior centers give it a try, with arrays of services that seem to fulfill seniors' every need. If you're new to town, there's no reason to feel disconnected. Just drop in to one of the following centers and you'll find a whole new world of friends and activities. Reno and Sparks each have a center and South Shore Lake Tahoe has two. The North Shore of Lake Tahoe area doesn't have a center, but people living there are always welcome at any of the centers listed below.

South Lake Tahoe Senior Center
3050 Lake Tahoe Blvd., South Lake Tahoe, Calif. • (530) 542-6094

You can take classes, stop by for lunch, get help with senior resources or just drop in to socialize at the South Lake Tahoe Senior Center. Owned by the City of South Lake Tahoe, the center is the focal point for senior activities in this area of South Shore Lake Tahoe. The welcome mat is always out for those who want to volunteer, and the center provides a variety of opportunities for getting involved. Recreational programs and activities include art workshops, water exercise, duplicate bridge, dancing, billiards, the writing club and stretch and tone classes. The center also sponsors daytrips and parties. Support services include health screenings, the mature driving program, senior peer counseling and

home delivered meals. Hours are 8:30 AM to 5 PM weekdays, with lunch served at noon. For assisted transportation through the local bus service, call the center and ask for details.

Sparks Senior Citizens Center
97 Richards Wy., Sparks, Nev.
• (775) 353-3110

Like its sister center in Reno, the Sparks Senior Citizens Center is a beehive of activity. Regular events include arts and crafts, card games, pool and billiards, exercise classes and dancing. Many of the same programs that are offered at the Reno facility are also available here (see our description above). Lunch is served weekdays at 11:30 AM and reservations must be made by 9:30 AM the same day in order to eat. The center doesn't provide transportation, but it's easily reached by Citifare bus. The hours for this comfortable, modern facility are 8 AM to 5 PM weekdays.

Tahoe–Douglas Senior Center
U.S. Hwy. 50, Zephyr Cove, Nev.
• (775) 588-5140

With a primary focus on social and recreational activities, Douglas County offers a limited senior program at the Tahoe–Douglas Senior Center. Since it's an all-volunteer facility, you're more than welcome to help out. Activities include arts and crafts, picnics, potlucks, daytrips around the area, card games and bingo. Hours depend upon the activities offered so be sure to call ahead for the schedule. For a small donation, the center also offers area transportation for doctor appointments and shopping.

Washoe County Senior Citizens Service Center
1155 E. Ninth St., Reno, Nev.
• (775) 328-2575

A multipurpose facility sponsored by Washoe County, the Washoe County Senior Citizens Service Center is a focal point where people can obtain information, services and access to community resources designed for older persons. When you visit the center, you're immediately aware of the high level of purposeful activity all around, from the enthusiastic exercise class in the multipurpose room to the quiet game of pool in the billiards room. The overall ambiance of this large, comfortable facility is that of a club or resort, where people gather to pursue a large variety of pleasurable activities. The ongoing programs include arts and crafts, creative writing, card games, exercise classes, support groups and a readers circle. Lunch is served weekdays and can be enjoyed either in the multipurpose room or on the sunny outdoor patio.

The Washoe County Library System maintains a full branch in the center, with a large selection of books (including large print editions), paperbacks, videotapes and newspapers. The Assistance League of Reno–Sparks sponsors the Senior Sampler Gift Shop, which sells items made by local senior crafters. And the American Association of Retired Persons staffs an information booth in the lobby to help inform seniors of AARP programs. Other programs that are managed from the center include Benefit Assistance, Daybreak, the Homemaker Program, Home Delivered Meals and the Senior Law Program. We tell you more about these in the Senior Services section of this chapter.

The center is open weekdays from 8 AM to 5 PM and occasionally after hours and on weekends for special events. Programs that are federally subsidized are free, but there are charges for meals, Daybreak and some recreational activities. The center doesn't provide transportation, but it's easily accessible by Citifare bus routes. If you're driving your own car, there's ample free parking right in front of the building.

Educational Opportunities

Lake Tahoe Community College
1 College Dr., South Lake Tahoe, Calif.
• **(530) 541-4660**
One does not live by physical activity alone — most of us need opportunities to explore our intellectual side as well. Retirement offers the chance for enriching educational experiences through classes and activities we probably didn't have time for during our working years. With its large variety of programs and classes, Lake Tahoe Community College is a

great place to get in touch with your cerebral self. As part of the California Community College System, the school makes it affordable and easy to enroll. California residents pay just $9 per credit and through its Good Neighbor Policy, people who've been residents of Nevada for at least one year pay $28 per credit. Non-Nevada out-of-state students pay $28 per unit for six or fewer credits and $83 per unit for more than six. Enrollment is open to everyone and courses are offered in art, business, computer science, health, humanities and social sciences. See our Education and Child Care chapter for a more detailed description of this school.

Sierra Nevada College
800 College Dr., Incline Village, Nev.
• **(775) 831-1314**
At $360 per credit, it's pricey and posh, but Sierra Nevada College gives residents of North Shore Lake Tahoe enriching opportunities for expanding their intellectual horizons. There's no break for seniors (although they're welcome in all classes), but you can audit courses for no credit for $125 per unit. The only accredited four-year private liberal arts college in Nevada, SNC offers courses in business, humanities, environmental science, visual and performing arts and teacher education. It also sponsors The Tahoe Forum, a program that brings well-known speakers to the area. See our Education and Child Care chapter for more details on the school.

Truckee Meadows Community College
7000 Dandini Blvd., Reno, Nev.
• **(775) 673-7000**
You can pursue a degree or just take classes for enrichment through Truckee Meadows Community College. See our Education and Child Care chapter for a full description of courses and programs. But TMCC goes above and beyond for seniors in its Silver College by offering free classes to Nevada residents who are 62 or older. Taught at its Old Town Mall campus at S. Virginia Street and Peckham Lane, the eclectic offerings at Silver College include Art Appreciation, Theater for Seniors, Religions, Computer I and II for Seniors, Drawing, Yoga and Golf. Community services classes are available at half price and

include Arts and Crafts, Money and Management, Photography and Family Issues.

For more information on classes or to register at Silver College, call (775) 325-2897. TMCC also has a satellite campus at Incline High School in Incline Village, Nevada. For assistance in courses offered in the North Shore Lake Tahoe region call (775) 673-7148 or (775) 832-4260.

University of Nevada, Reno
900 N. Virginia St., Reno, Nev.
• **(775) 784-1110**

The best things in life are free for people 62 and older at the University of Nevada, Reno: they don't have to pay tuition for regular university courses. If you've put off getting that first degree (or even second or third) because you didn't have the money for it, the university makes it easy for you by charging only for books and lab fees. Let your fingers do the walking through the catalogue and pick from a large variety of degree and nondegree programs. Check out our Education and Child Care chapter for more specific information.

UNR also offers free and minimal-fee classes through its ElderCollege program. Targeted to older lifelong learners, ElderCollege provides interactive educational opportunities, with members planning and conducting classes as well as simply taking them. The annual $35 membership in ElderCollege also entitles you to the benefits of UNR's Senior Sunshine Fund, which includes tickets to performing arts and athletic events at the university. For information on ElderCollege call (775) 784-8053 and for the Senior Sunshine Fund call (775) 784-4774.

Numbers You
Should Know

Adult Protective Services, (775) 688-2811
American Association of Retired Persons (AARP), (775) 328-2506
American Cancer Society, (775) 329-0609
American Lung Association, (775) 829-5864
Consumer Advisory Program Hotline, (775) 688-6128
El Dorado County Senior Information and Referral, (530) 621-6150
Eldercare Helpline, (800) 243-3638
Eldercare Locator, (800) 677-1116
Lend-a-Hand Senior Services, (775) 747-7285
Meals on Wheels South Lake Tahoe, (530) 573-3130
Nevada Bureau of Services to the Blind, (775) 688-1450
Nevada Division for Aging Services, (775) 688-2964
Northern Nevada Center for Independent Living, (775) 353-3599
Placer County Senior Information and Referral, (530) 886-4540
Reno Family YMCA, (775) 329-1311
Senior Connection, (775) 784-8090
Senior Nutrition Program El Dorado County, (530) 621-6150
Senior Nutrition Program Placer County, (530) 888-7137
Washoe Senior Options, (775) 982-5400
YWCA of Reno and Sparks, (775) 322-4531

Senior Services

Nonprofit organizations and governmental agencies in the Reno/Tahoe area offer a wealth of services designed specifically for seniors. We can't begin to list them all, but in this section we give you an overview of the kinds of programs older persons can take advantage of to enrich their retirement years.

Benefit Assistance Program
1155 E. Ninth St., Reno, Nev.
• **(775) 328-2590**

When seniors need a little extra help with their bills each month, Washoe County Senior Services can help through its Benefit Assistance Program. Based upon income and age criteria, older persons are eligible for rebates on property taxes, local telephone service, sewer fees, heating costs and TV cable fees. The program also distributes free medical equipment and food.

Community Home-Based Initiatives Program (CHIP)
445 Apple St., Ste. 104, Reno, Nev.
• **(775) 688-2964**

As an alternative to nursing home care, CHIP helps older persons maintain independence in their homes by providing nonmedical assistance. Attendants offer companionship in addition to help with personal care, shopping and housekeeping.

Daybreak
1155 E. Ninth St., Reno, Nev.
• **(775) 328-2591**

Operating seven days a week, Daybreak offers group care to people with physical or social disabilities. The program provides nursing services, needs assessment, rehabilitation, activities, meals and counseling. In addition to giving caregiving families a break, it helps participants overcome the social isolation that often accompanies illness. While fees vary from $35 per day for full-time to $17.50 for part-time, no one is denied participation because they are unable to pay.

Grandparents Raising Grandchildren
850 Mill St., Reno, Nev.
• **(775) 328-5400**

If your retirement lifestyle includes responsibilities for your grandchildren, you can find support and information through Grandparents Raising Grandchildren. This support group meets monthly to hear speakers, exchange child-care tips and discuss the problems and stresses grandparents experience.

Home Delivered Meal and Nutrition Programs
1155 E. Ninth St., Reno, Nev.
• **(775) 328-2581**

For older persons unable to take care of their own nutritional needs, the Home Delivered Meal Program is literally a lifesaver. To qualify, a person must be 60 or older and unable to cook and prepare food or to eat at a group location. Meals are delivered weekdays at no cost, but contributions are encouraged. Washoe County Senior Services also offers meals at its two senior centers and at ten additional satellite locations in the county.

Homemaker Program
1155 E. Ninth St., Reno, Nev.
• **(775) 353-3110**

If you're ill or disabled, it's frequently impossible to keep up on housekeeping chores. The Homemaker Program provides assistance with cleaning, meal preparation, shopping and personal care activities. The program is free to those 60 and older who need help because of a health-related situation.

Meeting Place
949 W. Moana Ln., Reno, Nev.
• **(775) 825-9423**

The Meeting Place provides an enriching program of learning and socialization for

---

INSIDERS' TIP

Citilift provides transportation in the Reno/Sparks area for disabled or older persons. For information call (775) 348-5438.

people who need supervision because of physical or memory impairments. The program consists of social and recreational activities, exercise, arts and crafts, memory retention programs and pet therapy.

Northern Nevada Ombudsman
445 Apple St., Ste. 104, Reno Nev.
• (775) 688-2964

Managed by the Nevada Division for Aging Services, the Northern Nevada Ombudsman program gives homebound seniors an advocate for voicing their concerns and complaints. The services are free and confidential to those who are 60 or older.

Saint Mary's Silver Connection
601 W. First St., Reno, Nev.
• (775) 688-6100

If you're 50 or older, staying healthy can be easy with a free membership in Saint Mary's Silver Connection. As part of Saint Mary's Health Network, the Silver Connection offers health screenings, educational programs and support groups that emphasize healthy habits and preventive medicine. Its monthly newsletter tells members about upcoming health-related events as well as the cultural activities, trips and free movies the program offers. The

Silver Connection also sponsors 50 Plus, a support group for widows and widowers.

Sanford Center for Aging
Univ. of Nevada, Reno, Reno, Nev.
• (775) 784-4774

Exploring innovative ideas for successful aging, the Sanford Center for Aging pursues programs in education, research, community outreach and service. Major outreach includes the Retired and Senior Volunteer Program, the *Sanford Center's Salute to Seniors* radio show, the Lake Tahoe Wellness Conference for Seniors and the Senior Sunshine Fund.

Senior Bridges
2385 E. Prater Wy., Ste. 202, Sparks, Nev. • (775) 356-1279

Intensive mental health treatment is available to seniors through the partial hospitalization program at Senior Bridges. Participants learn to deal with emotional problems and stress during the day, but return home at night to maintain involvement in the community.

Senior Law Program
1155 E. Ninth St., Reno, Nev.
• (775) 328-2592

It's hard to imagine you can get the exper-

This student is receiving the assistance of a Foster Grandparent Association volunteer.

tise of an attorney for free, but the Senior Law Program provides consultation and representation at no cost for residents of Washoe County who are 62 or older. Services are limited to elder rights law, government benefits and entitlements, consumer matters, real property and housing issues, and lifetime planning. Clients are expected to pay only for court costs and filing fees.

Senior Social Friends
97 Richards Wy., Sparks, Nev.
• **(775) 356-8123**

Many older persons find themselves alone after losing a spouse through death or divorce. Senior Social Friends helps older singles move on with their lives by supporting each other through social activities.

Washoe Senior Health Center
850 Mill St., Reno, Nev.
• **(775) 328-5420**

As part of Washoe Health System, Washoe Senior Health Center is a doctor's office just for people 65 or older. The center offers comprehensive care that also includes educational and preventive information. Patients receive a free membership in Washoe Senior Options, a senior-only program that sponsors social functions, trips and health and wellness services.

Working and Volunteering

American Association of Retired Persons Senior Community Service Employment Program
170 Terminal Way #282, Reno, Nev.
• **(775) 323-2243**

AARP's employment program can launch you on a second career with its counseling, training and information and referral service. The program is free for those who are 55 or older who also have limited income.

Foster Grandparent Program
1552 C St., Sparks, Nev.
• **(775) 358-2768**

You can profoundly enrich your life as well as that of your foster grandchild in the Foster Grandparent Program. Volunteers provide one-on-one daily attention to at-risk youth in schools, hospitals, drug treatment centers, day care centers and correctional institutions. You can apply if you're 60 or older, love children, meet certain income requirements and can volunteer 20 hours a week. Benefits include a small stipend, reimbursement of expenses, insurance and an annual physical.

Golden Opportunity
560 Mill St., Reno, Nev.
• **(775) 785-6106 ext. 127**

If "retirement" means continued involvement in the world of work, Golden Opportunity can help you develop your talents, learn new skills and find the right job to use them in. To qualify for the program, you must be 55 or older, meet financial guidelines and be seriously interested in working.

ProNet
(775) 688-1680

Although not just for seniors, we list this organization here because many older persons could benefit from their services. ProNet is a nonprofit organization that helps unemployed professionals find jobs. No-cost services include self-help networking, resources and training to assist in job hunting and workshops and programs to develop new job skills and to improve resumes.

Retired & Senior Volunteer Program of Washoe County
401 W. Second St., Ste. 102, Reno, Nev.
• **(775) 784-1807**

Volunteering where you can really make a difference is one of the most rewarding experiences many older persons discover in their

---

INSIDERS' TIP

Most Reno/Tahoe health clubs have fitness programs and classes designed specifically for older persons. Check local phone books for listings under "Health Clubs" and call for scheduled times and fees.

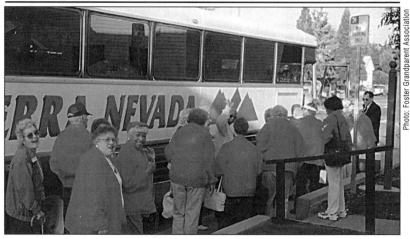

Reno/Tahoe has a variety of fine organizations that provide group activities for seniors and access to local facilities and services.

retirement. The Retired & Senior Volunteer Program of Washoe County (RSVP) actively recruits seniors 55 and older for a large number of local nonprofit and public agencies. With so many to choose from, you're sure to find the position that's just right for you. The program places volunteers in schools, museums, cultural events, hospitals, social agencies, parks and senior services. If you're newly retired and/or new to town, there's no better way to meet people with similar interests.

Senior Auxiliary Volunteer Effort (S.A.V.E.)
(775) 321-8312

If you've ever wanted to be a policeman, here's your chance. Sponsored by the Reno Police Department and the Retired & Senior Volunteer Program, S.A.V.E. is open to people 50 and older who want to help make their community a better place to live. Duties of the uniformed volunteers include checking on the vacant houses of people who are on vacation, fostering Neighborhood Watch and patrolling during daylight hours in specially marked po-

lice cars. The role of the volunteers is limited to observing and reporting.

Senior Companion Program
1552 C St., Sparks, Nev.
• (775) 358-2322

Many older persons delay or avoid living in nursing homes by using help provided by volunteers in the Senior Companion Program. Assistance is provided through home health care, hospitals, hospices, public housing and geriatric clinics. Volunteers are reimbursed for their expenses and receive insurance and an annual physical as a benefit. To qualify for volunteering, you must be at least 60 years old and agree to work 20 hours a week.

Fun and Fitness

Ballantine's Ballroom
2920 Mill St., Reno, Nev.
• (775) 324-1000

If you like to dance for fun and fitness, you're sure to find your comfort zone at

Ballantine's Ballroom. A popular dance hangout with the older crowd, Ballantine's offers ballroom and tap lessons as well as public dancing.

Incliners
Incline Village, Nev. • (775) 831-0362

With a whopping 800 members (almost 10 percent of the population of Incline Village, Nevada), the Incliners is the indisputable center of social activity for many older people living in Incline. Members meet twice a month for dinners and social events but also avidly pursue sports and hobbies together, such as tennis, golf, bike riding and bridge. Members must be 49 or older and be able to pay $10 in annual dues.

Newcomers Club of Reno–Sparks
(775) 828-5133

Although it's open to people of all ages, the Newcomers Club of Reno–Sparks has helped hundreds of older people transition into new lives in the Reno/Sparks area. With the motto, "There are no strangers here, only friends we have not met," it's hard not to feel welcome at the multitude of activities they sponsor. To be eligible for membership, you must be new to the area within a year of joining or have had a major lifestyle change, such as retirement, divorce or death of a spouse. More than 1,000 people are affiliated with the main umbrella group, which is made up of dozens of eclectic activity groups.

Over 50s Club
Kings Beach, Calif. • (530) 546-8535

For more than 30 years, seniors in the North Shore Lake Tahoe area have used the Over 50s Club as a focal point for socializing. They meet three times a month at the North Shore Community Center in Kings Beach, California, or at the Crystal Bay Club in Crystal Bay, Nevada, for potlucks, special events and gaming evenings.

Paradise Park Activity Center
2700 Paradise Dr., Reno, Nev.
• (775) 356-3176

The City of Reno offers a veritable smorgasbord of activities for seniors at the Paradise Park Activity Center, including exercise classes, quilting bees, dance workshops and card games. The parks and recreation department also welcomes suggestions for additional activities of interest to area seniors.

Senior Social Friends
2700 Paradise Dr., Reno, Nev.
• (775) 356-8123

Widows and widowers who've worked through the initial phase of grief recovery can take the first steps toward a new beginning through Senior Social Friends. The group meets several times a week at Paradise Park Activity Center. Call for times and information about specific activities.

Sparks Recreation Department Senior Softball Leagues
(775) 353-2376

You may love watching your grandchildren play ball, but how about playing yourself? Dust off your mitt and join in the fun with the Senior Softball Leagues. With names like Reno Rowdies and Super Seniors, the 18 teams comprise a large enthusiastic group of players that competes all year long. Sponsored by the Sparks Recreation Department, most league games take place on the Rail City's ball fields.

Where to Live

The choices of retirement or senior housing in Reno/Tahoe run the gamut, from private residences to apartments to full-service retirement homes with assisted living and nursing care. See our Real Estate and Neighborhoods chapter for an overview of housing and locales.

As one of the fastest growing areas in the country, it's hard to keep up with the increasing number of options. Although we can't list them all, in this chapter we give you examples of residential choices geared specifically to older persons: retirement communities and assisted living facilities. Rates are based upon single occupancy; facilities will charge several hundred additional dollars for a second occupant. For the assisted living facilities, we mention approximate rates, but they may vary depending on individual needs. For a complete listing of retirement living options, check in local telephone books under "Retirement."

Retirement Homes

Alterra Wynwood Retirement Residence
1900 E. Prater Wy., Sparks, Nev.
• **(775) 359-7700**

Spacious and impressive, Alterra Wynwood Retirement Residence feels just like home. Comfortable seating and lush green plants in the public areas create a cozy environment perfect for stimulating conversation or quiet reading. The tastefully decorated studio and one-bedroom apartments rent from about $1,500 to $2,200 a month. The rental fee includes scheduled transportation, meals, utilities, weekly housekeeping, linen service and cable television. A full-time activities director is in charge of the large variety of outings and events offered daily to residents. There's also a library, beauty shop and even an ice cream parlor.

Classic Residence by Hyatt
3201 Plumas St., Reno, Nev.
• **(775) 825-1105**

True to its name, Classic Residence by Hyatt is classic in every sense of the word. For retirees who can afford the best, it combines the ambiance of an exclusive country club with the warmth of a private home. If you've stayed at Hyatt resorts or hotels, you know the level of service and the elegant accouterments Hyatt provides.

Classic offers studio, one- and two-bedroom apartments, many with patio or balcony views of the Sierra Nevada mountains and the Washoe County Golf Course. Rates range from about $2,200 to $3,700 per month, with assisted living offered at additional cost. Monthly fees include meals, weekly housekeeping, scheduled transportation, apartment maintenance and concierge assistance. Classic even provides a moving coordinator to help with relocation details.

Amenities of the facility include the Wintergarden Lounge, library, arts and crafts studio, exercise room, beauty/barber shop, onsite banking, outdoor walking paths, free laundry facilities, parking, computer center, private dining room, billiards lounge and club room. Geared to active retirees, this facility goes out of its way to offer a large variety of cultural, educational, social and recreational outlets for residents.

Manor at Lakeside
855 Brinkby Ave., Reno, Nev.
• **(775) 827-3606**

Within easy walking distance of lovely Virginia Lake in Southwest Reno, the studio apartments at the Manor at Lakeside range in price from $1,100 to $1,300 per month. The monthly fee includes housekeeping, laundry, transportation, utilities and meals. Residents of the Manor have a full array of activities to choose from, including arts and crafts, exercise classes, local trips, social events and parties, discussion groups, card games and billiards. The facility also has a library, a beauty salon and free transportation service. If you're a pet owner, you'll be delighted to know the welcome mat is out for Fido or Fluffy also.

Odd Fellows Retirement Manor
1155 Beech St., Reno, Nev.
• **(775) 323-1911**

In a picturesque park-like setting near the University of Nevada, Reno, the Odd Fellows Retirement Manor has 118 private rooms that rent for $740 to $840 per month. Housekeeping, meals, activities and transportation are included. The university campus and nearby Dick Taylor Memorial Park offer enjoyable routes for daily walks.

Reno Camlu
1920 Harvard Wy., Reno, Nev.
• **(775) 825-2044**

Designed for carefree retirement living, Reno Camlu includes all the necessities for quality living in the rental payment. Studio apartments start at $1,125 and one-bedroom units at $1,350 per month, including weekly

INSIDERS' TIP

To find out how to file a state or federal charge of age discrimination call (202) 663-4900.

housekeeping and linen service, three daily meals, transportation, scheduled activities and satellite television. Residents can also take advantage of the on-site beauty and barber shop and the community visiting area. Since Reno Camlu is strictly a rental facility, residents are not required to sign leases or pay buy-in fees. Its location is especially convenient for shopping as it's right across from a large mall that has stores such as Costco, PetSmart, Office Depot and many other small retail establishments.

Tahoe Senior Plaza
1109 Third St., South Lake Tahoe, Calif.
• (800) 222-2469, Ext. 149

Opened in the spring of 1999, Tahoe Senior Plaza is a lovely mountain chalet with 44 one-bedroom apartments designed for independent living. Since the complex is federally subsidized housing for the elderly, residents must be at least 62 and meet certain income guidelines. Those accepted will pay rent equal to about 30 percent of their adjusted annual income. Because demand is high, it's necessary to place your name on a waiting list.

Assisted Living

Alterra Wynwood Assisted Living
2000 E. Prater Wy., Sparks, Nev.
• (775) 359-7733

Personalized service is the trademark at Alterra Wynwood Assisted Living since residents' preferences are an integral part of their care. Assistance with unscheduled needs is provided 24 hours a day and a licensed nurse is on staff every day. All of the apartments in this bright, modern facility have wall-to-wall carpeting and kitchenettes. Housekeeping and laundry service plus a full array of educational and social opportunities are included. Prices start at $2,400 per month.

Tahoe Manor Guest Home
586 Glorene Ave., South Lake Tahoe,
Calif. • (530) 542-2383

Tucked away in a forest of beautiful pinos, Tahoe Manor Guest Home is the only assisted living facility in the Lake Tahoe area. Its personal care program is designed to assist active, healthy seniors in adjusting to a slower pace of life while maintaining their independence. Services include three meals a day, daily housekeeping, laundry service, assistance with personal care, transportation and scheduled activities. The modern facility offers a beauty salon, recreational sitting room and a patio for lounging. Costs for government subsidized residents are $750, and it costs $1,325 for private-pay residents.

The Inn at Summit Ridge
4880 Summit Ridge Dr., Reno, Nev.
• (775) 787-3000

The Inn at Summit Ridge enables residents to age in place since it offers several levels of care depending upon individual needs. Monthly fees range from $1,890 to $3,600 and include meals, housekeeping and linen, basic utilities, scheduled transportation and assistance with daily activities. Residents can enjoy the beautifully landscaped courtyard, the library with its cozy fireplace, an elegant private dining room and the activities room with a big-screen TV.

Just a glance in local telephone books will show more than 800 physicians and surgeons practicing in every field of medical specialization.

Healthcare and Wellness

Because Reno/Tahoe is such an attractive place to live, it's not hard to understand why there's an abundance of doctors in the region. After all, if you can choose where to practice medicine, why not select a beautiful area with unlimited opportunities for recreation? Just a glance in local telephone books will show more than 800 physicians and surgeons practicing in every field of medical specialization. Almost any medical procedure you might need is available locally except organ transplants, which are routinely done in Sacramento, California, about two hours away by car.

In addition to the hundreds of medical doctors, about 100 podiatrists and doctors of osteopathy and more than 300 dentists have hung out their shingles here. Although most of these medical personnel practice traditional medicine, alternative care, such as acupuncture and homeopathy, is also available.

Since the Reno/Sparks area is the largest center of population, it serves the medical needs of not only its own residents but of people living in nearby rural communities in Nevada and California. And while Lake Tahoe has a high number of doctors per person and two small hospitals, the variety of medical care available in Reno and Sparks is much greater. Although the good news is the high quality and diversity of care available, the bad news is that it costs about 20 percent more than the national average.

You might not think that an area well known for its 24-hour lifestyle would be especially conscious of healthcare and wellness. Statistics also paint a rather grim picture, showing high rates for suicide, smoking and alcohol abuse, particularly in Reno and Sparks. But in spite of this, a healthy lifestyle is a priority for an increasing number of residents because they want to participate fully in the outdoor activities available in the area. Insiders also know that many people living at Lake Tahoe are sports enthusiasts who spend as much time as possible hiking, biking and skiing.

When not exercising outside, many people stay in shape at one of the more than 30 health clubs in the area. While some clubs are fitness studios emphasizing exercise machines and individual workouts, others are full-service health centers, with lap pools, childcare facilities, racquetball and tennis courts, tanning salons, massage therapy, clothing shops, restaurants, personalized training and a large variety of classes. And because Reno is a 24-hour city, you can work out around the clock in many of its health clubs. Before joining a club it's a good idea to shop around, since membership packages and prices vary a lot. Check local phone books under "health clubs" for complete listings.

But even athletes who are in good condition occasionally have accidents and get hurt. If that happens to you, you can take some comfort in knowing that the Reno/Tahoe area has attracted a number of athletically-inclined physicians who specialize in sports medicine. They understand not only the clinical aspects of sports injuries but the practical side as well, since it's likely they spend a lot of their free time hiking, biking and skiing. If you're looking for knee reconstruction or joint replacement, just let your fingers do the walking through the Yellow Pages, where you'll find a variety of highly qualified orthopedic surgeons listed. After all, with more than 20 ski resorts in the area, they have plenty of ski-related injuries to practice on.

While the variety of available medical care reflects in part the lifestyle of area residents and visitors, the medical community is further enriched by the University of Nevada School of Medicine in Reno. Established in 1969 by the Nevada State Legislature and funded in part by the late eccentric billionaire, Howard Hughes, the School of Medicine is integrated with local hospitals, clinics and physicians. More than 900 community physicians throughout the state are involved in its mission to provide medical education and training for Nevadans. The school is also an important center of medical research, focusing on problems that affect Nevada in particular. The University of Nevada, Reno also trains registered nurses in its Orvis School of Nursing; Truckee Meadows Community College, also in Reno, trains registered nurses as well as certified nursing assistants. The Reno/Tahoe area is also home to a number of licensed schools of massage.

In this chapter we give you a general overview of the kinds of healthcare offered in the Reno/Tahoe area. We tell you about the major hospitals, which are comprehensive healthcare delivery systems, as well as the smaller specialty hospitals and clinics. We tell you how to find a doctor, where to get emergency care, what support groups are available and where to get alternative medical care. And last, but not least, we tell you how to get medical attention for the family pet.

Hospitals

Reno

HealthSouth Rehabilitation Hospital of Reno
555 Gould St., Reno, Nev.
• (775) 348-5500

As the country's largest provider of ambulatory surgery, HealthSouth specializes in rehabilitative services. Their occupational rehabilitation program emphasizes structured returns to work and injury prevention. The Reno facility consists of a 60-bed inpatient unit and a transitional living apartment as well as outpatient services. Their diagnostic imaging center also has an Open MRI, which is especially appealing to patients who are claustrophobic.

Reno Veterans Affairs Medical Center
1000 Locust St., Reno, Nev.
• (775) 786-7200

Serving veterans in northern Nevada and northeastern California, the Reno Veterans Affairs Medical Center is a 110-bed general medical and surgical hospital with a 60-bed nursing home care unit. The VA is well known for its innovative geriatric health programs as well as research into diseases and geriatric rehabilitation. With more than 60 projects ongoing at any given time, the center conducts more research than all other hospitals in Nevada combined. The center has studied Alzheimer's, Parkinson's, kidney and cardiovascular diseases, hypertension, diabetes and breathing disorders. The VA also offers Home Based Primary Care to veterans needing care in their home environment and Contract Adult Day Health Care which helps delay admission to a residential care facility.

Saint Mary's Regional Medical Center
235 W. Sixth St., Reno, Nev.
• (775) 789-3000

The legacy of Saint Mary's Regional Medical Center was born when a group of Dominican nuns arrived in Reno in 1877 to open a school for local children. The sisters soon learned that early Reno not only lacked educational structures but needed healthcare facilities as well. To help address this need they built Sisters' Hospital in 1908, which was the forerunner of Saint Mary's.

With 367 beds and about 700 staff physicians, today the hospital is part of Saint Mary's Health Network, a large integrated healthcare delivery system. Specialty services offered by Saint Mary's include rehabilitation, home care, outpatient surgery, radiology, emergency care, surgery and heart services. The Center also operates Hospice of Northern Nevada, the Maclean Center for Addictions and Behavioral Health, the Parish Nurse Program to train volunteer nurses and the Silver Connection for those 50 and older, as well as health and wellness outreach for women and children. Because Saint Mary's is still operated by Catholic Sisters, the spiritual well-being of patients is part of the healing process. The inpatient hospital rooms at the center are especially appealing because all of them are spacious and private.

Washoe Medical Center
77 Pringle Wy., Reno, Nev.
• (775) 982-4100

Founded in 1862 to treat smallpox victims, Washoe Medical Center is northern Nevada's oldest healthcare facility. It is also Reno/Tahoe's largest and most comprehensive acute-care hospital, with the only Level II trauma center, bone-marrow transplant unit, pediatric intensive care unit and radiation therapy program in the area. It also has centers to treat diabetes, heart disease, cancer and substance abuse as well as dialysis, surgical and poison centers.

As part of Washoe Health System, Washoe Med (as it's known by Insiders) is home to an extensive variety of services designed not only to treat illness but to educate patients and their families and friends about wellness and preventive medicine. To increase awareness of prenatal issues, Washoe Med helps sponsor Baby Your Baby Day; to educate young people about the dangers of smoking it participates in the Blow Off Smoke Campaign; to help make children aware of healthful habits it

holds Kids at Heart Camp; and to emphasize women's health issues it sponsors Washoe Women's Day of Health.

Recognizing that healing has emotional as well as physical aspects, Washoe Med encourages loved ones to become part of the healthcare team with its Very Important Partners program and provides interaction with dogs through its Pet Therapy with K-9 Kare.

Because it's a large regional complex that serves people from outlying areas as well as locals, Washoe Med has amenities not found in all hospitals. You can rent a hotel room at the Washoe Inn, enjoy tasty meals in three restaurants and shop in the boutique, all within the medical campus. There's also covered parking, a chapel, a pharmacy and a dry cleaners. Washoe Health Resource Center provides a wealth of information about healthcare and wellness, with 400 books and periodicals and access to computers.

If you're more comfortable in a small hospital, Washoe Med may seem too large for you as it has 529 licensed beds. And if you prefer a private room, Washoe does not always provide one, but St. Mary's Regional Medical Center and Northern Nevada Medical Center will.

West Hills Hospital
1240 E. Ninth St., Reno, Nev.
• (775) 323-0478

A 95-bed private psychiatric facility, West Hills Hospital offers inpatient hospitalization and a variety of outpatient programs for people of all ages who have mental health problems. Patients work with a treatment team, consisting of a psychiatrist, social worker or counselor, psychiatric nurses and mental health technicians. The hospital has an extensive substance abuse program which is available on either an inpatient or outpatient basis.

INSIDERS' TIP

Operating from Reno hospitals, the Care Flight medical emergency helicopter is the busiest single helicopter medical air service in the country, averaging more than 100 flights per month. The isolation and inaccessibility of parts of the Reno/Tahoe area make the helicopter especially suitable for transporting critical patients to the medicl facilities they require.

Willow Springs Center
690 Edison Wy., Reno, Nev.
- **(775) 858-3303**

Willow Springs Center is a 74-bed residential treatment center for children and adolescents aged 5 to 17. Established in 1988, Willow Springs provides a long-term therapeutic environment for young people experiencing emotional and behavioral problems. It's affiliated with West Hills Hospital, a mental health facility also in Reno.

Sparks

Nevada Mental Health Institute
480 Galletti Wy., Sparks, Nev.
- **(775) 688-2001**

Operated by the State of Nevada, the Nevada Mental Health Institute offers psychiatric services, day treatment and case management. Treatment in its 74-bed adult psychiatric hospital includes diagnostic and therapeutic services. Program fees are on a sliding scale, depending upon eligibility.

Northern Nevada Medical Center
2375 E. Prater Wy., Sparks, Nev.
- **(775) 331-7000**

It's large enough to offer comprehensive medical services but small enough to add a personal touch to healing. Originally Sparks Family Hospital when it opened in 1983, Northern Nevada Medical Center is a 100-bed, acute-care hospital on 23 acres in Sparks. It has a 24-hour emergency room and complete surgical and diagnostic services, including a comprehensive same-day surgery program.

Although it sounds like a pizza delivery system, it's the only hospital that has a "15-minute ER Guarantee" that means your emergency room visit is free if you're not seen within 15 minutes by a nurse and 60 minutes by a doctor. The center also follows up almost all cases that come through the ER with a phone call home after the patient is released from the hospital. NNMC also boasts a preadmission program designed to familiarize patients with staff and hospital procedures before treatment. The Senior Bridges program at NNMC is nationally recognized and offers complete inpatient and outpatient psychological care for people 65 and older.

Tahoe Pacific Hospital
2385 E. Prater Wy., Sparks, Nev.
- **(775) 331-1044**

On the seventh floor of Northern Nevada Medical Center, Tahoe Pacific Hospital is a hospital within a hospital. Patients who are critically ill or who have suffered a serious injury are often referred to Tahoe Pacific for a long-term rehabilitative stay. The therapy department offers services in speech, occupational, physical and recreational rehabilitation. The hospital's working arrangement with NNMC permits use of their surgery, laboratory and radiology services on site.

North Shore Lake Tahoe

Incline Village Health Center
880 Alder Ave., Incline Village, Nev.
- **(775) 833-4100**

A division of Tahoe Forest Hospital District (which is based in Truckee, California), Incline Village Health Center is an eight-bed, acute-care hospital. It offers 24-hour emergency care, diagnostic services, outpatient surgery and inpatient observation. Because of its small size, the emphasis is on outpatient services. Through its Physician Finder referral system, the center provides access to more than 80 physicians who represent a wide variety of specialties. For information about these doctors, their locations and insurance accepted, patients can call (800) 733-9953, extension 483, or (530) 582-3483.

South Shore Lake Tahoe

Barton Memorial Hospital
2170 South Ave., South Lake Tahoe, Calif. • (530) 541-3420

Barton Memorial Hospital is living testimony to what a small community can do when it works together to meet a critical need. Prior to the hospital's opening in 1963, medical care was provided by a small number of local physicians. The nearest hospitals in Reno and Carson City, Nevada, were nearly an hour away when the roads were clear, and frequently were all but unreachable during periods of heavy snow. Realizing the necessity of having more accessible medical care, local residents worked to raise funds for the original 38-bed medical facility. Celebrities who regularly performed in the area even joined the effort, with the profits from Elvis Presley's benefit concert used to build the Intensive Care Unit.

Since those first frantic fund-raising days, Barton Memorial has expanded to an 81-bed acute-care facility with a medical staff of more than 100 and a support staff of about 200. The medical complex also includes a Skilled Nursing & Rehabilitation Center with 48 beds. Services include 24-hour emergency care with a trauma room, surgery, hospice care, home health and diagnostics.

Barton Memorial is an attractive, modern medical facility that is a source of great pride to those living in South Shore Lake Tahoe. It continues to be a not-for-profit hospital that is owned by the community.

Referral Services

If you're new to the Reno/Tahoe area or just visiting, the easiest way to find out about local doctors is to use the referral numbers below. Also note that most hospitals keep referral lists of physicians.

Direct Doctors Physician Referral, (800) 874-5775

Physician Finder, (530) 582-3483 or (800) 733-9953, extension 483

Saint Mary's Health Network, (775) 789-3627

Walk-in Clinics

The following clinics operate with extended hours and will accept patients with no appointments.

Medina Medical Center, 961 W. Fifth Street, Reno, Nevada, (775) 348-8800

Orchard Urgent Care, 2295 S. Virginia Street, Reno, Nevada, (775) 825-1551

Saint Mary's Family Walk-in Health Center, 6580 S. Virginia Street, Reno, Nevada, (775) 853-3333

Specialty Health Clinic, 350 W. Sixth Street, Reno, Nevada, (775) 322-2122

Stateline Medical Center, 176 U.S. Highway 50, Stateline, Nevada, (775) 588-3561

Tahoe Urgent Care Medical Clinic, 2130 Lake Tahoe Boulevard, South Lake Tahoe, California, (530) 541-3277

Truckee-Tahoe Medical Group, 945 N. Lake Boulevard, Tahoe City, California, (530) 583-5320

Washoe Urgent Care, 975 Ryland Street, Reno, Nevada, (775) 982-5210

Zephyr Medical Center, 195 U.S. Highway 50, Stateline, Nevada, (775) 586-8102

Alternative Medical Care

It wasn't that long ago that alternative medicine, such as acupuncture and homeopathy, was viewed by many people as nothing more than treatments of last resort, used when all traditional methods of treatment had failed. But today a growing number of people rely on alternative medicine for ongoing and preventive medical care.

The Reno/Tahoe area has a number of clinics and doctors that integrate scientific and natural medicine. Some services available include homeopathy, herbology, neural therapy, chelation, hormone management, Chinese herbal medicine, sclerotherapy, trigger point therapy and acupuncture. For up-to-date information about alternative treatments, check out the Alternative Medical Directory printed each week in the *Reno News & Review*. To find a listing of doctors and clinics, look under the subheading "Homeopathy" in the Physicians section of the Nevada Bell telephone book. You can also call the National Center for Homeopathy at (703) 548-7790 for referral and general information.

As a starting place, the following clinics offer some type of alternative medicine.

Bio Medical Health Center, 6490 S. McCarran Boulevard, Reno, Nevada, (775) 827-1444

Cancer Care Center, 521 Hammill Lane, Reno, Nevada, (775) 829-1009

Century Wellness Center, 380 Brinkby Avenue, Reno, Nevada, (775) 826-9500

Gerber Medical Clinic, 3670 Grant Drive, Reno, Nevada, (775) 826-1900

Spanish Springs Medical Group, 1015 Spanish Springs Road, Sparks, Nevada, (775) 359-3466

Triad Medical Center, 4600 Kietzke Lane, Reno, Nevada, (775) 829-2277

Women's Health Care, 1101 W. Moana Lane, Reno, Nevada, (775) 827-2449

Special Services and Support Groups

If you need a helping hand, or simply moral support, it's just a phone call away since several hundred organizations offer support services in the Reno/Tahoe area. We can't list them all, but we'll give you a sampling of what's available. If you don't find what you need, call the Crisis Call Center at (775) 784-8090; they keep a complete list of community resources.

Alzheimer's Association Northern Nevada Chapter
705 S. Wells Ave., Reno, Nev.
• **(775) 786-8061**

This association provides information, referral, support groups and free respite care for families affected by Alzheimer's.

American Red Cross
1190 Corporate Blvd., Reno, Nev.
• **(775) 856-1000**

In addition to emergency disaster relief, the American Red Cross offers a variety of community education programs about AIDS, first aid, safety and babysitting.

Association for Retarded Citizens–Washoe County Chapter
790 Sutro St., Reno, Nev.
• **(775) 333-9272**

Known as WARC by locals, the Association for Retarded Citizens evaluates, trains and provides work opportunities for retarded persons in its thrift stores. As a highly successful advocate for the mentally retarded, it also offers family counseling and community education programs.

Basic Recovery Associates, Inc.
604 Greenbrae Dr., Sparks, Nev.
• **(775) 358-4998**

Programs at Basic Recovery meet court requirements and include outpatient substance abuse treatment, DUI and traffic safety schools, anger management, parenting, money management and individual and family therapy. Fees are on a sliding scale.

Bridges in Consciousness
2850 Wrondel Way, Reno, Nev.
• **(775) 827-6788**

AIDS support and grief counseling are offered by this center.

CARE Chest of Sierra Nevada
5390 Riggins Ct., Ste. F, Reno, Nev.
• **(775) 829-2273**

People who have no insurance benefits or adequate financial resources for medications and medical equipment can obtain them at no cost through this program.

Catholic Community Services of Nevada–North
275 E. Fourth St., Reno, Nev.
• **(775) 322-7073**

This nonprofit organization offers emergency assistance on a variety of levels: clothing, housing, transportation and food.

Children's Cabinet, Inc.
1909 S. Rock Blvd., Reno, Nev.
• **(775) 856-6200**

A highly successful organization with a large umbrella of services for children and families, Children's Cabinet is well respected for its counseling, tutoring, parenting and substance abuse programs.

Children's Cabinet at Incline Village
893 Southwood Blvd., Incline Village, Nev. • **(775) 831-6200**

Through a variety of programs, this nonprofit is a centralized clearinghouse of information and services for children and families in North Shore Lake Tahoe.

Crisis Call Center
(775) 784-8090, (800) 992-5757

Established in 1966 as a suicide prevention hotline, Crisis Call Center is the longest continuously operating crisis line in the country. Highly trained volunteers answer more than 1,000 calls each month from those in need. The crisis line is staffed 24 hours a day and serves rural Nevada as well as the Reno/Tahoe area.

Foster Grandparent Program
1552 C St., Sparks, Nev.
• (775) 358-2768

Children and seniors lend each other a helping hand through this program. Older persons receive a stipend, transportation and meals in exchange for providing services to children with special needs.

Gamblers Anonymous–
South Lake Tahoe
(530) 573-2423

The program offers help to those addicted to gambling.

Gamblers Anonymous–
Reno/Sparks
(775) 356-8070

Individuals with gambling problems are offered support and counseling through this program.

Grief Recovery Outreach
Workshop (G.R.O.W.)
(775) 982-4385

Grief Recovery Outreach Workshop offers guidance, friendship and support for those beginning the healing journey of grief. Programs are available at various times throughout the fall, winter and spring at St. John's Presbyterian Church, Washoe Medical Center and St. Mary's Regional Medical Center. Call for specific times and dates.

Health Access Washoe County (H.A.W.C.)
1175 Harvard Way, Reno, Nev.
• (775) 329-6300

This community health clinic provides low-cost medical services to Medicare, Medicaid and uninsured patients.

I Can Cope
712 Mill St., Reno, Nev.
• (775) 329-0609

Offered by the American Cancer Society, the program offers support and counseling for individuals and families affected by cancer.

Nevada Hispanic Services, Inc.
190 E. Liberty St., Reno, Nev.
• (775) 786-6003

For the growing Spanish-speaking population, this agency provides interpretation and translation services, immigration assistance, job placement and youth programs.

Project Restart
624 E. Fourth St., Reno, Nev.
• (775) 324-2622

As its name suggests, Project Restart has a variety of programs to help at-risk people start over with training and job placement.

Reno/Sparks Gospel Mission, Inc.
145 W. Third St., Reno, Nev.
• (775) 323-1560

The Gospel Mission offers emergency food, clothing and shelter to anyone who has identification and is sober. Counseling is also available through their Christian Addiction Recovery and Education (C.A.R.E.) program.

INSIDERS' TIP

Don't be surprised if you see your aerobics instructor on stage downtown, as dancers from the shows frequently give exercise classes at local health clubs.

Nonprofits and support groups offer a variety of services in the Reno/Tahoe area, from crisis intervention to hospice to senior daycare.

Ronald McDonald House
323 Maine St., Reno, Nev.
- **(775) 322-4663**

The house provides a home away from home for families of children who are patients in any Reno hospital.

Saint Mary's Hospice
of Northern Nevada
1155 W. Fourth St., Reno, Nev.
- **(775) 789-3046**

Operated as part of Saint Mary's Health Network, the hospice provides medical and spiritual care for terminally ill patients and their loved ones.

Senior Law Project–
Washoe County
1155 E. Ninth St., Reno, Nev.
- **(775) 328-2592**

This project gives free legal help to those 60 and older who are residents of Washoe County in the areas of Social Security, government benefits, Medicare, Medicaid and landlord/tenant disputes.

Senior Daybreak
1155 E. Ninth St., Reno, Nev.
- **(775) 328-2591**

This program provides daycare for adults 18 or older as an alternative to institutionalization. It offers caregivers daytime relief with nursing and social opportunities for those with disabilities.

Survivors After Sexual Assault
(775) 784-8085

The program is a support group for survivors of sexual assault.

Survivors of Suicide
(775) 784-8085

Individuals who have survived the suicide of a significant other can join this self-help group.

Tahoe Youth and Family Services
1021 Fremont Ave., South Lake Tahoe, Calif. • (530) 541-2445

Programs provided by this nonprofit include youth and family counseling, a 24-hour runaway hotline and substance abuse counseling.

Womenspace Unlimited
3140 Lake Tahoe Blvd., South Lake Tahoe, Calif. • (530) 544-2118

Directed at women and families in crisis, Womenspace Unlimited offers counseling, emergency services and educational outreach.

Pet Care

If your pet needs medical attention, don't

panic: state-of-the-art medical care is available at the many veterinary hospitals in the Reno/Tahoe area. Many clinics offer 24-hour emergency care, house calls, surgery, boarding and even acupuncture. Some veterinarians specialize in just horses, cats or small animals; others treat all types of pets.

Since animals (like people) don't get sick at the most convenient times, it's a good idea to have a couple of emergency numbers handy. The **Animal Emergency Center** at 6427 S. Virginia Street in Reno, (775) 851-3600, has a doctor on the premises during nighttime hours, all weekend and 24 hours a day during holidays. The **North Hills Veterinary Clinic** at 1075 N. Hills Boulevard in Reno, (775) 972-5566, and **Incline Veterinary Hospital** at 880 Tanager in Incline Village, Nevada, (775) 831-0433, offer 24-hour on-call emergency care. In the South Shore Lake Tahoe area, most veterinarians rotate emergency duty so the answering service at any of their offices will refer you to the doctor on call. **Carson-Tahoe Veterinary Hospital** operates one of the few pet ambulances available in the country. Equipped much like a human ambulance, it will travel up to 400 miles from the area. For information call (775) 883-8238.

Emergency Numbers

Police, fire and ambulance: 911
Adult Protective Services: (775) 688-2811
Air Ambulance Network: (800) 327-1966
Care Flight medical emergency helicopter: (800) 648-4888
Child Find of America, Inc.: (800) 426-5678
Child Help, USA: (800) 422-4453
Child Protective Services Washoe County: (775) 328-2300
Committee to Aid Abused Women: (800) 500-1566
Compulsive Gambling Hotline: (800) 567-8238
Crisis Call Center: (775) 784-8090 or (800) 992-5757
Crisis Pregnancy Center–Reno: (775) 826-5144
Domestic Violence Hotline: (775) 883-7654
Federal Bureau of Investigation: (775) 323-7143
Hearing impaired emergency calls: 911, then tap space bar until someone answers
Missing Children's Hotline: (800) 235-3900
National Center for Missing and Exploited Children: (800) 843-5678
National Runaway Switchboard: (800) 621-4000
National Youth Crisis Hotline: (800) 448-4663
Nevada State Division of Forestry: (775) 883-3535
Nevada State Highway Patrol: Dial "0," ask for Zenith 1-2000
Planned Help for Pregnancies Life Line: (530) 581-5433
Planned Parenthood: (775) 688-5555
Poison Control Hotline: (800) 876-4766
Runaway Crisis Line–Tahoe: (530) 541-8500
Secret Witness Lake Tahoe: (530) 541-6800
Secret Witness Reno/Sparks: (775) 322-4900
Tahoe Women's Services: (530) 546-8474
Washoe Poison Center: (775) 982-4129
Women's Center–South Lake Tahoe: (530) 211-4444

The majority of both California's and Nevada's state budgets (about 53 percent of each) goes toward providing a quality education to students from kindergarten all the way through to obtaining a Ph.D.

Education and Child Care

We take education seriously here in the Reno/Tahoe area, from our children in preschools to our graduate students at universities. The majority of both California's and Nevada's state budgets (about 53 percent of each) goes toward providing a quality education to students from kindergarten all the way through to obtaining a Ph.D. Our commitment to better education grows stronger each year.

Both Nevada and California have mandated high school exit examinations which all seniors must pass in order to graduate with a high school diploma. And, at the K through 8 levels, standardized tests are being used by both states to evaluate student performance.

One problem that crops up each year is the large influx of new students. About 4 percent of the student body each year is new, putting a strain on the already overcrowded hallways of our schools. To help alleviate this problem, voters recently approved a $198 million bond issue to construct new schools in the Washoe County School District, one of the four school districts (two in Nevada and two in California) that cover the Reno/Tahoe area. As of May 1999, about 60,000 students attend school in the Reno/Tahoe area with about 6,000 teachers assigned to see to their educational well-being.

Even though the number of students in the Reno/Tahoe area continues to grow, private educational facilities in the area still number below 50. Most of these serve kindergart-

ners but private schools at the elementary, middle and high school levels can be found.

Some families prefer to home school their children, which is permissible as long as the curriculum is approved by the local school district.

Despite the area's commitment to education and the fact that the students' average scores on the ACT and SAT are among the best in the state (and above the national average), Nevada still ranks dead last among states sending their high school graduates on to college. Only 37 percent of Nevada's high school seniors enroll in institutions of higher learning, well below the national average of 62 percent. This low percentage can be explained by Nevada's stellar economy — high school graduates have no problem finding jobs here, and most of the jobs are in the service industry or the construction business where advanced degrees are not needed.

All this is a shame, because the university and community college system in the Reno/Tahoe area is one of the best in Nevada. (On the California side of the lake, there's only one community college; it's in South Lake Tahoe). In fact, in 1998, *U.S. News and World Report* ranked the University of Nevada, Reno as one of the top 100 colleges and universities in the United States.

This chapter begins with an overview of the public and private schools throughout the Reno/Tahoe area. Then we discuss the topic

INSIDERS' TIP

The oldest schoolhouse in Nevada is the Glendale School in Sparks, built in 1864. The building was used until 1958. It is now part of the Heritage Park and Museum in downtown Sparks.

of child care options in our area and give you a range of places to begin your search for those child-care services that best suit you.

Recess is over, so let's get back to school.

Education

Public Schools

Reno/Sparks and the Nevada-side of North Shore Lake Tahoe

Washoe County School District
425 E. Ninth St., Reno,
Nev. • (775) 348-8000

The Washoe County School District (WCSD) serves more than 52,000 students. Within the Reno/ Tahoe area, more than 3,100 teachers work in 58 elementary schools, 11 middle schools, 13 high schools and two special needs schools. The average student/ teacher ratio is 22.5 to 1 in the elementary grades, except first and second grades, where a state-mandated 16 to 1 ratio is maintained. To help remain in compliance with this state law, some first- and second-grade classrooms employ a team-teaching situation where two teachers are assigned to a class of 32 students. The middle-grade classrooms average a 26.2 to 1 student/teacher ratio and the high schools maintain a slightly higher ratio.

WCSD is the 90th largest district in the nation and with the addition of more than 2,000 students a year, overcrowding is a continual issue here. To meet the challenge of maintaining a reasonable student/teacher ratio, some elementary schools have volunteered to go on a year-round, single-track or multi-track schedule. And in 1998 voters okayed a $198 million school bond for the construction of three new high schools and two elementary schools.

Despite the fact that overcrowding is a

problem in WCSD, especially at the high school level (only one of the district's 13 high schools is below capacity), the *Reno-Gazette-Journal* continues to report that students consistently average higher on the SATs than the rest of Nevada and the nation. In 1998, the average SAT combined verbal and math score for students in the WCSD was 1,055, compared to the rest of the students in Nevada at 1,029 and the rest of the country at 1,016. All elementary school students are required by state law to take the TerraNova standardized test. In high school, seniors must pass state-mandated reading, writing and math examinations to receive a high school diploma, no matter what the student's overall grade point average is.

At the high school level, WCSD oversees the Glen Hare Occupational Center, which provides alternative classes to high school students. These classes include electronics, computer aided design, business systems, advanced child development and many other occupational specialties. The WCSD also began a magnet high school program for juniors and seniors. The school is located on the campus of Truckee Meadows Community College in Reno. At TMCC, high school students earn college credits while they finish their high school graduation requirements. In 1998, Nevada's first charter school, a state-funded contract school, opened its doors in Reno, giving high school students even more of a selection for their secondary education.

Even though the majority of WCSD's schools are located in the Truckee Meadows, the district is responsible for one high school, one middle school and one elementary school in Incline Village on the North Shore of Lake Tahoe.

To enroll a student in the WCSD, first contact the WCSD administration at the number listed to find out which school your home is zoned for. Then proceed to that school with the following documentation: your child's immunization record, proof of residency and proof of the child's identity. Contact the Washoe County Health Department at 1001

E. Ninth St., Reno, Nevada, (775) 328-2400, to set up a consultation appointment regarding the immunization record, since appropriate immunizations depend on the student's age. A utility bill, a rental agreement or a mortgage contract is acceptable as proof of residency. For child identification, a birth certificate, a passport or a baptismal certificate is sufficient. Another helpful document is a student's most recent report card to help place the student in the proper class or classes.

The WCSD provides bus service from K–12 if a student lives 2 miles or farther from his or her school.

Nevada law requires that every child between the ages of 7 and 17 attend school. Kindergarten is not mandatory but, as of July 1998, a student who does not attend kindergarten must be tested before entering the first grade.

California-side of North Shore Lake Tahoe

Tahoe-Truckee Unified School District
11839 Donner Pass Rd., Truckee, Calif.
• **(530) 582-7600**

The Tahoe-Truckee Unified School District is responsible for five schools located around the California-side of North Shore of Lake Tahoe.

Two elementary schools, one middle school and one high school are located in Tahoe City, California. The district is also responsible for one elementary school in Kings Beach, California. The total population of these schools tops just over 2,000 students. California mandates a 20 to 1 student/teacher ratio in its K–3 classrooms, and all elementary school students must take a standardized achievement test. High school students, in order to graduate, must take an exit examination.

To enroll a student in the TTUSD, first contact the district's administration at the number listed to find out which school your home is zoned for. Then proceed to that school with the following documentation: your child's immunization record, proof of residency and

proof of the child's identity. Required immunizations may be obtained from the county's health department or from a private physician. A utility bill, a rental agreement or a mortgage contract is acceptable proof of residency. For child identification, a birth certificate or a passport is preferred. Another helpful document is a student's most recent report card to help place the student in the proper class or classes.

The TTUSD provides bus service from K–12 if a student lives within the boundaries marked for his or her school, no matter the distance from the school. California law requires that children must attend school between first grade and their 18th birthday. Kindergarten is not mandatory.

South Shore Lake Tahoe

Douglas County School District
751 Mono Ave., Minden, Nev.
• **(775) 782-5134**

The Douglas County School District is responsible for three schools on the South Shore of Lake Tahoe on the Nevada side. The district's administrative offices are located over the mountains in the tiny Nevada town of Minden, so at times students, teachers and parents feel isolated from the rest of the school district, especially during the snow season.

The district maintains a high school and one elementary school in Zephyr Cove, Nevada, and a middle school at Stateline, Nevada. The total student population of all the schools is 915.

To enroll a student in the county's schools at the lake, proceed to your school with the following documentation: your child's immunization record, proof of residency and proof of the child's identity. A utility bill, a rental agreement or a mortgage contract is acceptable as proof of residency. For child identification, a birth certificate, a passport or a baptismal certificate is sufficient. Another helpful document is a student's most recent report card to help place the student in the proper class or classes.

The DCSD provides bus service from K–12 if a student lives 2 miles or farther from his or her school. Nevada law requires that every child between the ages of 7 and 17 attend school. Kindergarten is not mandatory but, as

Photo: Roger Brotherton

The Palmer School of Engineering is a prominent part of the top-ranked University of Nevada, Reno.

of July 1998, a student who does not attend kindergarten must be tested before entering the first grade.

Lake Tahoe Unified School District
1021 Al Tahoe Blvd., South Lake Tahoe, Calif. • (530) 541-2850

The fourth school district with jurisdiction around Lake Tahoe is the Lake Tahoe Unified School District located in South Lake Tahoe, California. This district has the responsibility of overseeing five elementary schools, one middle school and three high schools, all of which are located in South Lake Tahoe. The students number about 5,600 and the district employs about 300 teachers.

By California state law, the elementary schools must maintain a 20 to 1 student/teacher ratio in grades K–3, but district officials say this ratio is maintained throughout all the elementary grades. One of the three high schools is a transient learning center, where students who need more time adjusting to high school life attend classes usually taught by one teacher. And one of the high schools is a continuation high school that is attended by a small number of students who are having trouble in the traditional school system.

To enroll a student in the LTUSD, first contact the district's administration at the number listed to find out which school your home is zoned for. Then proceed to that school with the following documentation: your child's immunization record, proof of residency and proof of the child's identity.

Required immunizations may be obtained from the county's health department or from a private physician. A utility bill, a rental agreement or a mortgage contract is acceptable proof of residency. For child identification, a birth certificate or a passport is preferred. Another helpful document is a student's most recent report card to help place the student in the proper class or classes.

The LTUSD provides bus service from K–12 if a student lives within the boundaries marked for his or her school, no matter the distance from the school. California law requires that children must attend school between first grade and their 18th birthday. Kindergarten is not mandatory.

Private Schools

About 50 private schools operate in the Reno/Tahoe area. Within this total, 39 serve kindergartners and preschoolers, 18 serve elementary school students, 14 serve middle school students and nine serve high school students. Most of these educational facilities have religious affiliations and only a few are large facilities. Most are smaller schools that boast low student/teacher ratios. The majority of the schools are located in the Reno/Sparks area.

Tuition costs range from a low of about ₡1,400 per year to high of $8,500. The following is an alphabetical sampling of some of the leading private schools in the Reno/Tahoe area. To locate schools not listed here, refer to the Yellow Pages under "Schools—Private."

Bishop Manogue Catholic High School
400 Barlett St., Reno, Nev.
• **(775) 329-0011**

This is the only Catholic high school in the Reno/Tahoe area. It was established in 1948 and has always had an outstanding reputation in both academics and athletics. About 529 students attend Manogue. The school employs about 31 teachers and is also known for its honors classes in English, science, math and U.S. history. A dress code is enforced and an entrance examination is required. The school will move sometime in 2000 to new facilities south of Reno. Manogue advertises that it has no waiting list for admission.

Brookfield School
6800 S. McCarran Blvd., Reno, Nev.
• **(775) 825-0257**

Brookfield School is an independent private school with classes from preschool through 8th grade. The school is academically oriented and teaches French starting in first grade. It uses the LearnStar interactive learning method, the Spectra art program and the Suzuki violin method. The school has about 115 students and 15 teachers. Every year, the school holds a ski week and schedules trips to France and Washington, D.C. The school was founded in 1963 and requires an entrance examination. It is accredited by the National Independent Private School Association. This is one of the most expensive schools in the Reno/Tahoe area.

Calvary Baptist Church Schools
1881 Harvard Wy., Reno, Nev.
• **(775) 329-7775**

This Baptist-affiliated school provides religious education to about 120 students in grades K–8. The school is equipped with a computer lab and boasts a 17 to 1 student/teacher ratio. Tuition is moderately priced.

Cambridge Montessori School
627 Sunnyside Dr., Reno, Nev.,
• **(775) 746-8844**

Cambridge is affiliated with the American Montessori Society and teaches grades primary–8. The Montessori curriculum is hands-on and is tailored to each student's individual learning style.

This school was established in 1984, has an enrollment of about 78 students and employs 18 teachers. Its curriculum includes music, art, Spanish, computers and science. The school also provides before- and after-school care.

Church Academy
1205 N. McCarran Blvd., Reno, Nev.
• **(775) 329-6625**

This academy, established in 1979, is a nondenominational school providing religious education to 60 students in grades K–12. The school employs three teachers who instruct in multiage classrooms.

His Little School
445 E. Queen Wy., Sparks, Nev.
• **(775) 358-1102**

This is an independent, interdenominational school teaching grades K–8. The 88 students study religion, phonics-based reading, creative writing and computer science. The school has a before- and after-school care program. It was established in 1988.

Legacy Christian School
6255 Pyramid Hwy., Sparks, Nev.
• **(775) 424-1777**

One of the newest Christian schools in the area, Legacy is nondenominational and offers classes from K–12. The curriculum includes religious evangelical education, art and athletics. About 60 students attend the school, which employs about 14 teachers. The school was founded in 1997.

Lighthouse Baptist Christian Academy
2655 N. Rock Blvd., Sparks, Nev.
• **(775) 359-0150**

About 27 students attend this Baptist-affiliated school in grades K–12. The school's three teachers instruct classes in religion with additional emphasis on physical education and visual arts. This academy was founded in 1995.

Little Flower Catholic School
1280 Casazza Dr., Reno, Nev.
• **(775) 323-2931**

Little Flower is one of four Catholic elementary schools in the Reno/Tahoe area. The school teaches grades 1–8 and has an enrollment of about 280. The students receive computer training in all grades and receive instruction in health and nutrition from nursing majors at the local university. The school recently purchased new playground equipment. School uniforms are mandatory.

Mountain View Montessori
200 Island Ave., Reno, Nev.
• **(775) 322-6162**

This nondenominational school is affiliated with the Association Montessori International. The pre-school5th grade school teaches the self-paced Montessori curriculum and has mixed-aged classes. Courses include music, art, dance, drama, chess, skiing, computers, Japanese and Spanish. The school will add 6th grade next year. Its student population of 135 is served by 15 teachers.

Our Lady of the Snows School
1125 Lander St., Reno, Nev.
• **(775) 322-2773**

This is one of the four Catholic elementary schools in the area. The school teaches grades 1–8 and has an enrollment of 276. Our Lady of the Snows boasts a hands-on science curriculum and always wins numerous prizes at the Regional Science Fair. The school has an athletic program. And, as at most Catholic grade schools, uniforms are mandatory.

Reno Christian Academy
2100 El Rancho Dr., Sparks, Nev.
• **(775) 331-0909**

This K–12 nondenominational Christian school uses the Abeka Christ-centered, accelerated curriculum which includes traditional classes, religion, athletics and extracurricular activities. The school provides before- and after-school care. It was founded in 1990 and has 145 students and 18 teachers.

Reno Junior Academy
1090 Bresson Ave., Reno, Nev.
• **(775) 322-0714**

This Seventh-Day Adventist school instructs 85 students in grades K–11. The curriculum includes religious studies, community service projects, peer mentoring programs, distance learning and athletics. Each spring, students take weeklong field trips around the West.

The school uses the Internet for some higher-level courses. Reno Junior Academy is the oldest private school in the area; it was established in 1902.

St. Albert the Great Catholic School
1255 St. Albert's Dr., Reno, Nev.
• **(775) 747-3392**

This is the oldest and largest Catholic elementary school in the area. It was founded in 1955 and teaches 294 students in grades K–8. The school teaches the standard Catholic curriculum and boasts that every classroom is equipped with a computer. It has full-day kindergarten, prekindergarten and day care. Uniforms are mandatory.

St. Thomas Aquinas School
905 W. Lake Blvd., Tahoe City, Calif.
• **(530) 583-4253**

The only Catholic school at Lake Tahoe, St. Thomas Aquinas teaches grades K–12. The

INSIDERS' TIP

The PTA in Nevada is called the PFA (Parent Faculty Association).

small student population of 34 is taught by four teachers, including the school's principal. The school teaches the standard Catholic curriculum.

Sage Ridge School
2515 Crossbow Ct., Reno, Nev.
• (775) 852-6222

This school opened in the fall of 1998 and is the most expensive school in the area. The 6th–8th grade classes are taught using an integrated, universal curriculum that stresses liberal arts combined with technology. Every student is provided with a laptop computer. Sage Ridge likes to call itself "a liberal arts middle school." Classes at the school are 80 minutes long. So far 86 students are enrolled but the school has room for 108. The school plans to build additional facilities for grades 9 and 10 by the fall of 1999. And in 2001 it expects to expand to 11th and 12th grades.

Shepherd of the Mountains Lutheran School
955 W. Peckham Ln., Reno, Nev.
• (775) 827-4242

This K–8 school is affiliated with Wisconsin Synod Lutheran and provides religious education along with academic programs including art, science, math and spelling. The school has 37 students and three teachers and participates in SNCAL athletics.

Squaw Valley Academy
235 Squaw Valley Rd., Olympic Valley, Calif. • (530) 583-1558

The most prestigious school at Lake Tahoe, SVA is a boarding school that "provides a college preparatory curriculum in a structured environment." It boasts small classes and advanced placement courses. The coeducational school has 100 students and eight teachers and offers soccer, skiing, snowboarding, hiking and tennis as its extracurricular activities. It was founded in 1978 and is fully accredited.

Tahoe Montessori School
848 Glorene Ave., South Lake Tahoe, Calif. • (530) 544-1818

This is one of only two schools at Lake Tahoe that uses the Montessori curriculum.

The other is a preschool. This preschool–4th grade school offers year-round full- and part-time child care. It uses an individualized learning method and boasts a low student/teacher ratio. Summer programs are available at this nonsectarian, state-registered private school.

Wingfield Springs Community School
6360 Spanish Springs Rd., Sparks, Nev.
• (775) 626-8816

This independent school began in 1997 and teaches preschool through 1st grade. It plans to have students up through 3rd grade starting in the fall of 1999. The 42 students learn French and computers, as well as the standard subjects. It provides before- and after-school care and offers summer school. The school has eight teachers.

Colleges and Universities

The state-run University and Community College System of Nevada is comprised of two doctoral-granting universities, four community colleges and one environmental research facility. Of those, one university, one community college and the research facility are located in the Reno/Tahoe area on the Nevada side. On the California side of Lake Tahoe, only one community college affords students a chance at higher education.

In the private sector, five colleges offer accredited degree programs in the Reno/Tahoe area. These private colleges offer degree programs ranging from a BA in liberal arts to an MS in business administration.

Public Colleges and Universities

Lake Tahoe Community College
1 College Dr., South Lake Tahoe, Calif.
• (530) 541-4660

LTCC is one of California's 106 public community colleges. Founded in 1974, the college is Lake Tahoe's only two-year college. LTCC offers 20 majors and 15 courses resulting in certificates of achievement. The majors include Art, English, Fine Arts, Physical Edu-

Photo: Roger Brotherton

The campus of the University of Nevada, Reno contains both open spaces and traditional college architecture.

cation, Humanities, Natural Science and Criminal Justice.

About 3,000 students attend the college, seeking either an associate's degree or certificates of achievement. Like most community colleges in California, LTCC offers transfer, career education and occupational technologies programs.

The college has a child development center that is used as a lab for its early Childhood Education programs, a theater and a technology center. It participates in California's Golden Valley Conference in men's and women's cross-country running and women's volleyball.

LTCC recently expanded its vocational offerings by adding a nursing assistant program and a dental assistant program. Both programs usually have waiting lists for admittance. The college employs 36 full-time faculty and numerous part-timers, and offers both night and weekend classes to accommodate students who work (which is the majority of those who attend).

High school graduates are eligible for admission, as well as people 18 years old or older who are legal residents of the LTCC district. On special occasions, LTCC will admit students enrolled in grades 9–12 if they are recommended by their high school counselors.

Truckee Meadows Community College
7000 Dandini Blvd., Reno, Nev.
• **(775) 673-7000**

TMCC provides the Reno/Tahoe area with a wide variety of vocational, occupational and academic transfer degree programs. It has an enrollment of 10,000 for both credit and noncredit students who can participate in 51 accredited associate degree programs and 32 certificates of achievement.

The college's main campus on a hill overlooking Reno covers 63 acres and includes a new advanced technology center, library and child care center. The two-year college also provides satellite campuses on Edison Way and Old Town Mall in Reno, as well as a new location in Incline Village. Classes are also held in the district's high schools, giving students more than 40 different places to take classes at TMCC.

The college includes a Re-entry and Women's Center, distance learning facilities, state-of-the-art computer labs, Veteran's Upward Bound Program and Community Services Offices. The Institute of Business and Industry is part of TMCC's occupational education and business partnering mission.

The average TMCC student is 32 years old, working and in school part-time. TMCC conducts several courses at night and on the weekends to accommodate these working students.

If you are a high school graduate or have a GED or are 18 years old, you may attend TMCC. Juniors and seniors in high school may also apply to TMCC High School, which is a combination high school/community college. For more information on admissions, telephone TMCC's Administration Office at (775) 673-7042. TMCC has offered two-year programs ranging from casino operations to electronics technology since 1971.

University of Nevada, Reno
1664 N. Virginia St., Reno, Nev.
• (775) 784-4865

UNR is the oldest of Nevada's two universities and the only research institution. The campus was opened in 1885 as a land-grant institution and has grown from one building and 56 students to 200 acres and more than 12,000 students. Located within walking distance of downtown, but secluded on a tree-covered campus, the university is supported by ten schools and colleges which offer 70 undergraduate majors, 64 master's degree programs, 33 doctoral programs, a four-year medical school and a nationally recognized honors program.

UNR is fully accredited by the Northwest Association of Schools and Colleges and for the seventh consecutive year is ranked in the top 15 percent of America's public and private colleges. *U.S. News and World Report* always places UNR in the Top 100 schools (including Harvard and Yale) in its yearly "America's Best Colleges" issue. UNR's athletic teams receive regular regional and national attention.

UNR emphasizes a core curriculum of social sciences, natural sciences, mathematics, English, fine arts and diversity, with additional requirements according to students' majors.

The number of credits needed for graduation ranges from 128 to 134. The academic year is comprised of two 15-week semesters beginning in August and ending in May. The university also offers three summer sessions. More than 96 percent of the 650 full-time faculty hold the highest degree available in their fields. Some of the colleges include College of Arts and Sciences, Business Administration, Education, Engineering, Mines, the Reynolds School of Journalism, graduate school, medical school and continuing education. UNR is also the home of the National Judicial College and the National College of Juvenile and Family Court Justices.

Applications for admission should be received by UNR's Admissions and Records by March 1 for the fall semester and by November 1 for the spring semester. You can obtain an application packet from the Office of Admissions, (775) 784-6865.

Private College and Universities

Career College of Northern Nevada
1195 Corporate Blvd., Reno, Nev.
• (775) 856-2266

This trade and technical college has 250 students and provides training in electronics, data processing, word processing, medical and legal office management and microcomputers. It is accredited by the Accrediting Commission of Career Schools and Colleges of Technology. The college offers associate degrees in Occupational Studies in Electronics Engineering Technology and Occupational Studies in Computerized Business Management.

Morrison Business College
140 Washington St., Reno, Nev.
• (775) 323-4145

Morrison is a senior college, founded in 1902, which specializes in business education. The college offers programs in accounting, computer accounting, medical, legal assistant/paralegal, office administration, computer information systems and business management. The school boasts that its students can earn a specialized diploma in 6 to 9 months, an associate degree in 15 months and a bachelor's degree in 2 to 3 years. The college is accredited by the Accrediting Council for Independent Colleges and Schools.

Sierra Nevada College
(775) 831-1314, (530) 546-4545, (800) 332-8666

Sierra Nevada College is a four-year, nonprofit, independent liberal arts college. The coeducational college is located on the North Shore of Lake Tahoe and offers programs in more than 15 different fields from its departments of business administration, visual and performing arts, humanities and science, and teacher education.

Sierra Nevada College is best known in the area for its fifth-year teacher education program. This program prepares students for teacher certification or recertification in California and Nevada. The college is planning to offer a master's degree in education.

The student/faculty ratio is 15 to 1. More than 95 percent of the classes have fewer than 20 students. The college is accredited by the Commission on Colleges and Northwest Association of Colleges and Schools. Its ski business and hotel, restaurant and resort management major is one of the best in the U.S.

Even though the college is small (about 600 students), its ski teams (the college's only athletic teams) have earned national recognition. The men's ski team has won the Collegiate Ski Association's national title for the last eight years and the women's team has won the title six out of the last eight years.

The mailing address for Sierra Nevada College is PO Box 4269, Incline Village NV 89450.

University of Phoenix
5310 Kietzke Ln., Reno, Nev.
• (775) 828-7999

The University of Phoenix is a private bachelor's and master's degree granting institution with programs in business, management, education, computer information systems and counseling. Calling itself "a university created just for working adults," it offers undergraduate and graduate degrees in Business Management, Business Information Systems, Human Services, Business Administration, Organizational Management and Education Supervision.

The university's mission is to meet the higher educational needs of working adults. According to its plan, students attend classes one night a week and finish a course every five to six weeks. The university is accredited by the Commission on Institutions of Higher Education of the North Central Association of Colleges and Schools.

Child Care

The Reno/Tahoe area is jam-packed with things to do, places to go and people to meet, and at times moms and dads need to do some of these things alone, and so the need for child-care facilities arises. In the Reno/Tahoe area, about 145 day centers provide child-care services, about 15 agencies provide babysitter referrals and two handle nannies and au pairs.

Even though the Nevada side of the area is a 24-hour operation, there are no child-care centers that are open all night and only a handful of home-care facilities that offer overnight care. Casinos do not have child-care facilities for visitors but most will recommend babysitting services. The phone books for each of our geographical locations (Reno, Sparks, North Shore Lake Tahoe and South Shore Lake Tahoe) list child-care facilities, preschools, babysitters and nannies. But just because they are listed doesn't mean they are licensed. So how do Insiders pick their child-care providers? Carefully, and with an emphasis on the word licensed.

Quality Child Care

In order to choose a child-care facility wisely, you must first know what distinguishes a quality program from the others. According to the National Association for the Education of Young Children, the nation's largest organization of early childhood professionals, look for these characteristics in a child-care facility:

1. Children in the program are generally comfortable, relaxed, happy and involved in play and other activities.

2. Small groups of children are supervised by sufficient numbers of adults who have specialized training in early childhood development and education and first aid.

3. Adult expectations are varied appropriately for children of different ages.

4. All areas of a child's development are stressed equally.

5. The staff meets regularly to plan and evaluate the program.

6. Parents are welcome to observe, discuss policies, make suggestions and participate in the work of the program.

Also, the association recommends asking these questions when you visit a child-care setting to help make up your mind on the facility:

1. Are they licensed?

2. Do they charge for overtime when you are late?

3. Do they provide meals and snacks?

4. What kind of disciplinary methods are used?

5. How much training and experience working with children does the caregiver have?

6. What kind of turnover does the child-care program have?

7. What will your child be doing throughout the day?

8. Can you visit your child at any time?

9. Does the caregiver have a parent contract or written policies about fees, hours, holidays, illness and other considerations?

Finding the right caregiver can be challenging, but it is also one of the most important decisions you'll make. Be as well educated about the facilities and caregivers as possible and visit several child-care settings before choosing one. Also, never leave a child in a setting that you haven't personally visited, and always contact your local licensing agency to ask about the complaint history of the child-care provider that you are considering.

Child-care Facilities

Even though you'll find two of the major child-care chains here, most of the facilities in the Reno/Tahoe area are run out of private homes. Both chains and private facilities must follow the rules and regulations set down by Nevada and California law that are outlined below.

Rules, Regulations and Resources

On the Nevada side of the area, child-care facilities are licensed and regulated by the county upon recommendation of the state's Child Care Advisory Board and approval of the State of Nevada Bureau of Child Care Licensing, (775) 328-2327. On the California side, policies and procedures are regulated by the state's Health and Welfare Agency, Department of Social Services, Community Care Licensing Division, (916) 229-4530.

Nevada

On the Nevada side of the Reno/Tahoe area, state law requires that all child-care providers be licensed and it divides private caregiving operations into two categories. The first group is the family child-care home where a provider cares for up to six children. The second is a group child-care home where a provider cares for more than six but no more than 12 children. Each caregiver employee must obtain a work permit especially for child-care work from the appropriate sheriff's department. These employees must also be trained in CPR, policies, procedures and programs of the facility and the recognition of the symptoms of illnesses. Caregivers are also required to continue their training every year with a minimum of 12 hours related to courses in the field of developmentally appropriate practices for young children.

Several nonprofit agencies on the Nevada side of the Reno/Tahoe area provide free referral services for parents looking for child-care facilities. **The Children's Cabinet**, (775) 856-6210 or (800) 753-5500, provides resource and referral services to help parents in their search for child-care services. **The Community Services Agency**, (775) 786-6023, **The Division of Child and Family Services**, (775) 684-4416, and **The Washoe County Department of Social Services**, (775) 328-2327, will also provide you with a list of licensed child-care providers and will advise you if any complaints have been filed against a particular facility.

California

Private family child-care homes in California are divided into two categories: small family child-care homes with up to six children and large family child-care homes with up to 12 children. Each child-care facility must be in strict compliance with staffing ratios and capacity restrictions. The staff of these facilities receives training in preventive health practices, CPR, pediatric first aid, prevention of infectious disease, sanitary food handling, child nutrition, caring for children with special needs and reporting signs of child abuse. In addition to these training requirements, all employees who have frequent and routine contact with the children must also be fingerprinted for a thorough background check. Furthermore, the facilities are under strict fire-safety rules, and the state has the right to send inspectors in at any time without notice.

The state of California's **Community Care Licensing Division**, (916) 229-4530, can tell you about any complaints lodged against day-care facilities. Several nonprofit consumer assistance groups provide information about child-care facilities on the California side of the Reno/Tahoe area. The **Choices for Children–Resource Agency**, (530) 541-5848, in South Lake Tahoe, California, provides child-care referrals, parent and provider training, a resource library and a child-care food program. In the North Shore Lake Tahoe area, the **Tahoe-Truckee Children's Network**, (530) 581-4514 or (800) 618-5224, is a free community resource for parents. Serving North Lake Tahoe and Truckee, California, as well as Incline Village, Nevada, the network provides child-care referrals, parenting support and rec-

reation such as after-school sports. **The Children's Cabinet** in Incline Village, (775) 831-6200, is a centralized clearing house of information and direct services for children and families in the North Shore Lake Tahoe area.

Nannies and Babysitters

Local governments in the Reno/Tahoe area don't regulate nannies, nor will they refer you to any. Only two private companies work as placement agencies for nannies and au pairs: **Nanny Services of Nevada**, (775) 334-4725, and **AuPairCare**, (800) 428-7247.

Nannies can be hired for a few hours per day or can be contracted for the more traditional live-in arrangement. Even though not required by law, the more reputable ones will be CPR-certified and licensed. Nannies' rates vary from about $10 per hour for short stays to weekly rates beginning at $300 for those who live in.

About 14 babysitting agencies are listed for the Reno/Tahoe area (consult the Yellow Pages for your area) but like nannies, the local governments don't regulate or refer babysitters. The laws in both California and Nevada say that a license is required when caring for more than one unrelated family's child in the sitter's home, but if a sitter goes to the child's location, no license is required.

Babysitters can be your 13-year-old next-door neighbor or the 60-year-old professional. Either way, parents should always verify qualifications and check references. Babysitting rates vary and a small deposit may be required. It's a good idea to discuss fees and arrangements when first talking with the sitter, before you commit to hiring that person for the night or day.

Latchkey and After-school Programs

The problem of finding child-care services for those working parents with school-age children has been eased by a local youth watch program coordinated by the various parks and recreation departments of the towns and cities in the Reno/Tahoe area. These youth watch programs include: before- and after-school care for K–6th graders, summer programs for students in schools with traditional academic year schedules, and year-round break programs for those students in year-round schools.

The before- and after-school programs provide a fun and safe environment for your children when you have to be at work before school starts or you have to be at work when school ends. These latchkey programs give children time to do their homework, provide arts and crafts training and include special activities such as indoor and outdoor games. Rates vary but usually hover around $60 for before-school sessions and $120 for after-school sessions. Each session is about 23 days long.

The summer program hours vary but most begin at 7 AM and go until 6 PM. These programs cost anywhere from $60 to $80 per week. The activities offered include field trips, arts and crafts and special summer activities.

Because some of the elementary schools in the Washoe County School District have gone to a year-round schedule, the parks and recreation departments of Reno and Sparks have added year-round school break programs to their services. These are full-day programs, offered August through May, for youth in K–6th grades in year-round schools. Various field trips and group activities are planned. This is a week-by-week program that does not accept drop-ins. Rates vary from $60 to $75 per week.

For more information on any of the latchkey programs mentioned here, telephone the City of Reno Parks and Recreation Department, (775) 327-9159; the City of Sparks Parks and Recreation Department, (775) 353-2376; the City of South Lake Tahoe Recreation, (530) 542-6055; or the Town of Truckee, (530) 582-7720.

Most of the private schools in the Reno/Tahoe area (see our Education section earlier in this chapter) have preschool or prekindergarten programs, and the majority offer before- and after-school child-care programs. Consult with the individual school for specific information on programs and availability.

Also, the local YMCAs can provide some services in the area of child care. (Be aware, however, that students and/or families must be members.) Contact the Reno YMCA, (775) 329-6654, or the Sparks YMCA, (775) 685-9622, for further details.

Another agency that can provide after-school programs is the Boys and Girls Club. These clubs are scattered around the area and some have programs similar to the latchkey programs, offering games, arts and crafts and study hours. Contact these Boys and Girls Clubs for more information: Reno/Sparks, (775) 331-3605; Stateline, Nevada, (775) 588-0027; North Shore Lake Tahoe, (530) 546-4324; and South Shore Lake Tahoe, (530) 542-0838.

At one time, more than 80 newspapers dotted the scene from Virginia City to Lake Tahoe. These newspapers were the first written record of the area's flamboyant history and date back to 1859.

Media

The roots of the media in the Reno/Tahoe area go as deep as some of the silver veins did on the Comstock Lode. At one time, more than 80 newspapers dotted the scene from Virginia City to Lake Tahoe. These newspapers were the first written record of the area's flamboyant history and date back to 1859. Dan De Quille and Joe Goodman are recognized as pioneer journalists on Virginia City's *Territorial Enterprise*, the same newspaper that gave Mark Twain his literary start. Alf Doten and Wells Drury gave these pioneer writers on the old *Enterprise* all the competition they could handle as rival journalists on Gold Hill's *Daily News*. But now the days of newspaper competition in the area are all but gone, with only three dailies and a handful of weekly newspapers remaining.

Radio, on the other hand, seems to be thriving in the area: 30 radio outlets are crowded on the air waves between Reno and Lake Tahoe. Listeners have choices ranging from alternative rock to conservative talk and everything in between. Listeners also have the opportunity to tune in, somewhere on the AM or FM dial, almost every nationally syndicated program from Howard Stern and Don and Mike to G. Gordon Liddy and Rush Limbaugh. One of the most listened-to radio programs is the Art Bell Show, a late night talk-fest from southern Nevada broadcast in the north on KKOH-780 AM. Bell has a propensity for attracting guests who could give the writers on the *X-Files* nightmares. Bell has interviewed people who swear they have been abducted by aliens and those who know they can stop airplane engines by mental telepathy.

The area's television market sits at 118th in the nation, making it a middle-of-the-pack market. We have an affiliate for all the big companies here including NBC, CBS, ABC, WB, PBS, UPN and Fox. The three local news broadcasting stations have very competent personnel who provide the area with its only head-to-head news competition.

Newspapers

In bygone days, the Reno/Tahoe area grew legendary because of its intense newspaper rivalries. Today, Reno finds itself a one-paper town. The Gannett-owned *Reno Gazette-Journal* is the regional daily; it zones its inside local sections for the rural counties and Carson City. Even though Sparks has its own daily, the *Daily Sparks Tribune*, the small-circulation newspaper cannot compete with the much larger Gannett newspaper and doesn't try to. South Lake Tahoe's *Tahoe Tribune* is the lake's only daily newspaper, but several well-written weeklies keep the rest of the communities informed.

The area has only one alternative newspaper, the *Reno News & Review,* but readers can find a good assortment of out-of-area newspapers in stock at most local book and convenience stores. *The Wall Street Journal* and *The New York Times* offer home delivery, and *USA Today* can be found at almost every street corner and shopping center.

This section is divided into daily and weekly newspapers with a subheading for specialty magazines and periodicals. Most of the publications can be purchased through subscriptions or at newsstands. Many of the smaller products are free.

Dailies

Reno Gazette-Journal
955 Kuenzli St., Reno, Nev.
• **(775) 788-6200**

Reno's only daily newspaper, the *Gazette-Journal* reaches about 67,000 readers Monday through Saturday and about 85,000 on Sundays. One of the 82 newspapers owned by the Gannett Co., Inc., it constantly wins awards from its parent company's yearly in-house competitions and takes home its share of awards from the Nevada Press Association.

The *Gazette-Journal* acquired its hyphenated name from the merger of the *Reno Evening Gazette* and the *Nevada State Journal*, two of Reno's surviving newspapers. Both of these newspapers began printing in the 1870s and continued independently until 1939 when they were purchased by Speidel Newspaper, Inc. This newly founded Reno Newspaper Group continued to publish both the Republican evening *Gazette* and the Democratic morning *Journal* until 1977 when Speidel Newspapers merged with the Gannett Company, and the *Reno Gazette-Journal* was born.

Today, if someone asked a *Gazette-Journal* reader the newspaper's politics, the answer would definitely depend on which side of the political fence the reader was peeking over. The Republican readers curse the newspaper for being too liberal and the Democratic readers call it too conservative. In reality, the newspaper is slightly left of middle-of-the-road, endorsing more Democrats than Republicans.

Most criticism of the newspaper stems from the fact that it is a Gannett-owned product. *Gazette-Journal* critics condemn the newspaper for putting profit above good journalism and ridicule it for taking the path of least resistance with its editorials. Proponents of the newspaper say they like its community-oriented tradition and the way the *Gazette-Journal* concentrates on local news.

Generally, the front page consists of stories about the Reno/Tahoe area and Nevada, with one story devoted to national or international news. The *Gazette-Journal* relies on the Associated Press and the Gannett News Service for its national and international stories. Some of its best sections are sports, local news and "Sierra," a family, home and arts section. The newspaper's beat reporters do outstanding jobs covering the police and the courts, education and water issues. The newspaper began devoting more time and space in 1997 to hard-hitting investigative pieces but its forte is covering breaking news stories. The editors will throw all assets at their disposal to cover every angle when a breaking local story warrants.

The newspaper prints a *Best Bet* tabloid insert every Wednesday, covering the casino, entertainment and nightlife scenes. Sunday it produces *Calendar*, a weekly guide to the arts and entertainment outside of the casinos, and on Saturday, it distributes *HomeFinder*, a real estate guide to the area.

The *Gazette-Journal* is also home to Brian Crane, a nationally syndicated cartoonist and creator of the comic strip "Pickles." The newspaper also boasts of having the most loved and hated columnist in the Reno/Tahoe area. Corey Farley, a liberal opinionist, has been voted both the newspaper's best and worst columnist by the readers for the past several years.

Daily Sparks Tribune
1002 C St., Sparks, Nev.
• **(775) 358-8061**

This feisty little newspaper publishes daily except Saturday and holidays and has been Sparks's community newspaper since 1910. In no way does anyone see it as a rival to the bigger, more powerful *Reno Gazette-Journal*. Its niche is its exhaustive coverage of Sparks. Its small 6,000 circulation attests to the fact that the only readers who give a hoot about the paper are those living in Sparks's neighborhoods. The newspaper gives its readers a balanced coverage of Sparks's politics, police, courts and education, and it has a great sports section which includes good coverage of high school athletics.

The best way to describe its political leanings is independent. It doggedly nips at the heels of both Republicans and Democrats and has the most diverse collection of columnists, ranging from a Christian conservative to a socialist. This diversity makes the newspaper fun to read.

Some of the *Tribune*'s reporters have gone on to the *Reno Gazette-Journal*, the *Detroit Free Press* and New York newspapers.

The paper has been called the stepchild of the Tribune Publishing Company, which owns several other newspapers throughout the West. Its own advertising staff will tell you that the only thing that keeps the *Sparks Tribune* afloat is *The Big Nickel*. The paper publishes this free tabloid every Thursday; it's a classified ad publication with a 50,000 circulation.

The front page is devoted entirely to local news, and the newspaper uses the Associated Press for national and international news and sports on its inside pages. Its Sunday edition includes *Parade Magazine*.

Tahoe Daily Tribune
3079 Harrison Ave., South Lake Tahoe, Calif. • (530) 541-3880

This newspaper, printed Monday morning through Friday morning, is Lake Tahoe's only daily. It is a member of the Swift Newspaper Group, which also owns all the weekly newspapers scattered around the lake communities, and has a 9,600 circulation Monday through Thursday and a 10,500 circulation on Friday. In keeping with company policy, the *Daily Tribune* carries mostly local and community news. The *Daily Tribune* serves the Lake Tahoe area in El Dorado, Placer and Alpine counties in California and Carson, Douglas and Washoe counties in Nevada. On a typical news day, the newspaper runs about five local stories on the front page and devotes one page to regional, one page to national and one page to international news. The sports section runs Bay Area professional sports and national sports stories but tries to cover Lake Tahoe high school and local sports as well. The newspaper is served by the Associated Press.

Over the years, the *Daily Tribune* has become the media powerhouse of Lake Tahoe. Established in 1958, the newspaper aggressively promotes tourism to the area. Its political stand is middle-of-the-road, but it usually shies away from political controversy, concentrating instead on more feature-type stories about Lake Tahoe that visitors would enjoy.

The *Daily Tribune* also publishes *Action Magazine* (see subsequent entry).

Weeklies

Action Magazine
3079 Harrison Ave., South Lake Tahoe, Calif. • (530) 541-3880

The *Tahoe Daily Tribune* publishes *Action Magazine*, a weekly tabloid which serves as

Lake Tahoe's entertainment guide. This tab comes out on Fridays and covers the entertainment happenings around the lake. Its sections include music, sports, theater, hot spots and casino shows. It is a must-have for visitors and locals alike. The California Newspaper Publishers' Association voted the weekly tabloid the best entertainment guide in California. Circulation is about 22,000 for the free guide.

Ahora Spanish-English Newspaper
30 May St., Ste. 2, Reno, Nev.
• (775) 323-6811

Founded in 1983, this newspaper provides Reno/Tahoe's growing Spanish-speaking community with local, national and international news printed in both Spanish and English. The only Spanish newspaper in the area, it has a paid subscription of 620 and circulates about 11,300 copies free throughout Reno/Tahoe. This newspaper is published on Thursday.

Comstock Chronicle
800 Main St., Gold Hill, Nev.
• (775) 847-0765

The *Comstock Chronicle* is the only newspaper remaining in an area once teeming with daily newspapers. "The Voice of the Comstock" prints about 2,500 copies of its 12-page tabloid every Friday and concentrates solely on Virginia City/Gold Hill and Storey County news with an emphasis on local politics. In a county which boasts only 3,500 citizens, the *Chronicle* manages to reach about two-thirds of the population. Most of its journalists are freelancers and the newspaper rarely uses by-lines with its stories.

The opinion pages and Letters to the Editor are often controversial, making this section fun to read. The *Chronicle* still exudes the feistiness that once made the *Territorial Enterprise* and the Gold Hill *Daily News* legendary.

North Lake Tahoe Bonanza
917 Tahoe Blvd., Incline Village, Nev.
• (775) 831-4666

One of the four newspapers surrounding Lake Tahoe owned by the Swift Newspaper Group, this twice-a-week newspaper reflects the community-oriented area it serves. Founded in 1964, the *Bonanza* concentrates on local news, local sports and local politics. The front page is more likely to have a spread on the Incline High School graduation than a hard news story of a local burglary. The opinion page is lively with Letters to the Editor, tirades on local politics and explanations of local happenings. The newspaper has a circulation of 7,100 for its Wednesday and Friday editions in a town of about 9,400.

Reno News & Review
708 N. Center St., Reno, Nev.
• **(775) 324-4440**

The only alternative weekly in the Reno/Tahoe area, the *Reno News & Review* likes to take on the establishment and especially likes to badger the *Reno Gazette-Journal*. Its assistant editor says its alternative voice is not beholden to the powers that be and it covers everything, including stories that the mainstream media won't touch.

This every-Wednesday publication began in 1993 as *The Nevada Weekly* and was founded by former *Reno Gazette-Journal* reporters as an alternative source of news to the Gannett-owned Reno daily. They soon found out they were not financially equipped to go up against the Gannett Company. The founders sold the weekly to Chico Community Publishing, Inc., in 1995, and it became the *Reno News & Review*, joining the publishing company's two other alternative weeklies in Chico and Sacramento, California.

The weekly tabloid is progressive, spirited and targeted at the young-adult crowd. Stories often rake local politicians over the coals, take pot shots at the establishment and wreak havoc on corporate America. This newspaper prints about 27,000 copies each week and has an estimated readership of 63,000. It can be found all over the Reno/Tahoe area in the bright-red street racks at convenience and grocery stores, malls, gas stations, restaurants and just about anywhere else the Generation X crowd hangs out.

The Sierra Sun
11429 Donner Pass Rd., Truckee, Calif.
• **(530) 587-6061**

Another Swift Newspaper Group product, *The Sierra Sun* has been keeping the Truckee area informed since 1869. This Thursday publication concentrates, like the other Swift newspapers, on local and community news and with a circulation of 6,000 reaches about two-thirds of the population of Truckee. Stories range from the Boy Scouts' annual Pinewood Derby to opinion pieces on year-round education in local schools.

Tahoe World
241 N. Lake Blvd., Tahoe City, Calif.
• **(530) 583-3487**

The *Tahoe World* has the smallest circulation of the Swift Newspaper Group's weekly Lake Tahoe newspapers, but it didn't let that fact hamper it from winning the Best Weekly Newspaper Award in the California Press Association's 1997 Better Newspaper Contest. The *Tahoe World* covers community and local news on the western side of the lake and prints on Thursday, reaching about 5,800 readers. Like its sister weeklies around the lake, this newspaper concentrates on keeping its readers informed on all the local happenings. The newspaper coverage stretches from Tahoe City to Kings Beach. It began publishing in 1963.

Magazines and Other Print Media

Adventure West
924 Incline Wy., Incline Village, Nev.
• **(775) 832-3730**

This bimonthly magazine is distributed nationally to about 150,000 subscribers. It bills itself as "America's Leading Adventure Travel Magazine" and devotes its pages to describing and recommending adventure travel around Reno/Tahoe and the rest of western North America. Some of its sections include Travelogues, Adventure Directory, Regional Activities and Techniques on fishing, hiking, mountain biking, skiing and golfing.

Fun and Gaming
434 Washington St., Reno, Nev.
• **(775) 786-3594**

As the title suggests, this publication (distributed every Thursday) keeps Insiders abreast of the entertainment events and show schedules for the various casinos and lists the fun things to do in the Reno/Tahoe area. The magazine can be found in almost every casino, a few businesses close to the casinos and at the Reno/Tahoe International Airport. The publication has a 12-page special pullout during football season covering the betting odds on all NFL and college football teams. It also includes a dining and restaurant section and a map of the local area. Its circulation is about 30,000.

Nevada Farm Bureau Agriculture & Livestock Journal
1300 Marietta Wy., Sparks, Nev.
• (775) 358-3276

This monthly tabloid provides readers with news about Nevada's agriculture and farming. Produced by the Nevada Farm Bureau and circulated to farm bureau families, the newspaper's motto is: "All the News Farmers Can Use." Its circulation is about 2,100 and copies are available by subscription or from the farm bureau.

Nevada Magazine
1800 U.S. Hwy. 50 E., Ste. 200,
Carson City, Nev. • (775) 885-5416

Nevada Magazine is published by the state and reaches about 80,000 readers twice a month. Even though the magazine is not published in the Reno/Tahoe area, it devotes many articles and stories to the region. The publication is the state's official guide to recreation, travel, people, history and events in the Silver State. Its special section entitled "Reno/Tahoe Territory" keeps visitors in tune with what's happening in the way of performances, exhibits, festivals and celebrations. The best magazine for learning about the state's history, it has been published since 1940 and is available by subscription; it can also be found at bookstores around the area.

The Nevada Rancher
(775) 358-2681

This tabloid covers ranching and agricultural interests in Nevada and the West. It includes livestock events, a local calendar of events, feature stories, ranching news briefs, research articles, sales reports, 4-H happenings and Reno/Tahoe high school rodeo news.

Founded in 1970, this monthly publication reaches about 4,000 readers. It is available by subscription and distributes about 200 free copies to local feed and ranching stores.

North Tahoe/Truckee World
(530) 546-5995

This weekly magazine contains current events, entertainment, recreation and sightseeing information for the North Shore of Lake Tahoe. Both visitors and residents alike find this guide useful in planning weekends or vacations around the northern part of the lake. The circulation is about 20,000 and copies can be found at various business locations around the North Shore.

Northern Nevada Catholic
2995 Skyline Blvd., Reno, Nev.
• (775) 323-4044

The official community news publication of the Roman Catholic Church in northern Nevada, the publication reaches about 25,000 readers, 10 times per year. The newspaper can be found in all of the area's Catholic churches and also has a paid subscription readership. The tabloid prints official church news with stories, features and profiles.

Reno Informer
(775) 747-8833

The *Reno Informer* is the area's only gay and lesbian newspaper. First published in 1993, the newspaper has a print run of 6,000 copies, but its editor says its readership may be three times that number because the newspapers are passed along from reader to reader. Stories cover local gay and lesbian issues and events. It also has a list and map of gay and lesbian nightclubs and bars and businesses that are gay-friendly. The free newspaper is published the first week of every month and can be found in all of the gay and lesbian nightclubs and bars in the area.

The Senior Advocate
2995 Skyline Blvd., Reno, Nev.
• (775) 323-3006

One of two locally published newspapers for seniors, this publication is written and distributed by the Roman Catholic diocese of Reno, which also publishes the *Northern Ne-*

vada Catholic. This monthly publication goes out to 80,000 seniors and features local, state and federal news pertaining to older adults. The newspaper carries feature stories and legislative issues and has as its guest columnists both Nevada senators and congresspeople. The publication also carries sections on healthcare and Social Security subjects. Most of the newspapers are direct mailed to subscribers.

Senior Spectrum
(775) 348-0717

One of two publications devoted to the senior population in the Reno/Tahoe area, this monthly newspaper is dedicated to informing and entertaining the older crowd. The *Spectrum* is jammed with articles dealing with retirement, financial and legal advice, health and fitness, nutrition and columns by local doctors, lawyers and investment counselors. The newspaper includes some restaurant reviews and advertises some companies that give seniors discounts. A monthly calendar of events is included, as well as a classified ads section and feature stories about local seniors. The newspaper is distributed once a month and reaches about 40,000 readers. It began publishing in 1985.

Showtime Magazine
155 Glendale Ave., Ste. 11, Sparks, Nev.
• (775) 353-5100

This weekly magazine is available at all of the Reno/Tahoe hotel/casinos, some of the smaller motels, the area's visitor centers and the Reno/Tahoe International Airport. As the name suggests, the magazine deals with casino entertainment. It also has special sections on where to dine, special events and gaming tips and includes maps of Reno and Lake Tahoe. The magazine has a two-page quick-reference guide to all the casino entertainment for the week and prints about 20,000 copies. The publication is free.

Sunny Day Guide to Lake Tahoe
(757) 468-0606

This publication is printed for the Incline Village/Crystal Bay, North Lake Tahoe and Tahoe/Douglas chambers of commerce. The small magazine is filled with feature stories

about both the North Shore and the South Shore of Lake Tahoe and includes maps of the entire lake. It has a calendar of events, a casino chart, a beach chart and a list of almost every restaurant around the lake. It has special sections on shopping, lake activities, fishing and golfing. Almost every page offers a discount coupon to one of the many businesses around the area.

The Total Pack Edge
(775) 787-3343

This newspaper is published monthly from August through June plus three special editions per year and is strictly devoted to articles about University of Nevada, Reno athletics. The publication is independently owned and is not affiliated with the university. It derives its name from a play on words of UNR's mascot and team name — The Wolf Pack. The newspaper does an outstanding job covering the revenue-generating sports (football, basketball and baseball) but also devotes a lot of ink to the non-revenue-generating sports like skiing, swimming, tennis and golf. The 1997-98 school year was its first year of publication, and it garnered a good readership though most advertisers and sponsors bailed out after the football season. The paper can be found all over the area and often shares the news racks with the *Reno News & Review*.

Radio

The first radio station hit the Reno/Tahoe airwaves in 1928 and since then the radio market has bullied its way onto the scene with every type of programming from conservative talk to alternative rock. Now about 30 stations on both the AM and FM dials broadcast from Reno to the South Shore of Lake Tahoe.

If you check the pre-set channels on the car radios of the 16- to 21-year-olds, you will find most tuned to Alice (KLCA 96.5 FM — home to alternative rock) or Magic 95 (KNEV 95.5 FM) or K-Winds (KWNZ 97.3 FM), but the station that continually comes in first place with most of the area's listeners is KKOH 780 AM. The Arbitron ratings (radio's equivalent to TV's Nielsen ratings) continually give this conservative talk radio station the nod as the No.1 station across the radio dial. This radio station just celebrated its 70th anniversary, making it the oldest in the area, and features such shows as Rush Limbaugh, Mike Reagan and Paul Harvey.

The second most–listened-to station, according to the Arbitron ratings, is KBUL 98.1 FM with its pure country format — not a surprise to most Insiders since Reno/Tahoe is also the home to one of the biggest professional rodeos in the nation and features the Buck N' Ball (a combination rodeo and country-western dance) for a New Year's Eve celebration. KKOH, KBUL and Magic 95 are all owned by the Citadel Communications Corporation, giving this company three of the top five most–listened-to radio stations in the area.

Though not as popular as it is in the Las Vegas area, we do have one radio station devoted to keeping the sports bettors informed with its all sports talk radio format: KPLY 1270 AM.

A word of warning about radio stations here in the Reno/Tahoe area: they seem to change format and frequencies as often as two cherries pop up on the pay line of slot machines.

The following is a list of Reno/Tahoe radio stations categorized by format.

Adult Contemporary
KRLT 93.9 FM
KRNO 106.9 FM
KTHO 590 AM
KTHX 100.1 FM (The X)

Alternative/Classic Rock
KDOT 104.5 FM
KLCA 96.5 FM (Alice)
KNEV 95.5 FM (Magic 95)
KOZZ 105.7 FM
KRZQ 100.9 FM (Howard Stern)
KWNZ 97.3 FM (K-Winds)
KZZF 102.9 FM (The Zephyr)

Blues/Big Bands
KSRN 92.1 FM

Christian
KIHM 1590 AM

Country
KBUL 98.1 FM
KHWG 107.7 FM

Jazz
KUNR 88.7 FM (UNR campus)

News-Talk
KHIT 630 AM
KKOH 780 AM
KOWL 1490 AM
KPTT 1450 AM
KRNV 101.7 FM

Oldies
KCBN 1230 AM
KNHK 92.9 FM (The Hawk)
KODS 103.7 FM

Spanish
KQLO 920 AM
KXEQ 1340 AM (La Super Q)
KXTO 1550 AM

Sports
KPLY 1270 AM

Top 40
KRNG 101.3 FM (The Renegade)

Television

Reno/Tahoe television is slowly inching its way up the market-share ladder. Recently, it climbed to 118th in the nation, making it a middle-of-the-pack market. The area now has nine local TV stations broadcasting: ABC, CBS, Fox, NBC, PBS, UPN, WB, a public access channel and one Spanish-language station.

The ABC, CBS, and NBC affiliates in the area provide news broadcasts at least four

times per day, usually beginning at 6 AM, and provide the area's only head-to-head news competition. And the competition has been good for viewers. Each station has a bevy of reporters and camera technicians, minivans and satellite trucks which constantly roam the area providing excellent on-the-spot news coverage.

One local Spanish station provides a growing Latino population with national and local news. The addition of Sierra Nevada Cable Access Television (SNCAT) in 1997 gives the general community a place to go to produce hometown programs.

Cable companies in Reno/Sparks are as plentiful as the TV stations, but the two biggest are AT&T Cable Services and Quadravision. AT&T Cable Services, 9335 Prototype Way, Reno, Nevada, (775) 850-1200, carries more than 90 channels in its basic and premier-rate programming package. It recently began offering Digital Cable and offers music channels as well as several pay-per-view programs.

Quadravision, 1345 Airmotive Way, Reno, Nevada, (775) 686-5586, provides a line-of-sight antenna cable service that includes 22 channels plus two premium programs and a pay-per-view.

As far as Lake Tahoe is concerned, the following companies offer services: AT&T Cable Services, 520 National Avenue, Tahoe Vista, Calif., (530) 546-5915, or 924 Emerald Bay Road, South Lake Tahoe, California, (530) 544-4882; and Sierra Communications Systems, 2520 Lake Tahoe Boulevard, South Lake Tahoe, California, (530) 544-1040 or (800) 544-1043.

Almost every weekly and daily newspaper in the Reno/Tahoe area provides its readers with a television guide for the week. The publications carry the cable channel designations for all of the stations and most have special sections devoted to movies and sports.

The local stations are listed below in alphabetical order by station call letters.

KAME-UPN, Channel 21
KNPB-PBS, Channel 5
KOLO-ABC, Channel 8
KREN-WB, Channel 27
KRNV-NBC, Channel 4
KRXI-FOX, Channel 11
KTVN-CBS, Channel 2

KUVR-Spanish 68
961 Matley Ln., Reno, Nev.
• **(775) 327-6800**

The only local TV station broadcasting in Spanish, the programming carries only two local shows, both of them nightly news segments, one at 6 PM and one at 11 PM. Sayra Vasquez-Calmes and Carlo Vargas share the duties as news anchors.

SNCAT-Sierra Nevada Cable Access Television
4024 Kietzke Ln., Reno, Nev.
• **(775) 828-1211**

This is Reno's community access television. The station receives its revenue from local cable franchise fees and uses the money to help the general public produce TV programs. The station offers editing, video and producing classes, then helps students produce hometown programs. The station broadcasts city and county government meetings and also helps out the local university and community college by transmitting distant learning classes, enabling students in the rural counties to attend classes by video conferencing. The station's programming runs 24 hours a day.

The Reno/Tahoe area has been rich in religious diversity since the first pastors preached in mining camps, trading stations and farming communities in the 1800s.

Worship

Some locals say there's more praying in casinos than in churches, but whether it's true or not is anybody's guess. What we do know is that the Reno/Tahoe area has been rich in religious diversity since the first pastors preached in mining camps, trading stations and farming communities in the 1800s.

Bringing spiritual leadership to the early Reno/Tahoe pioneers presented unique challenges, however. In addition to contending with the expected hardships of frontier life, the first clergy were required to travel many miles to reach their flocks in the tiny scattered settlements. Conditions were often less than ideal for conducting church services since the early "towns" were sometimes nothing more than collections of tents or temporary structures. But the early preachers persevered, even saying their prayers from a pulpit in the local saloon if necessary. When the population boomed, particularly after the discovery of silver in Virginia City, Nevada, in 1859, the first churches were constructed. And as Reno/Tahoe became more settled, representatives from a variety of denominations arrived to help "civilize" the area.

The Mormons first arrived in 1851 when a group was dispatched from Salt Lake City to develop a settlement in the Carson Valley south of Reno. Known originally as Mormon Station, the community was later renamed Genoa after the Italian town where Christopher Columbus was born. The oldest town in Nevada, Genoa was the site of the first government that would later become the state of Nevada. (We tell you all about the sights in this charming historic town in our Daytrips chapter.) The Mormons continue to be a well-established religious group, with more than 20 congregations throughout the area.

The first Catholic church was built after Father H. P. Gallagher arrived in Genoa in 1860. With 16 churches today, Catholics are an important element of the religious scene in Reno/Tahoe. Counting 2,600 families as members, the largest congregation is at St. Therese Church of the Little Flower at 875 E. Plumb Lane in Reno. A modern circular structure built in 1977, the church is open and spacious, with lovely faceted stained-glass windows.

St. Thomas Aquinas Cathedral in Reno had humble beginnings as St. Mary's Washoe Mission. Established in 1871 as an independent parish, it was elevated to the status of cathedral in 1931 by Pope Pius XI. After fires destroyed earlier buildings, the church was relocated to its present structure at 310 W. Second Street in 1910. Constructed in Italian Renaissance style, the cathedral showcases exquisite stained-glass windows created by Hungarian artists, Isabel and Edith Piczek.

The Episcopalians arrived in the area in 1859, and though less numerous than some other denominations, seven churches still thrive. If you're looking for churches with a view, none is lovelier than St. John's in the Wilderness Episcopal Church at 1776 U.S. Highway 50 in Glenbrook, Nevada. Facing the eastern shore of Lake Tahoe, the window behind the pulpit presents an inspirational panorama of snow-dusted mountains and azure water. Trinity Episcopal Church at 200 Island Avenue in Reno also boasts a delightful setting since it's right on the Truckee River.

INSIDERS' TIP

The Flemish bells at Trinity Episcopal Church in Reno can be heard by passersby on every quarter hour. The donor requested in her handwritten will that the names of her friends be inscribed on each of the 35 bells.

Weather permitting, after the service, parishioners can enjoy refreshments on the front lawn of the church while watching the river flow by.

Another intriguing church on the Truckee River, the First United Methodist Church in Reno, dates from 1868 and has been in its present building at First and West streets since 1926. A charming ivy-covered stone building, its lighted tower is a well-known landmark in downtown. Like most churches, First United Methodist has beautiful stained glass windows in its sanctuary. But unlike any other church, the windows are framed by the Hosanna Arch, which contains the delicate sculptured faces of infants and children in the parish. If you're looking for coffee after services, you can head across the street for a gourmet blend at Java Jungle on the banks of the river.

Along with Protestants and Catholics, Jewish people also established early religious communities. The first B'nai B'rith lodge was founded in 1862 in Virginia City and the Chevrah B'rith Sholom in Reno in 1878. The first Jewish temple, Temple Emanu-El, was built in Reno in 1921. Today Jewish services are held in conservative Temple Emanu-El, reform Temple Sinai and orthodox Chabad in Reno and at Temple Bat Yam in Stateline, Nevada. The North Tahoe Hebrew Congregation meets at the North Tahoe Conference Center at 8318 N. Lake Boulevard in Kings Beach, California.

Bethel African Methodist Episcopal Church is the oldest African-American congregation in Nevada. Founded in Reno in 1910, it moved to its present building at 2655 N. Rock Boulevard in Sparks, Nevada, in 1993. Tracing its roots to the Free African Society Church founded in 1787, Bethel AME has experienced strong growth in recent years.

With more than 200 churches and synagogues, Reno/Tahoe is diverse in religious options. Just a glance in local phone books will show listings for every conventional denomination as well as some thought to be unconventional. In addition to all forms of Protestant, Catholic and Jewish congregations, you'll find listings for Baha'i, Buddhist, Eckankar and Muslim groups. Diversity doesn't stop with the variety of religious communities available but also extends to the language used in the services. An increasing number of churches offer services in Spanish because of the significant number of Spanish-speaking people living in the Reno/Tahoe area. With the overall growth in population, the demand for more and larger churches has also increased. New churches are springing up to accommodate the growing number of people who want to affiliate with a religious community.

If you're looking for specific information about church services, the quickest way to find out is to look under "Churches" or "Synagogues" in the local telephone books and to give them a call. Most churches have recorded messages about the times of services and activities. Church news is also printed in the Saturday edition of the *Reno Gazette-Journal*, the Friday edition of the *Tahoe Daily Tribune* and periodically in the *North Lake Tahoe Bonanza* and the *Tahoe World*.

Religious Unity and Outreach

While significant differences exist among the eclectic religious groups in Reno/Tahoe, in recent years unity has been a goal for many. Some churches foster cooperation by sharing facilities, trading clergy and having services together. With the theme "Unity Towards Evangelism," the Greater Reno Area Church Evangelistic project (GRACE) was founded in 1994. More than 70 members, comprised of churches, pastors and Christian leaders, have joined to mobilize church membership. Their mission is to foster pastoral and interchurch unity throughout the Reno/Sparks area. What

---

INSIDERS' TIP

You don't have to dress up to attend church services at Lake Tahoe. Those who come dressed for skiing, hiking or biking are welcome at area churches.

makes the GRACE project unique is that both charismatic and evangelical groups have come together in this cooperative effort.

While charity begins at home, with many religious groups reaching out to touch each other, it doesn't end there. The well-established tradition of helping those in need has expanded to comprehensive outreach programs that fill gaps left by governmental and non-profit agencies. Reno/Tahoe religious congregations are involved in a myriad of good works, extending helping hands to young and old, the disabled, the homeless, the hungry and almost anyone who has special needs. Virtually every religious group has organized programs that aid others in the community. They run shelters for the homeless, distribute food and clothing to the needy, offer support groups for those in crisis and provide spiritual counseling for those in prison. If you're looking for meaningful charity work in the Reno/Tahoe area, any one of the many churches can put you to work in a rewarding way.

Tying the Knot

Weddings have been big business in Reno/Tahoe for many years (see our History chapter for more details). Because of the exquisite scenery and the plethora of romantic locales for both the ceremony and the honeymoon, thousands of couples come to the area every year to tie the knot. With no waiting period or blood test required, it's easy to get married, even on the spur of the moment. Full-service wedding chapels will provide everything you need to make it romantic and legal, including the flowers, music, witnesses, minister, pictures and even a limousine to your wedding night hideaway. Some chapels are small and utilitarian, while others are large and elaborate. Many resorts have chapels with complete wedding services so see our Resorts chapter for more details. Most churches will also perform wedding ceremonies, but keep in mind that, unlike some wedding chapels, it can't be done at a moment's notice.

Wedding locations that are especially scenic include St. Francis of Assisi Catholic Church at Nev. Highway 431 and Kelly Drive in Incline Village, Nevada, (775) 831-0490, with its lovely view of Lake Tahoe behind the altar; St. John's in the Wilderness Episcopal Church at 1776 U. S. Highway 50 in Glenbrook, Nevada, (775) 882-8460; A Country Chapel at 3135 Lake Tahoe Boulevard in South Lake Tahoe, California, (530) 544-4944, with its charming Old Tahoe ambiance; and The Lakefront Wedding Chapel, the only chapel right on the shore of Lake Tahoe, at 3351 Lake Tahoe Boulevard, South Lake Tahoe, California, (530) 544-6119.

If you're looking for a more exotic locale than a church or chapel, that can be arranged, too. You can get married on a yacht through Woodwind Sailing Cruises, (775) 588-3000, on a paddle wheeler with Hornblower Cruises, (530) 541-3364 or in a country church at the Ponderosa Ranch in Incline Village, Nevada, (775) 831-0691. Since the possibilities for your perfect wedding are endless, we can't begin to give an exhaustive list. Check local telephone books under "Wedding Chapels," "Churches," and "Wedding Consultants" for complete information.

Index of Advertisers

Index

N